INTRODUCTION TO EVOLUTION

INTRODUCTION TO EVOLUTION

SECOND EDITION

PAUL AMOS MOODY

Howard Professor of Natural History and Zoology, University of Vermont

Harper & Row · Publishers

New York, Evanston, and London

B-R

TO MY WIFE JUD1TH

WITHOUT WHOSE COOPERATIVE SILENCE

THIS BOOK COULD NOT HAVE BEEN WRITTEN

CONTENTS

Organic evolution is the greatest general principle in biology. Its implications extend far beyond the confines of that science, ramifying into all phases of human life and activity. Accordingly, understanding of evolution should be part of the intellectual equipment of all educated persons.

As its name implies, this book is intended to form an *introduction* to organic evolution for readers who have not previously "met" the subject, and who have little or no background knowledge of biology in general. In writing I have constantly striven to render each subject understandable to such readers and to make my discussions elementary in the best sense of the word.

For the general reader and beginning student I distinguish sharply between textbooks and reference books. Reference books and advanced textbooks, with their encyclopedic treatment, exhaustive discussions, and detailed citations of literature, are essential tools for the scientist and the advanced student. But they are not suitable *introductions* to a branch of science. This function is served by the elementary textbook or "teaching book." The present volume is of this variety. In it the author serves as guide to a traveler in a strange country. On the basis of previous experience and greater familiarity with the terrain, the author guides his reader through the jungle of confusing facts and conflicting theories. The guide, not being all-wise, may make mistakes of judgment in selecting the path, but at least the reader will be more likely to reach his destination than he would have been without any guide at all. Having once mastered a route the reader will then be competent to explore other paths than those selected for him by his original guide. He will then, in other words, be in position to profit from reference books and research treatises. In the hope that readers will be stimulated to read more deeply in subjects which interest them I have included in the second edition more extensive lists of references than the first edition possessed.

Controversial subjects form an integral part of our discussion. I have not avoided them but have attempted always to distinguish clearly between fact and theory. In some cases I have pointed out what seems to me to be the conclusion justified by the evidence; in other cases I have indicated the wisdom of suspended judgment, awaiting further evidence. In the interest of clarity and of economy of the reader's time I have, in discussion of a given subject, included most readily understandable or most telling examples and supporting facts, without any pretense of exhaustive cataloguing. Teachers will, of course, augment my discussions as they think best.

As with the first edition, the main body of the first part of the book is concerned with the *facts* of evolution. This part is preceded (Chapter 2) by a brief discussion of the *theory* of how evolution occurs, and followed (Chapter 15) by a more complete summary of this subject. Chapter 15 is designed to serve (a) as a concluding chapter for those who desire but a brief summary of theory, and (b) as an introduction to the succeeding chapters in which theory is discussed in more detail for those who desire it. These later chapters have been completely reorganized and largely rewritten in the second edition. In response to many suggestions by users of the first edition a discussion of the principles of Mendelian inheritance and their chromosomal basis has been added (Chapter 17) to augment the discussion of population genetics (Chapter 19) and provide genetical foundation for understanding other causative factors in evolution. The second edition includes expanded discussions of some subjects included in the first edition (e.g., hybridization, speciation, and selective mating) as well as discussions of some subjects absent from the first edition (e.g., industrial melanism, mimicry, genetic assimilation and the Baldwin effect, and genetic homeostasis).

In each of the earlier chapters of the book I have attempted to bring the facts and interpretations up to date in the light of recent research. The discussion of the relationship between recapitulation and the origin of the Metazoa (Chapter 4) has been completely rewritten, as has the chapter on the evolution of man, a field in which discoveries of new fossils and more complete analyses of old ones lead to almost monthly changes in our knowledge and ideas. Some subjects have been augmented, for example, the evolution of the horse (by discussion of the brain and the springing mechanism of the foot), and the discussions of classification and geographic distribution (clines, rassenkreise, and zoogeographic "rules").

In a very real sense it is impossible to acknowledge adequately assistance given by others in preparation of this book. I am a debtor to countless scientists known and unknown to me. Science is "team play" at its best. It is a pleasure, however, to mention the names of certain individuals who have contributed directly to the immediate preparation of the volume. First among these I must mention Dr. Louise F. Bush, whose creative and interpretive drawings have added so much to the teaching value, as well as to the appearance, of the book. Most of the illustrations not borrowed unchanged from other sources are her work. I am also grateful to my colleague, Lyman S. Rowell, for two most useful drawings, to Dr. H. B. D. Kettlewell for two beautiful photographs of industrial melanism, and to L. W. Erbe for a photograph upon which the drawing of a tapir was based. Publishers and authors have been most generous in permitting me to borrow illustrations; for this I am grateful. The caption of each borrowed figure credits the source of the figure.

My indebtedness continues to many individuals who contributed in various ways to the first edition. Space limitations prevent mention of many of those to whom I am indebted, but because of the magnitude of their contributions it is a pleasure to recall the help offered by Joseph G. Baier, David W. Bishop, Charles F. Bond, Theodosius Dobzhansky, John T. Emlen, William K. Gregory, David Lack, John H. Lochhead, Ernst Mayr, Mabel L. Moody, Marjorie S. Murray, Carl T. Parsons, Henry F. Perkins, George Gaylord Simpson, and a geologist whose name was not divulged to me. It would also be a pleasure to list the names of those who, orally or in writing, have suggested changes for the second edition. James M. Barrett, Ross T. Bell, and Bobb Schaeffer are typical of many whom I should like to mention. While the persons listed have contributed greatly to whatever merits the book may possess, they are entirely without responsibility for its deficiencies.

It is my hope that readers of this edition will be as cooperative in sending me their constructive criticisms as were readers of the first edition.

An Explanatory Note for Students

The illustrations are numbered according to the system of including the number of the chapter in the number assigned the illustration. Thus, "Fig. 4.10" indicates that the figure in question is the tenth one in Chapter 4. The next illustration in that chapter is numbered "Fig. 4.11," and so on.

In most places the name of a contributor to evolutionary thought is followed by a date, usually in parenthesis—e.g., "Darwin (1859)." The date enables one to identify the publication referred to, listed with the author's name at the end of the chapter.

PAUL A. MOODY

Burlington, Vermont
December, 1961

INTRODUCTION
TO EVOLUTION

CHAPTER 1

EVOLUTION SEEN

IN PERSPECTIVE

Organic Evolution

Evolution means change. We speak of the evolution of the solar system, the evolution of the earth, the evolution of the airplane, the evolution of the automobile. In such cases we are referring to the changes which have occurred in solar system, earth, airplane, or automobile.

The evolution with which this book is concerned involves a special form of the broader meaning of the term: **organic evolution.** This subdivision of evolution deals with changes undergone by living things, plants and animals. For our purposes we may define organic evolution as the theory that plants and animals now living are the modified descendants of somewhat different plants and animals which lived in times past. These ancestors, in their turn, are thought of as being the descendants of predecessors which differed from them, and so on, step by step, back to a beginning shrouded in mystery.

In the above statement the words "modified descendants" deserve special emphasis. The word "modified" refers to the element of change which we have just mentioned as inherent in the whole idea of evolution. The word "descendants" introduces an idea not present in the broader use of the term "evolution." When we speak of the evolution of the automobile we have reference to the changes occurring in the transition from the "horseless carriage" of a bygone era to the model currently advertised. We do not think of the older automobiles as being the parents or ancestors of the newer ones in any literal sense. Makers of automobiles learn from experi-

1

ence gained with older models how to improve and modify their product so that later models are different from, and on the whole better than, earlier ones. But the later models are not literally the offspring of the earlier ones. Contrariwise, it is exactly this ancestor-descendant relationship which is visualized in the term "organic evolution." More recent animals are thought of as the direct genetic descendants of somewhat differing ancestors which formerly lived on the earth.

The reader will have noted that the definition of organic evolution just given differs from the popular conceptions of the meaning of evolution. If the proverbial "man in the street" is asked the meaning of the word, he is likely to reply, "Man came from monkeys." This exclusive preoccupation with man is perhaps natural in one but little acquainted with, or interested in, the remainder of the living world. To a biologist the evolution of man is but one portion of the vast drama of evolutionary change including all living things. Each animal alive today is the product of long evolutionary history.

Another shortcoming of the man in the street's definition lies in the fact that he pictures one modern form as descended from another modern form. Man and monkey are contemporaries, both products of long evolution. It is as incongruous to speak of one as the descendant of the other as it would be to speak of one member of the sophomore class in college as the descendant of another member of that class. What, then, is the evolutionary interpretation of the relationship existing between monkey and man? Rather than being a father-to-son relationship, it is more comparable to a cousin-to-cousin relationship. You and your cousin have a pair of grandparents in common. Modern man and modern monkey are thought of as having shared a common ancestor in the distant past. From this common ancestor both inherited some characteristics in which they still resemble each other. Was this common ancestor a man or a monkey? Neither. He was a form that had the potentialities of giving rise to a monkey, on the one hand, or of giving rise to a man, on the other. There is no evidence that any of the animals we know as monkeys have that potentiality.

Beginnings of the Evolution Idea

Many people seem to think that the whole idea of evolution started with a man named Darwin. This belief probably arose from the fact that Darwin's great book, *The Origin of Species,* published in 1859, was the first widely read book on evolution published in English. This classic in our field had two main objectives: to convince people that evolution is indeed a fact, and to present evidence in support of Darwin's theory of the means and methods by which evolutionary change occurs. This theory is called natural selection; it represents Darwin's special contribution to evolutionary thought. The fundamental concepts of natural selection are presented in Chapter 2 and are further elaborated in Chapters 15–21.

Ideas that by one means or another evolution does occur far antedated Darwin, however. In fact, such ideas are probably as old as human thought. As soon as man had attained sufficient intellect to observe the similarities and differences among the animals and plants surrounding him, and to speculate about them, he undoubtedly began to form crude ideas of evolution. Certain it is that by the time he had learned to record his thoughts so that posterity might read, concepts of evolution were present in his mind. Not that these early concepts correspond in detail with our modern ideas of evolution; far from it. They were highly speculative, frequently colored with mythology, and represented at their best what we may think of as "good guesses," since in part they were subsequently proved correct. But in them we see, though dimly, the outlines of the idea that the living world is one, and that living things change, giving rise to new forms.

The ancient Greek philosophers afford evidence of these early gropings for explanation of the earth and its inhabitants. Space forbids mention of more than a few of these pioneers in human thought. One was **Anaximander,** whose adult life spanned the first half of the sixth century B.C. According to Anaximander, men were first formed as fishes; eventually they cast off their fish skins and took up life on dry land. Here we have one of those "good guesses." As will be evident after perusal of Chapter 8, modern evidence supports the view that a distant ancestor of man was indeed a fish. How much credit should be accorded Anaximander for speculations which proved to contain this kernel of truth?

Xenophanes was in part a contemporary of Anaximander although, unlike the latter, he lived on into the fifth century B.C. Xenophanes is credited with being the first person to recognize that fossils, such as petrified bones embedded in rocks, represent the remains of animals that once lived. Today we take the idea for granted, but that fact should not lessen our appreciation of the insight shown by the first person to grasp it. Truth is "obvious" only after its discovery. Xenophanes also realized that the presence of fossils of marine animals on what is now dry land indicates that the ocean once covered the area.

The fifth century B.C. also saw the man who has been hailed by Osborn

(1896) as "the father of the Evolution idea": **Empedocles.** According to this philosopher, plants arose out of the earth, as did, subsequently, animals. Animals arose as unattached organs and parts which joined together in haphazard fashion. Most of these conglomerations were freaks and monsters incapable of living, but occasionally a combination of organs appeared which could function as a successful living organism. Such successful combinations survived and populated the earth, while the incongruous assemblages died. It is possible to see in this account the first glimmerings of the idea of the survival of the fittest, an idea which formed such an important part of Darwin's theory of natural selection twenty-three centuries later. But the danger is great of "reading into" such ancient writings ideas which were not actually in the mind of the author. Empedocles included man among the beings formed in the manner described.

The fourth century B.C. is memorable for the life and work of **Aristotle,** well termed by Locy (1925) "the greatest investigator of antiquity." Best known to us as philosopher, Aristotle possessed far more of the spirit of scientific research than did his predecessors, or than did most of his successors for centuries to come. Thus, within the limits of the materials and methods available to him he carried on investigations in such diverse fields as marine biology, anatomy, embryology, and the metamorphosis of insects. Although the accuracy of his scientific observation excites our admiration, we find less to admire in his speculations concerning evolution. There he failed to follow the ideal which he himself propounded: "We must not accept a general principle from logic only, but must prove its application to each fact; for it is in facts that we must seek principles, and these must always accord with facts." Yet our censure must be temperate, since the store of "facts" available to Aristotle was totally inadequate as foundation for the activity of his towering intellect.

We shall confine our attention to one contribution made by Aristotle to evolutionary thinking. He maintained that there is complete gradation in nature. The lowest stage is the inorganic. Organic beings arose from inorganic by direct metamorphosis. He conceived the organic world to consist of three states: (1) plants; (2) plant-animals, a transitional group in which he included sponges and sea anemones; (3) animals, characterized by feeling or sensibility. Within the animal group he constructed a genetic series leading from lowest forms up to man, placed at the apex. Hence, we may think of Aristotle as the father of those "family trees" which have been so conspicuous in writings on evolution ever since. It is to be noted, however, that his tree had no branches; it was a straight line from polyps to man. Nor did his tree contain any prehistoric animals; unlike Xenophanes. Aristotle failed to appreciate the true significance of fossils. More accurate diagrams of relationship were far in the future. The first tree of life to possess branches and to be influenced by appreciation of the importance of fossils was published by Lamarck in A.D. 1809 (in his *Philosophie Zoologique*).

One is tempted to remark at this point that thinking on evolution stood still during the more than 2000 years which separated Aristotle from Lamarck. Such a statement would be extreme, yet true in the main. In this long interim what of real significance for evolution was occurring? During this time science, in the modern meaning of the term, came into existence and developed. Little by little there was accumulated that body of facts which, as we have seen, Aristotle recognized as essential foundation on which to establish general principles. Without such a foundation thinking on evolution must have remained forever mere speculation. Accordingly, we can recognize the importance to evolution of developments occurring during these twenty centuries, while at the same time realizing that we lose but little when we omit discussion of evolutionary ideas prevalent during them. The foundations were not ready to receive the superstructure until the nineteenth century A.D.

No complete survey of the history of evolutionary thought is possible within the confines of this volume. Interested readers are referred to books listed at the end of this chapter. Our present aim has been to demonstrate that thinking about evolution is as old as human thought, and to mention a few of the first contributions to the subject. The contributions of Lamarck and Darwin receive further discussion in Chapter 15.

Evolution and the Church

The idea of evolution shares with various other scientific advances, such as the idea that the earth revolves, the distinction of having been opposed in times past by religious leaders. The latter were, of course, primarily interested in the application of evolution to man, or rather in making certain that evolution did not apply to man. It was felt that in some way man was degraded if one admitted any connection between him and the lower animals. Admittedly, also, the story of man's origin through evolution does not agree in detail with the story of his origin through special creation contained in the first chapters of Genesis. Wise churchmen like St. Augustine and St. Thomas Aquinas early recognized that these chapters, while expressing important religious truth concerning the Creator, should not be regarded as literal history. Unfortunately, both for religion and for science, the leadership of these men was but little followed.

The controversy which climaxed after the appearance of Darwin's *Origin of Species* has now largely subsided. For the most part the churches recognize evolution as the means by which the Creator works. Some portions of Protestant denominations, commonly called "fundamentalist," still deny the truth of evolution. There are fundamentalists in the Roman Catholic Church also. But that church does not officially oppose evolution, even of man, so long as no attempt is made to explain the origin of the human soul by this means. This is a restriction readily accepted by the present author since in his opinion the soul does not come within the province of science (see p. 219).

Plan of the Book

Evolution manifests itself in varied aspects of the living world—in structure, in chemical composition, in nature of life processes (metabolism), in embryonic development, in chemical nature of blood, in the manner in which animals are distributed over the earth and adapted to differing environments, in the classification of animals, in the remains of prehistoric animals preserved to us as fossils. In the next chapter we shall summarize some ideas of the nature and causes of evolutionary change, ideas which will be of use to us in understanding the varied manifestations of evolution. Then we shall consider the factual contributions to study of evolution made by various fields of biology. Finally, in Chapters 15–21 we shall discuss in more detail the means and methods by which evolutionary change occurs.

References and Suggested Readings

Darwin, C. *The Origin of Species by Means of Natural Selection.* 1859. Modern Library series, Random House, New York; or Mentor Book MT294, New American Library, New York.

Locy, W. A. *Biology and Its Makers.* New York: Henry Holt and Co., 1915.

Locy, W. A. *Growth of Biology.* New York: Henry Holt and Co., 1925.

Nordenskiöld, E. *The History of Biology.* New York: Alfred A. Knopf, Inc., 1928.

Osborn, H. F. *From the Greeks to Darwin,* 2nd ed. New York: The Macmillan Company, 1896.

CHAPTER 2

CHANGING ANIMALS

The Fact of Change

We have mentioned (p. 1) that organic evolution deals with changes undergone by living things, plants and animals. Some readers who are not used to thinking of these matters may feel that we are making an unwarranted assumption when we speak of animals *changing*. The fact that they do change has by no means always been recognized. Indeed, until quite recently in the history of human thought most people have believed that the animals living today were created as they now are, once and for all, as recorded in the first chapters of Genesis. This belief was championed by many eminent scientists of former times. Among these was Linnaeus, the eighteenth-century Swedish naturalist who founded the system of classification still used (see Chap. 14). Linnaeus assigned scientific names to great numbers of plant and animal species and genera. He believed that these species were for the most part the ones created as described in Genesis. As his knowledge expanded, however, he modified this view to the extent of conceding that new species might arise through hybridization (cross-mating) between the original species. In view of this widespread belief in the fixity of species, how is it that we now speak of animals as changing? In other words, what makes us think that the kinds of animals living today are not the kinds of animals which have "always" existed?

The direct evidence on the question just raised comes from the "record of the rocks"—from the remains of animals that formerly lived but are now known to us only as fossils. In fairness to Linnaeus we should recall that almost nothing was known about fossils in his day. As we shall see in later chapters (Chaps. 7–11), this geologic record demonstrates that hosts of animals not present in the modern world formerly lived. What became

of them, and what was their relationship to modern animals? According
to one point of view, formerly widely held, they became extinct, leaving no
descendants. Perhaps widespread calamities (such as floods) effected
wholesale removal of these ancient animals. And perhaps they were then
replaced either by new animals especially created for the purpose or by
animals that migrated in from regions of the earth untouched by the
catastrophe in question. This **theory of catastrophism** was prevalent among
biologists of past centuries. The eminent French biologist, Cuvier, whose life
spanned the close of the eighteenth century and the first part of the nineteenth, was one of its most powerful exponents.

We note that according to the theory of catastrophism the "new" animals inhabiting a given region after a catastrophe would not be the descendants of the "old" animals formerly found in the region. They would
be fresh creations, created either in the region in question or elsewhere.
This idea stands in direct contrast to the idea of organic evolution, which
holds that the "new" animals are modified descendants of certain of the
differing animals that formerly existed, in that region or some other. Not
that *all* the old animals left modified descendants; far from it. Evidence
indicates that only a small minority had that capability. The rest became extinct without issue.

The Changing World

Returning to our original question concerning the fact of changes in animals, we may note that we should expect such change even if the geologic
record did not afford a direct testimony of it. It is a truism that change is
the only unchanging aspect of our world. So far as we can judge this has
always been true. The physical world has undergone great changes. Periods of glacial cold have alternated with periods of tropic heat. The floors
of shallow seas have been elevated to form lofty mountain ranges, and the
latter have in turn been worn down to low hills and plains, and perhaps
eventually covered by the sea once more. Aquatic environments, the home
of great proportions of the animal kingdom, have undergone continual
change. The oceans have changed the least, yet even here changes have
occurred, as, for example, in temperature and in salinity. The oceans have
also fluctuated greatly in depth, particularly along the margins of continents. Elevation and subsidence of areas of the earth's crust have been
involved in this fluctuation as has, during glacial periods, the locking up of
vast quantities of the earth's water supply in polar icecaps and their extensions equator-ward. The environments of fresh-water animals have
been even more subject to change. Rivers and lakes are notably short-

lived, changing features of the landscape. Terrestrial environments, lacking the stabilizing influence exerted by a watery medium, are most variable of all. As a rule terrestrial animals face greater fluctuations in temperature, humidity, and other environmental factors than do aquatic animals.

What have such changes in the external world to do with changes in animals themselves? Simply this: if a species of animal is to succeed it must at all times be *adapted* to its environment. If the environment changes, as we have seen that it does repeatedly, the species must either adjust to that environmental change or die. The geologic record is full of examples of animals that could not adjust to changed conditions and hence became extinct.

We may well note at this point that change in one species will inevitably lead to changes in other species. Change in the organic environment of an animal may be at least as important as change in its physical environment. An animal may, for example, become adapted to a diet consisting of a certain plant, as the koala, the marsupial "teddy bear," is dependent upon a diet of eucalyptus leaves. If the climate changes so that the plant can no longer exist in the region, the animal must either change its food habits or become extinct in that region. If it becomes extinct, that fact will affect the fate of flesh-eating animals (predators) which had been dependent upon the plant eater as part of their food supply. And changes in numbers of predators will affect the numbers of other species of plant eaters preyed upon. So one change sets off a whole series of other changes, the effects expanding like the ripples started by one stone dropped in a quiet pond.

Thus we see that changes in the physical environment and changes in the organic environment make change in a species inevitable if it is to continue inhabiting this changing world. As we have intimated, these changes to be effective must *adapt* the species to live under the conditions in which it finds itself, or, alternatively, to live under some conditions available to it, by migration perhaps. In the following chapters we shall see examples of such adaptations in modern animals. We shall also note that despite changes necessitated by the requirements of life under particular conditions, species retain basic similarities of structure which can best be explained as indications of their ancestry. Both the adaptive changes and the basic similarities are important to the study of evolution.

Changing Genes

We have noted that the geologic record gives testimony that animals do change, and that the demands of living in a changing world insure that animals must change. We may now note that animals possess within themselves the seeds of their own changes. Nearly everyone in these days has at least heard of the units of heredity called **genes.** These submicroscopic structures are found in the nuclei of the myriads of cells composing our bodies and the bodies of other animals and plants. Genes are concerned in the determination of what an individual's characteristics shall be, and they form the principal hereditary link between one generation and the next. To a very large extent the characteristics of an offspring are determined by the genes which he receives from his parents: from his mother through the egg or ovum and from his father through the sperm cell which fertilizes that ovum. The point we wish to emphasize here is that genes are not unchanging units; they undergo changes called **mutations.** When a gene mutates, the result is a gene which conditions production of a changed characteristic. If, for example, the gene originally participated in production of brown eye color, the mutated gene might fail to play its role in formation of brown pigment, with the result that the eye would appear blue. This matter of mutation will be referred to in other connections later (pp. 336–338); at present we merely wish to point out that it provides animals with a means by which change can occur, and, indeed, inevitably will occur, since mutations arise "spontaneously" at a fairly constant, though slow, rate.

How do we know that animals have changed? We have the direct evidence afforded by the geologic record. Furthermore, we infer that changes must occur from the nature of the external world, coupled with the necessity placed upon animals of always maintaining adaptation to that world. And finally, we observe that the units of heredity, the genes, undergo mutation, thereby providing the raw materials of change.

Changes in Animals, and the Mechanisms of Evolution

We may appropriately inquire at this point: What happens to inheritable changes (mutations) after they appear? In later chapters (Chaps. 15–21) we shall discuss the nature of mutations and of the forces that play upon them. In the present connection it will be sufficient to state a few general principles which will be useful in the following discussions of the varied manifestations of evolution.

Natural Selection

Much of our thinking on the causes of evolutionary change has its roots in Darwin's great book, *The Origin of Species by Means of Natural Selec-*

tion, mentioned in the preceding chapter. Darwin introduced the term **natural selection** to convey the idea that nature exercises selection somewhat as an animal breeder does when he wishes to improve a stock of domestic animals. The breeder selects as parents of the next generation those individuals possessing qualities he wishes his stock to have. At the same time he prevents the reproduction of those individuals which lack the desired qualities. Thus selection by breeders (artificial selection) has two aspects, one positive, the other negative. Similarly, natural selection is both positive and negative in its working.

Directing attention first to the negative aspect, we can readily understand that if a bodily change is harmful, so that possessors of it are not so well adapted to life as they would have been without it, the change will be a handicap. Possessors of such a handicap may not live to maturity, or if they do live they may not reproduce. Or if they do reproduce they may not produce as large a proportion of the next generation as do their unhandicapped brethren. As a result the harmful change will tend to disappear in subsequent generations.

This negative aspect of natural selection is important to animals as a conservative or stabilizing force, insuring that undesirable changes are weeded out and discarded from the species. Negative selection (stabilizing selection of Schmalhausen, 1949) helps to keep the species always at its "adaptive peak" by preventing establishment of changes which would lessen perfection of adaptation to the environment in which the species lives. Negative selection is a preserver of the status quo; it is constructive insofar as deviations from the established norm would be detrimental to the species. But real progress is seldom achieved by enforcing conformity to established patterns. Accordingly we look to the positive aspect of natural selection for the means of progressive change.

If a bodily change is beneficial to its possessors, the latter will have an advantage over their fellows who lack the change. If conditions are such that competition is keen, this advantage may be sufficient to make a difference in ability to survive, or to produce offspring, or both. If it is, possessors of the change will produce more than "their share" of offspring. If these offspring inherit the change, the result will be that among them will occur a greater proportion of individuals possessing the change than possessed it in the parental generation. Let us suppose, for example, that under a certain set of circumstances it is beneficial to an animal to have long legs, the better to run away from enemies. If some members of the species have longer legs (the result of mutation) than do others, the longer-legged individuals may survive the ravages of their enemies better than do the shorter-legged members. There will be a tendency for the

long-legged individuals to become the parents of a larger proportion of the
next generation than do their shorter-legged fellows. As a result, long legs
will be possessed by larger numbers of the second generation than possessed them in the first. If this same trend continues for several or many
generations, eventually the whole population may come to possess the
beneficial change. This, in simplified, nontechnical terms, is the central
idea of the positive aspect of natural selection. More complete statements,
with discussion of the forces operative, will be found in the closing chapters of the book (pp. 450–507). The central idea, however, will be
found most useful in interpreting the manifestations of evolution discussed in the chapters immediately following this one.

We note that positive natural selection resembles positive artificial selection in that in both instances individuals possessing some special attribute
are favored to become parents of the next generation. In artificial selection the favored individuals are the ones possessing some quality desired
by the breeder. In natural selection the favored individuals are the ones
possessing some quality which renders them better adapted than their fellows for life under the circumstances in which they find themselves. In
both instances the desirable quality or change will be likely to be of more
frequent occurrence in the next generation than it was in the former.
Progress, in terms of more perfect adaptation to the conditions of life, is
the result.

Postadaptation and Preadaptation

Our discussion so far has emphasized more and more perfect adaptation
to a stable environment in which the species is already living. This type of
adaptation is called **postadaptation,** since the species has already entered
the environment, and additional adaptation merely perfects the animal
for living under the conditions prevailing. Much evolutionary change is
of this nature.

On the other hand, a bodily change may be of no particular benefit, may
indeed even be harmful, in the environment in which the species is living,
but would be beneficial in some other environment. If possessors of this
change can reach that other environment, they may thrive there, with the
result that the change may increase in frequency as generations pass in the
new environment. Eventually the change may characterize all inhabitants
of the new environment, becoming for this population "standard equipment." This phenomenon of a change which, though it may not be beneficial in the original environment, fits an animal to invade another en-

vironment is called **preadaptation** or **prospective adaptation** (Simpson, 1953).

Sometimes the change in question may be useful in the original environment and yet be of such a nature that it preadapts its possessor for life in another environment. Crossopterygian fishes (pp. 157–162), for example, had a fin adapted for locomotion in the water, yet the fin had within it a skeleton which could be made over to form a limb for locomotion on land. Thus we say that the skeleton of the crossopterygian fin (Fig. 8.18, p. 161) was preadaptive for life on land.

Apparently preadaptation has played an important role in progressive evolution, by which we mean the production of radical changes in animals, as contrasted with the perfecting of adaptation to the environment in which the animal is already living. To be sure, the perfecting of the adaptation of a species to its environment is in a sense progressive. Yet such a process, useful as it is, does not usually lead to radical change in structure. It is one thing for a fish to become more and more perfectly adapted for life in the water, quite another thing for it to climb out of the water and enter the new environment of air. Fishes (i.e., the Crossopterygii) possessing structures preadapted for life on land could make the change; other fishes could not.

Meeting Environmental Changes

Consideration of preadaptation has introduced a new factor into our discussion, that of change in the environment. In earlier pages of this chapter we noted that environmental change has occurred repeatedly throughout the history of the earth. How do species of animals meet such changes?

In the first place, species frequently meet changed conditions by succumbing to them—by becoming extinct. Such extinction may be world-wide, or it may involve only certain regions of the earth. Thus, for example, at the close of the Mesozoic era the dinosaurs became extinct throughout the earth. On the other hand, in much later times the camels, formerly inhabitants of North America, became extinct on that continent while remaining existent in Asia, Africa, and South America (llama) (Fig. 12.5, p. 271).

Another manner in which animals may meet change in the environment is by being sufficiently adaptable or versatile so that they can live under a great variety of conditions. While this seems not to have been a very common solution of the problem, various examples come to mind. The rats and mice that dwell with us in our houses as unwelcome guests originated in Asia but are so adaptable to all manner of conditions that they have become practically world-wide in distribution. Apparently cockroaches, which have survived virtually unchanged all the vicissitudes of the earth since the days before the great coal deposits were formed, owe their vast lease on life to a similar ability to adapt to whatever may befall them. Other examples might be cited but we may content ourselves by mentioning that man himself, thanks to employment of his intelligence, is the supreme example of ability to live under widely diverse conditions.

A third way in which animals may meet changes in environment is by undergoing changes themselves. This is the commonest method of solving the problem, by species that do succeed in solving it. In Chapter 15 we shall discuss a theory that changes in the environment directly produce or call forth appropriate corresponding changes in animals—the theory of the inheritance of acquired characters. Since, as we shall see, there is little positive evidence that this phenomenon does occur, we shall concentrate attention here upon **mutations** as a source of bodily change in animals. As we shall see later, there are other sources of genetic variability than mutations. But in order to present the principles of natural selection as simply as possible we shall concentrate on mutations in our present discussion.

As noted before, mutations are changes in genes that result in changes in the bodies of animals possessing the changed genes in appropriate proportion (see pp. 331–335). Mutations occur at random, without regard to the needs of individuals in which they occur. If the mutations are harmful in their effect, they will be eliminated by the negative action of natural selection discussed above. If, however, the mutations are beneficial, they will be preserved, and the number of individuals possessing them will be increased in subsequent generations by the positive action of natural selection. Recent experiments showing that natural selection actually does operate as we postulate are briefly discussed in Chapter 20. Positive selection of beneficial mutations may lead to more perfect adaptation to an existing environment, or, alternatively, to adaptation to new conditions if the environment changes.

We have seen that when the environment changes a species may become extinct. Sometimes, however, though most of the members of a species may fail to survive, a few members, usually the possessors of changes (mutations) adapting them to the new conditions, will survive. The surviving few will then become the progenitors of future generations, which will inherit the changed condition permitting life in the changed environment.

If a species becomes extinct, the result is an **environmental niche**—a possible place and means of livelihood—left vacant. There may be in the vicinity, however, some other species possessed of structures which preadapt it for life in the vacant "niche." For such a species the disappearance of the former species would be the opening of a door to opportunity. Sometimes the environmental niche remains vacant for a long time before a species appears that is adapted to occupy it. Thus Simpson (1953) has pointed out that the niche left vacant by the extinction of ichthyosaurs (reptiles, relatives of the dinosaurs, having highly fishlike body form; Fig. 3.5, p. 30) was unoccupied until the advent of dolphins and porpoises millions of years later.

Accordingly we see that possession of bodily changes, the result of fortunate mutations, may enable animals to meet changing environments in one of two ways. (1) In some cases possessors of changes among members of the species already present in the environment may be enabled to survive while their fellows cannot. (2) In other cases the species already present in the environment may become extinct, but other species possessing structures which preadapt them to life in the niche left vacant may be enabled to move in and occupy that niche.

A specific example may help to make clear the application of the general principles we have been discussing. We have already referred to the fact that the crossopterygian fishes gave rise to the first land vertebrates, the amphibians. This was one of the greatest changes to occur in the evolution of vertebrates. More information concerning it will be found in Chapter 8. This change occurred in the period of geologic time known as the Devonian (p. 137). Prior to that time all vertebrates had been water dwellers. Hence the dry-land environment was an unoccupied environmental niche, as far as vertebrates were concerned. As nearly as we can picture it from our great distance in time, the course of events ran somewhat as follows.

Elevation of the land was reducing more and more the size of the lakes and estuaries in which fresh-water fishes were living. During the dry seasons some ponds probably dried up completely, while others were reduced to stagnant pools of foul water, overcrowded with fishes. Under such conditions most fishes must have died, as they do when similar conditions arise today. But among the fishes in those Devonian ponds were some which were preadapted for invasion of the unoccupied environmental niche just across the water line. These were the crossopterygian fishes we have mentioned. Three of their most striking preadaptations were: (1) the skeletal structure of the fins, providing raw material for a limb that could support the body and accomplish locomotion when the body was no longer buoyed up by surrounding water (Fig. 2.1); (2) an air bladder connected to the mouth cavity and capable of being used as a simple lung for respiration in the air; (3) nostrils which opened from the exterior into the mouth cavity and thus made possible the breathing of air with the mouth closed or otherwise employed. (In most fishes the nostrils connect to closed pouches containing the sense organs of smell and do not open into the mouth cavity.)

We may picture some of these crossopterygian fishes as making use of their preadaptations to crawl from their fetid pools, probably at first in search of fresher and less crowded ones (Romer, 1959). Presumably the first overland excursions were brief. And probably very few of the crossopterygian fishes succeeded in making even this much departure from

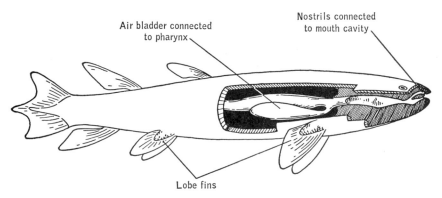

FIG. 2.1. Diagram of crossopterygian fish dissected to show three ways in which it was preadapted for life on land.

ancestral habits. Pioneering is seldom a mass phenomenon. Eventually, however, there must have arisen small populations of crossopterygian descendants increasingly emancipated from life in the water and finally making use of it only as a place to spawn and lay their eggs, as most amphibians do to this day. This increasing emancipation from life in the water would be accomplished by that postadaptation of which we have spoken. The principal mechanism involved in the change from water to air was doubtless the positive aspect of natural selection—the favoring of individuals possessing changes (arisen through mutation) which more adequately fitted them for life on land than their fellows.

"Many Are Called but Few Are Chosen"

We have stressed the point that the numbers of individuals involved in making the dramatic change from water to air were probably small. The great bulk of fishes, even of the crossopterygian fishes, stayed in the water, living and dying as might be determined by stringency of conditions confronting them. A few were the pioneers into the new environment outside the water.

As Simpson (1953) especially has pointed out, rates of evolutionary change vary greatly, from animal to animal and from time to time. We may be sure that the "chosen few" among crossopterygian descendants in the Devonian were in a highly unstable condition as regards adaptation. At first they must have been barely able to meet requirements of life in the new environment; life must have been a "nip and tuck" affair. Under such precarious conditions any slight improvement might have made an important contribution to survival and hence have been favored by natural selection. This fact, together with the small numbers of individuals involved, would have been conducive to rapid evolution. (The influence of numbers upon rates of evolutionary change is discussed in Chapters 19, 20, and 21.) Consequently the shift from water to land probably occurred quickly, in terms of geologic time.

One reason for mentioning here the small numbers of transitional forms and the brief span of the world's history in which they lived is to point out that these facts explain in large measure why we seldom find fossils of actual transitional forms between one major group of animals (such as fishes) and another major group (such as amphibians). Transitional forms are so seldom found, in fact, that one school of thought claims that they never existed, that one group arose from another by one sudden change ("systemic mutation" of Goldschmidt, 1940). This idea has been expressed by the striking statement: "The first bird hatched from a reptile's egg." It seems more likely, however, that Simpson is correct in postulating that transitional forms did occur but that they were so relatively few in number and occurred during such a brief interval of geologic time that chances of finding fossils of them are small. Moreover, in the following chapters we shall note examples of transitional forms whose fossils *have* been discovered. Chapter 7 presents additional information concerning reasons why the geologic record is incomplete.

Potentiality plus Opportunity

We may appropriately mention at this point an erroneous idea prevalent among many people who know little about evolution. This is the notion that if evolution is a fact all animals must be constantly tending to become "higher" animals, or, in its most exaggerated form, that all animals must be tending to become man. One sometimes hears the argument that evolution cannot be a fact, for if it were there would be no "lower" animals left—they would have all become men long since! Thoughtful consideration of the foregoing discussion will demonstrate the fallacy of such an idea. We have seen that animals are constantly tending to become *adapted* to the environment in which they live. Hence most fishes, either today or in Devonian times, may be thought of as tending to become "better" fishes; only a few, and that in one stage of the earth's history, became amphibians. Among the latter, in turn, only a few members of one group had the potentialities, and the opportunity, to become reptiles; the rest remained amphibians, becoming adapted to a variety of habitats. So it must have been always, and with all groups of animals. To only a minority of any group befell at once the potentiality and the opportunity for radical change into something different.

As we look about us today we see animals, each the product of long evolution, occupying each its own environmental niche in the world. The modern amoeba in its drop of water is admirably adapted to the conditions of life as it finds them. It is not tending to become a "higher animal." There already are higher animals filling the available niches. But hundreds of millions of years ago there were no higher animals; then some one-celled animals having the necessary potentialities were presented with the opportunity to enter the vacant "higher-animal niches" and did so. But still the "one-celled-animal niches" remained, and continued to be occupied by amoeba and its relatives to this day. Is not the modern amoeba as successful in being an amoeba as we are in being men?

In the following chapters we shall note many instances of preadaptation, as well as of the perfecting of adaptation of new structures once they have appeared (postadaptation). In later chapters will be found more complete discussions of the principles of evolutionary change sketched above with the broadest possible strokes. The details of theory can best be understood and appreciated after we have acquired a background of fact.

References and Suggested Readings

Darwin, C. *The Origin of Species by Means of Natural Selection.* 1859. Modern Library series, Random House, New York; or Mentor Book MT294, New American Library, New York.

Goldschmidt, R. *The Material Basis of Evolution.* New Haven: Yale University Press, 1940.

Romer, A. S. *The Vertebrate Story.* Chicago: University of Chicago Press, 1959.

Schmalhausen, I. I. *Factors of Evolution. The Theory of Stabilizing Selection.* Philadelphia: The Blakiston Company, 1949.

Simpson, G. G. *The Meaning of Evolution.* New Haven: Yale University Press, 1949.

Simpson, G. G. *The Major Features of Evolution.* New York: Columbia University Press, 1953.

CHAPTER 3

EVOLUTION AS SEEN IN

THE STRUCTURE OF MODERN

ANIMALS

Morphology

Structure is the easiest aspect of an animal to study. Perhaps it is for this reason that knowledge of animal structure dates from ancient times and was, indeed, the first aspect of biology to develop. The study of structure is called **morphology,** a word of slightly broader meaning than the more familiar term "anatomy," which is nearly synonymous. Biologists had not progressed far in the study of morphology before they were impressed by *similarities* among different animals and began to speculate as to the reason for these similarities.

Analogy

Why are different animals similar in structure? In the first place, we may note that there is no cause for surprise in the fact that animals living in the same environment or having similar methods of locomotion, obtaining food, and so on, resemble each other. Fishes and whales are both faced with the problem of moving rapidly through water. What could be more natural than that they both should have streamlined body forms and should be propelled by the thrust of powerful tails against the surrounding water? Or again, birds and bats utilize the air as a medium of locomotion. Both, therefore, possess wings which, like the wings of an airplane, support the body in the air and, unlike the wings of an airplane, serve as the means for forward propulsion. The reader can readily supply additional examples from his own observation. When animals live similar lives they usually resemble each other to some extent, the similarity being connected with the similar functions which their bodies serve. Similarity of structure connected with similarity of function is termed **analogy;** structures exhibiting it are said to be analogous.

Insects resemble birds and bats in the possession of wings. The insect wing somewhat resembles a structure molded in plastic. Both the wing and the outer covering (exoskeleton) of the body contain a complex material (nitrogenous polyssacharide) called chitin. The wing is stiffened by a series of hollow tubes, the "veins" (Fig. 8.21, p. 165). The whole forms a lifeless structure operated by muscles attached to its base.

The wings of bird and bat are quite otherwise (Fig. 3.1). The supporting surface of the bird wing is composed of feathers, that of a bat wing of a membrane formed of modified skin. The feathers, in the one case, and the membrane, in the other, are supported by an internal skeleton of bone, a very different material from the chitin of the insect. The skeleton of these wings forms a series of segments. The segment attached to the body is supported by a single bone (Fig. 3.1), the **humerus.** To the tree end of the humerus two bones attach, the **radius** and **ulna.** Next comes a group of little bones, the **carpals** (corresponding to man's wristbones), then the **metacarpals** (corresponding to the bones in the palm of man's hand), and finally the **phalanges** (corresponding to the bones in man's fingers). In the bat the first "finger," corresponding to the human thumb, is short and tipped with a claw, while the other four fingers have long slender metacarpals forming stiffening supports, like the ribs of an umbrella, for the wing membrane. In the bird the carpals, metacarpals, and phalanges are partly fused into an irregularly shaped bone serving to support the feathers of that part of the wing. We see, then, that the wings of insects are really very different from the wings of birds and bats. We may conclude that analogous similarities are on the whole rather superficial in nature.

Homology

In describing the skeleton of the wings of birds and bats, in the preceding paragraph, we have repeatedly referred to the skeleton of the human arm to make our meaning clear. It will already be evident, therefore, that considerable similarity exists between the skeletons of the arm of man and of the wings of bird and bat. The similarity is particularly clear in the

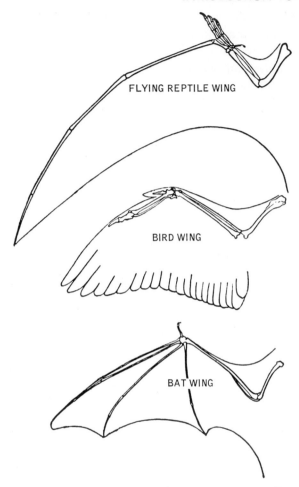

FIG. 3.1. Comparison of vertebrate wing structures. (By
permission from *The Dinosaur Book*, by Colbert, p.
100. Copyright, 1951. McGraw-Hill Book Company,
Inc.)

case of the bat. The similar segments found in arm and wings may be
listed as follows, starting at the shoulder (Fig. 3.2): (1) humerus,
(2) radius and ulna, (3) carpals, (4) metacarpals, (5) phalanges. Here
is similarity of structure not readily explained as connected with similar
function.

Fig. 3.2 presents, along with the forelimb of man, the limbs of four
mammals adapted for more or less rapid movement over the surface of
the earth. A glance at the figure suffices to reveal that dog, hog, sheep, and
horse all have their forelimb skeletons constructed of bones arranged ac-

cording to the same pattern. True, there are modifications. In the hog two of the "fingers" are much larger than the other two, whereas in the sheep only two are present, forming the support of the so-called "split hoof." The two remaining fingers are the third and fourth (in numbering, the human thumb is designated as I, the "index finger" as II, and so on). Digit III is the only one remaining intact in the horse; its enlarged fingernail forms the

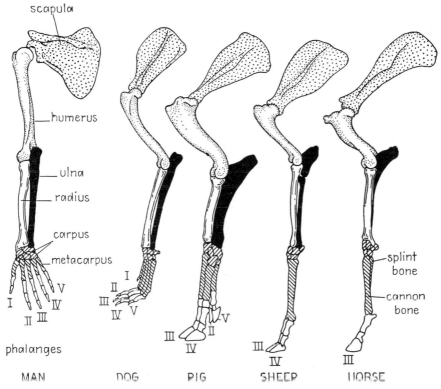

FIG. 3.2. Forelimbs of man and of several mammals variously adapted for walking and running. Roman numerals identify the five digits. (After Le Conte.)

solid hoof. In the horse the radius and ulna are fused together, and the metacarpal of digit III is greatly enlarged and elongated, forming the so-called **cannon bone.** Closely attached to the rear surface of the cannon bone are two slender bones known as the **splint bones;** they represent reduced metacarpals of digits II and IV.

Directing our attention to animals living in the water we note that whales, seals, and sea lions have their forelimbs modified into paddle-like flippers. Dissection of one of these flippers reveals that its skeleton is composed of the same five segments we have noted in the arm of man and

in the limbs of terrestrial mammals (Fig. 3.3). The segments are shortened but they are all there in the order listed above.

Thus we see that among birds and mammals limbs adapted for grasping, flying, running, and swimming are all constructed upon the same basic
pattern. They share a fundamental similarity of structure which is evidently entirely unconnected with the uses to which they are put. How can
we explain the origin of similarity of this kind, similarity which has no
relation to function—which, indeed, exists in many cases despite dissimilar functions?

One way in which we might answer this question is that of the biologist
who first called attention to the fact that a basic pattern underlies all these
forelimbs. That was Cuvier, the eminent French comparative anatomist of

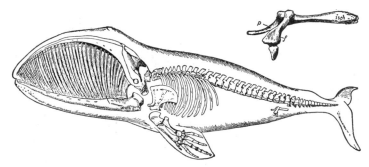

FIG. 3.3. Skeleton of a whalebone whale. The upper figure shows rudiments of the pelvic girdle and hindlimb; *p*, pubis; *isch.*, ischium; *f*, femur.
(After Romanes; from Guyer, *Animal Biology*, Harper & Brothers, 1948,
p. 123.)

the past century. Cuvier was not convinced of the truth of evolution. He
believed that each species of animal had been created separately, the idea
usually referred to as the theory of **special creation.** But if species were
separately created how could similarities between them arise? Obviously
they would be similar if they were *created* to resemble one another. More
specifically, we might assume that in shaping forelimbs the Creator used a
certain pattern; when he created the hand of man he modified that pattern
in a certain way; when he created the wing of a bat he modified the pattern in a different way; when he created legs adapted for rapid running he
modified the pattern in still a different way; and so on. According to this
theory there is no genetic relationship between man, bat, and horse; all
they have in common is that they were made by the same Creator. In
much the same way a dressmaker may use a pattern in constructing a
dress of silk and then, changing it somewhat if necessary, to construct a

housedress of cotton. The silk dress is not the "ancestor" of the cotton one, or even its "sister" or "cousin" in any literal sense. Similarly, according to the theory of special creation different species of animals are not genetically related to one another even though they may exhibit similarites of structure.

Most modern biologists do not find this explanation satisfying. For one thing, it is really not an explanation at all; it amounts to saying, "Things are this way because they are this way." Furthermore, it removes the subject from scientific inquiry. One can do no more than speculate as to *why* the Creator chose to follow one pattern in creating diverse animals rather than to use differing patterns.

Hence most modern biologists explain the origin of similarities which have no relation to similar functions in a different manner. They are convinced that the similarity exists because the animals concerned *inherited* the structure from an ancestor which they shared in common. We have seen that the vertebrate forelimbs, for example, appear to be modifications of a five-fingered **(pentadactyl)** limb having one upper-arm bone (humerus), two lower-arm bones (radius and ulna), wristbones (carpals), and metacarpals and phalanges arranged to form five fingers (Fig. 3.2). Why are such diverse limbs as those of man, bat, bird, whale, horse, and so on, all modifications of this pattern? The evolutionary explanation is that these animals all inherited the limb pattern from an ancestor which had that pentadactyl limb in more or less typical form. When the descendants of this ancestor took to life in the water, to locomotion through the air, or to running over hard ground they made over what they had in the way of limbs to serve the new functions. But despite the reconstruction necessary the indelible traces of the inherited pattern still remain. Thus, in contrast to the theory of special creation, the theory of creation by evolution maintains that different animals *are* related to each other in the sense of direct inheritance.

In our discussion we have noted two types of similarity. Similarity connected with similar functioning we have ascribed to analogy. We shall find useful a term for similarities not connected with similarities of function: the word **homology.** Two organs in different animals are analogous if they are used for the same purpose; two organs in different animals are homologous if they have the same fundamental structure, whether or not they are used for the same purpose.

These terms can be readily illustrated in connection with the forelimbs just discussed. We have seen that the wing of an insect is analogous to the wing of the bird; i.e., both wings are used for flight. The insect wing is not homologous to the bird wing, however, since the structures of the two wings differ greatly. The wing of the bird is analogous to the wing of the bat, since they are both used for flight. In this case, moreover, the two wings are also homologous, since they both have the same fundamental structure, both being modifications of the pentadactyl limb. For the same reason the leg of the horse is homologous to the wing of the bird, although the leg of the horse is not analogous to the wing of the bird, since the two limbs are used for such different functions. Thus organs in different animals may be analogous but not homologous, analogous *and* homologous, or homologous but not analogous.

According to the most generally accepted interpretation, homologous structures owe their fundamental similarities to common ancestry. They are indications, remaining in modern animals, of what the ancestors of these animals were like. In a sense, all modern animals are "made-over" animals—the made-over versions of their ancestors. And just as a made-over garment if examined closely may reveal some indications of its former state, so modern animals reveal to a discerning eye what the characteristics of their ancestors must have been. For this reason the discovery and analysis of homologous structures forms one of the most powerful tools used in tracing the evolutionary histories and relationships of animals.

In this discussion we have illustrated homology with examples in which the fundamental similarities are easily seen. In all fairness we should mention that tracing homologies is frequently difficult. For example, there is convincing evidence that the "hammer" and "anvil" (malleus and incus) of the chain of three little bones in our middle ear are homologous to two bones which formed the articulation of the lower jaw to the skull in our reptilian ancestors (quadrate and articular bones; see p. 190). In this case careful investigations of modern animals, of embryonic development and of fossil forms were all needed before the homology became evident.

Adaptive Radiation

The concept of adaptive radiation may be illustrated by the limb structure of mammals. Mammalian limbs, like those of other vertebrates aside from fishes, are modifications of the pentadactyl limb. Primitive, ancestral mammals are believed to have been short-legged, five-fingered creatures living on the ground but having limbs not strongly modified for any particular type of locomotion. Such animals are called **terrestrial** in Fig. 3.4; insect-eating (insectivorous) mammals such as the shrews form modern

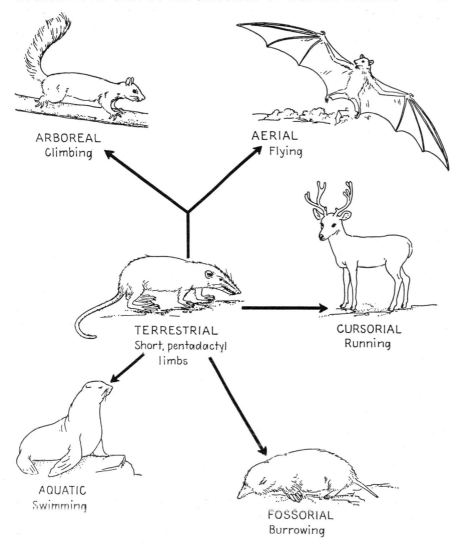

FIG. 3.4. Adaptive radiation in limb structure of mammals. (Modified after Lull, *Organic Evolution*, The Macmillan Company, 1947.)

representatives of them. Mammals possessing this primitive limb structure are placed in the center of the diagram. Of the lines radiating from this central point one leads to **arboreal,** a term for tree-dwelling forms, which in one way or another have adapted limbs for life in trees; squirrels, sloths, monkeys are among the examples. Another line leads to **aerial,** representing mammals adapted for flight. Only bats occupy the position at the terminus of this line, since they are the only truly flying mammals.

Somewhere along the line we should place such gliding forms as the wrongly named "flying" squirrel. It will be noted that the diagram represents the lines leading to arboreal and to aerial as not entirely independent. A single line is shown emerging from terrestrial and then dividing into the two branches. This arrangement was made to suggest the probability that the ancestors of flying mammals lived in trees, i.e., that life in trees preceded flight. Perhaps gliding formed the transitional type of locomotion between climbing and true flight.

Continuing around the diagram in a clockwise direction we come to the line ending in **cursorial.** This term refers to mammals, like horses and antelopes, which have developed limbs suitable to rapid movement over the surface of the ground. Part way along this line we should place animals with less strongly modified limbs, such as wolves, foxes, hyenas, lions.

A line leading downward ends with the term **fossorial,** applying to burrowing mammals. Some of these, like the moles, have modified their forelimbs into such specialized and powerful digging organs that they are poorly adapted for locomotion on the surface of the ground. Others, like pocket gophers and badgers, are expert diggers but have retained limb structures enabling them to move readily on the surface.

Finally, a line leads to the term **aquatic.** At the end of this line we find such mammals as whales and porpoises, with limbs so strongly modified for life in the water that they cannot move about on land. Part way along the line we should place seals, sea lions, and walruses, mammals with limbs strongly modified for life in the water yet retaining some ability to move about on land. Still nearer the center on this same line we should place such accomplished swimmers as otters and polar bears, mammals equally at home in water or on land.

All the mammals mentioned as belonging on one of the radiating lines have limbs more or less adapted for some particular mode of locomotion. All lines start from a common center representing the short, pentadactyl limbs of terrestrial mammals. From this center, evolutionary lines radiate out in various directions. Hence **adaptive radiation** is evolution in several directions starting from a common ancestral type.

What is the relationship of adaptive radiation to homology and analogy? All the limbs mentioned are homologous to each other, since they are all variations of the pentadactyl limb. But for the most part a given limb is only analogous to others on the same radiating branch of the diagram. Thus the leg of the antelope is analogous to the leg of the horse, since they have the same function. Furthermore, limbs of animals on one radiating branch of the diagram are not analogous to limbs of animals on other radiating branches. Thus the legs of antelopes and horses are not analogous to the legs of moles.

What does the diagram of adaptive radiation indicate as to the ancestry and evolutionary relationships of the animals included? In the first place we recall that, if the evolutionary interpretation is correct, possession of homologous structures is evidence of common ancestry. All the animals included in the diagram have modified pentadactyl limbs, hence they must be related to each other. Possession of this common limb pattern does not indicate *close* relationship, however, since the pattern is shared, not only by all mammals, but also by birds, reptiles, and amphibians—by all vertebrates except fishes, in other words.

What of the animals grouped together on one of the radiating lines? Are they related to each other? We have just noted that possession of the pentadactyl pattern indicates that they are distantly related, but does their position together on one of these lines indicate that they are closely related? The answer will be evident if we recall that the groupings on the radiating lines are based upon possession of *analogous* similarities, and that possession by two animals of analogous similarities is not in itself indicative of common ancestry.

Parallel Evolution

As examples of cursorial adaptation we have mentioned antelopes and horses. These two are placed on the same branch of the diagram because they have limbs serving the same function. But, as just mentioned, possession of analogous similarities does not indicate relationship. Both antelopes and horses are believed to have evolved from ancestors having short, pentadactyl limbs ("terrestrial," Fig. 3.4); both have achieved elongated, slender limbs adapted for rapid running. But the antelopes have developed two toes on each foot (after the manner of the sheep shown in Fig. 3.2), while the horses have developed but one toe (Fig. 3.2). Both have achieved the same goal but have done so separately and in differing ways. Thus the horse and antelope form an example of what is termed **parallel evolution**—two forms independently undergoing similar changes in the courses of their respective evolutionary histories. Another example of parallel evolution is afforded by the flipperlike forelimbs of seals and those of manatees and sea cows. Seals and sea cows are not closely related, but through parallel evolution they have developed similar forelimbs.

If forms which have independently developed similar adaptations are far removed from each other in the scale of relationship, their evolution toward the common adaptation is frequently termed **convergent evolu-**

tion, rather than parallel evolution. Thus the whales and their relatives and an extinct reptile, *Ichthyosaurus,* became extremely fishlike in general body form (Fig. 3.5). This attainment of similar form by animals as distantly related as are a reptile and a mammal forms an example of

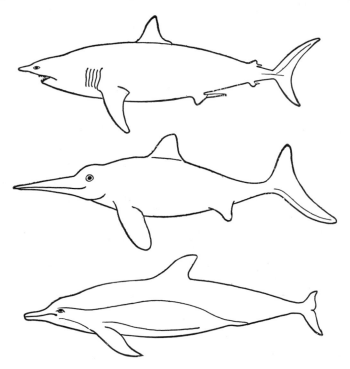

FIG. 3.5. Convergent evolution exhibited by a fish (shark), a reptile (*Ichthyosaurus*), and a mammal (dolphin), all strongly adapted for aquatic life. (From Lull, *The Ways of Life,* Harper & Brothers, 1947, p. 47.)

convergent evolution. The wings of bee, bird, and bat afford another example of convergence.

In summary we may point out that parallel and convergent evolution lead to production of analogous similarities. On the other hand, homologous similarities are indications of the persistence of ancestral structure throughout all the vicissitudes of evolutionary change.

Homology in Skull Structure

Use of forelimbs for illustrative purposes in the preceding discussion was dictated by the clarity with which the several points could be shown and by the relative ease with which the structures could be understood by readers unacquainted with details of vertebrate anatomy. Actually, however, our illustrative material might have been drawn from any portion of the body. All systems and parts of the bodies of vertebrates exhibit the fundamental similarities which we have designated as homologous. Thus, the skulls of vertebrates have received exhaustive investigation. Studies reveal that "from fish to man" a common pattern of bone arrangement is

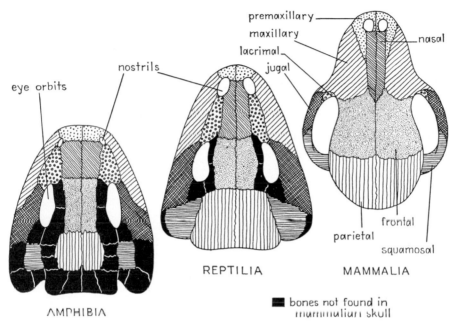

FIG. 3.6. Basic structural plan of the roof bones of the skull in amphibians, reptiles, and mammals. Bones present in mammals are named, others are shown in solid black. (After Zangerl, "The methods of comparative anatomy and its contribution to the study of evolution," *Evolution*, Vol. 2, 1948.)

found; evolution has consisted of gradual reduction in numbers of bones, through loss and through fusion of one bone with another, and of changes in function and in relative size. Fig. 3.6 illustrates the point that the skulls of amphibians, reptiles, and mammals are based upon this common pattern. The figure also demonstrates progressive reduction in number of bones and the corresponding increase in importance of such bones as the frontals and parietals as the brain underlying them increases in size. Why do skulls of such diverse animals give evidence of having been constructed on a common pattern? Because, if the evolutionary interpretation is correct, the diverse animals all inherited that pattern from a common ancestor.

We might continue to pile example upon example, but every reader who has taken a course in elementary zoology or in comparative anatomy can supply his own. Such courses are filled with examples of homology and, indeed, are constructed with the latter as a fundamental tenet. Why, for example, do students of comparative anatomy dissect the common cat? Not because they are particularly interested in cats as cats, but because the anatomy of the cat is to a considerable extent typical of the anatomies of all mammals, including man. By study of one mammal the student can learn much about all mammals, because of the fundamental similarities, homologies, found everywhere in mammalian structure.

Homology in Brain Structure

Although we have stated that homology characterizes all bodily systems, our examples thus far have been confined to the skeletal system. Fig. 3.7

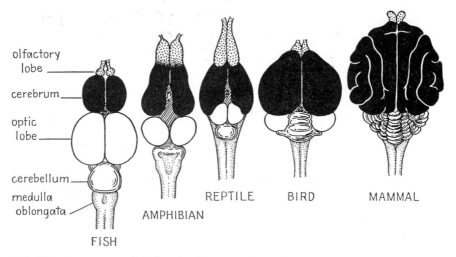

FIG. 3.7.   Comparison of the brains of a series of vertebrates. Dorsal view. (After Guyer, *Animal Biology*, Harper & Brothers, 1948.)

illustrates the point that the "soft parts" of the body present common patterning as well as do the "hard parts." It will be evident from the figure that brains of vertebrates, ranging from fishes to mammals, are constructed of similar series of parts: **olfactory lobes, cerebral hemispheres, optic lobes, cerebellum, medulla,** and other less prominent divisions and subdivisions. As we progress through the series some lobes become more prominent than others. In particular the cerebral hemispheres, much smaller than the optic lobes in fishes (Fig. 3.7), become in mammals the dominant portion of the brain, hiding the remains of the optic lobes beneath them so that the latter are not visible in the view of the mammalian brain shown in the figure. Despite the differences connected with differing functions, however, the common pattern of brain structure is clearly evident. The reader can now readily form his own conclusion as to the reason for this fact.

Homology in Invertebrates

Homology is by no means the exclusive attribute of vertebrates. Our concentration of attention upon vertebrates has been due to the fact that the structure of vertebrates is better known to the average reader than is the structure of invertebrates. The latter, however, also show common patterns of structure upon which are superimposed modifications connected with differing functions. One of the most instructive examples of this phenomenon is derived from the mouth parts of insects. This example gains added interest from the fact that it was known to Darwin and cited in his *Origin of Species*.

Insects considered most primitive by entomologists have mouth parts adapted for cutting and shredding plant tissues. The common grasshopper is a typical example (Fig. 3.8). Its mouth is provided with a pair of **mandibles** which act like jaws in cutting and biting. They move in a horizontal plane, in contrast to the vertical movement of the lower jaw of vertebrates. In the mouth there is a tonguelike structure called the **hypopharynx.** Accessory to the mandibles are two pairs of mouth parts unlike anything possessed by vertebrates. These are called, respectively, the **1st** and **2nd maxillae;** they aid in the process of conveying food into the mouth. They are provided with short, "feeler"-like processes called **palps.** In the grasshopper the pair of 2nd maxillae enter into the formation of a **labium** or "lower lip." There is present also a **labrum** or "upper lip."

Starting with the cutting or mandibulate pattern of mouth parts just described we can trace an adaptive radiation comparable to the one illustrated by vertebrate forelimbs. For example, the honeybee has adapted the mouth parts for its particular means of food gathering (Fig. 3.8). The mandibles continue to function as jaws but are used principally, not for cutting food, but for "working" the beeswax until it is pliable and in condition to be utilized in construction of honeycomb. Food consists of the nectar of flowers drawn up into the mouth through a pumplike arrangement consisting of a tube with a plunger within. The tube is not a solid structure

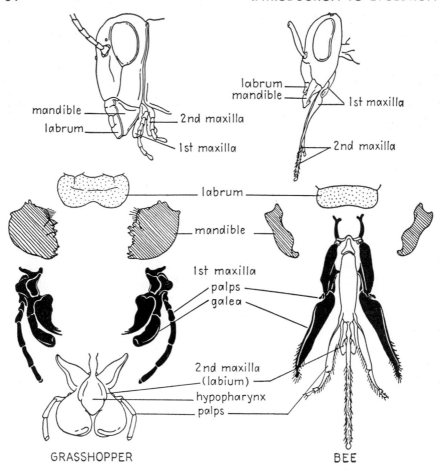

FIG. 3.8. Mouth parts of grasshopper and honeybee. Upper sketches show mouth parts in place in the head, lateral view. Lower sketches show mouth parts removed, front view.

but is improvised by bringing together the pair of 1st maxillae and the labial palps. The plunger within the tube is a tonguelike structure formed from a portion of the labium. A muscular sac at the upper end of the tube acts in sucking up liquids much as does the rubber bulb of a medicine dropper (pipette).

Butterflies and moths also have a tube through which nectar from flowers is drawn into the mouth (Fig. 3.9). As in bees, suction is produced by a muscular sac connected to the tube; there is, however, no plunger (tongue) in the tube. In many butterflies and moths the tube is long and slender and when not in use is coiled like a tiny watchspring under the animal's head. This slender tube is composed of the pair of 1st maxillae

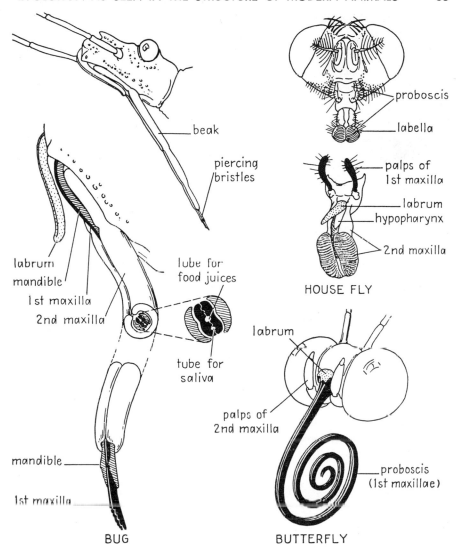

beak

piercing
bristles

labrum
mandible
1st maxilla
2nd maxilla

tube for
food juices

tube for
saliva

mandible

1st maxilla

BUG

proboscis

labella

palps of
1st maxilla

labrum
hypopharynx

2nd maxilla

HOUSE FLY

labrum

palps of
2nd maxilla

proboscis
(1st maxillae)

BUTTERFLY

FIG. 3.9. Mouth parts of bug, house fly, and butterfly. Upper drawing of the bug shows the beak attached to the head, with only the tips of the piercing bristles showing. Lower drawing shows a portion of the beak cut away to reveal the cross section, with an enlarged cross section of the bristles at the right. Mandibular bristles shown in diagonal shading; 1st maxillary bristles, solid black; 2nd maxillae, forming the beak, unshaded.

elongated, hollowed out on their adjoining surfaces, and held together by interlocking grooves and ridges. Mandibles and 2nd maxillae are rudimentary, except in one family of moths which have retained biting mouth parts, thereby adding evidence in support of the view that sucking mouth parts, possessed by other moths, are in reality "made over" from the biting and cutting type.

A third modification is possessed by the true bugs (Order Hemiptera). They have a proboscis somewhat like a hypodermic needle which they thrust through the skin of plant or animal to withdraw underlying juices (Fig. 3.9). Though the most notorious member of the group is the bed-bug, by far the larger number of true bugs suck the juices of plants and of other insects rather than the blood of vertebrate animals. Unlike a hypo-dermic needle the proboscis is not thrust through the skin by sheer force applied to it. The creature wielding it is too tiny for that. Rather, a hole is drilled for its insertion, the drilling being done by two pairs of sharp, piercing bristles (Fig. 3.9). The innermost pair of these is formed from the 1st maxillae, hollowed out on their adjoining faces to form the walls of two tubes. Plant and animal juices are sucked through the larger, dorsal tube; saliva may be forced outward into the puncture wound through the smaller, ventral tube (Fig. 3.9). On either side of the 1st maxillae are the mandibles, also modified to form piercing bristles. In drilling the hole the four bristles slide up and down independently, the mandibular pair be-ing the more active in the process. This hypodermic arrangement is en-cased for a portion of its length in a rostrum or beak formed of the 2nd maxillae (Fig. 3.9).

The two-winged flies, the housefly being the most familiar example, have a proboscis formed from labrum, hypopharynx, and labium (2nd maxillae) (Fig. 3.9). In some flies the proboscis terminates in a pair of broad, soft pads (labella) pierced by many pores which function in "sponging up" liquids; in biting flies the proboscis is modified for piercing.

We see, then, how a set of "standard parts" (labrum, mandibles, hypo-pharynx, 1st and 2nd maxillae) have been modified to serve such diverse food habits as cutting and shredding plant tissues, sucking nectar from flowers (by two different types of mechanism), piercing the skin to suck juices of plants or animals, and gathering liquid from the surfaces of food particles. Why are such diverse mechanisms based upon the same under-lying pattern? Evidently the basic pattern of mouth-part structure was in-herited from an ancestor shared by all these modern insects. As noted above, the mandibulate or cutting mouth parts represent the type from which all the others are believed to have arisen through adaptive radiation.

Serial Homology

Thus far we have spoken of the homology of an organ in one animal with an organ in another animal. We have said, for example, that the wing of the bird is homologous to the arm of man. There is another type of homology in which two or more structures *in one individual* are compared. Fundamental similarity of structure between one part of an animal and another part of the same animal is called **serial homology.**

An example of serial homology is seen in the arm and leg of man. The segment of each which is attached to the trunk has a single bone as skeletal support; in the arm this bone is called the humerus (Fig. 3.2); in the leg it is called the **femur.** In the succeeding segment of the arm and leg there are two bones, called radius and ulna in the arm, **tibia** and **fibula** in the leg. Then come a group of wrist and ankle bones, respectively, called carpals in the arm, **tarsals** in the leg. Next are the bones of the palm of the hand and the sole of the foot, metacarpals and **metatarsals,** respectively. Finally, the bones of fingers and toes are called **phalanges** in both cases. Evidently, then, our fore and hind limbs are modifications of the same fundamental pattern, modified for grasping and handling in the one case, for locomotion in upright posture in the other.

Much more elaborate examples of serial homology are afforded by the jointed appendages of invertebrates. Examination of the numerous appendages of a lobster or crayfish reveals that those in different parts of the body have much resemblance despite the fact that they are modified for a variety of functions (Figs. 3.10 and 3.11). The most conspicuous pair are the "pinchers" or **chelae,** used by the animal in grasping food and in fighting. Just behind the chelae are the four pairs of **walking legs,** used in slow locomotion along the bottom of the stream in which the animal lives. Behind the walking legs and attached to the abdomen are several pairs of **swimmerets** (XIV and XVI in Fig. 3.11; not shown in Fig. 3.10). These are small appendages; their name gives a false impression of their importance in swimming. In females masses of eggs become attached to them, hanging like tiny bunches of grapes while embryonic development progresses. In males the first pair of swimmerets (XIV in Fig. 3.11) is modified for the transference of sperm cells to the female. A broadly expanded, somewhat paddlelike structure will be noted at the end of the abdomen (Fig. 3.10). When the creature wishes to move rapidly it flexes or bends its abdomen powerfully, this terminal structure offering resistance to the water much as does an oar. As a result the body shoots backward with great speed. The terminal structure employed in this maneuver is composed of a flap (telson, Fig. 3.10) attached to the last segment of the body, augmented by flattened appendages on either side, the **uropods** (Fig. 3.10; XIX in Fig. 3.11).

Anterior to the chelae is found a succession of appendages modified for a variety of functions. Some of them, **maxillipeds** and **maxillae** (VII and

V, Fig. 3.11), aid in grasping food and conveying it to the mouth. One
pair, the **mandibles** (III, Fig. 3.11), crush the food. Two other pairs, the
antennae and **antennules** (II and I, Fig. 3.11), form sensory "feelers."

The great variety of functions served by the appendages of the crayfish
will be evident from the foregoing summary. Careful study reveals that

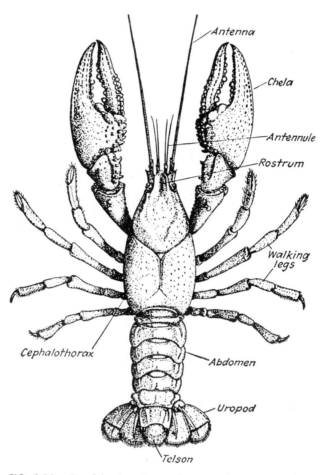

FIG. 3.10. Crayfish, dorsal view. (From Hagen, *Memoirs Museum of Comparative Zoology*, Harvard University.)

they are all modifications of a single pattern. We have spoken of a five-
fingered (pentadactyl) pattern underlying vertebrate forelimb structure;
similarly we might say that a two-fingered pattern underlies the structure
of crayfish appendages, as well as of those of all other members of Phylum
Arthropoda: crustaceans, spiders, insects, and their kin. This two-fingered
structure is called a **biramous appendage** and is well illustrated by the

typical swimmeret of a crayfish (XVI, Fig. 3.11). The basal portion of
the appendage, **protopodite,** is unpaired but may consist of more than one
segment. Attached to the protopodite are the two "fingers," each composed of several or many segments. The "finger" nearest the midline of
the body is called the **endopodite,** the lateral one the **exopodite.** The labeling of Fig. 3.11 indicates clearly how, starting from this primitive arrangement, appendages adapted for the wide variety of functions have
been derived by modification, and in some cases loss, of one or another of
the original parts.

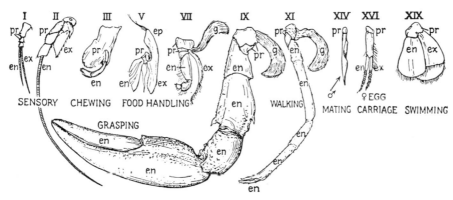

FIG. 3.11. Crayfish appendages; *pr,* protopodite; *en,* endopodite; *ex,* exopodite; *ep,*
epipodite; *g,* gill. (By permission from *General Zoology,* by Storer, p. 442. Copyright,
1943. McGraw-Hill Book Company, Inc.)

What are the implications of serial homology for evolution? It will be
noted that arthropods, such as the crayfish, have bodies composed of a
series of **metameres** or somites (this segmentation is particularly clear in
the abdomen of the crayfish, Fig. 3.10). Each metamere is provided with
a pair of jointed appendages, modifications of the biramous pattern. It
would seem that the common ancestor from which these arthropods inherited the arrangement described must have had a body composed of a
series of metameres, somewhat like the earthworm's, and had each metamere equipped with a pair of biramous appendages in typical form. In
descendants from this ancestor some of the metameres became fused together, to form a **cephalothorax** as in the crayfish (Fig. 3.10), or to form
separate head and thorax as in an insect. At the same time appendages
attached to different metameres of the body became modified to serve a
variety of functions. Thus, like homology in general, serial homology finds
its most reasonable explanation in a theory of descent with modification,
i.e., of evolution.

We are now in position to understand more concerning the significance of the arrangement of insect mouth parts discussed previously (pp. 33–36). It will now be evident, for example, that the mandibles and 1st and 2nd maxillae are paired appendages, modified biramous appendages. In the grasshopper one pair, provided by one metamere of the body, have become cutting mandibles. Since a pair of appendages consists of a right-hand appendage and a left-hand one, we can understand why it is that an insect has a right mandible or jaw and a left mandible instead of having an upper jaw and a lower jaw as we have.

A peculiarity of the sucking tubes or proboscises of such insects as bees and butterflies may have seemed odd to the reader—the fact that they are not tubes having solid and continuous walls but are composed of right and left components held together firmly enough to form a more or less watertight tube. The reason for this type of construction is evident if we conceive that ancestral insects were under the necessity of utilizing the raw materials at hand in evolving these tubes. The raw materials consisted of paired, biramous appendages which had already been modified as mouth parts for use with a diet of solid food. These paired elements then received additional modification to form tubes through which liquids could be drawn into the mouth. The resulting "peculiar" tube constructions are thus readily understandable upon a basis of descent with modification, whereas it would be difficult to form a rational explanation for them upon a basis of special creation.

Vestiges

Vestigial or rudimentary organs are parts of the body that are relatively small in size and have little, if any, ascertainable function. In every case of importance to the study of evolution they appear to represent useless remnants of structures or organs which are large and functional in some other animals.

The most familiar rudimentary organ in man is the **vermiform appendix** (Fig. 3.12). "Vermiform" suggests its wormlike appearance. The appendix attaches to a short section of the large intestine called the **caecum,** and the latter is located at the point where the large intestine is joined by the small intestine. The caecum is a short pouch, ending blindly except for the small opening into its extension, the appendix.

If we study the digestive systems of lower animals we discover that carnivorous (flesh-eating) mammals have the caecum reduced to a short, blind pouch much like our own. Cats, for example, have a short caecum,

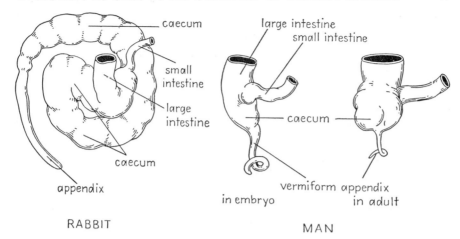

FIG. 3.12. Caecum and vermiform appendix in rabbit, in human embryo, and in adult man. (Rabbit, after Bensley, *Practical Anatomy of the Rabbit*, 7th ed., The Blakiston Company, 1945. Man, after Walter, *Biology of the Vertebrates*, The Macmillan Company, 1939.)

with no appendix at all. On the other hand, if we study herbivorous (plant-eating) mammals having simple stomachs more or less like ours we find that the caecum is a large pouch, in some cases as capacious as all the rest of the digestive system put together. In some herbivorous mammals it is broad throughout its length. In others it tapers to a point at its free end. The combined length of caecum and appendix in a rabbit, for example, is about 18 inches (Fig. 3.12). For the first 12 inches or so it is a broad, thin-walled pouch containing a spiral fold or valve which increases the internal surface. The terminal 5 or 6 inches of it has thicker walls and no spiral valve and corresponds to our appendix.

The large caeca of herbivorous mammals form storage compartments in which partly digested food remains while bacterial action takes place upon it. One of the most abundant constituents of plant tissue is cellulose. The digestive fluids of mammals contain no enzymes that digest this substance. For this reason man, for example, could derive no appreciable nourishment from a diet of paper, a product consisting largely of cellulose. Certain bacteria, however, can break down cellulose into chemical compounds which the body can utilize. In the caeca of herbivorous mammals such bacteria have time to act on the cellulose, thereby retrieving for the animal a portion of its diet which would otherwise be wasted. Accordingly the caecum is a valuable organ for herbivorous animals lacking the complicated stomachs of ruminants (e.g., cattle).

How do we happen to have a caecum and associated appendix? Our diet consists of both plant and animal material, but in the preparation of plant material for human consumption we eliminate most of the cellulose (in the "woody" portions). We do not use our caecum and appendix as a container for food undergoing bacterial action. Then why do we have them? The most reasonable explanation seems to be that we inherited them from some remote ancestor having a diet which necessitated such adjuncts to the digestive system. When the descendants of this ancestor eventually changed their food habits the caecum and appendix, no longer useful, decreased in size until they became mere remnants of the functional organs they once had been.

It is difficult to explain the presence of useless vestiges upon a basis of special creation without imputing to the Creator some lack of skill in planning or construction. Accordingly, opponents of the idea of evolution

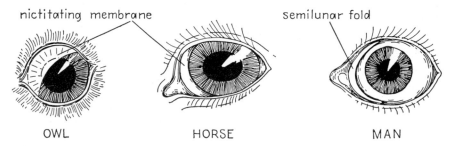

nictitating membrane   semilunar fold

OWL   HORSE   MAN

FIG. 3.13. Nictitating membrane (third eyelid) of owl and horse, and vestigial semilunar fold of man. (Mainly after Romanes, *Darwin and After Darwin*, 3rd. ed., Open Court Publishing Company, 1901.)

commonly maintain that organs like the appendix are not useless at all, that they have functions which we have never been able to discover. Clearly, "the burden of proof lies with the affirmative" in the matter of proving the usefulness of vestiges for which no functions have ever been discovered. Many readers can testify from personal experience that if the appendix has a function at all it is so unimportant that the advantages of having the organ removed far outweigh the disadvantages.

Other vestiges are found in the human body. For example, in the inner angle of each of our eyes there is a little fold of flesh called the **semilunar fold** (plica semilunaris) (Fig. 3.13). This corresponds to a structure which in many lower animals is a movable third eyelid, the **nictitating membrane,** lying under the other eyelids and sweeping across the eye from the inner angle outward. In many animals, as for example owls, the nictitating membrane is transparent, affording a means of cleaning and lubricating the surface of the eyeball without obstructing vision in the process, even for the fraction of a second necessary to wink the other two eyelids. In horses the membrane is well developed, containing cartilage. When the eye is strongly retracted the membrane extends across it for about an inch. The membrane is variably developed in other mammals and in lower vertebrates.

The tails commonly possessed by both wild and domestic mammals are familiar to everyone. A chain of vertebrae continuous with those comprising the remainder of the vertebral column forms the skeletal axis of the tail, attaching just behind the pelvic girdle (the bones to which the hind limbs articulate). In man a much reduced string of vertebrae, partly fused together, arises at this same point and curves forward, instead of extending out into an external tail. This structure, called the **coccyx**, is clearly homologous to a group of reduced tail vertebrae (Fig. 11.5, p. 230).

Everyone who has watched a horse on days when biting flies were bothersome is familiar with the way in which this animal can twitch certain areas of the skin. All observers of horses will recall also the manner in which the animal can move and turn its ears the better to hear sounds coming from different directions. Although we do not have these capabilities we commonly have rudimentary muscles connected with skin and ears. Generally these organs do not function, though some individuals can demonstrate ability to move the scalp or "wiggle" the ears.

Although the list of vestigial organs in man is long the above sample will suffice. We must not create the impression, however, that vestiges are the exclusive attribute of man. It may safely be stated that every specialized animal retains some rudimentary structures in its anatomy. Snakes, for example, are noted for lack of limbs, yet a few, such as boas and pythons, possess in appropriate position in the body tiny bones which seem to represent the last vestiges of pelvic girdle and hind limbs. Similarly, whales have no hind limbs, yet in the position where hind limbs if present would occur small bones are found which seem to represent rudiments of pelvic girdle and hind limbs (Fig. 3.3).

Vestigial structures in the leg of the horse have already been mentioned (p. 23): the splint bones representing the rudimentary metacarpals of digits II and IV. These vestiges are slender bones of variable development partly fused to the cannon bone (metacarpal of digit III) supporting the hoof. The lower end of each splint bone is bluntly pointed and without connection to other bones.

Birds are characteristically flying animals, yet a few are flightless. One of these, the kiwi of New Zealand, possesses useless vestiges of wings supported by tiny replicas of the usual bones of a bird wing (Fig. 3.1). Feathers covering the body conceal these rudimentary wings from view.

How are we to explain the presence of useless structures such as those described above? Are we to suppose that creatures were "deliberately" made with structures which would never be of use to them? Or does it seem more reasonable to conclude that the kiwi, for example, inherited its wings from an ancestor which was a flying bird and hence had use for wings?

As already mentioned, occasional biologists doubt that structures usually classed as rudimentary are in fact without function. It has been maintained, for example, that the small bones we have spoken of as rudimentary hind limbs in whales are not such at all, but are bones having the function of stiffening the walls of the anus, the posterior opening of the digestive tract. Most students of anatomy are not in accord with this view. Occasional mistakes may be made in labeling small organs as rudimentary, but it seems entirely unlikely that the percentage of error is high. To most biologists, therefore, the presence of small organs that seem to have no function in themselves but correspond to functional organs possessed by other animals indicates inheritance from common ancestry. Descendants having use for the organ in question retained it as a functional organ; in descendants having no use for it the organ became reduced in size. The culmination of this trend would be complete loss of the organ. Apparently some extinct flightless birds, such as the giant moa of Madagascar, attained this extreme. Possession of rudimentary organs may be regarded as a way station on the road to elimination of those organs.

References and Suggested Readings

Darwin, C. *The Origin of Species by Means of Natural Selection.* 1859. Modern Library series, Random House, New York; or Mentor Book MT294, New American Library, New York. (Note particularly Chap. 14.)

Dewar, D. *Difficulties of the Evolution Theory.* London: E. Arnold & Co., 1931.

Guyer, M. F. *Animal Biology,* 4th ed. New York: Harper & Brothers, 1948.

Lull, R. S. *Organic Evolution,* rev. ed. New York: The Macmillan Company, 1947.

Romer, A. S. *The Vertebrate Body,* 2nd ed. Philadelphia: W. B. Saunders Co., 1955.

Snodgrass, R. E. *Principles of Insect Morphology.* New York: McGraw-Hill Book Company, Inc., 1935.

Walter, H. E., and L. P. Sayles. *Biology of the Vertebrates,* 3rd ed. New York: The Macmillan Company, 1949.

Zangerl, R. "The methods of comparative anatomy and its contribution to the study of evolution," *Evolution,* 2 (1948), 351–374.

CHAPTER 4

EVOLUTION AS SEEN IN EMBRYONIC DEVELOPMENT

Homology in Embryos

In the preceding chapter we saw that similarities of adult structure not connected with similar habits and adaptations are most reasonably explained as the result of inheritance from common ancestry. In the present chapter we shall consider similarities existing among embryos.

It is a striking fact that there are not only many evidences of common patterns in the adult structures of diverse animals but evidences of common patterns in embryonic development. Indeed, the two phenomena are related, since embryonic development is the process by which adult structure is attained. We might anticipate, therefore, that similar final results would usually be achieved by similar developmental processes.

Some of these embryonic similarities are displayed in Fig. 4.1, which represents six stages in the embryonic development of six different animals, ranging from fish to man. Each sequence begins with a single cell, the **fertilized egg** or **ovum,** shown at the bottom of each of the six vertical columns. To facilitate comparison the ova are all drawn about the same size, although there are actually large size differences. Thus, the human ovum measures only about 1/250 of an inch in diameter while the ovum of a shark measures in the neighborhood of 2 inches. Each is a single cell, however, containing genetic contributions from both mother and father. Size differences depend mainly upon the amounts of food material—yolk—present. In the fish egg enough yolk must be provided to nourish the embryo until it is sufficiently developed to begin actively secur-

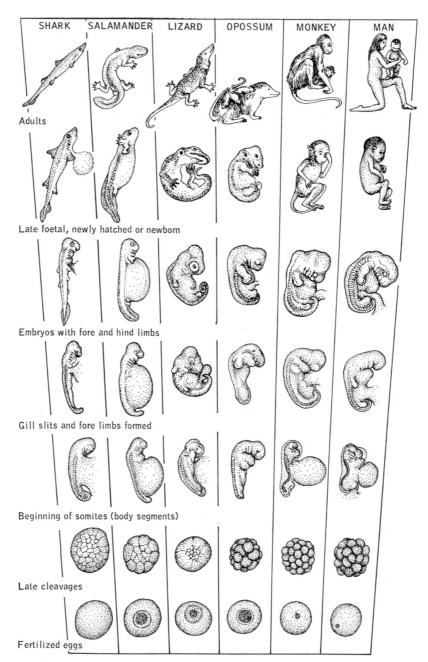

| SHARK | SALAMANDER | LIZARD | OPOSSUM | MONKEY | MAN |

Adults

Late foetal, newly hatched or newborn

Embryos with fore and hind limbs

Gill slits and fore limbs formed

Beginning of somites (body segments)

Late cleavages

Fertilized eggs

FIG. 4.1. Comparative embryology from fish to man. (Modified from Gregory and Roigneau, *Introduction to Human Anatomy*, 1934, p. 42, American Museum of Natural History.)

ing food for itself, whereas the mammalian embryo is nourished from the blood of the mother almost from the outset of development.

Inspection of Fig. 4.1 reveals the great similarity of the early embryonic stages of all the forms shown. The embryos in the second and third horizontal rows, from the bottom, are so similar that only an expert could tell them apart if they were misplaced. By the stage represented in the fourth row, the fish and salamander have acquired more identifying characteristics, but even in the stage represented by the fifth row the similarities of embryonic lizard, opossum, monkey, and man are most striking. We see, then, that the embryos of these diverse animals all follow a common pattern at first but progressively diverge from this pattern as they approach their respective adult morphologies. As von Baer, pioneer embryologist of the last century, expressed it, "During its development an animal departs more and more from the form of other animals" (as translated in de Beer, 1958).

Why do we find evidence of common pattern in embryonic development? This is the same question asked in the preceding chapter about common pattern in adult structure, and the answer is similar. The common pattern of embryonic development seems most reasonably explained as having been inherited from an ancestor common to all the animals possessing the similar embryonic developments. Explanations not involving common ancestry may take two forms. It may be maintained that the Creator created each species separately but saw fit to confer on different species similar processes of embryonic development. Or it may be maintained that mechanical and physiological necessities operating in development bring about the similarities—that there is, in effect, no other road which an ovum could follow in its development to the adult state. An apparent instance of this is discussed below (p. 68). Similar physical forces undoubtedly have similar effects in producing basic similarities among embryos. Yet detailed similarities in development, like those to be considered presently, seem not to be completely explained as the result of such similar forces.

Homology in Early Development

The earliest stages of embryonic development, even in much more diverse forms than those included in Fig. 4.1, which after all are all vertebrates, are remarkably similar—so much so that it is possible to design a "typical" diagram of early stages in development. Fig. 4.2 shows typical development of an ovum containing little yolk, as for example starfish

and sea urchin eggs among invertebrates, or amphioxus eggs in Phylum
Chordata. In its essential features, however, the sequence of changes
shown characterizes all animals. Fig. 4.2 is related to Fig. 4.1 in the following manner. Stage *a* of Fig. 4.2 represents a fertilized ovum like those
shown in the bottom row of Fig. 4.1. Stages *f* and *g* represent the stage
shown in the second horizontal row of Fig. 4.1. Thus stages *b* through *e*

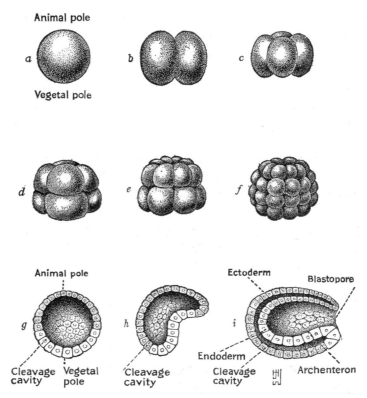

FIG. 4.2. Typical early embryonic development; *g, h,* and *i* are shown
cut in half. (From Guyer, *Animal Biology,* Harper & Brothers, 1948,
p. 476.)

stand in between the bottom and the second rows of Fig. 4.1, and stages
h and *i* are slightly later stages than the stage shown in the second row of
that figure.

Fig. 4.2 demonstrates that the fertilized ovum undergoes a series of cell
divisions. The original single cell divides into two (*b*), then each of these
two divides into two in turn, the result being a four-celled stage(*c*). The
cells continue to divide, so that we have successively an eight-celled stage
(*d*), a sixteen-celled stage (*e*), a thirty-two-celled stage, and so on. As

the process continues there comes into existence a ball of cells, more or less hollow in the center, called a **blastula;** g in Fig. 4.2 represents a blastula sliced open to reveal its internal cavity, the **cleavage cavity.** Essentially, a blastula is an embryo composed of a single layer of cells, as shown in the figure. This one-layered stage then proceeds to convert itself into a two-layered embryo, the **gastrula** (i). Gastrula formation occurs in a variety of ways, various expedients being resorted to if the presence of yolk impedes the process. Fig. 4.2 shows the relatively simple process possible when the cleavage cavity is not obstructed with yolk. One side of the blastula swings inward (h); this in-bending, accompanied by continued cell division, suffices to produce the condition shown at i.

With attainment of the gastrula stage an embryo shows forecasts of things to come. The cells remaining on the outside constitute a layer called the **ectoderm,** obviously in position to form the outer surface of the body. The cells which fold inward form a layer called the **endoderm** lining the newly formed cavity, the **archenteron.** The latter is the beginning of the digestive tract. The archenteron has but one opening to the exterior, the **blastopore.** In many invertebrates the blastopore becomes the mouth, at or near the anterior end of the body. In vertebrates, on the other hand, the region of the blastopore becomes the posterior or tail end of the body, though usually the blastopore itself does not remain as the posterior opening of the digestive tract, the anus.

Almost at once a third layer, the **mesoderm,** forms; although this is not shown in Fig. 4.2, it can be visualized as located in the remnant of the cleavage cavity, between the ectoderm on the outside and the endoderm on the inside.

The ectoderm gives rise to the external surface of the body, including such things as skin, scales, feathers, hair, and to the nervous system and the sensory membranes of the sense organs. The endoderm lines the digestive tract and gives rise to glands associated with digestion, such as liver and pancreas. The lungs of land-dwelling vertebrates also arise from the endoderm. The mesoderm forms almost everything else: muscles, bones, kidneys, connective tissue, and so on.

The pattern of development illustrated above may be said to consist of the following sequence: (1) single cell; (2) successive cell divisions to form clusters of two, four, eight, sixteen, and so on, cells; (3) a one-layered stage; (4) a two-layered stage; (5) a three-layered stage. The uniformity of occurrence of this pattern of development throughout the animal kingdom, from worms to man, is remarkable.

At least two factors must be operative in production of this uniformity.

In the first place, the number of ways in which an organism consisting of multitudes of cells arranged in layers can arise from a single cell must be limited. In part, then, the uniformity is imposed by those mechanical and physiological necessities mentioned previously (p. 47). Such necessities would operate to produce similarities in the broad outlines of development. Similarities in details of development, on the other hand, are more likely to have resulted from a second factor: inheritance from common ancestry.

Theory of Recapitulation or Paleogenesis

In its modern form this is the theory that the embryos of animals repeat some of the developmental stages passed through by embryos of their ancestors.

The recapitulation theory has had a stormy history. The fundamental idea stems from von Baer, whom we have already quoted. His theory had substantially the form we have stated: "The young stages in the development of an animal are not like the adult stages of other animals lower down on the scale, but are like the young stages of those animals" (de Beer's translation, 1958). Subsequently Ernst Haeckel formulated the theory to mean that the embryos of higher animals repeat the *adult* stages of their ancestors. This form of the theory was called the Biogenetic Law, and was summarized by the statement: "Ontogeny recapitulates phylogeny." Ontogeny is the life history of the individual, starting with the ovum; phylogeny, as the term was used by Haeckel, is the series of adult ancestors of the individual in question. Haeckel maintained that in some way the adult condition of an ancestor is pushed back into embryonic development so that embryos of descendants pass through that ancestral adult stage. We shall see presently, for example, that in one stage the human embryo strongly resembles a fish embryo. Haeckel would not have been satisfied with such a statement; he would have insisted that the human embryo at that stage resembles an adult fish. The recapitulation theory was a great stimulus to research in embryology, but as investigation led to more complete knowledge of the subject it became evident that Haeckel was wrong and that von Baer had been right. Embryos of higher animals repeat embryonic stages of their ancestors, not adult stages. The pros and cons of this intellectual conflict are ably set forth in de Beer's *Embryos and Ancestors* (1958).

Insofar as the recapitulation theory forms valid interpretation of facts, we may look to embryonic development for clues as to the course taken by evolutionary development. We may expect, for example, that two animals derived from a common ancestor will both retain some of the features of embryonic development occurring in the life history (ontogeny) of that ancestor. Furthermore, as noted in our discussion of Fig. 4.1, the more closely related two animals are, the greater will be the proportion of their ontogenies exhibiting similarities. Thus the human embryo and the monkey embryo are similar throughout much more of their development than are the human embryo and the fish embryo (Fig. 4.1).

De Beer (1958) states: "Similarity in ontogeny between any animals is a proof of their affinity, and no evidence as to the adult structure of the ancestor." The latter portion of the statement is intended as rebuttal of Haeckel's version of the recapitulation theory but is a bit extreme since after all embryos frequently do present some indication of the nature of adult structure toward which they are developing. We can learn from embryos something of the nature of the common ancestor in question. This matter will become clearer as we consider some examples from human embryonic development.

Recapitulation in Human Embryos

We turn now to some of the salient features of human embryonic development, emphasizing those which give evidence of recapitulation.

Each human being begins life as a single cell, the fertilized ovum. This was formed by the union of a sperm cell produced by the father with an ovum produced by the mother. The size of the fertilized ovum is near the limit of vision with the unaided eye. The first cell divisions with which the fertilized ovum begins its development are much like those diagramed in Fig. 4.2. As a result of repeated cell division a ball of cells is formed. This is similar to the blastula (Fig. 4.2) except that it is at first not hollow. As shown in Fig. 4.3 a cavity soon forms, following which an outer layer, the **trophoblast,** and an **inner cell mass** can be distinguished. At about this stage the embryo "burrows" into (really digests its way into) the wall of the uterus of its mother, where it comes in close contact with the latter's blood. This blood supplies the embryo with food and oxygen and removes waste products. The trophoblast forms the means of contact between the embryo and the maternal blood stream and contributes to the formation of the embryonic membrane known as the **chorion.** The embryo itself develops in the inner cell mass.

The inner cell mass soon becomes differentiated by the formation of two cavities separated by a double layer of cells (Fig. 4.3C). The upper cav-

ity is called the **amnion,** the lower one the **yolk sac,** and the double layer
separating them is referred to as the **embryonic disc.** The embryo itself
forms from this embryonic disc, the two layers of which are the ectoderm
and the endoderm. Hence this two-layered stage of the human embryo corresponds to the gastrula stage of typical development (Fig. 4.2), although
it differs from the typical form in appearance and in method of formation.

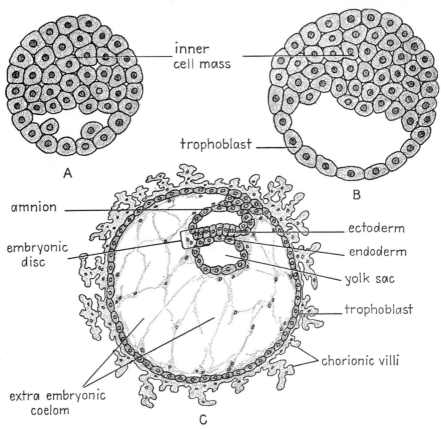

FIG. 4.3. Human embryonic development during the first week following fertilization.
(C, after Patten, *Human Embryology,* The Blakiston Company, 1946.)

There is interest in the fact that gastrulation and mesoderm formation in
the human embryo, as in the embryos of other mammals, are more like
these processes in large-yolked eggs (reptiles, birds) than they are like the
processes in small-yolked ones (e.g., Fig. 4.2). This is true despite the
absence of yolk. Why? (See discussion of the yolk sac, pp. 168–169.)

During the first few days the embryo grows with great rapidity (Fig.
4.4). In the figure most of the trophoblast has been removed, only the

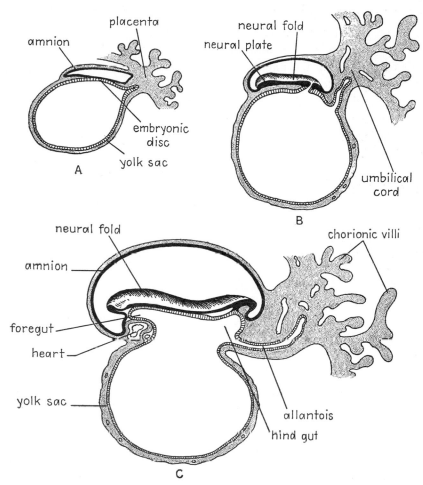

FIG. 4.4. Human embryonic development during the third week. Longitudinal sections through the embryo and membranes. Only half of the embryo is shown. Ectoderm indicated with solid black, endoderm with cross lines, mesoderm with fine dots. (After Arey, *Developmental Anatomy*, W. B. Saunders Co., 1947.)

portion, the **placenta,** most directly connecting the embryo to the wall of the uterus being shown. The embryonic disc becomes elongated, and the cavities above and below it become enlarged. Almost immediately the embryonic disc forms the beginning of the central nervous system. Two parallel **neural folds** are thrust up into the overlying amniotic cavity (Fig. 4.4 and Fig. 4.5A and B). If we think of the neural plate (that portion of the embryonic disc which does this) as a flat plain, the neural folds are like two parallel mountain ranges elevated above the surrounding country. If, now, we can imagine such mountain ranges as growing higher and higher, and then bending toward each other until their summits touch and fuse together, we have a metaphor for the process by which the neural folds form into a **neural tube.** As shown in Fig. 4.5C, fusion of the folds occurs first in the middle of the "back" of the embryo, progressing from that point toward the head or anterior end and toward the tail or posterior end (Fig. 4.5D) as though being closed by zippers. The neural tube is wider at the anterior end than it is in other regions of the body; this anterior portion will form the **brain,** the more posterior portions the **spinal cord.**

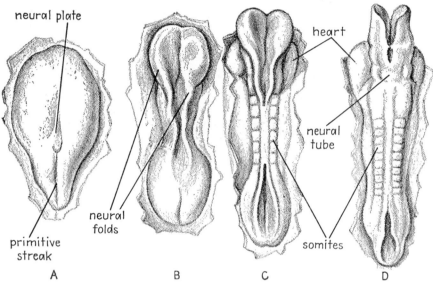

FIG. 4.5. Human embryonic development during the third and fourth weeks. Dorsal view, showing the "back" of the embryo. (After Arey, *Developmental Anatomy,* W. B. Saunders Co., 1947.)

From Fig. 4.4C, it will be noted that while the beginnings of the central nervous system are being thrust up into the amniotic cavity the under surface of the embryo is also changing. The upper part of the cavity which we have referred to as the yolk sac becomes partially separated from the lower portion. The upper part is the beginning of the digestive tract and corresponds to the archenteron of a typical gastrula; the anterior portion of the tract is the foregut, the posterior portion the hind gut (Fig. 4.4C).

The Human Yolk Sac

The lower portion of the cavity beneath the embryonic disc remains as the yolk sac. This is an appropriate time to inquire into its significance. Since there is no yolk to be contained, how do we happen to have it?

In examining the eggs of reptiles and birds we note that they are enclosed within leathery or brittle shells. Within these shells must be stored enough food, yolk, to nourish the embryo until it is ready to hatch and begin actively foraging for its food. Everyone is familiar with the large, yellow, globular yolk mass in a hen's egg, for example. The embryo develops on top of this mass, and early in its development encloses the yolk in a large yolk sac (Fig. 8.24, p. 169). All birds and reptiles do the same. Although mammalian embryos obtain their nourishment in an entirely different manner, nevertheless they develop yolk sacs connected to the digestive tract just as do reptile and bird embryos (Figs. 4.4, 4.9). Why? As in the cases of rudimentary or vestigial organs possessed by adults (pp. 40–44), the most reasonable explanation seems to be that mammals inherited these useless sacs from ancestors for which yolk sacs were functional organs. To be specific, it is believed that mammals inherited their yolk sacs from reptiles, since there are many reasons for regarding reptiles as ancestral to mammals. We may note in passing that mammals also inherited in greatly reduced form another embryonic structure of great value to reptile and bird embryos, the **allantois** (see pp. 169–170).

Somites in Human Embryos

On both sides of the neural tube **somites** develop (Fig. 4.5C and D). These are more or less cubical blocks of mesodermal tissue forming between the ectoderm and the endoderm; the ectoderm is molded over them so that their outlines are visible externally. The first ones form just posterior to what will be the head. Subsequently the number is increased by formation of somites posterior to these first ones (Fig. 4.5). Thus a row of somites arises on each side of the central nervous system.

Somites form, among other things, the beginning of the **muscular system.** Most of the muscles which later attach to the skeleton and make possible movements under conscious control (voluntary, striated muscles) develop from these somites, directly or indirectly. The adult muscles have the greatest diversity of size and shape, and utter lack of resemblance to the rows of blocklike somites from which they came. Such disparity between embryonic beginnings and adult structure clearly calls for explanation.

Since the muscular systems of all vertebrate embryos agree in beginning as rows of somites, this pattern is evidently an ancient one. The most primitive vertebrates, and those which we learn from the fossil record were first to appear, are the fishes. Fish embryos, like embryos of other vertebrates, develop rows of somites. Subsequently these somites develop into segmentally arranged muscles of the body wall, the **myotomes** (Fig. 4.6). Although the myotomes of fishes take the form of nested *V*'s or *W*'s, it will be evident that the change from the segmental blocks of the embryo is much less drastic than is the change by which rows of blocks are transformed into the muscles of the back and limbs of higher vertebrates, including man. Rows of segmental somites form a "reasonable" beginning for a muscular system which is to consist mainly of muscles divided into successive segments, as in fishes.

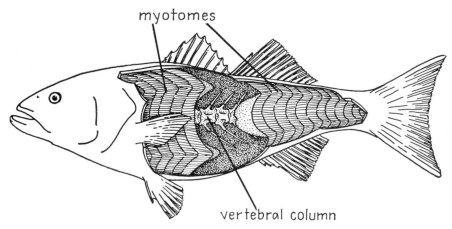

FIG. 4.6. Locomotor apparatus of a typical fish. (After Gregory and Roigneau, *Introduction to Human Anatomy*, American Museum of Natural History, 1934.)

At this point we may inquire into the utility to a fish of having muscles arranged as shown in Fig. 4.6. Fishes are propelled forward in the water mainly by undulations of the body which confer upon the large tail fin a sculling motion. Other highly aquatic animals are also propelled forward by undulations of the body. The most complete analysis of the mechanism involved was made by Coghill (1929) on the water-dwelling larvae of *Amblystoma,* a genus of tailed amphibians. Since these aquatic larvae also have muscular systems arranged in segments, they afford quite as good information on the advantages of that arrangement as would fishes.

Fig. 4.7 presents diagrams of the essential mechanism of swimming in *Amblystoma* larvae. The myotomes (somites) will be noted in parallel rows on both sides of the spinal cord. Each segment is separated from its neighbors before and behind by membranous partitions, the muscle fibers themselves attaching to these membranes. Thus when the muscle fibers in one myotome contract, the width of the myotome, i.e., the distance between anterior and posterior partitions, decreases. In the middle diagram of Fig. 4.7 the first six myotomes on the left side are represented as contracted. Since the contraction shortens them, the result is necessarily the bending of the head to one side, as shown. Now this "first flexure" starts to move posteriorly down the row of segments, by successive contraction of one somite after another down the length of the animal. At the same time myotomes between the flexure and the head of the animal relax in corresponding sequence. Thus the flexure "travels" down the length of the animal. When the first flexure nears the tail a second flexure forms on the *right* side just behind the head (Fig. 4.7, third diagram). Then this

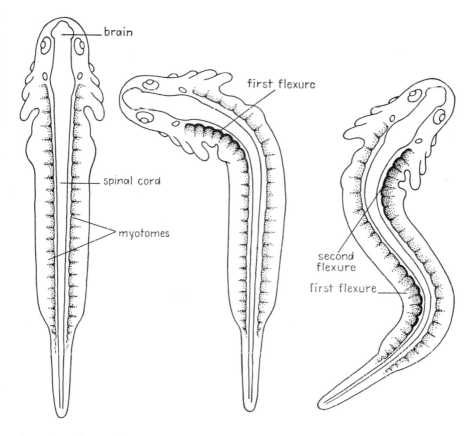

FIG. 4.7. Action of segmental body muscles in producing swimming movements. (After Coghill, *Anatomy and the Problem of Behaviour,* Cambridge University Press, 1929.)

second flexure "travels" down the length of the body. The combination of the two flexures throws the body into an *S* curve, as shown. The bends of the body travel backward, pressing against the surrounding water and sending the body forward. The result is comparable to that obtained from the thrust of a propeller blade. In rapid locomotion the successive right and left flexures follow each other with great rapidity.

Evidently a segmental arrangement of body-wall musculature is an efficient mechanism for rapid swimming. Fish embryos in process of developing such a mechanism start with rows of somites. But why do all other vertebrate embryos also follow this pattern regardless of whether or not the adults into which they develop are ever going near the water? The

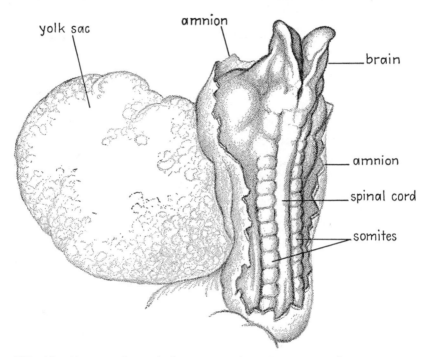

FIG. 4.8. Human embryo of about twenty days. Amnion partially cut away to reveal embryo. (After Corner, in *Contributions to Embryology*, Carnegie Institution of Washington, Vol. 20, 1929.)

most reasonable answer seems to be that this is an embryonic pattern inherited from aquatic ancestors, i.e., from fishes. We shall see that this is only one of many reasons for thinking that fishes are the ancestors, near or remote, of all vertebrates living on land.

While the neural tube and rows of somites have been forming in the human embryo (Fig. 4.8) other changes have also been occurring. The heart has started to form, for example (Fig. 4.9). As the body increases in size the embryo "bulges up" more and more into the cavity above the embryonic disc—the amniotic cavity. Soon this cavity would be filled but for the fact that it increases in size with enlargement of the embryo. The cavity contains a fluid, the **amniotic fluid,** surrounding the embryo and protecting it from injury (Fig. 9.12, p. 191). Soon the embryo is free from underlying tissues, remaining attached to the wall of the uterus by the stalklike **umbilical cord** (Fig. 4.10; and Fig. 9.12, p. 191). The umbilical cord ends in the **placenta,** the beginning of which was noted above. The cord contains blood vessels carrying the embryo's blood to and from the placenta, where it comes in close contact with the mother's blood, though

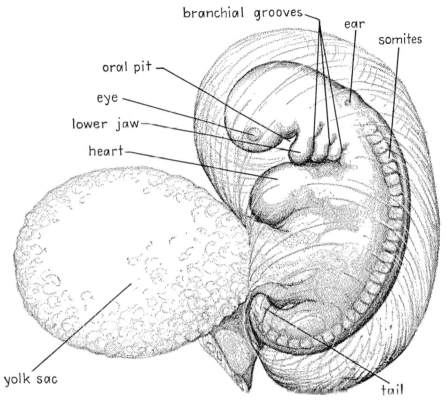

FIG. 4.9. Human embryo of the fourth week (3.9 mm. long). (Mainly after Patten, *Human Embryology,* The Blakiston Company, 1946.)

the two bloods are separated by thin membranes. "Buds" representing the beginnings of arms and legs have appeared, as have, also, the eyes (Fig. 4.10).

"Gill Slits" in Human Embryos

Figs. 4.9 and 4.10 give evidence of another new development, sometimes called "gill slits," although **branchial grooves** is a better term for them, since most of them do not form actual slits in the human embryo. They constitute a series of grooves in the lower head and neck region. On

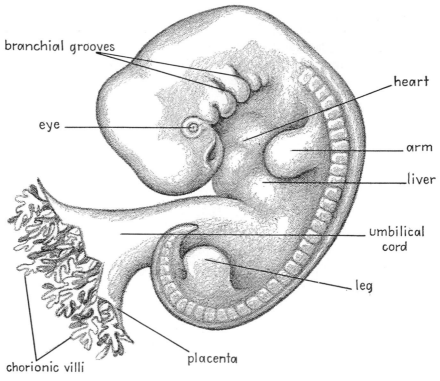

branchial grooves

heart

eye

arm

liver

umbilical
cord

leg

chorionic villi

placenta

FIG. 4.10. Human embryo at the end of the first month (7 mm.). (Mainly after Gilbert, *Biography of the Unborn*, The Williams & Wilkins Co., 1939.)

the inside of the body, in the wall of the digestive tract in the region called the pharynx, a corresponding series of **pharyngeal** or **gill pouches** develops. In fish embryos the grooves on the outside finally meet the corresponding pouches from the inside. A perforation then forms, converting the grooves into slits or clefts—openings directly from the pharynx to the exterior of the body. Typically five such gill clefts develop on each side of the head of fishes.

What is the function of the gill clefts in fishes? Fig. 4.11 presents diagrams of the head of a shark with portions of the surface cut away so that mouth, pharynx, and connected structures may be seen. As the fish swims, water is taken into the mouth and passes to the exterior through the gill clefts (note the arrows). As it passes through the clefts the water bathes the **gills** lining the walls of the clefts. The gills are soft fleshy structures with surfaces richly supplied with capillaries of the blood system. Since the blood in the capillaries is separated from the water passing through the clefts by only a thin membrane, means is provided for the taking on by the blood of oxygen from the water, and for the giving up to the water of

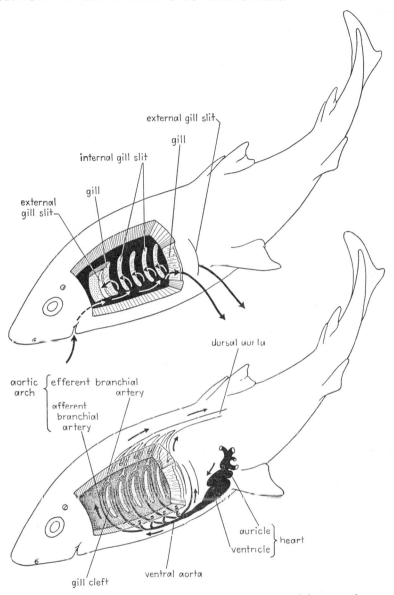

FIG. 4.11. Respiratory mechanism (upper diagram), and heart and aortic arches (lower diagram) of a fish (shark). A "window" has been cut into the pharynx. In upper diagram arrows indicate paths of water currents. In lower diagram arrows indicate direction of blood flow.

carbon dioxide carried by the blood. This is the mechanism by which the fish breathes; in other words, gill slits or clefts are part of the respiratory mechanism of fishes.

Why do the embryos of other vertebrates, such as reptiles, birds, and mammals, which never breathe by means of gills, start the process of developing a series of gill slits? As with the somites mentioned above, this seems another instance of inheritance of embryonic structure from aquatic ancestors, another indication that land-dwelling vertebrates are the descendants of fishes.

It is noteworthy that in the human embryo one of the gill pouches does become perforated, forming a passageway from the pharynx to the outside of the head. This passageway is divided into two portions, the external ear canal, leading from the outside of the head to the middle ear, and the Eustachian tube, leading from the middle ear to the throat (pharynx). The eardrum in the middle ear forms a thin partition between the two portions of a passageway which otherwise would directly connect the pharynx and the exterior as does a gill slit of a fish.

Aortic Arches

Mention was made above of the gills lining the walls of the gill clefts in fishes and affording the means by which blood is brought in close contact with the water passing through the clefts. Since gills have this function, obviously blood vessels must be provided for transporting blood to and from them. The arteries providing this transportation occur in characteristic arrangement (Figs. 4.11; 4.13B). The heart of a fish has one **auricle,** which receives blood from the **veins.** The auricle transmits the blood to the single **ventricle,** a muscular chamber that propels the blood forward through the **ventral aorta.** From the latter several branches pass the blood to the gills lining the gill clefts. These branches are called **afferent branchial arteries;** in the tissue of the gills they subdivide into a network of countless tiny **capillaries.** As noted above, it is while the blood is in these capillaries that it exchanges its carbon dioxide for oxygen from the water passing over the gills. The blood passes out of the capillaries into a series of **efferent branchial arteries,** all of which connect to the **dorsal aorta.** The latter has numerous branches conveying blood to all parts and organs of the body. From these parts and organs blood is returned to the auricle of the heart by the veins, thus starting the cycle anew. It will be noted that there are as many pairs of afferent and efferent branchial arteries as there are gill clefts. One afferent artery plus its corresponding efferent artery constitutes one **aortic arch.** Thus in Fig. 4.11 five aortic arches are shown.

We have noted that in the human embryo a series of gill or pharyngeal pouches forms although most of them do not perforate to form actual clefts (Fig. 4.12). Needless to say, also, actual gills never develop in the walls of these pouches. Nevertheless, it is a surprising fact that the embryo forms an arrangement of arteries as though it were getting ready to supply blood to such a series of gills. At this stage in its development the human heart has one auricle and one ventricle, as does the heart of a fish embryo or adult. Running forward from the ventricle is a single ventral aorta (Figs. 4.12; 4.13A); this gives rise to several aortic arches which

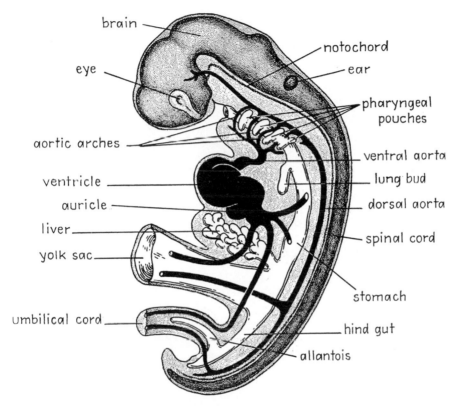

FIG. 4.12. Human embryo of 4 mm. dissected to show digestive tract and aortic arches. (After Arey, *Developmental Anatomy*, W. B. Saunders Co., 1947.)

pass between the successive pharyngeal pouches. The aortic arches are continuous vessels, not interrupted by series of capillaries as they would be if gills actually appeared. As in the fishes, the dorsal ends of the aortic arches connect to the dorsal aorta. Fig. 4.13A shows a human heart of this stage removed from the body, together with the accompanying ventral aorta and the bases of some of the aortic arches. Six pairs of aortic arches appear, although not all are fully developed at any one time.

The fidelity with which the human embryo, in common with embryos of other mammals, and of birds, reptiles, and amphibians, repeats the fish-

embryo stage of heart structure and arterial arrangement is amazing, affording one of the most beautiful examples of embryonic recapitulation.
In the fish most of the aortic arches persist to provide blood circulation
through the gills, as previously noted; the heart remains permanently in

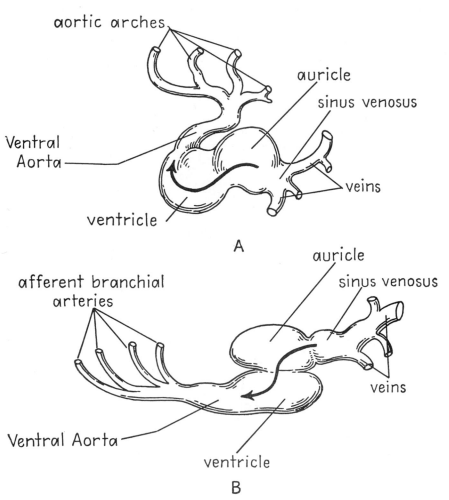

FIG. 4.13. Heart and aortic arches of, A, early human embryo (cf. Fig. 4.12) and, B,
fish (cf. Fig. 4.11). Arrows indicate direction of blood flow.

the single-auricle, single-ventricle state. The heart of the human embryo
soon develops two auricles and two ventricles, the extra one of each being
connected with a secondary circuit of circulation for the **lungs.** In the human embryo the six pairs of aortic arches have a varied fate. Three of
them disappear. Of the other three, one persists in connection with the

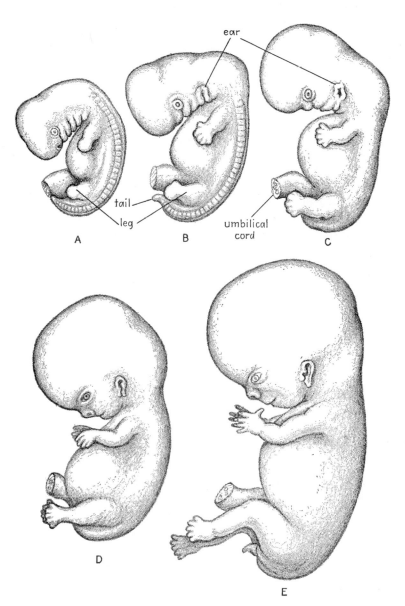

FIG. 4.14. Human embryos and fetuses. A, fifth week (10 mm.). B, sixth week (13 mm.). C, seventh week (15 mm.). D, seventh week (17 mm.). E, eighth week (23 mm.). (After Gilbert, *Biography of the Unborn*, The Williams & Wilkins Co., 1939; after His.)

system of arteries supplying blood to the head, another persists on the left side as the connection between the heart and the dorsal aorta, and the third forms the pulmonary arteries conveying blood to the lungs. Thus we see how arteries "designed" for one purpose are made over to serve other functions when the original function is discarded or becomes obsolete.

Our account of human embryology has brought us through only the first of the 9 months of prenatal development (Fig. 4.10). As we might anticipate, however, it is during this early period that the human embryo exhibits the greatest number of characteristics comparable to those of embryos of lower animals. Many more such examples of recapitulation might be included in our account, involving such diverse organs as kidneys; brains; the skeletal bars, which in fishes support the gills and in the embryos of higher animals appear only to be made over to serve a variety of other functions; and so on. We shall content ourselves with but one additional example: the **tail,** clearly shown in Fig. 4.10. At this stage the embryo seems prepared to provide us with as adequate a tail as that possessed by any lower mammal—our cat and dog companions, for example. The tail reaches its maximum length when the embryo is about 6 weeks old; at that time its length may be about one-sixth that of the embryo. Subsequently the tail shortens, except in rare cases (p. 76). Soon it is lost to view externally, persisting as the vestigial coccyx mentioned earlier (p. 43).

At the end of the first month of life the human embryo is only about a fourth of an inch long. It continues to grow and develop rapidly. By the end of the second month the developing individual has distinctly human appearance and arrangement of organs (Fig. 4.14). It is then no longer called an embryo; it has become a human **fetus.** For the many fascinating details of human development which could not receive attention in this brief account the interested reader is referred to textbooks of human embryology, especially to the highly readable *Biography of the Unborn* by Margaret Shea Gilbert.

Interferences with Recapitulation

In the foregoing pages we have described a few examples of ways in which embryos of higher animals resemble the embryos of lower animals, resemblances involving surprising detail in many instances. Nevertheless, a word of caution is in order about expecting too much of recapitulation. In the first flush of enthusiasm following enunciation of Haeckel's version of the recapitulation theory (p. 50) some biologists hailed the new idea as a means of solving all enigmas of animal relationships and evolutionary history (phylogeny). It was thought that if one studied the embryonic development of a given species intensively enough one could trace step by step the entire evolutionary history of that species. Hopes of doing this dwindled when it was finally realized that *adult* ancestral stages are not repeated by embryos, that the latter repeat embryonic conditions of their ancestors only. Despite this restriction, however, recapitulation has much to contribute to the study of evolution.

Why does not an embryo repeat all the embryonic stages possessed by its ancestors? The first answer is: **lack of time.** We have noted that most of the recapitulation by the human embryo is confined to the first month, practically all of it to the first two months, of life. How would it be possible in this brief span for the human embryo to retrace all the steps of human evolution, involving many millions of years?

Again, we must remember that the main "object" of an embryo is to become an adult as expeditiously as possible. Retracing ancestral history is purely secondary, of interest to inquiring biologists but not to the embryo itself. Accordingly we may expect that whenever ancestral stages can be condensed or entirely omitted by embryos such **omissions and condensations** will occur. The success of a species is dependent in part upon the efficiency with which its embryos can become adults, without waste of time or food supply. Inclusion of unnecessary embryonic stages would be wasteful in both respects and consequently a handicap to the species in life's competition. Thus we may look upon the examples of recapitulation remaining to us as the irreducible minimum of ancestral stages which nature has never found a way of eliminating or circumventing. It might seem, for example, to increase embryonic efficiency if the muscles of the human embryo could be formed in the first place as tiny miniatures of the adult muscles, the somite stage described above being circumvented entirely. But apparently this has not been possible or feasible. We may be reasonably certain that if it had been possible to omit somite formation we should not find the latter as a constant feature of embryonic development in amphibians, reptiles, birds, and mammals. But many other features of embryos of ancestral forms must have been lost to us because it *was* possible for the embryos of their descendants to omit them.

Why do embryos of higher animals ever find it necessary to retain structures characteristic of the embryos of their ancestors? The more we learn of forces operative in embryonic development the more we realize that the whole process is like a chain reaction, starting before fertilization of the ovum and proceeding in orderly sequence to the adult condition. One event initiates another; the latter initiates a third, and so on. We have experimental proof, for example, that the neural tube (p. 54) will not form unless the particular region of ectoderm from which it is to form has underlying it a **notochord.** The notochord is an unsegmented rod lying in the position which the backbone will eventually occupy (Fig. 4.12). The notochord appears very early in embryonic development and serves as an **organizer,** inducing formation of a neural plate and tube in the ectoderm lying over it. Experiments on embryos of lower animals indicate that if the notochord is removed no neural tube will develop. Now a notochord is found in all members of Phylum Chordata. In a few members of the phylum (e.g., *Amphioxus,* Fig. 5.5, p. 101) it persists throughout life, forming an elastic, stiffening rod down the back. In most members of the phylum, i.e., in vertebrates, it is eventually replaced by a vertebral column, a bony backbone. Thus the presence of a notochord in the embryos of higher vertebrates is an example of recapitulation of a structure present in the embryos of ancestors. Why does the notochord still continue to appear in embryos of these higher vertebrates? Probably because it is needed as an organizer to induce formation of the neural tube. Neural tube formation in the first ancestral chordates probably occurred under the influence of the notochord, and the connection of the latter with neural tube formation was so vital that embryos ever afterward must have notochords to induce formation of their neural tubes. The notochord also forms an axis around which the segmental bones comprising the vertebral column develop. It seems likely that the presence of the notochord is also essential to this process of backbone formation, though experimental evidence on the point is lacking.

Again, three kidneys are found in Phylum Chordata. The hagfish (Order Cyclostomata) has the kidney called the **pronephros.** Other fishes, and the amphibians, have as their kidney the **mesonephros.** But their embryos all develop a pronephros first; then the mesonephros develops and the pronephros disappears. Why does the pronephros develop at all? Although we have no direct experimental evidence upon which to base an answer, it seems probable that the pronephros serves as an organizer inducing subsequent formation of the mesonephros. One evident contribution is made by the pronephros to the mesonephros: the duct leading from the pronephros to the exterior is taken over by the mesonephros for the conveying of its waste products. In reptiles, birds, and mammals the kidney is the **metanephros.** But again the embryos faithfully recapitulate ancestral embryonic history, developing first a pronephros (which never functions as a kidney), then a mesonephros (which functions as a kidney for a time in the embryo), and finally a metanephros. Why is all this past history repeated? Why not develop the metanephros at once and have done with it? Probably we see here evidence of a chain reaction of the type mentioned above. It may well be that each kidney serves in turn as an organizer, inducing formation of structures which follow it in time of development.

In conclusion, we see that ancestral embryonic structures are retained when their retention serves some useful function in promoting embryonic development. This function is frequently that of organizers, making possible the forging of successive links in the chain reaction which constitutes embryonic development.

Another confusing aspect of embryonic development is the fact that the **time sequence** of stages is frequently modified or even reversed. The mammalian placenta, for example, is a relatively recent development in evolutionary history—the invertebrate, fish, amphibian, and reptilian ancestors of mammals all lacked it. Not until the mammalian status was reached, necessitating nourishment of the embryo within the uterus of the mother, did a placenta (Fig. 4.10) develop. We might expect, therefore, that the placenta would develop late in the embryonic life of mammals. But if that were the case how would the mammalian embryo obtain food during its earlier development? Since the mammalian ovum has no yolk, connection with the mother's blood stream must be made almost at once. Hence, as already noted, the placenta is one of the first features of a mammalian embryo to appear, despite its arising late in evolutionary history. This phenomenon illustrates the fact that an embryo must at all times be **adapted** to its embryonic environment and to the requirements imposed upon it of securing the necessities of life. Attainment of such adaptation has frequently destroyed recapitulation of ancestral embryonic stages or distorted the sequence in which the stages occur. In some cases the differing adaptations of embryos or larvae of two related forms may result in these young stages being more unlike than the adults are. This gives rise to exceptions to von Baer's principle (p. 50).

Recapitulation and the Origin of the Metazoa

In the examples of recapitulation by the human embryo we have seen that the repetition of stages confirms the idea that remote ancestors of man (and other mammals) were fishes, and that subsequently reptiles occupied a place in the lineage leading from fishes to mammals. It is noteworthy that this conclusion concerning the ancestry of mammals would have been reached even though mammalian embryos had not resembled fish embryos and reptilian embryos. Studies of anatomy and of the fossil record would by themselves have led to the conclusion; embryonic recapitulation adds welcome confirmatory evidence. In this and in many other instances embryology confirms conclusions based on other lines of evidence. When other lines of evidence are lacking, or contradictory, to what extent is it safe to draw conclusions as to ancestry from embryology alone? With due recognition of factors noted above that modify recapitulation, can we nevertheless use the embryonic record as a means of reaching conclusions concerning the nature of ancestors that are otherwise unknown?

One case in which such conclusions have been generally drawn, although not without dissent, is that of the origin of many-celled animals, the metazoa. Most biologists are agreed that the first animals were single-celled organisms, protozoa, and that many-celled animals evolved from these single-celled ones (see Boyden, 1953, for a dissenting view, however). But if so, what were the transitional stages in this evolution? Many, probably most, biologists conclude that embryonic development gives us clues to the answer.

Earlier in the chapter we noted that early embryonic developments of widely diverse organisms are homologous, that is, are so similar that a typical sequence of stages can be drawn (Fig. 4.2). Do these stages represent a case of recapitulation; do they give us clues as to the stages the metazoa passed through in their evolution from the protozoa? Striking parallels can be drawn between these stages and simple organisms living at the present time. In Fig. 4.15 the first vertical column represents the stages in typical embryonic development; the second column contains representative modern organisms that show comparable structures. In the top squares of each column are single cells, the ovum on the one hand, typical protozoa on the other. If this is a case of recapitulation, we have in the fact that all organisms begin life as a single cell (the fertilized ovum) confirmatory evidence that metazoa evolved from protozoa.

In the second squares of both columns of Fig. 4.15 we have small aggregates of cells: cleavage stages of embryonic development on the left, simple colonial organisms on the right. *Gonium* and *Pandorina* are representative organisms that consist of colonies of cells. They are frequently called colonial protozoa but since they possess chlorophyll they may be classed as plants. Perhaps they are best classified as Protista without assigning them to either the plant or the animal kingdom. At any rate it is the general level of organization rather than exact relationships that con-

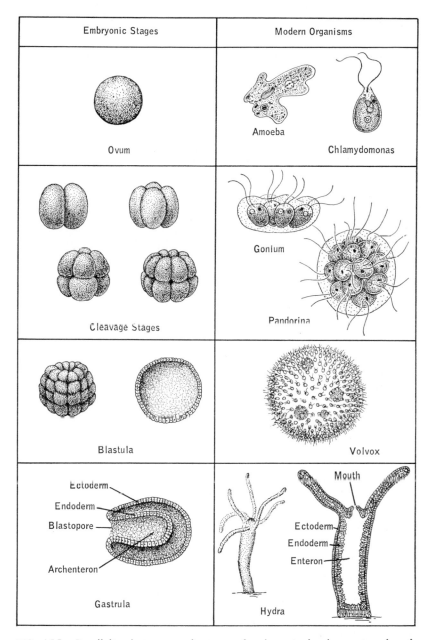

Embryonic Stages	Modern Organisms
Ovum	Amoeba Chlamydomonas
Cleavage Stages	Gonium Pandorina
Blastula	Volvox
Gastrula	Hydra

FIG. 4.15. Parallelism between early stages of embryonic development and modern organisms representing levels of organization which may possibly have characterized stages in the evolution of the metazoa.

cerns us. In these colonial forms each colony consists of four or more cells each of which is independent of the others except in locomotion; the colony moves as a unit. The species of *Gonium* shown, for example, consists of a colony of four cells bound together by a jellylike substance. When reproduction occurs each cell divides into two, and each of these daughter cells, in turn, divides into two. Thus four daughter colonies of four cells each arise; they are released from the surrounding jelly and take up independent existences. *Pandorina* and other colonial forms consist of larger numbers of cells—16, 32, 64, 128, and more. Like *Gonium* each of these larger colonies begins life as a single cell which divides and subdivides, stopping when the cell number appropriate to the species has been reached.

The third squares in both columns of Fig. 4.15 contain spherical aggregates of cells, the blastula of embryonic development on the left, a colonial organism called *Volvox* on the right. *Volvox* consists of thousands of cells bound together in a spherical colony. Like the blastula in embryonic development of higher animals it is a one-layered organism. The bottom squares of both columns (Fig. 4.15) contain two-layered organisms, the gastrula of embryonic development on the left, *Hydra,* representing Phylum Coelenterata (jellyfishes, sea anemones, corals, and their kin), on the right. *Hydra* is a simple fresh-water jellyfish consisting mainly of two layers of cells (ectoderm and endoderm); it is essentially a gastrula with tentacles. Like a gastrula it has a simple digestive cavity with but one opening to the exterior. This pattern is common to the coelenterates, though some differ from *Hydra* in appearance owing to the presence of great amounts of "jelly" between ectoderm and endoderm. This jelly (mesoglea) does in fact contain cells.

In the embryonic development of higher animals a third layer, the mesoderm, appears soon after the two-layered stage is attained. In parallel manner mesoderm is found in the phylum of animals usually placed next after Phylum Coelenterata in the classification: Phylum Platyhelminthes (flatworms), and in all subsequent phyla.

If the parallelism we have just traced represents a case of recapitulation the sequence of stages in the evolution of the metazoa was as follows: (1) single cells; (2) groups of cells aggregated into colonies; (3) spherical, one-layered colonies; (4) two-layered organisms (Phylum Coelenterata); (5) three-layered organisms (Phylum Platyhelminthes and higher ones). In other words, the protozoa were ancestral to the coelenterates, which in turn were ancestral to flatworms and higher phyla. Is such an interpretation correct? Since the writings of Haeckel most biologists have agreed that it is. But the long and careful studies of Hadži (1953) have thrown doubt on its correctness. Despite the striking parallels noted, we may not have here a case of recapitulation at all. The metazoa may have evolved by an entirely different process. Hadži presents reasons for concluding that protozoa of the type known as Infusoria (cilia-covered organisms like *Paramecium*) gave rise to very simple members of Phylum Platyhelminthes, the Acoela of Class Turbellaria. These minute worms have no digestive cavities and are provided with cilia. Some of the Infusoria have many nuclei in the single large cell. If a bit of cytoplasm around each nucleus became enclosed by a cell membrane a many-celled organism would result. Hadži visualizes the Acoela as arising from the Infursoria by such a process of cellularization (see de Beer, 1954). According to this view coelenterates are somewhat simplified descendants of flatworms (Platyhelminthes), not their ancestors. The simplification has been connected with adoption by coelenterates of an attached or sessile mode of existence.

Since there are no known fossils of the first metazoan animals, we have no direct evidence as to whether metazoa arose by aggregation of cells as seen today in colonial protozoans (Haeckel's view; reaffirmed by Marcus, 1958) or by cellularization of cilia-bearing protozoans (infusorians) as postulated by Hadži (1953). The embryonic development of higher animals seems to indicate that Haeckel was correct; yet in the absence of other evidence it is dangerous to conclude that the early stages of embryonic development necessarily represent recapitulation of what happened when the protozoa gave rise to the metazoa many millions of years ago.

Recapitulation Aids in Classification

Recapitulation is sometimes of aid in informing us of the relationships of animals when the adult structure leaves us in doubt. A case in point is presented by the **tunicates.** Members of the genus *Molgula* (Fig. 4.16) are small, soft-bodied, "spineless" creatures living in the sea. Their outer surface is a tunic (hence the name "tunicate") of cellulose. They live attached to rocks, the pilings of wharves, and the like. The tunic is pierced by two openings corresponding to the incurrent siphon ("mouth" in Fig. 4.16) and the excurrent siphon ("opening of atrium") of a clam or oyster. Sea water is sucked in through the incurrent siphon, is passed into a pharynx the walls of which are constructed to strain out tiny animals and plants suitable for food, and, after passing through the "pharyngeal gill

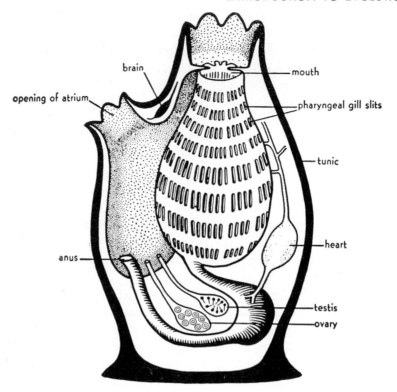

FIG. 4.16. Internal anatomy of an adult tunicate (*Molgula*). Diagrammatic. (From Buchsbaum, *Animals Without Backbones*, 2nd ed., University of Chicago Press, 1948, p. 316.)

slits," is ejected into the sea again through the excurrent siphon. This method of feeding is much like that of such molluscs as clams and oysters. Accordingly tunicates were at one time considered molluscs or close relatives of molluscs.

Later the young or larval stages of tunicates were discovered. Unlike the adult, the larva of *Molgula* (Fig. 4.17) is a free-swimming, tadpolelike creature. Its swimming tail is stiffened by a **notochord;** it has a pharynx pierced with **gill slits;** and it has a small **brain** and **spinal cord dorsal** in position. These are the most distinctive characteristics of Phylum Chordata (the phylum to which all vertebrates belong) and are most unlike structures possessed by members of Phylum Mollusca. Evidently, therefore, tunicates belong in Phylum Chordata. The larval condition appears to indicate that their ancestors were free-swimming chordates. The present mode of life of adult members of *Molgula,* unmoving, with a mollusclike method of feeding, must represent a specialized condition adopted by the

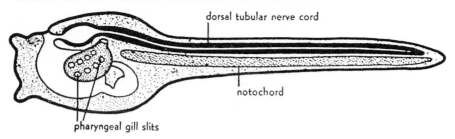

FIG. 4.17.   Internal anatomy of a larval tunicate (*Molgula*). Diagrammatic. (From Buchsbaum, *Animals Without Backbones*, 2nd ed., University of Chicago Press, 1948, p. 318.)

creature relatively late in its evolutionary history. The mode of life is an adaptation enabling it to occupy a particular niche in the economy of marine life. Adult *Molgula* is sometimes referred to as "degenerate." Since it seems, however, to be a successful animal, adequate to the requirements of life as it finds them, such anthropocentric aspersions are of doubtful wisdom.

Embryonic Vestiges

In the preceding chapter we called attention to rudimentary or vestigial structures (pp. 40–44). We found their presence in adult animals most reasonably explained as due to retention of reduced remnants of organs functional in ancestors. Embryos frequently commence the development of organs which will not appear in the adult. Such abortive beginnings may be thought of as embryonic rudiments or vestiges.

The tail of the human embryo mentioned above (p. 65) clearly falls in this category. Whalebone whales (Fig. 3.3, p. 24) do not have teeth in their jaws, yet in some species the tooth germs appear in the embryo, only to disappear. Insects never have paired appendages (pp. 37–39) attached to the body segments comprising the abdomen. Yet in the embryos of some beetles the beginnings of such appendages appear, to disappear later. The forelimbs of whales have been developed into flippers, while the hind limbs have been lost (except for vestiges of bone buried in the flesh, Fig. 3.3). Yet whale embryos develop fore- and hind-limb buds, as does the human embryo (Fig. 4.10); the hind-limb buds later degenerate. Sheep, in common with cows, deer, antelopes, and their kin, have no clavicle or "collarbone." Yet the beginnings of a clavicle appear in the sheep embryo and disappear later. Other examples might be given. The occurrence of such embryonic rudiments seems most reasonably explained as resulting from recapitulation of ancestral characteristics.

Reversions

In addition to the normally occurring embryonic rudiments embryos occasionally develop abnormal structures reminiscent of normal structures possessed by other, usually "lower," animals. Such abnormal structures are called **reversions** or **atavisms.** Occasionally, for example, a human baby is born with a short, fleshy tail protruding from the base of the spine. Since the vertebral column does not extend into the atavistic tail it is easily removed by a surgeon. Tails as long as 8 inches have been recorded.

We have mentioned the pharyngeal pouches, together with the fact that only one of them actually perforates to form an opening from the pharynx to the exterior (Eustachian tube plus external ear canal, pp. 61–62). Occasionally an additional one of these pouches will form an opening to the exterior. The result is a **cervical fistula,** an opening from the nasal cavity or throat to the surface of the head below the ear or to the surface of the neck, the exact position depending upon which of the pouches forms the fistula (Fig. 4.18). It will be recalled that in fishes all of the pouches open to the exterior in this manner to form the gill slits through which water passes in the process of respiration (Fig. 4.11). A cervical fistula, then, results from return by one pharyngeal pouch to embryonic procedures normal in a fish embryo.

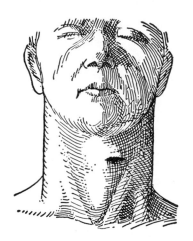

FIG. 4.18. Cervical fistula originating from the second pharyngeal pouch. (From Arey, *Developmental Anatomy,* W. B. Saunders Co., 1947, p. 179.)

Human beings, in common with other primates, are provided with one pair of mammary glands located in a pectoral position (on the chest). Many lower mammals, pigs and dogs being familiar examples, have a row of mammary glands extending along both sides of the chest and abdomen. Occasionally human beings are born with extra mammary glands or extra nipples, reminiscent of the condition normal in lower mammals.

One most interesting example of reversion is found in the horse. In a later chapter we shall note that some of the prehistoric horses regarded as ancestral to the modern horse had three toes on each foot (Fig. 10.5, p. 202). The third digit was enlarged to form a hoof but the second and fourth digits were also present, though of smaller size. We have already remarked (pp. 23 and 43) that the second and fourth digits of the modern horse have disappeared except for their metacarpals, which are present as the rudimentary splint bones. It will be recalled that the metacarpal of the third digit forms the large cannon bone, to which the phalanges of that digit articulate. Occasionally a horse is born with one of the splint bones also bearing phalanges. These phalanges are small but sometimes the terminal one bears a greatly reduced hoof (Fig. 4.19). The author's introduction to this phenomenon occurred when as a boy he was enticed by a lurid poster into a side show at a county fair to see an "eight-footed horse." Once inside he beheld a healthy horse quietly eating hay. The horse had the usual four hooves, but beside each one there dangled a tiny extra hoof, just as illustrated in the figure. The similarity of this abnormal structure to the structure normal for the foot of such a prehistoric horse as *Merychippus* (Fig. 10.5, p. 202) is evident.

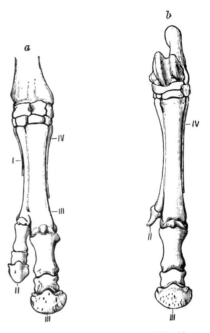

FIG. 4.19.   Forefoot (a) and hindfoot (b) of a multitoed modern horse. (From Lull, "The evolution of the horse family, as illustrated in the Yale collections," *American Journal of Science*, Vol. 23, 1907, p. 166.)

Conclusion

In this chapter similarities of embryonic development have been stressed. We have noted that all animals above single-celled protozoa are similar in the early stages of development, and that in general there is direct relationship between similarity of adult structure and the proportion of embryonic development which is similar in different animals. Thus, dissimilar animals are found to follow like paths of development for a time and then to diverge, each going its own way. The more dissimilar the animals the shorter the period of embryonic development which they share in common. Why do dissimilar animals share any similarity of embryonic development at all? The most reasonable explanation seems to be inheritance from common ancestry. In accordance with this view we may picture two species descended from a common ancestor. That ancestor had a certain pattern of embryonic development. Both species inherited the pattern. But each species proceeded to evolve in its own way; thus eventually each came to differ from the ancestor and from the other species. Consequently the later portions of the embryonic developments of the two species differ, even while both retain certain features of the pattern of early embryonic development inherited from the common ancestor. Evidently, then, recapitulation will occur in only those portions of embryonic development which two species share in common. The human embryo, for example, is never a fish or a fish embryo, yet it follows a course of development similar to that of a fish embryo up to a point representing the stage at which the line leading eventually to man diverged from the line leading eventually to modern fishes.

Embryonic rudiments and reversions add confirmatory evidence of inheritance of embryonic patterns from common ancestry.

References and Suggested Readings

Arey, L. B. *Developmental Anatomy,* 6th ed. Philadelphia: W. B. Saunders Co., 1954.

Barth, L. G. *Embryology,* rev. ed. New York: Henry Holt & Co., 1953.

de Beer, G. R. "The evolution of the Metazoa." In J. Huxley, A. C. Hardy, and E. B. Ford (eds.). *Evolution as a Process.* London: Allen & Unwin, 1954. Pp. 24–33.

de Beer, G. R. *Embryos and Ancestors,* 3rd ed. Oxford: Oxford University Press, 1958.

Boyden, A. A. "Comparative evolution with special reference to primitive mechanisms." *Evolution,* 7 (1953), 21–30.

Coghill, G. E. *Anatomy and the Problem of Behaviour.* Cambridge: Cambridge University Press, 1929.

Corner, G. W. *Ourselves Unborn.* New Haven: Yale University Press, 1944.

Gilbert, M. S. *Biography of the Unborn.* Baltimore: The Williams & Wilkins Co., 1939.

Hadži, J. "An attempt to reconstruct the system of animal classification." *Systematic Zoology,* 2 (1953), 145–154.

Marcus, E. "On the evolution of the animal phyla." *Quarterly Review of Biology,* 33 (1958), 24–58.

Romer, A. S. *Man and the Vertebrates,* 3rd ed. Chicago: Chicago University Press, 1941. (Note particularly Chap. 20.)

Smith, H. M. "Paleogenesis the modern successor to the biogenetic law." *Turtox News,* 34 (1956), 178–181, 212–216. Chicago: General Biological Supply House.

CHAPTER 5

EVOLUTION AS SEEN IN

CHEMICAL STRUCTURE

AND IN METABOLISM

Fundamental Unity of All Living Things

In the preceding chapters we have discussed examples of fundamental similarities of structure (homologies) in the gross anatomies of animals and in their embryonic developments. Homology goes much deeper than this, however. The most truly fundamental of all similarities are similarities of chemical structure and function (metabolism).

Chemists recognize the existence of slightly more than a hundred chemical **elements.** All things, animate and inanimate, are composed of one or more of these elements, combined together in varying ways and proportions. Of these one hundred elements, living things are constructed mainly of *four.* These four, carbon, hydrogen, oxygen, nitrogen, constitute about 99 percent of all living matter—plant, amoeba, or man. Here is fundamental similarity indeed!

Of the remaining elements, sulfur and potassium are always found in living organisms and hence, with the "big four" mentioned above, are always essential to life. Still other elements are essential to most, if not all, living things: copper, iron, cobalt, zinc, magnesium, manganese, calcium, sodium, and chlorine. Traces of other elements are found with variable frequency in the plant and animal kingdoms. These "trace elements" are frequently important despite their presence in but small quantity. They often contribute to such quantitatively small but nevertheless vital constituents as vitamins. But we note that living things are mainly composed of less than a fifth of the elements available in nature, and that of this small group four only are especially prominent. It may well be that this fundamental similarity of chemical structure running through the plant and animal kingdoms is basic to all other similarities.

There is interest in the fact that the chemical elements found in living things are among the most abundant of the elements found in nature. This would be expected if living matter originated from nonliving matter. In living things some elements, especially carbon and nitrogen, are present in greater abundance than they are in the nonliving world, while other elements, e.g., silicon, are present in much less abundance.

What do these chemical elements form in living organisms? The most plentiful compound is **water,** composed of hydrogen and oxygen in the proportion of two atoms of hydrogen to one of oxygen: H_2O. Water comprises from 70 to 90 percent or more, by weight, of living things. It is a most essential constituent, taking part in all life processes. Without it life could not exist. Dissolved in the water are various inorganic salts, such as sodium chloride ("table salt").

In addition to water and inorganic salts, the chemical elements found in largest amount in living things form three classes of organic compounds: **carbohydrates, fats,** and **proteins.** Carbohydrates (e.g., starches, sugars, and cellulose, the stiffening, fibrous material in plants) are composed of carbon, hydrogen, and oxygen, the latter two elements being present in the same proportions as they are in water. Fats are also composed of carbon, hydrogen, and oxygen, but the oxygen constitutes a smaller proportion of a fat molecule than it does of a carbohydrate molecule. Other elements, such as nitrogen and phosphorus, may also be present in fats. Proteins, familiar to us in "lean meat" (muscle), are the most complex substances known. They always contain carbon, hydrogen, oxygen, nitrogen, and sulfur. Phosphorus is also a frequent constituent, having a special duty to perform, as we shall see shortly. Other elements may be present.

Again we note the fundamental similarity of all living things, expressed in this case by the fact that they are all composed of proteins, carbohydrates, and fats, which combine to form the complex substance termed by Huxley "the physical basis of life": **protoplasm.** Protoplasm, "the living stuff," is observable with the microscope and is found to have many of the same physical and chemical properties in all living things. Actually, there are differences. The protoplasms of plant, amoeba, and man are not identical. But the similarities overshadow the differences, indicating again that all life is one.

Thus we see that the elements carbon, hydrogen, oxygen, nitrogen, and a few others combine to form proteins, carbohydrates, and fats. Proteins, carbohydrates, and fats combine to form protoplasm. What does protoplasm form? In almost all living things protoplasm is built into structural units called **cells** (Fig. 5.1). These are usually of microscopic size; they are

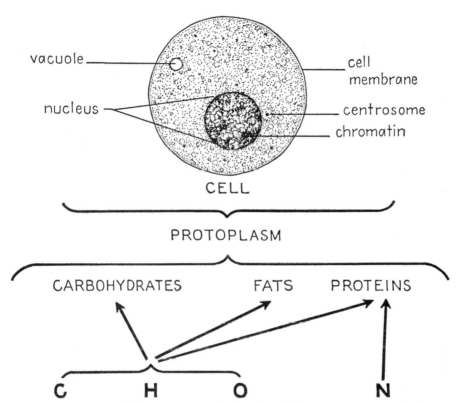

FIG. 5.1. Diagram of the manner in which carbon, hydrogen, oxygen, and nitrogen enter into formation of carbohydrates, fats, and proteins, and the latter in turn combine to form protoplasm, which is aggregated into cells.

the "building blocks" of which the tissues of plants and animals are constructed. An organism may consist of one cell (see Chap. 4), of several or many cells, or of millions of cells. In the latter instance the body is composed of specialized **tissues,** some serving purposes of digestion, some of secretion, some of sensory perception, some of conduction of nervous impulses, some of locomotion, and so on. But all of these specialized tissues are composed of cells. The cells vary in shape and other properties, but they are all so similar in fundamental plan that we can draw a diagram of a "typical" cell (Fig. 5.1) stressing the points shared in common. In

1838 and 1839 Schleiden and Schwann firmly established the truth that all plants and animals are composed of cells, plus structures, such as shell and bone, produced by cells. Organization of protoplasm into cells, then, is another fundamental similarity possessed by all, or almost all, living things (the question of whether or not the noncellular viruses are living is not of particular concern to our present discussion).

So far, we have been dealing with similarities of structure: chemical structure, submicroscopic and microscopic structure. Similarities of structure frequently entail similarities of function, similarities of the processes participated in by the similar structures—in other words: similarities of physiology. Since cells have the same fundamental structure throughout the plant and animal kingdoms we should not be surprised by the fact that the process of **cell division (mitosis)** is essentially similar throughout these kingdoms. Although there are many variations in detail, the fundamentals of the process can be incorporated into one diagram of "typical" mitosis (Fig. 5.2). Reduced to its essentials mitosis is a process by which the **chromosomes** of the nucleus are precisely duplicated so that each of the two daughter cells has chromosomes exactly like the other and exactly like those possessed by the cell which divided. Other constituents of the cell are divided with approximate equality, but the process has as its main "objective" *exact* duplication and distribution of the chromosomes. Why are the chromosomes so important? They contain the **genes,** already mentioned as the units of heredity (p. 10). Evidently precise distribution of such units of heredity is of first importance.

Though genes have never been seen with a microscope, much has been learned about them by indirect methods and by study of what they do and how they do it. They exercise control over processes going on within the cells. Since the body is composed of cells, all of which were derived from a single cell (fertilized ovum) by repeated cell divisions, this control is especially important in determining the nature of the individual. Both heredity (genes) and environment are important in determining this. Of the two, the genes are the continuing element; passed on from generation to generation they form the continuity between parents and offspring. As noted in Chapter 2, genes sometimes undergo change, called mutation, the altered gene having a different effect on the organism from that of the unaltered gene. Since the origin of change is one of the fundamental problems of evolution, we shall have much to say about mutations in our discussion of the principles of evolutionary change (Chaps. 15–21).

In a very real sense genes are the most fundamental units of living things. They form the principal connection between one generation and the next, and they are of prime importance in determining the nature of

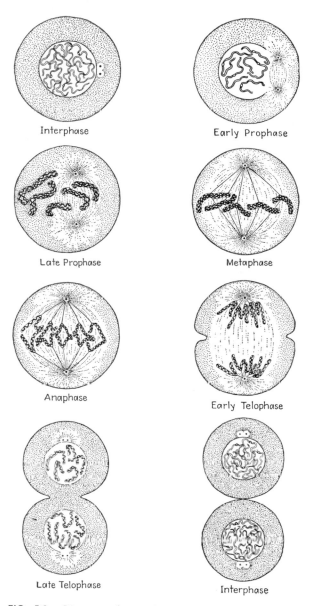

Interphase

Early Prophase

Late Prophase

Metaphase

Anaphase

Early Telophase

Late Telophase

Interphase

FIG. 5.2. Diagram of typical mitosis (cell division). Note the elaborate mechanisms insuring exact duplication of each chromosome, and exact distribution of the "daughter chromosomes" so that each cell receives one of each kind and thus has exactly the same number and kinds as the original cell had. In the first diagram (upper left) each chromosome is shown as having duplicated itself (indicated by the double lines showing parallel threads). Each chromosome shortens, by coiling, and secretes a matrix about itself prior to the actual separation of the daughter chromosomes (formed by the earlier duplication) in anaphase and later stages.

the organism in which they are found. Perhaps the first living things were essentially genelike in nature. While we may never know what form life first took, the viruses offer a possible clue, since they have some of the attributes we associate with living things (e.g., reproduction) combined with attributes more characteristic of nonliving material (e.g., the fact that some of them, at least, can be crystallized). It is suggestive that viruses and genes have many points in common: the chemical constituents are similar, nucleic acids playing an essential role; both are capable of reproduction (self-duplication); both influence the life processes of cells in which they are found; both undergo chemical change (mutation). But whatever may have been the nature of the first living entity, we see in genes the most fundamental units of life—the units basic to homologies of morphology (Chap. 3), of embryology (Chap. 4), of serology (Chap. 6), and of physiology.

Similarities and Dissimilarities in Metabolism

The processes of living, such as digestion and assimilation of food, respiration, production of energy, excretion, and so on, are included under the general term **metabolism.** Since plants and animals share so many similarities of chemical and physical structure we should expect to find similarities in the living processes in which these like structures participate. The expectation is justified, but added to the similarities we find differences no less interesting.

Turning first to the matter of nutrition we ask: How do living things obtain the carbon, hydrogen, oxygen, nitrogen, and so on, to build into proteins, carbohydrates, and fats? In the first place, some living things can make use of these elements as they occur in inanimate nature. These are the green plants. If a green plant has available a supply of water (containing hydrogen and oxygen in the same proportions found in carbohydrates), carbon dioxide (in the air), a variety of inorganic salts, and a source of nitrogen such as ammonia or nitrate, it can manufacture its own proteins, carbohydrates, and fats, including all needed vitamins. The wonderful synthetic ability of the green substance, **chlorophyll,** makes this process possible, utilizing energy from the sun. Living things which can thus derive all needed supplies from the inorganic world are called **autotrophic.** Autotrophic organisms are absolutely essential to the survival of organisms which lack the ability to manufacture some or all of their proteins, carbohydrates, and fats from inorganic ingredients. Such dependent organisms are called **heterotrophic.**

Heterotrophic organisms vary in their dependence upon other organisms for food. Many of them can manufacture all needed proteins, fats, vitamins, and so on, if they are provided with a source of carbon other than the carbon dioxide of the air. That is, they do not possess the green plant's ability to build carbohydrates from carbon dioxide and water but must obtain the needed carbon from carbohydrates (sugars, starches) manufactured by green plants. Most fungi are in this category. Given a source of carbon in the decomposition of organic matter, fungi can manufacture for themselves everything else they need. Thus the bread mold, *Neurospora,* can do this, except that it cannot manufacture its own biotin, one of the B group of vitamins. *Neurospora* must obtain its biotin already formed.

Animals are heterotrophic. With few exceptions they cannot manufacture from carbon dioxide and water any considerable proportion of the carbohydrates they need. Thus animals are "energy spenders" (Blum, 1955), obtaining their energy from carbon compounds built up, synthesized, by green plants. Animals vary in ability to manufacture other necessary materials, given a suitable source of carbon (in compounds furnished by plants). Most mammals, for example, can manufacture their own vitamin C (ascorbic acid), but the guinea pigs and the primates (monkeys, apes, and man) cannot.

Proteins are built up of organic compounds called **amino acids.** Amino acids, in turn, are manufactured from carbohydrates and some source of nitrogen, such as ammonia. Given these ingredients animals can manufacture some of the necessary amino acids and synthesize them into proteins. Green plants can synthesize *all* their proteins in this way. Animals vary in their ability to do so. There are about nineteen amino acids generally involved in the synthesis of one or another of the animal proteins. Of these nineteen, man, for example, can manufacture eleven for himself in quantities sufficient for his needs. The others must ordinarily be included, already formed, in his diet. White rats, the lower mammals whose dietary requirements have been most intensively studied, cannot manufacture two amino acids which man can manufacture. Despite differences, however, there is surprising similarity among animals, even among such unlike forms as insects, birds, and mammals, in the amino acids which can, and those which cannot, be synthesized by the animal itself. Or looking at the matter the other way around, there is surprising similarity among animals in dietary requirements—in the nature of materials which must be supplied already formed. Here again we see fundamental similarities indicating that all life is one.

But along with the resemblances we have noted differences. These express themselves in decreased ability to manufacture needed organic materials from inorganic sources. Apparently abilities possessed by ancestors have been lost by descendants in many cases. If green plants are abundant in the environment, why should an animal manufacture its own carbohydrates from carbon dioxide and water? The same question might be asked for any other ingredient in the diet. Evidently, then, unneeded capabilities have been lost by organisms. Such a loss would be favored by natural selection (Chap. 2), since wasted energy is always disadvantageous. In other words, the losses of synthesizing capability are examples of the trend toward *specialization* which we shall find appearing time after time in our study of evolution.

How do animals utilize proteins, carbohydrates, and fats contained in their food? Proteins are used in the body to form new tissue, both to increase the amount of tissue when the body is growing and to replace worn-out tissue. We obtain proteins from meat, eggs, cereals, and many other foods, but these proteins are not in a form to be used directly by our bodies. They must first be broken down into their constituent amino acids. Then these amino acids are synthesized into the precise proteins needed by the body for growth and repair. The breaking down of proteins into amino acids is one part of the process of **digestion** occurring in our stomach and small intestine. The process is made possible by the presence in these parts of the digestive tract of substances called **enzymes,** which act as catalysts. Proteins, being extremely complex chemical substances, are not split into amino acids at one step; a series of changes is involved. Each change in the process is made possible by presence of the appropriate enzyme. The point we wish to make here is that there is great similarity throughout the animal kingdom in these protein-splitting enzymes.

Carbohydrates and fats are used by the body as *fuel,* to provide energy for all phases of metabolism, energy for movement and activity, energy in the form of heat (especially in birds and mammals). Some carbohydrates, such as the "simple sugar," **glucose,** are comprised of small enough molecules so that they can pass unaltered through the membrane lining the digestive tract. They are then carried by the blood to the tissues of the body where fuel is needed. But starches, and many sugars, consist of larger molecules which must first be split into "simple sugars" before they can pass through the membrane. As in the case of proteins, this splitting of larger molecules into smaller ones is accomplished by enzyme action. And again there is great similarity throughout the animal kingdom in the enzymes concerned. The enzymes possessed by an individual species are closely correlated with the food habits of the species. Carnivores (flesh eaters) have mainly protein-splitting enzymes; herbivores (plant eaters) have mainly carbohydrate-splitting ones; omnivorous feeders like ourselves are well supplied with all kinds. In other words, the differences which exist are connected with the *adaptation* of animals for different diets.

We have mentioned that proteins are utilized for growth and repair of tissues. Suppose an animal eats more protein than is needed for growth and repair; what happens to the excess? We recall that the protein is split into amino acids. Amino acids not needed for synthesis of new proteins are broken down still further, in higher vertebrates mainly by the liver. The products formed are carbohydrates (simple sugars) and ammonia. This is just the reverse of the process mentioned on page 85 by which amino acids are manufactured in the first place. The carbohydrates derived from this process are used as fuel, just as any other carbohydrates are. The ammonia formed is a waste product, and being toxic (poisonous) it must be eliminated from the body as efficiently as possible (see below).

Fuel for Life's Fires

Every process connected with the business of living requires the expenditure of energy, whether in locomotion of the body as a whole, in the use of muscles in work and play, or in the less obvious activities such as the secretion of glands, the activity of the nervous system, and all the other processes involved in metabolism: digestion, respiration, excretion, and so on. No cell of the body can carry on its activities without using energy. Thus it becomes important to inquire into the means by which the cells obtain the needed energy.

The sun is the ultimate source of energy for life on this earth. We have seen that green plants are capable, through photosynthesis, of combining carbon dioxide and water to form carbohydrates. The simplest chemical formulation we can write for this reaction is the following:

$$6 CO_2 + 6 H_2O \rightarrow C_6H_{12}O_6 + 6 O_2$$

(For the benefit of readers unfamiliar with even elementary chemistry we translate as follows: "Six molecules of carbon dioxide combine with six molecules of water to form one molecule of glucose plus six molecules of oxygen.") The oxygen is liberated into the atmosphere; the carbohydrate (glucose) is the product in which we are interested at present. It may be stored in the plant tissues, or, more commonly, molecules of this "simple sugar" may be combined to form more complex sugars or starches or may enter into the formation of amino acids and hence of proteins.

We should note particularly that this reaction occurs only under very special conditions. If we mix carbon dioxide and water in a test tube they do not combine to form glucose. Why not? The fundamental reason is that the combining of carbon dioxide and water to form a carbohydrate requires appropriate application of energy. The forming of carbohydrate is an "uphill reaction," and energy is required to drive anything uphill, as everyone knows. Where can the needed energy be obtained and how can it be applied? Green plants have the ability to harness energy from the sun's radiations for this particular synthesis. Actually, then, a molecule of glucose contains not merely carbon, hydrogen, and oxygen; it also contains a certain amount of energy which was not present in the carbon dioxide and water from which it was formed. In carbon dioxide and water molecules the atoms are bound together by electrical forces of relatively little energy. In glucose, however, the atoms are bound together in a more complex manner. The accompanying diagram shows the arrangement of atoms in a molecule of one form of glucose. The five carbon

$$
\begin{array}{c}
\text{CH}_2\text{OH} \\
\text{H} \quad \text{C}\!-\!\!-\!\!-\text{O} \quad \text{H} \\
\text{H} \\
\text{C} \quad \text{OH} \quad \text{H} \quad \text{C} \\
\text{HO} \quad \text{C}\!-\!\!-\!\!-\text{C} \quad \text{OH} \\
\text{H} \quad \text{OH}
\end{array}
$$

atoms and one oxygen atom are joined together in a hexagonal ring. The connecting lines of the ring represent bonds holding the atoms together. These are called covalent bonds. They result from the pairing of an electron from one atom with an electron from its neighbor in the ring. In a sense the atoms "hold hands" by means of their electrons. Energy is expended in building this chemical structure, and this energy must be obtained from a source, the sun, outside the plant itself. The "locked-up" energy contained in such molecules is of paramount importance for animals.

As we have seen, animals are ultimately dependent upon plants for food. Animals eat plants, and the carbohydrates manufactured by the latter are digested and transported to the cells of the body. In this way animal cells are supplied with fuel. In the animal cells the chemical reaction given above is reversed:

$$ C_6H_{12}O_6 + 6\ O_2 \rightarrow 6\ CO_2 + 6\ H_2O $$

One molecule of glucose combines with six molecules of oxygen (obtained from the air through respiration). The products obtained are six molecules of carbon dioxide, six molecules of water, *and* the energy "locked up" in the process of building the glucose molecule in the first place. Since energy was required to build this molecule, energy is released when the molecule is finally broken down. Part of the free energy can then be used by the animal cells for carrying on their life processes. Thus in a roundabout way each cell of the animal body receives energy from the sun.

Our account of the transfer of energy from sun to animal cell is greatly oversimplified. Every stage of the process is enormously complex. The manufacture of glucose by green plants involves many steps, including intermediate products having complex chemical composition. The $6 CO_2 + 6 H_2O$ forms the beginning of a series of substances; $C_6H_{12}O_6$ is the culmination of this series. Included in the series are substances which do not appear in the final product. Of these we may mention particularly enzymes and coenzymes (see below), without which the synthesis could not be accomplished. Formation of energy-rich carbohydrate from energy-poor carbon dioxide and water is complex and difficult business.

Complexity also characterizes the release in animal cells of energy stored in the carbohydrate molecules. The simple formula given above conveys the impression that the process is much like burning coal in a steam engine. In the engine coal unites with oxygen (burns), with resultant production of heat (energy). Similarly, our formula shows glucose uniting with oxygen, with release of energy. While this is true, it is again an oversimplification. Between the glucose-plus-oxygen on the one hand and the carbon dioxide-plus-water on the other at least twenty-five intermediate steps occur. In a muscle cell, for example, free energy is transferred from the glucose to complex organic constituents of the muscle cell itself. Many intermediate products are involved in the chemical transformations by which, in a series of steps, free energy from the glucose is transmitted to the contractile mechanism of the muscle cell, making possible contraction of the latter. It is important to note that each of the steps involves the action of an *enzyme*. Previously we noted enzymes concerned with the digestion of food. But enzyme action is of much more general occurrence. So far as we can tell, every chemical change in metabolism is activated—catalyzed—by an enzyme. Enzymes are usually, if not always, protein in nature and hence in themselves extremely complex substances. Not only is an enzyme needed for each chemical transformation, but frequently one or more complex substances necessary for the activity of an enzyme must also be present. These are called coenzymes.

Thus by a series of steps involving enzymes and coenzymes are accomplished chemical transformations making possible transfer of free energy from glucose to cell mechanisms. The sequence of chemical events is extremely complicated. Prominent among the intermediate substances involved are phosphorus-containing derivatives of adenylic acid. The element phosphorus plays a particularly important role in the mobilization and transport of the free energy required for cellular activity. Readers with some knowledge of organic chemistry will find in textbooks of biochemistry and physiology (e.g., Harrow and Mazur, 1958) details of the process. Here we wish to emphasize one point. Insofar as our knowledge enables us to reach a conclusion, these complex metabolic processes, with their enzymes and coenzymes, are fundamentally similar in all animals. Indeed, we may extend this statement to plants since, aside from their unique capability of photosynthesis, plants are much like animals in metabolic processes. There are many variations on the theme, but the theme itself underlies all variations. No more convincing evidence of the fundamental unity of all life could be found.

The Origin of Life

Our brief discussion of the building of energy-rich compounds (e.g., glucose) from energy-poor ones (e.g., carbon dioxide and water) raises an interesting question concerning the origin of life on earth. We noted that enzymes are necessary in the manufacture of carbohydrates by green plants. We also noted that enzymes are proteins, and proteins have much more complex chemical structure than do carbohydrates. Now, proteins are built of amino acids, and the latter in turn are formed in part of carbohydrates. Yet in photosynthesis carbohydrates cannot be formed unless proteins are already present to serve as enzymes! Here we seem in danger of becoming involved in a vicious circle of the "which came first, the hen or the egg" variety. What we really wish to know is this: Back in the beginning when there were no proteins to serve as enzymes how were the first energy-rich compounds manufactured from energy-poor ones?

Undoubtedly the appearance of the first life on this planet was preceded by a long period of chemical evolution, a period during which chemical compounds were being formed and rebuilt under the influence of radiations from the sun, of temperatures then prevailing, and of other conditions found at the time. We may feel sure that carbon-containing compounds were among those formed in this way. They would have been relatively simple, energy-poor carbon compounds. How could free energy be applied to them to build them into carbohydrates and proteins? Blum (1955) has suggested that the origin of life may have been a very gradual process, so that it might be difficult to draw a precise line between non-living and living. This author suggests the possibility that adenylic acid compounds containing phosphorus may have made possible a first step in this gradual process. We recall that such compounds are essential for the transport of free energy in living cells. These compounds incorporate in their structure "energy-rich phosphate bonds"; when the bonds are broken energy is released to be utilized by the cell. Perhaps such adenylic acid compounds, formed in the days of inanimate chemical evolution, provided the free energy needed for the first step in transforming energy-poor carbon compounds into energy-rich ones. We may imagine that, following such a beginning, the process of developing compounds increasingly rich in energy progressed step by step until eventually the first proteins appeared. With the appearance of proteins the way would have been open for the gradual development of increased complexities of structure and function. Especially important would be the development of some form of photochemical reaction by which the sun's radiations could be harnessed to provide energy for building energy-rich compounds in quantity needed if life was to progress beyond the first simple beginnings. The photochemical reaction eventually evolved was, as we have seen, the photosynthesis carried on by green plants. It is significant that blue-green algae, single-celled plants capable of this synthesis, are among the first living things of which we have fossil evidence (p. 138).

The mystery of the origin of life has such appeal that many scientists have theorized about it. We have touched on the matter only as it involved the initial mobilization of free energy in days before the advent of photosynthesis. Readers are referred to Blum (1955), Oparin (1957), and Wald (1954) for further discussion of this fundamental problem and for references to other writings on the origin of life.

Disposal of Nitrogenous Wastes

Ammonia is a nitrogenous waste product continually formed in all animals. It is derived not only from the splitting of excess proteins taken in as food but also from the breaking down of proteins from worn-out tissues of the body. The problem of ridding the body of this toxic waste product is faced by all animals.

It is relatively simple for aquatic animals. Ammonia is highly soluble in water, so animals living in water readily lose their ammonia to it. Hence, a large proportion of the nitrogenous wastes of aquatic animals is excreted as ammonia. Among vertebrates this is true of most fishes, which excrete ammonia mainly through their gills.

The land dwellers cannot rid themselves of ammonia so easily. Accordingly we find that the amphibians have a different method of dealing with the problem. They convert the ammonia into **urea** (by combining it with carbon dioxide). Urea is readily soluble in water and differs from ammonia in being relatively nontoxic. Thus it can be stored in the body and eventually excreted by the kidney in the urine.

It will be recalled that typical amphibians, such as frogs, have a life history which includes a tadpole stage. The tadpole is a larva living in the water, using gills for respiration, and in general leading a fishlike existence. Interestingly enough, frog tadpoles also resemble fishes in excreting most of their nitrogenous wastes in the form of ammonia. Then, upon metamorphosis into the adult form, the change to the urea-forming mode of excretion is made. Here evidently is an example of recapitulation (see Chap. 4), in this case **biochemical recapitulation.**

A slightly more complex situation is presented by the vermillion-spotted newt (*Triturus*). Nash and Fankhauser (1959) found that young larvae, living in the water, excrete most of their nitrogen as ammonia but that the proportion so excreted decreases as time for metamorphosis approaches. By the time of metamorphosis about 80 percent of the nitrogen is excreted as urea, and the proportion increases to 87 percent during terrestrial life (the "red eft" stage). Eventually the newts return to the water to live as adults. In these aquatic adults partial return to the larval pattern of excretion occurs: 26 percent of the nitrogen is excreted as ammonia, 74 percent as urea.

Passing on to more completely terrestrial vertebrates, we find reptiles, birds, and mammals faced with the problem of conserving the body's water supply. How can the body be rid of nitrogenous waste products without undue loss of water in the process? There are two general solutions to the problem. Most mammals have retained the process of converting ammonia into urea, which is conveyed by the blood to the kidney. The tubules of the mammalian kidney have developed a special portion (Henle's loop) which serves the purpose of removing water from the urine, leaving the latter highly concentrated. Mammalian urine, then, contains a maximum of waste carried by a minimum of water.

Birds and most reptiles solve the problem somewhat differently. They convert ammonia into **uric acid,** an almost insoluble compound. The urine is added to the feces, and the water is reabsorbed into the body in the posterior portion of the digestive tract. In many lizards, snakes, and birds the urine is a semisolid mass of uric acid crystals, excreted with almost no loss of water.

It is interesting that some turtles have been found to excrete nitrogenous wastes both in the form of urea and in the form of uric acid. Since turtles are a very ancient group of reptiles (see Fig. 9.3, p. 177) this fact may indicate that early reptiles could accomplish both types of excretion. At any rate, the urea-forming system was doubtless inherited from amphibian ancestors. The latter also doubtless passed on the same method of excretion to the reptiles that were the ancestors of mammals (Fig. 9.3). Apparently the uric acid system was the "new development" which eventually came to characterize more highly specialized reptiles (e.g., lizards and snakes) and birds.

Needham has stressed the importance of embryonic needs in the development of the two systems of nitrogen excretion. From our discussion of the human embryo and its contact with the mother's blood stream we appreciate that urea formed in the embryo is readily transferred to the mother's blood and excreted by her kidneys. Things are quite otherwise for reptile and bird embryos. Locked away in their eggshells (Fig. 8.24, p. 169) these embryos must "live with" their waste products until hatching time. Tissues of most animals cannot thrive in a high concentration of urea. Nitrogenous wastes in bird embryos are converted into insoluble uric acid and then stored in the embryonic sac known as the allantois. In this manner the tissues are freed of soluble nitrogenous wastes that might interfere with normal metabolism—clearly an adaptation to the needs of life within an eggshell. How the turtles with their urea excretion fit into this picture is not clear. Some turtle eggs are laid in moist sand; possibly urea in solution can be passed out through the eggshell under such conditions. The matter merits further investigation.

At this point mention is appropriate of a sequence of events in the chick embryo that has frequently been cited as an example of biochemical recapitulation. Needham (1931) pointed out that in this embryo the total amount of ammonia relative to dry weight of the embryo reaches a peak on about the fourth day, that the relative concentration of urea is highest on about the ninth day, following which the concentration of uric acid becomes maximal. These facts have been interpreted to indicate that the chick embryo exhibits biochemical recapitulation: first excreting ammonia like a fish, later excreting urea like an amphibian, and then attaining the uric acid excretion which will characterize it as an adult. Reinvestigation of the problem by Fisher and Eakin (1957) has cast doubt on the correctness of this interpretation. These investigators found that at no time does the chick embryo actively excrete ammonia, though a low and fairly constant concentration of it is present in both embryonic tissues and yolk. They also found that the urea arises entirely from the amino acid arginine, and that in urea excretion the liver and kidney do not function in the manner characteristic of amphibians and mammals. Furthermore they found that as soon as the kidney starts functioning (at about the fifth day), the excretory product is uric acid as in adult birds. Evidently, then, the chick embryo does not recapitulate ancestral modes of excretion.

Turning to the invertebrates for a moment, we note that insects differ from most other invertebrates in the high proportion of nitrogenous waste excreted as uric acid. Like terrestrial vertebrates, most insects are faced with the problem of conserving the body's supply of water.

The Internal Environment

We have noted a variety of fundamental similarities (homologies) in chemical structure and in metabolism. Perhaps no similarity is more striking than the similarity in composition of the blood plasmas of varied animals. The plasma is the fluid portion of blood. It contains proteins in solution; the similarities and dissimilarities of some of these form the basis of the serological tests to be discussed in the next chapter. But aside from its proteins, plasma is essentially a salt solution. Salts of sodium, potassium, calcium, and magnesium are predominant. Of these salts our friend of the dining table, sodium chloride, occurs in greatest abundance. At this time we are particularly interested in the fact that the relative proportions of these various salts are strikingly similar in the blood plasmas of most animals, not only vertebrates but also most invertebrates, insofar as the latter contain body fluids correctly described as blood. Here is another of those fundamental similarities running through the animal kingdom.

An additional point of interest is the fact that the relative proportions of the various salts in blood plasma resemble the proportions with which these salts occur in *sea water*. This similarity may be of significance. There are various reasons for believing that life began in the sea—that the first organisms developed in the environment formed by a dilute salt solution, which is what sea water is. Even today marine protozoa live completely immersed in such a salt solution, and in such simply constructed creatures as sponges and jellyfishes (Porifera and Coelenterata) all tissues, internal as well as external, are bathed by sea water. These animals have no blood of their own, but sea water serves the same purpose, conveying to the cells such needed materials as oxygen and carrying away waste products of cell metabolism. As we intimated earlier, the "living stuff," protoplasm itself, has as its basis a salt solution. Apparently protoplasm originated in an environment of salt water. And apparently, also, protoplasm can exist only in an environment of salt water. Furthermore, the salt concentration and the proportions in which the various salts occur can seemingly vary only within fairly narrow limits if protoplasm is to survive.

We may picture, then, what probably occurred when in the course of their evolution animals became so complex in structure that some parts were no longer bathed directly by sea water. These parts would need a carrying agent to bring such essentials as oxygen and digested foodstuffs to them and to remove waste products. So some of the sea water was "bottled up" within the organism and became the blood. Mechanisms for propelling the blood throughout the body developed. In this way even the cells of innermost tissues of the body continued to live in an environment like that of the sea water in which life began.

If our interpretation is correct, animal bloods are similar in salt composition and concentration because life originated in an environment of salt water having about this composition and concentration and can continue to exist only in such an environment. The blood provides the cells with an "internal environment" reminiscent of the external environment prevailing when life began. Although some cells have become adapted for life in fluids of quite different concentrations, it is still true on the whole that "la fixité du milieu intérieur est la condition de la vie libre" (Claude Bernard). Constancy of internal environment is a necessary condition for life. This fact is reflected in another of the fundamental similarities uniting varied members of the animal kingdom.

Osmotic Regulation

The necessity for maintaining a relatively constant internal environment has presented organisms with serious problems as they have invaded differing external environments. A major factor is the phenomenon of **osmosis**. Some membranes, including the living membranes of plants and animals, are said to be differentially permeable; some substances pass through them more readily than do others. If, for example, a differentially permeable membrane has salt solution on one side of it and pure water

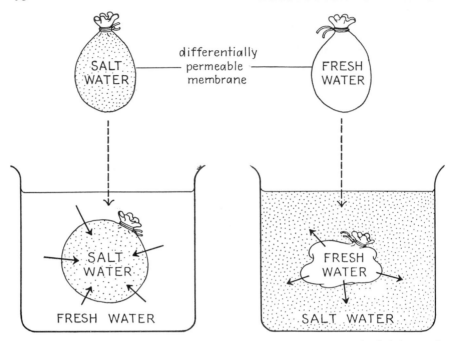

FIG. 5.3. Effects of osmotic pressure on two closed bags composed of differentially permeable membrane: left, a bag containing salt water, immersed in fresh water; right, a bag containing fresh water, immersed in salt water.

on the other, the pure water will pass through the membrane more readily than will the salt solution. Suppose we take a bag of differentially permeable membrane, fill it with salt solution, close it tightly, and then immerse it in pure water. We shall find that water passes *into* the bag through the membrane more rapidly than salt solution passes out of the bag through the membrane. The net result will be an increase in volume of the solution in the bag. If, as we have stipulated, the bag is tightly closed, an increase in volume of its contents will result in its becoming distended (Fig. 5.3). In other words, a pressure will develop inside the bag. This is known as **osmotic pressure,** and under some circumstances it may develop considerable strength—sufficient to burst our bag, perhaps. If we reverse our experiment, placing pure water in the bag and immersing the bag in salt solution, we shall find the greater movement of material in the opposite direction: the contents of the bag will become less and less, as it loses its water to the outer salt solution (Fig. 5.3). Note that in both cases water passes through the membrane *from* a region in which there is much water but little or no salt *to* a region in which there is less water in proportion to the concentration of salt. In other words, the water moves from a region in which *it* is present in relatively higher concentration to a region in which it is present in relatively lower concentration.

An organism such as a fish is in a real sense a salt solution enclosed within a bag of differentially permeable membrane. So long as the salt concentration on the outside is the same as the salt concentration on the inside there will be no osmotic effect of the kind just discussed. But suppose the fish lives in fresh water; then we have the situation described above of a differentially permeable membrane enclosing salt solution and immersed in water (Fig. 5.3). The result will be movement of water *into* the fish through its exposed membranes. If this movement were unopposed, the fish would become distended and water-logged, and might even burst, like our hypothetical bag. Obviously, what is needed is a means of ridding the animal of excess water—a means of "bailing out." The kidneys of fishes provide such a means. The kidneys of fresh-water fishes extract fluid from the blood, passing to the exterior quantities of dilute (hypotonic) urine (Fig. 5.4A).

We usually think of the kidney as an organ for ridding the body of nitrogenous wastes (see above) since that is its primary function in man and other mammals, but this is not true of fishes; in them the kidney functions little, if at all, in excretion of such waste products. We recall from our preceding discussion that nitrogenous wastes of aquatic animals are largely in the form of ammonia, and that this is passed from the blood to the surrounding water, primarily through the gills in the case of fishes.

Fresh-water fishes are faced with still another problem, that of conservation of the *salts* of blood and protoplasm (see above). The urine contains salts. How can a fresh-water fish excrete quantities of urine without seriously depleting the body's supply of salts? The problem is partially solved by the fact that the tubules of the kidney have developed sections where salts are reabsorbed from the urine back into the blood. Thus the urine reaching the exterior has a lower salt concentration than does the blood (that is what we mean when we say that the urine is "hypotonic"). But some salts are lost; the loss is made up by salts contained in food eaten by the fish, and by special secretory cells located on the gills (Fig. 5.4). These cells have the power to extract salts from the surrounding water and pass them into the blood; even "fresh" water contains some salts, though they are in low concentration.

The osmotic problem faced by fishes living in the ocean differs from that faced by fresh-water fishes. The salt concentration of the blood plasma of bony fishes is only about one quarter to one third that of sea water (Robertson, 1957). This fact may be taken to indicate that ancestors of marine bony fishes lived in fresh water, where a salt concentration less than that of sea water (in which, as we have seen, life began) was acquired. When some of the descendants of these ancestral fresh-water fishes returned to the ocean they were faced with the problem of living in a medium having greater salt concentration than did their own body fluids. They were in the position of bags of differentially permeable membrane enclosing a dilute salt solution and immersed in a more concentrated salt solution (Fig. 5.3). The contents of such a bag would decrease as water passed out-

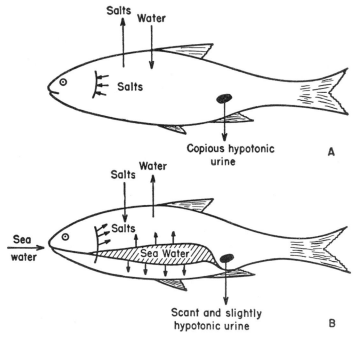

FIG. 5.4. Diagram of osmotic regulation in bony (teleost) fishes. A, fresh-water species. B, marine species. (After Baldwin; from Florkin and Morgulis, *Biochemical Evolution*, Academic Press, Inc., p. 84.)

ward through the membrane. In other words, strange as it may seem, marine fishes have to fight desiccation or drying out, owing to loss of water through exposed membranes.

How could marine descendants of fresh-water fishes meet the problem? From their fresh-water ancestors they inherited kidneys which excreted quantities of water. But marine fishes need to conserve water! Such kidneys would prove a liability. So we find that in marine bony fishes the kidneys are greatly reduced in structure and excrete but small amounts of urine. But since even that amount of water loss must be compensated for, marine fishes swallow ("drink") sea water, and the latter is absorbed, salts and all, into the blood (Fig. 5.4B). That practice restores the needed water, but it also gives the body a greater quantity of salts than is needed. Thus there is the further problem of ridding the body of excess salts. The kidney is of little help here, since its function has been much reduced in the interest of water conservation. The problem is solved by secretory cells in the gills which have the function of passing salts from the blood into the surrounding water (Fig. 5.4). Note that they function in just the opposite way from the secretory cells in the gills of fresh-water fishes.

The method described above of solving the osmotic problems of marine life is that of bony (teleost) fishes. For cartilaginous fishes (sharks, dogfishes, etc.) the problem was solved in an entirely different manner. Their internal concentration was raised to meet the concentration of the surrounding sea water and thus prevent unfavorable osmotic effects. This change was brought about in a most curious way. The salt concentration was not substantially increased; rather the *urea* concentration was increased. Whereas most fishes excrete their nitrogenous wastes as ammonia, sharks and their allies convert the ammonia to urea and then retain a high concentration of the latter within the body. This is a unique means of protecting these fishes from the desiccating effect of water loss to the surrounding sea water through exposed membranes.

Fresh-water fishes also gave rise to amphibians, the first terrestrial vertebrates, ancestors of reptiles, birds, and mammals. Earlier in the chapter we noted that water conservation is a primary problem of land dwellers. This being true, a kidney excreting large quantities of dilute urine would be as much a detriment to land dwellers as it is to marine teleost fishes. Accordingly, the amphibian kidney has some ability to absorb water from the urine back into the blood. Some of the salt supply is also salvaged in this way. In addition salt is obtained in the food. But amphibians are only incompletely terrestrial animals; many of them live their lives in fresh water and are much like fresh-water fishes in matters of osmotic regulation. Other amphibians must stay in a moist environment, never having evolved skin coverings effective against desiccation. As noted previously, however, these amphibians no longer excrete most of their nitrogenous wastes as ammonia, as did their fresh-water fish ancestors. They convert the ammonia to urea and use the kidney as the principal means of ridding the body of the urea.

What was the *original* function of the vertebrate kidney? We have two opposite points of view; at the present time we can not decide which is correct.

1. Romer (1959) has concluded that geological and other evidence indicates that the first vertebrates (jawless fishes called ostracoderms, Fig. 8.14, p. 159) lived in fresh water. If so the vertebrate kidney functioned first as an organ for ridding the body of excess water, and only later took on functions of excretion.

2. Robertson (1957) has concluded that the geological and other evidence indicates that the first vertebrates were marine, and that the kidney was primarily an excretory organ. Its microscopic structure resembles that of excretory tubules found in some invertebrates, in fact. According to this point of view the ridding of the body of excess water came as a later function of the organ. Robertson's opinion is that some marine vertebrates, notably cyclostomes (lamprey, hagfish) and cartilaginous fishes such as sharks did not have fresh-water ancestors; yet all have well developed kidneys.

Both authors quoted agree, however, that evidence supports the view that bony fishes and amphibians had fresh-water fishes in their ancestry. Hence an organ that functioned in connection with osmotic regulation in ancestors assumed (or resumed?) the function of excretion in descendants.

The excretory function of the kidney, once inaugurated, or resumed, became its main function. Reptiles, birds, and mammals develop horny scales, feathers, hair, etc., with the result that water loss through the skin is minimal. And water loss through the kidneys in birds and mammals is reduced by development of a special section of the kidney tubules (loop of Henle) which reabsorbs back into the blood much of the water in the urine. Salts are also salvaged by regions of the tubules. Thus these truly terrestrial animals excrete a concentrated (hypertonic) urine, ridding the body of a maximum amount of waste dissolved in a relatively small amount of water. As already mentioned, reptiles and birds which convert nitrogenous wastes into relatively insoluble uric acid attain the peak of water conservation in the excretory process (pp. 92–93).

The solutions of problems of osmotic regulation afford striking examples of adaptation to environmental requirements, as well as an example of evolution of function in an organ of the body, the kidney. Structural changes in the kidney accompany the functional changes, but the details are beyond the scope of the present brief discussion.

Biochemical Evidence of Vertebrate-Invertebrate Relationships

Phylum Chordata includes all vertebrates, possessing a vertebral column ("backbone") as adults, and a few animals that lack a vertebral column but do possess a notochord in some stage of development (the protochor-dates). Of this latter group the tunicates were mentioned in the preced-ing chapter (pp. 73–75). Also included among the protochordates are the lancelet, *Amphioxus,* and the somewhat wormlike group typified by *Balanoglossus* (Fig. 5.5). Each of these three groups has at one time or

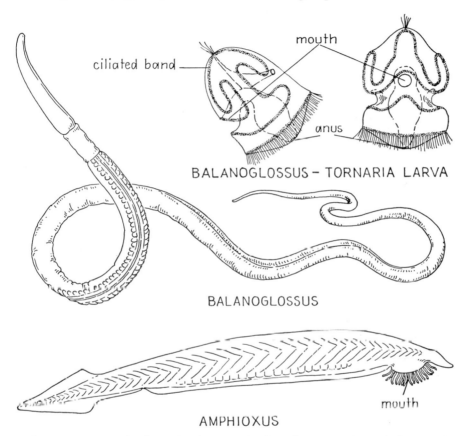

FIG. 5.5. Two protochordates: *Amphioxus* and *Balanoglossus,* together with the tornaria larva of the latter.

another been proposed as possible ancestors of vertebrates. But if one of them is ancestral, from what group of invertebrates did it arise in its turn? Phylum Chordata is singularly isolated among the phyla; none of the other phyla possess structural features which approach those of chor-dates at all closely. Consequently, the evolutionary origin of vertebrates is a much debated point. One clue is furnished by the fact that *Balanoglos-sus* passes through a most unchordatelike larval stage (Fig. 5.5). Its larva resembles nothing encountered elsewhere in Phylum Chordata, but it does resemble the larvae of members of Phylum Echinodermata. This phylum includes starfishes, brittle stars, sea urchins, and their spiny allies. There is little about the adults to suggest relationship to, and possible ancestry of, vertebrates. Yet because of the striking larval similarities, especially in the mode of development of the coelom (body cavity), the most widely accepted theory of vertebrate origin is that some echinoderms, or a group ancestral to echinoderms, gave rise to the group of protochordates of which *Balanoglossus* is a survivor, and that this group gave rise to vertebrates. *Amphioxus* is more like vertebrates than are the other protochordates; it may be a survivor of a group in the ancestral line or allied to it.

Within the last few years unexpected corroboration of this theory has come from the field of biochemistry. A complicated series of chemical reactions is involved when muscles contract. Involved in one step of the process are chemical compounds known as phosphagens (recall the importance of phosphorus in transport of free energy in muscle cells, p. 90). In the muscles of vertebrates the phosphagen present has in its composition the substance called **creatine,** the compound being known as creatine phosphoric acid, or phosphocreatine, or, for brevity, PC. On the other hand, the muscles of most invertebrates have a phosphagen containing the substance called **arginine,** the resulting compound being known as arginine phosphoric acid, or phosphoarginine, or PA.

Here we have a clear-cut chemical distinction: vertebrates all have PC; most invertebrates have PA. How do the protochordates fit into the picture? *Amphioxus* resembles vertebrates in having PC only. Some species of tunicates appear to have PA only, others PC only (Morrison, Griffiths, and Ennor, 1956). *Balanoglossus* possesses both PA and PC. Thus these protochordates, taken collectively, seem to link vertebrates with invertebrates. Turning to the latter we ask: Is PC possessed by any groups of invertebrates? Some echinoderms possess PC, and some segmented worms (Phylum Annelida) have a substance which is similar and may be the same. Some echinoderms possess PA only, at least one possesses PC only, others possess both PA and PC, as does *Balanoglossus*. These facts strengthen the idea that the group represented by *Balanoglossus* is the connecting link between invertebrates and vertebrates. There is also the possibility that, as suggested by Prosser (1960), PC has arisen more than once, by parallel evolution in independent evolutionary lines (see below). Yet the distribution of PA and PC, particularly when taken together with similarity of larvae, suggests that echinoderms are at least closely related to the ancestors from which the chordates arose. It is entirely possible, of course, that both echinoderms and chordates arose from a common ancestral group no longer existing. Parenthetically it is interesting to note that precipitin tests (Chap. 6) also indicate that echinoderms are the invertebrates most closely allied to Phylum Chordata (Wilhelmi, 1942).

Chemical Mutations

Florkin and Morgulis (1949) have called attention to the fact that phosphoarginine and phosphocreatine have similar chemical structures. One could give rise to the other by chemical changes of no great magnitude. Such changes could arise in evolutionary history through one or more gene mutations. The sequence would be: (1) change in gene, with (2) resulting change in the chemical compound whose nature was determined by that gene. Such mutations evidently occurred in the line leading to vertebrates, changing some, and eventually all, of the PA production to PC production. These mutations may also have occurred in other lines, as, for example, in the ancestry of the few annelid worms mentioned above as possessors of PC or a closely allied compound.

Another example of chemical mutation cited by Florkin and Morgulis is that of a peculiar respiratory pigment found in the blood of certain families of annelid worms. The respiratory pigment in our own blood is **hemoglobin,** the red substance in our red blood cells. Hemoglobin consists of an iron-containing compound (heme) combined with a protein (globin). Hemoglobin carries oxygen from the lungs to cells in need of it. All vertebrates possess hemoglobin, as do a large number of invertebrates. Included in this group are many annelid worms, such as the common earthworm. But three families of annelid worms have a blood pigment which is *green,* rather than red. It is called **chlorocruorin.** A member (*Serpula*) of one of these three families possesses both chlorocruorin and hemoglobin. Although the two substances have contrasting colors, the chemical differences between the iron-containing portions of them are of a minor nature. There are also differences in the amino acids comprising the protein portion. But so far as the iron-containing component is concerned, a relatively small genetic change, perhaps even a single mutation, could have produced the observed chemical alteration.

Actually, all mutations (except chromosomal aberrations—see p. 396) are "chemical mutations" in the sense that they are chemical changes in genes, resulting in chemical changes in bodily materials and processes controlled by those genes. Even mutations having structural changes as their most conspicuous effects are chemical mutations in this sense. The structural change has as its basis some change in chemical metabolism operative during embryonic development, and this change in turn is preceded by chemical change in a gene. This fact suggests the question: How do chemical changes in genes cause changes in bodily processes? There is evidence that genes control the nature of *enzymes,* those catalystlike substances essential to all living processes. When a gene changes, the enzyme it conditions is modified accordingly, and hence the bodily process controlled by the enzyme is altered.

While all mutations are chemical mutations in the sense just stated, the chemical mutations we stress at this point are those having as their principal effect an observable change in the chemistry of the body. Many additional examples are known. A change in a gene which conditions the production of pigment material, melanin, results in the gene's failing in its function. Presumably the changed gene fails to produce an essential enzyme. Consequently, if an individual inherits such a changed gene from both parents, he will have no pigment, i.e., he will be an albino. Research with the bread mold, *Neurospora,* mentioned previously, has brought to light mutations which cause failure in the synthesis of one or another of the amino acids, vitamins, and other organic substances which normal *Neurospora* can manufacture for itself (see Beadle, 1946). These are all mutations having as their outward manifestations changes in the chemistry of the organism.

Retinal Pigments, an Evolutionary Enigma

The retinas of our eyes contain two kinds of light-sensitive cells, the rods and the cones. The rods function in dim light, the cones in bright light. The rods contain a sensitive pigment commonly called "visual purple" but better termed **rhodopsin.** It is rose-colored, rather than purple, and it bleaches rapidly when exposed to light. Its properties are important in the visual process.

Rhodopsin is found in the eyes of marine fishes, frogs, turtles, birds, and mammals. Evidence, direct and indirect, also indicates its presence in eyes of invertebrates. In fresh-water fishes, however, it is replaced by a different substance, one actually purple in color, called **porphyropsin.** Both rhodopsin and porphyropsin are formed in part from vitamin A, different forms of the latter being involved in the two instances. Vitamin A belongs to the class of compounds known as carotenoids, a group of fat-soluble pigments varying from yellow to red and occurring widely in both plant and animal tissues. The principal pigment in carrots is one of them. Wald (1946) has presented evidence that response to light throughout both plant and animal kingdoms depends upon one compound or another in this group. Apparently we have here another example of far-reaching chemical homology uniting widely diverse living things.

Aside from this broad homology, however, is the interesting question of why fresh-water fishes have a different carotenoid, porphyropsin, than do other vertebrates. Added significance is given the question by the fact, mentioned earlier, that fresh-water fishes are believed to have been ancestral to both marine bony fishes and land vertebrates. This being the case, and assuming that ancestral fresh-water fishes resembled modern ones in this respect, both the line leading to marine bony fishes and the line leading to land vertebrates (amphibians and their descendants) apparently underwent an evolutionary change (chemical mutation or mutations) from porphyropsin to rhodopsin. This would afford another example of parallel evolution. It is interesting that the chemical difference between the two types of visual pigment is small. The molecule of rhodopsin incorporates one more atom of hydrogen than does the molecule of porphyropsin, or, to put it differently, the ring structure of the porphyropsin molecule has one more double bond than does that of rhodopsin (Wald, 1958).

We may well ask: why did the chemical change in visual pigment occur at all? Perhaps the porphyropsin system may be, in some way still unexplained, an adaptation for life in fresh water. Evidence comes from investigation of various animals. For example, the sea lamprey (a cyclostome) spends most of its adult life in the ocean but spawns, and undergoes early development, in fresh water. Wald (1958) reported that young lampreys on their way downstream to the ocean have rhodopsin in their retinas, while older lampreys on their way upstream to spawn have porphyropsin. It is as though the pigment had changed in anticipation of the environment to which the lamprey was going. Wald has regarded this change as biochemical metamorphosis.

As we noted previously (p. 92), the newt *Triturus* spends its larval period in the water and then emerges on land for a sort of adolescent period (the "red eft" stage); after two or three years it returns to the water to live as an adult. During the red eft stage it not only excretes most of its nitrogenous wastes in the form of urea (Nash and Fankhauser, 1959) as other land-dwelling amphibians do, but it also possesses a preponderance of rhodopsin in its retina, although porphyropsin is also present (Wald, 1958). When the newt has undergone a sort of second metamorphosis and returned to the aquatic environment for its adult life, porphyropsin is found to be the only visual pigment in its eyes (and the proportion of nitrogenous wastes excreted as ammonia has increased, as noted previously). The changes in both visual pigments and nitrogen excretion may be adaptations to the resumed aquatic life.

In some cases the environment in which the animal was spawned seems to determine which substance shall be present or predominate. Thus fresh-water eels spend most of their lives in fresh water but migrate into the sea to spawn. They have both substances but the rhodopsin predominates. At the time of migration from fresh water to the sea, in fact, all detectable pigment may be rhodopsin. Salmon also possess both substances, but in their case the porphyropsin predominates. They spend most of their lives in the sea but spawn in fresh water.

Bullfrogs were found by Wald to exhibit an interesting recapitulation of the change from porphyropsin in fresh-water fishes to rhodopsin in their descendants, the amphibians. Bullfrog tadpoles possess the porphyropsin system, with only a trace of rhodopsin. Thus, living in fresh water, they resemble fresh-water fishes. At the time of metamorphosis from tadpole to adult the eyes develop the rhodopsin characteristic of land vertebrates. Here we have another instance of biochemical recapitulation, although there may be nothing mysterious about it beyond the mystery of why porphyropsin should be adaptive for life in fresh water, rhodopsin for life in the air. Still other cases were given by Wald (1958) who stressed the point that the change in visual pigment is only one of several biochemical changes undergone during metamorphosis. Further research may reveal that the chemical change in visual pigment is only a more or less incidental accompaniment of more profound biochemical changes undergone by animals as they adapt to life in fresh water, on the one hand, or to life in the ocean or on land, on the other. (Yet there are a few wholly marine fishes that have porphyropsin!) Obviously we must await the results of further research before making any sweeping generalizations about the adaptive significance of these substances.

Conclusion

In this chapter we have discussed some of the fundamental similarities (homologies) exhibited in the chemical structure and metabolic processes of living things. We have also considered some of the evolutionary changes which have modified basic patterns as organisms have become adapted to differing environments. We see that adults and embryos have changed during their evolutionary histories not only in morphology but also in physiology. The fact that our knowledge of the morphological changes is more complete than our knowledge of the physiological and biochemical changes merely reflects the present stage in the history of science. Morphology and embryology are old branches of biology; physiology and biochemistry are youngsters. As they "grow up," our knowledge of biochemical evolution will increase vastly.

References and Suggested Readings

Baldwin, E. *An Introduction to Comparative Biochemistry*, 3rd ed. Cambridge: Cambridge University Press, 1949. (A most readable and stimulating little volume.)

Beadle, G. W. "Genes and the chemistry of the organism," *American Scientist*, 34 (1946), 31–53. Also in G. A. Baitsell (ed.). *Science in Progress*, Vol. 5. New Haven: Yale University Press, 1947. Pp. 166–196.

de Beer, G. R. *Embryos and Ancestors*, 3rd ed. Oxford: Oxford University Press, 1958.

Blum, H. F. "Perspectives in evolution," *American Scientist*, 43 (1955), 595–610.

Blum, H. F. *Time's Arrow and Evolution*, 2nd ed. Princeton: Princeton University Press, 1955.

Fisher, J. R., and R. E. Eakin. "Nitrogen excretion in developing chick embryos," *Journal of Embryology and Experimental Morphology*, 5 (1957), 215–224.

Florkin, E., and S. Morgulis. *Biochemical Evolution*. New York: Academic Press, Inc., 1949.

Harrow, B., and M. Mazur. *Textbook of Biochemistry*, 7th ed. Philadelphia: W. B. Saunders Company, 1958.

Krogh, A. *Osmotic Regulation in Aquatic Animals*. Cambridge: Cambridge University Press, 1939.

Morrison, J. F., D. E. Griffiths, and A. H. Ennor. "Biochemical evolution: position of the tunicates," *Nature*, 178 (1956), 359.

Nash, G., and G. Fankhauser. "Changes in the pattern of nitrogen excretion during the life cycle of the newt," *Science*, 130 (1959), 714–716.

Needham, J. *Chemical Embryology*. 3 vols. Cambridge: Cambridge University Press, 1931.

Nigrelli, R. F. (ed.). "Modern ideas on spontaneous generation," *Annals of the New York Academy of Sciences*, 69 (1957), 255–376.

Oparin, A. I. *The Origin of Life on the Earth*, 3rd ed. New York: Academic Press, Inc., 1957.

Prosser, C. L. "Comparative physiology in relation to evolutionary theory." In S. Tax (ed.). *Evolution After Darwin*. Vol. 1, *The Evolution of Life*. Chicago: University of Chicago Press, 1960. Pp. 569–594.

Prosser, C. L., and F. A. Brown, Jr. *Comparative Animal Physiology*, 2nd ed. Philadelphia: W. B. Saunders Co., 1961.

Robertson, J. D. "The habitat of the early vertebrates," *Biological Reviews*, 32 (1957), 156–187.

Romer, A. S. *The Vertebrate Story*. Chicago: University of Chicago Press, 1959.

Smith, H. W. *From Fish to Philosopher*. Boston: Little, Brown & Co., 1953.

Wald, G. "The chemical evolution of vision," *The Harvey Lectures,* Series 41, pp. 117–160. Lancaster, Pa.: Science Press Printing Co., 1946.

Wald, G. "The origin of life," *Scientific American,* 191 (1954), 45–53.

Wald, G. "The significance of vertebrate metamorphosis," *Science,* 128 (1958), 1481–1490.

Wilhelmi, R. W. "The application of the precipitin technique to theories concerning the origin of vertebrates," *Biological Bulletin,* 82 (1942), 179–189.

CHAPTER **6**

EVOLUTION AS SEEN IN

SEROLOGICAL TESTS

The Precipitin Test

Serological tests depend upon the faculty possessed by the body of protecting itself against foreign invaders. When bacteria and viruses gain entrance into the body the latter responds with a defense mechanism consisting of the formation of substances called **antibodies.** When, for example, a person has smallpox his body forms antibodies against smallpox virus. The antibodies react with the virus, aiding the body to recover from the attack. If subsequently the virus again seeks to enter his body it will be met by the antibodies already formed, ready to neutralize or otherwise destroy it. We say that such a person has become immune to smallpox.

As everyone knows, it is not necessary actually to contract smallpox to become immune to it. By the process of vaccination a little of the virus, so treated that it has lost its virulence and cannot cause the disease, is introduced into a person's blood stream. The body reacts against the virus, forming antibodies which will later prove of protective value if an active virus is encountered.

The protective mechanism just mentioned is called into action not only by harmful organisms but also by any foreign substance of a protein nature. A substance which will induce the formation of antibodies is called an **antigen.** If, for example, serum (the fluid portion) of the blood of a horse is inoculated into a rabbit, the latter's defense mechanism will be called into play, resulting in the formation of antibodies against horse serum. The antibodies are themselves protein substances, and many of

109

them are found in the blood serum of the animal which produced them. Such an antibody-containing serum is called an **antiserum.** Thus, if some of the blood serum from a rabbit inoculated as described above is removed and mixed with horse serum, the antibodies will react with the horse serum to form a white precipitate. Hence antibodies of this kind are called **precipitins,** and the serological test making use of them is called the **precipitin test.**

In most of the precipitin tests of interest to the study of evolution, domestic rabbits have been used as antibody producers, partly as a matter of convenience, partly because rabbits produce antibodies more readily than do some other laboratory animals.

Homology of Serum Proteins

As an example of the application of the precipitin test we may consider the results of tests performed with antibodies formed by rabbits inoculated with human serum (Fig. 6.1). If the inoculation is properly done the rabbit will form antibodies against the human serum. Blood is then withdrawn from the rabbit and the serum is removed from the blood cells. The antiserum so obtained will be found to contain antibodies specific for human serum. As shown in the figure, if a little of the antiserum is mixed in a test tube with human serum a white precipitate will form and will settle to the bottom of the tube.

The test is continued by mixing in another test tube some of the antiserum, containing antibodies against human serum, with some chimpanzee serum. Will antibodies formed against human serum react with chimpanzee serum? Reaction will depend upon whether or not the proteins of chimpanzee serum are sufficiently similar in chemical structure to those of human serum so that antibodies formed against the one will react with the other. As the diagram shows, most tests performed as indicated, without additional refinements, fail to distinguish chimpanzee serum from human serum, the same amount of precipitate being formed in both tubes. In other words, chimpanzee serum and human serum seem almost exactly alike in chemical structure.

The test shown in the diagram continues by the mixing of a third sample of rabbit antiserum, containing antibodies against human serum, with baboon serum. Will reaction occur in this tube? Again the answer will depend upon whether or not baboon serum is sufficiently similar to human serum so that antibodies formed against the latter will react with the former. In agreement with tests which have been performed, the figure indicates that a smaller amount of precipitate is formed in this tube than was formed in the other two. Evidently, then, baboon serum contains some proteins similar to those in human serum; presumably, however, the greater proportion of the baboon's serum proteins are unlike those found in man.

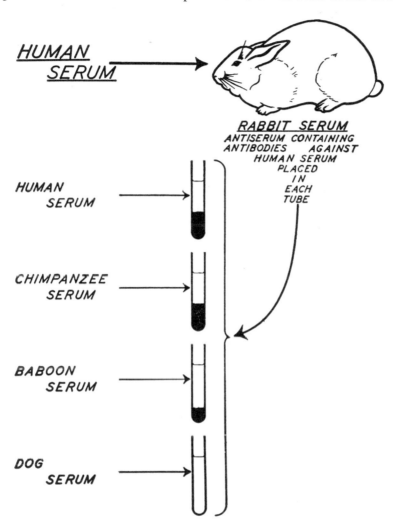

HUMAN
SERUM

RABBIT SERUM
ANTISERUM CONTAINING
ANTIBODIES   AGAINST
HUMAN SERUM
PLACED
IN
EACH
TUBE

HUMAN
SERUM

CHIMPANZEE
SERUM

BABOON
SERUM

DOG
SERUM

FIG. 6.1. Principle of the precipitin test applied to investigation of animal relationships.

The diagram includes an additional test tube—one in which antiserum, containing antibodies against human serum, is mixed with dog serum. No precipitate is shown. The proteins of dog serum are so unlike those of human serum that antibodies formed against the latter usually fail to react with the former. Sometimes if an antiserum is very potent a small reaction occurs. It may well be that all mammals have some small amount of chemical similarity in their serum proteins.

The results just described are typical of tests employing antibodies against human serum. Many other species might be and have been included, but the principles involved are well exemplified by the test as described.

We have seen that chimpanzee serum is so like human serum as to be nearly or quite indistinguishable from it (without introducing special refinements into the test), while baboon serum is less like human serum than chimpanzee serum is. How is the similarity between human serum and chimpanzee serum to be explained? As with morphological similarities (Chap. 3) there are two possible explanations. We may hold that the similarity is more or less a coincidence, or occurred because a common chemical pattern for blood proteins was followed in creation. But according to the explanation most satisfactory to modern biologists the similarity is the result of inheritance from common ancestry. Both man and chimpanzee inherited their serum proteins from a form ancestral to both of them, and the proteins have behaved as conservative characteristics, becoming but little altered in the subsequent evolutionary history of man, on the one hand, and of the chimpanzee, on the other.

The evolutionary explanation for the origin of the similarity between human serum and baboon serum follows similar lines. In the distant past (probably as long ago as the Oligocene period—p. 137) the baboon, an Old World monkey, and man shared a common ancestor. From that ancestor both inherited a certain pattern of serum structure. But in subsequent evolutionary history the pattern has been modified so that today there is less similarity between baboon and human serum than between chimpanzee and human serum. It may be that man and the chimpanzee shared a common ancestor more recently than did man and baboon. This possibility would accord well with one school of thought concerning human evolution (Chap. 11). On the other hand, some students of the subject maintain that man is not more closely related to the great apes (including the chimpanzee) than he is to the lower monkeys. Do the serological findings contradict this latter view? Such is the usual conclusion, but in all fairness we should point out that it is not the only possible one. We should remember that evolution does not occur at a constant rate in all evolutionary lines. Perhaps for some reason the serum proteins in the line of ancestry leading to the baboon have changed at a more rapid rate than have the serum proteins in the lines leading to man and the great apes. Or possibly the changes in serum proteins in these latter two lines have been of similar nature although independent in occurrence, affording an example of parallel evolution (see p. 29).

If the evolutionary explanation for the similarity in serum structure is the correct one, serological tests form a means of measuring the degree of relationship of animals to one another. The principle involved is that the degree of chemical similarity is proportional to the degree of relationship. Closely related forms will have serum proteins much alike; more distantly related forms will have serum proteins less alike. On the whole, tests actually performed seem to support this principle, despite the possibility that occasional similarity between sera may be due to convergent or parallel evolution, as some similarities in morphology are (Chap. 3). Moreover, it is to be noted in passing that parallel evolution may indicate relationship of the forms concerned. Evidence shows that the nature of serum proteins is controlled by the units of heredity, the genes. We have noted that genes occasionally undergo chemical alteration (mutation). The variety of mutations possible to any one kind of gene is limited. Thus if two forms inherit a certain gene from a common ancestor that gene may later undergo the same mutation in both forms, the resultant changes being similar in nature though independent in occurrence. Thus parallel evolution may indicate possession by the forms concerned of similar or identical genes, inherited from a common ancestor. The importance of such independent recurrence of mutations in different though related forms receives additional emphasis in our discussion of the cell proteins determining the blood groups (pp. 121–125).

Measuring the Precipitin Test

If serological tests are to be utilized for measuring animal relationships, some method of measuring the precipitate formation must be adopted. Various methods have been employed. The volume of precipitate settling to the bottom of the tube may be measured in a special calibrated tube of small diameter. Or the Kjeldahl test may be employed to determine the amount of nitrogen present in the precipitate—the amount of nitrogen being proportional to the amount of precipitate. The most widely used method consists of making serial dilutions of the serum (antigen) to be tested (Fig. 6.2). Our diagram is based on data obtained in a study of the relationships of a number of mammals to the sheep. Inoculation of a rabbit with sheep serum causes production of antibodies against sheep serum. A small quantity of the rabbit serum containing antibodies against

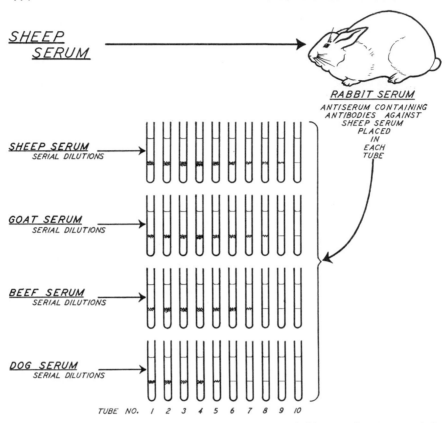

FIG. 6.2. Principle of the precipitin test, employing serial dilutions of antigen, and the interfacial reaction.

sheep serum is placed in the bottom of each of a series of test tubes. Each tube then receives a small quantity of a dilution of sheep serum. The first tube in the series receives sheep serum diluted 1:100 with physiological salt solution. The second tube receives a 1:200 dilution of the sheep serum. In succeeding tubes sheep serum in dilutions of 1:400, 1:800, 1:1600, 1:3200, 1:6400, 1:12,800, and so on, is added. The diluted serum is added carefully so that it will not mix with the antiserum already present. Thus a sharp interface is left between the two; at this interface a ring of precipitate forms. Such a "ring test" is more delicate than the form of the test described previously, in which the solutions are mixed and the precipitate settles to the bottom of the tube.

After the rings have had time to form, the highest dilution in which ring formation occurs is determined by inspection. This dilution is called the **end point** of the reaction. In Fig. 6.2 the end point of the **homologous reaction** (that with serum of the kind originally inoculated into the rabbit —sheep serum in this instance) is shown as being 1:25,600. Although this is a hypothetical example, the results shown are in keeping with those of tests actually performed.

The figure shows a similar ring test of the reaction of antibodies against sheep serum when tested with goat serum. A series of dilutions of goat serum is prepared and overlayered above the antiserum in a series of tubes, as was done with the sheep serum in the preceding test. In this case the highest dilution in which a ring forms is indicated as being 1:12,800. The ratio of the two end points gives a quantitative statement of the amount of similarity in serum proteins and hence of the degree of relationship of the two species. By custom the homologous end point (1:25,600 in this case) is regarded as 100 percent. The end point obtained with the goat serum (1:12,800) can then be expressed as 50 percent, a value slightly lower than that usually obtained in actual tests of sheep-goat relationships.

The test is repeated, using the same antiserum, with a series of dilutions of beef serum. The end point with the latter is shown as being 1:6400. This corresponds to 25 percent of the homologous end point. Thus, insofar as one can draw conclusions from a single series of tests, the goat is twice as closely related to the sheep as is the beef animal.

Tests utilizing dilutions of dog serum are shown as yielding an end point of 1:1600—6.25 percent of the homologous end point. This indicates that the dog is much less closely related to the sheep than the beef animal is.

Serology Supplements Morphology

The order of relationship indicated in the test just described (Fig. 6.2) is in accordance with expectation based on morphological studies of the animals mentioned. This fact is reflected in the classification of the latter. The sheep, goat, and beef are included in one order, Order Artiodactyla—even-toed hoofed mammals. The dog, on the other hand, is a member of Order Carnivora, along with most other flesh-eating mammals.

Indeed, from the pioneer investigations of Nuttall (1904) to the present most serological results have served to confirm the generally accepted classification of animals based on morphology. This is what would be expected if both morphological and serological similarities are attributable to inheritance from common ancestry. The fact that serological results confirm relationships as determined by morphology when these relationships are clear and firmly established gives confidence in the validity of serological results in cases where morphology does not by itself afford clear and unequivocal evidence as to relationships.

The whales afford a case in point. To which of the terrestrial mammals are they most closely related? Simpson (1945) states concerning them, "Because of their perfected adaptation to a completely aquatic life, with all its attendant conditions of respiration, circulation, dentition, locomotion, etc., the cetaceans are on the whole the most peculiar and aberrant of mammals. Their place in the sequence of cohorts and orders is open to question and is indeed quite impossible to determine in any purely objective way." Perhaps serological tests may afford the objective determination sought. Nuttall inoculated a rabbit with whale serum and used the resultant antiserum in tests with sera from a considerable array of mammals. Strongest reactions were obtained with the sera of other whales. Some reactions of medium strength occurred with sera from representatives of Order Artiodactyla—even-toed mammals. Sera of other mammals gave less reaction or no reaction at all.

Tests by Boyden and Gemeroy (1950) strengthened the evidence of serological relationship between whales and artiodactyls. These investigators employed a modification of the serial-dilution method described above (Fig. 6.2). In each tube the antigen dilution was *mixed* with the antiserum instead of being overlayered above it. The amount of turbidity or cloudiness which developed in each tube in 20 minutes as a result of antigen-antibody reaction was measured with a photoelectric instrument called the Libby Photronreflectometer. Such turbidity formation precedes the settling of precipitate to the bottom of the tube as shown in Fig. 6.1. With the instrument mentioned it is possible to measure the amount of reaction in all the tubes of the series of dilutions. The measurement used in statement of relationships is, accordingly, based on the sum of the reactions in all the tubes, instead of being based merely upon the magnitude of the greatest dilution in which a reaction (ring) can be seen, as in the interfacial test (Fig. 6.2). Using antisera prepared against whale serum, and checking the results with reciprocal tests employing antisera prepared against beef serum, Boyden and Gemeroy found clear indication that whales are more similar serologically to artiodactyls than they are to any other order of mammals. This might mean that whales sprang from primitive artiodactyl stock or that both arose from the same ancestral Condylarthra (pp. 195–196). We shall not know until the fossil record of whale evolution becomes more complete than it is at present. At any rate, serological tests have here helped to fill a gap in our knowledge of relationships.

Rabbits and Rodents

Similar uncertainty exists concerning the relationships of hares and rabbits to other mammals. These animals are like rodents (rats, mice, squirrels, beavers, woodchucks, etc.) in possession of a gnawing arrangement of the front or incisor teeth. Two upper incisors are greatly enlarged so that they resemble small chisels. A similar pair of chisel-like lower incisors meets the upper pair to make possible efficient gnawing. Because hares and rabbits, on the one hand, and rodents, on the other, possess this arrangement the two groups were for many years both included in Order Rodentia. The practice widely adopted today, however, is to emphasize the many morphological features by which rabbits differ from rodents, and accordingly to place hares and rabbits in the separate Order Lagomorpha. Even today, however, the separation of lagomorphs and rodents into separate orders is not always followed, despite the fact that no forms intermediate between lagomorphs and rodents are known from the fossil record, and that representatives of both orders are known from as ancient times as the Paleocene (p. 137), these ancient representatives being as distinctly rodents, on the one hand, and lagomorphs, on the other, as are their modern descendants.

Among biologists who agree to the separation of Order Lagomorpha from Order Rodentia there is disagreement as to whether or not lagomorphs are more closely related to rodents than they are to some other orders of mammals. For example, it has long been recognized that lagomorphs resemble artiodactyls in some morphological features.

It occurred to the author that this was a question upon which serological tests might shed light. Accordingly with his graduate students he carried on an investigation employing both the ring tests and the turbidity (photronreflectometer) tests described above. Since the rabbit was to be one of the subjects of investigation it could not also be employed as antibody producer. Male domestic fowl were found to serve this purpose admirably. Being birds, they may be considered equally removed from all mammals and hence in a position to afford the proper "serological perspective."

An example of results obtained with the turbidity test is presented in Fig. 6.3. The numbers along the base of the graph represent the tubes in the series of dilutions. Tube 1 contained whole serum as antigen. Tube 2

contained antigen (serum) diluted 1:1; tube 3 antigen diluted 1:2; tube 4
antigen diluted 1:4; and so on in doubling dilutions. The antiserum added
to each tube had been obtained by pooling antisera from four cocks all of
which had been inoculated with domestic rabbit serum. The numbers
along the left side of the graph represent the turbidity developed (in terms
of galvanometer readings of the photronreflectometer). The solid line of

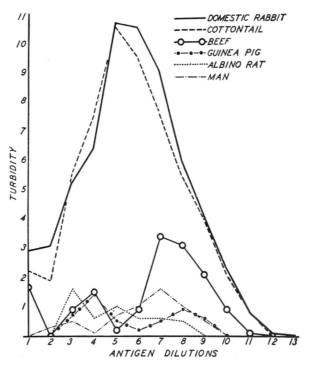

FIG. 6.3. Serological relationships of lagomorphs to several other mammals. Turbidity (photronreflectometer) tests.
(From Moody, Cochran, and Drugg, "Serological evidence
on lagomorph relationships," *Evolution*, Vol. 3, 1949,
p. 28.)

the graph connects points representing the turbidity formed in each of the
tubes of the homologous series, i.e., the series containing successive dilutions of domestic rabbit serum. It will be noted that this curve includes a
greater area than do any of the other curves. The curve representing the
reaction obtained with the other lagomorph included in the study, the cot-
tontail rabbit, is second in magnitude. The other curves subtend much
smaller areas. Of these the reaction with beef serum, representing Order
Artiodactyla, is greatest, the reactions with the sera of representatives of

Order Rodentia (albino rat, guinea pig) and of the representative of Order Primates (man) being of less magnitude.

The accompanying bar graph (Fig. 6.4) summarizes the results of the test shown in Fig. 6.3 and of another test performed with antiserum obtained at another time from the same four cocks. It is evident that the results to date confirm the wisdom of separating lagomorphs from rodents

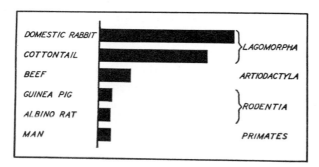

FIG. 6.4. Relative serological relationships of several mammals to the domestic rabbit. Turbidity (photronreflectometer) tests. (From Moody, Cochran, and Drugg, "Serological evidence on lagomorph relationships," *Evolution*, Vol. 3, 1949, p. 30.)

and suggest that lagomorphs are not more closely related to rodents than they are to other orders of mammals. It is tempting to see in these results evidence of greater affinity between lagomorphs and artiodactyls than exists between lagomorphs and any other order studied. Such a conclusion, while suggested, would be premature, however; more tests and tests including representatives of a greater number of orders of mammals are needed before we can state with certainty that lagomorphs are more closely allied to one order than they are to any other one.

Porcupines

Porcupines live in North and South America and in Africa. Though they both have quills, New World and Old World porcupines differ in many respects. For example, African porcupines have much the larger quills. African porcupines burrow in the ground; American porcupines live in trees. Nevertheless, skeletal similarities result in their traditionally being classed together as "hystricomorph" rodents, a term which also includes a variety of other South American rodents, such as guinea pigs, agoutis, pacas, and capybaras (Fig. 12.1, p. 260). Evidence indicates that porcupines appeared in the Old World and in South America in Oligocene times but that none lived in North America until the Pliocene (p. 137). If the porcupines had a common origin how did some of them reach South America and others Africa without passing through North America? While it is possible, as suggested by Darlington (1957), that both they and monkeys may have passed through North America without leaving fossil evidence as yet discovered, the question remains a troublesome one. Land bridges from Africa to South America, rafting across the Atlantic Ocean, and island-hopping via Antarctica have all been invoked in attempting to explain this peculiar distribution.

But perhaps the African and American porcupines are not closely re-lated at all. Perhaps they both evolved independently from rodents known to be widely distributed before the first porcupines appeared (Wood, 1950). If so, we may expect that they would be quite unlike serologically. Moody and Doniger (1956) investigated the question, using (1) antisera formed against North American porcupine serum, and (2) antisera formed against African porcupine serum. All tests agreed in indicating that the porcupines are but distantly related to each other, as distantly as either is to guinea pig and agouti, in fact. Apparently, then, New World and Old World porcupines developed their quills independently by parallel evolution. Quills are modified hairs; various other relatively unrelated mammals have developed quills and spines from hair (e.g., the European hedgehog, and the spiny anteater of Australia, Fig. 12.2, p. 262).

Musk Ox

The musk ox, shaggy denizen of Arctic regions, is obviously a member of the family of artiodactyls to which cattle, bison, buffaloes, sheep, and goats belong: Family Bovidae. But is it more closely related to cattle and bison or to sheep and goats? On the one hand, it has sometimes been re-garded as an arctic bison, and hence closely related to cattle. On the other hand, fossil evidence seems to indicate that it is more closely related to goats than to cattle and their allies. Serological tests (Moody, 1958) indi-cate that its relationship is to sheep and goats rather than to cattle. Fig. 6.5 indicates this and also demonstrates the value of *reciprocal* tests in serologi-cal studies. An antimusk-ox serum gave a large reaction with sheep and goat sera, little with beef and bison sera. An antigoat serum gave large re-action with musk-ox serum, thus confirming the test with antimusk-ox serum. Finally, an antibeef serum gave small reaction with musk-ox serum, thereby confirming the small reaction given by the antimusk-ox serum

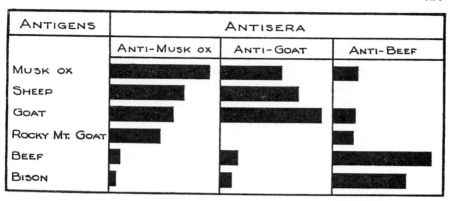

FIG. 6.5. Serological relationships of the musk ox to other members of Family Bovidae. Turbidity (photronreflectometer) tests. Abscissal scale is in percentage, the strength of the homologous reaction with each antiserum being designated as 100 percent. (Drawn by Melton M. Miller, Jr.; from Moody, "Serological evidence on the relationships of the musk ox," *Journal of Mammalogy,* Vol. 39, 1958, p. 557.)

when tested with beef serum. Incidentally, the tests also indicated the known close relationship to each other of sheep and goats, as well as that of beef and bison.

Serology could make valuable contributions toward solving many other enigmas of relationship. Serological investigation of the interrelationships of marsupials (see pp. 261–264) has been made by Wemyss (1953), and of flesh-eating mammals, Order Carnivora, by Leone and Wiens (1956) and by Pauly and Wolfe (1957).

New techniques employing the separation of proteins migrating in an electric field (electrophoresis) are being developed and will doubtless contribute to future studies of animal relationships (Woods, *et al.,* 1958; Sibley and Johnsgard, 1959).

Blood Groups

Nearly everyone is acquainted with the fact that all human beings belong to one or another of four blood groups. The latter are designated as group A, group B, group AB, and group O. The group to which one belongs depends upon the presence or absence in his red blood cells of two protein substances (antigens) designated A and B. The presence of these antigens can be detected by serological means. Persons who belong to group A have substance A only in their cells. Persons belonging to group B have substance B only. Both substances are present in the red blood cells of persons belonging to group AB; neither substance is present in the cells of members of group O. Knowledge of these blood groups has contributed greatly to the safety of blood transfusions, as well as to tests used in courts of law in cases of disputed paternity of children.

From the standpoint of evolution antigens A and B are of interest because of their distribution. In the first place we note that no human racial or ethnic group is characterized by the presence or absence of A or B. The nearest approach to an exception to this statement is afforded by the American Indians, some of whom show a high percentage (98 percent) of group O (i.e., lack of both A and B). Antigens A and B do occur in a small proportion of the Indian population, however (see p. 251), and evidence from the mummies of the cliff-dwelling Indians of the Southwest indicates that the antigens were present in Indians living in prehistoric times.

While A and B are both present in members of all races, there are interesting differences in their proportional distribution. For example, the distribution of blood groups among white Americans or western Europeans is approximately as follows: group O, 47 percent; group A, 43 percent; group B, 7 percent; group AB, 3 percent. Proportions vary, since no sample of population tested is ever completely homogeneous, but the percentages given are sufficiently exact for our purpose. Thus, about 46 percent of our population possesses A, alone or combined with B, while only about 10 percent of our population possesses B, alone or combined with A. Among Chinese the percentages are about as follows: group O, 30 percent; group A, 25 percent; group B, 35 percent; group AB, 10 percent. In contrast to western Europeans, therefore, only about 35 percent of Chinese possesses A, alone or combined with B, whereas about 45 percent possesses B, alone or combined with A. Populations distributed between the two geographic extremes on the continent of Eurasia show intermediate conditions. The latter are distributed in such a way that a gradient is followed by each antigen. Thus as one travels eastward across Eurasia the proportion of substance A encountered in the populations decreases while the proportion of B increases. The significance of this striking trend is in doubt, but the trend is probably connected with the past migrations of peoples, whatever may have been the origin of the differences between the geographic extremes.

Data concerning blood groups have been collected for great numbers of ethnic and national groups (see pp. 251–252; also Wiener, 1943, and Boyd, 1950). In some cases the nature of the blood group proportions in a given population has aided anthropologists in determining the relationships of that population to others (see also discussion of human races, pp. 250–255).

Blood cell substances A and B are not confined to man. Among the great apes, for example, the antigens are distributed as shown in Table 6.1. Although the numbers tested are small, one contrast to the distribution in man seems striking. Apparently species differences in possession of one or another of the antigens occur among apes. Thus, chimpanzees seem never to have developed substance B, and the two species of gorillas seem to differ in which of the antigens is present, although here the numbers are too small to afford confidence in conclusions. It is interesting that group O, a large group, frequently the predominant one, in human populations is so poorly represented among the apes. Perhaps the presence of A or B or both, not their absence, was the original condition among ancestral pri-

TABLE 6.1. Distribution of Blood Groups in
the Great Apes[a]

	A	B	AB	O
Gibbon	1	5	1	—
Orang-utan	7	8	4	—
Chimpanzee	109	—	—	15
Gorilla				
Lowland species	—	13	—	—
Mountain species	2	—	—	—

[a] Numbers are actual numbers of individuals tested.
Based on data in Wiener, 1943; Wiener and Gordon, 1960.

mates. This suggestion, advanced by Wiener, contrasts with the idea frequently expressed that group O was the original condition from which groups A and B arose by mutation.

Wiener and Gordon (1960) called attention to an interesting difference between the blood groups of man and chimpanzee, on the one hand, and of the gorilla, on the other. In man and chimpanzee the A and B substances, when present, are found in the red blood cells, as we have noted. In the gorilla, however, these antigens may be present in the cells of organs and in secretions (as they may also be in man) but are *absent* from the red blood cells. This absence of A or B from blood cells, even when present in other cells, distinguishes the gorilla from man and chimpanzee and suggests to these authors that the chimpanzee is more closely related to man than is the gorilla.

A contrast should be noted between the distribution of antigens A and B and that of the serum proteins discussed earlier in the chapter. In general the serum proteins which we noted as chemically similar in man and some lower mammals (e.g., chimpanzee) are uniformly distributed. That is, all men, and all chimpanzees, possess them. Although as noted above antigens A and B seem to be distributed among apes in somewhat this manner, among human beings they are so variably distributed that the brothers and sisters in one family may differ in possession of them. This does not mean that their distribution is a haphazard matter. Far from it. Antigens A and B follow rigidly the rules of inheritance first discovered by Mendel in his experiments with garden peas and subsequently named "mendelian" inheritance. In other words, these antigens depend upon the genes. As mentioned above, the genes occasionally change, undergoing mutation. The distinctive properties of substances A and B probably originated as mutations, as did the absence of either which characterizes people belonging to group O. From what we know of rates of mutation in lower animals we surely need not assume that the mutation producing O, for example, occurred just once in evolutionary history, and that all animals and human beings inherited the lack of antigens A and B from the one ancestor or ancestral group. Such a view might lead to the absurd conclusion that people who belong to group O are more closely related to chimpanzees than are people who belong to group B (Table 6.1)!

What, then, is the basic similarity between man and the other mammals which is expressed in common possession of the blood group antigens? It is a basic similarity of germ plasm, demonstrated by the fact that genes possessed by man and at least his nearest relatives are so similar that when they undergo mutation the products of the latter are identical or closely similar. Here is another example of that parallel evolution already mentioned (p. 29). Doubtless such basic similarity of germ plasm underlies all the morphological and serological similarities which we have called homologies and interpreted as indicative of evolution. But in the case of the blood groups the relationships between genes and their products (antigens A and B) are more direct and clearly evident than are relationships between genes and many of the other characteristics of animals. Hence antigens A and B afford more distinct evidence of fundamental similarities existing between germ plasms than is supplied by characteristics whose genetic basis is not so thoroughly known.

Other Antigens in the Red Blood Cells

Antigens A and B are not the only antigens which have been identified in red blood cells. Another pair of substances have been designated M and N. These are similar to A and B in many ways although they are separate from the latter in inheritance. Like A and B they are also variably present in other primates. Among the substances present in the red blood cells we may mention the one termed "Rh." This has received much publicity because of its clinical importance in connection with certain diseases of the newborn. The fact that it is shared by human beings with at least one species of lower primate is reflected in its designation; "Rh" is derived from "Rhesus," the name of the monkey commonly used in experimental laboratories.

Our knowledge of the distributions of antigens M, N, and Rh serves to corroborate conclusions reached from study of substances A and B relative to similarity of the germ plasms of different animals, including man. Such similarities of cellular antigens we interrupt as being based on inheritance from common ancestry. A like explanation seems to account for the similarities of *serum* antigens discussed in earlier portions of this chapter.

References and Suggested Readings

Boyd, W. C. *Genetics and the Races of Man*. Boston: Little, Brown & Co., 1950.

Boyden, A. "Systematic serology: a critical appreciation," *Physiological Zoology*, 15 (1942), 109–145.

Boyden, A., and D. Gemeroy. "The relative position of the Cetacea among the orders of Mammalia as indicated by precipitin tests," *Zoologica*, 35 (1950), 145–151.

Darlington, P. J., Jr. *Zoogeography: the Geographical Distribution of Animals*. New York: John Wiley & Sons, Inc., 1957.

Leone, C. A., and A. L. Wiens. "Comparative serology of carnivores," *Journal of Mammalogy*, 37 (1956), 11–23.

Moody, P. A. "Serological evidence on the relationships of the musk ox," *Journal of Mammalogy*, 39 (1958), 554–559.

Moody, P. A., V. A. Cochran, and H. Drugg. "Serological evidence on lagomorph relationships," *Evolution*, 3 (1949), 25–33.

Moody, P. A., and D. E. Doniger. "Serological light on porcupine relationships," *Evolution*, 10 (1956), 47–55.

Nuttall, G. H. F. *Blood Immunity and Blood Relationship*. Cambridge: Cambridge University Press, 1904.

Pauly, L. K., and H. R. Wolfe. "Serological relationships among members of the Order Carnivora," *Zoologica*, 42 (1957), 159–166.

Sibley, C. G., and P. A. Johnsgard. "An electrophoretic study of egg-white proteins in twenty-three breeds of the domestic fowl," *American Naturalist*, 93 (1959), 107–115.

Simpson, G. G. "The principles of classification and a classification of mammals," *Bulletin of the American Museum of Natural History*, 85 (1945), 1–350.

Wemyss, C. T., Jr. "A preliminary study of marsupial relationships as indicated by the precipitin test," *Zoologica,* 38 (1953), 173–181.

Wiener, A. S. *Blood Groups and Transfusion,* 3rd. ed. Springfield, Ill.: Charles C. Thomas, 1943.

Wiener, A. S., and E. B. Gordon. "The blood groups of chimpanzees. A-B-O groups and M-N types," *American Journal of Physical Anthropology,* 18 (1960), 301–311.

Wood, A. E. "Porcupines, paleogeography, and parallelism," *Evolution,* 4 (1950), 87–98.

Woods, K. R., E. C. Paulsen, R. L. Engle, Jr., and J. H. Pert. "Starch gel electrophoresis of some invertebrate sera," *Science,* 127 (1958), 519–520.

CHAPTER 7

EVOLUTION AS SEEN IN THE

GEOLOGIC RECORD: NATURE

OF THE RECORD

In earlier chapters of this book we have seen evolution manifested by similarities among living animals in chemical composition, structure, metabolic processes, embryonic development, and serological properties of the blood. If our conclusion based on what we might term circumstantial evidence is correct, in times past animals must have existed that were the common ancestors from which modern animals inherited the similarities revealed by morphology, physiology, embryology, and serology. Can we find positive evidence that such animals actually did exist? If so our accumulated circumstantial evidence will be greatly strengthened by what we may regard as direct evidence. This direct evidence is supplied by the geologic record.

Fossils

The geologic record or "record of the rocks" resembles records written by man in that it must be *read*. Before we can read a record we must learn the language in which it is written. The geologic record is written in the language of **fossils.** Any type of remains of a prehistoric animal may be considered a fossil. Accordingly, fossils take many forms. The most usual type consists of **petrifactions** of the harder parts of the animal's body— bones and teeth in the case of vertebrates, shells of molluscs, exoskeletons ("shells") of arthropods (lobsters, crayfishes, spiders, insects, and their relatives).

After an animal dies its flesh is destroyed by predatory animals, scavengers, insect larvae, bacteria, and so on. These destructive forces also act upon bones and shells, but more slowly. Occasionally such "hard parts" lie in surroundings which protect them from complete destruction, particularly if the animals lived in the water or, in the case of terrestrial animals, if the bones or shells were swept into a body of water by a river at time of flood. The organic matter in bone or shell gradually disintegrates, leaving the structure somewhat porous. Water seeps into the interior of the bone, and minerals dissolved in the water are slowly deposited there. Thus the porosities gradually become filled with deposits of such materials as lime and silica. The portions of the original structure composed of inorganic materials frequently remain substantially as they were in life. In this way even fine details of internal structure may be preserved.

At times the original material of the bone or shell is dissolved away entirely and replaced by other materials. Thus the calcium carbonate composing a shell may in some cases be replaced by silica. The replacing material may preserve the details of the original structure with great fidelity, or, on the other hand, it may preserve only the general form of the original. An example is afforded by the remarkably complete and uninjured invertebrate fossils now being recovered from limestone rock deposits in the Glass Mountains of Texas. Advantage is taken of the fact that the original materials of shells and exoskeletons have been replaced by silica in the manner just described. Pieces of limestone bearing the fossils are immersed in large vats of muriatic acid. The limestone dissolves, in a reaction familiar to every student of high school chemistry, freeing the silicified fossils, intact and undamaged.

Under exceptionally favorable circumstances replacement of the type under discussion may even result in preservation of some of the internal organs ("soft parts") of an animal.

Natural preservatives have sometimes helped to save animal materials from destruction. Thus the bones of animals which became mired in the asphalt or tar pits at Rancho La Brea in California are in a fine state of preservation owing to the preservative action of the crude asphaltic oil. In Poland skeletons of the woolly rhinoceros, with some of the flesh and skin preserved, have been found buried in oil-soaked ground.

Not infrequently the buried body and skeleton of an animal disintegrate entirely. If the surrounding material is sufficiently firm a cavity may remain having the exact outlines of the structure which disappeared. Such a cavity is called a **mold.** It may be filled by natural deposits, forming a **natural cast** of the form of the original object. Or if a natural cast does not form, the mold when discovered may be filled with plaster of Paris or some plastic compound to produce an **artificial cast.** Perhaps the best-known examples of the use of this technique are the casts produced of people who perished in the eruption of Vesuvius which buried Pompeii under many feet of volcanic ash in the year A.D. 79. Such molds and casts reveal the shape but not the internal structure of the original object. Natural and artificial casts of the interior of the brain cavities of extinct animals form the only material available for study of the brains of these animals. Casts of such soft-bodied creatures as jellyfishes form almost our only source of information concerning members of these groups. Molds and casts of the burrows made by prehistoric animals frequently reveal something of the nature of the latter.

Similar to molds are **impressions** sometimes left by vanished objects or parts of the body upon the surrounding material. The impression is made while the latter is soft—much as one leaves an impression on softened sealing wax with a signet ring. Thanks to such impressions we know something of the shapes and venations of prehistoric leaves, of the feathers of extinct birds, of the wing membranes of flying reptiles, of the skin surface of dinosaurs, and so on. Footprints of extinct animals are also impressions affording much valuable information about the animals which made them.

Occasionally the disintegrating soft parts of a body leave behind a thin **film of carbon.** Because of this we know, for example, the exact body outlines of the extinct swimming reptile, *Ichthyosaurus* (Fig. 3.5, p. 30).

Among the most perfect fossils known are the insects preserved in **amber.** When a biologist wishes to preserve an insect permanently in suitable condition for detailed study with a microscope he embeds it in balsam on a glass slide. Balsam is the pitch or resin from coniferous trees. Millions of years ago insects became entangled and entombed in soft, sticky resin exuding from pine trees, just as their modern descendants may be observed to do today. The resin hardened and eventually changed to amber, preserving the minutest details of structure of the contained insects.

A few extinct animals are known from **frozen specimens** in which the flesh as well as the bones has been preserved in remarkably fresh condition for thousands of years. This type of specimen has occurred principally in northern Siberia where the ground remains permanently frozen. The woolly mammoth is the animal best known from such specimens.

There are other types of fossils but the ones mentioned are most common and most generally useful. Usually fossils are more or less distorted or destroyed by forces operating on the rocks in which they are embedded. It will be evident that, even when fossils are in the most favorable condition possible, much experience and knowledge of anatomy, of both living and extinct animals, are necessary to enable the investigator to interpret correctly the portions of animals remaining for his study.

"Pages" in the Geologic Record

We have seen that reading the geologic record consists of placing correct interpretation upon a variety of fossil remains of animals previously existing on the earth. But if the history of life on earth is to be understood, the separate events comprising that history must be arranged in correct sequence and relationship. Printed records are firmly bound so that the pages follow one another in correct sequence to provide the reader with a coherent and connected account. But in the geologic record, how are we to tell which is "page 1," which "page 2," which "page 3," and so on?

The "leaves" comprising the geologic record "book" are layers of rock, called **strata.** A stratum consists of more or less solidified material which was originally deposited by a carrying agent such as water or air. By far the larger proportion of the known strata was deposited on what was then the floor of shallow extensions of the sea. In such shallow seas multitudes of animals live, many of them species with calcareous shells or skeletons. As generation follows generation the shells and skeletons settle to the bottom to form a layer of ever increasing thickness. As time goes on the deeper portions of this deposit are subjected to the pressure of overlying portions, with the result that the deposit becomes more or less solidified and consolidated into rock—limestone in the present example. If a river empties into this region of the shallow sea, deposits of material transported by the river mingle with the remains of marine animals. The river brings the products of erosion of the neighboring land, such as silt and clay, and mingled with them the remains of aquatic and terrestrial animals, particularly when the river is at flood stage. So through hundreds and thousands of years the sediment accumulates and gradually becomes consolidated into **sedimentary rock.**

Geologic changes in that region of the earth may eventually result in a change both in the animals inhabiting that section of shallow sea and in the materials being brought down by the river. The deposit following such a change will, naturally, be of somewhat different nature from the deposit formed before the change. Such changes account in part for the stratified or "layer-cake" appearance of deposits, so evident in such places as the walls of the Grand Canyon of the Colorado River. The many strata visible there afford us information concerning successive changes in that region of the earth for many millions of years.

How, then, do we tell which is "page 1," which "page 2," and so on in our geologic record "book"? As a general principle we may state that the oldest strata are the deepest ones, and that as we proceed upward in such a series of layers as that displayed in the walls of the Grand Canyon the strata are successively younger and younger in age. This time sequence follows naturally from the manner in which the material is deposited, as just described.

Disturbance of the Record

Interpretation of the sequences of events in the geologic record would be relatively simple if confusing and destructive forces were not at work. One destructive force is **erosion,** which removes many "pages," entire "chapters" even, from the record. For hundreds of thousands or millions of years a certain region is covered by shallow sea and receives successive deposits. If the earth's crust is sinking slowly, as portions of the Atlantic coastline of North America are known to be doing today, the deposits may eventually total thousands of feet in thickness. Finally we may picture a great upheaval occurring in that region, with formation of a mountain range. In the process the deposits formed in the bottom of the sea are thrust up into the air, thousands of feet up perhaps. This sort of thing has happened time and again in the history of the earth. Indeed, if it had not happened we should know relatively little of the past history of the earth, since obviously deposits are almost inaccessible to human study as long as they are buried under the sea. Yet as soon as the strata are exposed to the air in this fashion the forces of erosion start to tear them down, and the rivers to transport the products of their destruction to the neighboring sea, thereby initiating the formation of new deposits in that sea. Thus the substances composing the earth's crust are being constantly "reworked"— portions exposed to the air being eroded away, the products of this erosion going into the formation of new deposits which will eventually form new sedimentary rocks.

As erosion continues on the newly formed mountain range entire strata may be worn away, and eventually entire groups of strata. This process is going on in our present mountain ranges; since it is slow geologists have ample opportunity to study the strata before they disappear. But consider all the strata which were destroyed before there were any geologists—or any men at all, for that matter. We are told that at one time the Appalachian chain, including the Green Mountains of Vermont, the White Mountains of New Hampshire, the Berkshires, the Alleghenies, the Blue Ridge, and so on, was higher than the present Rocky Mountains. How many "chapters" of the geologic record were destroyed as these mountains were being worn down to their present height!

Fortunately strata lost by erosion in one part of the country may be preserved in another region. But it is not possible to fill in all the gaps in the record by comparing different regions of the earth's surface. Gaps are frequently left in the records of animal life, since a species of animal found in one part of the country at a certain time might not have been an inhabitant of another part of the country at that same time.

We may suppose that after millions of years of erosion our mountain range is reduced to a row of low hills. Finally another change in the earth's crust occurs and the region is dropped below sea level again, the hills being submerged. Then this newly formed sea floor will begin to collect deposits again, as did the floor of this region when we first began our story of it. The new deposits will be laid down immediately on top of whatever deposits were left by the preceding erosion. If eventually the region is again lifted into the air where geologists can study it they will find the old deposits, left from the preceding period of erosion, and immediately on top of them the new deposits. No remains will be left of the, perhaps, thousands of feet of deposits which were eroded away. The result is much like a book which has Chapter 15 following immediately after Chapter 3. Fortunately geologists are astute in detecting such **unconformities** in series of strata, but detecting the presence of a gap does not necessarily enable one to fill in the lost history.

Another source of difficulty in interpreting the geologic record lies in the fact that at times older rocks may come to lie *above* younger ones. Fig. 7.1 demonstrates graphically one way in which this comes about. The upper diagram shows a series of strata deposited smoothly, as described in our hypothetical example. Obviously the older layers are at the bottom of the series. Then a mountain range is formed by folding of the earth's crust. The fold is accompanied by a strong thrust, from the west in the example diagramed, which displaces a section of the crust toward the east, actually sliding it over the strata already present in that region, as shown in diagram 4 (Fig. 7.1). Such an **overthrust** may extend for many miles. As a result older strata are found to lie over younger ones. The land surface is subsequently sculptured by erosion, many of the signs of the phenomena which produced the observed sequence of strata being obliterated. Prolonged study involving large areas suffices to reveal the true explanation,

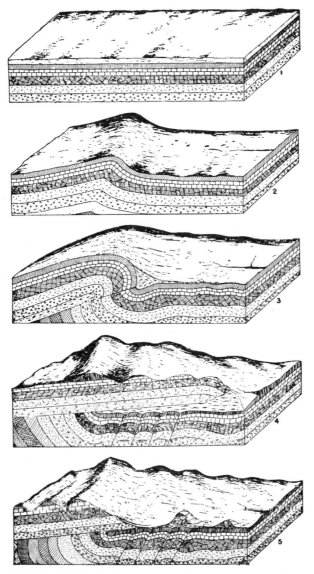

FIG. 7.1.   Folding followed by overthrust, one way in which the time sequence of strata is disturbed. (By permission from *Historical Geology*, by Hussey, p. 306. Copyright, 1947. McGraw-Hill Book Company, Inc.)

although the latter may not be evident if study is confined to a small area.

Over much of the earth—in fact all localities lacking high mountains or deep canyons—the number of strata exposed on the surface in any one locality is strictly limited. In more level regions one or a few strata will be found exposed for study. Younger strata are lacking because (1) none were ever deposited in that particular region, or (2) they were formed but were subsequently removed by erosion. Older strata may be buried from view, if present at all. Because of the vagaries of the raising and lowering of different portions of the earth's crust no one area has beneath it strata representative of all past periods in geologic history.

The question may arise as to how geologists determine the age of, for example, a single stratum found exposed in a given region when the strata immediately older and younger are not available for study. To solve the problem requires the most painstaking comparison of the rock in this locality with rock in other localities where the relationships among neighboring strata are more evident. The comparison involves details of the rock structure itself, as well as distribution of "key fossils" which serve to distinguish rocks formed at one time from those formed at other times and characterized by other key fossils. Always when possible reference is made to a region where the stratum in question can be found in undisturbed position relative to strata deposited before and after it.

Incompleteness of the Geologic Record

In the foregoing discussion we have attempted to gain some insight into the manner in which the relative ages of rocks are determined, as well as into the difficulties attendant upon the making of such determinations. We may now inquire into the reasons for the incompleteness of the record of past life on the earth.

Of the animals living at any one time in the history of the earth how many will be known to geologists a million or more years later? In the first place we may subtract most of the animals having no "hard parts." This will include most of the protozoa, though some of them, notably the foraminiferans, produce calcareous shells. These shells, though individually of minute size, in the aggregate have produced thick deposits of limestone. Most of the coelenterates and worms will also fail to leave fossil remains. Among the coelenterates the corals are an exception to this statement since their calcareous skeletal supports form another important source of limestone.

Of the animals possessing hard parts, how many will be known to geologists a million or more years later? The chances of fossilization vary greatly. Evidently, from the foregoing account, animals living in the ocean have the best chance of being preserved as fossils. Animals inhabiting fresh water have, perhaps, the next best chance, while terrestrial animals have the least chance. In order to be preserved as a fossil the body of a horse, for example, must be prevented from complete destruction. Not only the softer portions of the body but also the skeleton will disintegrate in a few years if exposed to action of predatory animals, scavengers, insect larvae, bacteria, and the erosive forces of the weather. A dry climate favors preservation of bones, but even dry bones disintegrate in time. Hence it is necessary that the bones be protected by being covered. Wind-blown soil, such as that which produced the thick deposits of clay known as loess, may provide the protective covering. Or if the animal becomes mired in a bog or in quicksand the bones may gradually sink and be covered. The fossils in the Rancho La Brea asphalt pits are a special case of this procedure. Or if the bones happen to lie in the flood plain of a river they may be covered by a deposit of soil left by the river when it overflows its banks in time of flood. Or the river, in flood stage, may sweep the bones into a lake or into the sea, where they will be mingled with the remains of aquatic animals. Thus, one of the most productive sources of fossils of Tertiary mammals is the White River Bad Lands of South Dakota and Nebraska. The material of these beds was laid down as a delta by rivers flowing from the Black Hills, mountains formerly much higher than they now are. Mammalian remains were swept down by the rivers and became embedded in the delta.

We see, then, that the chances are against an animal's hard parts' being fossilized, particularly if the animal is a land dweller. Of the animals which are fossilized, how many will be known to geologists a million or more years later? A first hazard facing these fossils consists of the chemical and geologic processes at work on the deposits in which the fossils are embedded. We have seen (p. 128) that the original material of the fossil is more or less completely replaced by minerals transported by water permeating the deposit. The deposition of minerals may follow faithfully the original structure, or the process of replacement may more or less completely obliterate that structure. If later deposits are piled on the one in question fossils in the latter are almost certain to be crushed and distorted. The consummation of such destruction is reached if the deposit finally comes to lie deep in the earth's crust with thousands of feet of other deposits above it. As a result of the tremendous pressure and accompanying heat the deposit may be so altered that all fossils in it are destroyed. Later the various minerals will recrystallize in the crystalline forms characteristic of each. Rock that has undergone this process of internal alteration through heat and pressure followed by recrystallization is called **metamorphic rock.** We have mentioned limestone as a prominent sedimentary rock rich in fossils; when limestone is subjected to the process described the product is marble. Metamorphism is a most efficient eraser of fossils.

Of the fossils which escape the destruction just described, how many will be known to geologists a million years or more later? It is evident that deposits which remain deeply buried under younger strata or under the sea will remain largely unknown. Some exception to this statement is afforded by mines, in the walls of which fossils may be found. Our knowledge of animals contemporaneous with the vegetation which entered into formation of coal depends to considerable extent upon fossils collected in connection with the mining of coal. Borings for artesian wells and oil wells reveal something of fossils in the strata through which they pass. But on the whole locating fossils depends largely upon their being exposed on the surface of the earth. Erosion acts on fossil-bearing rocks, wearing away the surrounding rock and exposing the fossil. If the latter happens to fall under the eye of a geologist, well and good, but if not, erosion will eventually destroy it along with the enclosing rock. Erosion is continually exposing fossils in this way. Most of them are probably never seen by geologists. The earth is a big place, and geologists are few in number and strictly budgeted in time and funds. These same reasons explain why it is not feasible to start digging more or less at random on the chance of uncovering fossils. In some places where fossils are known to be particularly abundant such a process may be practicable, as, for example, in the Rancho La Brea tar pits. But generally, owing to the scattered distribution of fossils, it would be far too costly of time and money.

While we have by no means enumerated all the reasons why our knowledge of past life on the earth is incomplete, we have emphasized some of the main forces operating to deprive us of such knowledge. The wonder is, not that the geologic record is incomplete, but that it is as complete as it is.

The Geologic Time Scale

The "chapters" of the geologic record are arranged in chronological sequence, the result being the geologic time scale (Table 7.1). The time scale is arranged to agree with the fact that, when undisturbed, older strata lie beneath younger ones. Thus we begin to read the chart at the *bottom* instead of at the top.

The total span of geologic time is divided into five large divisions, called **eras** (first column of Table 7.1). The oldest era, Archeozoic, is placed at the bottom of the chart. The boundaries of the successive eras are deter-

TABLE 7.1 Geologic Time Chart

[Quaternary]	RECENT	Modern genera and species of animals. Dominance of man.
[Tertiary]	PLEISTOCENE	Many large mammals of types now extinct. Prehistoric men.
CENOZOIC	PLIOCENE MIOCENE	During these periods mammals increased in specialization, many groups attaining their maxima.
	OLIGOCENE EOCENE PALEOCENE	In these periods ancestral representatives of most modern orders of mammals appeared. Archaic mammals attained their maximum in Eocene; most became extinct at its close.
	CRETACEOUS	First flowering plants (angiosperms); deciduous trees first abundant. Dominance of dinosaurs. Marsupial and placental mammals.
MESOZOIC	JURASSIC	Maximum of ammonites. Belemnites. Insects abundant, including social insects. Dominance of dinosaurs. First birds: Archaeopteryx. Early mammals; Pantotheria.
	TRIASSIC	Maximum of labyrinthodont amphibians. First dinosaurs. Mammal-like reptiles: Therapsida.
	PERMIAN	Expansion of ammonites. Last of trilobites. Expansion of reptiles: Cotylosauria, Therapsida.
	PENNSYLVANIAN	Luxurious vegetation, forming coal. First insect fossils. Many labyrinthodont amphibians. First reptiles.
	MISSISSIPPIAN	Foraminiferans, spiny brachiopods, and crinoids abundant. Few corals and trilobites. Many shell-crushing sharks. Amphibians.
PALEOZOIC	DEVONIAN	Brachiopods, corals, and crinoids abundant. Trilobites declining. First ammonites. Terrestrial plants and animals, spiders. Dominance of fishes. First amphibians.
	SILURIAN	Corals, brachiopods, and crinoids abundant. Trilobites beginning to decline. Eurypterids prominent. Scorpions and millipedes. Ostracoderms and placoderms.
	ORDOVICIAN	First corals, crinoids, nautiloid cephalopods, ostracods. Graptolites, brachiopods, snails, and trilobites abundant. First vertebrates.
	CAMBRIAN	Dominance of trilobites. Brachiopods. Calcareous sponges. Many other invertebrates; no vertebrates. Cephalopods appeared near its close.
PROTEROZOIC		Few fossils: annelid worm burrows, calcareous deposits by algae. Graphite.
ARCHEOZOIC		Calcareous deposits by algae 2,600,000,000 years old; graphite.

mined by occurrence of major geologic revolutions, such as extensive mountain formation.

Most of the eras are subdivided into **periods** (second column), separated from one another by geologic phenomena of less magnitude than those which mark the ends of eras. The oldest period within an era is placed at the bottom of the sequence of periods comprising the era.

Dating the Past

Table 7.1 contains no statement of lengths of time involved. A recent estimate of the length of time which has elapsed between the present and the beginning of each of the last three eras is as follows (Kulp, 1961):

Beginning of Cenozoic Era	63 million years ago
Beginning of Mesozoic Era	230 million years ago
Beginning of Paleozoic Era	600 million years ago

We must recognize that these figures are rough approximations only. The difficulties of estimating geologic time in terms of years are so great that wide differences of opinion are inevitable. Yet within the last few years more accurate and quantitative methods than any previously available have been developed. These methods depend upon "clocks" which the rocks themselves contain in the form of radioactive elements (isotopes). One of the most important, and the first to be utilized, is uranium. At a constant rate, uranium emits helium and is transformed into lead. The age of some rocks can be determined by comparison of the proportions of un-decayed uranium and of lead present in the rock. The method is applicable only to rocks which contain uranium, of course; unfortunately the sedimentary rocks richest in fossils usually do not contain this element. Uranium tests indicate that the earth may be as old as 4500 million years (Patterson, Tilton, and Inghram, 1955). The oldest known fossils are those of algae found in rocks some 2600 million years old (Holmes, 1954). Hence for nearly two billion years of its existence the earth was probably not populated with living organisms. Recently other physicochemical methods of dating fossils and archeological discoveries have developed so rapidly as to give great promise for the future of accurate dating of prehistoric life. Of these the most accurate method depends upon the determination of the rate at which radioactive "heavy carbon" atoms in a given sample of material are losing their radioactivity. Heavy carbon has an atomic weight of 14, instead of the "normal" 12. Atoms of carbon 14 are formed in the earth's upper atmosphere by the action of cosmic rays on nitrogen atoms. These radioactive carbon atoms lose their radioactivity spontaneously by a sort of disintegration. As old ones are disintegrating new ones are being formed by the cosmic rays. The result is an equilibrium in the atmosphere. The equilibrium is at about one radiocarbon atom for a trillion "normal" carbon atoms. These carbon atoms are found in the carbon dioxide of the atmosphere. The equilibrium point represents a concentration at which radiocarbon in the carbon dioxide disintegrates at the same rate that new radiocarbon atoms are being formed. As a result the concentration of radiocarbon remains constant and has done so for a long period of time.

As we have seen (Chap. 5), plants use carbon dioxide in the manufacture of carbohydrates; animals obtain the latter by eating plants. Thus during their lifetimes plants and animals are constantly acquiring radiocarbon atoms along with "normal" ones, and the relative numbers of the two kinds are probably the same in the body as in the atmosphere. Radiocarbon atoms steadily lose their radioactivity in the body, as they do outside of it. But since new radiocarbon atoms are constantly being taken in as part of the food, the concentration of these "heavy carbon" atoms in the body of plant or animal remains about constant as long as the plant or animal lives. After death no more carbon enters the body, and the radiocarbon already present steadily disintegrates. Hence the amount of radiocarbon present diminishes steadily, a diminution accompanied by a concomitant decrease in the rate of atom disintegration in the tissue. The fewer the radiocarbon atoms present, the smaller the number of them undergoing disintegration at any one time. Thus if we take a piece of ancient wood or bone and measure the rate at which carbon 14 is now disintegrating we can estimate the age of the material, since we know the rate at which disintegration occurs in living wood or bone. When this technique has been applied to materials of known age the demonstrated accuracy has been such as to give confidence in determinations made on materials of unknown age. (See Libby, 1956.)

The carbon 14 method is applicable only to organic materials still containing carbon; it cannot be used on fossils in which all organic matter has been replaced by minerals. Since the amount of radiocarbon present decreases steadily with time, the method can probably never be used on material older than about 70,000 years. Accurate dating within that time span will prove most valuable, however. Among the early inhabitants of North America, for example, were makers of a particular type of stone arrowhead (probably used on darts rather than arrows), the so-called Folsom points. Pieces of burned bone found with some of these points give a carbon 14 date of 9,883 years, indicating that these early Americans lived about 10,000 years ago (Sellards, 1952).

Other physicochemical methods will doubtless be developed to supplement the carbon 14 method. One such method already being employed depends upon the rate at which fluorine becomes incorporated into bones during fossilization. Although variables in the process have yet to be explored, the test gives promise of usefulness. Utilization of this method contributed significantly to proof that the "fossils" called "Piltdown man" were a hoax (Weiner, Oakley, and LeGros Clark, 1953).

Visualizing Geologic Time

Unavoidably our ideas of time are conditioned by the length of the human life span and its subdivision into periods (infancy, youth, etc.) and years. The term "one million years" is so far outside our experience as to be meaningless to us. Multiples of a million years are, if anything, even less meaningful. We may have the vague impression that a million years is "a very long time," and that a thousand million years is "a very, very long time." But in other connections a thousand years also seems "a very long time." Indeed, all periods longer than a human lifetime or two have a tendency to fade into "a-very-long-time" vagueness for us.

But we *can* grasp the meaning of the length of a year and of its subdivisions into months, weeks, days, hours, minutes, and seconds. Consequently James C. Rettie (1950) rendered a signal service by picturing geologic time in subdivisions of a year. He imagined a moving picture taken of earth by inhabitants of another planet, using a super-telephoto lens and a time-lapse camera. This imaginary film was taken at the rate of one picture per year for the last 757 million years. When it is run in a projector at normal speed (twenty-four pictures per second), twenty-four years of earth history flashes by each second. Since the author has the film run continuously twenty-four hours a day, about two million years of past history are shown on the screen each day. To show the entire 757 million years requires running the film continuously for one full year. The author starts the show at midnight of one New Year's Eve and runs it without interruption until midnight of the next New Year's Eve.

For many fascinating details of this movie readers are referred to the original article or to the reprint of it in *Coronet* magazine (March, 1951). We have space for but a few high spots.

Throughout January, February, and March the movie runs on without showing any signs of life upon the earth. Single-celled organisms appear

early in April, many-celled ones later in that month. Late in May come the
first vertebrates. It is the middle of July before the first land plants begin to
pave the way for animal life on land. Late August arrives before the first
land vertebrates, the amphibians, put in an appearance. The first reptiles
appear by the middle of September. Among these the dinosaurs dominate
the scene through the remainder of September, through October and much
of November, about seventy days. In the meantime the first birds and first
mammals appear. The raising of the Rocky Mountains near the end of
November signals the end of the great era of reptilian domination.

As the movie runs on into December we see the mammals dominant;
they undergo their great evolutionary developments. Christmas arrives:
the movie shows us the Colorado River beginning to cut its Grand Canyon.
We have the vaguely uneasy realization that the year is nearing its close,
yet we have seen no signs of man. Day follows day until we reach the last
day of the year. Suddenly about noon of December 31 the movie shows
us the first men. During the afternoon the glaciers push southward from
the polar regions, and then retreat, four successive times. By suppertime
man is still not much in evidence. By about 11 o'clock in the evening varied
"Old Stone Age" men become quite prominent in the picture, and by 11:45
men who make more refined stone implements and cultivate the soil ap
pear. Five or six minutes before the end of the picture we see the dawn of
civilization. One minute and seventeen seconds before the end the Chris-
tian era begins. Twenty seconds before the end Columbus discovers America. Seven seconds before the end the Declaration of Independence is
signed.

Many aspects of this wonderful imaginary movie are worth pondering.
Life has existed on earth for some eight months of the movie's year; man
has been here for about twelve *hours* of that year. The dinosaurs dominated the movie for seventy days; man has dominated it for about half of
one day, so far. (Yet sometimes we look condescendingly upon the dinosaurs as "unsuccessful" animals! If the movie continues into the future
will it show us here seventy days from now?) Man has been in existence
for about twelve hours of the movie, but for only about five or six *minutes*
has he had any civilization which we consider worthy the term. This is
sometimes a comforting thought when we become impatient with the
"slow" progress made by mankind in adopting various desirable reforms
—such as the abolition of war. In speaking of this progress as "slow" we
are using human lifetimes as our yardstick. Any progress made since the
dawn of civilization has been dazzlingly swift, measured in terms of man's
total existence on earth.

References and Suggested Readings

Dunbar, C. O. *Historical Geology.* New York: John Wiley & Sons, Inc., 1949.

Holmes, A. "The oldest dated minerals of the Rhodesian shield," *Nature,* 173 (1954), 612–614.

Hussey, R. C. *Historical Geology,* 2nd ed. New York: McGraw-Hill Book Company, Inc., 1947.

Knopf, A. "Time in earth history." In G. L. Jepsen, E. Mayr, and G. G. Simpson (eds.). *Genetics, Paleontology and Evolution.* Princeton: Princeton University Press, 1949.

Kulp, J. L. "Geologic time scale," *Science,* 133 (1961), 1105–1114.

Libby, W. F. "Radiocarbon dating," *American Scientist,* 44 (1956), 98–112.

Patterson, C., G. Tilton, and M. Inghram, "Age of the earth," *Science,* 121 (1955), 69–75.

Rettie, J. C. "The most amazing movie ever made." In R. Lord, and K. Lord (eds.). *Forever the Land.* New York: Harper & Brothers, 1950. Reprinted in *Coronet,* 29 (1951), 21–24.

Sellards, E. H. "Age of Folsom man," *Science,* 115 (1952), 98.

Simpson, G. G. *The Meaning of Evolution.* New Haven: Yale University Press, 1949.

Weiner, J. S. *The Piltdown Forgery.* New York: Oxford University Press, 1955.

Weiner, J. S., K. P. Oakley, and W. E. LeGros Clark. "The solution of the Piltdown problem," *Bulletin of the British Museum (Natural History), Geology Series,* 2 (1953), 141–146.

Zeuner, F. E. *Dating the Past,* 3rd ed. London: Methuen & Company, 1952.

CHAPTER 8

EVOLUTION AS SEEN IN THE GEOLOGIC RECORD: PRE–CAMBRIAN AND PALEOZOIC ERAS

Since so little is known of Archeozoic and Proterozoic life, it is sometimes convenient to refer to these eras collectively by the term "Pre-Cambrian." Cambrian rocks are the earliest ones in which abundant fossils are found (Table 7.1, p. 137).

Beginnings

In a sense the geologic time scale may be thought of as starting with the beginning of the earth. How long ago did that event occur? The question cannot be answered with exactness, though recent estimates indicate that the earth may be in the vicinity of 4500 million years old (p. 138).

Although it is not within our province to discuss the various theories of the earth's origin, we may state that at one time the planet was evidently extremely hot, with temperatures above the melting point of rock. As the earth cooled the molten materials solidified into the original **igneous rocks.** During all this time conditions on the planet were unsuitable for life. Accordingly a very long period must have elapsed between the beginning of the earth and the beginning of life on the earth.

Conditions Necessary for Life

Both the time and the manner of the beginning of life are shrouded in mystery. We may be reasonably sure that life did not originate until climatic conditions arose bearing resemblance to those pertaining today.

Suitable conditions for life are rather narrowly delimited. Extreme cold and extreme heat render life impossible. Abundant water is necessary to life. An abundant supply of carbon in usable form is also essential. As noted previously (Chap. 5), carbon is the fundamental structural element in all living things. Animals are dependent upon plants for their supply of carbon. Plants are dependent upon the carbon dioxide in the atmosphere for their carbon. Animals obtain their carbon by eating the plants, or by eating other animals which have eaten plants. Thus life as we know it would be impossible without carbon dioxide in the atmosphere, and without sunlight.

With very few exceptions all living things depend upon oxygen in the atmosphere, including atmosphere dissolved in the water of streams, lakes, and oceans. The oxygen combines with (oxidizes) carbon-containing compounds, a chemical reaction which releases heat and energy. An analogy is the burning (oxidizing) of coal, relatively pure carbon, under the boiler of a steam engine to produce heat and energy. Almost all of the processes within the bodies of animals, as well as the outward activities of these animals, are entirely dependent upon this source of energy. Without it they would be as dead as a steam engine without a fire. Thus life would be impossible in the absence of an atmosphere containing oxygen.

Again, if pressure of the atmosphere and force of gravitation diverged widely from those actually found to prevail on the earth, life as we know it could not exist. Our discussion of the requirements for life might be greatly expanded, but the points enumerated will suffice to demonstrate that conditions on the earth must have approached those prevailing in modern oceans before life could have come into existence at all.

How did life originate on this planet? There is a certain fascination in speculating on this perhaps forever unsolvable mystery. In Chapter 5 we discussed attributes which first living things must have possessed, together with some ideas concerning the form taken by these first possessors of life. Whatever the sequence of events leading to its origin, life *did* originate; that is evident. Hence its subsequent evolution may be traced, despite the fact that the earliest chapters of the story are unknown and the later ones are incomplete.

ARCHEOZOIC ERA

There are at least two reasons why the earliest chapters of the history of life on this planet are unknown. In the first place, the earliest forms of life probably lacked those "hard parts" which we have seen to be most readily preserved as fossils (Chap. 7). Viruses, bacteria, most one-celled plants and animals, and most coelenterates (e.g., jelly-fishes) are notably lacking in structures likely to be preserved as fossils. Some or all of these are the forms we should expect to have been present in the early days of life on the planet. In the second place, most of the Archeozoic rocks were later subjected to metamorphism; hence most fossils present were destroyed (p. 135). As noted previously, however, fossils of **algae** have been found in rocks approximately 2600 million years old (p. 138). Since these simple plants doubtless possessed the power of photosynthesis (p. 84), this method of capturing energy from the sun and utilizing it in synthesis of organic compounds has existed on the earth for over two billion years (Briggs, 1959).

In addition to these fossils, indirect evidence that life was present in Archeozoic oceans is furnished by deposits of **graphite** in rocks of this era. Graphite, the "lead" of our pencils, is composed of carbon, as is coal. In later periods of earth history deposits of carbon in the form of graphite and coal represent the remains of vegetation. Accordingly we may reasonably conclude that Archeozoic graphite was also derived from simple plant life, probably in the main from algae.

The presence of iron ore in Archeozoic rocks is also sometimes considered evidence of the existence of life, since iron ore frequently represents the result of bacterial action. Since, however, iron ore may be deposited by processes that do not involve the action of living things, the evidence here is not so conclusive as it is in the case of graphite.

Limestone in deposits of this era may also have been derived from living organisms. The fossils of algae, mentioned above, are of this nature. Some of the limestone deposits from later periods represent the massed shells of such protozoans as foraminiferans and the skeletons of such coelenterates as corals. Yet some limestone is of inorganic origin and hence the mere presence of limestone does not prove that life existed at the time the deposit was formed.

PROTEROZOIC ERA

Like rocks of the preceding era, many Proterozoic rocks were subjected to metamorphism, with consequent destruction of any fossils they may have contained. Since there are, however, large deposits of unmetamorphosed Proterozoic rocks, the scarcity of fossils in the latter is somewhat surprising. The most abundant fossils from this era consist of globular masses of limestone representing the remains of colonies of **algae.** Many of these deposits are of large size, analogous in numerous ways to the coral reefs in our present oceans.

Animal fossils from this era are conspicuous by their rarity. Fossils of radiolarians and foraminiferans (protozoans which secrete shells of silica and calcium carbonate, respectively) have been reported, as have also fossils of brachiopods (see p. 147), the spicules of sponges, and even the impression of a jellyfish. While there is every reason to expect that such animals would have been living in Proterozoic oceans, confirmation of the reported fossils themselves seems to be lacking, in some cases at least.

The fossils most generally accepted as derived from a Proterozoic animal consist, not of the remains of the animals themselves, but of casts of the homes of the animals. In the bottoms of shallow portions of modern oceans **annelid worms,** marine relatives of our common earthworm, live in burrows. These burrows are not temporary affairs like the tunnels of earthworms but have definite walls secreted by their inhabitants. Casts which seem to have been formed in burrows of this type are found in Proterozoic deposits.

If we are correct in interpreting the Proterozoic worm burrows as evidence that annelid worms existed in this era, we must conclude that much evolution had occurred prior to this time. Annelid worms are placed well up in the scale of invertebrate animals. They have considerable complexity of structure. Evidently, therefore, an extensive evolutionary history leading up to them must have taken place prior to and during the Proterozoic era. Unfortunately a fossil record of that history was for the most part never formed or has been irrecoverably lost. This statement applies equally to the other phyla of invertebrates. Yet although fossil remains of them are so scanty it is likely that most of the invertebrate phyla were represented in late Proterozoic seas. One reason for thinking so lies in the wealth of invertebrate life found in the seas of the next era.

PALEOZOIC ERA

The beginning of the Paleozoic era is known to us from the earliest deposits bearing abundant fossils. It will be noted (Table 7.1, p. 137), that this era is much the longest of the ones following the Proterozoic, and that it is divided into seven periods, of which the Cambrian is the first or oldest.

Cambrian Period

Between the rocks remaining to us from the Proterozoic era and the first ones representing the Cambrian period occurs a gap in the geologic record representing in all probability a lapse of many millions of years. In view of these lost chapters in the record we need not be surprised that the story of animal evolution does not commence in the Cambrian where it left off at the end of the Proterozoic era. In place of the paucity of fossils characteristic of Proterozoic rocks we find in Cambrian deposits abundant fossils, particularly in the later deposits of the period. Cambrian oceans teemed with a wide variety of invertebrates.

One reason for the increase in completeness of record may lie in the fact that in the interim between Protero-zoic and Cambrian, animals possess-ing hard parts (shells and exoskele-tons) increased greatly in numbers. **Brachiopods** constituted an impor-tant portion of the Cambrian fauna. These animals are enclosed within shells consisting of two portions or valves. Unlike the shells of bivalve molluscs, such as clams, the two valves are unequal in size (Fig. 8.1). Molluscs themselves are represented in Cambrian seas by a few **snails** and, near the close of the period, rare **cephalopods** (p. 151).

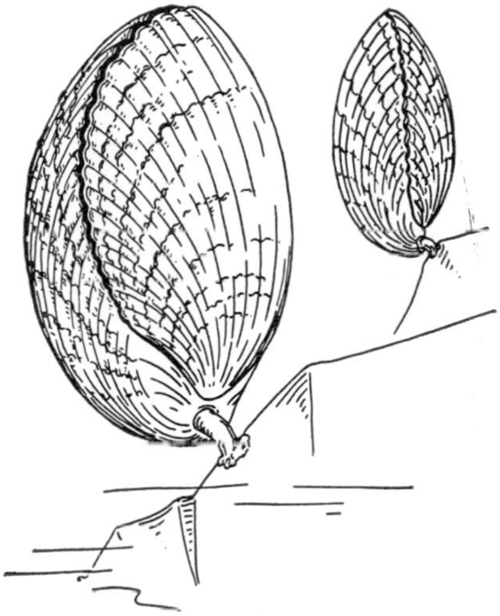

FIG. 8.1. Brachiopods, attached to rocks by their pedicles. Note the larger size and differing shape of the half-shell pierced by the pedicle. (Mainly after Dunbar, *Historical Geology*, John Wiley & Sons, Inc., 1949.)

Worm burrows, recalling those of the Proterozoic, are abundant in some Cambrian deposits.

The dominant animals in the Cam-brian seas were the **trilobites,** consti-tuting some 60 percent of the known inhabitants of those seas. They were small animals for the most part, ranging between one and four inches in length, the giant among them being 18 inches long. The examples presented in Fig. 8.2 are typical. Fig. 8.3 shows a trilobite with such structures as antennae and appendages restored to the appearance presented in life.

The first thing to note about trilobites is that they are members of Phylum Arthropoda, to which such creatures as lobsters, crayfishes, spiders, and insects also belong. The general similarity to a lobster, for instance, is evi-dent in the shell-like exoskeleton, the segmented body, and the jointed ap-pendages. Arthropods form the "highest" (most complex and specialized) phylum of invertebrates. Thus in the first geologic period that we know from adequate fossil material the highest invertebrate group of animals is represented. This fact indicates that a great proportion of the evolution of invertebrates had already occurred, although our records of its history are almost entirely lacking. Since trilobites appeared on the scene with such apparent abruptness their origin is uncertain. It seems reasonable to believe that they evolved from annelid worms, the other great group of invertebrates having segmented bodies. Evidence that annelid worms were present in the Proterozoic will be recalled.

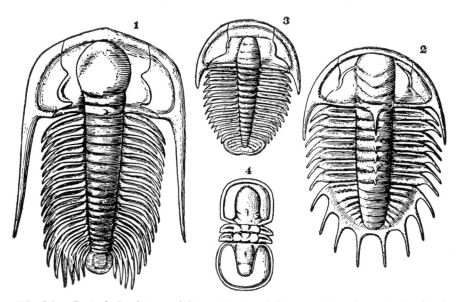

FIG. 8.2. Typical Cambrian trilobites. (Reprinted by permission from *Textbook of Geology, Part II, Historical Geology,* by Louis V. Pirsson and Charles Schuchert, published by John Wiley & Sons, Inc., 1915, p. 595.)

Our knowledge of life in Cambrian seas would be confined almost exclusively to shells and exoskeletons were it not for a most fortunate and unusual fossil discovery in the Burgess shale of British Columbia. The fossils consist of thin carbon films (see p. 129) showing in amazing detail the structures of the animals from which they were formed. Both hard and soft parts are shown by these carbonaceous films. Among the remains are trilobites preserved with their limbs and antennae, delicate arthropods like the modern brine shrimp, annelid worms complete with setae (bristles) and details of the internal organs, sponges, and such soft-bodied creatures as jellyfish. One of the most interesting members of the assemblage is an onychophoran. The onychophorans are peculiar, wormlike arthropods exemplified by the modern *Peripatus* (Fig. 8.4). Their particular interest

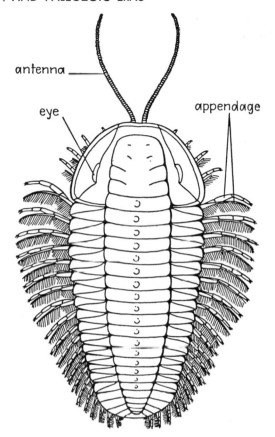

FIG. 8.3. Trilobite anatomy. (After Beecher.)

lies in the fact that they combine characteristics of arthropods with those of annelid worms. Thus they strengthen the evidence that arthropods evolved from annelids. Hence the finding of onychophorans living as contemporaries of the first arthropods (trilobites) is of much interest.

Thanks to the rare fortune of the Burgess shale fossils we know that the Cambrian seas supported a wealth of invertebrate life of kinds not ordinarily preserved as fossils. Perhaps we should have inferred that this world of soft-bodied marine animals existed, but certainty is more satisfying than inference.

In conclusion we note two general facts about Cambrian animals. They all lived in the ocean; none were land dwellers. They were all invertebrates; no representatives of Phylum Chordata, comprised of the vertebrates and their kin, were present at this stage in the world's history.

The Cambrian was a very long period, even for a geologic period. It is

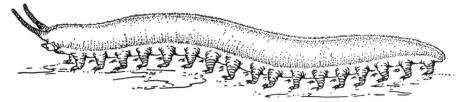

FIG. 8.4. *Peripatus,* an onychophoran.

variously estimated to have been of 60 to 100 million years in duration. Comparison of earlier Cambrian fossils with later Cambrian fossils reveals the fact that much evolutionary change occurred during the course of this long period.

Ordovician Period

The oceans continued to support varied invertebrate life. Space will permit us merely to note changes which occurred in that fauna as time went by.

The first **corals** appeared among the coelenterates in the Ordovician period. We noted above evidence that jellyfishes were present in the Cambrian period. Apparently, however, no coelenterates in that period developed the ability to secrete calcium carbonate, thereby forming what is for the coral animal at once its skeleton, its apartment house, and its memorial monument. Each of the pits or hollows on the surface of a piece of coral represents the point of attachment of a tiny sea anemone-like coral animal (Fig. 8.5). One generation builds upon the foundations laid down by its predecessors. Hence coral rock, built up at times into great reefs in the ocean, is the result of coöperative action of countless hordes of coelenterates over great periods of time. Much limestone originated in this way.

Colonial animals called **graptolites** were a most characteristic feature of the oceans during this period (Fig. 8.6). Small forms without means of locomotion, they achieved world-wide distribution through the action of ocean currents, in which they floated. While their relationships are uncertain, they are probably best regarded as coelenterates, though some investigators have considered them to be lowly members of Phylum Chordata (protochordates, pp. 100-101).

Phylum Echinodermata came into prominence at this time. This spiny-skinned tribe was represented only by tiny cystoids in the Cambrian; in the Ordovician **crinoids** and even a rare **starfish** appeared. Crinoids or sea

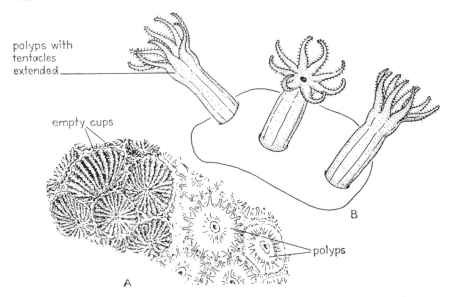

polyps with
tentacles
extended

empty cups

polyps

A

B

FIG. 8.5. Coral. A, coral animals (polyps) seen from above, and, at left, the empty cups remaining after their death. B, coral polyps of a species suggestive of *Hydra*, a free-living coelenterate (Fig. 4.15, p. 71).

lilies look not unlike flowers growing in the ocean (Fig. 8.7). The stem or stalk attaching the creature to the ocean floor is composed of piled rings fastened together. These rings, freed by disintegration of crinoid stems, are immensely abundant in many Ordovician rocks.

Brachiopods continued abundant throughout the Ordovician. Snails, relatively rare in the Cambrian, became abundant in Ordovician oceans. Among the molluscs the greatest prophecy of things to come was presented by the occurrence of **cephalopods.**

Cephalopods are the group of molluscs to which squids, octopi, and nautili belong. The chambered nautilus (Fig. 8.8) of our modern oceans presents a structure not unlike that of its Ordovician ancestors. The animal itself is soft-bodied and unsegmented; it possesses a pair of eyes and a cluster of extensible, sucker-bearing arms or tentacles around the mouth. As shown in the figure, the animal lives in the outermost compartment of its tapered shell. When it grows it moves outward, adding to its shell and secreting behind it a wall or **septum.** Thus the shell eventually consists of a series of chambers or compartments, evidence of successive stages in the growth of the animal (Fig. 8.8). Where each septum joins the side wall of the shell a line of attachment, called a **suture,** is formed. In the earliest

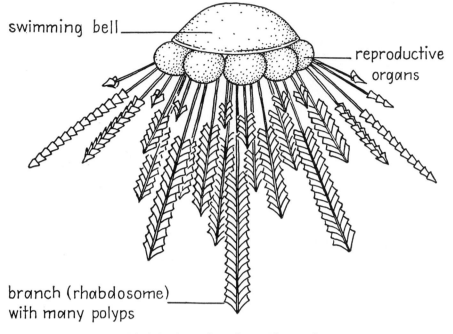

swimming bell

reproductive organs

branch (rhabdosome)
with many polyps

FIG. 8.6. Graptolite colony. (After Bassler.)

cephalopods the suture lines were smooth curves (Fig. 8.8). In later periods cephalopods having suture lines following complex configurations
were found, as noted below. Cephalopods having smoothly curved suture
lines are called **nautiloids.** Interestingly enough, both our modern
nautili and these earliest cephalopods were of this type. The principal difference between the shells of Ordovician nautiloids and those of their
modern descendants relates to the coiling of the shell. Some of the Ordovician cephalopods had straight shells (Fig. 8.9), others were loosely coiled,
while still others were closely coiled like those of modern nautili. In Fig.
8.9 the smooth sutures are visible in places where the outer surface of the
shell has been chipped away. Cephalopods included the largest animals
living in Ordovician seas; some of the straight-shelled forms reached a
length of 30 feet.

Many other invertebrates were present in the Ordovician. Among them
were the **bryozoans,** lowly animals which have constituted an important
agent of limestone formation in oceans ever since their first appearance.
Among the other invertebrates we should not forget the trilobites, which
as in the Cambrian formed an important constituent of the fauna, the great
variety of forms suggesting adaptations to many conditions of aquatic life.

Ostracods, tiny crustaceans enclosed in bivalved shells, first appeared in this period.

The most portentous occurrence in the Ordovician was the appearance of the first vertebrate members of Phylum Chordata. Bony scales have been found in deposits of this period, indicating the presence of armored vertebrates. We have no further knowledge concerning the possessors of these scales but they may have been ancestral to ostracoderms, jawless fishes, whose remains are found in Silurian deposits.

Silurian Period

During the Silurian period some of the invertebrate groups previously present expanded greatly in numbers of kinds and of individuals while other groups declined. Of the groups which expanded we may mention the corals, the brachiopods, and the crinoids, all of which were extremely abundant. Graptolites, on the other hand, had declined from their abundance in Ordovician seas, and trilobites also were beginning to decline. Some of the Silurian trilobites developed quite bizarre shapes and spines (Fig. 8.10). This type of specialization is frequently ascribed to racial "senescence" or "old age." Apparently it forms one indication that a group has become highly specialized for a particular mode of life and has correspondingly lost that plasticity which

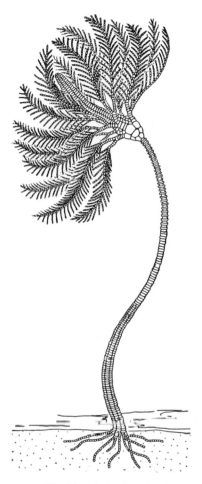

FIG. 8.7. A simple crinoid.

would enable it to adapt to other modes of life should conditions change. The spines in this instance may have served for protection from predators, if there were any present capable of preying on trilobites.

The most characteristic invertebrates of Silurian times were the **eurypterids** or "sea scorpions" (Fig. 8.11). They were a group of arthropods that had made a small beginning in the Cambrian but did not constitute an im-

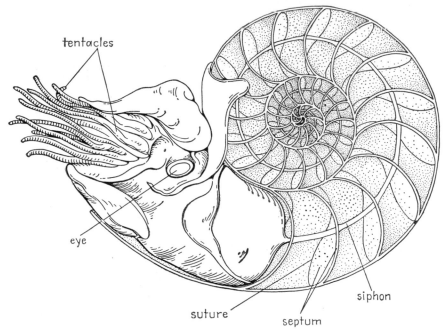

tentacles

eye

suture

septum

siphon

FIG. 8.8. Pearly nautilus, with shell cut longitudinally to show internal chambers. (After Hancock.)

portant feature of the fauna until the Silurian. These remarkable arthropods were small for the most part, though one had a body length of 7 feet and was probably the largest arthropod that ever lived.

Closely similar to eurypterids in many ways, and probably descended from them, were **scorpions** not unlike those of the present day (Fig. 8.12). These and **millipedes** existing at the time may have been terrestrial, thereby earning the distinction of being the first known animals to live on land. The evidence is inconclusive, however. Similarly, evidence is indecisive as to whether or not terrestrial plants existed at this time, though their occurrence seems not unlikely in view of the great numbers of them found in the next period. From our earlier discussion of the dependence of animal life upon plant life (p. 84) it will be evident that no considerable development of terrestrial animals could be expected prior to development of terrestrial plants.

Vertebrates are represented in Silurian deposits by remains of **ostracoderms.** These were little creatures with jawless mouths, their nearest modern relatives being lampreys and hagfishes. They became much more abundant in the next period. **Placoderms,** the first fishes possessing jaws, were probably also present at this time (see p. 156).

Devonian Period

As intimated above, terrestrial plants were abundant in the Devonian period. Some of these displayed the interesting transitional stages by which water-dwelling plants were able to make the change to life in the air. Forests of seed ferns existed at this time, some of the individual plants reaching a height of over 40 feet and having a trunk diameter of 3 feet.

Remains of terrestrial animals are relatively few. Several species of spiders, a mite, and the first air-breathing snails are included in the group, as are also the first terrestrial vertebrates, the primitive amphibians known as **labyrinthodonts,** to be discussed more fully later.

Invertebrate marine life continued abundant. Brachiopods reached their zenith; corals and crinoids occurred in profusion. Trilobites, on the other hand, continued to decline. Doubtless they were the prey of cephalopods and fishes. In addition to nautiloids, cephalopods were represented by a group in which the suture lines (p. 151) presented a wavy or "loop-and-saddle" appearance (Fig. 8.13). These

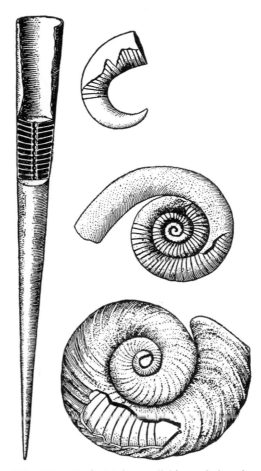

FIG. 8.9. Ordovician nautiloid cephalopods. (Reprinted by permission from *Textbook of Geology, Part II, Historical Geology,* by Louis V. Pirsson and Charles Schuchert, published by John Wiley & Sons, Inc., 1915, p. 626.)

were the first **ammonites,** a group which underwent extensive development in later periods.

The Devonian is frequently called "the age of fishes." We have noted that ostracoderms were found in the Silurian, and may have originated in

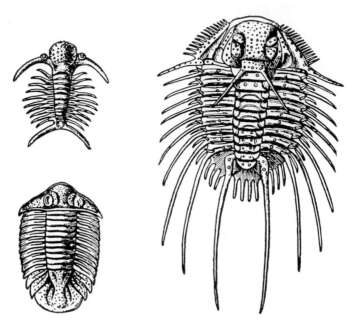

FIG. 8.10. Silurian trilobites. (Reprinted by permission from *Text-book of Geology, Part II, Historical Geology,* by Louis V. Pirsson and Charles Schuchert, published by John Wiley & Sons, Inc., 1915, p. 667.)

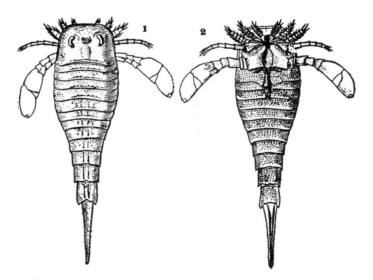

FIG. 8.11. Silurian eurypterid. 1, dorsal view. 2, ventral view. (Reprinted by permission from *Textbook of Geology, Part II, Historical Geology,* by Louis V. Pirsson and Charles Schuchert, published by John Wiley & Sons, Inc., 1915, p. 675.)

the Ordovician. Much more complete remains of them are found in Devonian deposits (Fig. 8.14). Like modern cyclostomes (lampreys and hagfishes) they had mouths without jaws, and they had no paired fins. Some
of them had a pair of movable flippers attached just behind the head but
these did not correspond to the pectoral fins of true fishes. The name
"armored fishes" is based on the armor plate of fused scales covering the
head and part of the body. This armor may have served as protection from
predatory eurypterids (Romer, 1959) or it may have served to reduce the
amount of body surface exposed to unfavorable osmotic action.

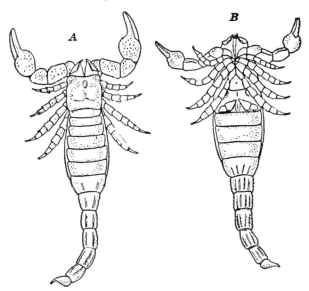

FIG. 8.12. Scorpions of Silurian age. A, dorsal view of
one species; B, ventral view of another. (After Pocock; reprinted by permission from *Textbook of Geology, Part II,
Historical Geology,* by Louis V. Pirsson and Charles Schuchert, published by John Wiley & Sons, Inc., 1915, p. 670.)

Ostracoderms were the forerunners and probably the ancestors of higher
types of fishes which appeared in the Devonian. Among these were the
placoderms (Fig. 8.15), the first fishes to possess jaws. The term "placoderm" as used here includes the acanthodians, which are sometimes regarded as a separate group. Placoderms form a varied assemblage but the
anatomy of some of them suggests that they were the ancestors of two
great groups of fishes appearing about this time: (1) **Chondrichthyes,** fishes
with cartilaginous skeletons, such as dogfishes and sharks; and (2) **Osteichthyes,** fishes with skeletons composed mainly of bone, such as sturgeon,
gar pike, trout, salmon, perch, bass, tuna.

An aberrant group of placoderms was noteworthy for producing the largest animal of the time, *Dinichthys* ("terrible fish"). This somewhat sharklike animal reached a length of 20 or 30 feet. It appears to have inhabited brackish and salt water. The head and forepart of the body were covered with armor; the armor plates covering the jaws took the place of teeth in forming a shearing device.

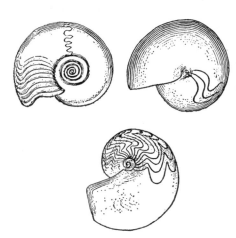

FIG. 8.13. Devonian ammonites (goniatites) showing wavy suture lines. (Reprinted by permission from *Textbook of Geology, Part II, Historical Geology*, by Louis V. Pirsson and Charles Schuchert, published by John Wiley & Sons, Inc., 1915, p. 709.)

We have noted that Chondrichthyes (sharks and dogfishes) have skeletons of cartilage. Consequently prehistoric representatives are known mostly from such hard parts as teeth, spines, and scales. In the case of *Cladoselache* (Fig. 8.16), however, we are more fortunate; the outline of the body and some details of skin and muscles were preserved in the fossilization.

Turning to the Osteichthyes, we note that they are commonly divided into two subclasses. **Subclass Actinopterygii** (ray-finned fishes) includes most of the forms we are familiar with as food and sport fishes. **Subclass Sarcopterygii** (Romer, 1959) (fleshy-finned fishes) includes the lungfishes (Dipnoi) and the Crossopterygii, a group represented by the ancestors of the first amphibians and by the coelacanth fishes. (The Sarcopterygii are often called Choanichthyes, meaning the fish with nostrils, but since coelacanths lack internal nostrils the name is not particularly appropriate.) Because of their ancestral position, the **Crossopterygii** (lobe-finned fishes) are of particular interest to us. Each pectoral and pelvic fin had a thickened, fleshy base (Fig. 8.17). Within these fleshy bases in such a species as *Eusthenopteron* were skeletal elements capable of developing into the stiffening supports for limbs of terrestrial vertebrates (Fig. 8.18).

Crossopterygians, like lungfishes and like some modern actinopterygians such as the gar pike, had air bladders connected to the pharynx. Such a connection makes possible filling of the bladder with air from the exterior. Thus, gar pikes and some modern lungfishes, when the surrounding water becomes stagnant and unfitted for respiration by means of gills, rise to the surface and gulp in air. Their air bladders function as lungs.

Accordingly we see that Crossopterygii of Devonian times possessed a mechanism capable of developing into the respiratory system needed by terrestrial vertebrates—an example of preadaptation (pp. 12–16). In

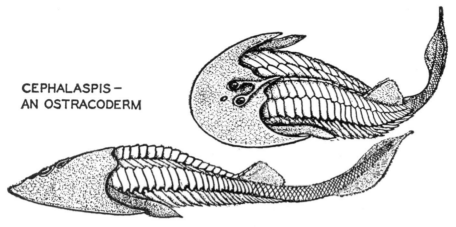

CEPHALASPIS –
AN OSTRACODERM

FIG. 8.14. An ostracoderm (armored fish), *Cephalaspis;* length one foot or less. (By permission from *Comparative Anatomy,* by Neal and Rand, p. 24. Copyright, 1936. McGraw-Hill Book Company, Inc.)

many of the modern bony fishes, on the other hand, the air bladder has no opening to the pharynx; gas pressure in the bladder is regulated through action of the blood system. Thus the bladder serves as a swim bladder, a

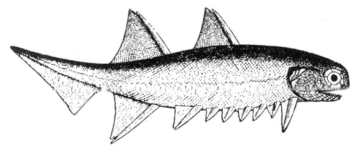

FIG. 8.15. A placoderm (acanthodian) fish (*Climatius*) from the Devonian; length about 3 inches. (From Romer, *Vertebrate Paleontology,* University of Chicago Press, 1945, p. 41.)

hydrostatic organ enabling the fish to adjust to varying pressures at different depths.

Ancestral crossopterygians also shared with lungfishes another feature useful for respiration in air. The external nostrils, instead of opening into blind pouches as they do in most fishes, connected to openings in the roof of the mouth. Thus terrestrial descendants of the Crossopterygii could breathe through the nose, with the mouth closed.

The nearest living relative of these ancestral crossopterygians is the coelacanth fish, *Latimeria*, discovered in 1938. Previously the coelacanths were known only from fossils; they were thought to have become extinct

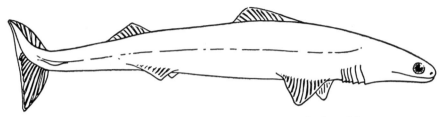

FIG. 8.16.   A Devonian shark, *Cladoselache;* length about 3 feet.

at the close of the Cretaceous period. Then in the winter of 1938–1939 a specimen was caught off the coast of South Africa. Intensive search for other specimens was fruitless at first, but since 1952 several specimens have been obtained near the Comoro Islands off Madagascar. The drama of discovery connected with the first and second specimens makes a fascinating story as told by the scientist most concerned, Dr. J. L. B. Smith

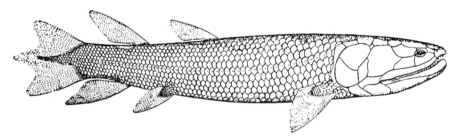

FIG. 8.17.   Crossopterygian fish, *Eusthenopteron;* length about 2 feet. (Reprinted by permission of the publishers from Percy Edward Raymond, *Prehistoric Life,* Cambridge, Mass.: Harvard University Press, 1939, p. 98.)

(1956). The modern coelacanth differs from ancestral lobe-finned fishes by having only a vestige of an air bladder (Millot, 1954), and no internal nostrils. Yet the creature is of great interest because of the strong possibility that it has retained many primitive characteristics of tissues and internal organs, and hence may give us clues as to the nature of these features in the ancestral Crossopterygii. The lobe fins are of especial interest; they have complex musculature, and observation of living specimens indicates that the fins are capable of a great variety of movements (Millot, 1955).

"It is plain that the fish can crawl about, in the water at least" (Smith, 1956).

The Crossopterygii gave rise to the first amphibians, the **labyrinthodonts.** A few remains indicate that the transition occurred in the Devonian. These first amphibians were long-bodied, weak-limbed creatures, somewhat "lizardlike" in appearance (Fig. 8.19). The lobe fins inherited from their crossopterygian ancestors had been transformed to serve as supports for the body in a medium, air, which did not buoy up the body as had

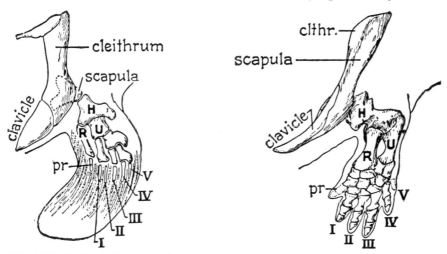

FIG. 8.18. Skeletal elements in the fin of the crossopterygian fish, *Eusthenopteron* (left), and in the limb of the Paleozoic amphibian, *Eryops* (right). H, humerus. R, radius. U, ulna. (After Gregory; by permission from *General Zoology*, by Storer, p. 201. Copyright, 1943. McGraw-Hill Book Company, Inc.)

the water of the old environment. Fig. 8.18 shows the skeletal elements in a typical crossopterygian fin and in the limb of an early amphibian.

We may note in passing that the idea that Devonian Crossopterygii used their fins to crawl out on land does not seem improbable in view of the nature of the coelacanth fins and the fact that in certain parts of the world today some fishes (e.g., "climbing perch") use their fins in just this manner, even climbing trees in search of insects.

The air bladder, inherited by amphibians from crossopterygian ancestors, served as simple lungs, and, as we have seen, the nostrils were arranged to permit breathing with the mouth closed.

The labyrinthodonts retained many features of their crossopterygian ancestors. Their name refers to a complicated pattern of infolding which characterized the arrangement of the enamel of the teeth. A similar arrangement characterized the enamel patterns of crossopterygian teeth. The dorsal surface of the skull of labyrinthodonts was composed of a mosaic of small bones fitted together edge to edge. The first diagram in Fig. 3.6 (p. 31) represents this mosaic pattern. These bones correspond in detail to the bony plates covering the heads of the Crossopterygii (Fig. 8.17). These and other similarities cannot be mere coincidence; they leave no doubt that amphibians arose from Crossopterygii.

Although these first amphibians possessed many preadaptations for life in the air, it is likely that most of them spent the greater portion of their lives in the water, as many amphibians do to this day (Romer, 1959). They had one great advantage over most fishes, however: they *could* leave the

FIG. 8.19. A labyrinthodont amphibian, *Diplovertebron;* about 2 feet long. (Reprinted by permission of the publishers from Percy Edward Raymond, *Prehistoric Life,* Cambridge, Mass.: Harvard University Press, 1939, p. 111.)

water when necessity arose. Under what conditions would it have been desirable to do so? Apparently they did not leave to escape predatory animals. In their fresh-water environment the ancestors of amphibians were the largest animals present. Abundant food supply on land can hardly have been the explanation since these animals were carnivorous, and prospective prey in the form of animals living on land was, as we have seen, much less abundant than was prey living in the water. The most generally accepted answer to the question is based on the idea that the ancestors of amphibians lived in pools that dried up periodically, as do the pools in which some lungfishes live today. Under conditions of overcrowding in stagnant water, followed perhaps by complete evaporation of that water, a premium would be placed on being able to breathe air directly and to move about on land, perhaps at first in search of a neighboring pool having better living conditions. Animals able to survive such stringent conditions were on their way to becoming true land dwellers. Thus, as so often happens, progress occurred under the lash of adversity.

We may note that amphibians have never completely conquered the terrestrial environment. Their method of locomotion on land is inefficient. They are not provided with skins which prevent undue loss of water from the body by evaporation. And perhaps most important of all, most of them must return to the water to lay their eggs. A few have developed a variety of expedients to avoid returning eggs to the water, but none of these expedients hold promise of general usefulness, as did the method developed by the first reptiles (pp. 168–169).

In the water amphibian eggs develop much as do fish eggs, and the aquatic larvae, "tadpoles," have many of the characteristics of fishes, thus, incidentally, affording an example of recapitulation (p. 50). Interestingly

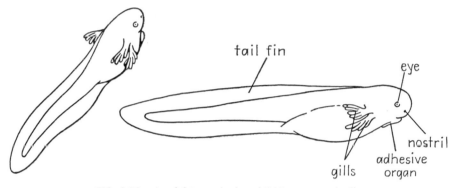

FIG. 8.20. Amphibian tadpole exhibiting external gills.

enough, the "external gill stage" of an amphibian larva (Fig 8.20), the stage in which branching, frondlike gills project laterally from the surface of the head, is similar to stages in the development of some modern remnants of ancient groups of fishes: *Polypterus,* and some of the Dipnoi, lungfishes. If we ever learn of the larval development of the Crossopterygii we shall probably find that the latter had an "external gill stage" too.

Mississippian Period

The Mississippian period and the one following it have frequently been regarded as subdivisions of one period called Carboniferous. The Mississippian period is frequently called Lower Carboniferous, the Pennsylvanian period Upper Carboniferous. The name "Carboniferous" refers to the formation of coal. In the Mississippian, however, little or no coal was formed.

Extensive limestone deposits of this period were formed principally, not from coral reefs, for corals were relatively scarce, but from vast numbers of foraminiferans and crinoids. Crinoids reached the peak of their development in the seas of this period. Brachiopods having long spines radiating from their shells were also characteristic of these seas. Trilobites, on the other hand, were rare. Their continued decline may be explained in part by the presence of some 300 species of sharks having flat, "pavement" teeth adapted for crushing the shells of molluscs and arthropods.

Fossils of terrestrial life of the time are relatively few in deposits remaining to us. Skeletons of small, salamanderlike amphibians have been found, as have casts of amphibian footprints.

Pennsylvanian Period

The great coal deposits remain to us as memorials of the Pennsylvanian period. Vast expanses of lowland were for long periods of time but slightly elevated above sea level, and hence were perennial swamps. In these swamps, encouraged by a mild climate, flourished luxuriant plant growth whose carbon later became fossilized as coal. A Pennsylvanian forest would have looked strange indeed to modern eyes. Deciduous trees, the type most familiar to us, were lacking, as were true conifers, although a forerunner of the latter having bladelike leaves was found. The least strange plants would have been the ferns, though we are scarcely accustomed to the sight of ferns with fronds 5 or 6 feet long and trunks 50 feet high. Otherwise the plant life was quite unlike anything which meets our eyes. The largest trees, and among the most common ones, were the scale trees, so called because the surface of the bark had a pattern resembling the pattern of scales on a snake's skin. The patterning was produced by scars left by the bases of closely set leaves. Trunk diameters of 6 feet and heights of 100 feet were found. Vast canebrakes of scouring rushes, similar to their modern relative *Equisetum* ("horsetails") but reaching heights of one hundred feet, added to the luxuriant plant growth destined for conversion into coal.

Insect life flourished. Predecessors of the Pennsylvanian insects are still unknown. Future discoveries may help to fill this gap in our knowledge, revealing the ancestry and early evolution of the group. Most of the Pennsylvanian insects were of archaic types not now living, though one struck a distinctly modern note: the cockroach (Fig. 8.21). Although cockroaches constitute only about 1 percent of modern insect faunas, they formed about 60 percent of insects living in Pennsylvanian times. Some reached a length of 4 inches. They were strikingly similar to their modern descendants in structure. It is a remarkable fact that while some animals are undergoing

great evolutionary changes others continue virtually unchanged for millions of years. Dynasties of animals wax and wane, but the cockroach
goes on forever.

Large size characterized many Pennsylvanian insects. Thus one of a
group of insects closely resembling modern dragonflies had a wingspread
of about 34 inches, making it the largest insect ever recorded.

Aside from cockroaches the most numerous insects were of a group now
extinct, the **Paleodictyoptera** (Fig. 8.21). These insects are of interest as
the ancestors of all other winged insects.

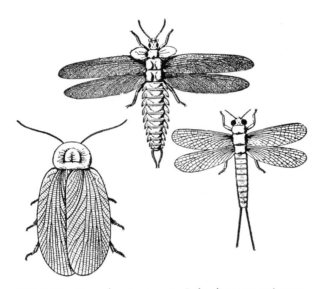

FIG. 8.21. Pennsylvanian insects. *Paleodictyoptera* (upper,
and lower right). Cockroach (lower left). (Reprinted by permission from *Textbook of Geology, Part II, Historical
Geology, by Louis V. Pirsson and Charles Schuchert, pub-*
lished by John Wiley & Sons, Inc., 1915, p. 752.)

We recall that amphibians first appeared during the Devonian period,
apparently having evolved from crossopterygian fishes (pp. 159–163). We
have noted that these early amphibians were of a group known as labyrinthodonts (sometimes called Stegocephalia). The Pennsylvanian period
saw expansion of this group, some eighty-eight species being known. Somewhat lizardlike in appearance, the labyrinthodonts had relatively large
heads, which were frequently broad and flat (Fig. 8.19). A third or pineal
eye commonly occurred between, and slightly behind, the more usual pair.
This was evidently another inheritance from crossopterygian ancestry.
Limbs were short, extending laterally from the body (Fig. 8.19) and form-

ing a rather inefficient locomotor apparatus wherein an undue proportion of muscular energy was expended in raising the body off the ground. This inefficiency was probably mitigated by the fact that labyrinthodonts spent a great portion of their lives in the extensive swamps of the period, where water supported much of the weight of the body. Many of these amphibians were small, only a few inches long. At the other extreme were animals about 10 feet long, and one, known only from its footprints, which probably weighed at least five or six hundred pounds.

The first **reptiles** appeared in the Pennsylvanian period. Since fossils of reptiles are exceedingly rare in deposits of the period we shall postpone further discussion of them until our consideration of the next period, the first period having reptiles as prominent members of the fauna.

Permian Period

The marine animals of the Permian period were similar to those of the two preceding periods, though changes were occurring gradually. The crinoids, for example, which had reached a peak of abundance in the Mississippian, had become relatively rare by Permian times. The close of the period saw the last of the trilobites. When the curtain had arisen on the Paleozoic era some 300 million years previously the trilobites had occupied the center of the stage, dominating the scene. It is perhaps fitting that their extinction marked the closing act of the Paleozoic drama.

Brachiopods, particularly spiny-shelled ones mentioned as abundant in Mississippian seas, continued as prominent members of the marine fauna in the Permian but declined markedly by the end of that period, many forms becoming extinct.

Contrariwise, the cephalopods with wavy and contorted suture lines, the **ammonites,** underwent progressive evolution during the Permian. Many new forms appeared, foreshadowing the great expansion of this group during the following era.

Turning to life on land, we find that the plants characteristic of the Pennsylvanian period lived on into the Permian. As the period advanced, however, the extensive swamps basking in mild climate disappeared from large portions of the earth. More arid conditions arose, accompanied by cold in winter. In widespread regions of the Southern Hemisphere extensive glaciers were formed. Thus the luxuriant vegetation of the coal deposits was replaced by hardier plants over much of the earth. True conifers became the leading type of forest tree.

Permian insects were quite unlike those of the preceding period. They averaged smaller in size; cockroaches formed a decreased proportion of them. New orders appeared: mayflies, dragonflies, beetles, among them.

Labyrinthodont amphibians continued as inhabitants of moister portions of the environment. Deposits containing their fossils indicate that as the country became more arid they concentrated their habitations in and around rivers and streams. Although a variety of forms appeared, the general description given above continued to characterize the group.

The most exciting occurrence in the Permian was the progressive development of **reptiles.** Although, as we have seen, they arose in the Pennsylvanian period, it was not until Permian times that reptiles formed a prominent part of the vertebrate fauna. The first reptiles were the **cotylosaurs**. In shape and bodily characteristics cotylosaurs closely resembled labyrinthodont amphibians (Fig. 8.22). In fact the resemblance was so

FIG. 8.22.   A Permian cotylosaur reptile, *Limnoscelis;* length about 5 feet. (Romer, 1959, considered that this creature was amphibious and had webbed feet.) (After Case, *Publication No. 207,* Carnegie Institution of Washington, 1915.)

great that concerning one creature living at the time, *Seymouria* (Fig. 8.23), there is still uncertainty as to whether it was a reptilelike amphibian or an amphibianlike reptile. Concensus leans toward the latter interpretation today. Its skull was much like that of the labyrinthodonts but many features of the remainder of its skeleton resembled those of primitive reptiles. If we knew what kind of an egg it laid (see below) we could be more certain as to whether it was an amphibian or a reptile. But our chief interest lies in the fact that the existence of such a form demonstrates the close relationship of labyrinthodonts to cotylosaurs. Cotylosaurs are believed to have arisen from labyrinthodonts.

Did the first reptiles live in the water or on land? Romer (1959) has concluded that they spent most of their lives in the water, as their amphibian ancestors had done, but that unlike the latter they laid eggs on land, as aquatic turtles do today. He pointed out the advantages of laying eggs on land, especially lessened danger of having the eggs and young eaten by predatory fishes, insect larvae, and the like, and lessened danger of destruction through drying in a climate characterized by alternating wet and dry seasons, as the latter part of the Paleozoic seems to have been. It is interesting to note in this connection that many modern amphibians manage to lay their eggs on land, employing a variety of protective devices. But none of these devices are as successful as the ones incorporated into the reptilian egg.

FIG. 8.23. A Permian vertebrate, *Seymouria,* combining characteristics of both amphibians and reptiles; length about 20 inches. (Mainly after Case.)

This important change was made possible by enclosure of each egg within a protective capsule containing enough nourishment to last the embryo until it had reached a stage when, as a newly hatched young, it could move about on land and secure its own food. Fig. 8.24 shows the arrangements by which this result is achieved for bird embryos; the reptilian egg is identical in its main features. The capsule mentioned is composed of a **shell** and **shell membranes;** the shell of reptilian eggs is pliable, in contrast to the brittleness of birds' egg shells. The embryo itself is enclosed within a bladderlike membrane called the **amnion.** This serves as a container for the **amniotic fluid** in which the embryo floats. The fluid protects the embryo from mechanical injury and from drying. Thus the embryos of reptiles and birds resemble those of fishes and amphibians in that all develop while submerged in liquid. In the case of fishes and amphibians the liquid is the water of streams and ponds; in the case of reptiles and birds the liquid is the fluid bottled up within the amnion. One may speculate that, since the embryos of ancestors had "formed the habit of" developing in liquid, if descendants were to avoid laying their eggs in water they would be under necessity of providing a substitute liquid in which embryonic development could occur. Incidentally, we may here appropriately recall the many respects in which the embryos of higher vertebrates resemble the embryos of fishes (see Chap. 4).

The **yolk** of the reptilian or avian egg constitutes the store of food men-

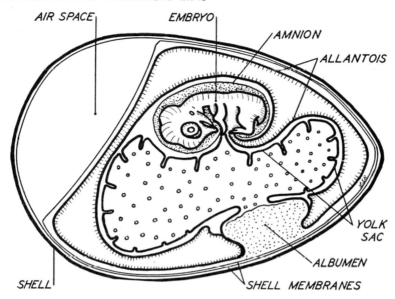

FIG. 8.24.   Embryo of a bird, together with shell, shell membranes, and embryonic membranes. (Drawn by Lyman S. Rowell.)

tioned above. Water for the needs of the embryo is present in the yolk and also in the **albumen** ("white") of the egg. Early in development an outgrowth from the body of the embryo surrounds the yolk with a **yolk sac.** This, like the digestive system of which it is an outgrowth, is lined with endoderm. The endoderm cells digest the yolk. The products of this digestion are picked up by the blood, flowing in the network of blood vessels which permeate the walls of the yolk sac, and transported to the embryo as nourishment is needed.

Oxygen is another necessity for the embryo. Oxygen is abundant in the air surrounding the egg, but a means must be provided for securing it and transporting it to the embryo. The shell and shell membranes are sufficiently porous to permit air to enter. The blood serves as agent of transportation, in this instance through a network of blood vessels in the walls of an embryonic membrane called the **allantois** (Fig. 8.24). Like the yolk sac, the allantois grows out from the embryo; it spreads around underneath the shell membranes, where blood in its blood vessels can pick up oxygen from air diffusing through. Waste products of embryonic metabolism, principally uric acid (p. 93), are stored in a portion of the allantois, to be discarded when hatching time arrives.

Thus we see that by means of elaborate arrangement of shell, shell membranes, yolk sac, amnion, and allantois, reptiles and their descendants the

birds avoided the necessity of laying their eggs in the water as their ancestors had always done. This was one of the greatest achievements in the
entire history of vertebrate evolution.

What other advances over their amphibian ancestors did the reptiles
achieve? Like amphibians, reptiles are "cold blooded," meaning that they
have but little ability to regulate their body temperature. Reptiles achieve
more of such regulation than do amphibians, but to a considerable extent
body temperature fluctuates with fluctuations of the surrounding temperature.

Most modern amphibians lack scales on their skin, while reptiles have
coverings of horny scales. This difference in body covering aids reptiles in
living in drier habitats than are possible for amphibians, since the scaly
covering decreases water loss by evaporation from the surface of the body.
It is noteworthy that when scales are present in amphibians, as they were
in labyrinthodonts and are in reduced form in the modern limbless caecil-
ians, they are of the bony type characteristic of fishes. Apparently such
scales were inherited from the crossopterygian ancestors of amphibians but
have been lost by most modern representatives of the latter. Horny scales
of the type characterizing the surface of reptilian skin formed a "new"
evolutionary development.

Reptiles have larger brains than have amphibians, the enlargement of
the cerebral hemispheres in particular forming a portent of better things
to come.

Reptiles differ from modern amphibians by having one occipital condyle, the bony knob by which the skull is articulated to the first ver-
tebra of the backbone. Modern amphibians have two occipital condyles,
but labyrinthodonts had only one. Apparently, therefore, a single condyle was the primitive condition, retained by reptiles but not by later
amphibians.

Reptiles are distinguished from amphibians by other differences in skeletal details, including number of joints characteristic of fingers and toes.
Nevertheless it is difficult to pick out one diagnostic characteristic by
which the anatomy of all reptiles differs from the anatomy of all amphibians.

The cotylosaur reptiles are of greatest interest to us because they were
the ancestors of higher reptiles and, indeed, the distant ancestors of birds
and mammals. During the Permian and the early part of the Triassic (Table 7.1, p. 137) the cotylosaurs and their immediate descendants formed
a diversified group of reptiles. A few Permian reptiles were surprisingly
specialized. One of the commonest, *Dimetrodon,* is sometimes called a

"finback" because of the enormous elongation of the neural spines projecting up from its backbone (Fig. 9.3, pelycosaurs, p. 177). Too slender to serve for protection, these spines apparently supported a membrane that stretched down the back like an enormous fin. But of what use to a land animal is a fin? Speculations are as varied as they are ingenious; perhaps the best idea is that the membrane served in connection with control of body temperature, since it presented a considerable area of skin to the surrounding air. In another species each spine was provided with a series of transverse "yardarms" somewhat after the manner of a mast on a square-rigged sailing vessel, or of a telegraph pole.

Among the Permian reptiles a group of particular interest are the **therapsids,** or mammal-like reptiles (Fig. 8.25). Although they formed a

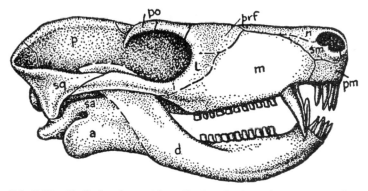

FIG. 8.25. Skull of a therapsid reptile, *Bauria*, lateral view. *a,* angular; *d,* dentary; *l,* lacrimal; *m,* maxilla; *n,* nasal; *p,* parietal; *pm,* premaxilla; *po,* postorbital; *prf,* prefrontal; *sa,* surangular; *sm,* septomaxillary; *sq,* squamosal. (After Broom and Boonstra; from Romer, *Vertebrate Paleontology,* University of Chicago Press, 1945, p. 289.)

diversified group, collectively the therapsids foreshadowed most of the distinguishing characteristics of the skeleton of mammals. While reptilian teeth are typically simple cones, therapsids developed teeth resembling the incisors, canines, premolars, and molars of mammals (Fig. 8.25). Like mammals they developed two occipital condyles in place of the single condyle possessed by other reptiles. Compared to other reptiles, they had a smaller number of bones in the skull, approaching the mammalian number. The pineal opening, the site of the third or pineal eye in many reptiles, had disappeared. The opening in the temporal region of the skull posterior to the eye (temporal fossa) was arranged as it is in mammals, and frequently the bony bar separating it from the orbit of the eye had disappeared (Fig. 8.25), as it has in many mammals.

The lower jaw of reptiles consists of several bones fastened together, whereas the mammalian lower jaw consists of a single pair of bones, the right and left **dentaries.** In therapsids the dentaries formed most of the jaw, the other bones being reduced in size (Fig. 8.25). The secondary or "hard" palate separating the mouth cavity from the nasal cavity above it was present in therapsids, as it is in mammals. The limbs were developed for better locomotion than characterized other reptiles, the body being lifted higher from the ground and the limbs being placed more directly beneath, instead of spread out at the sides as were the limbs of other Permian reptiles.

In short, the Permian therapsids were acquiring the characteristics which were to prove of such value to their descendants, the mammals.

References and Suggested Readings

Briggs, M. H. "Dating the origin of life on earth," *Evolution,* 13 (1959), 416–418.

Colbert, E. H. *Evolution of the Vertebrates.* New York: John Wiley & Sons, Inc., 1955.

Dunbar, C. O. *Historical Geology.* New York: John Wiley & Sons, Inc., 1949.

Hussey, R. C. *Historical Geology,* 2nd ed. New York: McGraw-Hill Book Company, Inc., 1947.

Millot, J. "New facts about coelacanths," *Nature,* 174 (1954), 426–427.

Millot, J. "First observations on a living coelacanth," *Nature,* 175 (1955), 362–363.

Moore, R. C. *Introduction to Historical Geology,* 2nd ed. New York: McGraw-Hill Book Company, Inc., 1958.

Raymond, P. E. *Prehistoric Life.* Cambridge, Mass.: Harvard University Press, 1939.

Romer, A. S. *Vertebrate Paleontology,* 2nd ed. Chicago: University of Chicago Press, 1945.

Romer, A. S. *The Vertebrate Story.* Chicago: University of Chicago Press, 1959.

Simpson, G. G. *The Meaning of Evolution.* New Haven: Yale University Press, 1949.

Smith, J. L. B. *The Search Beneath the Sea. The Story of the Coelacanth.* New York: Henry Holt & Co., 1956.

CHAPTER 9

EVOLUTION AS SEEN IN THE

GEOLOGIC RECORD:

MESOZOIC ERA

The 160 million years or more comprising the Mesozoic era are sometimes called the "age of reptiles," since during this time the group of reptiles called dinosaurs held undisputed sway over living things on the surface of the earth, while other reptiles dominated the sea, and still others the air. Instead of discussing each of the periods of the era (Table 7.1, p. 137) successively we shall discuss Mesozoic life under four main headings: (1) culmination of cephalopods; (2) evolution of dinosaurs and their relatives; (3) origin of birds; (4) origin of mammals.

CULMINATION OF CEPHALOPODS

Ammonites

Ammonites were the dominant invertebrates of Mesozoic seas. We recall that they first appeared in the Devonian (p. 155), probably as descendants of the nautiloids, which had existed from Ordovician times (p. 152). The nautiloids were characterized by straight or smoothly curved suture lines, formed by junctures of the septa with the side wall of the shell (Fig. 8.9, p. 155). Ammonites, on the other hand, had suture lines of some complexity. The Devonian ammonites (goniatites) had suture lines with a "loop-and-saddle" configuration (Fig. 8.13, p. 159). Their descendants in later periods of the Paleozoic retained suture lines of com-

FIG. 9.1.   Ammonite shell, showing complex suture lines. (Courtesy of Ward's Natural Science Establishment, Inc., Rochester, N.Y.)

parable complexity. The Mesozoic, however, saw an "outburst" of ammonite evolution, accompanied by great increase in complexity of suture lines. More than 6000 species of ammonites have been described from Mesozoic deposits. Most of these were relatively small, with shell diameters averaging not over 4 inches. Yet some Mesozoic ammonites attained large size; shell diameters of 5 feet were not uncommon, and some species were 10 feet in diameter.

For the most part each individual turn or volution of the coiled shell was high and narrow in cross section. Lightness of structure characterizing many ammonite shells suggests that their inhabitants were active animals, perhaps good swimmers. A variety of knobs, spines, and ridges ornamented shells of a number of species. Many had a trap-door-like arrangement (operculum) by which the opening of the shell could be closed when the body and tentacles were completely withdrawn into the shell. But in numerous ways the most remarkable feature of Mesozoic ammonites was the complexity of fluting of the margins of the septa. The intricacy of these lines suggests the tracery of frost patterns on a windowpane, or the outlines of a fern frond (Fig. 9.1).

The Jurassic period (Table 7.1, p. 137) saw the culmination of the ammonites. They continued into the Cretaceous in diminished numbers. During the later stages of their evolution bizarre shell forms occurred. Some shells showed a partial or complete tendency not to coil. Depending upon the degree of this tendency, loosely coiled, bent, or straight shells resulted.

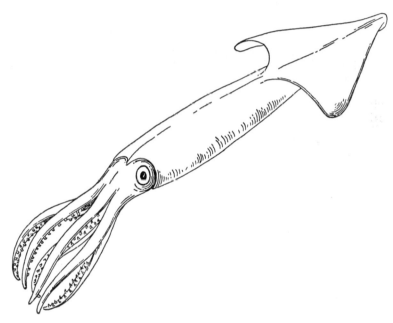

FIG. 9.2. Belemnite, restored; length 5 or 6 feet. (Mainly after Hussey, Historical Geology, McGraw-Hill Book Company, Inc., 1947.)

Some shells showed coiling of the first portion to be formed, followed by subsequent formation of a straight shell section. The tendency of any group of animals to develop such an assemblage of bizarre and atypical forms is sometimes called racial "old age" or "senescence" (p. 153). Terming it so gives no adequate explanation for its occurrence, however. Yet such diverse animals as trilobites, ammonites, and dinosaurs exhibited the tendency. No ammonites survived the close of the Mesozoic.

We should note that the more conservative group of cephalopods, the nautiloids, did not share the extinction of their relatives the ammonites. We recall that the nautiloids were the first cephalopods to appear (p.

152); they are still represented by a few species dwelling in modern seas, including the pearly nautilus (Fig. 8.8, p. 154).

Belemnites

The modern squids and octopi had a host of Mesozoic relatives, the belemnites. In general appearance they resembled the modern squid (Fig. 9.2). Their cigar-shaped internal skeletons are extremely abundant in Mesozoic deposits. They ranged in length from a few inches to 5 or 6 feet. Fortunate occurrence of fossils having the outlines of the body indicated by a carbonized film informs us that there were six tentacles and that the latter were provided with hooks, in place of the sucking discs possessed by modern squids. Remnants of the "ink" by means of which belemnites, like modern squids, formed a "smoke screen" to facilitate escape are preserved with rare fossils.

The internal skeletons of belemnites were divided into chambers suggestive of those of the uncoiled nautiloids (Fig. 8.9, p. 155) that were probably their ancestors. There are indications that the internal skeleton was a remnant of an external, chambered shell possessed by nautiloid, or possibly ammonoid, ancestors.

EVOLUTION OF DINOSAURS AND THEIR RELATIVES

On preceding pages we have traced the rise of land-dwelling vertebrates from crossopterygian fishes. We noted that the immediate descendants of the latter were the labyrinthodont amphibians, which, in turn, gave rise to the cotylosaur reptiles. All this occurred before the beginning of the Mesozoic. As noted on page 170, cotylosaurs are important as the ancestors of higher reptiles (Fig. 9.3).

The cotylosaurs had skulls solidly roofed in the region back of the eyes, the temporal region. From the cotylosaurs arose several lines of descendants, each line characterized by presence or absence of one or both of two openings in the temporal region: the **temporal fossae.** The **Therapsida** or mammal-like reptiles have already been mentioned (p. 171); they had a single temporal fossa—a single opening on each side, placed posterior to the eye and rather widely spaced from the midline of the skull. Therapsid and other reptiles so characterized are classed together as **Synapsida** (Fig. 9.4).

Another line is known as the **Diapsida** because of the possession of two

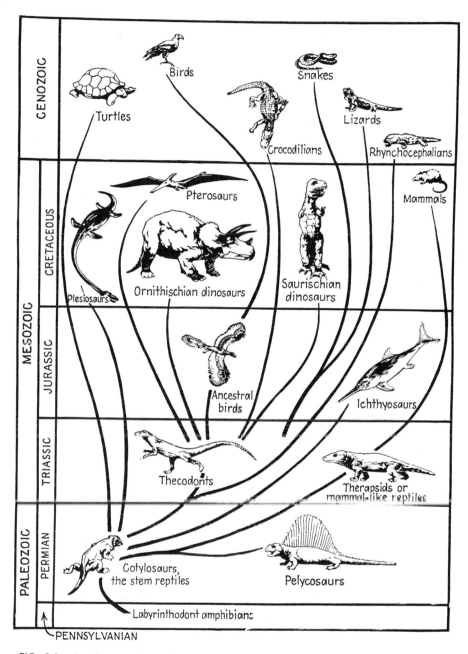

FIG. 9.3. Family tree of reptiles. (By permission from *The Dinosaur Book*, by Colbert, p. 52. Copyright, 1951, McGraw-Hill Book Company, Inc.)

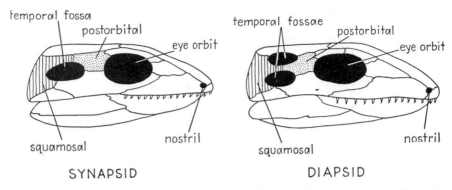

FIG. 9.4. Basic structural plans of the skulls of Synapsida and Diapsida. Note the single temporal fossa in the synapsid skull, the two temporal fossae in the diapsid skull. (After Colbert, *The Dinosaur Book,* McGraw-Hill Book Company, Inc., 1951.)

temporal fossae on each side of the skull—one near the midline, the other more lateral in position. The two are separated by a bridge of bone (Fig. 9.4). To the diapsid line belong the dinosaurs.

Thecodonts

Diapsid ancestors were found in the Permian. They resembled lizards in having long bodies and slender limbs. Their descendants in the Triassic were the **thecodonts,** direct ancestors of the dinosaurs (Fig. 9.3). Most of the thecodonts were small reptiles. They had narrow skulls which lacked a pineal opening but preserved the diapsid characteristic of two temporal openings on each side. The most distinctive characteristic of these reptiles, however, lay in their method of locomotion. Instead of walking or running on all four legs, as a dog does, they adopted a bipedal (two-footed) type of locomotion, running on the two hind legs as do many birds, e.g., robin and ostrich. The hind legs were elongated, forming a support upon which the body was balanced as on a fulcrum (Fig. 9.3). The body projected forward from this fulcrum, its weight counterbalanced by a long tail projecting backward. The forelimbs, freed from locomotor duties, were available for use in grasping and handling. Since all the weight of the body was concentrated on the hind legs, the attachment of the latter to the body was of necessity greatly strengthened. This involved strengthening of the pelvic girdle and of its attachment to the vertebral column, as well as the development of a more perfect ball-and-socket joint for attachment of the leg to the pelvic girdle. The legs no longer sprawled broadly at the sides of the animal, as they had in many earlier reptiles, but were placed well under the body, with knees turned forward, a position better calculated for efficient support of weight.

The body form resulting from this adaptation of the thecodonts for a bipedal gait provides the key to an understanding of dinosaur structure. The inheritance from thecodont ancestry was never completely obliterated, even in those dinosaurs which became huge in size and returned to a four-footed or quadripedal locomotion. The thecodont body plan is, as Colbert (1951) has said, "the blueprint to dinosaurian body form."

Orders of Dinosaurs

The dinosaurs arose from thecodonts in the Triassic and continued as the dominant land animals throughout the remainder of the Mesozoic. In reality the dinosaurs did not constitute a single group; from the first they were divided into two great orders, the **Saurischia** and the **Ornithischia.** These names refer to the most clear-cut distinction between the two: the

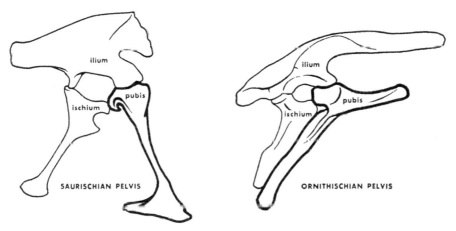

FIG. 9.5. Pelvic girdles of saurischian and ornithischian dinosaurs. (By permission from *The Dinosaur Book,* by Colbert, p. 65. Copyright, 1951. McGraw-Hill Book Company, Inc.)

structure of the pelvic girdle. The Saurischia retained a triradiate arrangement of the pelvic bones similar to that of their thecodont ancestors (Fig. 9.5). The **ilium** was the bone attaching the girdle to the vertebral column. To the ilium attached two bones, the **pubis,** extending ventrally and anteriorly, and the **ischium,** extending ventrally and posteriorly (Fig. 9.5). The socket (acetabulum) for the head of the femur was located at the junction of these three bones. Since the ischium and pubis on one side of the body were usually attached to the corresponding bones of the other side, a firmly braced tripod for attachment of the legs to the body was achieved.

The pelvic girdle of the Ornithischia differed from that of the Saurischia mainly in the structure of the pubis. This bone possessed two prongs (Fig. 9.5), one extending anteriorly, the other posteriorly and ventrally, parallel to the ischium. The arrangement of the posterior prong resembled that of the pubis in birds, hence the name Ornithischia ("bird hips").

Saurischia

The Saurischia include the dinosaurs most like their thecodont ancestors. These are the **Theropoda,** which, like the thecodonts, were carnivorous and bipedal. They ranged in size from small animals to *Tyrannosaurus,* the largest carnivorous land animal that ever lived (Fig. 9.6). This Mesozoic

FIG. 9.6. *Tyrannosaurus* attacking the horned dinosaur, *Triceratops.* (Restorations by Charles R. Knight; courtesy of the American Museum of Natural History.)

menace was about 50 feet long and 18 to 20 feet tall as he stood on his tremendous hind legs. The forelegs were tiny in proportion to the 8- to 10-ton bulk of the creature; each foreleg retained but two functional digits, armed with hooked claws. The lower jaw was hinged to the huge skull in a manner to give the animal a mouth of inordinate gape. The jaws were armed with rows of pointed teeth, some of them 6 inches long. This enormous engine of destruction was obviously well equipped to prey upon its giant herbivorous contemporaries.

The largest herbivorous dinosaurs belonged to a second division of the Saurischia, the **Sauropoda.** These creatures departed from the characteristics of their thecodont ancestors by returning to a four-footed or quadripedal locomotion and modifying the conical teeth of their carnivorous ancestors. Despite the return to quadripedal locomotion, however, the forelegs of most of them remained shorter than the hind ones—a telltale trace of their thecodont ancestry. The heads of sauropods were absurdly small for animals of such great bulk. The teeth were reduced in size and number. This relatively ineffectual dental armament suggests dependence upon a soft type of water vegetation for food. Indeed, it is thought that these giants spent much of their lives in lagoons and swamps. The nostrils of some of them were located high up on the head, seemingly to

FIG. 9.7. *Brontosaurus,* one of the largest dinosaurs. (Restoration by Charles R. Knight; courtesy of the American Museum of Natural History.)

make breathing possible while the mouth was engaged in underwater feeding. Also, the bulk was so great that it is difficult to see how the legs could have furnished adequate support, for protracted periods of time, without the aid of buoyancy provided by surrounding water. The weight of an animal varies in proportion to the cube of its length, while the strength of a pillarlike leg increases in proportion to its cross section, which increases only by squares. Thus, as Romer (1945) has pointed out, if a reptile doubles its length its weight is increased about eight times while the strength of its legs is increased but four times. The largest species of sauropods had weights ranging from 30 to 50 tons. It seems that much of the support for this weight must have been supplied by water in which the giants spent the greater portion of their lives.

Brontosaurus, one of the largest dinosaurs, reached a length of about 80 feet and weighed some 30 tons. Much of the length is attributable to the long neck and tail (Fig. 9.7). The small head contained a brain disproportionately small even for a reptile, a class not noted for its brain development.

Ornithischia

Whereas the Saurischia had their major period of expansive evolution during Jurassic times, living on into the Cretaceous as indicated in Fig. 9.3, the other great order of dinosaurs had their greatest period of development during the Cretaceous. The Ornithischia were on the whole more specialized than were the Saurischia. One indication is seen in the fact that the Ornithischia departed from the thecodont pattern of pelvic structure, while the Saurischia retained this pattern (Fig. 9.5).

All of the Ornithischia were herbivorous. Their teeth were somewhat leaf-shaped, with serrated edges. Most of the Ornithischia lacked teeth in the front of the mouth. Presumably this toothless region was covered with a horny beak somewhat like that possessed by turtles.

A majority of the Ornithischia forsook the bipedal gait of their thecodont ancestors, though in most of these secondarily quadripedal forms the disproportionate length of the hind legs betrayed their ancestry. Among the bipedal ornithischians the forelegs were never so greatly reduced in size and function as they were among the saurischian bipeds.

The Ornithischia fall naturally into four groups or suborders:

1. The **Ornithopoda** include all the bipedal Ornithischia and some of the quadripedal ones. Best known among them are the bipedal, duckbilled dinosaurs. About 30 feet in length, these dinosaurs had long, powerful hind legs and reduced forelegs. The toothless beak was flattened and widened to form an oversized duckbill, probably used for underwater feeding much as a duck employs its bill. Mummies show us that the skin was covered with small scales and that there was webbing between the toes, indicative of life in swampy regions or along the margins of pools or lakes.

2. The **Stegosauria** or plated dinosaurs possessed a double row of projecting plates down the back, and spikelike spines on the tail (Fig. 9.8). We may imagine that the thrashing about of that tail must have afforded persuasive discouragement to carnivorous dinosaurs in search of prey. Although *Stegosaurus* was quadripedal, bipedal ancestry had left its mark in the disproportionately short forelegs (Fig. 9.8). The skull was inordinately small, housing a brain about the size of a walnut. This in an ani-

FIG. 9.8. *Stegosaurus*, the plated dinosaur; length about 20 feet. (From Lull, *Organic Evolution*, p. 484. Copyright 1945 by Richard S. Lull. Used by permission of The Macmillan Company, publishers.)

mal bigger than an elephant! In the region of the hind legs was found an enlargement of the spinal cord about twenty times as large as the brain. It would seem that the brain must have served principally in connection with the sense organs of the head and with the activities of the small, weakly toothed mouth, leaving coördination of the remainder of the body to the spinal cord. Many other dinosaurs also had sacral enlargements of the cord greater than their brains. The Mesozoic era is not memorable for intellectual activity.

3. The **Ankylosauria** were heavily armored dinosaurs somewhat reminiscent of turtles or of armadillos in the completeness of their armor plate. They have been called the "tanks" of the Mesozoic battlefield.

4. The **Ceratopsia** or horned dinosaurs owe their name to possession of a

horn over each eye and a horn on the nose (Fig. 9.9). They possessed a parrotlike beak and a great frill of bone projecting backward over the neck. While this doubtless served to protect the neck, its principal function was probably to afford attachment for powerful muscles supporting the heavy head. The head in giant ceratopsians constituted an unusually large proportion of the body. The massive structure and armament of the "busi-

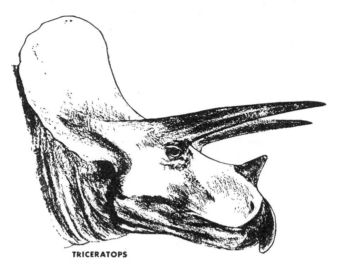

TRICERATOPS

FIG. 9.9. Head of *Triceratops*, a giant horned dinosaur. Skull about 8 feet long. (Restoration by John C. Germann; by permission from *The Dinosaur Book*, by Colbert, p. 82. Copyright 1951. McGraw-Hill Book Company, Inc.)

ness end" of a horned dinosaur give us some conception of what was required for successful living in a world inhabited by such carnivores as *Tyrannosaurus* (Fig. 9.6).

The ceratopsians were the last dinosaurs to appear on the scene. Their entire evolution was confined to the Cretaceous period. We may note in passing that the famous dinosaur eggs which have received so much publicity were laid by a small, ancestral member of the group, *Protoceratops*. Two of the eggs were found to contain bones of unhatched embryos.

Extinction of the Dinosaurs

For at least 160 million years the dinosaurs were "lords of all they surveyed." Then "suddenly," in the geologic sense, they all became extinct. Not one dinosaur fossil has ever been found in deposits more recent than those of Mesozoic age. Why this mass extinction of creatures which had been successful for so long?

Many answers to the question have been proposed. Most of them relate in some way to the drastic geologic changes which marked the close of the Mesozoic. At this time the Rocky Mountains were formed, an occurrence which resulted in extensive changes in the flat interior of North America. The inland seas disappeared and the swampy lowlands became greatly restricted. This change must have affected adversely the many dinosaurs which lived amphibious lives or preyed upon those that did. The plant life changed; herbivorous dinosaurs may not have been able to modify their food requirements correspondingly. The climate became colder. Dinosaurs, like modern reptiles, probably had little ability to control their body temperatures. It is noteworthy that the few reptiles which today live in cold climates must undergo long periods of dormancy—hibernation. Perhaps dinosaurs could not hibernate successfully. A contrast in this respect is afforded by mammals, already present in Mesozoic times. Their greater metabolic activity and accompanying warm-bloodedness were great assets in a world grown colder. Despite their somewhat larger brains and higher metabolism the mammals of the time were too small to have constituted a direct menace to the ruling reptiles. Perhaps, however, they contributed to the decline of the latter by eating their eggs.

Why did the dinosaurs become extinct? We have indicated that many factors doubtless contributed to their downfall. They were well adapted for life in the Mesozoic world, but they were not adaptable enough to meet the altered requirements for successful living in the Cenozoic world.

Conquest of the Sea

Not all the reptiles of this golden age of reptilian life were dinosaurs. Several groups of reptiles returned to the sea for a home. Of these aquatic reptiles two are shown in Fig. 9.3: **plesiosaurs** and **ichthyosaurs.** Both developed a somewhat fusiform body shape, but the plesiosaurs had long neck and tail, while the ichthyosaurs had a fishlike absence of neck and a fishlike fin on the tail. The limbs of plesiosaurs were paddlelike, those of ichthyosaurs were more like the paired fins of fishes in external appearance. The ichthyosaurs even resembled fishes to the extent of developing a dorsal fin (Figs. 3.5, p. 30, and 9.3). Plesiosaurs probably swam rather slowly by an oarlike action of their limbs. Ichthyosaurs must have propelled themselves by undulation of the body, as does a fish (pp. 56–58), using the limbs as rudders. Thus the ichthyosaurs were much the more rapid and agile swimmers of the two, occupying the niche in Mesozoic marine life held by porpoises and dolphins in modern seas.

Conquest of the Air

Another group of Mesozoic reptiles became adapted for flight. These were the **pterosaurs** (pterodactyls), descended like the dinosaurs from the thecodonts (Fig. 9.3). Pterosaurs developed membranous wings supported by a modification of the pentadactyl limb unlike that of either birds or bats (Fig. 3.1, p. 22). The fourth finger of the hand became greatly elongated, forming support for the front margin of the wing (Fig. 9.10). The first three

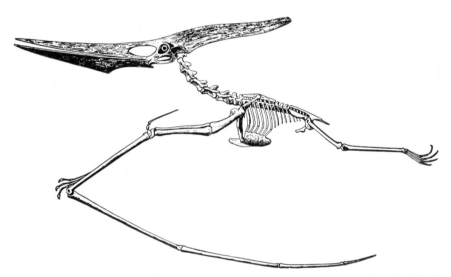

FIG. 9.10. The most specialized pterosaur, *Pteranodon*. (From Eaton, *Memoirs of the Connecticut Academy of Arts and Sciences,* 1910, Vol. 2, pp. 1–38.)

fingers bore claws by which the creature could cling to rocks or to the limbs of trees. Pterosaurs had small bodies relative to wingspread (Fig. 9.10); this spread reached 27 feet in the largest species. The bones were hollow, and consequently light. The sternum or breastbone was relatively large, furnishing attachment for breast muscles connected to the wings. This motor mechanism was probably not of sufficiently great development to provide for strong and sustained flight. It is thought that pterosaurs used their wings largely in gliding and soaring, launching themselves, perhaps, from the tops of cliffs. The pterosaur brain was large for a reptile, the sense of sight being strongly developed, as in birds. Possibly pterosaurs were warm-blooded; it is difficult to see how a really cold-blooded animal could maintain the activity necessary for flight.

We may well note at this point that comparison of ichthyosaurs with fishes and dolphins (Fig. 3.5, p. 30), and of pterosaurs with birds and bats, presents some of the most beautiful examples available of that *convergent evolution* discussed in an earlier chapter (p. 29). It would be difficult to find a more fascinating aspect of evolution than that afforded by study of the variety of ways in which a given problem (e.g., flight) has been solved independently by differing groups of animals. Some solutions are better than others. Thus, it has been pointed out that the pterosaur wing, consisting of an unbroken expanse of membrane supported only along its outer edge, would not lend itself to agile maneuvering in flight. Also, a tear in it would be more disastrous than would a tear in a bat's wing, since the latter is supported by four elongated fingers instead of only one (Fig. 3.1, p. 22). As compared to the attainments of birds and bats, only partial success crowned pterosaur invasion of the air.

ORIGIN OF BIRDS

The thecodonts have claimed our attention as ancestors of the two orders of dinosaurs, and of pterosaurs. Birds also arose during the Mesozoic from this same bipedal stock (Fig. 9.3). Indeed, the term "glorified reptiles" frequently applied to birds suggests the fact that they are similar to reptiles in many ways.

The principal distinguishing characteristic of birds is possession of **feathers.** But the structure and development of feathers reveal that they are modified reptilian scales. Birds are **warm-blooded,** a condition, as mentioned above, which is really necessary if an animal is to be capable of sustained flight. Unlike pterosaurs, birds have an **insulating body covering** of feathers; this aids greatly in prevention of loss of heat from the body surface. Modern birds, like pterosaurs, have the light construction afforded by **hollow bones.** In flying birds the **sternum** or breastbone is greatly enlarged to provide anchorage for muscles operating the wings. We have seen that pterosaurs also showed development of this kind. Both birds and pterosaurs have, or had, **"eye brains"**—brains showing pronounced dominance of visual areas, with reduction of the portions connected with the sense of smell. Birds have a system of **air sacs** connected to the lungs. Mayr has suggested that these serve principally as an internal ventilating system, dissipating the heat generated by the vigorous metabolic activity necessary to flight. Birds have well-developed legs, with structure similar to that of the legs of some of the bipedal dinosaurs. Pterosaurs, on the other hand, had very weak legs. The wing surface composed of feathers is much more efficient, maneuverable, and readily repaired than was the flying mechanism of pterosaurs.

Discussions of evolution in former years frequently included mention of "missing links." The term was used in various senses but always included the idea of a form standing midway between two groups of animals now clearly separate from each other. In most cases such exactly intermediate forms have not been preserved to us, but the Jurassic birds, *Archaeopteryx* and *Archaeornis,* form a fortunate exception to this lack. They are clearly birds, since the imprints of the feathers are preserved in the *Archaeopteryx* fossils (Fig. 9.11). Yet they are so reptilian that if the imprints of the feathers had not been preserved they would probably have been classified as small, bipedal dinosaurs. Relative to body size the wings were small, and three of the digits of each hand persisted, armed with claws. Thus the forelimbs were probably used for climbing as well as for flight. Indeed, the small wingspread suggests that gliding from a height was a more probable activity than was sustained flight.

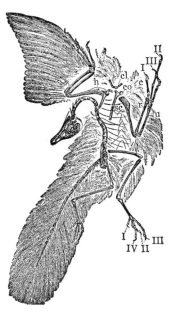

FIG. 9.11. *Archaeopteryx, a Jurassic toothed bird. cl, clavicle; h, humerus; r, radius; sc, scapula; u, ulna. (After Steinmann-Döderlein; from Guyer, Animal Biology, Harper & Brothers, 1948, p. 615.)*

The tail was long, with a row of feathers along either side of the slender chain of vertebrae (Fig. 9.11), and clearly reminiscent of thecodont ancestry (Fig. 9.3). This tail is strikingly unlike that of modern birds. In them the bony portion of the tail is very short; length of tail is due entirely to length of feathers. Finally we may note that the jaws of these Jurassic birds, as well as the jaws of Cretaceous birds, were equipped with teeth. In this respect again they resembled reptiles more than they did modern birds, since the latter are always characterized by toothless, horny beaks. It is interesting that the Jurassic birds did not possess the hollow bones characteristic of modern birds, on the one hand, and of pterosaurs, on the other. Apparently birds and pterosaurs, both descended from thecodonts, developed hollow bones independently and at widely differing times. Seemingly we have here another example of that *parallel evolution* which we have discussed in other connections.

ORIGIN OF MAMMALS

It is fitting that our discussion of the Mesozoic should conclude with the origin of the animals which were about "to inherit the earth."

We noted (p. 171) the occurrence in the Permian period of therapsid or mammal-like reptiles. It will be recalled that these reptiles approached mammalian structure in many ways (Fig. 8.25, p. 171), including the following: (1) teeth differentiated into incisors, canines, premolars, and molars; (2) two occipital condyles; (3) reduction in number of skull bones; (4) single temporal opening (fossa) having boundaries similar to those of the mammalian temporal fossa; (5) lower jaw in which the dentary bone was predominant; (6) presence of a secondary or "hard" palate; (7) limbs arranged for more efficient locomotion than that characterizing most reptiles.

These therapsid reptiles are regarded as the ancestors of mammals (Fig. 9.3). The therapsids themselves continued into the Triassic but only a few remnants of the group persisted until the Jurassic. Animals which were clearly mammals occurred in the Jurassic. Evidently, then, mammals arose from their therapsid ancestors late in the Triassic or early in the Jurassic.

Unfortunately the fossil record is most fragmentary at this point. Also, it is difficult to decide whether the remains which have been found are those of advanced therapsid reptiles or those of early mammals. This uncertainty is hardly surprising in view of the fact that the therapsids had already approached closely to mammalian skeletal structure. The problem arises as to where to draw the line between therapsid reptiles and mammals. The decision would be much easier if we knew more of these Triassic animals than is revealed by their skeletons. Did they have hair like a mammal or scales like a reptile? Did they lay eggs like a reptile or were the young born as in a mammal? (The diagnostic value of this point is somewhat lessened by the fact that a small group of living mammals, the monotremes—duckbilled platypus and spiny anteater—lay eggs much as do reptiles.) Were the young nourished with milk secreted by mammary glands of the mother? Were they warm-blooded? These and other mammalian characteristics we should wish to know about. Since such knowledge is denied us, however, we must draw what conclusions we can from the skeletons.

Accordingly, a general practice has been to draw the line between therapsid reptiles and mammals at that point at which the lower jaw came to consist of but one pair of bones, the right and left dentaries, articulating directly to the skull. We have seen that reptiles have several bones in each half of the lower jaw (p. 172). The dentary is the principal tooth-bearing bone but the connection of the lower jaw to the skull is made by one of the other bones, the articular, which is hinged to the quadrate bone of the skull. In therapsid reptiles the bones other than the dentary became progressively reduced in size, while the dentary itself became progressively larger, and extended back toward the squamosal bone of the skull (Fig. 8.25, p. 171; in this lateral view the quadrate is hidden by the squamosal, "sq," and the articular bone of the lower jaw is posterior to the surangular, "sa"). Eventually the dentary became hinged to the squamosal, and the articular and quadrate bones, greatly reduced in size, lost their function of hinging the jaw and became the malleus and incus ("hammer" and "anvil") of the chain of three little bones in the middle ear. Animals having the dentary articulating directly with the skull in this way are mammals. Interestingly enough, Mesozoic vertebrates have been found having two jaw articulations side by side: articular with quadrate, dentary with squamosal. Were such creatures reptiles or were they mammals? If as we have stated animals having the dentary hinged to the squamosal are mammals, they were mammals (Simpson, 1959). But in calling them so we are drawing an arbitrary line.

This difficulty of distinguishing certain therapsid reptiles from mammals is highly significant. It arises from the existence of a series of transitional stages linking typical reptiles to typical mammals. Such a series of transitional stages occasions no surprise if mammals evolved from reptiles by gradual process of change but would be entirely inexplicable if mammals had been separately created.

Evidence accumulates that several groups of therapsid reptiles gave rise to descendants that would be regarded as mammals by the criteria mentioned (Olson, 1959; Simpson, 1959). Some of the lines became extinct; one apparently led to modern monotremes, and another to the Pantotheria (see below) and thence to marsupials and placentals.

Undoubted mammals lived in the Jurassic, but they were not a prepossessing tribe compared to the ruling reptiles of the time. All of them were small, most of them of the sizes of mice and rats. One species approached the cat in size and apparently in carnivorous food habits, while one herbivorous species resembled a woodchuck in many ways. One hopeful portent for the future was presented by the brains of these early mammals. Although small and primitive, judged by modern standards, nevertheless the brains were a considerable improvement over the brain equipment of reptiles.

Mammalian fossils of Cretaceous age are somewhat more abundant and complete than are those of Jurassic age. By the close of the Cretaceous the two main groups of mammals, the marsupials and the placentals, were in existence. They seem to have arisen, probably independently, from one of the groups of mammals living in the Jurassic, the **Pantotheria.**

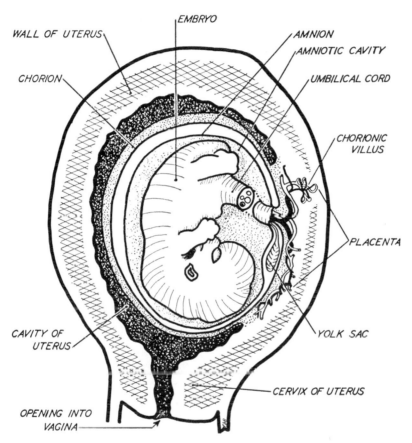

FIG. 9.12. Human embryo, with placenta and embryonic membranes, in position in the uterus of the mother. (Drawn by Lyman S. Rowell.)

Marsupial and placental mammals differ in many respects. The names suggest their differences in the reproductive process. The embryos of placental mammals undergo a relatively long period of development within the uterus of the mother, being nourished by the mother through the **placenta** (Fig. 9.12). As noted previously (p. 59), blood vessels from the embryo pass through the umbilical cord to the wall of the uterus, where they come in close contact with the mother's blood. The embryonic blood vessels in this region give rise to a series of **chorionic villi** (Fig. 9.12); each of these villi is bathed in blood of the mother, thereby providing a means for ready interchange of oxygen, food, and waste products.

In marsupials, on the other hand, the placenta is absent or poorly developed. The young are born in an extremely immature, almost embryonic, condition. They complete their development while housed in a pouch, or marsupium, on the abdomen of the mother. Marsupials also differ from placentals in a number of distinctive skeletal features.

The opossum is the only modern, North American marsupial. Interestingly enough, marsupials similar to the opossum were living in the North America of Cretaceous times. Thus the opossum possesses unique value in studies of mammalian evolution owing to its position as the most truly primitive living mammal. In Australia, geographically isolated from the rest of the world from late Cretaceous times, marsupials were free from the competition of placental mammals and evolved into a great variety of forms: kangaroos, wombats, bandicoots, koalas, and so on (see pp. 262–264).

Placental mammals of Cretaceous age are at present known mainly from fossils collected in Mongolia. These mammals were small insect-eaters, as had been their Jurassic ancestors, the pantotherians. Thus they were the ancestral forms of **Order Insectivora.** To this order belong such modern mammals as shrews, moles and hedgehogs (*not* porcupines!). Early, relatively unspecialized insectivores have long been regarded as the ancestors from which other orders of placental mammals arose. Their position in the center of our diagram illustrating adaptive radiation among mammals will be recalled (Fig. 3.4, p. 27). The fossil record of the earliest placentals confirms the ancestral position of the insectivores.

References and Suggested Readings

Colbert, E. H. *The Dinosaur Book,* 2nd ed. New York: McGraw-Hill Book Company, Inc., 1951.

Colbert, E. H. *Evolution of the Vertebrates.* New York: John Wiley & Sons, Inc., 1955.

Lull, R. S. *Organic Evolution,* rev. ed. New York: The Macmillan Company, 1945.

Olson, E. C. "The evolution of mammalian characters," *Evolution,* 13 (1959), 344–353.

Romer, A. S. *Vertebrate Paleontology,* 2nd ed. Chicago: University of Chicago Press, 1945.

Romer, A. S. *The Vertebrate Story.* Chicago: University of Chicago Press, 1959.

Simpson, G. G. "Mesozoic mammals and the polyphyletic origin of mammals," *Evolution,* 13 (1959), 405–414.

CHAPTER 10

EVOLUTION AS SEEN IN THE

GEOLOGIC RECORD:

CENOZOIC ERA

We have seen that the end of the Mesozoic was marked by momentous changes in the surface of the earth, including the elevation of our Rocky Mountains. As a result the continent of North America attained nearly the outlines and general appearance it has today. Geologic changes during this era were largely connected with wearing down of mountains, followed by their reelevation through regional uplift. These phenomena were particularly characteristic of western North America. Then in the Pleistocene period the face of the northern portions of the continent was altered by the action of great glaciers, sweeping southward from arctic regions.

The Cenozoic era is divided into a succession of periods: Paleocene, Eocene, Oligocene, Miocene, Pliocene, Pleistocene, Recent (Table 7.1, p. 137). These subdivisions of the time scale are frequently termed "epochs," since they are of a somewhat different order of magnitude from the periods into which the Paleozoic and Mesozoic eras are divided. For the sake of simplicity, however, we shall refer to these Cenozoic divisions also as periods. They are represented by series of strata occurring in the order given and marked by the progressive evolution of animals, particularly of mammals. Indeed, the Cenozoic is sometimes called "the age of mammals."

The periods were of unequal duration. As noted earlier (p. 138), the Cenozoic is estimated to have lasted from about 63 million years ago until the present. The intervening time was divided approximately as follows (Kulp, 1961):

Pleistocene and Recent	1 million*
Pliocene	12 million
Miocene	12 million
Oligocene	11 million
Eocene	22 million
Paleocene	5 million

* Note added in 1963: now thought to be at least 3 million.

While these estimates are based on the most accurate determinations available, later research and further refinements in methods of dating rocks will undoubtedly necessitate their revision. But they probably are of the correct "order of magnitude."

As indicated in Table 7.1 (p. 137), the first five periods are frequently grouped together into a unit of the time scale called the "Tertiary," the Pleistocene and Recent being relegated to a comparable unit called the "Quaternary." This practice is being gradually abandoned, but the terms are still widely used, especially "Tertiary," a convenient collective title for designating all of the Cenozoic preceding the ice ages (Pleistocene).

Climatic Changes

During the first two periods of the Cenozoic the climate of much of North America was mild. Much of the interior of the continent was a flat lowland enjoying a subtropical climate resembling that of Florida. Palm trees grew as far north as Minnesota and the Dakotas; crocodiles throve in these same regions. Figs and magnolias grew in Alaska. Temperate climates extended as far north as Greenland, where such trees as giant redwoods, beeches, and elms were found.

With the beginning of the Oligocene the climate slowly became cooler, particularly in the interior of the continent. Palms and large crocodiles disappeared from northern regions, though small alligators lived in Nebraska as late as Miocene times, along with plants similar to those found at present in our Gulf states. Local arid regions began to appear on the leeward side of newly elevated mountains. The moisture carried by westerly winds was condensed and precipitated as rain on the windward, western slopes of the mountains, as is the case today. The process culminated with the great regional uplift of the Cordilleran ranges in Pliocene and Pleistocene times. The widespread aridity of western North America followed that geologic occurrence.

The glaciation occurring in the Pleistocene has already been mentioned.

Actually there were four successive glaciations during this period. Four times glaciers centering around the Hudson Bay region swept down over the northern tiers of states, extending into Pennsylvania, southern Ohio, and Illinois. During such times reindeer lived as far south as southern New England, and such an arctic animal as the musk ox ranged through Kentucky, Arkansas, and Texas. Each glaciation was followed by an interglacial period during which the climate in a given region was as mild as, if not milder than, it is today. The interglacial periods lasted for many thousands of years; the shortest is estimated to have been of 135,000 years' duration. Some 10,000 years are estimated to have elapsed since the last glaciation (Libby, 1956). Thus it may well be that we are at present living in an interglacial period, that the Recent period of our time chart (Table 7.1, p. 137) really forms part of the Pleistocene. The extensive ocean ice of the arctic regions and the glaciers covering Greenland and the antarctic continent remind us that glaciation is not far away. Indeed it has been estimated that a lowering of average annual temperature by only 5° C. would bring the ice sheets down upon us again. Will the glaciers return? Only our remote descendants will be able to answer that question with certainty.

MAMMALIAN EVOLUTION IN THE CENOZOIC ERA

Disappearance of the dinosaurs at the end of the Mesozoic left a clear field for mammalian expansion. We have already noted the occurrence in Cretaceous times of both marsupial and placental mammals (p. 191). A few of the Cretaceous mammals persisted into the Paleocene, notably opossumlike marsupials, and insectivores. We recall that the latter are the group of placental mammals from which the other orders of placental mammals are believed to have arisen. Among these other orders, representatives of carnivores, primates, and ungulates lived in Paleocene times. The carnivores (flesh eaters) and ungulates (hoofed animals) living at this time were quite unlike their modern relatives, however. Most of them belonged to groups which underwent a relatively rapid evolution during the Paleocene and Eocene and then disappeared. Thus they are sometimes called **"archaic mammals"** to distinguish them from the "progressive mammals" whose development was slower but led to modern types of mammals. Most of the archaic carnivores belonged to a group called **Creodonta,** most of the archaic ungulates to a group called **Condylarthra.**

During the Eocene the archaic mammals had their brief period of ascendancy. Some of the archaic ungulates became quite large. The culmination in this direction was reached by the horned mammal, *Uintatherium* (Fig. 10.1). This creature was elephantine in size, though not in details of structure. Creodonts, the archaic carnivores, somewhat resembled wolves, weasels, cats, hyenas, and the like.

The end of the Eocene saw the extinction of the archaic mammals. Apparently they were not able to compete successfully with the more progressive mammals developing around them. Lull (1945) has pointed

FIG. 10.1. *Uintatherium,* an archaic hoofed mammal. (After Osborn.)

out that, as compared to the latter, archaic mammals were deficient in structure of teeth, feet, and brain. In these features the archaic mammals were conservative and inadaptable, unable to change with changing conditions.

Turning to the more progressive mammals, we find that the first rodents and first lagomorphs appeared late in the Paleocene. The beginning of the Eocene saw ungulates of the two orders existing today: Perissodactyla (odd-toed) and Artiodactyla (even-toed). Members of the Condylarthra were probably ancestral to these two orders. Indeed, representatives of most of the orders of mammals appeared in either the Paleocene or the Eocene, thus laying the foundations for evolution of these orders during succeeding periods of the Cenozoic. Within the orders evolutionary changes ran somewhat parallel courses. Ancestors in each were relatively small, and were not specialized for particular types of food or for particular types of locomotion. In general, descendants of these ancestors attained larger size and became more or less highly specialized in leg and tooth structure. As samples of such evolutionary histories we shall summarize those of horses and elephants (proboscideans). We choose these in preference to others partly because of general interest in the end products of the evolution, partly because of the fact that the fossil record is more complete for them than it is for many other familiar mammals.

EVOLUTION OF THE HORSE

Adaptations of the Modern Horse

Horses belong to the order of odd-toed ungulates, Perissodactyla. In Chapter 3 we noted the limb adaptation of horses for rapid running on hard ground (pp. 23–28). We recall that digit III is greatly enlarged and elongated, its "fingernail" having become the hoof. The other digits have disappeared, except for the splint bones representing rudiments of metacarpals (or metatarsals) of digits II and IV. The metacarpal (or metatarsal) of digit III has become the powerful cannon bone of the slender lower leg of the horse. Since the muscles are concentrated in the proximal (attached) region of the limb, being connected to the bones they move by slender tendons, the entire structure forms a light, rapidly swinging pendulum, admirably adapted for swift movement.

One of the most striking adaptations of the horse's foot for rapid running consists of a set of spring ligaments on the posterior surface of the foot. Fig. 10.2 shows the arrangement of some of the principal ligaments of the forefoot. It will be noted that a large interosseous tendon (ligament) arises from the posterior surface of the cannon bone and ends in movable sesamoid bones which form a pulley arrangement back of the fetlock joint. As shown, various ligaments connect these sesamoid bones to the phalanges of the hoof (sesamoid ligaments). The whole arrangement is elastic and may be compared to a powerful rubber band. When the weight of the horse is placed upon the foot the toe is bent upward and the ligaments are stretched. The tension so developed tends to spring the foot back into its original position (to flex it), and so to propel the horse forward. Thus the impact of the foot upon hard ground is translated into upward and forward propulsion as from a springboard. Camp and Smith (1942), to whom we owe much of our knowledge in this matter, state that "the action resembles that of a boy jumping on a pogo-stick; the harder the impact, the higher the bounce—up to the capacity of the apparatus."

The automatic springing action of the ligaments is augmented by the contraction of the flexor muscles of the leg, the tendons of which are also attached to the phalanges (in the diagram these tendons are not shown, though the cut ends at the attachments of one of the principal ones, Flexor digitalis profundus, are indicated). Near the upper ends of these tendons check ligaments connect to adjacent bones. Thus when tension is placed on these tendons, as for example by impact of the foot on hard ground, these check ligaments may be stretched, reinforcing the action of

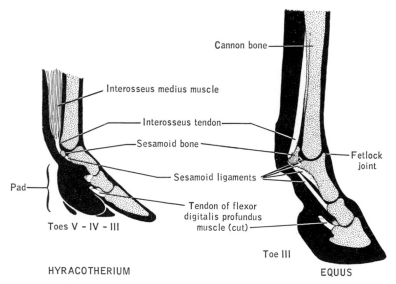

FIG. 10.2. Pad-supported forefoot of *Hyracotherium* compared with the spring-ing mechanism in the foot of the modern horse. The pad in *Hyracotherium* is shown in black, as are the tips of digits IV and V. Tendons and ligaments are shown in white; bones are dotted. (Modified from Camp and Smith, "Phylogeny and functions of the digital ligaments of the horse," *Memoirs*, University of California, Vol. 13, 1942.)

the ligaments shown in Fig. 10.2 and preventing injury to the latter by over-stretching (sprain).

Horses obtain their food by grazing—feeding on such vegetation as grass covering the surface of the ground. If a long-legged animal is to do this, some means must be provided for getting the mouth down to the ground. Lengthening the neck would accomplish the result, and to a moderate degree the neck of the horse has been lengthened. But a horse has a large and heavy head; there would be obvious mechanical dis-advantage in perching it on the end of a really long neck. To a considerable extent the problem has been solved for the horse by lengthening the anterior part of the skull itself. The portion of the skull anterior to the eyes has been elongated into the well-known muzzle (Fig. 10.3D). One result of this elongation has been the production of a gap in the tooth row between the incisor (front) teeth and the grinding battery composed of

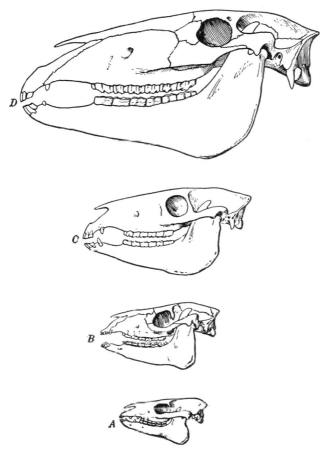

FIG. 10.3. Series of horse skulls in ascending geologic order. A, *Hyracotherium* (Eohippus). B, *Mesohippus*. C, *Merychippus* (*Protohippus*). D, *Equus*. (From Scott, *A History of Land Mammals in the Western Hemisphere*, p. 283. Copyright 1937 by American Philosophical Society. Used by permission of The Macmillan Company, publishers.)

premolars and molars. This toothless gap is called the diastema (Fig. 10.3D). It is utilized by man as a convenient location for the bit used to control the movements of the horse.

The grinding battery composed of premolar and molar teeth is an adaptation for the chewing of harsh grasses, containing silica. This food material is so abrasive that it wears away teeth that chew it, and it must be eaten in large quantities to provide the required nourishment. The problem is solved by developing teeth which continue to grow as fast as they are worn away. As shown in Fig. 10.4, each individual grinding tooth is long or high-crowned (hypsodont). Until the horse becomes rather old the molars do not develop pronged roots, as do our own molar teeth, but continue to grow as the surface is worn away. This surface has exposed on it a complicated pattern of lines of hard enamel (Fig. 10.4). The enamel pattern is set in a matrix of softer dentine and cement. The latter wear away more rapidly than does the enamel, with the result that the surface is continually maintained in a roughened condition reminiscent of the surface of a millstone, the ridges of hard enamel protruding above the dentine and cement. In this manner the horse is provided with a self-sharpening, self-renewing grinding mechanism for use on the harsh material comprising its diet.

If space permitted, other adaptations of the horse might be enumerated, but our purpose will be served by concentrating attention on those just discussed: (1) enlargement and elongation of digit III, with loss of other digits and development of a spring mechanism; (2) elongation of the preorbital portion of the skull; (3) development of premolars and molars into high-crowned, continuously growing grinders. To these should be added the large size characteristic of most varieties of horses.

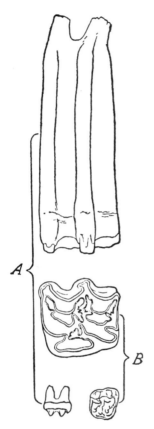

FIG. 10.4. Molar teeth of modern horse and of *Hyracotherium*. A, teeth in lateral view. B, Crowns of the teeth. (After Osborn; reprinted by permission from *Textbook of Geology, Part II, Historical Geology,* by Louis V. Pirsson and Charles Schuchert, published by John Wiley & Sons, Inc., 1915, p. 932.)

Hyracotherium

Having reviewed the characteristics of the modern horse we turn our attention to the characteristics of the first horse of which we have any knowledge: *Hyracotherium* (also called Eohippus). This animal lived in North America in Eocene times, migrating to Europe during that period. Although *Hyracotherium* was definitely horselike in many ways it differed greatly from our modern horse. In the first place, it was small, about the size of a fox terrier dog. Its legs were short and had four toes on the front feet, three on the hind (Fig. 10.5A). We note, however, that digit III already showed incipient signs of predominating. Through study of the scars left on the foot bones by attachments of ligaments and tendons,

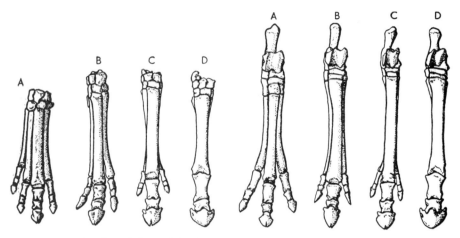

FIG. 10.5. Forefeet (left) and hind feet (right) of four horses. A, *Hyracotherium*. B, *Miohippus*. C, *Merychippus*. D, *Equus*. Not drawn to scale. (A, after Cope; B and C, after Osborn; from Romer, *Vertebrate Paleontology*, University of Chicago Press, 1945, p. 422.)

Camp and Smith (1942) came to the conclusion that *Hyracotherium* did not have the springing mechanism characteristic of the modern horse (see above). Instead the foot must have been supported by a pad (Fig. 10.2) as in many forest-dwelling animals, including the tapir, a distant relative of the horse. It will be noted from the figure that the interosseous tendon is shown arising from a muscle instead of attaching directly to the back of the cannon bone as it does in the modern horse. Most mammals, including other hoofed forms than *Equus,* have such a muscle. Indeed, occasional horses have muscle tissue in this tendon. Apparently reduction of fleshy fibers, virtually changing the tendon to a ligament, has been one of the evolutionary changes in the evolution of the springing mechanism. "Muscular tissue, by weakening the tendon, would tend to enfeeble this [springing] action" (Camp and Smith, 1942).

The preorbital portion of the skull was not elongated; the orbit of the eye was in the middle, measuring from front to rear (Fig. 10.3A). The molar teeth were not high-crowned, continuously growing grinders. In fact they were much like human molar teeth (Fig. 10.4). They had low crowns, developed pronged roots, and had surfaces covered by rounded tubercles or cusps much as do our own molar teeth.

Another most unhorselike characteristic of *Hyracotherium* was its brain. Studies of casts of the interiors of skulls (endocranial casts) have revealed that the cerebral hemispheres were small and smooth; they did not cover the olfactory bulbs anteriorly or the midbrain posteriorly as did the cerebra of later horses (Edinger, 1948). In fact, as Fig. 10.6 shows, among brains

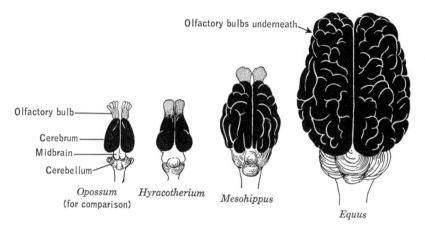

FIG. 10.6. Horse brain evolution. Comparison of the brain of *Hyracotherium* with that of the opossum and with the brains of *Mesohippus* and *Equus*. The horse brains, based on endocranial casts, are drawn to scale; *Hyracotherium* and opossum brains are of about the same size. (After Edinger, *Evolution of the Horse Brain*, Memoir 25, Geological Society of America, 1948.)

of living mammals the one most similar to the *Hyracotherium* brain is that of the opossum, a marsupial which has retained an almost reptilian brain configuration. Evidently, in the early stages of horse evolution brain development lagged behind evolution of the limbs. We shall see that this also appears to have been true of human evolution (Chap. 11).

Hyracotherium was a forest dweller, a browser subsisting on soft vegetation quite unlike the food of its plains-dwelling descendants. Its spreading toes formed better support on the soft forest floor than does the single hoof of its modern descendant. It probably escaped its enemies by hiding, as do most forest-dwelling, herbivorous animals, instead of by running away, as must inhabitants of treeless plains.

From Hyracotherium to Equus

We have sketched above the beginning and the ending of horse evolution. What occurred in the millions of years separating *Hyracotherium* from its modern descendant, *Equus?* Fortunately the intervening history is well documented by numerous fossils showing the transitional stages of the changes in body structure required to transform the ancestor into its modern descendant. Space limitations prevent more than a brief glance at a few of the main stages, but the interested reader may obtain more detailed information by consulting references at the end of the chapter.

Fig. 10.7 summarizes some of the events in this evolutionary history. The diagram is designed to emphasize the point that at various times in the history of horses evolutionary radiations occurred, several or many forms arising from an ancestor. Thus *Hyracotherium* in the Eocene gave rise to several somewhat differing forms, among them the line which led to *Mesohippus* in the Oligocene.

Mesohippus was of the size of a small dog, different species varying from 18 to 24 inches high at the shoulder. Each foot had three toes, but digit III was the largest and strongest of the three (as in *Miohippus,* Fig. 10.5B). A small nodule of bone representing metacarpal V remained in the forefoot. The metacarpals and metatarsals of the three functional digits (II, III, IV) were elongated, as compared to the corresponding bones of *Hyracotherium,* an indication that the legs were beginning to lengthen. This point is not well shown in Fig. 10.5, where all the feet are shown reduced to the same absolute length instead of being drawn to scale. As compared to *Hyracotherium, Mesohippus* had a slightly greater development of the ligaments that were to develop into a spring mechanism in its descendants, but like *Hyracotherium* (Fig. 10.2) it doubtless depended upon a pad under the toes for support of the body's weight.

The preorbital portion of the skull of *Mesohippus* had begun to elongate, a larger diastema being present than was present in *Hyracotherium* (Fig. 10.3B). The molar teeth were low crowned, but the premolars, except for the first one, already resembled molars in structure. From this point on in horse evolution the premolars and molars combined to form the dental battery.

As indicated in Fig. 10.6, the brain of *Mesohippus* was markedly different from that of *Hyracotherium*. The opossumlike configuration had been lost. The cerebral hemispheres had enlarged and become convoluted so that the brain assumed much the appearance of a small horse brain.

Miohippus was much like *Mesohippus* but of larger size. The low-

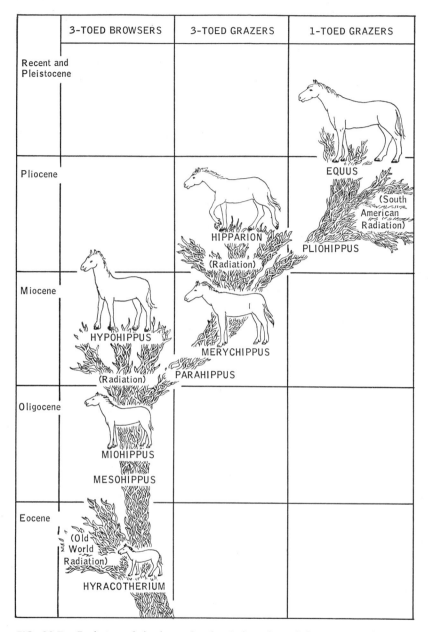

FIG. 10.7. Evolution of the horse family. Only a few of the many evolutionary lines and of the known representatives in those lines are included. (Modified from Simpson, *The Meaning of Evolution*, Yale University Press, 1949, p. 134.)

crowned teeth and the spreading, three-toed feet indicate that these were forest horses living on soft vegetation—three-toed browsers like their ancestor, *Hyracotherium*.

In Fig. 10.7 *Miohippus* is shown as an ancestor for several radiating lines. Of these the line involving the least change led to *Hypohippus,* a "forest horse" living in Miocene and early Pliocene times. This three-toed browser was much like an enlarged version of *Miohippus*.

Parahippus, another descendant of *Miohippus,* presented in its various species a nearly complete spectrum of transitional stages between its ancestor and *Merychippus,* i.e., between "three-toed browsers" and "three-toed grazers" (Fig. 10.7). The teeth were becoming high-crowned grinders (hypsodont). The legs were becoming longer, and digit III was becoming more predominant than it had been in the forest-dwelling ancestors.

As indicated in Fig. 10.7, *Merychippus* was a three-toed grazer adapted for life on the western plains which arose in the Miocene as a result of widespread continental elevation. The elongated legs, the predominance of digit III (Fig. 10.5C), the elongation of the preorbital portion of the skull (Fig. 10.3C), and the high-crowned molar teeth all point in this direction. Interestingly enough, the milk teeth ("baby teeth") of *Mery-chippus* were low-crowned like those of Oligocene horses, thus affording us a prehistoric example of recapitulation (Chap. 4). As might be anticipated, *Merychippus* showed an increased development of the ligaments mentioned above as forming a spring mechanism in the foot of the modern horse. The relatively short side toes (II and IV) probably did not touch the ground most of the time, serving as support only "when the foot was under great pressure or sunk into sand or mud" (Camp and Smith, 1942). There was probably no foot pad of the type found in *Hyracotherium* and *Mesohippus.*

It is also significant that during the course of the Miocene *Merychippus* underwent striking evolution of the cerebral hemispheres of the brain. Later specimens exhibited the fundamental pattern of fissures (convolutions) which was to characterize later horses, e.g., *Equus,* Fig. 10.6 (Edinger, 1948).

Merychippus is shown (Fig. 10.7) as the center of another radiation. Some descendants continued as three-toed grazers, e.g., *Hipparion.* On the other hand, *Merychippus* was ancestral to horses which reduced the number of digits on each foot to one—the line leading through *Pliohippus* to *Equus.* This loss of the side digits was a most striking evolutionary change. Why did it occur in the *Equus* line but not in the other lines? Did the side digits have a function in the three-toed forms, even the ones in which these digits were short relative to digit III? This question is usually answered in the negative but Simpson (1951) has challenged such a conclusion. He pointed out that when a horse is galloping and lands on its middle toe, this toe is bent strongly upward. As noted above, under such great pressure the side toes of, for example, *Merychippus* would touch the ground. Simpson has suggested that the side toes may have had "an essential function to act as buffers to stop the bending of the middle toe at this point and to lessen the danger of spraining the elastic ligaments by stretching them too far." If this is correct, why did the side toes disappear in the line leading to *Equus?* Perhaps because other structures took over the function of preventing spraining of the spring mechanism. We have mentioned that in *Equus* the tendons of long flexor muscles are connected to adjacent bones by check ligaments. These assist the other elastic ligaments and form part of the spring mechanism, especially under powerful stress. Perhaps the safety factor provided by these check ligaments was not present in the three-toed horses. This is a point on which we do not have information, however. We may note in passing that the horse has paid a price for its highly specialized springing foot. Lameness connected with injury to the elastic ligaments is common.

Some species of *Pliohippus* had tiny side toes, though in other species these were represented only by splint bones, as in *Equus*. *Pliohippus* attained the size of a modern pony, some 40 inches (10 hands) high. The trends for increase in the preorbital length of the skull and increase in size and complexity of the molar teeth continued.

The transition from *Pliohippus* to *Equus,* the genus to which modern horses, asses, and zebras belong, was a small one, involving further increase in size and some changes in anatomical details. The first representatives of *Equus* appeared in late Pliocene times; during the Pleistocene the genus achieved world-wide distribution. Although North America has provided the stage for the greater part of their evolution, horses became extinct on this continent by the close of the Pleistocene. This extinction is difficult to explain. By the time man later reintroduced horses into America conditions on our western plains were highly favorable for them.

EVOLUTION OF PROBOSCIDEANS

The living representatives of Order Proboscidea are the Asiatic and the African elephants. The two differ somewhat in struc-

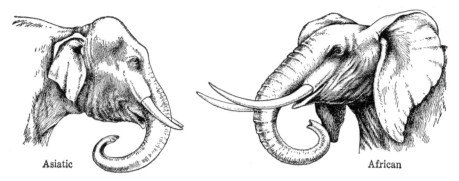

Asiatic   African

FIG. 10.8. Comparison of the heads of Asiatic and African elephants. (From Guyer, *Animal Biology*, Harper & Brothers, 1948, p. 91.)

ture, the most obvious difference to a casual observer being in the size of the ears (Fig. 10.8). The great palm-leaf-like ears of African elephants stand in marked contrast to the ears of Asiatic elephants. Asiatic elephants have long been domesticated and used as work animals; they are the species commonly seen in circuses.

Elephantine Adaptations

Huge bulk is always brought to mind by mention of elephants, and indeed many of the bodily adaptations of elephants are connected with their large size. To support the weight of the body the limbs have a strong, pillarlike construction. The feet have retained the full complement of five toes, but much of the weight is supported, not by the toes, but by a pad of elastic tissue which forms both the sole of the short, broad foot and a sort of functional "rubber heel."

Since the body is supported high above the ground on long legs, the elephant, like the horse, is faced with the problem of reaching the ground for feeding. We have seen how the problem was solved in the horse (p. 198). In the elephant the solution was entirely different. Here the head is so heavy that any lengthening of the neck would be a great mechanical disadvantage. Accordingly, elephants are characterized by short necks. Nor is the preorbital portion of the skull lengthened, as it is in the horse. Instead we find the development of the organ which gives the order its name: the proboscis or trunk. This versatile organ consists of the nose and upper lip greatly elongated. As everyone who has fed peanuts to elephants knows, the two nostril openings are at the tip of the trunk, along with a fingerlike projection (African elephants have two of them) by means of which small objects may be picked up.

The development of a proboscis has a peculiar effect upon the topography of the skull. In most mammals the external nares, bony openings in the skull at the base of the nostrils, are at or near the anterior tip of the skull. In mammals that develop a proboscis the nares recede from the tip; in elephants they have receded so far up the front of the skull that they appear to be located in the middle of the forehead (Fig. 10.9). Presumably this recession of the nares is connected with the necessity for firm anchor-

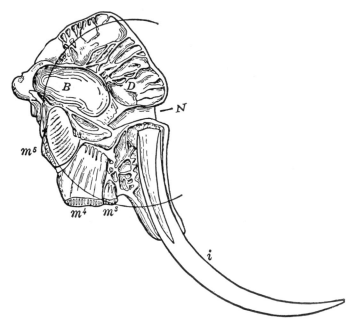

FIG. 10.9. Skull of elephant, sectioned longitudinally. *B*, brain cavity. *D*, diploë (air cells). *i*, incisor (tusk). m^3, m^4, m^5, molars. *N*, nares. (From Lull, *Organic Evolution*, p. 561. Copyright 1945 by R. S. Lull. Used by permission of The Macmillan Company, publishers.)

age for the powerful musculature of the proboscis. Owing to this effect of proboscis development upon skull topography it is possible to estimate from the structure of the skull the size of proboscis possessed by a prehistoric proboscidean.

Another characteristic of the elephant skull is development of extensive air cells or diploë (Fig. 10.9). While these serve to lighten the skull their principal function is probably connected with support of the heavy head. It will be noted from the figure that an elephant's "high forehead" is not caused by brain development but by the presence of these diploë. The skull is hinged to the vertebral column by the occipital condyles, which thus constitute the fulcrum of a lever system. Increasing the height of the head above these condyles increases the surface for, and the mechanical advantage of, the muscles and ligament which support the head. The importance of achieving such mechanical advantage is evident when we recall that the two tusks together may weigh over 400 pounds and be 9 or 10 feet in length, though the average size is not so great as this.

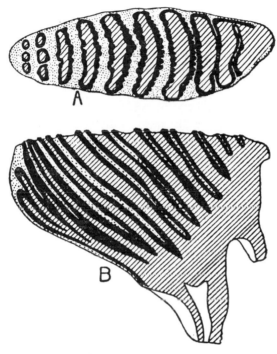

FIG. 10.10. Molar tooth of elephant. A, crown view. B, longitudinal section. Black, enamel. Oblique lines, dentine. Dots, cement. (From Lull, *Organic Evolution,* p. 563. Copyright 1945 by R. S. Lull. Used by permission of The Macmillan Company, publishers.)

The tusks are formed from the right and left second upper incisor teeth. The ivory composing them consists of the dentine material of the teeth, no enamel being present except for a small area on the end of the tusk when it first erupts. A large, open pulp cavity in the base of each tusk provides for continuous growth.

Nothing about an elephant is more unique than its molar tooth structure and the system of molar replacement. Each individual molar is large, consisting of several flattened plates arranged vertically and fastened together by cement. Each plate or lamella has a core of dentine surrounded by enamel. The composite structure produced by cementing together such lamellae presents a broad grinding surface on which transverse ridges of enamel rise above the general surface, owing to the more rapid wearing away of the softer dentine and cement (Fig. 10.10).

As everyone knows, most mammals have, during the course of their lifetimes, two sets of teeth: the "milk teeth" or deciduous teeth and the permanent teeth. The permanent teeth replace the milk teeth *vertically;* a permanent premolar in the upper jaw, for example, develops above the corresponding premolar of the milk set and eventually replaces that tooth by moving down into the position formerly occupied by it. Thus, early in life a typical mammal has a complete set of milk teeth all in use at one time, later in life a complete set of permanent teeth all in use at one time. Arrangements are quite otherwise in elephants. While some of the molars are identified as milk teeth, others as permanent teeth, the individual teeth succeed each other in series, one at a time, rather than as complete sets. Thus typically at any given time only four molars are in use, one in the upper jaw and one in the lower jaw on each side. As the molars wear out they are replaced by others, but replacement is *longitudinal,* not vertical; the new molar is pushed forward from the rear of the jaw. Fig. 10.9 shows this method of replacement in the upper jaw. In the figure the third molar (m^3) is present as a worn-out remnant; the fourth molar is shown as the functional one, and the fifth molar is shown forming above and behind the fourth one, as a reserve to replace the latter when it in turn wears out.

Moeritherium

Having reviewed some of the distinctive characteristics of elephants we turn our attention to the earliest known ancestral proboscidean, *Moeritherium.* As in the evolution of the horse, our starting point is a relatively small animal showing only the beginnings of the specializations of its descendants and living early in the Cenozoic era. *Moeritherium* lived in Africa in late Eocene and early Oligocene times. It was about the size of a modern tapir, perhaps 3 feet in height, and probably had a tapirlike short proboscis (Fig. 10.11), as indicated by slight recession of the nasal openings of the skull. The second upper incisors were beginning to form tusks (Fig. 10.12). Short tusks on the lower jaw will also be noted; they projected forward in a somewhat spoutlike fashion. They are unlike

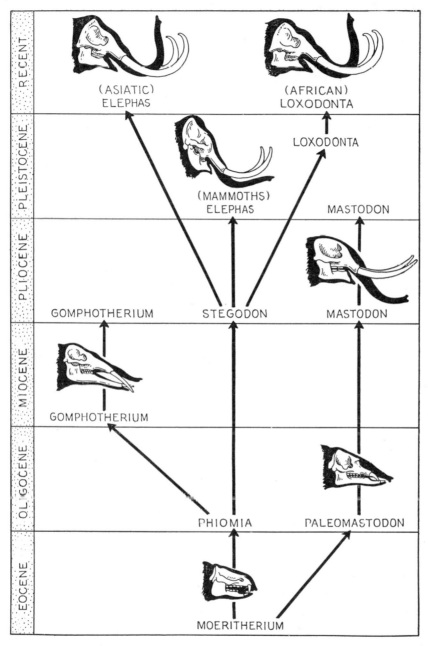

FIG. 10.11.   Abbreviated chart of proboscidean evolution. (Mainly after Lull, *Organic Evolution*, The Macmillan Company, 1945; sketches after Scott.)

anything found in modern elephants but anticipate later developments in some of the other proboscideans. *Moeritherium* had slight formation of air cells, diploë, in the posterior region of the skull. The molars were low-crowned, possessed two transverse crests each, and occurred in rows as in most mammals. The longitudinal method of molar replacement came much later.

Phiomia and Paleomastodon

The relationships of the various prehistoric proboscideans to each other are not entirely certain. In broad outline the arrangement shown in Fig. 10.11 is substantially correct. The Oligocene proboscideans, *Phiomia* and *Paleomastodon*, were larger than *Moeritherium* and had attained limb structure quite like that of modern elephants. The lower jaw had become considerably elongated (Fig. 10.13), and the second upper incisors formed downwardly curving tusks. Recession of the nasal openings indicates that a short proboscis was present (Fig. 10.11). Lull suggests that the trunk developed originally for the purpose of reaching beyond the elongated lower jaw. The molar teeth were more complicated in structure than were those of *Moeritherium,* having on their surfaces three transverse crests, with some accessory cusps. The posterior portion of the skull was heightened by the presence of air cells in the bone.

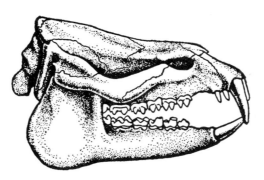

FIG. 10.12. Skull of Moeritherium. (After Andrews; from Romer, *Vertebrate Paleontology,* University of Chicago Press, 1945, p. 409.)

Lack of space prohibits mention of all the varied and interesting proboscideans that roamed the earth in Cenozoic times. In the main we shall content ourselves with pointing out three principal evolutionary lines. One side line is of sufficient interest to deserve passing attention, however. That line, not indicated in Fig. 10.11, culminated in *Dinotherium,* a proboscidean lacking upper tusks and having lower tusks curved downward and backward in most unusual fashion (Fig. 10.14). The molar teeth, low-crowned with but two or three cross ridges (Fig. 10.14), were relatively unspecialized. A diet of soft, succulent vegetation seems indicated. Some specimens exceeded modern elephants in size. *Dinotherium* ranged widely over

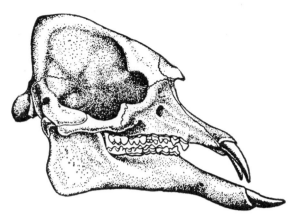

FIG. 10.13. Skull of *Phiomia*. (After Andrews; from
Romer, *Vertebrate Paleontology*, University of Chicago
Press, 1945, p. 409.)

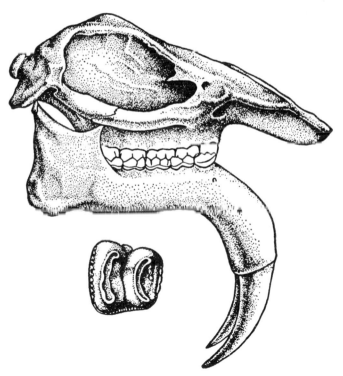

FIG. 10.14. *Dinotherium:* skull and surface of molar tooth. (After
Gaudry and Andrews; from Romer, *Vertebrate Paleontology*, University of Chicago Press, 1945, p. 411.)

Eurasia and Africa, the last survivors being found in African Pleistocene deposits.

Gomphotherium

One group of proboscideans specialized in elongation of the lower jaw. Typical of this group is the Miocene form, *Gomphotherium* (Fig. 10.15). The most extreme lower jaw recorded was six feet and seven inches in length. While some of the jaws were very slender, approaching the

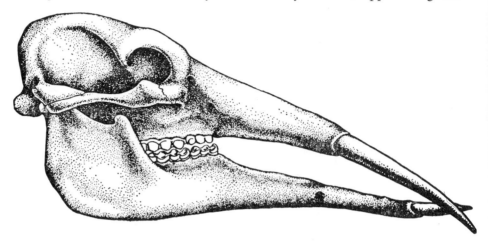

FIG. 10.15.   Skull of *Gomphotherium*. (From Romer, *Vertebrate Paleontology*, University of Chicago Press, 1945, p. 409.)

mechanical limit, jaws of other species formed a shovel-like arrangement which may have been of use in digging for food. The molar teeth were large, but were low-crowned, with long roots. The largest species of *Gomphotherium* had a height of about 7 feet and was massively built. *Gomphotherium* is of interest as the first proboscidean to reach North America, presumably as a migrant from Asia.

Mastodons

Another line of proboscideans culminated in the mastodons (Fig. 10.16). These were creatures of elephantine size that roamed North America until postglacial times, as judged by the fact that their bones are found near the surface in bogs and swamps. The mastodon lower jaw was short (Fig. 10.16), usually without tusks, although rudimentary lower tusks are found in some specimens. The upper tusks were large, sometimes attaining a length of 9 feet, and curved upward. The skull contained an extensive

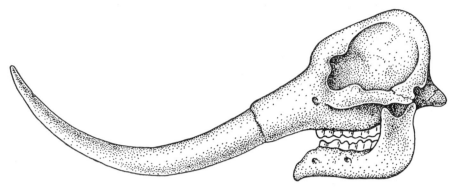

FIG. 10.16. Skull of *Mastodon*. (After Lull, *Organic Evolution*, The Macmillan Company, 1945.)

development of air cells but they were arranged in such a manner that the "highbrow" appearance of true elephants did not result. The molar teeth were low-crowned, long-rooted, and had on the surface three or four transverse crests, without cement in the intervening valleys (Fig. 10.17). We note that this tooth structure contrasts sharply with that of elephants (Fig. 10.10). But two fully formed molars occupied each jaw at any one time. Judging by stomach contents found associated with some American mastodon specimens, the latter were forest dwellers, including in their diet twigs of such coniferous trees as hemlock and spruce.

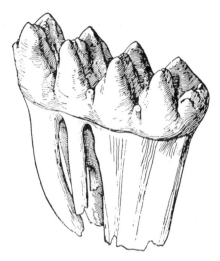

Mammoths and Elephants

True elephants, including the Asiatic and African species and the extinct mammoths, are believed to have arisen from the Asiatic form, *Stegodon* (Fig. 10.11). In structure of molar teeth *Stegodon* presented a condition somewhat transitional between the structures of mastodon and of elephant teeth. The transverse crests were more numerous than they were on mastodon teeth, yet the amount of cement between the crests was not so great as it was in elephant teeth. Ele-

FIG. 10.17. Molar tooth of *Mastodon*. (From Scott, *A History of Land Mammals in the Western Hemisphere*, p. 417. Copyright 1937 by American Philosophical Society. Used by permission of The Macmillan Company, publishers.)

phants and mammoths are characterized by the massive molar structure previously described, by the longitudinal method of molar replacement, by possession of a short, high skull and a short, tuskless lower jaw. We may note in passing the interesting fact that the fetus of the elephant has a long lower jaw. As development continues the jaw becomes relatively shorter (de Beer, 1958). Here is another example of recapitulation (pp. 50–51). Probably if we could but learn of them we should find that the fetuses of all proboscideans had long lower jaws. The adult *Moeritherium* retained the jaw in about its fetal proportions. In some of the proboscideans (e.g., *Gomphotherium*) the adult jaw became still further elongated, while in others it became relatively shorter.

During Pleistocene times a variety of mammoths ranged widely over the earth, including regions with climates not suitable for the two modern elephants. Thus the *woolly mammoth* wandered into arctic regions. This mammoth is perhaps the most completely known of all prehistoric mammals, owing to the happy fact that complete carcasses have been found in the permanently frozen gravels of northern Siberia. Thus the "soft parts" usually unavailable for study in fossil animals have been preserved along with the bones. Thanks to this fortunate preservation, we know that this mammoth was covered with coarse, dark brown hair, having a maximum length of 20 inches, and with a dense undercoat of woolly hair about an inch long. The creature has added interest for us because of cave paintings and carvings of it made by our prehistoric relative, Cro-Magnon man (p. 245). Presumably these mammoths served as a source of food for men of the time.

Although the height of about 9.5 feet attained by the woolly mammoth did not equal the height of large Asiatic elephants today, some other mammoths exceeded the latter. The imperial mammoth, for example, was 13.5 feet high at the shoulder. This mammoth and some of its American contemporaries were characterized by extreme spiraling of the tusks. Since the spiral tusks continued to grow throughout life, in some old individuals the tips actually crossed each other, producing a condition in which the tusks were effective neither for digging nor for fighting.

References and Suggested Readings

de Beer, G. R. *Embryos and Ancestors,* 3rd ed. Oxford: Oxford University Press, 1958.

Camp, C. L., and N. Smith. "Phylogeny and functions of the digital ligaments of the horse." University of California, *MEMOIRS,* 13 (1942), 69–123.

Colbert, E. H. *Evolution of the Vertebrates.* New York: John Wiley & Sons, Inc., 1955.

Dunbar, C. O. *Historical Geology.* New York: John Wiley & Sons, Inc., 1949.

Edinger, T. *Evolution of the Horse Brain.* Geological Society of America, *MEMOIR* 25, 1948.

Hussey, R. C. *Historical Geology,* 2nd ed. New York: McGraw-Hill Book Company, Inc., 1947.

Kulp, J. L. "Geologic time scale," *Science,* 133 (1961), 1105–1114.

Libby, W. F. "Radiocarbon dating," *American Scientist,* 44 (1956), 98–112.

Lull, R. S. *Organic Evolution,* rev. ed. New York: The Macmillan Company, 1945.

Osborn, H. F. *Equidae of the Oligocene, Miocene and Pliocene of North America,* iconographic type revision. New York: American Museum of Natural History, *MEMOIRS,* Vol. II, Pt. I, 1918.

Romer, A. S. *Vertebrate Paleontology,* 2nd ed. Chicago: University of Chicago Press, 1945.

Romer, A. S. *The Vertebrate Story.* Chicago: University of Chicago Press, 1959.

Scott, W. B. *A History of Land Mammals in the Western Hemisphere,* rev. ed. New York: The Macmillan Company, 1937.

Simpson, G. G. *The Meaning of Evolution.* New Haven: Yale University Press, 1949.

Simpson, G. G. *Horses.* New York: Oxford University Press, 1951. (Authoritative account of horse evolution.)

CHAPTER 11

EVOLUTION AS SEEN IN THE

GEOLOGIC RECORD:

EVOLUTION OF MAN

Pope's dictum that "the proper study of mankind is Man" may be taken as symbolic of the enhanced interest most people feel in members of their own species, as compared to their interest in other portions of the animal kingdom. Probably it is only natural that the subject of the evolution of man arouses more widespread interest than does, for example, that of the evolution of the horse. Yet it is unfortunate that the "man in the street" thinks of evolution only in terms of its bearing upon the question of man's ancestry, instead of recognizing that man's evolution is one scene in a much vaster drama. But perhaps our criticism of the average citizen's myopic vision should be mitigated by the realization that he is occasionally encouraged in this restricted view by those who should know better.

The foregoing is not intended to belittle man or the importance of his evolution, but to suggest the perspective in which all evolution should be viewed. Many animals have arisen through evolution, among them man. The same principles at work in the production of other animals operated in the production of man. Man is the finest product which has yet arisen through the evolutionary process. But that is not to say that the evolutionary process was set in motion in the first place for the express purpose of producing man.

Why is man the finest fruit on the tree of life? The very fact that he can ask the question suggests the answer. Man is the only product of the evolutionary process to develop the mentality to wonder about himself and his origin, and to acquire some measure of knowledge in the matter. The human mind, then, is the greatest achievement of the evolutionary process. His mind enables man to wonder and, within limits, to know and understand. To a considerable and increasing extent, also, man's mind enables him to control his environment instead of being controlled by it as other animals are. Nor should we forget the emotional and aesthetic attributes of mind, attributes which have underlain some of the noblest achievements of our race.

The Human Brain

Because of the preeminent position accorded the human mind, and because of the close association between mind and the functioning of the brain, we shall place emphasis on the development of the brain in our discussion of the evolution of man. Brain development affords some clue to mind development. It is noteworthy in this connection that the outstanding achievement of human evolution was the development of the brain. We have seen that birds specialized in developing wings, horses in developing legs for running, elephants in developing tusks and trunk and giant molars. Man specialized in developing brain. Accordingly, the unique features of man's evolution are largely concerned with the evolution of this brain. It will occupy the center of the stage in the following discussion.

Before proceeding further a word is in order concerning an omission which will be troubling some readers. We have accorded preeminence to the human mind but have said nothing about the human soul. The reason for the omission lies in the fact that the soul is outside the province of science. Science deals with phenomena which can be detected, studied, and measured by use of scientific instruments. The soul is not amenable to this approach. It cannot be seen, or weighed, or analyzed chemically; nor can it be studied—as yet, at least—by the methods of the psychologist. Thus discussion of the soul would be out of place in a book of science. This may not always be true, but for the present we must look to religion and philosophy for knowledge of the soul.

Pre-Primate Ancestry

Man is clearly a mammal. Hence the evolutionary history which we have traced for mammals in general is also his evolutionary history.

Briefly, we recall that the sequence, subsequent to attainment of vertebrate status, was as follows: crossopterygian fishes, to labyrinthodont amphibians, to cotylosaur reptiles, to therapsid reptiles, to primitive mammals of group Pantotheria, to mammals of Order Insectivora.

Order Primates

We have noted that the Insectivora constitute the group of mammals from which the other orders of placental mammals are believed to have arisen. Among these other orders is Order Primates, the order to which man belongs, in company with tree shrews, lemurs, tarsiers, monkeys, and apes. These forms are grouped together in one order because they possess in common a number of anatomical features. Yet the order is not characterized by any one big specialization as are many other orders of mammals. Thus, members of Order Artiodactyla (e.g., deer, antelope) are specialized for running on two toes of each foot, members of Order Carnivora (e.g., cats, dogs) for flesh eating, members of Order Chiroptera (bats) for flying, members of Order Cetacea (e.g., whales, porpoises) for swimming, and so on. Members of Order Primates exhibit a trend toward freeing of the forelimbs from locomotor duties, making possible their employment for other purposes, notably the grasping and handling of objects. The lower primates show only the beginnings of this trend, which reaches its culmination in man. The trend was doubtless of highest importance in human evolution, being closely connected with development of the upright posture which forms one of man's most distinctive attributes. This emancipation of the hands from duties of locomotion was probably an essential prerequisite for the great development of the brain mentioned above as man's crowning achievement.

The trend toward emancipation of the forelimbs from locomotor duties and employment of these limbs for grasping and handling is reflected in a number of bodily features characterizing members of Order Primates. Thus, the thumb and great toe are more or less opposable to the other digits; flattened finger nails have largely replaced the claws possessed by other mammals; and the eyes are directed anteriorly instead of laterally. Obviously, anteriorly directed eyes are in much better position to see and examine objects held in the hands than are laterally directed eyes. As the forelimbs have lost locomotor duties the hind limbs have assumed more and more complete responsibility for body support and locomotion when primates walk on the ground. This fact is reflected in the plantigrade walking position of the feet, with the sole of the foot nearly flat on the ground for its entire length.

Primates are also characterized by many other features, such as posses-sion of a single pair of mammary glands, usually pectoral (on the chest) in position, complete separation of the eye orbit from the temporal fossa by a partition of bone, and so on. The sample given is sufficient to emphasize the many features shared by man with his fellow primates.

Beginnings of Primate Evolution

The Order Primates is conveniently divided into two suborders: Suborder Prosimii (tree shrews, lemurs, tarsiers) and Suborder Anthro-poidea (monkeys, apes, men) (Simpson, 1945). Among the prosimians the **tree shrews** (Fig. 11.1) are the most primitive, resembling both insectivores and primates in structure. Indeed they were formerly classed as members of Order Insectivora. It seems highly probable that tree shrews living in early Cenozoic times were at once the descendants of true insectivores and the ancestors of higher primates.

The immediate descendants of these tree shrews were **lemurs** and **tarsiers,** both represented by numerous forms in early periods of the Cenozoic era. Lemurs are small animals resembling monkeys in many ways, as, for example, in having hands tipped with flattened nails instead of claws. Even so, some lemurs have a specialized claw on one digit of each hand. The faces of lemurs project into unmonkeylike muzzles, however, suggesting the faces of little dogs (Fig. 11.1). Tarsiers are represented today by only one form, the spectacled tarsier, found in some islands of the East Indies. This animal is remarkable for its enormous eyes and concomitant development of the visual regions of the brain (Fig. 11.1).

Did tarsiers evolve from lemurs or did they arise directly from tree shrews? Authorities differ on this question. But significantly, in the case of some of these early Eocene prosimians "it is a matter of great difficulty to decide whether they should be classified as lemurs or tarsiers" (Le Gros Clark, 1949–1957). This suggests their close relationship. On the other hand, some of the Eocene tarsiers resembled monkeys in dentition and skull characteristics and hence may well have been ancestral to higher members of the order. At any rate it is clear that early Cenozoic prosimians were the ancestors of higher primates.

Monkeys, Apes, and Men

Suborder Anthropoidea is divided into two groups: (1) New World monkeys, and (2) Old World monkeys, apes, and men. Man resembles

FIG. 11.1. Representative modern primates. A, tree shrew (*Tupaia*). B, lemur (*Galago*). C, tarsier (*Tarsius*). D, macaque monkey (*Macaca*). E, gibbon (*Hylobates*). F, chimpanzee (*Pan*). (Drawn by Maurice Wilson; from Le Gros Clark, *History of the Primates*, British Museum [Natural History], 1949, Frontispiece.)

Old World monkeys and apes, as contrasted with New World monkeys, in having a narrow nose, with nostrils close together, in having two premolar teeth (instead of three) on each side of both jaws, in having a bony canal connecting his external ear with the middle ear, and in numerous other features. Man and apes lack an external tail; most monkeys of the Old World have tails, although the latter are frequently more or less shortened and in any event never develop the prehensile capabilities of the tails of New World monkeys, which serve as veritable fifth limbs.

In many ways man is similar in structure to the great apes, particularly to the chimpanzee and the gorilla. Clearly, none of these forms are the *ancestors* of any of the others, for they are all contemporaries. The chimpanzee and gorilla are as completely "modern" in their own ways as man is in his. They may be our distant cousins; they are certainly not our grandparents. One's cousin is not one's ancestor.

Granted that modern monkeys, apes, and men are related, how close are the relationships among the several groups, and when did the evolutionary line leading to each begin to diverge from the evolutionary lines leading to the others? Unfortunately the fossil record is most incomplete on these points. Fossils are few and fragmentary. And the very fact that similarities among the forms in question are so great renders interpretation and evaluation of fossil remains difficult. We should not be surprised, therefore, that specialists in the field disagree sharply. In the present state of knowledge dogmatic statements are not in order. Our wisest course is to present the points on which there is general agreement and to state the bases of disagreement on questions still undecided. In so doing we shall be reflecting the fact that science itself undergoes continual evolutionary change. Much of its fascination lies in the challenge of the still unanswered questions.

Fig. 11.2 presents in diagrammatic form some of the best current thinking concerning the evolution of Old World monkeys, apes, and man. The diagram may be likened to a river flowing from bottom to top and dividing into numerous channels as it progresses, like a river flowing through its delta. At the bottom of the diagram we note the Eocene prosimians mentioned above; from them arose the Oligocene ancestors of Old World primates. New World monkeys are not shown; New World and Old World forms may have originated from different groups of Eocene prosimians, but we must await discovery of additional fossils before we can be sure of relationships involved.

In the Oligocene period the diagram includes a most interesting little fossil known as *Parapithecus*. This creature is known from a single lower jaw, less than two inches in length, found in Egypt. This tantalizing fossil

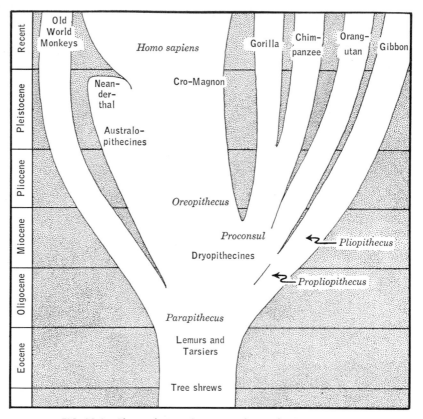

FIG. 11.2. The evolution of primates during the Cenozoic era.

belonged to a creature which some writers call a monkey and others an ape. Since the jaw and teeth are quite unspecialized, along lines of specialization followed by either later monkeys or later apes, we may be wise not to try to classify the creature as either the one or the other. From our standpoint *Parapithecus* is most interesting as evidence that there existed in Oligocene times primates so primitive in structure that they could have been the ancestors both of later Old World monkeys and of apes (Gregory, 1951; Colbert, 1955).

The Old World monkey "channel" of the diagram is shown separating from the rest of the "river" during the Oligocene. The same is true among the apes for the "channel" leading to the gibbon (Fig. 11.2). Not only is *Parapithecus* a probable ancestor of the gibbon, but two other fossils, *Propliopithecus* from the Oligocene and *Pliopithecus* from the Miocene, indicate something of the subsequent course of gibbon evolution. Modern gibbons, at home in southeastern Asia and the East Indies, are slender-bodied, long-armed specialists in brachiation (swinging through the tree-tops by their arms) (Fig. 11.1).

During Miocene and on into Pliocene times there lived in various parts of Africa, Europe, and India a varied assemblage of apes classified together in the subfamily **Dryopithecinae.** Collectively they are believed to have included the ancestors of the modern orang-utan, chimpanzee, and gorilla. Of these the orang-utan, inhabitant of the rain forests of Sumatra and Borneo, is so unlike his African relatives that he is believed to have gone his separate way since early Miocene times. Others of the Dryopithecinae were ancestral to the African apes: gorilla and chimpanzee. In particular, one of the group named *Proconsul,* living in Africa in early Miocene times, shows characteristics indicating its probable ancestry of these apes. The chimpanzee and gorilla are so similar that they are thought to have diverged from a common ancestor fairly recently, in early Pleistocene or late Pliocene, as Fig. 11.2 indicates.

Ancestry of Man

Having established the probable ancestries of monkeys and apes we come now to the question of the ancestry of man. This portion of our diagram (Fig. 11.2) is represented by a broad "channel" which to be more realistic should be subdivided into an interlacing network of smaller channels twisting, turning, dividing, and recombining in most complicated fashion (cf. Fig. 11.16). Names have been placed at various points along this channel to *Homo sapiens* The names represent progressive levels of development toward the *Homo sapiens* stage and in some instances, at least, may well represent actual ancestors. It will be noted that the name of *Parapithecus* is so placed as to indicate that this monkey-ape was ancestral to man. Our limited knowledge of *Parapithecus* indicates that it was so primitive in its primate characteristics that it represents a stage in evolution in which Old World monkeys, apes, and ancestors of man were not clearly separated. Indicating that it was ancestral to all three is in accord with the view that man shared common ancestry with monkeys and apes. This is the most widely held view, though a few investigators have maintained that man is not related to monkeys and apes, but has followed a separate evolutionary line springing directly from tarsiers and lemurs.

What of other human ancestors in the Oligocene? Were there forms ancestral to both men and apes? Or had the ancestral line leading to man already separated from that leading to apes? Until more Oligocene fossils are found we can not answer these questions.

Passing on to the Miocene and Pliocene we note the Dryopithecinae, ancestral to orang-utan, chimpanzee, and gorilla. Were they also ancestral to man? This question has been answered both "yes" and "no." The diagram indicates the possibility that they may have been but also indicates, by the open channel to the left of the name "Dryopithecinae," that other, still-unknown Miocene forms *may* have been ancestral, either to the exclusion of the Dryopithecinae or in addition to them.

The question of the ancestral position of the Dryopithecinae is of interest since it involves the whole question of man's relationship to the *apes*. Among living primates the chimpanzee and gorilla are man's closest relatives, as judged by many similarities of structure of both skeleton and "soft parts," and including such things as the type of placenta and the results of serological tests (see pp. 111–113). But there are also differences. Some of

FIG. 11.3. Gorilla. (Drawn by Maurice Wilson; from Le Gros Clark, *History of the Primates*, British Museum [Natural History], 1949, p. 34.)

the most striking of the differences are connected with the manner in which apes travel through the trees. Modern apes are strongly specialized for arm-swinging, for **brachiation.** True, the massive gorillas no longer spend much time in the trees, but their anatomy bears incontestable evidence that their immediate forebears were brachiators. Among the special-

izations for brachiation are elongation of the forelimbs, reduction of the
thumb so that the other fingers of the hand function as a sort of hook on
the branches of trees, and shortening of the hind limbs (Figs. 11.1 and
11.3). Many correlated changes in muscles, muscle
attachments, and joint structure are also entailed.
If the body is heavy, great enlargement of the musculature of the shoulders and arms is necessitated.

Man is not a brachiator. Is he descended from
ancestors who were? Relative to trunk height both
modern apes and man have long arms (Washburn,
1950). Man differs from modern apes, however,
in that his legs are longer than his arms; in this
respect, as in some others, man resembles Old
World monkeys more than he does the modern
apes (Straus, 1949). In this connection it is of
great interest that Miocene apes such as *Proconsul*
also had forelimbs shorter than hind limbs (Simons,
1960). Since this was true of *Pliopithecus* as well,
the fact suggests that elongation of the arms was a
later acquisition in lines leading to modern apes
specialized for brachiation, and that in the lines
leading to man the primitive relationship of shorter
arms than legs was retained.

Authorities differ as to whether *Proconsul* itself
should be regarded as ancestral to man. If it was a
brachiator it was not a highly specialized one. In
fact, its arms possessed a sufficiently generalized
structure (Fig. 11.4) so that both the arm structure
of man and that of the specialized brachiators
among later apes might have been derived from it
(see Napier and Davis, 1959; Le Gros Clark,
1960). On the other hand, its teeth were somewhat
specialized, suggestive of the teeth of its descendants, the chimpanzee and gorilla. But if it was not
ancestral to man, some other members of the
Dryopithecinae may have been. Future discoveries
will doubtless afford much interesting information
on this point.

Great interest has been aroused recently by
studies of a fossil primate known as *Oreopithecus*

FIG. 11.4. Arm skele-
ton of *Proconsul* (cf.
Fig. 3.2). Based on a
reconstruction by J. R.
Napier and P. R. Davis.
(From Le Gros Clark,
*The Antecedents of
Man,* Edinburgh Uni-
versity Press, 1959, p.
216.)

(Fig. 11.2) which lived in late Miocene or early Pliocene times, some 13 million years ago. Many fossils of this form have been found in a lignite mine in Tuscany, Italy. Preliminary studies seem to indicate that *Oreopithecus* resembled man, and differed from apes and monkeys, in so many characteristics that it belongs in the same family with man, Family Hominidae (Hürzeler, 1958). (Apes, fossil and living, are placed in Family Pongidae.) If this interpretation is correct *Oreopithecus* "represents our first glimpse of a Tertiary hominid of any sort" (Straus, 1957). The teeth are unlike those of both monkeys and apes; rather they resemble human dentition in some respects. The canine teeth were relatively small, the face was short, and the pelvis was so broad as to suggest that the creature might have walked upright (Simons, 1960).

If further investigation firmly establishes the position of *Oreopithecus* in Family Hominidae, that fact will not in itself indicate that *Oreopithecus* was ancestral to later members of the family. We recall that the "channel" of human evolution has many subdivisions some of which (probably the majority of them) terminated without giving rise to new forms. This is as likely to be true of human evolution as it is demonstrably true of the evolution of, for example, the horses and the proboscideans (pp. 204 and 211). But human evolution may well have gone through a stage in which the actual ancestors resembled *Oreopithecus* in many respects.

Were there other members of Family Hominidae living in the Pliocene? Doubtless, but we must await further discoveries before we know anything of their nature. As indicated in our diagram (Fig. 11.2), the next known hominid fossils come from Pleistocene deposits—the australopithecines from South Africa.

Characteristics of "Homo sapiens"

Before we discuss the characteristics of Pleistocene hominids it will be useful to call attention to the characteristics of the species of man living at the present time, our own species. Doing so conforms with our practice of enumerating the characteristics of *Equus* before describing those of *Hyracotherium, Mesohippus,* and so on, and of describing the structure of modern elephants before discussing ancestral proboscideans. What are the characteristics of *Homo sapiens* for the evolution of which we should be watching as we study hominid fossils?

For the most part we shall concentrate upon anatomical characteristics which affect the skeletal system and hence can be studied in fossils.

1. *Brain.*   The large brain of *Homo sapiens* causes the brain case or

cranium of the skull to have an average capacity of about 1350 cc. Normal human brains vary greatly in size, however, with the result that cranial capacities vary all the way from 900 to 2300 cc. (Le Gros Clark, 1959). And, significantly, within this range there is no correlation between brain size and degree of intelligence. As extremes among notable men of letters we may cite Anatole France, with a brain volume of 1100 cc., and Jonathan Swift, with a brain volume of about 2000 cc.

The large size of brain, particularly of the frontal lobes of the cerebral hemispheres, has resulted in development of a relatively high forehead.

2. *Upright Posture.* The upright posture of *Homo sapiens* entails a whole series of anatomical changes as compared to the structure of primates which do not have this posture. The skull is balanced on the upper end of the vertebral column instead of projecting anteriorly from it. This change, plus, probably, other factors such as expansion of the brain case, has resulted in the shifting forward of the foramen magnum (the opening through which the spinal cord exits from the skull and enters the vertebral column), changing from the posterior position it occupies in forms which walk on all fours. Apes, with their partially upright posture, show an intermediate condition in this respect (Fig. 11.5).

The upright posture in *Homo sapiens* is made possible by a lumbar curve in the vertebral column—a forward bending of that column in the "small" of the back. Apes lack such a curve (Fig. 11.5).

One of the greatest changes in the skeletal system connected with upright posture concerns the pelvic girdle. In *Homo sapiens* the ilium bones are expanded to form a sort of basin supporting the internal organs of the body cavity. In forms which do not walk upright the ilia lack this supportive function and have a much more elongated shape (Fig. 11.5).

The legs of *Homo sapiens* are elongated, with relatively straight bones in upper and lower segments, and they terminate in a characteristic foot, most of the lower surface of which is in contact with the ground (plantigrade).

3. *Teeth and Associated Structures.* Of the numerous distinguishing characteristics possessed by the teeth of *Homo sapiens,* we shall list only a few outstanding ones, emphasizing those in which human teeth and jaws contrast with those of apes.

Homo sapiens differs from apes in the arrangement of the teeth. In apes the incisors are large and the front of the jaw is broad in consequence (Figs. 11.6 and 11.7). The canines are large, projecting tusks; and the premolars and molars extend backward from them in straight rows. The whole effect is that of a straight-sided "U." By contrast the human tooth row resembles a smoothly rounded parabola without sharp bends (Fig. 11.6); the incisors are small and the canines are not large and projecting as they are in apes. In apes there is characteristically a gap or diastema between the incisor teeth and the canine tooth on each side of the upper jaw; the canine tooth of the lower jaw fits into this space when the mouth

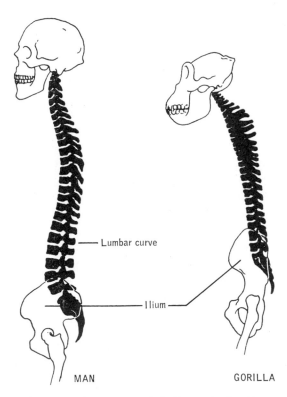

FIG. 11.5. Comparison of skull, vertebral column, and pelvis of man and gorilla. (Redrawn from Boule and Vallois, *Fossil Men*, The Dryden Press, 1957, p. 74, by permission of Henry Holt & Co., Inc.)

is closed. *Homo sapiens*, lacking the projecting canines, also lacks this "simian gap" in the upper tooth row.

In apes the first premolar teeth in the lower jaw have a cutting edge, are sectorial. In *Homo sapiens* the first lower premolar does not have this character.

A characteristic of the jaw of modern apes related to the large incisor and canine teeth is the development of a reinforcing ledge of bone extending backward from the symphysis of the jaw (Fig. 11.7). This "simian

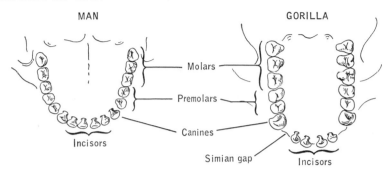

FIG. 11.6. Upper dental arches of man and gorilla. (Modified from Weidenreich, *Apes, Giants, and Man,* University of Chicago Press, 1946, p. 9.)

shelf" is lacking in men, both *Homo sapiens* and his predecessors, and in many, at least, of the Dryopithecinae (e.g., *Proconsul,* Fig. 11.7).

Another result of the small teeth in modern *Homo sapiens* is that the tooth row is short, as compared to that of apes and some of the earlier hominids. The longer tooth row possessed by these latter causes the face

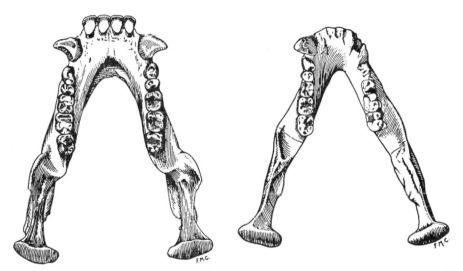

FIG. 11.7. Lower jaws of chimpanzee (left) and of *Proconsul* (right). (From Le Gros Clark, *History of the Primates,* British Museum [Natural History], 1949, p. 59.)

to protrude into a sort of muzzle—to be *prognathous.* The face of modern *Homo sapiens,* on the other hand, does not project in this fashion; the profile is more nearly vertical, or *orthognathous.*

In apes and earlier hominids with their long tooth rows the upper edge of the lower jaw extends forward further than does the lower—there is no projecting chin. In modern *Homo sapiens* with his shortened tooth row, the lower margin of the jaw extends forward as a chin (see Fig. 11.15). This chin may have evolved as an external buttress against the active stresses to which the broad human jaw is subjected in use (Du Brul and Sicher, 1954).

Modern *Homo sapiens* lacks heavy ridges of bone projecting over the eyes (supraorbital torus) possessed by apes and earlier hominids. In apes the eyebrow ridges are part of a series of ridges providing attachment (origin) for powerful chewing muscles. In modern *Homo sapiens* the chewing apparatus is reduced and the skull is expanded, providing origin for the chewing muscles without development of the ridges.

In summary we may characterize the striking features of the skeletal anatomy of modern *Homo sapiens* as follows: (1) cranial capacity varying from 900 to 2300 cc.; (2) high forehead without projecting eyebrow ridges; (3) upright posture, reflected in structure of skull, vertebral column, pelvis, and legs; (4) dental arch a smoothly rounded parabola; (5) canine teeth not projecting beyond the level of the other teeth; (6) no simian gap; (7) first lower premolar not sectorial; (8) lower jaw with a projecting chin; (9) no simian shelf; (10) face orthognathous.

Having reviewed some of the skeletal features of the end-product of human evolution we now turn our attention to earlier hominids, discussing them in chronological order, starting with the beginning of the Pleistocene period.

Australopithecines

The first known fossil of these primates was the skull of a child discovered in South Africa in 1924 (for a fascinating account by the discoverer see Dart, 1959). Dr. Dart christened the owner of this skull *Australopithecus africanus,* a name which taken literally signifies that it belongs to a different genus and species from *Homo sapiens.* (The name written first and capitalized is that of the *genus;* the name written second and not capitalized is that of the *species,* see p. 308.)" Australopithecus" means "southern ape"; this original child and fossils of adults subsequently discovered were grouped together into a subfamily, Australopithecinae, of Family Pongidae (apes). Subsequent discoveries and thorough investigation revealed, however, that these South African forms have many characteristics of man combined with an ape-sized brain and some other ape-like characteristics. Their resemblance to apes has been emphasized by some writers (e.g., Zuckerman, 1954), their hominid characteristics by

others (e.g., Le Gros Clark, 1955). The controversy as to whether they are
apes or men is in itself interesting. Suppose that remains of an actual
"missing link" between apes and man were to be discovered: we may be
sure that it would be so like an ape in some respects that some investigators
would classify it as such, and so like man in other respects that other investigators would classify it as human. Here are the australopithecines in
the midst of just such a controversy! Because, as we shall see, the char-

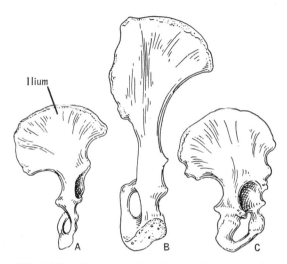

FIG. 11.8. The right pelvic bones of: A, *Australopithecus;* B, chimpanzee; C, *Homo sapiens* (Bushman). (After Broom and Robinson, "Further evidence
of the structure of the Sterkfontein ape-man *Plesianthropus,*" Transvaal Museum, *MEMOIR 4,* p. 60.)

acteristics they share with *Homo sapiens* are so fundamental and significant we shall consider them as primitive hominids.

The australopithecines (sometimes called "South African ape-men or
man-apes") were of small stature, averaging in the neighborhood of 4 feet
tall. One point of great significance about them was the fact that they
walked nearly or completely upright. The vertebral column had a distinct
lumbar curve. As shown in Fig. 11.8, the pelvic girdle was strikingly like
that of *Homo sapiens,* with its broadly expanded ilium, and unlike that of
apes. Four specimens of the pelvis are known; they all agree in indicating
that their owners had upright posture, although this was perhaps not as
perfected as that of modern man (Le Gros Clark, 1959). The position of the
foramen magnum well forward under the base of the skull is also indicative
of upright posture.

The teeth were strikingly human. Australopithecines agreed with *Homo sapiens* (p. 232) in that (1) the dental arch was a smoothly rounded parabola (Fig. 11.6), (2) the canine teeth did not project beyond the level of the other teeth, (3) there was no simian gap, and (4) the first lower premolar was not sectorial.

We conclude, therefore, that the upright posture and the character of the teeth warrant the inclusion of the australopithecines in Family Hominidae. What were their most striking differences from *Homo sapiens* himself? The skulls of these little people were notable for large jaws and teeth and

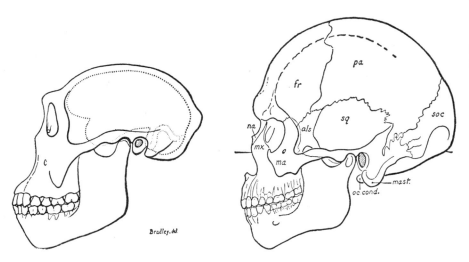

FIG. 11.9. Restored skull of an australopithecine (*Australopithecus*) (left) compared to a modern human skull (Tasmanian aboriginal). *als*, alisphenoid. *fr*, frontal. *ma*, malar. *mast.*, mastoid process. *mx*, maxilla. *na*, nasal. *oc. cond.*, occipital condyle. *pa*, parietal. *soc*, supraoccipital. *sq*, squamosal. (From Gregory, *Evolution Emerging*, Vol. 2, p. 977. Copyright 1951, by American Museum of Natural History. Used by permission of The Macmillan Company, publishers.)

small brain cases. The teeth were actually larger than those of modern man. As a result of the tooth and jaw development the face was prognathous and lacking a chin (Fig. 11.9). Eyebrow ridges projected over the eyes.

The small, flat brain case stood in marked contrast to the large face. Casts of the interior of the skulls reveal that the brain was of human form but was so small as to be outside the range for normal brains of *Homo sapiens*. Australopithecine brain capacity ranged from about 450 cc. up to 700 cc. (Le Gros Clark, 1959). We have seen that the smallest normal capacity for *Homo sapiens* is about 900 cc. Indeed the australopithecine brain size is comparable to that of apes. The range for the gorilla is 415 to 655 cc. Yet a gorilla with a brain of 650 cc. weighs four or five times as much as did these early men. Evidently the lightly built australopithecines with their small brains represent an evolutionary trend quite unlike that which culminated in the bulky gorilla.

Were the small brains of the australopithecines sufficiently developed to make possible any culture worthy the name? Recent findings of crude stone implements with the fossils of *Zinjanthropus* (see p. 237) corroborate previous fragmentary evidence that australopithecines made simple stone tools. Dart (1956, 1959) has suggested that the australopithecines may have fashioned implements and weapons of bone. Rather interestingly, quantities of baboon skulls fractured in such a way as to suggest that the creatures were killed by skillful blows on the head, have been found with australopithecine remains.

The australopithecines are now known from the remains of many individuals, exhibiting considerable variation in structure. Robinson (1956) distinguished two main types and called them genera (plural of "genus"): *Australopithecus* and *Paranthropus*. He stated that "there is greater difference between them than between the gorilla and the chimpanzee." *Paranthropus* had massive jaws and grinding teeth with accompanying heavy musculature; it was probably herbivorous. *Australopithecus* was more lightly constructed; its teeth suggest an omnivorous diet. Le Gros Clark (1955, 1959), on the other hand, recognized the variability encountered but suggested that it may have been no greater than that found within our own genus, *Homo*. Accordingly he placed all australopithecines in one genus: *Australopithecus*. We note that both of these authors would place the australopithecines in one or more genera distinct from genus *Homo*. But is even this taxonomic distinction justified? If they were men should they not be placed in the genus with other men, just as all types of dogs are placed in genus *Canis*? Mayr (1950) suggested that they be classified as *Homo transvaalensis*. Such differences of opinion are inevitable. In part they stem from differences of opinion as to what is to be included in the term "man"; in part they form an aspect of the unresolvable controversy between the "lumpers" and the "splitters" in taxonomy, i.e., those who emphasize similarities and classify similar forms together despite differences considered to be minor, and those who emphasize differences, separating animals into distinct categories on the basis of even small differences.

Whatever their exact relationships and classification, the australopithecines tell us much about the early stages of human evolution. We have seen that the primates as a whole are characterized by varying degrees of emancipation of the forelimbs from the duties of locomotion (p. 220). The various primates vary in the extent of this emancipation, and the brachiators among them have in a sense reversed the trend, although most of them have done so without serious loss of ability to use the hands in grasping objects. The lower monkeys, arboreal but not brachiators, possess hands adapted for grasping and handling objects, as everyone who has visited a zoo knows. They also foreshadow to some extent an upright posture of the trunk as they move through their arboreal habitat. The ancestor of man must have been such an arboreal (and brachiating?) primate who for some reason forsook life in trees for life on the ground. In response to the needs of the new environment, the tendency to upright posture bequeathed him by his tree-dwelling ancestors became perfected. Furthermore, the attainment of erect locomotion removed the last necessity for the employment of the hands in locomotion, leaving them free for other duties, notably the handling of objects. The latter led directly to the use of tools, the basis of all man's later achievements. Man without tools would be a most undistinguished member of the animal kingdom. Tools, developed and employed by the human brain, have made possible the development of civilization. To a very considerable extent man's cultural attainments have been, and continue to be, measured by the tools employed, as implied in our designation of cultures as "Old Stone Age" (Paleolithic), "New Stone Age," "Bronze Age," "Iron Age," "Age of Steam," "Age of Electricity," and so on. Accordingly the importance of the changes which paved the way for development of the ability to use tools can not be exaggerated. The primary change making this possible was attainment of upright posture, which, as the australopithecines and perhaps even *Oreopithecus* show us, came at the dawn of human evolution and *preceded* the great development of brain which was later to characterize man. Hands free to use tools came first; brain development adequate for making effective use of those hands in devising, using, and perfecting tools came later. Probably the brain development never would have occurred had not the hands been available first. In this connection it is interesting to recall that in the evolution of the horse, brain development lagged behind adaptive changes in the limbs. *Hyracotherium* with its almost reptilian brain had nevertheless begun the evolutionary changes in the limbs which were to characterize horse evolution (pp. 202–203; Fig. 10.6).

Were the australopithecines ancestral to later men, including eventually *Homo sapiens?* We have enumerated above many bodily characteristics of

Homo sapiens also shared by the australopithecines. The differences largely relate to large jaws and teeth and small brains. While it seems evident that the australopithecines demonstrate for us a stage passed through by man in his evolution, very possibly the actual specimens being discovered in South Africa were not members of a population which was literally ancestral to later men. But similar forms, living perhaps in other regions and as yet undiscovered, very likely were the actual ancestors. In this connection we should like to learn more of australopithecines living in regions other than South Africa. In 1959 the skull and tibia of an australopithecine were found in Tanganyika, thereby extending the known range of the group into East Africa. Called *Zinjanthropus boisei* by its describer, L. S. B. Leakey (1959), this fossil differs from those of the South African forms in some respects and may approach the structure of modern man more closely than do these latter. Interestingly, the bones came from a Lower Pleistocene campsite and were accompanied by stone tools and the bones of animals used as food.

More recently Dr. Leakey has discovered remains of two more individuals, a child and an adult, in the same region. Preliminary reports indicate that these remains are older, but more manlike, than those of *Zinjanthropus,* from which they differ in various ways. Interestingly enough, the canine teeth resemble those of *Proconsul*. In this fascinating field further discoveries, filling gaps in knowledge and changing ideas, may be expected almost daily.

Turning to regions outside Africa, we may note that Robinson (1956) considered that a hominid known from fragmentary remains found in Java and customarily called *Meganthropus* was actually an australopithecine; Le Gros Clark (1955), on the other hand, considered that it was a Pithecanthropus. Perhaps this difference of opinion is in itself revealing of the manner in which the australopithecines approached Pithecanthropus in structure. At any rate, our ignorance of the distribution of australopithecines outside Africa is as yet almost complete.

The actual ancestors of later men may have lived at an earlier time than did the known specimens of australopithecines. The latter are considered to date from the early Lower Pleistocene; Robinson (1956) stated that they "must also have been living in the Pliocene," but no Pliocene fossils of them are known. The remains of the next succeeding type of man, Pithecanthropus, are found in deposits considered to be from the beginning of the Middle Pleistocene (Le Gros Clark, 1959). Thus some hundreds of thousands of years may have intervened between the known australopithecines and Pithecanthropus. If the actual ancestors were older than the known specimens still more time for evolution of Pithecanthropus from australopithecine-type hominids would have been available.

Pithecanthropus

Our discussion of the australopithecines has indicated that early in the Pleistocene human evolution had progressed to acquirement of upright posture (perhaps even foreshadowed long before in *Oreopithecus*) and essentially human dentition. Upright posture freed the hands from locomotor duties and made possible, at least potentially, the use of tools. The brain, however, was still abnormally small for a primate that could be called human. In subsequent evolution to the *Homo sapiens* stage the brain increased in size, and the jaws and teeth decreased. What fossil remains do we have indicating the steps in this process?

Long before the first australopithecines were discovered unusual human remains had been found on the Asiatic island of Java. Here, in 1891, Dubois collected a skullcap with a few associated teeth and bones, notably a femur. The original owner of these bones was named *Pithecanthropus erectus,* meaning "erect ape-man." For years a controversy as to whether the creature was ape or man raged around these meager fossils. Fortunately he and his fellows are now known from portions of four skulls and some additional bones. More recently similar fossils were found in a cave near Peiping, China. Here a total of fifteen skulls and skull fragments have been found (Weidenreich, 1943, 1946). These fossils were named *Sinanthropus pekinensis* but subsequent investigation revealed that they are so similar to the Javan fossils that they certainly should be included in the same genus. Accordingly they have been renamed *Pithecanthropus pekinensis*. But here, even more than in the case of the australopithecines (p. 235), we are confronted with the question as to whether in reality these men should not be included in the genus of men, *Homo*. Mayr (1950) suggested that they be classified as *Homo erectus*. What name shall we use for them, then? In order to have a distinctive title without prejudging the outcome of the taxonomic controversy we shall follow the usage of Brown (1958) in employing the name Pithecanthropus without italicizing it; in this way we use it as a common or vernacular name rather than as a technical generic name.

Like the australopithecines, Pithecanthropus walked upright; he was slightly taller than the former, averaging in the neighborhood of 5 feet in height. The limb bones are indistinguishable from those of *Homo sapiens*. The brain size was somewhat increased over that of the australopithecines.

The cranial capacity of three of the Javan skulls ranged from 775 to 900 cc. while the Peiping specimens showed a still greater capacity, ranging from 850 to 1300 cc. (Le Gros Clark, 1949–1957). Thus the known brain sizes nearly bridge the gap between the australopithecines and modern man. Perhaps no australopithecine brain was quite as large as the smallest pithecanthropine brain, but the largest cranial capacity of Pithecanthropus was nearly as large as the 1350 cc. which constitutes the average of modern cranial capacities. The average of all known pithecanthropine specimens was about 1000 cc. In part this small average size was probably a reflection of small body size, but it is to be noted that the modern Bushman, who has about the same body size, has a cranial capacity of around 1300 cc. (Le Gros Clark, 1949–1957). The evidence is that the Javan representatives with their smaller brains lived somewhat earlier than did the slightly larger-brained pithecanthropines from China.

The small brain was housed in a flattened skull with little or no forehead and with brow ridges projecting "to form a prominent and uninterrupted shelf of bone overhanging the eye sockets" (Le Gros Clark, 1959; Fig. 11.10). The brain case was broadest at

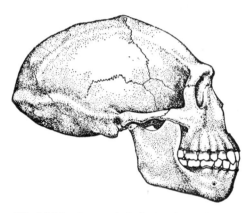

FIG. 11.10. Restored skull of *Pithecanthropus* from Java. (After McGregor and von Koenigswald, from Romer, *Vertebrate Paleontology*, University of Chicago Press, 1945, p. 357.)

the level of the ears and was pointed in back, rather than broadly rounded. The bones of the brain case were of extraordinary thickness, averaging 9.7–10 mm., as compared with 5.2 mm. for the thickness of corresponding bones in the skull of modern man (Weidenreich, 1943). We may note that this thickness was not an essentially apelike characteristic, since modern apes are not thicker skulled than are modern men.

As in the australopithecines, the teeth were large, the face prognathous and chinless. The molar teeth were so like those of the australopithecines as to be almost indistinguishable (Le Gros Clark, 1955).

Was Pithecanthropus confined to Asia? Recently three fossil jaws and a parietal bone almost indistinguishable from those of Pithecanthropus were found in Algeria. The name *Atlanthropus* has been given these fossils but they are probably better regarded as North African Pithecanthropus.

Le Gros Clark (1959) also suggested that the European Heidelberg jaw, long a bone of contention, may have belonged to a pithecanthropine, but other investigators see Neanderthal affinities in this jaw (Fig. 11.11), and at any rate far-reaching conclusions based upon one jaw are dangerous.

Thus we see that in about the middle of the Pleistocene, some half-million years ago, there lived in Asia and probably other regions people who walked upright, as did the South African australopithecines, but who were larger in body and brain than were the South African forms. Judged by modern human standards their brains were still small, however. Were these small brains indicative of markedly low intelligence? To answer this question we would wish more information about their culture than is available to us. Evidence from the caves in which the remains of the Peiping men were found indicates that these people manufactured stone tools of quartz and that they used fire. They were hunters, and judged by the cracked bones and skulls found associated with their remains they regarded brains and bone marrow as especial delicacies. There is some evidence that human brains and marrow were as welcome articles of diet as were those portions of lower animals. Le Gros Clark (1949–1957) sug-

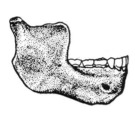

FIG. 11.11. The Heidelberg jaw. (From Romer, Vertebrate Paleontology, University of Chicago Press, 1945, p. 357.)

gested that their habits may have been somewhat similar to those of head-hunters of modern times in Borneo and elsewhere, and that they may have been almost as advanced culturally as are some of the less civilized peoples of today. But they were back near the beginning of being human; as Gregory (1951) expressed it, "Whatever the inherent possibilities of the Javan and Peking people's brains may have been, their bank of learning and tradition was still in a relatively early stage of accumulating a favorable balance."

Transitional Forms

We have now reached about the midpoint of the Pleistocene in time, and in human development we have reached a stage in which the brain averaged smaller than that of *Homo sapiens* though some individual brains were within the range of variation exhibited by the latter. Teeth were still large and jaws were chinless. Skulls were flattened and had heavy eyebrow ridges. This brings us to a portion of the Pleistocene from which human remains now known are few and fragmentary. But such as they are they exhibit trends from the Pithecanthropus-stage toward the two types of men found in later portions of the Pleistocene: Neanderthal man and *Homo sapiens* of modern type.

The two oldest of these remains come from Steinheim in Germany and Swanscombe in England. The **Steinheim** skull is fairly complete. Its cranial capacity is estimated at about 1100 cc.; it had heavy eyebrow ridges but a higher forehead than Pithecanthropus had (Fig. 11.12). In most respects it resembles the skull of *Homo sapiens* (Le Gros Clark, 1955). The same is true for the **Swanscombe** "skull," known only from three bones forming the roof and back of the brain case. The bones are unusually thick. The cranial capacity is estimated to have been about 1320 cc. Thus we see that living in the interval between the second and the third of the four glaciations in the Pleistocene (2nd Interglacial) there were men resembling *Homo sapiens* but of such unspecialized nature that they may well be representative of a varied population ancestral to both *Homo sapiens* of modern type and to Neanderthal peoples.

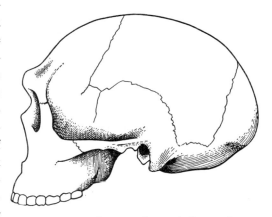

FIG. 11.12. The Steinheim skull (partly restored). Approximately one-third natural size. (From Le Gros Clark, *The Fossil Evidence for Human Evolution*, University of Chicago Press, 1955, p. 64; by courtesy of the British Museum [Natural History].)

Moving along in time to the interval between the third and fourth glaciations (3rd Interglacial) we find the **Fontéchevade** skulls from southern France. Parts of two skulls were found under a layer of stalagmite deposit in a cave. The bones, like those of the Swanscombe fossil, are unusually thick. The cranial capacity is estimated to have been greater than 1400 cc. The evidence is that, unlike the Steinheim (and perhaps Swanscombe) skull, these skulls lacked heavy eyebrow ridges. Interestingly enough, however, heavy eyebrow ridges did characterize another skull known from this period: the **Ehringsdorf** skull from Germany (Fig. 11.13). This skull had a fairly high forehead, however. Thus it resembled Neanderthal man in brow ridges and *Homo sapiens* in forehead.

We have mentioned only four of the fossils known from the second and third interglacial periods. Those we have mentioned suffice to indicate that during these periods there lived a varied assemblage of people capable in the aggregate of having been the ancestors of both Neanderthal man and

Homo sapiens of modern type. Classification of such transitional forms is difficult. Those most closely resembling *Homo sapiens* are sometimes called "presapiens" (cf. Vallois, 1954) but there is no clear indication that they constituted populations actually differentiated from their "pre-Neanderthal" contemporaries. In fact, as noted above, some *individuals* seem to have combined characteristics of both Neanderthal man and typical *Homo sapiens*. Sometimes these early peoples not clearly differentiated as either Neanderthal or *Homo sapiens* are called "early Neanderthals"

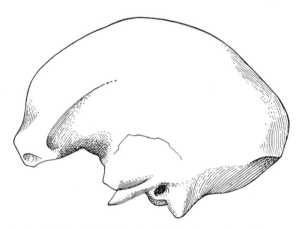

FIG. 11.13. The Ehringsdorf skull. Approximately one-third natural size. (From Le Gros Clark, *The Fossil Evidence for Human Evolution*, University of Chicago Press, 1955, p. 68; by courtesy of the British Museum [Natural History].)

and are represented as ancestral to both later or "classic" Neanderthals and to *Homo sapiens* (Howell, 1957). But it would seem as logical to call them "early *Homo sapiens*" and to represent them as ancestral to classic Neanderthals and to later *Homo sapiens* (essentially the view of Le Gros Clark, 1955).

In sum, these transitional forms seem best left unclassified. Like the australopithecines and like Pithecanthropus they exhibited great variability. Apparently wide variation in structure has always characterized man. From this varied assemblage of people two fairly distinct types emerged: Neanderthal man and *Homo sapiens* of modern type.

Neanderthal Man

During the first portions of the fourth or last glaciation, distinctive groups of people collectively known as Neanderthal man lived in Europe.

Known remains of these people are more numerous than are those of the men discussed above: between eighty and ninety individuals are represented by skeletal remains of varying completeness.

Neanderthal men whom we may regard as typical had brains at least as large as those of modern man, averaging about 1400 cc. In a sense, however, their brains were large in the wrong places. The lower and posterior portions of the brain were large, the upper and anterior portions being less well developed. Since the upper and anterior portions of the cerebral hemispheres seem to be most closely associated with higher mental processes, it is possible that the somewhat old-fashioned Neanderthal brain was connected with a degree of intelligence less than that of modern man. At any rate, the peculiarities of the brain affected the shape of the skull (Fig. 11.14). The forehead was low and slanting, and heavy eyebrow ridges projected over the orbits of the eyes. As in Pithecanthropus, the greatest width of the skull was at the level of the ears, the skull tapering upward from that point. By contrast, the large cerebral hemispheres of the modern human brain cause the skull to bulge above the level of the ears, the greatest width of the skull occurring at this higher level.

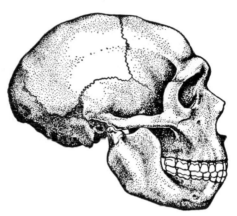

FIG. 11.14. Skull of Neanderthal man. (After McGregor; from Romer, Vertebrate Paleontology, University of Chicago Press, 1945, p. 357.)

The bones of the brain case averaged about 7.2 mm. in thickness. We note that this thickness is intermediate between that of the skulls of Pithecanthropus and of modern man (p. 239). The teeth were large, and there was no chin.

The Neanderthal peoples were shorter than are most modern groups; the men seem to have averaged a little over 5 feet in height, the women somewhat shorter. This small stature was due in part to the short legs, in which the shortness of the lower leg (shin) was particularly marked. They were stout, powerfully built people. Early restorations seemed to indicate that these people did not have a fully upright posture but later investigations have shown this interpretation to have been incorrect, having arisen from the fact that the first specimen restored was pathological, the skeleton of an individual suffering from severe arthritis (Straus and Cave, 1957).

They had stocky chests, broad shoulders, and large hands, though the fingers were short.

The Neanderthal culture was of the Old Stone Age type known as Mousterian; chipped flint tools and crude carvings remain as evidence. Some of the skeletons give evidence of reverent burial and are accompanied by ornaments and flint tools; the implication would seem to be that these people had some form of belief in immortality of the spirit.

Neanderthal peoples are best known from Europe. Fossils from other portions of the globe indicate that people of this general type, but differing in details, were living in such diverse places as Palestine (Mount Carmel), Rhodesia (**Rhodesian man**), South Africa (**Saldanha man**), Iraq (**Shanidar man**), and Java (**Solo man**). While these remains exhibit "neanderthaloid" characteristics, some of them also resemble typical *Homo sapiens* in certain respects, thereby again emphasizing the human variability mentioned previously. The skeletons found in caves on Mount Carmel in Palestine are interesting in that both neanderthaloid and *Homo sapiens* characteristics are represented. The various skeletons are sometimes regarded as having belonged to members of a single population. These people have been variously considered to be (1) hybrids between typical Neanderthals and typical *Homo sapiens* or (2) intermediate forms in the ancestry of typical Neanderthals, representing stages by which the earlier transitional forms (pp. 240–242) gave rise to the classic Neanderthals. It is possible, however, that the skeletons do not represent members of a single population but that "an early variety of modern man lived side by side, so to speak, with a Neanderthal variety" (Stewart, 1960).

This raises the question as to whether or not a distinct line can be drawn between Neanderthal man and *Homo sapiens*. Because typical Neanderthal peoples are possessed of a set of distinctive characteristics, most investigators conclude that while Neanderthal man should be placed in the same genus with ourselves he should be regarded as a separate species, i.e., that he should be classified as *Homo neanderthalensis*. In view, however, of the varying combinations of characteristics noted above, as well as of the possibility that Neanderthal peoples and *Homo sapiens* might have intermarried if they came into contact, a minority of investigators place Neanderthal man in our own species, *sapiens* (Mayr, 1950). If desired he may be regarded as constituting a separate subspecies in that species and be called *Homo sapiens neanderthalensis*.

The "extreme" or "classic" Neanderthals (i.e., those most unlike modern *Homo sapiens*) apparently lived only in Europe and became extinct there before the end of the last glacial period. They were succeeded by men of a very different type: Cro-Magnon man. What happened to the Neanderthal people? Were they conquered and exterminated? Or did they intermarry with the Cro-Magnon people and thus disappear as a separate type? Both possibilities have been suggested, but actually our ignorance on the subject is complete, for as Howell (1957) stated: "there is no clear-cut evidence which would indicate that the classic Neanderthals either (1) lived contemporaneously with the earliest of the Cro-Magnon people . . . or (2) that they interbred with the latter people."

Cro-Magnon Man

The successors in Europe of Neanderthal man were so like modern Europeans that the skeletons are indistinguishable. Thus they represent typical *Homo sapiens;* all the characteristics of this species listed previously (p. 232) apply to them. They differed from Neanderthal man in stature: males averaged over 6 feet in height, females about 5 feet and 5 inches. In contrast to neanderthalian structure, the lower or shin segment of the leg was long, indicating swift-footedness. The skull was of modern type, with high forehead, no heavy eyebrow ridges, and a distinctly jutting chin (Fig. 11.15). Unlike the faces of all his predecessors, the face of Cro-Magnon man was orthognathous. Teeth and jaws were

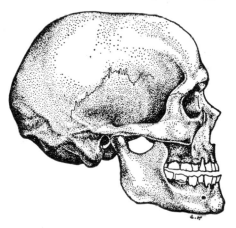

FIG. 11.15.   Skull of Cro-Magnon man. (After McGregor; from Romer, *Vertebrate Paleontology*, University of Chicago Press, 1945, p. 357.)

like those of modern man. Comparison of the skull of Neanderthal man (Fig. 11.14) with that of Cro-Magnon man (Fig. 11.15) will make these differences clear.

The Cro-Magnon people were characterized by a rather high type of Old Stone Age culture known as Aurignacian. In addition to stone, bone was used as material for manufacture of implements. These people buried their dead with elaborateness. But the Aurignacians are best known for the expertly drawn, colored pictures of contemporary mammals found on cave walls in France and Spain. These marvelous examples of primitive art are located in regions of the caves that are perpetually dark: the artists must have employed artificial illumination.

Cro-Magnon man probably reached Europe as an invader, coming, according to the prevalent idea, from Asia. Carbon-14 dating of objects from the Aurignacian culture indicates that these people lived in Europe some 27,000 years ago, well before the end of the last glaciation.

Eventually the Aurignacians were replaced by people having a different Old Stone Age culture, the Magdalenian. The Magdalenians lived in Europe some 15,000 years ago, and in turn were replaced by a succession of people of other cultures: the Mesolithic peoples who developed agriculture and domesticated animals, and the Neolithic (New Stone Age) peoples who advanced still further in perfecting tools and in communal living. It is generally believed that these later peoples constituted additional waves of invaders, probably from Asia, but we have little real knowledge of their origin, or of the evolutionary history of the modern races which in time replaced these older cultural groups.

All of these people were *Homo sapiens* of the modern type, judging from their skeletons. Variations in structure occurred, but these variations did not surpass the range of variation exhibited by modern man.

By 10,000 years ago, and probably before that date (perhaps as long ago as 37,000 years in the case of America: Krieger, 1957), *Homo sapiens* had reached such out-of-the-way regions of the world as Australia and North America.

Human Evolution

How shall we picture the evolution of man? It is frequently diagramed as a tree with limbs, branches, and twigs. But such a picture makes no provision for the diversity of men living at any one time, with the complexities introduced by migrations and gene exchange between populations that intermarry. A twig arises from one branch, not several branches, whereas a descendant may have drawn his genes from several ancestral groups. The tree as a means of picturing human evolution has outlived its usefulness. Fig. 11.16 is an attempt to avoid these shortcomings by picturing human evolution in terms of a pattern of interlacing, interweaving lines. The intent is to convey the impression of many ancestral lines crossing and recrossing as new forms arose, differentiated, combined characteristics by mating with other populations, and passed on their genes to descendants in varying proportion. The thought is that no one hominid living at a certain time was the ancestor of all hominids living at a later time, but that, rather, each later hominid received his collection of genes from varying predecessors, some of whom contributed more than others. As we have stressed

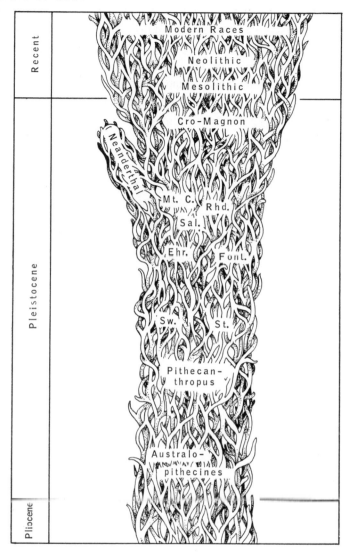

FIG. 11.16. Diagram of human evolution during the Pleistocene.
Ehr., Ehringsdorf; *Font.,* Fontéchevade; *Mt. C.,* Mt. Carmel; *Rhd.,*
Rhodesian; *Sal.,* Saldanha; *St.,* Steinheim; *Sw.,* Swanscombe.

repeatedly, the more we learn of hominids the more we appreciate that
they have always been a variable lot. Like the time-honored tree, our diagram is hypothetical, but it seems to represent better than does the tree
what we are learning both about the history of man's evolution and about
the factors and forces operative in evolution in general.

At various points in the ascending pattern (Fig. 11.16) we have inserted the names of known fossil forms. These are placed to represent successive *stages* in human evolution, with the additional probability implied that they may have contributed some of the genes possessed by their successors. Thus, the australopithecines may have contributed some genes to Pithecanthropus, but so also may some other ancestors as yet unknown to us (not all the lines leading to "Pithecanthropus" emanate from "Australopithecines"). Similarly, Pithecanthropus is generally regarded as ancestral to the mid-Pleistocene forms exemplified by the Swanscombe and Steinheim fossils, but it may or may not have been the only ancestor of these forms. And, as we have noted above, these and later "transitional forms" doubtless contributed both to the ancestry of Neanderthal man and to that of *Homo sapiens* of modern type.

The diagram does not indicate the *extent* of time during which each form lived. The australopithecines, for example, may have arisen in the Pliocene, and they probably lived on as contemporaries of the earliest representatives of Pithecanthropus.

The Human Species

As mentioned earlier, we regard all modern peoples as belonging to one species, *sapiens,* of one genus, *Homo.* What is a species? In Chapter 14 we shall discuss the attributes of this unit of classification. At present we shall confine ourselves to a definition generally acceptable in the light of modern biological knowledge, that of Mayr (1942, 1950): "Species are groups of actually or potentially interbreeding natural populations, which are reproductively isolated from other such groups." Reproductive isolation is discussed in Chapter 20 (pp. 471–473). Briefly, two populations are said to be reproductively isolated from each other if they *do not* interbreed, and hence exchange genes, even when they have opportunity to do so. The red squirrels and gray squirrels in our woods form an example of two species in one genus; although they may live together in the same woods they do not interbreed. They are reproductively isolated from each other.

What is the situation of the modern races of man? Each race is certainly composed of actually or potentially interbreeding populations. Are the races reproductively isolated from each other? Clearly there are no anatomical or physiological incompatibilities separating them. As we shall note later, however, reproductive isolation may at times have a psychological basis. Observation seems to indicate some limited measure of psychological isolation among human races, since members of one race usually *prefer* to marry members of the same race rather than members of other races. Exceptions are common, however. In the absence of social taboos, as, for example, in Hawaii, Jamaica, and many other parts of the world, racial hybridization is frequent and biologically normal. It is upon this basis that we conclude that all living peoples belong to one species.

Parenthetically it will be well to note a dissenting opinion on the statement just made. As we shall see in our discussion of classification (pp. 314–320), the "biological definition" of the word "species" given above is not accepted by everyone. Different species usually differ *structurally,* as well as in the matter of reproductive isolation. If one stresses structural differences and minimizes the importance of reproductive isolation one may conclude that the different races are so different structurally that they should be considered separate species. From time to time various students of human evolution have adopted this view (see Gates, 1948), but most investigators conclude that all modern peoples belong to but one species.

Turning our attention to the prehistoric men, we ask: how should they be classified? As noted previously, Cro-Magnon man has long been considered a member of our species, *sapiens.* In addition we have noted earlier peoples (such as Swanscombe, Steinheim, Ehringsdorf, and Fontéchevade) who had so many *sapiens*-like attributes that placing them in our own species seems justified (Le Gros Clark, 1955, 1959). Actually we can, of course, have no direct knowledge of the matter of reproductive isolation in their cases, but structurally they were so like typical *sapiens* that reproductive isolation from the latter seems unlikely.

As we have seen, some of the Pleistocene peoples combined Neanderthal-like characteristics with *sapiens*-like ones. What shall we say of them? Would they have been reproductively isolated from their more *sapiens*-like contemporaries? And what of the typical or "classic" Neanderthal peoples themselves? Would they have been reproductively isolated from peoples combining Neanderthal-like and *sapiens*-like characteristics, and from *sapiens*-like people? We can not answer these questions with certainty. As noted previously, classic Neanderthals are usually placed in their own species on structural grounds, and called *Homo neanderthalensis.* But perhaps all these late Pleistocene men constituted "actually or potentially interbreeding natural populations" and hence should be considered members of but the one species, *Homo sapiens* (Mayr, 1950).

And what of the various forms that collectively we have called Pithecanthropus, living in earlier Pleistocene times? They are so unlike *Homo sapiens* that they are usually placed in a separate genus (*Pithecanthropus*) from him, though, as noted previously, Mayr (1950) suggested that the differences are not sufficient to warrant separation at the species level, and suggested *Homo erectus* as a suitable name.

Going back to the earliest Pleistocene we find still less agreement concerning the australopithecines. They are customarily separated from *Homo sapiens* by placing them not only in a different species, but also in a different genus and even in a different subfamily (Australopithecinae). This subfamily is usually divided into two or more genera (p. 235). On the other hand, Mayr (1950) suggested that all of them be included in our own genus and in one species, and called *Homo transvaalensis*. Grouping them in one species suggests the unlikelihood that they would have been reproductively isolated from each other.

It will be noted that according to the suggested classification, all *men* of whatever geologic age would be placed in genus *Homo* (Mayr, 1950; Brown, 1958). Variation within the genus would be recognized by separating the various forms, especially those living at different times, into different species. Men living at any one time would usually be considered to belong to one species, though there would be exceptions. Thus, as we have noted, australopithecines and Pithecanthropus may have lived as contemporaries during portions of their respective existences. Probably they were so unlike that they would not have intermarried if they had come into contact with each other, and hence the placing of them in separate species (*H. transvaalensis* and *H. erectus*) would be justified.

Races of Homo sapiens

We have noted that modern men are usually considered to belong to one species, despite racial differences.

What is a race and how does it differ from a species? This question will receive further attention in our discussion of classification (pp. 320–323), where the point is made that race is equivalent to the subdivision of a species known as a *subspecies*. Here we may note that races or subspecies differ from species by the absence of that reproductive isolation forming an important hallmark of species. In addition to reproductive isolation, one species differs from another in some of its genes. The difference in genes usually manifests itself in differences in visible structure and characteristics, although not always. Similarly, one race differs from another in some of the genes present, but in this case the differences are usually less than they are between species. Indeed, the differences between races are more likely to take the form of variations in *frequencies* of occurrence of certain genes than they are to manifest themselves in the form of possession of certain genes by one race, with absence of those genes in another.

Thus races usually differ from species in two ways: (1) absence of reproductive isolation and (2) smaller amount of genetic difference. Both these attributes are complex variables, since there are degrees of reproductive isolation as well as degrees of genetic difference. As noted above, it is largely because of the absence of reproductive isolation that we conclude that the races of man *are* races and not species, despite the genetic differences between them.

The next point is of such great importance for the understanding of what races are, and what they are not, that we regret lack of space to discuss it in greater detail than will be possible here. *The differences between races are of the same kind as the differences between groups of people within races.* Much of our deplorable race prejudice would disappear if people generally could come to understand that fact, with all its implications. In recent years a great volume of evidence has been amassed on this point (see Boyd, 1950; Cold Spring Harbor Symposia on Quantitative Biology, Vol. 15, 1950; Dobzhansky, 1950; Dunn, 1951). A few brief examples must suffice us here.

The blood groups are the human characteristics most thoroughly analyzed as to genetic basis. As we saw earlier (pp. 121–122), racial groups differ in the *proportions* in which these blood groups occur (i.e., in the gene frequencies involved). So do populations *within* racial groups. Most American Indians, for example, exhibit a high percentage of individuals belonging to group O. Yet the Blackfoot and Blood tribes in Montana have an unusually high proportion of members belonging to group A. Contrariwise, groups of people usually considered to belong to different races may be quite similar in their blood group distributions. Thus while a high proportion of group B characterizes Asiatic peoples it is also characteristic of Abyssinians, and of Pygmies in the Congo. Eskimos, Portuguese, and Australian aborigines resemble one another in blood group distributions. We have picked a few examples at random, many others will be found in the references cited in the preceding paragraph. Similar differences and diversity exist in the distributions of the other blood cell substances (M, N, Rh, etc.). A point of great importance for us is the fact that there is no correlation between the distributions of these various substances—they vary in frequency independently of each other, and of such characteristics as skin color.

Another genetically determined trait concerns ability to taste the organic compound phenylthiocarbamide (PTC). Populations in different parts of the world differ in the proportion of persons able to taste this substance. Variability in this regard is independent of the variability in distribution of the several blood group substances.

Most persons think first of skin color when they think of racial differences. But here also there is great variability in amount of skin pigment present in different members of a single racial group. There is also great similarity in this respect among members of some diverse racial groups. Some inhabitants of India, for example, have darker skins than do some inhabitants of Africa. And again, variability in skin color occurs independently of variability in blood groups, tasting ability, and so on. Even hair form (straight, wavy, curly, kinky) is independent of skin color in inheritance, and most importantly, there is no correlation between any of these characteristics and such attributes as mental ability.

In bodily proportions variability within racial groups resembles variability between racial groups, and there is no correlation with blood groups, skin color, hair form, tasting ability, and so on. Thus we think of Scandinavians as tall and long-headed (dolichocephalic) although not all of them are, by any means. Exceptionally tall and long-headed are the Watusi tribe in eastern Africa, while their "next-door neighbors," the Pygmies, form a marked contrast in both respects.

Space permitting, we might add to the list indefinitely. The point we wish to make will be evident from these few examples, however: In the matter of genetic difference a race is only a "constellation of characters," in Boyd's phrase (1950). Races present mosaics of characteristics varying independently in their distribution. A population is called a race if it differs from some other population in relative frequencies of blood group genes, in proportion of individuals possessing the "taster" gene, in frequency of the genes controlling skin color, of the genes controlling hair form, of those controlling eye color, of those controlling stature, of those controlling head shape, and so on. Populations *within* a single race differ in these same ways. Thus races blend imperceptibly into each other and no sharp lines can be drawn between them. As Dobzhansky (1950) stated, "It is most important to realize that the differences between the 'major' human races are fundamentally of the same nature as the relatively minute differences between the inhabitants of adjacent towns and villages."

Accordingly we note that races are populations characterized by certain *frequencies* of the genes. Contrary to older ideas, there is no such thing as a racial "type" which all members of a race tend to approximate. The "typical Negro" or "typical Mongolian" has no more actual existence than does the "average man" about whom we sometimes read. No *individual* ever is "average"; each individual differs from every other in some respects ("identical" twins most closely approach an exception to this statement). We find the same situation when we attempt to classify *individuals* as belonging to one race or another. John Doe, for example, has dark brown skin and kinky hair; he belongs to blood group A, is Rh-positive, round-headed, and a "taster." Richard Roe has dark brown skin and wavy hair; he belongs to blood group B, is Rh-negative, long-headed, and a "non-taster." Despite all the differences between them people generally would classify them both as of the same race on the basis of their one point of similarity: dark brown skin (particularly if their ancestors came from the same continent). A third individual, George Goe, has little skin pigment, has wavy hair, belongs to blood group B, is Rh-negative, long-headed, and a "non-taster." Despite the many similarities between George and Richard people generally would probably not classify them as belonging to the same race, their decision being based on the point that George has little skin pigment while Richard has much.

Of course our imaginary example is oversimplified; many more characteristics than these are involved in classifying people, and the matter of geographic origin is also considered important. As will be noted below, each race probably originated as a group of people isolated geographically from other groups. Eventually the groups expanded and migrated (sometimes unwillingly, as in the case of African slaves migrating to the United States), thereby coming into contact with other groups. Intermarriage between groups occurred. But despite such intermingling attempts are made to classify people by the geographic origin of their ancestors. Thus if some of the ancestors of John Doe and Richard Roe of our preceding paragraph came from Africa, John and Richard would be called Negroes. On the other hand, if John's ancestors came from India and Richard's ancestors came from Africa, John and Richard would be considered to belong to different races. The artificiality of this whole system of classifying people is emphasized by the fact that individuals are not necessarily classified on the basis of the geographic origin of the *majority* of their ancestors. The extreme of absurdity is reached in the case of people most of whose ancestors were European, a minority having been African; such people by custom are classified as Negroes!

As indicated, our greatest lack of perspective concerns skin pigmentation inherited from African ancestors. Of all the genetic characteristics by which individuals differ from one another, why should skin color be the one about which we become emotional? It would be just as sensible for blood group A people to develop a "race prejudice" against blood group B people! The principal difference is that the one characteristic is exposed on the surface for everyone to see, while the other is hidden away, detectable only by serological tests. But the one difference is no more "important" than the other. As a matter of fact, of the genetic characteristics we have mentioned the most "important" is Rh, since in a small proportion of marriages incompatibility in this regard reduces the number of living off-spring producible. There might be some justification for Rh-negative women to develop "race prejudice" against Rh-positive men, and vice versa; in a certain proportion (frequently exaggerated in the public press) of marriages between such individuals difficulty in producing normal chil-dren arises. But there is no justification for race prejudice based on skin color differences.

The idea that there once existed certain so-called "pure races" was for-merly widely prevalent. A corollary was that the great human diversity observed today arose through intermarriage of these "pure races." From our discussion it will be evident that increasing knowledge of early and pre-historic men affords no evidence of "pure races." In fact, quite the opposite is the case: The more we learn of our predecessors on this planet the more we understand that they were always a highly diversified lot of people. We have seen that "racial" differences in the Pleistocene period were at least as great as they are today. Furthermore, we have emphasized the fact that the genes possessed by modern races were undoubtedly derived from a mixed ancestry of Pleistocene peoples (pp. 246–248 and Fig. 11.16).

An attempt to visualize the processes at work may help to unify points included in the preceding discussions. When the ancestors of man first descended from the trees, assumed upright posture, and began to use tools they were probably few in number. As they succeeded in their new en-vironmental niche they increased in numbers and migrated out into new territories. These first men were hunters and their social organization was undoubtedly that of small, roving bands and nomadic tribes. As groups of people became separated from each other opportunity was presented for gradual development of genetic diversity. Certain mutations would have occurred in some isolated groups but not in others. By chance some muta-tions would have been lost in some of the groups in which they occurred and would have become established in some other isolated groups (genetic drift, pp. 349 and 439). Mutations which conferred some advantage on their possessors would have been favored by natural selection (pp. 10, 351, 450). For example, if some groups entered regions characterized by high intensity of sunlight, mutations increasing the amount of pigment in the skin might have been of advantage (protection from harmful concen-trations of ultraviolet rays) and hence might have been favored by natural selection. Thus in such a region the population might eventually have be-come quite dark in color. If, conversely, other groups entered environments having sunlight of low intensity, mutations decreasing pigmentation of the skin might have been favored by natural selection, since maintenance of a certain level of ultraviolet irradiation of the skin is important in providing the body with vitamin D. Consequently in this region a lightly pigmented population might have evolved.

Many of the differences between races are adaptive in this manner, or were adaptive under the conditions in which the races originated. The exact nature of the adaptation has, however, not been analyzed in most instances. Such racial characteristics as are not adaptive may have become established in these isolated populations by chance, as noted above. The net result of these processes was development of diversity among geographically isolated peoples—the production of geographic races.

When these diverse peoples came into contact with each other (migration, conquest) they exchanged genes, as discussed previously (pp. 244–248) and diagramed in Fig. 11.16. Some of the combinations of characteristics thus arising may have proved superior to the characteristics of one or both of the parental populations. If so, natural selection would have favored the new combinations at the expense of the old. Particularly, natural selection seems to have favored the development of bigger and better brains, as we have noted. Such development was of first importance in enabling man to devise tools and to improve them—in other words, in enabling him to become increasingly a civilized man.

If our interpretation is correct, then, modern races are descendants of ancient races, but probably no one modern race is the descendant of any one ancient race alone. Our inability to draw any clear-cut lines between races gives added confidence that such is the case. The genes have been continually "reshuffled" as time, in geologic copiousness, has gone by.

We have sketched in broadest outline the probable course of race formation and racial change, stressing (1) geographic isolation; (2) mutations, and their fate as determined by chance and by natural selection; (3) exchange of genes between populations. These are among the important factors operative in animal, as well as human, evolution. They receive further amplification and discussion in Chapters 15–21.

References and Suggested Readings

Boule, M., and H. V. Vallois. *Fossil Men*, 4th ed. New York: Dryden Press, 1957.

Boyd, W. C. *Genetics and the Races of Man.* Boston: Little, Brown & Co., 1950.

Broom, R., and J. T. Robinson. "Further evidence of the structure of the Sterkfontein ape-man, *Plesianthropus.*" Transvaal Museum, *MEMOIR* 4. Pp. 11–83. (8 plates.)

Broom, R., and G. W. H. Schepers. *The South African Fossil Ape-Men, the Australopithecinae.* Transvaal Museum, *MEMOIR* 2, 1946.

Brown, W. L., Jr. "Some zoological concepts applied to problems in evolution of the hominid lineage," *American Scientist,* 46 (1958), 151–158.

Colbert, E. H. *Evolution of the Vertebrates.* New York: John Wiley & Sons, Inc., 1955.

Dart, R. A. "Cultural status of the South African man-apes," *Annual Report for 1955, Smithsonian Institution.* Washington, D.C., 1956. Pp. 317–338. (4 plates.)

Dart, R. A. *Adventures with the Missing Link.* New York: Harper & Brothers, 1959.

Dobzhansky, Th. "On species and races of living and fossil man," *American Journal of Physical Anthropology,* 2 (1944), 251–265.

Dobzhansky, Th. "The genetic nature of differences among men." In S. Persons (ed.). *Evolutionary Thought in America.* New Haven: Yale University Press, 1950. Pp. 86–155.

Du Brul, E. L., and H. Sicher. *The Adaptive Chin.* Springfield, Ill.: Charles C. Thomas, 1954.

Dunn, L. C. *Race and Biology.* United Nations Educational, Scientific and Cultural Organization (Unesco) Publication 995, 1951.

Gates, R. R. *Human Ancestry from a Genetical Point of View.* Cambridge: Harvard University Press, 1948.

Gregory, W. K. *Evolution Emerging,* 2 vols. New York: The Macmillan Company, 1951.

Howell, F. C. "The evolutionary significance of variation and varieties of 'Neanderthal' man," *Quarterly Review of Biology,* 32 (1957), 330–347.

Hürzeler, J. "*Oreopithecus bambolii* Gervais. A preliminary report," *Verhandlungen der Naturforschenden Gesellschaft in Basel,* 69 (1958), 1–48.

Krieger, A. "Early man," *American Antiquity,* 22 (1957), 321–323.

Leakey, L. S. B. "A new fossil skull from Olduvai," *Nature,* 184 (1959), 491–493. (Description of *Zinjanthropus.*)

Le Gros Clark, W. E. *History of the Primates.* London: British Museum (Natural History); Chicago: University of Chicago Press, 1949–1957.

Le Gros Clark, W. E. *The Fossil Evidence for Human Evolution.* Chicago: University of Chicago Press, 1955.

Le Gros Clark, W. E. "The crucial evidence for human evolution," *Proceedings, American Philosophical Society,* 103 (1959), 159–172. Condensation in *American Scientist,* 47 (1959), 299–313.

Le Gros Clark, W. E. *The Antecedents of Man.* Chicago: Quadrangle Books, Inc., 1960.

Mayr, E. *Systematics and the Origin of Species.* New York: Columbia University Press, 1942.

Mayr, E. "Taxonomic categories in fossil hominids," *Cold Spring Harbor Symposia on Quantitative Biology,* 15 (1950), 109–118.

Napier, J. R., and P. R. Davis. "The fore-limb skeleton and associated remains of *Proconsul africanus,*" *Fossil Mammals of Africa,* 16 (1959), London: British Museum (Natural History). Pp. 1–69. (10 plates.)

"Origin and Evolution of Man," *Cold Spring Harbor Symposia on Quantitative Biology,* 15 (1950).

Robinson, J. T. *The Dentition of the Australopithecinae.* Transvaal Museum, *MEMOIR* 9, 1956.

Romer, A. S. *Vertebrate Paleontology,* 2nd ed. Chicago: University of Chicago Press, 1945.

Romer, A. S. *The Vertebrate Story.* Chicago: University of Chicago Press, 1959.

Simons, E. L. "New fossil primates: a review of the past decade," *American Scientist,* 48 (1960), 179–192.

Simpson, G. G. "The principles of classification and a classification of mammals," *Bulletin, American Museum of Natural History,* 85 (1945), 1–350.

Stewart, T. D. "Form of the pubic bone in Neanderthal man," *Science,* 131 (1960), 1437–1438.

Straus, W. L., Jr. "The riddle of man's ancestry," *Quarterly Review of Biology,* 24 (1949), 200–223.

Straus, W. L., Jr. *"Oreopithecus bambolii,"* *Science,* 126 (1957), 345–346.

Straus, W. L., Jr., and A. J. E. Cave. "Pathology and the posture of Neanderthal man," *Quarterly Review of Biology,* 32 (1957), 348–363.

de Terra, H. "New approach to the problem of man's origin," *Science,* 124 (1956), 1282–1285. (Concerning *Oreopithecus.*)

United Nations Educational, Scientific and Cultural Organization. *Statement on Race.* Unesco Publication 769, 1950; also in *The Race Question,* Unesco Publication 791.

Vallois, H. V. "Neandertals and Praesapiens," *Journal of the Royal Anthropological Institute of Great Britain and Ireland,* 84 (1954), 111–130.

Washburn, S. L. "The analysis of primate evolution with particular reference to the origin of man," *Cold Spring Harbor Symposia on Quantitative Biology,* 15 (1950), 67–78.

Weidenreich, F. "The Skull of *Sinanthropus pekinensis;* a Comparative Study on a Primitive Hominid Skull" *Palaeontologia Sinica,* N. S. No. 10, 1943; whole series No. 127.

Weidenreich, F. *Apes, Giants and Man.* Chicago: University of Chicago Press, 1946.

Zuckerman, S. "Correlation of change in the evolution of higher primates." In J. Huxley, A. C. Hardy, and E. B. Ford (eds.). *Evolution as a Process.* London: Allen & Unwin, Ltd., 1954. Pp. 300–352.

CHAPTER 12

EVOLUTION AS SEEN IN THE GEOGRAPHIC DISTRIBUTION OF ANIMALS: CONTINENTS

Almost everyone knows that if he wishes to hunt lions he should go to Africa, and if tigers are his objective he must travel to India. But of those who know this, how many ever stop to wonder *why* lions are more common in Africa than they are in India, and why tigers are not found in Africa? As a result of studies by persons who have wondered about such things, a subdivision of biology known as geographic distribution or zoogeography has developed.

Zoogeography is concerned with the manner in which animals are distributed over our planet and attempts to explain the observed distributions. We shall commence our discussion of the subject by considering some of the peculiarities encountered in the distribution of animals on the larger land masses of the earth, the continents.

Africa and South America

The two large continents crossed by the equator are South America and Africa. Both have extensive tropical regions. Both extend southward into the Temperate Zone. Both have lowland jungles; extensive river systems; broad, dry plains; and high mountains. In short, both present much the same variety of habitats for living things. We might anticipate, therefore, that both continents would be populated with the same, or closely similar, animals. Such an expectation would differ widely from actuality, however.

In Africa we find **lions, elephants, rhinoceroses, hippopotami,** many kinds of **antelopes, giraffes, zebras, hyenas, lemurs, baboons, monkeys** with narrow noses and nonprehensile tails, **chimpanzees,** and **gorillas,** to enumerate only a random sample.

In South America we find not a single one of the animals just listed. South America has **monkeys,** to be sure, but they are quite unlike their African relatives; many have broad noses and other distinguishing features, including prehensile tails which serve as a fifth limb as they swing through trees. In South America are (Fig. 12.1) (1) **tapirs,** representing the odd-toed, hoofed mammals; (2) a group of rodents of which the **capybara, agouti,** and **paca** are perhaps the best known (our guinea pig is a domesticated relative); (3) **mountain lions** (panthers), **ocelots,** and **jaguars** as representatives of the cat family; (4) **llamas, guanacos, vicuñas,** and **alpacas** as representatives of the camel family. There are also **deer** (absent from Africa except in the neighborhood of the Mediterranean Sea), **armadillos,** many species of **opossums, giant anteaters, raccoons, spectacled bears, chinchillas, peccaries,** and **sloths,** those slow-moving arboreal animals which hang beneath the branches of trees instead of traveling on their upper surfaces. Furthermore, before white men overran the earth the two continents differed as markedly in their human populations as they did in their lower animals. The greater part of Africa was inhabited by various types of Negroes, while South America was inhabited by various types of Indians.

While we have stressed the differences between the mammalian faunas of these two continents, we do not wish to convey the impression that no groups of animals have representatives in both. Such widely ranging animals as bats, rats, mice, squirrels, hares and rabbits, and members of the cat, dog, weasel, and swine families occur in both continents. Despite this fact, however, differences outweigh similarities.

Why do these geographically similar continents differ so markedly in their animal populations? We shall defer the answer to this question until we have gained a more comprehensive view of animal distribution on other continents. We may note in passing, however, that for some people the answer is simple and clear. It is possible to be satisfied with the explanation that these continents have their present inhabitants because the latter were created in place, so to speak. Lions were created in Africa, not in South America; jaguars were created in South America, not in Africa, and so on. For people contented with this explanation the final answer has been given and there is nothing left to explain. Such an "explanation" removes the whole matter from the field of scientific inquiry.

FIG. 12.1. Typical South American placental mammals. Not drawn to scale.

In this connection we may note an interesting relationship between the distinctiveness of animals and the length of time they have occupied a given continent. This is particularly evident in South America, as pointed out by Simpson (1950), who called the relationship **faunal stratification.** The fossil record shows that armadillos and sloths, for example, occurred in South America as long ago as the earliest Cenozoic. There are no sloths anywhere else in the world, and no armadillos either, except as they later spread northward in the Americas. These forms are representative of the oldest "stratum."

An intermediate stratum is exemplified by the New World monkeys, which, as we have seen, are unlike the Old World forms in many respects. They have lived in South America since mid-Cenozoic.

As examples of a later stratum Simpson cited the field mice, which are closely allied to those of North America. They have formed part of the South American fauna since late Cenozoic times only.

Thus we see as a general trend a relationship between the length of time an animal has inhabited a given continent and the amount of differentiation that animal has undergone. Such a relationship is eloquent of evolution. If animals were created as they are and remained unchanging such a relationship would be meaningless, or would have to be ascribed to mere coincidence. We shall return to this relationship between elapsed time and amount of differentiation when we discuss the organisms of oceanic islands (see especially pp. 292–293).

Australia

The Tropic of Capricorn crosses not only southern Africa and South America but also the continent of Australia. The animal inhabitants of that isolated continent are most unlike those of either of the other two continents crossed by the Tropic. Everyone knows of the Australian kangaroos, for the young of which a fur-lined pouch on the abdomen of the mother serves as nest and living perambulator. The kangaroos belong to the subdivision of Class Mammalia characterized by possession of such a pouch, or marsupium, and hence called **marsupials** (see p. 192). Africa has no marsupials; South America has opossums and some tiny creatures known as caenolestids. In passing we might note that marsupials are also absent from Asia, and only one species, the so-called Virginia opossum, occurs in North America. How does it happen that marsupials are found only in such widely separated regions of the earth as America and Australia? The question suggests something of the complexity of problems confronting zoogeographers but belongs properly in a later portion of this discussion (pp. 265–267).

Before the coming of man, with his intentional and unintentional introduction of foreign species, Australia apparently had only bats, rats, and mice as representatives of **placental mammals** (pp. 191–192), the group which predominates in other regions of the globe. A dog, the dingo, is also present but may have been introduced by early man.

The Australian realm is unique as the home of the only living representatives of the group of mammals which lay eggs, the **monotremes** (p. 189). These representatives are the duckbilled platypus (*Ornithorhynchus*) and the spiny anteater (*Echidna*) (Fig. 12.2).

Aside from this sparse representation of placental mammals and monotremes, Australia is populated by an odd assemblage of marsupials (Fig.

FIG. 12.2. Monotremes. *Echidna* (spiny anteater), left; and *Ornithorhynchus* (duckbilled platypus), right.

12.3). In many ways they parallel the adaptations of placental mammals in the rest of the world, affording striking examples of that parallel evolution which we have stressed in other connections. Thus we find **kangaroos** of assorted sizes and means of livelihood. Most of them are terrestrial, though the **tree kangaroo** has forsaken life on the ground for life in trees. The **great red kangaroo** is the closest Australian approach to the swift-moving, grazing animals of other continents (deer, antelope, horses, and so on).

The **koala,** a slow-moving, nocturnal marsupial which has captured the popular imagination as a living "teddy bear," lives in eucalyptus trees, feeding on the leaves. **Marsupial moles** burrow in the ground just as do true moles in other parts of the world. **Wombats** are marsupials which have developed rodentlike teeth and have habits much like those of our woodchucks. Some **phalangers** resemble squirrels, while the **flying phalanger**

FIG. 12.3. Typical marsupials of the Australian region. Not drawn to scale. (Mainly after Troughton, *Furred Animals of Australia*, copyright 1947, Charles Scribner's Sons.)

resembles a flying squirrel in having membranes stretched between fore and hind limbs to provide planes useful in gliding.

Of the other marsupials of Australia and neighboring Tasmania we may mention **hare wallabies,** little kangaroolike creatures with habits much like those of our rabbits, the **Tasmanian wolf,** a carnivorous marsupial resembling true wolves in many respects, the **Tasmanian devil,** a carnivorous creature reminiscent of our badgers, and the **banded anteater,** a small marsupial with pointed snout and long, sticky, extensible tongue, the hallmarks of anteaters of whatever relationship the world over. In sum, the marsupials of the Australian region furnish a most striking example of that *adaptive radiation* discussed in an earlier chapter (pp. 26–29).

Eurasia and North America

The foregoing discussion reveals that the three continents of the Southern Hemisphere present marked contrasts in animal inhabitants. In the Northern Hemisphere, however, we find the contrasts much less striking.

The faunas of Eurasia and North America abound in animals which are either identical or closely similar. Confining our discussion to mammals, we may mention such widely ranging groups as deer, cats, wolves, foxes, otters, weasels, badgers, moles, shrews, rats, and mice. Many of these are found not only in the two northern continents now under consideration but also in many other regions of the earth. Restricting our attention to mammals more distinctive of the two northern land masses, we may mention some of the hoofed animals common to both: (1) **bison,** sometimes called buffalo in this country; (2) the large deer called **moose** in this country, elk in Europe; (3) the **wapiti,** frequently called elk in this country, closely similar to the stag of Europe (see comments on "common" names! p. 308); (4) **reindeer** or caribou; (5) the North American **mountain goat,** closely akin to the chamois of Europe; (6) the **mountain sheep** or bighorn.

Bears afford another example of the similarity of mammalian life on the two northern continents. Aside from one species inhabiting the Atlas Mountains of North Africa, and the peculiar spectacled bear living in the Andes of South America, bears are confined to these northern continents. Among the various species the **polar bear** is familiar to all as a denizen of circumpolar arctic regions.

Both northern continents have beavers, lynxes ("bobcats"), varying hares (brownish gray in summer, white in winter), and those odd little relatives of hares and rabbits, the pikas or conies. The list might be greatly extended, as well as expanded to include birds and other animals, but the examples cited will suffice to demonstrate the far-reaching similarities characterizing the faunas of these northern continents.

In the preceding paragraphs we have presented evidence that the three continents in the Southern Hemisphere differ markedly in their animal inhabitants, whereas the two great land masses in the Northern Hemisphere are closely similar in this respect. Can we now find some reasonable explanation for the contrasted situations in the two hemispheres?

Accessibility

As we examine a map, preferably a globe, we are struck by the fact that the three southern continents are widely separated from one another by expanses of ocean, whereas the northern land masses are nearly in contact, being separated from each other by only the 56 miles of Bering Strait. Perhaps, then, accessibility forms the clue we are seeking. This seems all the more likely when we realize that Bering Strait is shallow as well as narrow, and that there is every reason to believe that in various past geologic periods the region lay above sea level to create a continuous bridge of land between North America and Asia. A similar bridge may have existed between Europe and North America, perhaps by way of Iceland and Greenland, but the evidence for it is less conclusive than is the evidence for the Alaska-Siberia connection. The latter must have made possible extensive migrations between Eurasia and North America, which would explain in large measure the great similarities of animal life observed to occur in these two great land masses.

Turning to the Southern Hemisphere, we note that *inaccessibility* characterizes the three southern continents. Widely separated from one another, such connections as they have are with northern continents.

Of the three, Australia is the most completely isolated. Perhaps it was at one time connected to the continent of Asia by a land bridge of which the East Indian islands to the northwest represent the unsubmerged remnants. But the connection, if it ever existed, must have been extremely ancient. While only shallow ocean separates many of these islands (e.g., Borneo, Sumatra, Java) from Asia, there are deeper stretches between Australia and the islands mentioned. Evidence seems to indicate that Australia has been isolated from Asia since at least Cretaceous times (p. 137).

Did the ancestors of the monotremes and marsupials reach Australia by land before the present isolation of the continent occurred? Such an explanation is possible, though, as Simpson (1943, 1953) has pointed out, it may be more probable that these ancestors reached Australia by being transported from island to island across intervening ocean. Methods by which such transport might occur are discussed in the following chapter. "Island hopping" involves a large element of chance. The chances are against the dispersal of any terrestrial animal in this manner. As we have seen (p. 191), marsupial and placental mammals arose at about the same time. Why did the marsupials and not the placentals reach Australia originally? Simpson (1953) has suggested that this outcome was determined by chance. Once having chanced to arrive, the early marsupial immigrants were afforded opportunity for the remarkable adaptive radiation described above.

Until man began his introduction of placental mammals, among the latter only fliers, bats, and such accomplished stowaways as rodents had been able to reach the island continent. Even the rodents were few in number. Simpson (1943) stated that their immigration could not have occurred before the Oligocene; most probably it began in the Miocene, with occasional rodent immigrants arriving at later dates. At any rate, these rodent immigrations must have been unaided by any direct land connections.

Some reader may suspect that the reason higher mammals were not more abundant in Australia was because this continent was not suited to them. We should point out, therefore, the marked success some species of placental mammals have had following introduction by man. Rabbits, for example, introduced by man, have in some regions increased in numbers so prodigiously as to become a serious economic liability, as well as to cause extinction in those regions of marsupials dependent upon the food supply the rabbits have successfully monopolized. A similar situation prevails in New Zealand, where animals introduced originally for sport have thrived so mightily that the forest is being destroyed. The worst offender is the European red deer. Clark (1949) estimated that in 1942 there were at least 90,000 of them on South Island, another 10,000 grazers being composed collectively of fallow deer, Virginia deer, thar (a beardless wild goat from the Himalayas), chamois, wapiti, and moose. Wild pigs, goats, and sheep add to the destruction. In some regions overpopulation is so great that the forest resembles a trampled cattle yard, all young growth being destroyed and even adult trees suffering devastation. Evidently, then, inaccessibility rather than unsuitability is the key to explanation of the original unique fauna in the Australian region.

To a considerable extent the same explanation applies to the peculiarities of the South American fauna. The connection of this continent to North America is the tenuous Isthmus of Panama. At various times in geologic history that isthmus has been submerged, leaving South America isolated from its northern neighbor. During most of the Tertiary, South America was cut off in this manner. We recall that this period saw the evolution of the placental mammals (Chap. 10). The fact that the evolution of South American mammals followed its own course, largely independently of that of the rest of the world, is doubtless attributable to the fact that during long periods South American forms had no contact with those on other continents. Thus in isolation interrupted only occasionally the peculiar guinea-pig-like rodents (cavy, agouti, capybara, paca, and their kin), the distinctive South American monkeys, the porcupines, the armadillos, the sloths, the anteaters, the opossums, and many other unique animals were free to undergo adaptive radiation only slightly less striking than that of Australian marsupials.

In somewhat similar manner the animals in the regions of Africa south of the Sahara and adjoining deserts have undergone independent evolution in at least partial isolation. The animals of northern Africa more closely resemble those of Europe than they do those of central and southern portions of the continent. This again is understandable upon a basis of accessibility, since at various times the barrier presented by the Mediterranean Sea has been bridged—at the narrow Strait of Gibraltar, for example. On the other hand, the deserts form an effective barrier to dispersal of mammals adapted for life in forests, or for life on open plains which are not deserts.

We have been developing the idea that accessibility and inaccessibility play major roles in the distribution of animals. If an animal is to live in a certain region, (1) it must be able to reach that region, and (2) the region must be suitable for the existence of that animal. The second point is so self-evident as to need little elaboration. Obviously, for example, animals like frogs which have no adequate means of preventing loss of water from the body cannot live in deserts. Or again, since frogs and toads burrow into the soil to hibernate through the winter, they are not found in regions so far north that the subsoil remains frozen throughout the year. Examples of limitation of distribution by unsuitability of environments might be multiplied almost endlessly. But from the standpoint of the present discussion chief interest lies in the observed fact that animals do not inhabit all regions suitable to them. We cannot conclude that because an animal is not found in a given region the latter is necessarily unsuitable for it. If animals were separately and specially created, failure to find an animal in every region suited to it would be mysterious, to say the least. If, on the other hand, animals have evolved from predecessors which differed in structure and, frequently, in place of origin, failure to find an animal in a region suited to it but inaccessible to it is exactly what we should expect.

Centers of Dispersal

There emerges from our discussion a picture of new forms arising from old ones in certain regions and then migrating out from the "old home" in search of new worlds to conquer. We must hasten to add that this migration and "search" are not to any considerable extent voluntary activities of individual animals. Rather they represent slowly developing changes involving many generations and produced by many factors, including eventual overcrowding of what we have spoken of as the "old home" but what is more accurately termed the **center of dispersal.**

As examples of dispersal from such a center we may cite the evolutionary history of placental mammals. We recall that the evolution and dispersal of placental mammals occupied the center of the stage during the Cenozoic era (Chap. 10).

If we look at the continents of Eurasia and North America on a map drawn with the North Pole as a center (Fig. 12.4), we note that these lands form the greater portion of a circle around the pole and if Bering Strait were dry land would form one continuous land mass. Lowering the level of the ocean, or raising its floor, by only 150 feet would provide a dry-land connection across the strait. This land connection is believed to have arisen at various times in the past, most recently during the Pleistocene period when much water was locked up in continental glaciers. Most of Alaska seems to have remained free of glaciers. Hence during various periods of Pleistocene glaciation the land bridge could have afforded passage into the New World to such creatures as bison, musk oxen, goats, moose, woolly mammoths, and mastodons. Man himself probably also utilized this bridge, which was last open for the period between 25,000 years and about 10,000 years ago (Hopkins, 1959).

Most students of geographic distribution agree that this circumpolar land mass has provided the route by which animals have been distributed to the continents of the world. This land mass forms a hub from which three great spokes radiate southward, to terminate, respectively, in South America, Africa, and southeastern Asia with its adjoining islands (Fig. 12.4). What was the point of origin and center of dispersal for modern orders of mammals? Matthew (1939) concluded that these orders originated in the North Temperate zone with its variable climate. Thus most of the evolution of the horse occurred in North America, as did that of the camels (see below). Other examples might be given. On the other hand, Darlington (1957) marshalled evidence that animals, including mammals, are on the whole more diverse and numerous in kinds in the tropics than they are in temperate zones. He concluded that "the main center of dispersal of mam-

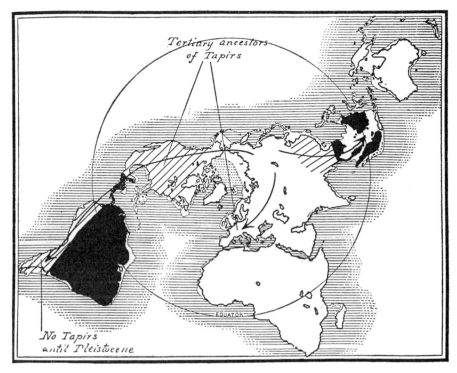

FIG. 12.4.   Geographic distribution of tapirs. Present range shown in solid black; range during Pleistocene shown in diagonal lines. Arrows radiate from center of dispersal. (From Matthew, *Climate and Evolution*, Special Publications of New York Academy of Sciences, Vol. I, 1939, p. 71.)

mals seems therefore to have been the main part of the Old World and especially the tropical part of it." He concluded that the Old World tropics was also the center of dispersal of fresh-water fishes, amphibians, reptiles, and birds.

If dispersal from a center is an actuality we should expect to find evidence of it in the fossil record. Fortunately that expectation is realized, despite the imperfections of the known portions of the record. From many possible examples we shall cite only two. They are of particular interest since they involve striking examples of *discontinuity* in the ranges of living animals.

Tapirs

The first example is that of tapirs, animals with which most readers are not likely to be familiar. Tapirs are the least specialized of the odd-toed hoofed mammals (Order Perissodactyla); they have four toes on each forefoot, three on each hindfoot, being reminiscent of the Eocene peris-sodactyl *Hyracotherium* in that respect. In general appearance they some-what resemble very large pigs. Their most unusual feature is a nose and upper lip drawn out into a short, flexible proboscis, a sort of incipient ele-phant's trunk (Fig. 12.1). But perhaps the most remarkable thing about them is their distribution. They live in only two regions: (1) Central and South America and (2) the Malay Peninsula and adjacent islands such as Sumatra and Borneo. Fig. 12.4 reminds us that these areas, shown in solid black, are about as distant from each other as two points on this earth can be. How does it happen that tapirs are found in these two widely separated areas?

If we are not satisfied with the explanation that the tapirs were created in the two regions mentioned, and not elsewhere, we find no clue to the an-swer to our question in the living animals themselves. When we turn to the fossil record, however, the explanation becomes clear. As indicated by the diagonally shaded portions of the map, during Pleistocene times tapirs ranged all over North and South America, and through considerable por-tions of Europe and Asia. In preceding Cenozoic periods ancestral tapirs lived in Europe and North America, where they were found as long ago as the Oligocene. Interestingly enough, tapirs did not reach one of their two modern havens, South America, until the Pleistocene. This fact correlates well with the isolation of that continent from North America during long periods of the Tertiary. Tapirs apparently never reached Africa.

Evidently, then, the present widely separated regions inhabited by tapirs represent isolated portions of a once widespread range. For some reason tapirs disappeared from the intervening regions. Doubtless changing en-vironmental conditions, coupled with competition from animals better fitted for them, were factors in causing this disappearance.

Camels

Camels and their South American relatives supply another example of discontinuity in modern range, explicable by reference to the fossil record.

Of the camel-like inhabitants of South America, the llama and alpaca are domesticated animals derived originally from wild, camel-like forms inhabiting the continent before the coming of man. The llama (cf. guanaco, Fig. 12.1) is smaller than a camel and lacks the characteristic hump of the latter, but its undoubted relationship to camels is revealed by many anatomical features. The limbs of the camel family are character-istic, being elongated and having two equally developed toes. All traces of lateral digits have been lost; i.e., no "splint bones" are present as they are in the horse (p. 23). The digits of the one-humped Arabian camel spread widely, offering effective support on soft desert sands. The feet of the two-humped Bactrian camel of central Asia, as well as those of the llama, are harder and less spreading, adapted for firmer and rockier terrain.

Camels and their South American relatives have a highly discontinuous distribution (Fig. 12.5). As shown by the solid black areas of the map, true

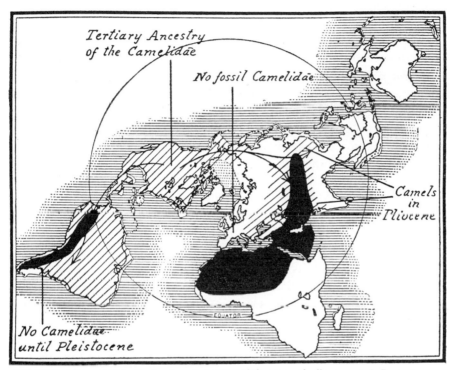

FIG. 12.5. Geographic distribution of the Camelidae (camels, llamas, etc.). Present range shown in solid black; range during Pleistocene shown by diagonal lines. Arrows radiate from center of dispersal. (From Matthew, *Climate and Evolution*, Special Publications of New York Academy of Sciences, Vol. I, 1939, p. 76.)

camels inhabit Africa, to the southern edge of the Sahara desert, Arabia, and the highlands of Asia. Llamas and their relatives inhabit the highlands of South America. The discontinuity between these ranges is almost as great as that between the two parts of the range of tapirs. As in the case of the latter, the explanation of the situation becomes evident when the fossil record is consulted. During Pleistocene times camels ranged over North and South America, Northern Africa, and most of Asia. Apparently they first reached the Old World in the Pliocene but did not reach South America until the Pleistocene. Again we note the effect of the isolation of the latter continent during most of the Tertiary.

Rather surprisingly, perhaps, for an animal we do not usually associate with our own country, the major portion of camel evolution occurred in North America. Here the fossil record dates back to the Eocene, to a little animal, *Protylopus,* which was in a stage of evolution comparable to that of *Hyracotherium* in the horse line. The subsequent evolutionary history of camels is almost as completely documented by North American fossils as is the evolution of the horse.

Evidently, therefore, North America was the center of camel evolution and dispersal. Camels reached the Old World across the Bering Strait land bridge, and South America across the Isthmus of Panama, when the latter was elevated above the sea in Pleistocene times (see arrows on the map, Fig. 12.5). Subsequently, camels became extinct in their center of dispersal, North America. As for the disappearance of the horses (p. 206), the reason is not known, although the same factor or factors may well have operated in both instances.

Barriers

The examples cited above reveal a common pattern underlying much of evolution and dispersal. An animal arises by evolution in a certain region. Typically it then attempts to expand its range, under pressure of factors such as overpopulation in the original center. Whether or not it succeeds in expanding its range, and the extent of expansion, depends upon many factors.

First among such factors we may mention **physical barriers.** Bodies of water are barriers to land-dwelling animals, the effectiveness of the barrier depending upon the attributes of the particular animal in question. Conversely, dry land is a barrier to the dispersal of aquatic animals. High mountain ranges, deserts, open plains (to forest dwellers), forest (to dwellers on open plains), as well as such climatic factors as intolerable extremes of temperature and many other physical factors serve as barriers to the dispersal of one animal or another.

No less effective are **biological barriers.** Among examples of these we may mention absence from a given region of food suitable to the species in question, presence in a given region of competitors for the same food supply or nesting sites, presence in a region of predatory animals, and the like.

The action of barriers may be nearly or quite complete, as in the case of the barrier to amphibian dispersal presented by sea water, or the barrier may be only partially effective. The degree of effectiveness depends not only upon the nature of the barrier itself but also upon the nature of the animals concerned. In general, a species can surmount a barrier in one of two ways: (1) by being adaptable to a variety of living conditions or (2) by giving rise to new forms adapted to conditions unsuitable for the parent species itself.

Adaptability is a most valuable attribute. Animals possessing it can extend their ranges into regions which offer conditions of life differing from those in the center of dispersal. Animals possessed of a generous measure of this quality range widely and change but little in response to the varying habitats they enter. In this way the various species of Old World rats and mice, for example, have achieved distribution as world-wide as that of man himself. And man is the star example of a form able to surmount all barriers to dispersal by virtue of adaptability.

Lack of adaptability, on the other hand, hinders, when it does not prevent, such dispersal. Furthermore, it may lead to extinction of a species in its home area if conditions in that area change sufficiently. The geologic record affords many examples of such extinctions. Between the extremes are found intermediate degrees of adaptability, contributing to the varying degrees of success with which animals meet changing conditions, either "at home" or as the species attempts to extend its range into new areas.

Animals which do not possess adaptability enabling them to live in a wide variety of habitats may be able to solve the problem of invading new and differing regions in a different manner. They may be able to give rise to new forms capable of living under conditions which the original species could not tolerate. This solution is a much more common occurrence than is the possession of the high degree of adaptability or versatility just discussed. Evidence that evolution of new forms has occurred is provided by the observation that *as animals have radiated out from their center of dispersal they have frequently become modified in various ways so that they are no longer identical with each other or with their ancestors.* The camels are a case in point. The llama, the Bactrian camel, and the Arabian camel differ somewhat from one another, and each differs somewhat from the camels which formerly inhabited North America, their center of dispersal (Fig. 12.5). Such differences, superimposed on fundamental similarities and correlated with the distribution of the forms concerned, offer eloquent testimony of evolution.

Continuous Ranges

While tapirs and camels afford examples of marked discontinuity in geographic range, the distribution of many groups of animals is more or less continuous, related forms being found in regions between the center of dispersal and outlying areas. Such a situation is no less interesting for the study of evolution than is discontinuity of range. In fact, in his brief auto-biography, Darwin mentioned this fact of "the manner in which closely allied animals replace one another in proceeding southwards over the Continent" (South America) as one of the three observations which most strongly directed his thinking into evolutionary lines.

In his *Origin of Species* Darwin wrote, "The naturalist, in traveling, for instance, from north to south, never fails to be struck by the manner in which successive groups of beings, specifically distinct, though nearly related, replace each other. He hears from closely allied, yet distinct kinds of birds notes nearly similar, and sees their nests similarly constructed, but not quite alike, with eggs colored in nearly the same manner."

This observation of Darwin's suggests a frequently observed phenomenon: that related races or species may be observed to vary in a regular way as one progresses from one part of their geographic range to another. For example, in the common zebra inhabiting the southern half of Africa the black striping of the legs steadily decreases (and in a form now extinct eventually disappeared) in a progressive series from north to south (Fig. 12.6). Such a character gradient has been called by Julian Huxley a **cline.** Multitudes of examples might be cited (for comprehensive summaries see Goldschmidt, 1940, and Huxley, 1942). A typical example comes from the work of Alpatov, who investigated honeybees throughout European Russia. He found that from north to south the tongue increases in length, the abdomen becomes lighter in color, and the wax gland decreases in size (Goldschmidt, 1940). These changes were observed to occur in a regular gradient, intermediate localities having bees with intermediate characteristics. In this case at least some of the changes observed may be connected with adaptation of the bees to different conditions. The nectar-secreting flowers in southern Russia may differ from those in northern Russia sufficiently to necessitate the longer tongue observed, for instance. We might well expect that when over a wide territory the climate and other environmental factors change gradually, the nature of the organisms inhabiting the successive parts of the territory would change gradually also. This is not to suggest that all characteristics observed to form clines are adaptive in nature. Some may be neutral (nonadaptive). In the absence of any evidence to the contrary, for example, we might suspect that the striping of the legs of the zebras noted above is such a neutral trait. Such phenomena as the gradual dispersion of genes from a center of dispersal could give rise to clines even when the resulting variation in characteristics

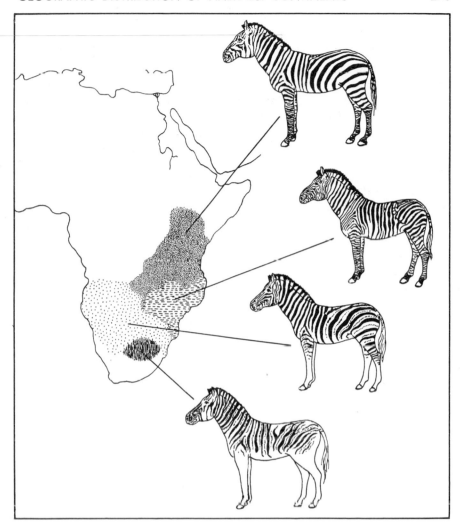

FIG. 12.6.   Cline exhibited in the striping of the legs of the common zebra (*Equus burchellii* or *quagga*) in the different portions of its range in Africa south of the Sahara Desert. (Striping patterns redrawn from Cabrera, "Subspecific and individual variation in the Burchell zebras," *Journal of Mammalogy*, Vol. 17, 1936, pp. 89–112.)

would be of no value to the organism in aiding its adaptation to the environment.

Frequently, however, clines do involve adaptive changes; this fact is reflected in what have come to be called the zoogeographic rules. **Bergmann's rule** states that in warm-blooded animals the body size increases with decrease in average temperature. This means in the northern hemisphere that body size increases in the northern parts of the range, as compared to the size exhibited in the southern portions. Thus our common deer averages larger in the northern parts of its range than it does in the southern. The same is true of many other mammals and birds. Large size in a cold climate has adaptive value in preventing loss of body heat. Since the mass of a body (e.g., a sphere) increases as the cube of the diameter while the surface area increases only as the square, larger bodies have *relatively* less area through which to lose heat than do smaller ones. Hence it is of value to a warm-blooded animal in a cold climate to be large.

Loss of heat through exposed areas of limbs, tail, and ears would also be disadvantageous to an animal in a cold climate. **Allen's rule** states that such exposed portions of the body decrease in size with decrease of aver-

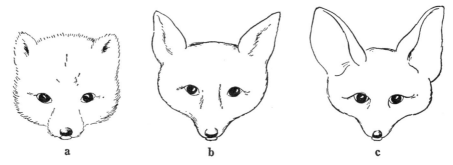

      a   b   c

FIG. 12.7. Head of arctic fox (a), red fox (b), and desert fox (c). (From Guyer, *Animal Biology*, Harper & Brothers, 1948, p. 175; redrawn from Hesse, Allee, and Schmidt, *Ecological Animal Geography*, John Wiley & Sons, Inc., 1937.)

age temperature. Comparison of the size of ears of an arctic fox, a fox of the temperate woodlands, and a desert fox illustrates the principle (Fig. 12.7). Of course the large ears of the desert fox may also have some positive adaptive value for that species.

Gloger's rule states that "among warm-blooded animals those living in warmer and moister climates develop more melanin pigment [are darker than are animals in cold, dry climates], whereas forms in dry, hot climates have more yellow and red pigment" (Goldschmidt, 1940). There are other trends sometimes stated as "rules,"—e.g., within bird species the number of eggs in a clutch increases from south to north. All of these rules are generalizations, and all have their exceptions. They describe tendencies exhibited in general by many clines.

The existence of clines themselves is perhaps the most interesting fact for our present purposes. They demonstrate a pattern of variability exhibited by species. This variability throughout a geographic region is most eloquent of evolution, as Darwin recognized. The phenomenon is exactly what we should expect if dispersal from a center, accompanied by evolutionary change, is a fact. If, on the other hand, all these neighboring, slightly differing, forms were separately created, what a vast multitude of separate creations must have occurred!

The variability of species just mentioned forms the basis upon which species are commonly divided into geographic races or subspecies (see pp. 320–327 for additional discussion).

Conclusions

We have seen that similar continents are not necessarily populated with similar animals. Similarity among continents in animal inhabitants depends far more upon the accessibility of those continents to the same animals than it does upon mere similarity of living conditions. Accordingly, the faunas of northern continents are more similar to each other than the faunas of southern continents are similar to each other or to the faunas of the northern continents. This relationship is explained by the relative accessibility of all parts of the Northern Hemisphere, contrasted with the relative inaccessibility of the main land masses in the Southern Hemisphere.

The role played by accessibility is entirely understandable if animals are found where they are, not because they were created on the spot, but because they could get there. Presumably some animals originate in a certain region and never disperse far from their point of origin. But such a stay-at-home history is the exception, not the rule. Most animals have attempted to expand their ranges, the attempts meeting with greater or less success depending upon the barriers encountered and upon the versatility and adaptability of the organisms themselves.

As animals move into new regions success is frequently achieved by adoption of bodily changes in structure and function. The changes may be great enough so that the resulting forms can no longer be considered to belong to the same species as the stock from which they arose. Such new races or species will, however, retain many points of similarity to each other and to the parent form. Since, at first at least, these kindred species occupy adjoining territories, the phenomenon of similar species replacing each other as one travels across the face of a continent arises. Eventually the original and derived species may become extinct throughout a considerable portion of their range, leaving remnants widely separated from each other, as in the cases of tapirs and camels. In such instances the original range can frequently be reconstructed by reference to the fossil record. All of these phenomena have significance if animals originate in separate regions (centers of dispersal) and then spread into those territories accessible to them, undergoing evolutionary change as their ranges expand into new environments.

References and Suggested Readings

Clark, A. H. *The Invasion of New Zealand by People, Plants and Animals. The South Island.* New Brunswick, New Jersey: Rutgers University Press, 1949.

Darlington, P. J., Jr. *Zoogeography: the Geographical Distribution of Animals.* New York: John Wiley & Sons, Inc., 1957.

Darwin, C. *The Origin of Species by Means of Natural Selection,* 1859. (Obtainable in the Modern Library series, Random House, New York; and as Mentor Book MT294, New American Library, New York.)

Darwin, C. *Autobiography.* In F. Darwin. *The Life and Letters of Charles Darwin,* Vol. 1, Ch. 2, and *Charles Darwin, Autobiography and Letters,* Ch. 2. New York: D. Appleton & Co., 1888 and 1892. Also in F. Darwin (ed.). *Charles Darwin's Autobiography.* New York: Henry Schuman, Inc., 1950.

Goldschmidt, R. *The Material Basis of Evolution.* New Haven: Yale University Press, 1940.

Hopkins, D. M. "Cenozoic history of the Bering land bridge," *Science,* 129 (1959), 1519–1528.

Huxley, J. S. *Evolution—the Modern Synthesis.* New York: Harper & Brothers, 1942.

Matthew, W. D. *Climate and Evolution,* 2nd ed. New York: New York Academy of Sciences, 1939.

Simpson, G. G. "Mammals and the nature of continents," *American Journal of Science,* 241 (1943), 1–31.

Simpson, G. G. "History of the fauna of Latin America," *American Scientist,* 38 (1950), 361–389.

Simpson, G. G. *Evolution and Geography.* Eugene, Oregon: Oregon State System of Higher Education, 1953.

Solecki, R. "How man came to North America," *Scientific American,* 184 (1951), 11–15.

Wallace, A. R. *The Geographical Distribution of Animals,* 2 vols. New York: Harper & Brothers, 1876.

CHAPTER 13

EVOLUTION AS SEEN IN THE GEOGRAPHIC DISTRIBUTION OF ANIMALS: OCEANIC ISLANDS

Animal distribution on continents is highly complex. The situation observed at present is the result of long series of changing events stretching back through the dim vistas of geologic time. Continents present a multiplicity of varied habitats open to animals capable of occupying them. Periods of isolation of continents, or portions of continents, resulting from submergence of intervening land, alternate with periods of connection, when the intervening land is again above sea level. Changing climates over great portions of the earth, extinction of previous inhabitants, appearance of new forms—these and many other factors operating through the ages have rendered the continental zoogeographic record intricate and difficult to decipher. Accordingly, zoogeographers turn to oceanic islands as a means of studying factors operating in evolution and distribution under simpler conditions. Oceanic islands may be thought of as affording the zoogeographer an approach to laboratory experimentation. Unfortunately biologists were not on hand to record the birth and subsequent population of the oceanic islands upon which we must depend at present for most of our knowledge of the subject. Consequently inferences must be drawn as to the beginnings of most of the "experiments." Nevertheless, the inferences can in many cases be made with considerable confidence. Thus oceanic islands have always held particular fascination for students of geographic distribution.

Continental Islands

Islands in the oceans of the world are classified into two categories: continental islands and oceanic islands. **Continental islands** are those which were at some time in the past connected to a continent; **oceanic islands** are those which have never been connected to a continent. For the most part, the former are located on the continental shelves of the continents nearest them; they are usually connected to the neighboring continent by shallow ocean, 100 fathoms (600 feet) or less in depth. (Note that in Figs. 12.4 and 12.5, pp. 269 and 271, certain regions of the ocean bordering continents and lying between them and neighboring islands have been left unshaded. These are the regions which are 100 fathoms or less in depth.) The maps indicate, therefore, that if the land were raised, or the ocean lowered, by 100 fathoms many islands would be connected to continents near them. For example, the British Isles would be connected to Europe (Fig. 12.5); Borneo, Sumatra, Java, and neighboring islands would be connected to southeastern Asia; New Guinea would be connected to Australia; Ceylon would be connected to India; Japan would be connected to Asia; and so on. All these, then, are continental islands, since there is no doubt that the ocean level has in times past fluctuated at least as much as the amount indicated.

In plant and animal life, continental islands are characterized by resemblance to the continent to which they were formerly joined. Naturally the resemblance is greatest if the connection to the continent was recent in geologic time, less if the connection was more remote in time, permitting the appearance meantime of new forms on the continent, and perhaps also on the island. Of particular interest in comparision to the fauna of oceanic islands is the fact that continental islands possess amphibians and also the large mammals characteristic of the neighboring continent. Thus, the mammals of the British Isles are in the main identical with those of Europe; and Borneo, Java, and Sumatra have tapirs, rhinoceroses, deer, wild dogs, members of the cat family, and other mammals found on the neighboring Asiatic mainland. It is most unlikely that such a mammalian fauna would have reached these islands except over dry land.

Nature of Oceanic Islands

Typical oceanic islands are not located on continental shelves. Most of them are far from any continent, with hundreds or thousands of miles of deep ocean in between. Most of them are the summits of mountain peaks rising from the ocean floor through thousands of feet of water and thence on up into the air. Most of them are volcanic, many still actively so.

FIG. 13.1.   Birth of a volcanic island. One of a group of new volcanic Islands pushing its way up from the sea floor 200 miles south of Tokyo, Japan. Seen from the USS *Norton Sound* (AV-11), Lat. 31–57 N., Long. 140–01 E. (Official Department of Defense photo.)

A dramatic view of the birth of such an island is shown in Fig. 13.1. Here the summit of a submerged volcanic mountain is caught in the act of breaking the surface of the Pacific, like a giant erupting tooth. From such beginnings oceanic islands are built. Perhaps the one shown in the picture may not develop into a large island; it may remain a small "bird rock," so called because the principal inhabitants are sea birds which use the small island for nesting. On the other hand, it may continue to thrust itself upward until it becomes a towering mountain rivaling Mauna Kea in the Hawaiian group. Mauna Kea rises 31,750 feet above the ocean floor and hence is the world's highest mountain, measured from base to summit.

How Oceanic Islands Are Populated

What animals and plants inhabit oceanic islands? The latter are populated by forms able to reach them by means other than passage across dry land. This statement follows from our definition of an oceanic island (p. 280). We must hasten to add, however, that there have been in the past, and are today, students of island life who believe that many of the islands usually considered oceanic nevertheless at one time or another were connected to continents, either by land bridges or by having actually constituted a portion of the continent. According to the latter view the island subsequently became detached from the continent and drifted away from it. This would be a very different method of oceanic island formation from the one described above. It forms part of the theory of "continental drift," according to which all the continents and islands at one time were gathered together into one continuous land mass. Eventually the parts of this mass separated from each other and drifted away, leaving the oceans in between.

The whole matter is highly controversial; evidence for and against each theory would be out of place in an elementary discussion (see Darlington, 1957, pp. 606–613). The author will assume responsibility for the statement that the evidence for such drift is to his mind unconvincing, being derived mainly, not from the researches of geologists, where one would naturally look for it, but from the researches of students of plant and animal distribution. Some students of distribution find explanation of observed facts difficult without assuming the occurrence of such original unity and subsequent separation of the land masses of the earth. Since, however, there are still many unknown factors involved in the dispersal of animals and plants, it seems wiser to admit gaps in our knowledge of how living things reach out-of-the-way places, and to seek to fill those gaps, than it is to postulate movements of continents and islands like pieces on a chessboard. This postulate may form an easy way out of a dilemma, but the easy way is frequently not the correct way.

Accordingly, our discussion of the means by which oceanic islands receive their inhabitants will dispense with floating continents, as well as with land bridges and sunken or "lost" continents sometimes postulated where vast depths of ocean are now found. We fully realize that some students of the subject will disagree with us.

Harmonic and Disharmonic Faunas

Faunas of oceanic islands usually present internal evidence of not having arisen by migration over land. The animals are usually a rather haphazard assemblage. Such a fauna is frequently spoken of as disharmonic, in contrast with the harmonic faunas of continents and continental islands. In **harmonic faunas** the various habitats and means of livelihood (environmental niches) are uniformly filled by animals, each adapted for its particular niche. In **disharmonic faunas** many environmental niches remain unexploited or are filled by animals which in a harmonic fauna have different habits and means of livelihood. Under island conditions animals have sometimes "improvised" means of exploiting environmental niches foreign to them on continents. Examples are given later in the discussions of the Galápagos and Hawaiian faunas.

Disharmonic faunas seem, then, to indicate absence of land connection. Where land connections occur, to continental islands, harmonic faunas are transferred from continents to islands more or less intact, except as island conditions may be unsuitable for this or that species. It is highly unlikely, for example, that a land bridge would be used by one species of tree snail and not by other animals inhabiting the original home of that snail. Yet land bridges have been postulated to explain just such arrival of single species on oceanic islands.

Not all faunas of oceanic islands are disharmonic. Some of the larger and older islands and archipelagos, like the Hawaiian Islands, have faunas which are quite harmonic. In such cases, however, it is evident that the harmonic fauna is not like that of any continent but is an evolutionary achievement that occurred on the islands themselves. It occurs on islands and archipelagos large enough to provide considerable diversity of habitat and ancient enough so that time has been provided for evolutionary change.

Absence of amphibians is particularly characteristic of most oceanic islands. Neither amphibian eggs nor adults can survive immersion in sea water. Transportation on rafts or by other means which avoid contact with sea water is possible and doubtless accounts for the presence of amphibians on those oceanic islands that do possess them. If land bridges had occurred, on the other hand, there is no reason why amphibians might not have traversed them, as in fact they must have done in populating continental islands, where they are usually abundant.

Absence of mammals, particularly of larger species, is also characteristic of oceanic islands. Had land bridges existed, at any time subsequent to the Cretaceous period at least (p. 137), such regularly observed absence would be inexplicable, since most of the islands prove to be entirely suitable to mammalian life once mammals are introduced by man or some other agency. We have seen that continental islands, e.g., Borneo, have abundant mammalian faunas which reached them over land connections.

Means of Dispersal to Oceanic Islands

If, then, we discount land connections as means by which animals reach oceanic islands, what other means are available?

Transportation by **wind** may well be the most important means of populating oceanic islands. The efficacy of this means will be at once apparent in the cases of plants which produce microscopic seeds and spores. Dust from the explosive volcanic eruption which destroyed a large part of the island of Krakatoa in 1883 encircled the globe, remaining suspended in the atmosphere for many months. Hence there is no difficulty in accounting for dispersal of seeds and spores which rival dust particles in minuteness.

Even larger seeds may be carried by winds and air currents. Thus Glick (1939) in connection with trapping insects in airplanes at high altitudes caught plant seeds at altitudes as great as 5000 feet. He concluded that transportation by prevailing winds in the upper air currents forms the most important means by which seeds reach oceanic islands. There seems no reason why this same method of transport may not be effective for animals and animal eggs which resemble seeds in diminutiveness, providing only that the animals or eggs can withstand conditions encountered in the upper atmosphere. Few people realize the vast multitude of minute land snails living all around us. Many of these snails are less than a millimeter in diameter and weigh less than one milligram. It should occasion no surprise that most oceanic islands possess such tiny snails and that in some cases snails found on these islands are hundreds, or even thousands, of miles distant from their nearest relatives.

The same situation applies to small insects. One investigator, Elton, has observed that aphids and flies are blown across the 800 miles between Europe and Spitzbergen (Zimmerman, 1948). In the investigation mentioned previously, Glick trapped thousands of specimens at heights up to 14,000 feet. Included were flightless larvae and nymphs, wingless adults, mites, and spiders. Significantly, the forms taken at greatest heights were weak fliers, while the stronger fliers, having heavier bodies, were found at lower altitudes. Thus for the most part transportation through the higher atmosphere was being accomplished with relatively little cooperation on the part of the insect.

Storms which reach hurricane intensity have great carrying power. Zimmerman states that a wind of 75 miles per hour has a lifting force of 16 pounds per square foot and that hurricane winds may exceed twice that velocity. The same author also records hurricane action which tore large sheets of iron roofing from a church on an island in Samoa and deposited it on another island 6 miles distant. We should not be surprised, therefore, that large insects and birds may be carried great distances by winds. Insects such as butterflies, grasshoppers, and beetles have been found as far as 1000 miles from their homes, and land birds are blown far out to sea. Zimmerman records that a pair of North American kingfishers flew ashore on Hawaii a few years ago. Many additional examples might be given, serving to support the view that windstorms transport small objects for long distances and blow flying animals far from the regions they normally inhabit and to which, if undisturbed, they would confine their flights.

A second means by which plants and flightless animals can reach oceanic islands is through **transportation by some animal capable of flight.** Examples have been observed occasionally for many years, and the matter was discussed by Darwin. Birds may carry mud and included small objects, attached to their feet or feathers. Zimmerman records that a mallard duck shot in the Sahara was found to have snail eggs on its feet. The same author states that he picked a living bark beetle from the feathers of an owl. Seeds may pass undamaged through the digestive tract of a bird. Accordingly, migratory birds, or birds blown by storms from their normal ranges, may account for occasional introductions of plants and animals on oceanic islands.

But neither winds nor migrating birds can afford means of transportation for such creatures as land mammals and reptiles. Although land mammals are few on oceanic islands, such reptiles as lizards and geckos are common. For larger land animals, therefore, some means of transportation across the ocean itself must have been operative. Such means are afforded by **natural rafts and "floating islands."** In times of flood large masses of earth and entwining vegetation, including trees, may be torn loose from the banks of rivers and swept out to sea. Sometimes such masses are encountered floating in the ocean out of sight of land, still lush and green, with palms 20 to 30 feet tall. It is entirely probable that land animals may be transported long distances in this manner. Mayr (1940) recorded that many tropical ocean currents have a speed of at least 2 knots; this would amount to 50 miles in a day, 1000 miles in three weeks. Heyerdahl's (1950) balsa raft, the "Kon-Tiki," carried six men from South America to a South Sea island, a distance of 4300 nautical miles, in 101 days. This is an average of 42.5 miles per day. Since a sail was used the steady trade winds augmented motive force provided by ocean currents.

Probably reptiles are more likely to withstand the vicissitudes of travel by natural rafts than are mammals, though the latter have occasionally been seen on rafts of this type. In this connection we may well recall that man has, from prehistoric times, traveled from island to island and from continent to island by boats and ships. He has intentionally transported some land animals in his boats, but in addition to these he has undoubtedly transported unintentionally an indeterminable number as stowaways. This fact adds difficulty to the problem of determining which mammals, for example, inhabited a given island before the coming of man. In the case of the Galápagos Islands there seems no doubt that rice rats, small rodents of South American relationship, were present before the advent of human visitors; but Gulick (1932) has concluded that "this may count as the only unequivocal instance of a mammal that has preceded man across an appreciable stretch of ocean." If such is the case natural rafts need have accounted for but little mammalian distribution, even that of small mammals. We noted earlier that large land mammals, for which natural rafts would afford inadequate means of transportation, are conspicuously absent from oceanic islands while conspicuously present on continental islands.

We note that all the means of dispersal just discussed are accidental, involving a large element of chance. It is significant that chance is just the factor which seems to have been operative in the production of the disharmonic floras and faunas characteristic of oceanic islands. The objection may be raised that the means postulated are too meager to have accounted for observed populations on oceanic islands. Yet the original number of immigrants may have been small, and their arrivals widely spaced in time. In the long stretches of geologic time even very improbable events, if they are not impossible, may occur. Thus Zimmerman (1948) concluded with regard to the rich and varied insect population of Hawaii "that over a period of several millions of years, only about 250 overseas stragglers succeeded in becoming established in the several thousand square miles of the Hawaiian Islands—perhaps only one successful colonization per 20,000 years!"

Some of the smaller oceanic islands bear evidence of relatively recent formation. This fact precludes the possibility that they were ever connected to continents or other islands by land bridges. Thus they may be considered to provide test cases of the efficacy of the accidental means of dispersal described above. One such island in the Pacific is Henderson, located some

150 miles north and east of its nearest neighbor, Pitcairn. Henderson is about 2.5 by 5 miles in extent; its greatest elevation is between 75 and 100 feet above sea level. It is certainly a young island, its age numbered in thousands of years rather than in hundreds of thousands. It appears to have risen sterile from the sea, like the island shown in Fig. 13.1. Zimmerman recorded that today it is densely covered with tangled tropical jungle. The Bishop Museum expedition of 1934 found more than 250 species of plants, mostly native, as well as an endemic genus or subgenus of rail, endemic insects, and endemic land snails. (Endemic species, genera, etc., are those occurring nowhere else than in the region under discussion.) Zimmerman concluded, "Thus, all of the major elements of the Polynesian terrestrial biota have succeeded in being transported across the sea, colonizing this tiny bit of isolated land, and have not only established themselves there but have evolved into new forms quite distinct from their forebears."

Thus far in our discussion of oceanic islands we have summarized the general characteristics of their animal life and discussed the means by which animals reached them. With these facts in mind we shall now turn our attention to a particular group of islands which have long held special interest for biologists, partly no doubt because it was the peculiarities of the animals inhabiting these islands which gave impetus to Darwin's thinking upon the subject of evolution. We refer to the Galápagos Islands, which Darwin visited in 1835 in connection with his circumnavigation of the globe as naturalist on H.M.S. *Beagle*.

GALÁPAGOS ARCHIPELAGO

The Galápagos archipelago is located on the equator about 600 miles west of South America (Fig. 13.2). There are five large islands in the group, with nineteen smaller ones and forty-seven rocks. The islands are of volcanic origin; some of the volcanoes are still active. The topography is rough and mountainous, the highest mountain rising more than 4000 feet above the sea. The lower regions of the islands are dry and barren, with a rough, inhospitable surface reminding visitors of an unfinished planet. Darwin (1839) wrote, "Nothing could be less inviting than the first appearance. A broken field of black basaltic lava, thrown into the most rugged waves, and crossed by great fissures, is every where covered by stunted, sunburnt brushwood, which shows little signs of life." Elsewhere he expressed himself still more feelingly: "The country was compared to what we might imagine the cultivated parts of the Infernal regions to be." To the hostility of the terrain to shoe leather is added the inhospitable nature of the vegetation: tree cactus, prickly pear cactus, thornbushes.

As one progresses inland and upward from the coast on the three highest islands extensive areas of open country are found. Humid forests

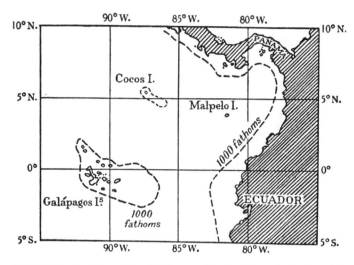

FIG. 13.2. Position of the Galápagos Islands. (From Lack, *Darwin's Finches,* Cambridge University Press, 1947, p. 2.)

occur in the interiors of the larger islands. Altogether, then, the archipelago exhibits considerable variety of habitat.

Despite the fact that the islands are directly under the equator, the climate is not excessively hot. The ameliorating effect of the cold Peruvian current sweeping northward along the coast of South America accounts for this fact in large measure.

Reptiles

The archipelago receives its name from the **giant land tortoises** which form some of the most distinctive inhabitants. These huge reptiles, weighing up to 500 pounds, were formerly abundant but are now becoming scarce. Their tameness, coupled with their ability to stay alive for months in the holds of buccaneer and whaling vessels, furnishing a supply of fresh meat in prerefrigeration days, contributed to their downfall. Darwin recorded, "It is said that formerly single vessels have taken away as many as seven hundred, and that the ship's company of a frigate some years since brought down in one day two hundred tortoises to the beach." The size and strength of the creatures is indicated by the fact that people can ride on their backs, a pastime indulged in by Darwin, who wrote, "I frequently got on their backs, and then giving a few raps on the hinder part of their shells, they would rise up and walk away;—but I found it very difficult to keep my balance."

Two other distinctive reptiles of the Galápagos Islands are the **land, and marine iguanas.** These big, lizardlike creatures are from 3 to 4 feet long. They contribute much to the feeling experienced by visitors of having stepped back into Mesozoic times. Formerly both varieties were extremely abundant. The marine iguanas are still found in large numbers, but the terrestrial iguanas are now nearly extinct. Yet of the latter Darwin wrote, "I cannot give a more forcible proof of their numbers, than by stating that when we were left at James Island, we could not for some time find a spot free from their burrows on which to pitch our single tent." That was in 1835.

The land iguanas are rather brightly colored, brownish red above, yellow underneath. The marine iguanas, on the other hand, are black. Both species are vegetarians, the marine form living on green algae, the land form on a variety of plant material, such as cactus, and the leaves of acacia trees.

The marine iguana is particularly remarkable as being the only known lizard to lead an aquatic existence. As adaptations for this mode of life it has partially webbed feet and a laterally flattened tail. It swims by serpentine movements of the body and tail, after the manner of the most accomplished swimmers in all classes of vertebrates, except birds. It seems reasonable to infer that when ancestral iguanas reached the islands they increased greatly in numbers until eventually the available food supply on land was inadequate to support further expansion. Under such conditions the pressure on the food supply would have been relieved if some of the iguanas proved capable of taking advantage of the algae abundant in neighboring shore waters. We may well imagine that the splitting of the iguana stock into the two forms found today occurred under such an impetus.

The roll of terrestrial reptiles on these islands is completed by mention of the fact that there is one genus each of snake, small lizard, and gecko.

Mammals

The disharmonic nature of the fauna is still further attested by the mammals, or rather by the lack of them. There is one genus of **bats** and one of

rice rats. As noted before, the latter rodents were evidently the only terrestrial mammals to reach the archipelago prior to the coming of man. Intentionally and unintentionally man has introduced cattle, horses, donkeys, pigs, dogs, goats, and black rats. These have run wild over the islands. That they have found the new home congenial is affirmed by the statement of Lack (1947): "The characteristic music of the Galápagos forest is not the song of birds but the braying of donkeys."

It is particularly significant that before these introduced species arrived there were no large, herbivorous mammals on the islands. The environmental niches usually filled by grazing and browsing mammals (e.g., deer, moose, antelope, and so on) were not filled by mammals. Probably it was owing to this fact that the reptiles were able to undergo the remarkable developments we have just noted. Darwin was impressed with this thought: "When we remember the well-beaten paths made by the thousands of huge tortoises—the many turtles—the great warrens of the terrestrial [iguana]— and the groups of the marine species basking on the coast-rocks of every island—we must admit that there is no other quarter of the world where this Order replaces the herbivorous mammalia in so extraordinary a manner." It was as though this isolated region, being free of mammalian competitors, afforded the reptiles one last chance for an adaptive radiation recalling, though dimly, the Mesozoic "golden age" of reptiles.

Other Animals and Plants

The small number of land insects and of land molluscs, as well as the great gaps in the expected types of plants, also bear witness to the disharmonic nature of the fauna and flora. Many widespread plant groups are notably absent, among them conifers and palms, as well as several important families characteristic of tropical America. The islands are old enough so that the environmental niches left vacant have been filled, at least partially, by plants which did succeed in reaching the islands. Thus, the typically low-growing prickly pear cactus has, on Galápagos, become a tree. We have noted previously (p. 283) that the filling of environmental niches by forms other than those normally filling them on continents is characteristic of floras and faunas of oceanic islands.

How Were the Islands Populated?

How did plants and animals reach the Galápagos Islands? Were the latter ever connected to America? At the present time no answer can be given to which all students of the islands will agree. The depth of the ocean between the islands and South America is greater than the depth of a section of the ocean extending northeast to Cocos Island, in the direction of Central America (Fig. 13.2). The view that the islands were once connected to Central America has received favorable discussion by Beebe (1924).

To many other students of the subject the amount of vertical movement of the crust necessary to form a dry-land connection to America seems unlikely, during that portion of geologic time concerned in the distribution of immediate ancestors of the plants and animals inhabiting Galápagos. Also, as we have seen, the flora and fauna are notably disharmonic, a fact favoring the view that immigration across the ocean was the means of population. The affinity of the Galápagos fauna to that of Central America is attested by many investigations. C. T. Parsons (personal communication) is of the opinion that ancestral forms were carried by the Panamanian current, which swings south to include the archipelago every few years. "This current washes up many floating plants and brings much rain which would enable many plants and animals, thrown up on the usually barren shore, to gain a foothold."

Opponents of the view that plants and animals reached the archipelago by transportation across water have raised particular objection to the suggestion that land iguanas and land tortoises could have reached the islands in this way. Yet lizards, the group to which iguanas belong, have colonized most of Polynesia, including very isolated islands. Apparently they can be carried long distances on floating vegetation, or even perhaps floating in the water themselves. Much remains to be learned about the means of dispersal possible to any particular animal. Tortoises have been observed to float and survive for long periods in sea water. Simpson (1943) has pointed out that the great land tortoises probably reached both South America and the Galápagos Islands in this manner, since they first appeared in South America in Miocene times, when that continent was not connected by land with North America. Some other islands (e.g., the Mascarene Islands in the Indian Ocean) also have giant land tortoises despite the fact that no evidence exists of former land connection to a continent.

While the affinities of the Galápagos fauna are almost exclusively with the American fauna, one Polynesian form is included. This is a land mollusc, unrelated to those in America and apparently derived from islands at least 3000 miles to the west. It seems wiser to state that we do not know the means by which this creature reached the islands than to postulate a far-flung land bridge for its exclusive use.

"Darwin's Finches"

No group of Galápagos animals is of more interest to students of evolution than are the birds, partly because of the role played by these birds in influencing the thinking of Darwin. He was particularly impressed by the varied adaptations exhibited by the unique finches of the archipelago. In commemoration of this fact, the most recent investigator of the Galápagos finches, Dr. David Lack (1947), has had the happy inspiration to term them "Darwin's finches." To his book of that title we are indebted for much of the following material on Galápagos birds.

As is true of other animals, the affinities of the birds on the archipelago are with American forms. There is, however, great variation in the degree of similarity between the island forms and their continental relatives. Thus, the **cuckoo** of the islands is identical with a South American species, and the single **warbler** is very similar to one living in Ecuador. The **martin** is regarded as belonging to a separate subspecies of a species mainly inhabiting the continent. The **tyrant flycatcher** is a distinct species, but closely related to an American species. The **mockingbird** differs so much from American mockingbirds that it is placed in a separate genus from the latter. Furthermore, the Galápagos mockingbird has become differentiated into nine island forms, "two of which are sufficiently distinctive to be treated as separate species, the other seven being treated as subspecies of a third species" (Lack, personal communication). Similarly, the **vermilion flycatcher** has differentiated into three island races. Finally, **Darwin's finches** are so different from any existing American finch that, as stated by Lack, "there is considerable doubt as to their nearest mainland relative."

Thus we see all degrees of similarity between island and mainland species: from identity of characteristics to widely differing traits. How can these facts be explained?

In the first place, how does it happen that Galápagos birds resemble American ones at all? Surely this resemblance must mean that the Galápagos birds are the more or less modified descendants of American species. If the birds had been especially created to live on the Galápagos Islands it is difficult to see why they should have been created to resemble birds living on the neighboring continent, rather than to resemble birds created to live on other islands, e.g., other islands in the Pacific, or the Cape Verde Islands near the coast of Africa. The Cape Verde Islands resemble the Galápagos Islands in many respects, yet, in the words of Darwin (1839), "the aboriginal inhabitants of the two groups are totally unlike; those of the Cape de Verd Islands bearing the impress of Africa, as the inhabitants of the Galápagos Archipelago are stamped with that of America." Such relationships of island faunas to those of neighboring continents are to be expected if evolution is a fact but are inexplicable upon any other basis.

In the second place, what is the significance of the fact that some Galápagos birds resemble American species more closely than do others? Lack is doubtless correct in explaining this fact upon a basis of the differing lengths of time during which the different species have been inhabiting the archipelago. Thus the cuckoo is probably a relative newcomer, so recently arrived that it has not had time to develop differences from its South American ancestors. The mockingbird, on the other hand, arrived much earlier, a fact evidenced by its greater degree of difference from mainland mockingbirds as well as by its differentiation into separate species and races on the various islands. Undoubtedly animals differ in rate of evolutionary change; conclusions correlating degree of difference with length of time during which isolation has been operative are probably valid in the main, however. (See discussion of faunal stratification, p. 261.)

Following this line of thought we conclude that the ancestors of Darwin's finches were very early migrants to the archipelago, perhaps the first birds to reach it. These finches differ greatly from any other living finch and have developed many island forms.

Finches belong to the largest family of birds, the Fringillidae, which includes many of our most common birds—among them our captive songster, the canary, the many species of sparrows, the goldfinch, the grosbeaks, and the cardinal. In the words of Chapman (1920), birds of this family "generally agree in possessing stout, conical bills, which are admirably adapted to crush seeds." With this fact in mind we direct our attention to Darwin's finches, characterized by Lack as follows: "Darwin's finches are dull to look at, not only in their orderly ranks in museum trays, but also when they hop about the ground or perch in the trees of the Galápagos, making dull unmusical noises. Only the variety of their beaks and the number of their species excite attention—small finch-like beaks, huge finch-like beaks, parrot-like beaks, straight wood-boring beaks, decurved flower-probing beaks, slender warbler-like beaks; species which look very different and species which look closely similar."

How did such diversity arise? When the finches first reached the islands they found many "unfinchlike ecological niches" open to them. Probably at first they had few, if any, enemies, though there are now two species of owls which prey upon them. Under such conditions the numbers of finches would have been limited only by the available food supply. Since the quantity of seeds available would have been limited, as numbers of finches increased a premium must have been placed upon ability to utilize sources of food not usual for finches. Absence of competitors for these other sources of food made possible a diversity of food habits which finches do not achieve on continents. For example, continents possess woodpeckers, specialists in boring into bark and wood of trees after insect larvae. Consequently no continental finch would be likely to take up this mode of gaining a living; woodpeckers already have a virtual monopoly on it. Yet on the Galápagos Islands, in the absence of woodpeckers, a finch did develop this woodpeckerlike method of feeding, as we shall see presently.

As indicated above, the chief differences between the various forms of Darwin's finches are differences in the beaks. The plumage of related species of these rather drab little birds is very similar. In fact, Lack presents evidence that the birds themselves depend upon the shape of the beak in recognizing members of their own species and distinguishing members of other species. To a considerable extent, also, differences in the beak are associated with the differing food habits mentioned previously. Small beak differences (e.g., those exhibited by different species within one subgenus) do not seem to be thus associated with food habits, however. The beaks display much variation; perhaps the struggle for existence on these islands has not been sufficiently rigorous to result in the rigid standardization usually characterizing continental species.

Adaptive Radiation of Finch Beaks

In the following series of sketches we present some of the prinicipal beak modifications connected with differing food habits.

The ground finches (Subgenus *Geospiza*) have heavy finchlike beaks (Fig. 13.3). Seeds form the chief item in their diet, although they are not narrow specialists in the matter. As the three sketches in the figure indicate, great differences in size of beak are found among the ground finches. To a considerable extent the large ground finches eat the same food as do the smaller ones, yet Lack presents evidence that the larger ones can eat larger seeds than can the smaller ones. In correlation with this fact the larger finches mainly ignore small seeds, such as those of grasses, which form the staple diet of the small ground finches. Thus competition between the various ground finches is reduced and they are able to occupy the same habitat.

The cactus ground finch (Fig. 13.4) has a long, somewhat decurved beak and a split tongue. It probes the flowers of the prickly pear cactus tree for nectar. It also feeds on the soft pulp of this cactus and on a variety of other food items.

The vegetarian tree finch (Fig. 13.5) has a short, thick, somewhat

FIG. 13.3. Beaks of three species of ground finches (Subgenus Geospiza). (From Lack, Darwin's Finches, Cambridge University Press, 1947, p. 57.)

parrotlike beak. Leaves, buds, blossoms, and fruits form its main items of diet.

The insectivorous tree finches (Fig. 13.6) have beaks much like the beak of the vegetarian tree finch. They live chiefly on beetles and other

FIG. 13.4. Beak of the cactus ground finch (Geospiza scandens). (From Lack, Darwin's Finches, Cambridge University Press, 1947, p. 57.)

FIG. 13.5. Beak of the vegetarian tree finch (Subgenus Platyspiza). (From Lack, Darwin's Finches, Cambridge University Press, 1947, p. 57.)

insects, although they are not averse to young leaves, buds, and nectar in season.

One of the most remarkable of the finches is the woodpecker finch mentioned previously. Its beak is stout and straight, similar to that of tree finches, but longer (Fig. 13.7). Almost completely insectivorous, it searches bark and leaf clusters and bores into wood like a woodpecker. When a woodpecker has exposed an insect it uses its long tongue to extract the insect from the crack or hole. This finch, lacking the long tongue, picks up a small stick or cactus spine, holds the latter lengthwise in its beak and probes out the insect, dropping the stick and seizing the insect as it emerges. This remarkable practice affords almost the only known exam-

FIG. 13.6.   Beaks of two insectivorous tree finches (Subgenus *Camarhynchus*). (From Lack, *Darwin's Finches*, Cambridge University Press, 1947, p. 57.)

ple of the use of a tool by a bird (Fig. 13.8). Clearly we have here an example of an animal which has "improvised" a means of entering an environmental niche foreign to it on continents of the world (see p. 283). This finch is also the only one to climb up and down vertical trunks and branches like a woodpecker.

The warbler finch (Fig. 13.9) is so much like a warbler that its true relationship was formerly not recognized. Its beak is slender and warblerlike. It searches leaves and bushes for small insects and sometimes catches the latter on the wing like a true warbler. Nectar and young leaves are also eaten.

FIG. 13.7.   Beak of the woodpecker finch (Subgenus *Cactospiza*). (From Lack, *Darwin's Finches*, Cambridge University Press, 1947, p. 57.)

Thus Darwin's finches afford another beautiful example of adaptive radiation, made possible in this instance by absence of enemies and competitors on a group of oceanic islands.

As Darwin stated in *The Voyage of the Beagle,* "Seeing this gradation and diversity of structure in one small, intimately related group of birds, one might really fancy that from an original paucity of birds in this archipelago, one species had been taken and modified for different ends."

DREPANID BIRDS OF HAWAII

In concluding our discussion of the light shed on evolution by the inhabitants of oceanic islands we shall cite another remarkable example of adaptive radiation among birds. The Hawaiian Islands are the home of a distinctive group of birds called "sicklebills," "honey creepers," or, better, "drepanids," from the name of the family to which they belong: Drepaniidae (Drepanididae). The fact that they are thus placed in a sepa-

FIG. 13.8.   The woodpecker finch and its stick. (Drawn by Roland Green from photographs by R. Leacock; from Lack, *Darwin's Finches*, Cambridge University Press, 1947, p. 59.)

rate family by themselves reflects their dissimilarity to all other birds. There is, indeed, considerable doubt as to their closest continental relatives. Present evidence suggests that their ancestors were allied to the honey creepers of tropical America (Family Coerebidae).

The Hawaiian Islands occupy an isolated position in mid-Pacific, far from any continent. North America is about 2000 miles away, Japan more than 3000 miles. The archipelago is even remote from other large oceanic islands. The view is sometimes advanced that the Hawaiian Islands were once joined to a still-existing continent or to a mid-Pacific continent which later sank below the waves. The more widely held view, however, is that the islands, of volcanic origin, rose directly from the ocean floor and were never connected to other bodies of land.

FIG. 13.9.   Beak of the warbler finch (*Certhidea*). (From Lack, *Darwin's Finches*, Cambridge University Press, 1947, p. 57.)

As would be expected in truly oceanic islands far from a continent, the number of land birds in the Hawaiian Islands is small. Also this avian fauna would be disharmonic were it not for the fact that the archipelago is old enough so that a secondary harmony of its own has had time to develop

(p. 283). We have seen that the ancestors of Darwin's finches reached the Galápagos archipelago so early that a wide variety of environmental niches was open to them. The same seems to have been true of the ancestors of the drepanids; it is probable that they were the first land birds to reach the Hawaiian archipelago. In these earlier times the drepanids, like Darwin's finches, were relatively free from both enemies and competitors. Thus they spread over all the islands suitable to them and became adapted for a wide variety of foods. As in the case of Darwin's finches, these adaptations must have arisen when available food supply, rather than enemies or competitors, formed the important factor tending to limit population size. Thus a premium would have been placed on ability to utilize foods different from those being eaten by the majority of the population. Such an interpretation, at least, gives us a reasonable explanation for the development of the amazing variety of beaks exhibited by the drepanids (Fig. 13.10).

The beak form believed to be most like that of the ancestral drepanid is possessed today by such a species as *Loxops virens* (Fig. 13.11). This relatively unspecialized little bird lives largely on nectar and insects obtained from the blossoms of flowering trees, such as the ohia. These flowers have short corollas, hence the nectar is easily reached. Berries are also eaten.

Nectar feeding is believed to have been the original food habit of ancestral drepanids. Beaks such as those already mentioned are entirely adequate for obtaining nectar from flowers having short corollas, especially when the tongue is tubular, and frayed at the end into a brushlike tip, as is the typical drepanid tongue. The effect is that of being provided with a built-in soda straw.

A unique group of plants belonging to the Lobelia family developed in Hawaii. Lobelias assume many forms, some herbs, some shrubs, still others small trees. The lobelia blossoms have long, curved, tubular corollas (Fig. 13.12). Hence the nectar is relatively inaccessible. Feeding on nectar from these tubular blossoms are found drepanids with one of the most remarkable of the beak adaptations. The extreme form of this adaptation is exhibited by the genus *Drepanis* (Fig. 13.10). Such long, slender, strongly curved beaks are obviously well adapted for reaching the bottom of tubular corollas. The significance of the common name "sicklebill" is readily apparent when we look at this form. The foreheads of birds having it are frequently observed to be plastered with the pollen of the lobelia flowers. Thus the visits of the birds aid in the reproduction of these plants.

Some readers may feel that birds with such slender, sickle-shaped beaks have paid a very high price for ability to reach the bottom of long, tubular

Susan Williamen-Ellis

FIG. 13.10. Adaptive radiation among the drepanids of Hawaii. (After Keulemanns; from Lack, *Darwin's Finches,* Cambridge University Press, 1947, p. 153.)

flowers. Obviously such a beak can be used for sucking nectar from short flowers also, yet its sphere of usefulness is definitely restricted. It is used at times for capturing small insects, but it is not good for cracking seeds, or for boring into bark and wood, or for eating fruits. Its possessor is, then,

highly adapted for one mode of feeding and is likely to remain a successful member of the fauna only so long as that mode of feeding is open to it. It affords us an example of a high degree of specialization, spelling success so long as the environment remains unchanged but carrying with it the threat of extinction when the environment changes.

FIG. 13.11. Beak of *Loxops vi-rens*. (After Rothschild; from Amadon, "Ecology and the evolution of some Hawaiian birds," *Evolution*, Vol. 1, 1947.)

Is there no other way in which the nectar at the base of long, tubular flowers can be reached than by developing a slender, curved beak useless for almost everything else? Flowers are not very substantial structures. Why not pierce a hole through the base of the corolla and reach the nectar directly? Bumblebees do it, why not birds? As a matter of fact *Loxops virens* (Fig. 13.11) has been observed to obtain nectar or insects from lobelia blossoms in this manner. Thus this species has achieved the result without sacrificing what may be termed an "all-purpose" beak. It is probably no accident that members of this species are among the most abundant and widespread of the drepanids, while the possessors of the slender, curved beaks are among the rarest. "It is frequently of greater value to be adaptable than it is to be highly adapted." (See p. 13.)

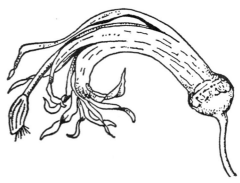

The Family Drepaniidae is divided into two subfamilies. *Drepanis* belongs to one of

FIG. 13.12. Curved flower of the lobelia, *Clermontia grandiflora*. (After Porsch; from Amadon, "The Hawaiian honeycreepers [*Aves, Drepaniidae*]," *Bulletin of American Museum of Natural History*, Vol. 95, 1950.)

these. Birds with long, curved beaks are also found in the other subfamily. *Hemignathus obscurus* is an example (Fig. 13.13). Its beak is believed to have evolved from a shorter, decurved beak such as that possessed by modern *Loxops virens* (Fig. 13.11). Comparison of the two figures will reveal that the principal evolutionary change was elongation. The beak of *Hemignathus obscurus* is used mainly for probing bark cavities in search of the insects which form the principal article of diet. But the beak is also used

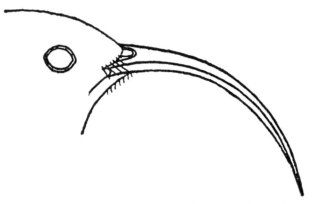

FIG. 13.13.   Beak of *Hemignathus obscurus*. (After Rothschild; from Amadon, "Ecology and the evolution of some Hawaiian birds," *Evolution,* Vol. 1, 1947.)

at times for obtaining nectar from the tubular blossoms of lobelias. Amadon (1950) suggested that the long, curved beaks of *Drepanis* and *Hemignathus* form an example of parallel evolution, the beak of *Drepanis* having

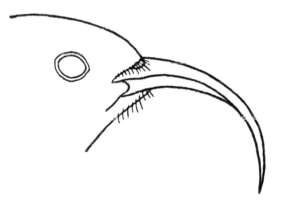

FIG. 13.14.   Beak of *Hemignathus lucidus*. (After Rothschild; from Amadon, "Ecology and the evolution of some Hawaiian birds," *Evolution,* Vol. 1, 1947.)

evolved as an adaptation for the obtaining of nectar from long, tubular flowers, while the beak of *Hemignathus* evolved as a forcepslike device for probing after insects living in bark cavities.

We note (Fig. 13.13) that the lower mandible of *Hemignathus obscurus* is slightly shorter than the upper one. In the related species *Hemignathus lucidus* the lower mandible is only about half as long as the upper one (Fig. 13.14) but is somewhat heavier in structure than is the lower mandible of *H. obscurus*. The feeding habits of these two species are similar, but the heavier lower mandible possessed by *H. lucidus* increases its ability to chip and pry away loose pieces of bark in search of insects. This species sometimes eats nectar, but less frequently than does *H. obscurus,* a fact doubtless correlated with the decreased efficiency of a beak of this type for nectar gathering. The next species we shall mention has a still more highly modified beak and is never observed to feed on nectar.

The culmination of this evolutionary trend toward shortening and strengthening the lower mandible is attained in *Hemignathus wilsoni* (Fig. 13.15). In this species the lower mandible is straight and heavy, enabling the bird to fill a woodpeckerlike environmental niche. Like woodpeckers, and like the "woodpecker finch" of the Galápagos Islands, these birds climb up and down vertical trunks and

FIG. 13.15. Beak of *Hemignathus wilsoni*. (After Rothschild; from Amadon, "Ecology and the evolution of some Hawaiian birds," *Evolution*, Vol. 1, 1947.)

branches. The straight lower mandible is used mainly to open the burrows of wood-boring insects. While holding the curved upper mandible to one side, the bird pounds vigorously with the sharp lower mandible, boring a hole and exposing the insect larva. Then the upper mandible, so slender that its tip is slightly flexible, is used as a probe to remove the insect. The slender tongue, which can be extended to the length of the upper mandible, aids in the process of extraction. The two mandibles also cooperate in prying loose bits of bark in search of insects concealed beneath. Perkins (1903) stated that this species feeds on insects inhabiting dead wood only, since it lacks the stout beak and huge muscles which enable *Pseudonestor* to excavate borers from live wood.

It is noteworthy that these three species have retained tubular tongues, thus betraying their nectar-eating ancestry.

Of the drepanids which have forsaken the ancestral diet of nectar, some have developed heavy beaks useful in cracking solid seeds and nuts. In

these heavy-beaked drepanids the tongue has largely lost its tubular character. The extreme was represented by *Psittirostra kona* (Fig. 13.16).
which lived mostly on the hard nuts of the bastard sandalwood tree. Perkins wrote, "As the dried fruit . . . is excessively hard, it is probable that
nothing short of the extremely powerful jaws . . . and their great muscles would be able to crack them. In cracking them a sound is produced,
which is audible at some distance, and as it is incessant when the bird is
feeding, by far the most easy way to get sight of this, is to listen attentively
for the sound."

Another extreme adaptation by the heavy-beaked group of drepanids is
represented by *Pseudonestor* (Fig. 13.17). Its beak suggests that of a
diminutive parrot and is used to expose the larvae, pupae, and immature

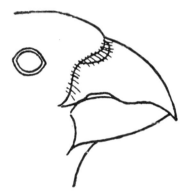

FIG. 13.16. Beak of *Psittirostra
kona*. (After Rothschild; from Amadon, "Ecology and the evolution of
some Hawaiian birds," *Evolution*,
Vol. 1, 1947.)

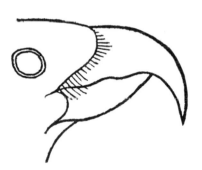

FIG. 13.17. Beak of *Pseudonestor*.
(After Rothschild; from Amadon,
"Ecology and the evolution of some
Hawaiian birds," *Evolution*, Vol. 1,
1947.)

stages of wood boring beetles. Perkins described the use of the beak as
follows: "The branch is gripped by the curved upper mandible and the
lower one opposed to it, and the burrow of the larva is exposed, either by
the act of closing the beak or by wrenching with it, the somewhat slender
tongue assisting in extracting the prey." The bird's equipment is powerful
enough to operate on hard wood.

Our brief survey of this remarkable group of Hawaiian birds has included mention of but a few of the thirty-nine drepanids found in the
islands. We have selected for mention the extremes of adaptation to different types of food. The species not mentioned possess beaks which fill
many of the seeming gaps between the conservative ancestral type (Fig.
13.11) and these extremes. As intimated above, such extremes of adapta-

tion to a particular environment are not without danger to the species. Thus Gulick (1932) wrote concerning these birds:

Adaptation has become completely and narrowly specialized for feeding upon the nectar, seeds, and insects of their Hawaii. And by the same token, all but a few of them are now ready to pay the penalty of over-specialization in a restricted environment. Such as are not exterminated by enemy pests like the mongoose [introduced by man], that they know not how to evade, are doomed to disappear whenever cattle destroy the particular environmental combination on which they depend. The Hawaiian woodlands, alive with song in 1850, are today already largely silent, except to some degree on the single island of Hawaii, where the destructive forces seem to have moved a little less rapidly.

And Lack, referring to the world's largest museum collection of Hawaiian birds, commented somewhat sadly, "The drawers of the Rothschild collection contain more representatives of some of the Hawaiian sicklebills than are alive in the islands today."

Conclusion

We have dwelt at some length on the inhabitants of oceanic islands because they afford examples of evolutionary change occurring within relatively recent times and under conditions still largely observable. The islands themselves are geologically young; hence any observed evolution of their inhabitants must have occurred within a relatively short span of time. Thus, basing his conclusion on the opinion that the Hawaiian Islands are of Pliocene and later age, Amadon (1947) estimated that about 5,000,000 years were available for the evolution of the drepanid birds. Although by human standards this is a very long time, it is but a small portion of geologic time, or even of that part of geologic time which has elapsed since the first birds appeared (p. 187). And the Hawaiian Islands are among the older oceanic islands.

Owing to their isolation, oceanic islands develop disharmonic floras and faunas. Taking advantage of environmental niches left vacant in such disharmonic faunas, animals reaching larger and older archipelagos early in their history underwent adaptive radiation quite unlike that possible to their relatives on continents. Hence oceanic islands have become the settings for some of the most vivid examples of evolution-in-action available to us.

References and Suggested Readings

Amadon, D. "Ecology and the evolution of some Hawaiian birds," *Evolution,* 1 (1947), 63–68.

Amadon, D. "The Hawaiian Honeycreepers (Aves, Drepaniidae)," *Bulletin of the American Museum of Natural History,* 95, Article 4 (1950), 155–262. Plates 9–15.

Beebe, W. *Galapagos: World's End.* New York: G. P. Putnam's Sons, 1924.

Bryan, W. A. *Natural History of Hawaii.* Honolulu: privately published, 1915.

Chapman, F. M. *Handbook of Birds of Eastern North America,* rev. ed. New York: Appleton-Century-Crofts, Inc., 1920.

Darlington, P. J., Jr. *Zoogeography: the Geographical Distribution of Animals.* New York: John Wiley & Sons, Inc., 1957.

Darwin, C. *The Voyage of the Beagle.* 1839. (Available in Everyman's Library, No. 104, E. P. Dutton & Co., Inc., New York; and as Bantam Book FC11, Bantam Books, Inc., New York.)

Darwin, C. *The Origin of Species by Means of Natural Selection.* 1859. Modern Library series, Random House, New York; or Mentor Book MT294, New American Library, New York.

Eibl-Eibesfeldt, I. *Galapagos.* New York: Doubleday & Co., Inc., 1961.

Glick, P. A. "The distribution of insects, spiders and mites in the air," *U. S. Department of Agriculture, Technical Bulletin* No. 673, 1939.

Gulick, A. "Biological peculiarities of oceanic islands," *Quarterly Review of Biology,* 7 (1932), 405–427.

Heyerdahl, T. *Kon-Tiki. Across the Pacific by Raft.* Chicago: Rand McNally & Co., 1950.

Lack, D. *Darwin's Finches.* Cambridge: Cambridge University Press, 1947.

Mayr, E. "The origin and history of the bird fauna of Polynesia," *Proceedings of the Sixth Pacific Science Congress,* 4 (1940), 197–216.

Perkins, R. C. L. *Vertebrata.* In D. Sharp (ed.). *Fauna Hawaiiensis.* Vol. I, part IV. Cambridge: Cambridge University Press, 1903. Pp. 365–466.

Simpson, G. G. "Turtles and the origin of the fauna of Latin America," *American Journal of Science,* 241 (1943), 413–429.

Simpson, G. G. "History of the fauna of Latin America," *American Scientist,* 38 (1950), 361–389.

Wallace, A. R. *Island Life.* New York: Harper & Brothers, 1881.

Zimmerman, E. C. *Insects of Hawaii.* Vol. 1, *Introduction.* Honolulu: University of Hawaii Press, 1948.

CHAPTER 14

EVOLUTION AS SEEN IN THE CLASSIFICATION OF ANIMALS

Man is characteristically the collecting and classifying member of the animal kingdom. Whether it be stamps, antique automobiles, buttons, Chinese porcelain, coins, books, tapestries, or works of art, there seems to be an innate tendency in human nature leading to the acquisition of objects of interest. For some the acquisition is in itself sufficient satisfaction, but for most people, possessed of more tidy minds, accumulation must be accompanied by classification and cataloguing—the putting of everything "in its place." We are so constituted that we feel ill at ease when surrounded by chaos. We are not satisfied until we can introduce organization into the unorganized, "put things to rights," and arrange things so that they "make sense." Much the same urge which leads one person to collect stamps leads another to collect animals. And for both, satisfaction is only complete when the items collected are properly filed and classified. Without this underlying human urge the great biological collections which are the pride of our museums and universities would never have come into existence.

Basis of Classification

Biological classification doubtless had its inception in the desire of the human mind to put things "in their places," as suggested above. A fundamental object of any system of classifying—library books, stamps, or animals—is to arrange in orderly sequence, to place like with like. Thus in the library the books on photography are side by side in one place, books on ceramics in another, biographies in still a third. *Similarity*, then, of one kind or another, is the basis of all classification. In the case of animals, similarity of *structure*, morphology, has traditionally been the basis upon which classifications have been built. More recently physiological and serological similarities have begun to contribute to classification, but it still remains true that most of the generally recognized classification is firmly grounded in morphological similarity. Morphologically similar animals are placed near together in classification; morphologically dissimilar animals are placed farther apart.

Classifications of one kind or another are probably as old as man's curiosity about his fellow inhabitants on this planet. During the centuries of the infancy of biology many classifications were suggested. Indeed, so many biologists created so many classifications that the resulting confusion finally became a stumbling block in the way of further scientific progress. It was the genius of the Swedish biologist, **Linnaeus**, born in 1707, that he was able to devise a system of classification which all biologists would agree to use and which was so logically developed that today, despite expanding horizons of biological knowledge, it still serves the needs of science. Addition and amplification have been necessary, but no fundamental reorganization. Linnaeus laid the foundations well.

Binomial System of Nomenclature

The basis of the Linnaean system is the conferring of two names upon each kind of animal. Hence this is a *binomial* system of nomenclature. Thus Linnaeus named the domestic dog *Canis familiaris*. The second name of the two designates a unit of classification called the **species**, while the first name of the two designates a larger unit of classification, usually including more than one species, called the **genus**. An analogy lies in the practice of writing the name of a human individual with the surname first, the given name second, e.g., Smith, John. The individual named is one of the Smiths, the particular one of them he is being John. Similarly the common dog belongs to the genus of dogs, *Canis*, his particular species being *familiaris*. The prairie wolf or coyote belongs to the genus *Canis* also, but not to the same species; his species is *latrans*. Thus he is known to science as *Canis latrans*. Similarly, the jackal of Africa belongs to the same genus but to a different species; he is *Canis aureus*.

A few conventions will be noticed in the binomial system. The names are always in Latin or in Latinized form. While this practice strikes most American college students as needlessly cumbersome, it insures uniformity of naming in writings of biologists of all nationalities. Although Latin is no longer regarded as the universal language of scholarship, knowledge of it is sufficiently widespread in all nations to render its use in forming names generally acceptable. With names agreed upon in this fashion, a biologist in one country, even though he be writing in Russian or Chinese, can be sure that biologists in other countries will know exactly what animal he is discussing. Such understanding would probably not ensue if the Russian biologist were to employ the Russian name of the animal.

"Common" or vernacular names are notoriously variable even within the confines of one continent and one language. Consider, for example, the big American member of the cat family known to biologists as *Felis concolor*. According to Seton (1929) that mammal is called in various parts of America by the following "common" names: panther, puma, mountain lion, painter, cougar, catamount, brown tiger, varmint, sneak-cat, red tiger, silver lion, purple panther, deer-killer, Indian devil, mountain devil, mountain demon, mountain screamer, king-cat. When we add to these the varied names for the animal in the Central and South American languages and dialects the confusion is truly appalling. We return to the simple appellation, *Felis concolor,* with a distinct sense of relief.

Another convention is that the scientific name of an animal is usually italicized (indicated in handwriting or typing by an underline). By convention, also, the name of the genus begins with a capital letter, the name of the species with a "small" (i.e., lower-case) letter. Frequently a name or initial, not italicized, will follow the name of the species, thus: *Canis familiaris* L. This name or initial designates the name of the biologist who conferred the name in the first place. Since Linnaeus himself gave names to so many animals and plants, L. is sufficient to remind the reader that the name derives from the founder of the system himself.

Family

We have seen that the dog, the coyote, and the jackal are all grouped together in the genus *Canis* because they are all so very doglike in structure and characteristics. We are reminded again that classification is based on similarities. There are other mammals which are somewhat doglike but not sufficiently so to be included in genus *Canis*. For example, the foxes are placed in genus *Vulpes*. The common red fox is *Vulpes fulva*.

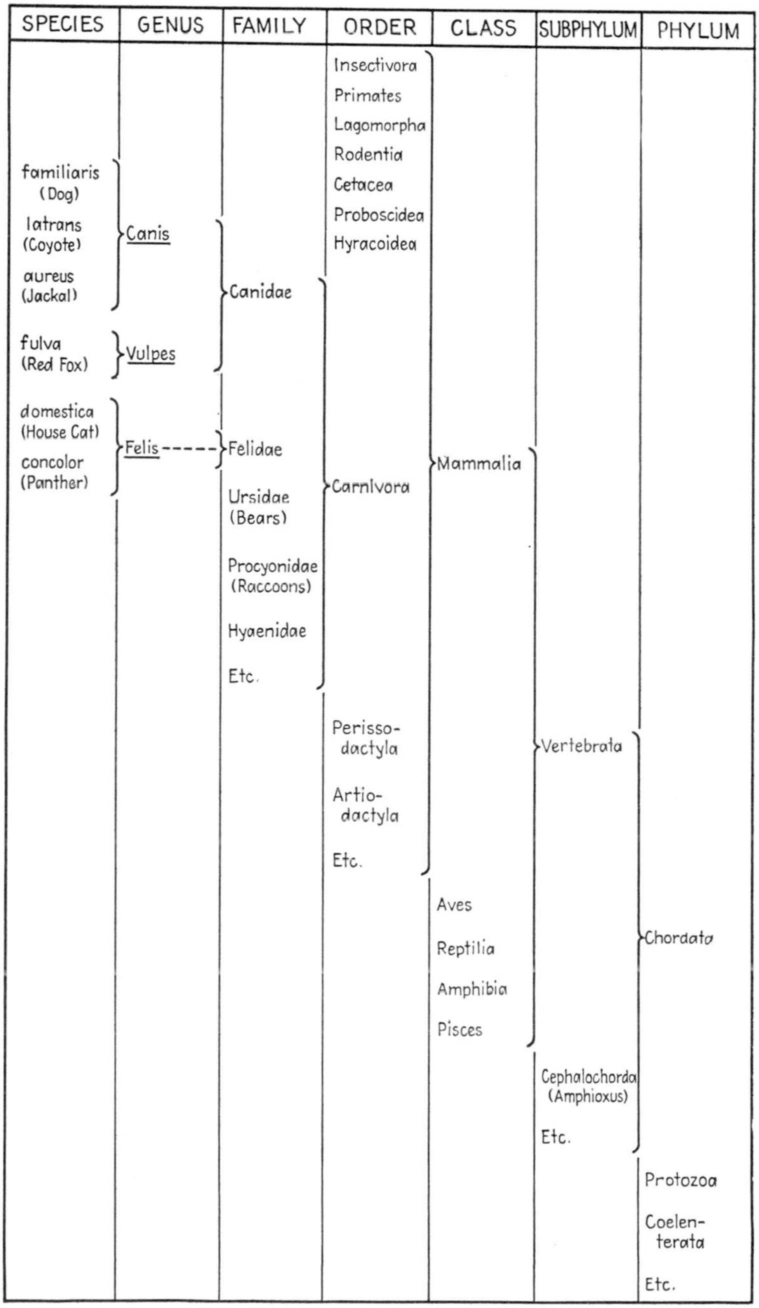

SPECIES	GENUS	FAMILY	ORDER	CLASS	SUBPHYLUM	PHYLUM
			Insectivora			
			Primates			
			Lagomorpha			
			Rodentia			
familiaris (Dog)			Cetacea			
latrans (Coyote)	Canis		Proboscidea			
aureus (Jackal)			Hyracoidea			
		Canidae				
fulva (Red Fox)	Vulpes					
domestica (House Cat)						
concolor (Panther)	Felis - - - - -	Felidae		Mammalia		
			Carnivora			
		Ursidae (Bears)				
		Procyonidae (Raccoons)				
		Hyaenidae				
		Etc.				
			Perisso-dactyla		Vertebrata	
			Artio-dactyla			
			Etc.			
			Aves			Chordata
			Reptilia			
			Amphibia			
			Pisces			
					Cephalochorda (Amphioxus)	
					Etc.	
						Protozoa
						Coelen-terata
						Etc.

FIG. 14.1.   Scheme of classification, using common carnivorous mammals as examples in the three lower categories.

The more or less doglike animals comprising genus *Canis* and genus *Vulpes,* and some others, are grouped together into a higher category in our classification known as the **family.** The particular family concerned here is named Canidae (Fig. 14.1). Another convention is evident at this point: the names of families always end with "-idae."

Order

Another family somewhat related to the Canidae is that called Felidae, including all the catlike animals. This family, like the former, is composed of several genera (plural of "genus"), each of which is subdivided into species. The genus *Felis* has already been mentioned; in addition to the species *concolor* within it, we may call attention to the species name of the common house cat: *domestica.* Thus our pet is known to science as *Felis domestica.* Other families include the Ursidae (bears), Procyonidae (raccoons), Hyaenidae (hyenas).

All the animals mentioned in the preceding paragraph are alike in some respects, some of the most striking similarities being connected with the nature of their diet. They are all carnivorous—flesh eaters. This fact is recognized in classification by grouping these families together into a larger unit of classification, the **order.** They all belong to Order Carnivora (Fig. 14.1).

Class

A dozen or so other orders of mammals rank along with the Carnivora. For example, Order Rodentia (gnawing animals) and Order Lagomorpha (hares and rabbits) were mentioned in connection with serological studies (pp. 117–119). Human beings, apes, and monkeys are included in Order Primates (pp. 220–221); elephants belong to Order Proboscidae (pp. 206–207), whales to Order Cetacea, even-toed hoofed animals to Order Artiodactyla, odd-toed hoofed animals to Order Perissodactyla, and so on.

Members of all orders just mentioned, and of some not mentioned, have several characteristics in common. They have hair, they are warm-blooded, the young develop in the uterus of the mother and then are born (as contrasted with being hatched from eggs). Following birth the young are nourished with milk secreted by mammary glands. Because of these and other similarities the orders are grouped together into a larger category of classification called the **class** (Fig. 14.1). The particular class with which we are concerned is Class Mammalia. Other classes are: Class Aves (birds), Class

Reptilia (lizards, snakes, crocodiles, etc.), Class Amphibia (salamanders, newts, frogs, toads), Class Pisces (fishes), and so on.

Subphylum

Members of all the classes mentioned above have a few fundamental similarities in common; for example, they all possess a backbone or vertebral column. Hence they are all grouped together into Subphylum Vertebrata (Fig. 14.1). Vertebrates, members of this subphylum, possess a vertebral column as adults, but during embryonic stages this bony column is preceded by an unsegmented, elastic rod called a *notochord* (p. 68). A few animals possess a notochord throughout life. These and a few aberrant forms which have a notochord only during larval existence (p. 74; Fig. 5.5, p. 101) either are grouped together into one subphylum, or are placed each in a separate subphylum of its own. Thus in Fig. 14.1 we have shown *Amphioxus,* the form with the persistent notochord, as having its own subphylum: Cephalochorda.

Phylum

The subphyla to which we have alluded combine to form Phylum Chordata (Fig. 14.1); the name refers to possession of a notochord at some time during life. Examples of other phyla are: Phylum Arthropoda (insects, crustaceans, etc.); Phylum Mollusca (snails, clams, oysters, and all kinds of "shell fish"); Phylum Protozoa (one-celled animals, or small animals lacking cellular structure, depending upon one's point of view).

Ascending Categories

Thus we see that the classification of the dog consists of an ascending series of more and more inclusive categories (Fig. 14.2). Or the classification may be looked at from the other point of view, as a descending series of categories, each one subdivided in turn until the smallest unit, the species, is reached. Fig. 14.2 shows the "steps" involved whether we travel them upward or downward. All of the categories named in the figure are subdivided, thereby increasing the number of "steps" in the series. Thus orders are divided into suborders, families into subfamilies, and so on. This added complexity is not important to the present discussion, however, although one subdivision, the subspecies, will receive special attention presently (pp. 320–326). Every animal can be classified in a manner similar to that employed above for the dog. We see that the higher or more inclusive categories are shared by large numbers of animals. Thus a dog and its master both belong to Phylum Chordata, Subphylum Vertebrata, and Class Mammalia (Fig. 14.1). The "parting of the ways" comes at the level of orders. While the dog belongs to Order Carnivora, its master belongs to Order Primates. Within the Order Primates, man is classified as belonging

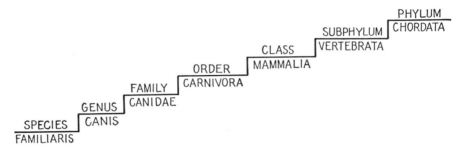

FIG. 14.2. Classification viewed as a series of steps.

to Family Hominidae. Man's genus in this family is called *Homo;* his species within the genus, *sapiens*. Hence *Homo sapiens* is his scientific name, as mentioned previously.

Classification Reflects Evolution

Having reviewed the general principles followed in classifying animals, we may next ask: what has this classification to do with evolution? As already noted, the system was designed by Linnaeus as a logical method of classifying and cataloguing, a method to be adopted by biologists of all countries, thereby eliminating the confusion which had existed up to that time. The Linnaean system has served this purpose admirably.

Linnaeus was not convinced of the truth of evolution. He believed that the species he named had been created as he found them. This view of the fixity of species was the one commonly held by biologists of his day, although, as we saw in Chapter 1, ideas of evolution had existed long before the eighteenth century. Nevertheless, it was not until the nineteenth century, bringing the writings of Darwin, that belief in evolution became really common. It may be of interest to note in passing that before the end of his life Linnaeus modified his views sufficiently to think it probable that some new species might have arisen by crossing or hybridization of the species originally created.

As we have seen, the Linnaean system is based on similarity. Animals similar in structure are classed together; animals dissimilar in structure are separated. Characteristics used in classifying are the fundamental similarities which we termed homologous in Chapter 3. Failure to distinguish homologous similarity from analogous similarity (i.e., that connected with similar function, pp. 20–26) results in errors of classification. Such an error was formerly made when whales were classified as fishes rather than as mammals.

To Linnaeus, two species which were similar in structure and therefore to be classed in the same genus were not *related* to each other in any sense of inheritance. In creating each separately the Creator had seen fit to make them similar to each other, just as a carpenter may see fit to build two houses which are much alike. The houses are not "related"; neither, to Linnaeus and most of his contemporaries, were the species.

Conceivably, then, fundamental similarities may be shared by two species because these species were created to resemble each other, no genetic relationship being present. On the other hand, fundamental similarities may be shared by two species because these species were derived from a common ancestor, or because one species was the ancestor of the other. Common inheritance as the explanation for similarity accords with the evolutionary interpretation, a matter we discussed at some length in Chapter 3 (see especially pp. 25–26). According to this view, a classification based on fundamental similarities, as the Linnaean system is, becomes a classification reflecting the actual *relationships* of the animals classified. The species included in one genus are similar because they are related to each other; they inherited their similarities from a common ancestor. Two genera included in one family have many characteristics in common; these were inherited from a predecessor ancestral to both genera. And so on step by step through the classification. Creatures as diverse as a fish and a man are included in one phylum, to pass to the "top" of our classification. Fish and man have some characteristics in common, notably possession of a notochord during some stage of life. Why do they and all other members of Phylum Chordata have this notochord? If the evolutionary explanation is correct they have it because they inherited it from an ancient form which once lived on this planet and was the remote ancestor of all of them.

It is customary today to refer to the classification of animals as a "natural system of classification." By this is meant a system based on the true (i.e., genetic) relationships of the animals classified. A natural system may be contrasted with an "artificial system" of classification having as its sole objective the cataloguing of plants and animals as a librarian classifies and catalogues books. The system as devised by Linnaeus was essentially an artificial system. But the similarities forming the basis for the cataloguing are now regarded as indicative of genetic relationship—related animals being classified together, unrelated ones separated from each other. Hence the artificial system has become a natural system *if* we agree that fundamental similarities of structure derive from common ancestry, the evolutionary explanation.

WHAT IS A SPECIES?

Students of evolution lay particular emphasis upon the small unit of classification mentioned above, the species. This is reflected in the fact that Darwin named his great treatise on evolution *The Origin of Species*. It is felt that if the origin of separate species can be accounted for, the origin of genera, families, orders, and so on, can be explained by the further application of the principles discovered or by extensions of those principles. To a considerable extent two new species arising from one original parent species would constitute the first step in evolutionary change. Two men walking down a road come to a fork in that road; one man follows the road to the right, the other man the road to the left. For a little while the two men are near together even though they may eventually have diverged so that they are thousands of miles apart. Similarly, two groups of animals starting on divergent courses of evolution would at the outset be very similar, similar enough to be regarded as two species in the same genus, even though their remote descendants may be "poles apart" in structure. Accordingly, if we can account for the first step in developing diversity of structure, the step which produces enough diversity to separate groups into distinct, though related, species, we have gone far toward an understanding of the causes of evolution. The species, then, occupies a key position in thinking on evolution. It is important that we inquire into the nature of the species with a view to determining what is involved in the origin of species.

What is a species? We asked that question earlier, in our discussion of human evolution (pp. 248–250). There we noted two attributes of species: (1) some degree of structural difference and (2) reproductive isolation. From differences of opinion concerning the relative importance of these two attributes arises most of the controversy over definition of the word. To focus attention upon the contrasting points of view we shall quote two proposed definitions. The first is that of Tate Regan, quoted with approval by various subsequent authors (e.g., Gates, 1948): "A species is a community, or a number of related communities, whose distinctive morphological characters are, in the opinion of a competent systematist, sufficiently definite to entitle it, or them, to a specific name." We note in this definition entire emphasis upon "distinctive morphological characters." We also note a point mentioned in our earlier discussion—the great amount of individual subjective judgment which admittedly enters into decisions as to what constitutes "sufficiently definite" morphological differences.

The second definition is that of Mayr (1942) quoted earlier: "Species are groups of actually or potentially interbreeding natural populations, which are reproductively isolated from other such groups." This definition places complete emphasis upon reproductive isolation, since the latter is felt to be primary. Given reproductive isolation, "distinctive morphological characters" will usually arise in due course (pp. 487–489).

These two definitions represent the extremes of a series. Many writers on the subject have proposed definitions of the word "species," most of them combining the two attributes of structural difference and reproductive isolation in various manners and degrees. Instead of proposing a definition of our own we shall discuss the various attributes which usually characterize species.

At the outset we may note that it is by no means necessary to assume that all species have "actually" the same properties or attributes, quite aside from differing human judgments in the matter. Among the one-celled animals (Protozoa), for example, "the species" may well be quite a differently constituted unit from "the species" among mammals. Indeed, it could hardly be otherwise. Despite differences, however, species do in general have some attributes in common. Accordingly we shall list some of the attributes which *on the average* are found to be characteristic of the species as a unit both of classification and of evolution.

In the first place, a species is a group of animals all of which usually possess some distinctive characteristic or characteristics. The characteristic is usually morphological, a visible structure, although some species are known which are not visibly distinguishable from each other. In such cases the "distinctive characteristic" is chemical or physiological. When, as in most instances, the distinctive characteristics are structural, the difference in structure between two closely allied species need not be great. Indeed, the difference is frequently quite small. The Florida tree snails, popular with many people because of the bright colors and varied patterns of the shells, may afford us an example here. These ornate snails all belong to one genus, *Liguus,* divided into several species. Two of the principal species are distinguished from each other by the fact that the apex of the coiled shell of one species is pink in color, while the apex of the shell of the other species is white. One authority on these snails commented, "This may seem like a trivial character on which to found a species, but it is the only constant one" (Simpson, 1929). Great variety in color pattern is found within the white-tipped species; the same is true within the pink-tipped one. The color of the tip, then, is the distinctive characteristic which makes possible classification of the varying forms into the two species.

Turning to a very different type of animal, we have an example of species differences between the two species of "deer mice" or "white-footed mice" inhabiting Vermont. These familiar inhabitants of woods and fields have large eyes and ears and long tails. Body and tail are dark-colored above but white on the under surfaces; the feet are white. Both species belong to genus *Peromyscus*. One belongs to species *maniculatus,* the other to the species *leucopus*. Although the two species are much alike there are a number of small differences between them. The hair clothing the back of *leucopus* is reddish brown, while the color of *maniculatus* is more predominantly gray, mixed with brown. Compared to *leucopus, maniculatus* has a longer tail, with a more sharply defined black stripe running the length of its upper surface, a more slender skull, with smaller molar teeth. Thus we see again that the characteristics distinguishing one species from its allies are usually small. Magnitude is not the important point; it is sufficient that the characteristic, though small, be possessed by all members of the group in question.

As a second attribute of species we return to the matter of *reproductive isolation*. As indicated in our discussion of human evolution (pp. 248–250), there is great difference of opinion as to the importance to be accorded this attribute. No statement we can make will be immune to criticism. Hence we shall make the statement which seems most generally applicable, admitting that there are exceptions to it. Members of separate species are usually reproductively isolated from each other, meaning that they usually *do not* interbreed or hybridize if and when they come into contact with each other. The wording "do not" was chosen deliberately. In many cases members of different species *cannot* interbreed. In the two species of *Peromyscus* inhabiting Vermont, for example, there is no evidence that it is possible for interbreeding to occur, either in a state of nature or when members of the two species are kept together in cages. On the other hand, many cases are known of species which *can* interbreed but do not do so under natural conditions. Referring to *Peromyscus* again, we find that our species *leucopus* ranges southward into Virginia. Another species, *gossypinus,* is found in the south Atlantic states, ranging northward into Virginia. In the Dismal Swamp of Virginia the ranges of the two species overlap so that members of both live together there. From a study of the mouse population of that swamp Dice

(1940) has concluded that there is no evidence that the two species breed together and produce hybrids—this despite the fact that when mice of the two species are kept together in laboratory cages they readily produce healthy and fertile hybrid offspring. Why do they not hybridize under natural conditions? It does not seem too anthropomorphic to conclude that when given a choice each prefers members of its own species to members of the other. Accordingly we conclude that where morphological or physiological barriers to interbreeding do not exist, psychological barriers may operate to the same end (see pp. 471–473).

We readily appreciate that this failure of species to interbreed (reproductive isolation) is important for the maintenance of the species as a discrete unit. Without this tendency not to hybridize, whenever two species came into contact interbreeding would tend to combine the two species into a varied hybrid population, an amalgamation in which the species concerned would become inextricably combined, losing identity and individuality. Although this process doubtless occurs at times, the fact that species in general maintain their individuality indicates that such interbreeding is not the usual situation.

As intimated above, the statement that members of different species do not interbreed is subject to exceptions. When hybrids between species are produced, however, they commonly, but not invariably, have lowered fertility or are completely sterile. Thus, despite the production of hybrids, the reproductive isolation of the species is maintained. Obviously a sterile hybrid population could not perpetuate itself and become a "melting pot" into which the two parent species would sink.

At times, on the other hand, hybridization may play an important role in evolution just as it does in the breeding programs by which man improves his domesticated animals and cultivated plants. Hybrids possess new combinations of characteristics arising from their mixed ancestry. In cases in which they are viable and fertile, such hybrids may under some circumstances enjoy advantages not possessed by either parent species, and hence be favored by natural selection (see further discussion on pp. 477–481).

In one way or another, the integrity of species is maintained by reproductive isolation. Without the latter there would be no species. Hence the justification for the primacy given reproductive isolation in Mayr's definition of species quoted above. Further discussion of the importance of reproductive isolation and of the mechanisms by which it arises will be found in Chapters 20 and 21.

We should note in passing, however, that the definition of "actually or potentially interbreeding populations, which are reproductively isolated from other such groups" has significance only for organisms that reproduce sexually. Plant and animal groups in which reproduction is asexual are not "interbreeding populations." In some cases a single individual may give rise to a whole line of descendants (a **clone** or **biotype**), all just like the original individual except as new mutations may from time to time introduce changes. Since interbreeding is absent, no test of reproductive isolation is possible. Classifying asexual organisms into species must therefore be based upon possession of distinctive characteristics as mentioned above. This is one reason why a species definition suitable for a majority of organisms is nevertheless not suitable for others (many plants and protozoans, for example).

Another attribute of species refers to the range or territory occupied. *Usually two closely allied species do not occupy the same territory, though frequently their territories will adjoin.* From the preceding discussion we can appreciate the fact that two closely allied species will usually be very similar to each other in appearance and habits. This implies that they will be likely to depend upon the same or similar food supply, seek the same home or nesting sites, and so on. Thus if they occupied the same territory they would usually be in direct competition. Such competition doubtless occurs and is important in promoting evolutionary change, yet in groups of species in a state of approximate equilibrium at a given stage in evolutionary history, direct competition is reduced when territories occupied by allied species are separate. An example may be found in the two species of *Peromyscus* inhabiting Vermont. *Peromyscus leucopus* occupies wooded lowlands and the lower portions of the mountain slopes; *maniculatus* occupies the higher portions of these mountains. While the two species both live in the state of Vermont, they actually occupy separate, though adjoining, territories.

In the case just mentioned, the wooded lowlands differ from the higher portions of the mountains not only geographically but also by environmental differences. Sometimes closely allied species may occupy the *same* territory if their environmental (ecological) requirements differ. We noted earlier (p. 294 and Fig. 13.3, p. 295) that three species of ground finches are enabled to live together on the Galápagos Islands because each species specializes in eating seeds of a certain size. Thus direct competition is reduced and we have an exception to the general rule that closely allied species do not usually occupy the same territory.

A corollary of the reproductive isolation mentioned earlier lies in the fact that when the territories occupied by two species do overlap there is generally no interbreeding between the species (recall the two species of *Pero-*

myscus inhabiting the Dismal Swamp). As a result, *forms intermediate in structure or transitional between the two species are not usually found.* The body structure of one species is usually separated from the structure of neighboring species by a "bridgeless gap." The word "usually" is important in this statement, since many exceptions occur.

We may summarize our discussion of the species as a unit of classification and evolution by listing the following attributes which *in general* characterize species: (1) members of a species possess in common distinctive characteristics; (2) intermediate or transitional forms are not usually found; (3) members of separate species do not usually interbreed, or if hybrids are produced they are usually sterile; (4) allied species usually have separate, though frequently adjoining, territories.

It is safe to surmise that any population of animals having all four of the attributes just listed will be considered a distinct species by all biologists. Disagreement enters when a group has some of the attributes but not all.

Finally, we may mention the practical difficulty of applying the yardstick of reproductive isolation to populations which are separated geographically (are **allopatric**). *If* such populations came into contact in nature *would* they interbreed? One method of answering the question is to attempt artificial hybridization between them. But here the evidence is one-sided. If the two populations will not interbreed in the laboratory (assuming that each population will breed within itself under such circumstances), that fact would be considered evidence that the populations are in fact separate species. Suppose, however, that the populations *do* interbreed in the laboratory: that fact is not in itself evidence that the populations should be considered to belong to one and the same species. For in a state of nature they might not interbreed, and if they *did* not they would be as reproductively isolated as though they *could* not. For this reason, and because many animals will not breed in captivity anyway, the experimental approach to the question has limited usefulness. Hence frequently the question can not be answered directly. Accordingly, systematists attempt to solve the dilemma by deciding whether or not the amount of morphological difference between the two populations is great enough so that they probably would not interbreed *if* they did come into contact naturally. But this brings us back to the variable of differences in judgment between individual biologists as to how much morphological difference is necessary if populations are to be regarded as separate species. Truly there is no royal road to classification. Nature is enormously complex. The complexity of the problems presented affords much of the challenge and fascination in science. If all the problems were easy "there would be no fun in science," as one biologist remarked to the author. Clearly the study of species is in no immediate danger of being shorn of "fun."

For discussion of forces and factors operative in species formation see Chapter 21.

SUBSPECIES OR GEOGRAPHIC RACES

We have referred several times to a division of the species called the subspecies. This smallest unit of classification corresponds to a "race" or "variety." We noted earlier that human races correspond to this category in classification (pp. 250–255).

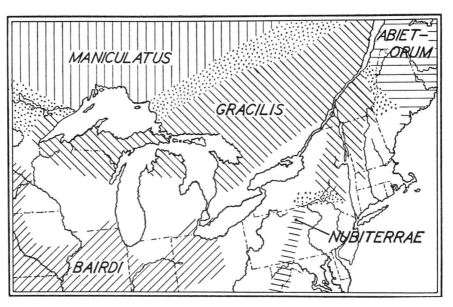

FIG. 14.3. Distribution of *Peromyscus maniculatus gracilis,* with portions of the ranges of neighboring subspecies (geographic races). Dots indicate areas of intergradation. (After Osgood, 1909.)

Increasingly the practice is followed of adding the name of the subspecies to the scientific name of an animal, thereby converting the name from a binomial to a trinomial. The name applied to the deer mouse inhabiting the mountains of Vermont then becomes *Peromyscus maniculatus gracilis.* From Fig. 14.3 we note that this subspecies ranges west to the Great Lakes. South and west of the latter another subspecies is found: *Peromyscus maniculatus bairdi*. North of Lake Superior and on into Canada is found the subspecies from which came the first specimen of *Peromyscus maniculatus* known to science. This specimen is called the "type specimen," and its subspecies is the type subspecies, being given the name *Peromyscus maniculatus maniculatus*.

Returning momentarily to our earlier analogy between scientific names and human names, we see that the name of the subspecies corresponds in a sense to a "middle name." Thus in a large city there may be so many John Smiths that it is necessary to distinguish between them in some way. Accordingly a metropolitan directory may list: "Smith, John Gregory; Smith, John Stuart; Smith, John Wilber," and so on.

One of the most distinctive attributes of subspecies is the fact that they occupy distinct territories, hence the appropriateness of the name **geographic race.** For example, the species *Peromyscus maniculatus* is divided into many subspecies scattered over the face of North America in such manner that a map of their distribution resembles a patchwork quilt. Fig. 14.3 shows the range of the subspecies *gracilis* mentioned above, together with portions of the ranges of other subspecies found in the northeastern part of this continent. We note that the map indicates certain regions in which intergradation occurs. This is a common feature of areas in which two subspecies come into contact.

Ordinarily members of different subspecies within one species are completely interfertile and hybridize readily whenever they come into contact. This condition stands in direct contrast to that noted previously as prevailing in regions in which the territories of two different *species* come into contact or overlap. Mechanisms of reproductive isolation which keep species separate have on the whole not developed between subspecies. Our discussion of lack of reproductive isolation between human races will be recalled in this connection (pp. 248–250). The principal factor operating to keep subspecies separate is a geographic one; different subspecies live in separate regions and hence for the most part do not come into contact with each other. So long as this condition prevails each subspecies maintains its integrity.

For the most part subspecies differ from one another in one or more structural features. Usually the differences are less than those found between two related species. Indeed, the visible differences may be so small that only an expert can see any difference at all, and frequently an expert must have a considerable number of specimens for comparison before he can be sure which of two subspecies is represented. One reason for this state of affairs is the fact that, as stressed earlier in our discussion of human races (pp. 251–254), subspecies frequently differ from each other in the *frequencies* with which certain genes (and hence characters) occur rather than in possession of certain genes by all members of one subspecies and absence of those genes from all members of a second subspecies. Varying distributions of the blood group genes in different human races furnish an example (pp. 251–252). "Races may be defined as populations which differ in the frequencies of some genes" (Dobzhansky, 1950).

Frequently the differences between subspecies seem to be more or less chance differences of no particular significance in the lives of the organisms (nonadaptive traits). At times we may consider differences nonadaptive merely through ignorance of their real significance, but there is no reason to doubt that populations may come to possess characteristics which are actually nonadaptive (see discussion of genetic drift, pp. 439–447). On the other hand, differences between subspecies may at times be clearly adaptive. A most interesting case of this in *Peromyscus* is afforded by a race of mice inhabiting Santa Rosa Island off the coast of northern Florida, near Pensacola. This long, narrow island running parallel to the shore and separated from it in places by only a quarter of a mile of water is covered with an exceptionally white sand. Living on the island is the lightest-colored race of *Peromyscus* known: *P. polionotus leucocephalus*. "In this race, most of the hair is white from base to tip, while the pigment of the skin is greatly reduced" (Sumner, 1932). Such a white race living in regions of white sand affords an excellent example of protective coloration, the protection in this case being against predators that use their sense of sight in locating prey, especially owls. We shall describe later (pp. 364–365) experiments which demonstrated that in actuality being light colored on a light-colored background does protect mice from predation by owls. We may picture this white race as having arisen during the past few thousand years by the action of natural selection favoring genes and mutations tending to lighten the color of the mice inhabiting the island. We may note in passing that *leucocephalus* is not an albino, differing from normally pigmented mice by a single gene as albinos commonly do. From the results of breeding experiments Sumner (1932) concluded that *leucocephalus* differs from the fully pigmented *polionotus* (see below) by a number of genes having additive effects (multiple genes or polygenes, pp. 391–394).

The race *leucocephalus* was evidently derived from the somewhat similar race on the neighboring mainland: *Peromyscus polionotus albifrons*. This race lives on the beaches and is light in color but not so light as *leuco-*

cephalus. Further inland live mice which are still darker in color and are named *Peromyscus polionotus polionotus*.

"The Subspecies Versus the Cline"

In the above example we note a regular progression in pigmentation: (1) in the interior a dark-colored form; (2) on the beaches a lighter-colored form; (3) on the neighboring island a still lighter form. As noted earlier (p. 274), such a gradient, or progressive pattern of change, across the face of the country is called a **cline.** Actually this cline has more than the three steps indicated, since Sumner found that intermediate forms between race *polionotus* and race *albifrons* occurred as he collected specimens nearer and nearer the coast of the mainland. This being the case, can we really draw a line between *P. polionotus polionotus* and *P. polionotus albifrons?*

Two points of view are possible: (1) subspecies *polionotus* and subspecies *albifrons* are realities; they interbreed when they come into contact, producing intermediate forms; (2) *Peromyscus polionotus* is not divided into subspecies but is characterized by ordered variability of hair color in the form of a cline. In our earlier discussion of clines (pp. 274–275) we noted the cline exhibited by zebras in the striping of the legs (Fig. 12.6, p. 275). The cline is an observable fact. The zebras are commonly considered to be divided into subspecies, partly upon the basis of this striping, but the difficulty encountered in delimiting the subspecies is reflected in the fact that no two investigators seem able to agree on how many subspecies there are or what shall be considered to constitute each one (cf. Cabrera, 1936; Rząśnicki, 1951). This is an extreme case; the confusion arises in part from the fact that no two individual zebras are alike in markings.

Wilson and Brown (1953) have stressed the view that subspecies are artificial creations of biologists' minds. Frequently a species with wide distribution may exhibit clines in a number of characteristics, e.g., coat color, ear size, foot length, tail length. From locality to locality the variability in one characteristic does not parallel variability in another one; the variabilities are independent, not concordant as we should expect them to be if subspecies (representing a certain coterie of characteristics) were realities. Nevertheless, considerations of practical usefulness will doubtless continue to cause biologists to designate as subspecies populations living in certain territories and characterized on the average by certain "constellations of characteristics." To some extent this involves putting nature in a strait jacket and drawing lines where there really are none, a fact which is of itself eloquent of the occurrence of evolution.

Subspecies and Microgeographic Races

Another difficulty in identifying subspecies or geographic races is the fact that they possess no clear-cut lower limit. They grade insensibly into **microgeographic races,** local races inhabiting small areas, e.g., one pond or one wood lot (Wilson and Brown, 1953). For example, Dice (1937) investigated populations of *Peromyscus* inhabiting wood lots only 3 or 4 miles apart but separated by cultivated land. He found statistically significant dif-

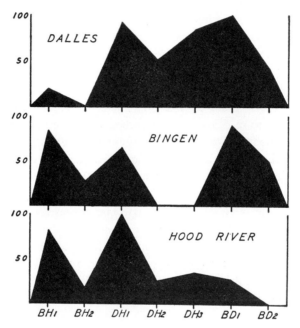

FIG. 14.4. "Profiles" representing the distribution of seven red-blood-cell antigens in three stocks of *Peromyscus*. Ordinate scale represents percentages of individuals possessing the respective antigens designated on the abscissa. (From Moody, "Cellular antigens in three stocks of *Peromyscus maniculatus* from the Columbia River valley," *Contributions from the Laboratory of Vertebrate Biology, University of Michigan*, No. 39, 1948, p. 13.)

ferences between these various subpopulations in a variety of bodily and skeletal measurements and in hair color. The present author made a serological study of three populations of *Peromyscus maniculatus* living a few miles apart in the Columbia River valley (Moody, 1948). He identified seven antigens in the red blood cells somewhat comparable to the A and B substances in human blood cells (p. 121). As the profiles in Fig. 14.4 indicate, the three populations differed from one another in percentage of individuals possessing each of the seven antigens. This is the same sort of racial difference we noted in percentages of individuals belonging to the different human blood groups. Whenever genetic tests are made a genetic basis for cellular antigens is always disclosed. Hence we may feel confident that Fig. 14.4 represents genetic difference between populations of wild animals living only a few miles apart.

Many other examples of microgeographic races might be cited (see Dobzhansky 1950, p. 168 ff.). Microgeographic races are of great interest since they represent subpopulations of a type postulated as important in the process of species formation (see speciation, pp. 484–491).

Microgeographic races are not clearly distinguishable from geographic races (subspecies). In fact the three populations of Columbia River valley mice analyzed serologically may be considered to represent different subspecies at least in part (Dice, 1949). Again we see in this difficulty in drawing lines eloquent testimony to the fact of evolutionary change.

Evolutionary Significance of Subspecies

We have presented several contrasts between species and subspecies: (1) Members of different species do not ordinarily interbreed when they come into contact; members of different subspecies within one species ordinarily do so. (2) Different species frequently occupy separate territories, but the latter may overlap, in which case intermediate forms are usually not found; different subspecies occupy separate territories which do not overlap, and if the territories come into contact intermediate or transitional forms are frequently found. (3) Structural differences between species are usually greater than those between subspecies.

We should note, however, that exceptions are found to every one of the above statements. In practice, then, it is frequently difficult to be sure whether two groups of animals should be classed as belonging to two subspecies in one species or whether they should be regarded as two distinct species in one genus. Thus again the judgment of the individual biologist comes into play, and with it opportunity for much disagreement in details of classification.

The principal interest in the subspecies or geographic race from the standpoint of evolution lies in the fact that it seems to represent a small step in the development of diversity. Most clusters of subspecies (Fig. 14.3) probably arose when descendants from some parental stock migrated out from a center of dispersal (pp. 268–272). As animals spread out over the country groups of them became separated from each other by distance and sometimes by geographic barriers. These separate groups, being out of contact with each other, gradually came to develop differences, so that each was no longer quite like the original parent stock or, on the other hand, quite like the other groups. (Recall our discussion of the processes involved in the evolution of the human races, pp. 250–255.) Each group would then rank as

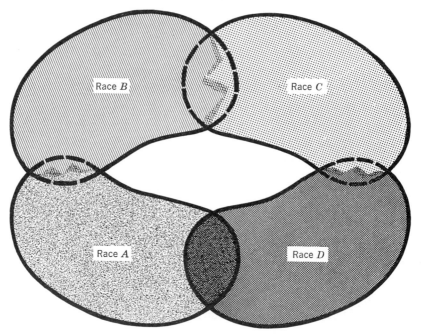

FIG. 14.5. The ranges of four geographic races forming a Rassenkreis. Where the ranges come into contact interbreeding occurs in three cases, but it does not occur in the area where Race D comes into contact with Race A.

a separate subspecies or geographic race. If now the groups became progressively more and more different in structure, and if, especially, these differences finally became sufficient to prevent interbreeding whenever members of different groups came in contact, the groups would be considered to have reached the rank of separate species. In brief, according to this view, the subspecies is a step in the development of the species.

We have referred to "clusters" of subspecies; sometimes these form more or less circular mosaics covering a certain geographic area. Such a mosaic or circle of races has been termed by Rensch (1960) a **rassenkreis.** Suppose, for example, that a rough circle is formed by races A, B, C, and D

(Fig. 14.5). Race A interbreeds with race B where their ranges come into contact. Race B interbreeds with race C, as does race C with race D. But race D does *not* interbreed with race A where their ranges come into contact. Are race D and race A to be considered separate *species* because they are thus reproductively isolated from each other? Perhaps not so long as the circle of interbreeding forms (races B and C) connecting them exists. But if races B and C were not known (had become extinct before biologists investigated the situation) probably race A and race D would be considered separate species. We mention this matter (1) to illustrate the fact that subspecies are not in all cases clearly distinguishable from species, and (2) to indicate one way in which species may arise from subspecies. (For further examples and discussion see Rensch, 1960, p. 23 ff.; Goldschmidt, 1940, p. 117 ff.; Lack, 1947, Fig. 23, p. 127, and accompanying text.)

We do not wish to give the impression that all subspecies are on the way to becoming species. For most subspecies, conditions will probably never be favorable for further development. Opportunity will not knock on their doors. But for a minority, conditions will favor further evolution leading to the formation of new species, and even perhaps eventually to new genera, families, and so on.

In subsequent chapters we shall discuss in more detail the processes involved in subspecies and species formation, as well as in the production of the major adaptive changes which usually distinguish members of different higher categories (e.g., different orders).

Conclusion

Let us return for a moment to the question of the manner in which classification supports the idea of creation by evolution, as contrasted with the idea of special creation. We have seen that classification is based upon similarity, primarily morphological similarity. To most biologists it seems more reasonable to explain fundamental similarities as based upon inheritance from common ancestry than as being due to the fact that separately created animals were created to be similar, or created according to similar patterns. Again, the difficulty of defining a species, of separating one species from another, and of telling whether a certain group is a species or a subspecies seems to indicate a web of interrelationships in nature, interrelationships most readily explained as arising by divergence from common ancestry. If each species were separately created it should be much easier than it is to draw sharp lines between them, and to draw sharp lines between species and subspecies.

References and Suggested Readings

Cabrera, A. "Subspecific and individual variation in the Burchell zebras," *Journal of Mammalogy*, 17 (1936), 89–112.

Dice, L. R. "Variation in the wood-mouse, *Peromyscus leucopus noveboracensis*, in the northeastern United States," *Occasional Papers, Museum of Zoology, University of Michigan*, No. 352, 1937. Pp. 1–32.

Dice, L. R. "Relationships between the wood-mouse and the cotton-mouse in eastern Virginia," *Journal of Mammalogy*, 21 (1940), 14–23.

Dice, L. R. "Variation of *Peromyscus maniculatus* in parts of western Washington and adjacent Oregon," *Contributions, Laboratory of Vertebrate Biology, University of Michigan*, No. 44 (1949), 1–34.

Dobzhansky, Th. "The genetic nature of differences among men." In S. Persons (ed.). *Evolutionary Thought in America*. New Haven: Yale University Press, 1950. Pp. 86–155.

Gates, R. R. *Human Ancestry from a Genetical Point of View*. Cambridge: Harvard University Press, 1948.

Goldschmidt, R. *The Material Basis of Evolution*. New Haven: Yale University Press, 1940. (Includes detailed discussion of subspecies formation.)

Huxley, J. (ed.) *The New Systematics*. Oxford: Oxford University Press, 1940.

Lack, D. *Darwin's Finches*. Cambridge: Cambridge University Press, 1947.

Mayr, E. *Systematics and the Origin of Species*. New York: Columbia University Press, 1942.

Mayr, E. "The bearing of the new systematics on genetical problems. The nature of species." In M. Demerec (ed.). *Advances in Genetics*, Vol. II. New York: Academic Press, Inc., 1948.

Mayr, E. (ed.). *The Species Problem*. Washington, D.C.: American Association for Advancement of Science, 1957.

Moody, P. A. "Cellular antigens in three stocks of *Peromyscus maniculatus* from the Columbia River valley," *Contributions, Laboratory of Vertebrate Biology, University of Michigan*, No. 39 (1948), 1–16.

Osgood, W. H. "Revision of the mice of the American genus *Peromyscus*," *North American Fauna*, No. 28. Washington, D.C.: U.S. Government Printing Office, 1909.

Rensch, B. *Evolution Above the Species Level*. New York: Columbia University Press, 1960.

Rząśnicki, A. "Zebras and quaggas," *Annales Musei Zoologici Polonici*, 14 (1951), 203–252. (16 plates.)

Seton, E. T. *Lives of Game Animals*, 4 vols. New York: Doubleday & Company, Inc., 1929.

Simpson, C. T. "The Florida tree snails of the genus *Liguus*," No. 2741, *Proceedings of the U.S. National Museum*, Vol. 73, Art. 20, 1929.

Simpson, G. G. "The principles of classification and a classification of mammals," *Bulletin of the American Museum of Natural History*, 85 (1945), 1–350.

Simpson, G. G. *Principles of Animal Taxonomy*. New York: Columbia University Press, 1961.

Sumner, F. B. "An analysis of geographic variation in mice of the *Peromyscus polionotus* group from Florida and Alabama," *Journal of Mammalogy*, 7 (1926), 149–184.

Sumner, F. B. "Genetic, distributional, and evolutionary studies of the subspecies of deer mice (*Peromyscus*)," *Bibliographia Genetica*, 9 (1932), 1–106.

Wilson, E. O., and W. L. Brown, Jr. "The subspecies concept and its taxonomic application," *Systematic Zoology*, 2 (1953), 97–111.

CHAPTER 15

MEANS AND METHODS OF EVOLUTIONARY CHANGE

The Problem

In preceding chapters we have noted evolution manifested in many guises.

We have seen numerous examples of relatively unspecialized animals which have given rise to descendants specialized for some particular mode of life. We have seen that frequently several lines of descendants have arisen from one ancestral group, and have termed this phenomenon adaptive radiation.

We have noted independent occurrence of similar evolutionary trends, and have termed this parallel evolution when the independent evolution occurred in two related groups of animals, convergent evolution when it involved two relatively unrelated groups.

We have observed the complexity of human evolution and suggested that isolated human populations developed differing characteristics while isolated, and that these characteristics were variously combined and recombined when subsequently the populations came into contact through migrations and conquests.

We have emphasized that the past and present geographic distribution of animals suggests that a form originates in a certain region (its "center of dispersal") and as descendants spread out from this center they undergo modification, so that eventually they differ from one another and from the parent form.

We have noted ways in which animals finding themselves on oceanic islands have been able to exploit environmental niches they would never have entered on continents.

We have seen that the formation of geographic races (subspecies) represents one of the first steps in development of that diversity which is a hallmark of evolutionary change, and that formation of the greater diversity characterizing species seems to be a later step in the same process.

All of these evolutionary manifestations require explanation. It is one thing to note their occurrence, another to explain the means by which they occur. Although the manifestations are varied, explanation of them obviously has a common denominator. In every case we are called upon to explain *diversity—how it arises and how it is preserved and perpetuated.* For evolution is the process by reason of which descendants differ from their ancestors.

We now direct our attention to the various factors contributing to the production of change in animals and hence to the origin of diversity. In Chapter 2 we sketched broadly some of the principal factors involved. In this chapter and the following ones we shall discuss these in more detail and introduce others not mentioned previously. Rereading of Chapter 2 will form appropriate introduction to the subject matter of these chapters.

SHUFFLING THE GENES

It is common observation that no two individuals are alike. Even so-called "identical twins," if observed closely enough, will be found to differ in some respects. And the extreme diversity among the population at large needs no emphasizing. The same diversity exists in the subhuman portions of the animal kingdom. If "every mouse looks like every other mouse" to us it is because we have not observed mice closely enough to be familiar with their distinguishing features. Recall the comment made by many Americans that all Chinese look alike, and the similar comment of Chinese newly come to this country that Americans are difficult to recognize because they all look alike. The individual differences are there; the difficulty in recognizing them lies in faulty observation, based on inadequate past experience.

What is the basis of this diversity among individuals? Insofar as it is of hereditary nature it arises in good part as the result of the operation of the mechanisms of inheritance.

On an earlier page (p. 10) we mentioned the units of heredity called **genes.** These are contained in **chromosomes** found in all cells composing the body. The chromosomes occur in pairs, one member of each pair being inherited from the father, the other from the mother. When germ cells are formed by an individual the members of each pair of chromosomes separate from each other; each germ cell receives one member only of each pair of chromosomes (Fig. 15.1). Since genes are contained in the chromosomes, genes also occur in pairs, and each germ cell receives but one member of each pair (Fig. 15.1). The genes composing any pair may be alike, or they may differ. Thus, to use a familiar example which somewhat oversimplifies actual conditions, a person may inherit a gene for brown eyes from each of

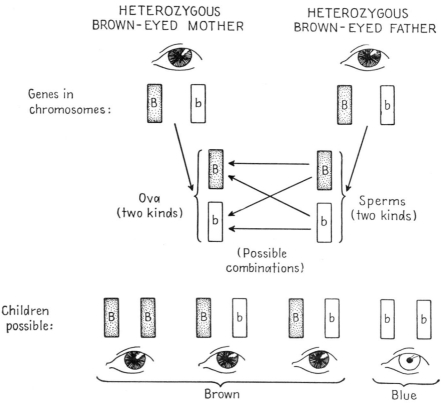

FIG. 15.1. Mendelian inheritance of eye color in a family in which both parents are brown-eyed but heterozygous. Brown color is shown as dependent upon a single gene which is dominant to the gene for blue color—somewhat of an oversimplification.

his parents. He will, of course, be brown-eyed. Another person may inherit a gene for blue eyes from each of his parents; he will have blue eyes. A third person may inherit a gene for blue eyes from one parent, a gene for brown eyes from his other parent. What will be the color of his eyes? Experience demonstrates that it will be brown. But it can be shown that the gene for blue eyes in such an individual is not destroyed or altered in any way by its contact with the gene for brown eyes. The gene for blue eyes simply does not produce any visible characteristic when the gene for brown eyes is also present. Hence we say that the gene for blue eyes is **recessive,** the gene for brown eyes **dominant.** A recessive gene, then, is one that does not produce a visible effect in an individual who also possesses the corresponding dominant gene. As a consequence, an individual must inherit a recessive gene from *both* of his parents if he is actually to exhibit the characteristic which that recessive gene produces.

It follows that there are two kinds of brown-eyed people in the world. If we let *B* represent the gene for brown eyes, *b* the gene for blue eyes, we can represent the two kinds of brown-eyed people as follows: (1) *BB*, (2) *Bb*. Both types are said to have the same **phenotype:** the same visible, bodily expression of the gene *B*. But they differ in **genotype:** in genetic constitution. Members of the first type have inherited the gene from both of their parents. Members of the second type have inherited a brown-eye gene from one parent, a blue-eye gene from the other. (Actually there are more than these two kinds of brown-eyed people, since more than one pair of genes are involved in producing the varying shades of brown eyes observable. But for present purposes concentration of attention on the one pair of genes will suffice.) Following this scheme, blue-eyed people have the formula *bb,* the gene for blue eyes having been received from both parents. Blue-eyed people, and brown eyed people of the first type (i.e., *BB*), having both members of the pair of genes alike, are said to be **homozygous.** Brown-eyed people of the second type (*Bb*), having one gene for brown eye, one gene for blue eye, are said to be **heterozygous.**

Now suppose that two heterozygous brown-eyed people marry (*Bb* × *Bb;* Fig. 15.1). The mother produces some ova which contain *B*, some ova which contain *b*. Similarly, the father produces sperm cells which contain *B*, others which contain *b*. What kinds of children are possible? A *B*-containing ovum may be fertilized by a *B*-containing sperm cell; the resulting child will have the *BB* combination and will be brown-eyed. Or a *B*-containing ovum may be fertilized by a *b*-containing sperm cell; the result will be a brown-eyed child (*Bb*). A heterozygous brown-eyed child will also result from the combination of a *b*-containing ovum with a *B*-containing sperm cell. Finally, a *b*-containing ovum may be fertilized by a *b*-containing sperm cell, the result being a blue-eyed child. This latter result is the most interesting from our present standpoint since it illustrates the mechanism by which children frequently differ from their parents. In general terms, heterozygous parents can transmit to their offspring recessive genes which have no visible effect in the parents themselves. Some children, receiving two such genes from their parents, will consequently differ from the latter in the characteristic concerned.

So far we have concentrated upon but one pair of genes, *B* and *b*. Another pair of genes, carried in a different pair of chromosomes, has to do with the color of the hair, determining whether it shall be red or some one of the other shades characteristic of human hair (we shall group them together under the term "non-red"). Accordingly, if parents are heterozygous for *both* these pairs of genes they can have children who have (1) blue eyes and red hair, (2) brown eyes and red hair, (3) blue eyes and non-red hair, (4) brown eyes and non-red hair. Other pairs of genes in other chromosomes are concerned with curliness of the hair. Thus heterozygous parents may have children who have (1) curly red hair and blue eyes, (2) curly non-red hair and blue eyes, (3) straight red hair and blue eyes, (4) curly non-red hair and brown eyes, (5) straight red hair and brown eyes—and so on; the reader can complete the series for himself. If such an amount of diversity is possible on the basis of just three pairs of genes, what a vast amount must be possible on the basis of the approximately 24,000 pairs of genes which each human being is estimated to possess!

One source of diversity in a population, then, lies in the mechanism of inheritance by which thousands of pairs of dominant and recessive genes are reassorted and reassembled generation after generation. The process is analogous to the shuffling of playing cards. How many different "hands" is it possible to obtain from one pack of fifty-two cards? How many different kinds of individuals can arise by the shuffling and "dealing" of many-times-52 pairs of differing genes?

A little thought will convince one that the diversity arising from the process just described is primarily a matter of *new combinations*—new combinations of characteristics already in existence. Shuffling and dealing cards results in new combinations of cards, not in new cards; the latter are still the familiar aces, kings, jacks, and so on. To a considerable extent the "shuffling and dealing" of genes occurring in the production of each new generation is primarily a matter of producing new combinations of old characteristics. For the most part the combinations are new, the individual characteristics entering into the combinations are not. Yet the analogy to playing cards is not perfect, since genes do influence each other. The presence of one gene causes another gene to produce a different result from that which it would produce if the first gene were not there. Because of this interaction of one gene with another the diversity actually produced by the shuffling described above is greater than it would be if the genes were entirely independent in their activities. Nevertheless, much of the diversity produced by the mechanism of heredity is a diversity of new combinations of old characteristics.

In our discussion of blood groups (pp. 121–125) we noted that the red blood cell substances A and B are present in varying proportions in different human populations and in different species of apes. Being gene determined, these substances afford excellent examples of the type of diversity we are discussing. We noted much the same type of diversity in our brief discussions of human races (pp. 250–255), and of the characteristics which distinguish *Peromyscus leucopus* from *Peromyscus maniculatus* (p. 316). In these latter instances the genetics of the differences has not been analyzed as it has in the case of the blood groups, but we may feel confident that an underlying diversity of genes (and of chromosome structure) forms the basis for the observed diversity of adult characteristics. Much evidence of this has been accumulated in animals whose genetic constitutions have been more thoroughly analyzed than have those of man, apes, and *Peromyscus*.

Interbreeding of Populations

We have seen that much diversity is possible as a result of the shuffling and recombination of different genes possessed by members of one population. Suppose that in addition two different populations, having somewhat differing genes, come into contact so that the members interbreed. Such an occurrence will greatly increase the possibilities for diversity. Examples spring to mind of individuals in such crossroads of the world as Hawaii who exhibit a combination of characteristics inherited from, for example, Polynesian, Japanese, and Irish ancestors. Indeed, on an earlier page we surmised that interbreeding of originally separate human populations has occurred repeatedly during the course of human evolution, and that the occurrence explains much concerning the origin of observed diversity of mankind past and present (pp. 246–248).

Significance for Evolution

Of what significance for evolution is this recombining of genes? In Chapter 2 we noted that the positive aspect of natural selection consists of the favoring of animals possessed of hereditary characteristics that are beneficial, either in the environment in which the animal finds itself or in some other environment open to it. The cumulative result of this favoring is postadaptation in the former case, preadaptation in the latter. While our earlier discussions concentrated attention on single hereditary characteristics, we readily appreciate that the same principles apply to *combinations* of characteristics. Animals having beneficial *combinations* of characteristics will be favored by natural selection over those having less favorable combinations.

Indeed, natural selection always operates on whole animals, never on separate parts of animals. Hence in a given environment the successful animal will be the one that combines the greatest number of qualities tending to adapt it to the environment in question. Accordingly, the shuffling of the genes is a means of producing a continuous supply of new combinations to be "tried out" by natural selection. Deleterious combinations are weeded out; beneficial combinations are favored. In this way progress, in terms of adaptation to environment, is made.

But continual reshuffling has its drawbacks as well as its utility. Once a beneficial combination of genes is formed will it not be broken up again in the very next generation by continuation of the shuffling process which created it? It is a matter of common observation that children do not inherit all the characteristics of one parent. A particularly gifted parent seldom if ever can endow a son or daughter with all the attributes which combined to produce his own unusual talent. To a considerable extent this recombining of characteristics does serve to break up favorable combinations.

There are, however, hereditary mechanisms tending to decrease the frequency of such dissolution of combinations. We have mentioned the fact that genes are contained in visible structures called chromosomes. One chromosome contains many genes, and the genes in one chromosome tend to stay together in inheritance. The tendency is, however, counteracted by processes making possible exchange of genes between chromosomes. These processes (crossing over and translocation, pp. 395–398) contribute to the reassorting of genes but they act with relative slowness. More, they are sometimes prevented or still further slowed by other genetic factors (such as the presence of inversions—see pp. 397–398). The subject is a complicated one, involving for its understanding considerable knowledge of the mechanisms of heredity; these receive further attention in Chapter 17. The point we wish to make here is that mechanisms preventing, or at least hindering, the breaking up of beneficial combinations of genes do exist.

In summary, in the reassorting and recombining of genes lies a means whereby natural selection is provided with raw materials in the form of varied combinations of hereditary characteristics. The diversity is increased whenever populations having somewhat different genes interbreed. We must next inquire how the differing genes arise in the first place.

NEW GENES FROM OLD

As noted earlier (Chaps. 2 and 5), genes occasionally undergo a change called **mutation.** In its commonest form this is a chemical change in the gene; as a result the changed or mutant gene has an effect different from that of the unchanged gene. In the fruit fly, *Drosophila,* for example, a dominant gene producing red eye color undergoes mutation, changing to a recessive gene which fails to produce the necessary pigment. Eyes of flies homozygous for this new gene remain white. We should note carefully that the primary change occurs in the genes. As a result of a change in a gene a change is later found in the bodies of all offspring containing the altered gene if the latter is dominant, or of all offspring homozygous for the altered gene if the latter is recessive. Since they arise as changes in genes, all mutations are, by definition, inheritable.

Spontaneously occurring, inheritable changes were known long before we knew anything of genes. Darwin mentioned "sports" of this kind in his *Origin of Species,* including among them the Ancon ram, a male sheep which appeared in the flock of Seth Wright, a Massachusetts farmer, in 1791. Its legs were much shorter than those of other sheep. This characteristic proved an advantage to the farmer, since short-legged sheep were less able to scale the stone-wall fences of the day than were other sheep. The ram passed on the new characteristic to his offspring and thereby became the sire of a short-legged race of sheep once common in New England. Here, then, was the appearance of a new, inheritable characteristic. While Darwin recognized that such "sports" occurred he placed little importance upon them, believing them to be too rare to be of much significance.

It remained for the Dutch botanist De Vries to focus attention upon the importance of mutations. Studying the evening primrose, *Oenothera lamarckiana,* De Vries observed that in a population inhabiting a field near Amsterdam individuals occasionally appeared which differed markedly from their fellows. Some were larger, some smaller; there were differences in flowers, in leaves, and in many other characteristics. When De Vries grew offspring from seeds produced by these unusual plants he found that the characteristics were inherited and that consequently new varieties of several kinds were produced. Here, then, was a species of plant which seemed to be caught in the act of producing new varieties or, as he called some of them, "elementary species." On the basis of these studies De Vries advanced his "mutation theory" of evolution. While later investigation has revealed that the phenomenon of occurrence of mutations does not in itself constitute a complete theory of evolutionary change, De Vries deserves much credit for focusing attention upon such inheritable changes in structure.

Subsequent to the investigations of De Vries many mutations have been discovered in other plants and in animals. Most of our modern science of genetics grew out of analysis of the mechanisms involved in inheritance of mutations. Details may be sought in books dealing with genetics; it must suffice us to note some of the attributes of mutations which render them valuable "raw materials" for the construction of evolutionary change.

Of primary importance is the fact that mutations are inheritable changes. As noted above, they are inheritable because they are (1) changes in the germ plasm (genes) followed by (2) changes in the bodies of offspring arising from the altered germ plasm.

What is the nature of this change in the germ plasm? Two main types of change may be distinguished. The most common type, and the one of greatest significance in the evolution of animals, is called **gene mutation.** It is the type mentioned in the first paragraph of this section—a chemical change in a single gene. As a result of its changed nature the gene then produces something other than it produced previously—black body color instead of gray in an insect, for example. By far the most common gene mutations involve the change of a dominant gene to a recessive one, although the reverse sometimes occurs.

Aside from changes in individual genes, changes in numbers and arrangements of genes sometimes occur through what are called chromosomal mutations or, better, **chromosomal aberrations.** Chromosomes are bodies in the nuclei of cells; unlike the genes within them, they are visible with the ordinary compound microscope. As noted previously (p. 336), each chromosome contains many genes—a thousand or so, frequently. Chromosomal aberrations arise in various ways: Chromosomes break into fragments which later join together but in arrangements different from the original ones. Small chromosomes fuse together to form large ones. Chromosomes increase in number, by addition of one or two extra chromosomes or, on the other hand, by addition of multiples of the number originally present. Discussion of the processes and of their effects upon inheritance will be found in books on genetics. Chromosomal aberrations seem to be of considerable importance in plant evolution (see pp. 418–420). The "mutations" of the evening primrose discovered by De Vries were later found to be mainly of this type. For further discussion of the mutation process see Chapter 17.

Mutations vary greatly in magnitude of effect produced. The change in length of legs in the Ancon ram and the changes observed by De Vries in the evening primrose were large changes. Subsequent research has shown, however, that by far the most abundant mutations produce only small changes.

What Causes Mutations?

We have spoken of mutations as being "spontaneous"; they arise unexpectedly for reasons which we do not know. The darkness of our ignorance on the subject is being dissipated, however, through discoveries of means by which the rate of mutation can be increased. In forms investigated intensively mutations have been observed to occur spontaneously at an extremely low but relatively constant rate. For example, a given mutation will occur spontaneously in one of a million individuals of the fruit fly, *Drosophila*. Muller has discovered that the rate can be greatly increased by bombarding the parents with X rays. Apparently the X rays penetrate to the germ plasm and there induce mutations, both gene mutations and chromosomal aberrations. Subsequently, other radiations, such as ultraviolet light, have been found to produce similar effects. The same is true of some chemicals, notably such carcinogenic (cancer-inducing) chemicals as mustard gas. The number of chemicals and physical forces found to induce mutation will undoubtedly increase as investigation continues.

We should note that present methods of inducing mutations are "shotgun" methods; the investigator never knows in advance which genes will be affected. He cannot single out a particular gene and cause it to mutate at will. Obviously such an ability would be highly desirable. There is some evidence that antibodies (p. 109) are among the substances capable of inducing mutations. Since antibodies have a degree of specificity, they may possibly be more selective in their action than are the radiations and chemicals just mentioned. Antibodies formed against lens proteins of the eye, for example, might react selectively with genes concerned with lens formation, causing mutations in those genes only (see discussion of experiments of Guyer and Smith, pp. 344–345). Only the future will disclose whether control of the mutation process in this way can actually be achieved, however. In the meantime it is important to note that radiations, some chemicals, and antibodies form examples of environmental agents which can cause inheritable changes in germ plasm. It is to be emphasized that these agents act on the germ plasm *directly,* not through the intermediacy of body tissues which have been subjected to change.

We know that our bodies are constantly being subjected to bombardment by radiations in extremely low concentrations—by cosmic rays, for example. Is it possible that such radiations induce "spontaneous" mutations? While there is no reason to doubt that such natural radiations have an effect on the germ plasm, their concentration is so low that they can hardly account for the observed rates at which mutations occur. Other forces must also be involved.

Another property of mutations is the fact that as far as we know at present they occur in random or haphazard fashion without regard to usefulness or the needs of the organism. This randomness has caused some biologists to conclude that mutations do not afford likely materials for constructive evolutionary change. We shall see, however, that the objection is not insuperable.

Are mutations *always* random, at all times and under all circumstances? Or can such factors as antibodies direct the course of mutation (see above, and pp. 345–346)? It would be worth much to be able to answer these questions.

A word of qualification is necessary in referring to the mutation process as random. Mutations are random in the sense that they may occur when they are not "needed," and may fail to occur when they are "needed," but their randomness has limits. As emphasized by Blum (1955, Chap. 9), the kinds of mutation which any one gene is capable of producing are limited by the physical and chemical structure of the gene itself and by its thermodynamic properties. Randomness occurs within definite limits. Such limitations on the mutation process impose limitations on the course of evolution itself, helping to determine what directions evolution can take and what directions it cannot take.

Inheritance of Acquired Characters

The foregoing discussion has stressed the fact that mutations are inheritable changes arising in the germ plasm (genes) and that these germinal changes later express themselves in altered body structure of subsequent generations. The sequence of events is important: (1) change in the germ plasm, (2) change in the body, of later generations.

Exactly the reverse sequence of events has sometimes been postulated as a factor in evolution: (1) change in the body, followed by (2) corresponding change in the germ plasm. In fact, this idea represents a distinct theory of evolution termed **Lamarckism,** after its originator, the French biologist Lamarck, who lived from 1744 to 1829 and hence preceded Darwin.

The essence of Lamarckism is the idea that changes acquired or developed by individuals during their lifetimes are transmitted to their offspring; this is the so-called "inheritance of acquired characters." We know that as organs or parts of the body are used they develop and increase in strength and size. Thus the college sprinter has at the peak of his training more powerful muscles than he would have had if his most strenuous sport had been bridge. Conversely, organs or parts of the body degenerate if unused. The powerless leg muscles of a person bedridden for a protracted period form a case in point. Lamarck's thesis was that bodily changes of this kind are passed on to offspring, who therefore are different from what they otherwise would have been. We see readily that this theory, if correct, provides a simple and direct means for the production of diversity.

An example may help to make the application clear. We have seen that the ancestors of the modern horse left the woods and took to life on the dry plains of the West (pp. 201–206). The change was accompanied by change in length and structure of the legs, making possible increased speed in running over hard ground. In line with Lamarck's theory we may postulate that the first ancestral horses to venture forth on the plains were chased by predatory animals, packs of wolves, perhaps. In running to evade these predators they would have increased the power of their legs (as our college sprinter increases the power of his by practice). Any gains in muscular strength and efficiency, and in length, of leg acquired in this manner would, according to the theory, be passed on to the offspring of the animals which acquired them. Thus the offspring would begin life with better legs for running than their parents had had when they began life.

But still the chase by predators would continue. By continued use of their legs for running away, the horses of this second generation would add another increment of strength and length, which would be passed on to the third generation. And so on, generation after generation, each generation improving on its heritage slightly and passing its gains on to its offspring. An analogy would be increase in a family fortune passed on from father to son in pre-inheritance-tax days, each generation adding to what had been received from its immediate predecessor. So after many generations the elongated and efficiently muscled legs of the modern horse evolved, *if* the Lamarckian explanation is correct.

The Lamarckian theory appeals because of its directness and relative simplicity. Biologists confronted with manifold instances of animals, past and present, adapted to their particular needs and environments with exquisite nicety find in the theory a satisfying means of visualizing how perfect adjustment between animal and environment can be achieved. What more natural than to suppose that whales developed the perfection of their streamlining through the action, for millions of years, of water pressure against their bodies as they swam? May it not be that the water molded the body gradually, the changes in shape, once acquired, becoming hereditary? Such a direct process of evolution is easy to visualize and has a forthrightness about it which to many biologists seems lacking in the means and methods of evolution to be described presently. But should we expect nature to be simple and forthright?

We return to the central question: *Are* characteristics developed by an

individual during its lifetime inherited by its offspring? Our everyday observations would lead us to answer in the negative. It is fortunate, for
example, that mutilations are not inherited. A man who loses a finger need
not fear to father a family lest his children be born with fewer than the
usual number of digits. Weismann, the German critic of Lamarckism, removed the tails from mice for many generations. Of course the mice in the
last generation were born with as long tails as the mice of the first generation had had at birth. Such evidences against Lamarckism have been
criticized on the ground that the mutilation is something done to an animal,
something in which the animal does not participate actively. Developments
produced by the activity of the individual do not seem to offer more convincing evidence in support of Lamarckism, however. If our hypothetical
college sprinter continues training after he leaves college and marries will
his sons be born with more highly developed leg muscles than they would
otherwise have had? We know that they will not. Is the son of a concert
pianist born with more skill in his fingers than would have been his if his
father had been a lawyer? While we know that aptitude for music is inherited, we are equally certain that the son will have to begin with simple
finger exercises just as his father did before him, despite the years of training the father received before the son's birth.

In this connection we may well consider a series of experiments which
have been interpreted as demonstrating inheritance of effect of training.
McDougall (1938) trained white rats in performance of a simple problem:
escape from a tank of water following a certain route. The trained rats were
mated and offspring were raised. The offspring, in turn, were taught the
problem; they then became the parents of a third generation. And so on for
forty-five generations. McDougall found marked and progressive decrease
in number of errors made in learning the problem as generation followed
generation. Taken at its face value, this finding would seem to indicate that
offspring were really profiting from training given their parents, that an
acquired character (training) was being inherited.

This experiment has been repeated by Agar and his colleagues (1954),
whose final report records results for fifty generations, covering a period of
twenty years. They started with a single pair of albino rats of the Wistar
strain. The offspring from this pair were divided into two groups. Members
of one group were trained and then used as parents of a second generation.
Members of the other group were not trained but were used as parents to
start a control line running parallel with the trained line. In each generation
some of the rats in the trained line were trained, and then mated to produce

the next generation. In each generation some of the rats in the control line remained untrained and were mated to produce the next generation in that line, while other rats were trained, to provide a measure of learning ability in the control line in the generation concerned. In the control line trained rats were never used as parents.

The investigators found that during the first fifteen or sixteen generations the number of errors in *both* trained and control lines decreased progressively. The causes of this decrease are obscure, but it was certainly not due to inheritance of the effects of training, since parents in successive generations of the control line were not trained at all. The greatest deficiency of McDougall's experiments was lack of a control line. In the light of this recent investigation, therefore, there remains no reason to consider that his results afford evidence of inheritance of the effects of training.

The experiments of Agar and his colleagues continued beyond the sixteenth generation. In later generations the number of errors fluctuated; generations in which few errors were made were followed by generations in which the number of errors was larger, and vice versa. The noteworthy fact is that *both* trained and control lines fluctuated similarly. Factors affecting both lines must have been operative. The experimenters concluded that environmental factors (such as seasonal fluctuations in temperature) and fluctuations in the health and vigor of the rat colony from year to year were reflected in the observed variations in speed of learning. At any rate, clear evidence was obtained against the hypothesis that the effects of training are inherited.

Through the years many experiments of varying kinds have been performed as attempts to demonstrate inheritance of acquired characters, and results of some of them have been interpreted as affording evidence of it. Nevertheless, deficiencies in planning or technique, overlooked sources of error, possibility of interpreting experimental data in more than one way have invalidated all experiments known to the author.

The line of attack which came nearest to yielding an exception to this last statement deserves special attention. From an a priori standpoint it seems difficult to visualize a mechanism by which changes in the body *can* be transferred to the germ cells and thus become inheritable. The germ cells are shut away in one small organ of the body (ovary in females; testis in males). How can changes in the body get to them? Since they are supplied with blood as are the other parts of the body, it is conceivable that substances carried by the blood might serve as "go-betweens," conveying to the germ cells the effects of changes in the body. Years ago it occurred to

Guyer that antibodies (pp. 109–110) might function in this way. Perhaps antibodies, if produced by changes in the body, would react with the germ cells in such a way as to change the latter.

In their experiments Guyer and Smith (1918–1924) concentrated attention on the crystalline lens of the eye. In earlier experiments a solution of lens substance (obtained from rabbits) was inoculated into fowls. The fowls formed antibodies against the foreign substance (p. 109). The fowl serum containing these antibodies was inoculated into pregnant rabbits. Some of the offspring of the latter were born with degenerate or malformed eyes. It looked as though the anti-lens antibodies had interfered with eye formation in the developing embryos. Had an inheritable change been produced in these embryos? When the young were raised and bred it was found that the eye defects were indeed inherited by subsequent generations. The nature of inheritance approximated that characteristic of recessive genes. Of particular significance was the fact that *males* passed the defect on to their offspring. If only females had done so the "inheritance" might have resulted from direct transference of antibodies from the blood of a mother to the blood of her offspring, since the two bloods are in close contact during all embryonic development. But no such close contact exists between a father and his developing offspring; his sole contribution to the latter is a sperm cell, consisting almost wholly of chromosome material. Hence anything a father passes on to his offspring must be contained in his germ plasm.

Was this, then, a case of inheritance of acquired characters, the acquired character being eye defect? Inheritance of acquired characters in the Lamarckian sense would involve a change in the body which would then be transferred to the germ plasm. In the present instance it is possible that the outside agent, the antibodies, acted on the eyes of the embryos *and* on the genes of those embryos directly. If so this would not constitute inheritance of acquired characters in the strict sense.

Guyer and Smith performed one experiment which came closer to meeting specifications for a demonstration of inheritance of acquired characters. They took advantage of the fact that the crystalline lens is not in contact with the blood stream, and that an individual will form antibodies against the lens material of his own eye if his blood is artificially brought into contact with that lens material. This contact was made when the lens of the eye of an anesthetized *male* rabbit was broken up by means of a needle; surrounding blood vessels then penetrated the damaged area. The male was subsequently mated to a normal female. Seven young were born to this pair of parents; four of the young had defective eyes. Unfortunately the experiment was terminated by a fatal epidemic before the inheritance of the defect by later generations could be proved. But the defects were similar to those whose inheritance had been proved in previous experiments. Here, then, was an instance in which an external agent (the experimenter's needle) produced a change in the body (destruction of the lens) which was then apparently transferred to the male rabbit's germ cells, presumably through the agency of antibodies. Taken at its face value, was this an instance of inheritance of acquired characters in the Lamarckian sense? Perhaps the antibodies had induced the formation of *mutations* in the genes controlling eye formation, as mentioned previously (p. 339). If so, would this condition constitute inheritance of acquired characters? If antibody formation resulted from a change in the body, and then the antibodies induced changes in the genes concerned with the characteristic in question, we should have something which to all intents and purposes would be inheritance of acquired characters. But the foregoing statement begins with "If"; indubitable proof that such a sequence of events can actually occur is lacking, though its possibility is suggested by these pioneer experiments of Guyer and Smith, supplemented by investigations of others on antibody induction of mutations.

Critics of the experimentation of Guyer and Smith have not been lacking. Other investigators have repeated the experiments, usually with some variations, and have not obtained the same results. One objection raised is that since rabbits sometimes carry recessive genes for eye defects, perhaps the stock used by Guyer and Smith was thus contaminated, the defects coming to light just at the time of experimentation but not because of the experimental procedures. Guyer has replied in rebuttal that control animals from the same stocks as the experimental animals did not show eye defects. He recorded seeing one rabbit with defective eyes among a total of 2000 individuals. Nevertheless, future experimenters must employ highly inbred stocks so that all recessive genes will be brought together in homozygous state and thus betray their presence by producing visible effects.

What is our verdict concerning the efficacy of inheritance of acquired characters as a means of producing new characteristics? Evidently we must bring in the Scotch verdict of "not proven." But it will be well to leave our minds open to the possibility that, in the particular circumstances in which antibodies may serve as intermediaries between change-in-body and the germ plasm, something amounting to inheritance of acquired characters may yet be demonstrated. If later investigation proves the occurrence of mutation directed by antibodies, mutations and acquired characters will at long last have been brought together into one synthetic theory of evolution. (See also "Genetic assimilation of acquired characters," pp. 420–424.)

WHAT HAPPENS TO MUTATIONS?

If we regard mutations as the raw material of evolutionary change, we may next inquire how that raw material is utilized. What happens to mutations once they occur? Our answer will be far from complete even though most of the remainder of this chapter and the greater part of the following chapters will be devoted to it. Incompleteness of the answer will arise in part from the fact that this is a relatively new field of investigation, in part from the fact that full understanding of what is known necessitates a more thorough knowledge of the science of genetics than is presumed of readers of this book.

At the outset we should recall two facts about mutations: (1) Most of them involve a chemical change in a single gene; (2) the changed gene usually behaves as a recessive in inheritance. When an individual inherits a changed gene from one parent and an unchanged gene from the other parent (i.e., is heterozygous), he actually exhibits the characteristic produced by the unchanged gene (the dominant gene). Suppose, for example, that in one member of a population of animals one gene undergoes mutation. For purposes of illustration we may say that the members of this population all possess a certain pair of dominant genes which we shall designate as AA. In the germ plasm of one member of this population a mutation occurs, changing one of the A's to a. The individual will then produce some germ cells containing A, some containing a. But the other members of the population will still produce only germ cells containing A. Consequently the fertilized ova from which the next generation arises will all be either AA or Aa, the latter being in exceedingly small minority. If A is completely dominant to a, both these types of offspring will actually *exhibit* the characteristic produced by the gene A. In other words, the new mutation a, while present, will not produce any visible effect. Evidently this situation could continue for many generations; so long as an a-containing germ cell always combines with an A-containing one the new mutation will continue to be "covered up" by the original characteristic (produced by A). Only when eventually two Aa individuals chance to mate together will an aa individual arise (by fertilization of an a-containing ovum from one parent by an a-containing sperm cell from the other). The aa individual will, of course, exhibit the new characteristic. We see, then, that mutations may remain hidden for many generations following the time of actual change in the gene concerned.

Evidence accumulates, however, that many, if not most, mutations are not completely recessive but rather exhibit some degree of dominance (see Muller, 1950). That is, they produce some effect in heterozygous individuals. In terms of our example: *Aa* individuals are not exactly like *AA* individuals in characteristics. The *a* gene in the heterozygote modifies the action of the *A* gene. When this is the case a new mutation will make its presence felt at once, even before any *aa* individuals appear. If the effect of the *a* gene, in combination with the *A* gene in a heterozygote, is beneficial, natural selection will favor the heterozygotes; if the effect of the *a* gene is harmful, natural selection will tend to eliminate the heterozygotes. In the former instance the frequency of the *a* gene in subsequent generations will tend to increase; in the latter instance the frequency will tend to decrease.

As we shall discuss more fully later (pp. 457–469), evidence is being obtained that in a state of nature organisms are heterozygous for many pairs of genes, and that in many cases the phenotype (p. 333) of heterozygotes is superior to the phenotype of homozygotes (e.g., *Aa* is superior to *AA* and *aa*). When this is so, what gene *a* produces when combined with *A* is more important than what it produces when combined with another gene of its own kind (*a*). Thus completely recessive genes, "covered up" in heterozygotes as mentioned above, may turn out to be the exception rather than the rule.

Natural selection can act on new mutations which have phenotypic effect in heterozygotes. This includes not only the partially recessive genes just mentioned but also changes of normally present recessive genes to completely dominant ones (e.g., change of gene *a* to gene *A*). In our present state of knowledge such mutations seem to be rarer than do mutations of dominant genes to genes having some degree of recessiveness or, to express it differently, somewhat lessened dominance, as described above. The Ancon ram (p. 337) may have constituted an example of a completely dominant mutation, since all offspring seem to have exhibited the shortened legs.

Returning to our recessive, or largely recessive, mutation *a,* we may now inquire: After the gene *a* has become widely enough distributed in the population so that *aa* individuals occasionally arise, what will happen to these individuals and to the "new gene" itself?

Genetic Equilibrium

Our answer to the question just raised will involve further consideration of the action of natural selection, but before we discuss the latter it will be well to consider forces acting on mutations in the absence of, or in addition to, natural selection. Unlike natural selection, these forces operate without regard to considerations of usefulness or harmfulness of the mutations concerned. They depend upon the operation of the laws of chance or probability in the "shuffling of the genes" discussed in an earlier section of this chapter.

In that discussion we noted the manner in which pairs of genes are reassorted generation after generation. The genes of heterozygous brown-eyed parents (Fig. 15.1), for example, are separated and then combined in various ways in their children and grandchildren. The genes remain the same (except for the rare occurrence of new mutations) but they are reassorted generation after generation to produce a collection of homozygous brown-eyed individuals, heterozygous brown-eyed individuals, and blue-eyed individuals. Suppose that in a given population there are a million B (brown-eye) genes and a thousand b (blue-eye) genes. These will be combined in pairs in homozygous brown-eyed individuals (BB), heterozygous brown-eyed individuals (Bb), and blue-eyed individuals (bb). If these individuals marry at random so far as eye color is concerned (e.g., if there is no tendency for brown-eyed people to prefer brown-eyed mates, or for blue-eyed persons to prefer other blue-eyed persons) the number of B genes and the number of b genes will tend to remain constant generation after generation. The genes will be "shuffled" and recombined but the numbers of the two kinds of genes present will tend to remain the same, just as the numbers of aces, kings, queens, jacks, and so on, in a deck of cards remain the same despite the varied assortments of them which may be dealt as hands during a long evening of play.

The tendency of gene frequencies to remain in equilibrium in succeeding generations finds mathematical expression in the Hardy-Weinberg law, discussed at greater length on pages 427–435. Our present purpose will be served by calling attention to the existence of this tendency to establishment and maintenance of **genetic equilibrium.** This equilibrium will tend to be maintained generation after generation unless disturbed (1) by fresh mutations from the dominant gene to the corresponding recessive one, or vice versa; (2) by natural selection; (3) by chance (see below).

If the dominant and recessive genes are both common in the population the contrasting characteristics produced will both occur commonly, as is the case with blue and brown eyes in many parts of the world. If, on the other hand, one gene, for example the recessive one, is rare, most members of the population will exhibit the characteristic produced by the dominant gene and only occasional individuals will show the recessive characteristic. Thus among sheep, although the predominant color is white, black individuals appear now and then. Occasional appearance of albinos in almost all species of higher animals affords another example. Other examples will be found in the discussion of polymorphic species (pp. 375–376). In this connection we should stress the fact that there will be no tendency for the recessive gene, though rare, to "die out." This fact is particularly pertinent to our discussion in view of the fact that all "new mutations" are rare at first.

The question under discussion is, What will happen to new mutations when they occur? We may now conclude that they will be incorporated into the genetic structure, the "gene pool," of the population, and that there will be a tendency for establishment of an equilibrium between the number of "new" genes and the number of "old" ones.

Genetic Drift

The genetic equilibrium just described is most effectively maintained when the size of the population is *large*. When the population is small, *chance* may cause radical deviations from the expected equilibrium. In a small population, confined, for example, to a small island, or to one mountain valley, or to one pond (in the case of an aquatic form), one of two things may happen: By the action of the laws of chance the gene *a* may be lost entirely, or, contrariwise, the gene *A* may be lost entirely, all members of the population coming eventually to have the new characteristic, i.e., to be *aa*. This phenomenon is known as "scattering of the variability" or **genetic drift.** Our knowledge of it is based largely upon the mathematical studies of Professor Sewall Wright and others in the field of population genetics. Without recourse to mathematics we may cite a simple example illustrative of the fundamental idea involved. We noted previously that a heterozygous individual (*Aa*) will produce two kinds of germ cells, some containing the dominant gene (*A*), some the recessive gene (*a*). These two types of germ cells will be produced in about equal numbers; hence *on the average* about half of the individual's offspring will be expected to receive gene *A* from him, about half will be expected to receive gene *a* from him (cf. Fig. 15.1). But that statement is true only if the individual contributes genes to large numbers of offspring. Suppose, by contrast, that an *Aa* individual is the parent of just two offspring living to maturity. It might easily happen that in both cases an *A*-containing germ cell would be involved. Thus as far as that one *Aa* parent is concerned the *a* gene is lost right there; none of the next generation will inherit *a from him*. Alternatively, of course, this single *Aa* individual might contribute only gene *a* to each of his two offspring. If this happened the frequency of gene *a* would be increased, that of gene *A* diminished. This example merely illustrates the way in which chance, involved here in determining just which germ cells shall actually be used, produces an effect upon the eventual fate of a new mutation. More complete discussion of the subject will be found in the following chapters.

As a result of genetic "drift," then, a new mutation arising in a small population either may be lost or, alternatively, may become the prevailing characteristic of the population. Our discussion of species and subspecies in the preceding chapter pointed out the fact that differences between related species or subspecies are usually small; frequently they involve characteristics which seem unimportant to the animals concerned. Insofar as they really are unimportant, characteristics may become established in a population largely as a result of this phenomenon of drift. We should note that breeding populations of animals are usually small. Physical barriers divide animals into small groups, as do intervening regions lacking food, shelter, or other factors necessary to the life of the animal in question. The effect is enhanced by the tendency of most animals to establish home areas from which they rarely wander, particularly during the breeding season. Various factors combine to insure that even what seems to be a widely ranging group is actually composed of many rather small subgroups which constitute the population units of significance in mate selection. Even in man propinquity is an important factor in determining whom a given person will marry. Thus animals exhibit small size of breeding population—the situation most conducive to the operation of genetic drift. Hence we conclude that many of the "unimportant" or "indifferent" characteristics distinguishing one species or subspecies from its neighbors may have arisen as mutations which eventually became established by operation of the laws of chance in the phenomenon of genetic drift.

We should not leave this subject without a word of caution about classifying characteristics as "unimportant" and "indifferent." Although many characteristics probably "make no difference" to their possessors, intensive study of some mutations has shown that they have several effects on their possessors aside from the visible change by which the gene is identified. For example, the first mutation observed in *Drosophila* goes by the name of "white eye." It changes the color of the eye from red to white, but it also changes the color of the testicular membrane, changes the shape of the spermatheca, and affects the length of life. So while it may be a matter of indifference to a fly whether its eyes are red or white, some of these other changes may well be of importance to the individual. Genes which affect more than one characteristic are called **pleiotropic.** Another example is Keeler's (1942) discovery that in rats genes which change color of the hair change the animals' disposition, increasing or decreasing tameness. Castle (1941) has shown that the gene which produces brown pigmentation in rats, mice, and rabbits accelerates growth and thus results in attainment of increased body size. Hence although brown color might be of no consequence to a mouse, the gene in question might be favored if it were of advantage to the mouse to be large. Examples might be added indefinitely. The more we learn about genes the more of them we discover to have effects in addition to the one which originally attracted our attention. Although the point is not established as yet, it may be that all genes have several effects, some of them indifferent or unimportant, some of them important, under certain circumstances at least.

Thus chance, operating particularly in small populations, may alter the genetic equilibrium which would otherwise prevail. An even more potent cause of genetic change in populations is natural selection. We have referred to its action repeatedly in earlier discussions (pp. 10–18); now we shall consider in more detail the factors involved.

NATURAL SELECTION

In Chapter 2 we noted that the concept of natural selection was Darwin's great contribution to thinking on evolution. In *The Origin of Species by Means of Natural Selection* Darwin compared the selective action of nature to selection employed by man in improving strains of plants and animals (artificial selection). When a breeder of cultivated plants or of domestic animals wishes to improve them he selects the individuals showing the desired qualities to be parents of the next generation and prevents individuals lacking the desired characteristics from contributing to the next generation. Thus Luther Burbank when developing improved varieties of plants, such as stoneless plums and spineless cactus, raised seedlings in large numbers. From these he selected only a few which to his practiced eye offered promise of possessing the qualities he desired. The rest of the seedlings were immediately burned; as many as 50,000 condemned plants might be destroyed after a single selection.

It was Darwin's thought that nature selects animals and plants in much the same manner, preserving those individuals which have characteristics best fitting them for life in the particular environment in which they find themselves and eliminating individuals less adequately equipped. If such natural selection does indeed occur, what is the driving force back of it and by what means is it accomplished?

Tendency to Rapid Increase in Numbers

The driving force, according to Darwin, is provided by the tendency of all living things to increase their numbers rapidly. A few examples will typify prevailing situations in most animals. Fishes are noted for the laying of large numbers of eggs. A 25-pound carp in an Iowa lake was found to contain 1,700,000 eggs; the similar prodigality of the salmon in egg production is common knowledge. One female toad may lay as many as 12,000 eggs. It has been calculated that one pair of houseflies breeding in April would have by August, if all eggs hatched and all resulting individuals lived to reproduce in their turn, 191,010,000,000,000,000,000 descendants. Turning to animals which breed more slowly and have longer intervals between generations, we may quote Darwin's statement concerning elephants: "The elephant is reckoned the slowest breeder of all known animals, and I have taken some pains to estimate its probable minimum rate of natural increase; it will be safest to assume that it begins breeding when thirty years old, and goes on breeding till ninety years old, bringing forth six young in the interval, and surviving till one hundred years old; if this be so, after a period of from 740 to 750 years there would be nearly nineteen million elephants alive descended from the first pair." Other examples might be quoted almost endlessly.

Limiting Factors

Why, in actual fact, do we not find our lakes choked solidly with fish, our fields carpeted with toads, the earth overrun with elephants, and so on? Because there are for each species certain checks or limiting factors opposing such increase in numbers.

One of the most important of these checks is **limited food supply.** Darwin himself was greatly influenced in his thinking by the essay of Malthus on population. It was the thesis of Malthus that population tends to increase in geometric ratio (e.g., by successive multiplication) while the food supply tends to increase in arithmetic ratio (e.g., by successive addition). Hence the population tends to increase at a more rapid rate than does the food supply available to that population. Whatever the truth of this much debated generalization, there is no doubt that limited food supply is an important factor in preventing unlimited increase in numbers of individuals in a given species.

Predatory animals constitute another check on population size. If the lions were exterminated on the plains of Africa the zebra population would doubtless increase rapidly for a time, until a new limit imposed by available food, and perhaps disease, was reached.

Disease is another limiting factor; epidemics occur among animals, particularly if they become overcrowded.

Space restrictions form another check on unlimited increase. Not only does overcrowding favor disease and starvation, but a certain amount of "elbow room" is required if animals are to live and reproduce normally. In many species the home or nest is surrounded by a certain area of home territory over which the occupant of the nest dominates and in which all other members of the same species and sex are treated as intruders. The density of population which a given region can support is determined in part, not by the amount of "standing room" available, but by the number of these home territories which can be provided without undue disturbance of the normal living and reproductive habits of the species in question.

Under the term **inanimate environment** we may include such limiting factors as climate, seasonal changes, and catastrophes of various kinds. Drought and severe heat in summer and severe cold in winter are examples. It has been estimated that during a severe winter half the wild horses inhabiting the southeastern region of the state of Washington perish. This example may suggest the questions: Is it purely a matter of chance which ones perish and which ones survive? What determines which of these horses shall live, which die? And we are led to the next element in the process of natural selection.

"The Struggle for Existence"

We have seen that in each generation each species attempts to produce many more individuals than can hope to live to maturity under the limiting conditions prevailing. The result is a competition among the offspring for food, mates, home territories, and the like, and a striving to survive the aggressions of predatory animals, disease, and the severities of inanimate nature. This process was called by Darwin "the struggle for existence." In this "struggle" what determines which individuals shall succeed, which fail?

We may answer this question by stating that those individuals will succeed which have favorable or advantageous inheritable variations of structure, physiology, and so on. Those individuals will fail which lack such variations or which have unfavorable or harmful ones. In this statement we have mentioned that the variations must be inheritable; while it is true that noninheritable, favorable variations might enable an individual to survive, such variations have no "future" so far as improvement of the species is concerned. (See, however, the "Baldwin effect," pp. 420–425.) The inheritable variations arise as new mutations and as new combinations of genes originating in various ways (pp. 396–402). Darwin himself placed great stress on the importance of variations, including individual differences, and he recognized that to be useful in evolution they must be inheritable. He was well acquainted with the fact that variation is universal, that "no two individuals are alike." In his day it was not known to what extent these differences between individual and individual are inheritable, to what extent they are caused by environment and hence not inheritable.

The fact that many of the little variations in structure are not inheritable was brilliantly demonstrated by the Danish geneticist, Johannsen. He chose to work with the characteristic of weight, in beans. Taking advantage of the fact that beans are self-fertilizing, he established a number of **pure lines,** each descended from one bean. In general, pure lines descended from heavy beans had greater average weight than did pure lines descended from light beans. Since each pure line bred true to a certain average weight generation after generation, hereditary factors must have been involved in the differences in weight. Since in any one pure line, descended from one bean, the hereditary factors must have been identical in all individuals, why were not all individuals identical in weight? Because superimposed upon the identical heredity were the effects of differences in environment (in sunlight, moisture, food supply, etc., available to individual plants and branches as they grew). When Johannsen took the heaviest beans in a certain pure line and raised progeny from them he found that the average weight was the same as that of the pure line itself, or the same as he obtained when he took a light bean from the same pure line and raised progeny from it. In brief, selection *within* a pure line was not effective in producing change. Of the many implications of Johannsen's work the one of most significance for us is the demonstration that many observed variations in structure are produced by environment, and that selection based on these environmentally induced variations does not result in changes in the resultant progeny. To be effective, selection, either by man or by nature, must utilize inheritable variations, i.e., mutations.

What Constitutes Success in the "Struggle for Existence"?

Darwin laid most stress upon survival; individuals having favorable inheritable variations survive, while their less highly endowed contemporaries perish. This phenomenon has been termed "the survival of the fittest." The "fittest" were thought of as those individuals which possess inheritable characteristics enabling them to succeed in the "struggle for existence" in the particular circumstances and environment in which they find themselves. Since they are the survivors, the "fittest" then become the parents of the next generation, members of which inherit the favorable characteristics from their parents.

A moment's reflection, however, will convince us that survival in itself is not the only, or even the chief, concern. The real point is not survival but *contribution to the next generation*. Obviously a dead animal cannot become a parent, but some living animals cannot, or do not, become parents either. So far as contribution to evolution is concerned, a living animal which does not reproduce might just as well be dead. Indeed, from the standpoint of his species it would probably be better if he were dead, since he consumes food without making any contribution to the species in return. This statement must be qualified for species in which individuals live together in societies. In such species individuals which do not reproduce may nevertheless contribute to the success of the species by rendering essential services to the society of which they are a part. Notable examples are such social insects as ants and bees, and man himself (see discussion of the role of cooperation, pp. 520–522). It is the social unit as a whole whose success is measured in terms of contribution to the next generation. Thus, be it on the individual or on the social level, success in the "struggle for existence" means success in contributing to the next generation. Included among the determinants of this success are all factors favoring effective reproduction. The reproductive process is a complicated one, subject to many influences. Fertility is affected by the health and well-being of the individual, and these in turn depend upon a variety of physiological, and even psychological, factors. In the "struggle for existence" premium is placed, then, both on characteristics which make for survival and on characteristics which make for high fertility.

A somewhat extreme example may help to emphasize the point. Imagine two competing groups of animals, each group consisting at the outset of

1000 young individuals. Of group A, 800 individuals survive to maturity; of group B, only 500 individuals survive. But in group A the reproductive rate is such that each individual is replaced by one descendant, whereas in group B each individual is replaced by two descendants. Which is the more successful group? Obviously group B is, since in the next generation it will number 1000 individuals, while group A will number only 800.

The most successful individuals or groups are those which contribute their genes in greatest number to the building of the next generation.

"Individuals having most offspring are the fittest ones" (Lerner, 1959). It is well to remember that this is what "fittest" means in natural selection theory, and all that it means. Much mistaken thinking to the contrary notwithstanding, "fittest" does not mean "strongest" or "fastest" or "healthiest" or "most intelligent." Of course individuals or societies lacking in all such traits may not be likely to leave the most offspring. But the measure of their fitness is not possession of the attributes listed; it is the leaving of offspring.

Nature of "the Struggle for Existence"

The phrase "struggle for existence" is unfortunate. It carries too many overtones of "Nature red in tooth and claw." True, predatory animals do play a part in reducing the number of surviving members of a population, and hence in determining which members shall contribute most to the next generation. But competition for available food supply is also a factor, operating principally in times of exceptional stringency, as, for example, during droughts, floods, exceptionally severe or prolonged winters, or as a result of extreme overpopulation of a given territory.

So far we have stressed competition between individuals in the same species (for food, territory, etc.): **intraspecific competition.** We should also note that **interspecific competition** occurs and may at times be important in evolution. Two closely related species (recently arisen from a common ancestral species, perhaps) may compete for the same food supply. If this competition is keen it may lead to changes in the two species so that competition will be lessened. Thus two species of ground finch living on the same Galápagos island may come to differ from each other in beak size by virtue of the fact that it is advantageous for one to specialize on large seeds, the other on small seeds. Or alternatively, one species may be so much more efficient than the other in utilizing the food supply that the less efficient species becomes extinct (at least in the territory originally shared in common). (See Hardin, 1960.)

Many important characteristics are less obviously related to struggle and competition than are the examples we have given. Resistance to disease is highly important. Any structural or physiological improvement contributing to vitality and fecundity will tend to confer a differential advantage on some individuals as compared to others. Ability to produce large numbers of viable offspring confers an advantage, particularly in species in which the parents do not care for the young after hatching or birth. Alternatively, increased perfection of postnatal care confers advantages in species which produce few offspring per parent. In the former instance more than the laying of large numbers of eggs is involved. The eggs must be viable, and they must be efficiently fertilized. Young which develop quickly have an advantage over those which develop slowly. When two competing strains differ in speed of individual development, that strain which produces mature offspring in less time will, other things being equal, contribute more of its genes to future generations than will a strain in which sexual maturity is attained more slowly. Offspring of the first strain may already have mated in their turn before offspring of the second strain have matured sufficiently to do so.

These examples are given to emphasize the fact that complex and subtle factors are involved in determining which individuals shall contribute most to the next generation. The familiar matters of escape from predators and competition for food are but two among many important factors.

Essence of Natural Selection

A brief statement of natural selection may help to bring our discussion into focus. Reduced to its essentials, *natural selection results from the cumulative action of all forces tending to insure that individuals possessing one genetic constitution shall leave larger numbers of offspring than will individuals possessing some other genetic constitution.* Thus if a mutation contributes in any way to the leaving of larger numbers of offspring it will be perpetuated in increased proportion in the next generation, since it will be carried by those "larger numbers of offspring." Contrariwise, if the mutation interferes in any way with the leaving of larger numbers of offspring it will be perpetuated in decreased proportion in the next generation, since it will be carried by but a decreased number of individuals in that generation.

We readily appreciate that if natural selection continues for several generations, individuals lacking the favorable mutation may be completely eliminated, with the result that the mutation becomes "standard equipment" for the entire population.

It will be evident, moreover, that these principles apply not only to individual mutations but also to those combinations of mutations (genes) discussed earlier in the chapter (pp. 334–336).

Origin of Races and Species

So far we have not accounted for a great amount of evolutionary change; we have shown how a population might come to possess a new mutation or combination of mutations. But we have noted previously that one mutation is usually a small change. Few, if any, races or subspecies differ from each other by a single mutation. How can we account for the origin of larger differences such as those distinguishing separate races and, especially, separate species, genera, and so on? *Addition* of one mutation to another probably accounts for many of these larger differences. Our hypothetical population acquires a certain favorable characteristic, as described above. In later generations a second mutation arises which is an improvement on, or addition to, the first one. Natural selection now works on this second mutation until some generations later the whole population comes to possess it. Thus step by step through the long expanses of geologic time greater and greater evolutionary change is produced by natural selection. The change as we have described it will be in the nature of more perfect *adaptation* to the environment in which the animals are living, i.e., *postadaptation* (pp. 12–13).

Continuing with our hypothetical population, let us suppose that the animals' environment changes—(1) as a result of geologic change in the region or (2) as a result of the animals' migration into a different region from that formerly inhabited. Now a premium may be placed on different characteristics from those formerly favored. As a result different mutations will prove advantageous in the "struggle for existence," and in consequence the population will gradually come to differ from its ancestors living under the conditions formerly prevailing. Thus diversity arises between a population living in one set of environmental conditions and ancestral or "sister" populations living in other environments. The amount of diversity will at first be slight, but it may increase until the populations become separate subspecies, and even eventually separate species, genera, and so on.

Earlier in this chapter we saw how the evolution of the long legs of the horse might be explained according to Lamarck's theory of the inheritance of acquired characters (p. 341). It may help to fix in mind the essentials of natural selection if we ask how the same evolutionary change can be explained by the theory of natural selection.

As before, we may postulate that the first ancestral horses to venture forth from the woods onto the plains were chased by predatory animals. The action of the predators would constitute one of the checks upon the too rapid increase in numbers of these ancestral horses. In the resulting competition to survive and leave progeny which individuals would succeed? If among the population of ancestral horses a mutation arose producing longer legs (just the reverse of the Ancon ram mutation), possessors of that mutation might be able to run faster than could their fellows. If so, a disproportionately large number of horses *not* possessing the mutation would become food for the predators before they had opportunity to mate and reproduce. Thus the horses having the mutation for longer legs would produce more than "their share" of offspring, with the result that more of the next generation would inherit longer legs than possessed them in the parental generation. If selection continued in the same way for several generations the shorter-legged horses might disappear entirely, leaving the field to the possessors of the longer legs. If, now, a second mutation occurred, increasing the length of the legs still more, possessors of that second mutation would be favored in the "struggle for existence," with the result that some generations later all horses would have the second mutation, possessors of the first mutation having been eliminated. And so step by step the progressive lengthening of leg observed in the evolution of the horse might be explained through the operation of natural selection on successive mutations. (For an alternative explanation for this example see pp. 412–413.)

In the preceding example we have kept the account as simple as possible in attempt to paint the broad outlines of the picture without including confusing details. Actually the situation at any time would have been much more complex, many factors in addition to length of leg entering into the determination of which individuals should contribute most to subsequent generations (see pp. 356–357).

A Glimpse of Variables in the Process

We have seen that mutations occur at definite, though usually low, rates. Different mutations have different rates of occurrence (**"mutation pressures"**). Thus the rate at which the raw materials of evolutionary change are supplied varies for different mutations.

The intensity of natural selection (**"selection pressure"**) varies greatly from time to time and from place to place. Under some conditions "the living is easy"; under others survival and reproduction are extremely difficult.

What we may call the **varying effects** of the mutations submitted to the action of natural selection constitutes another variable factor. Although most mutations are recessive, some of them produce detectable effects in individuals heterozygous for them, as noted previously (p. 347). Thus an individual heterozygous for a recessive mutation (*Aa* in constitution) may have lowered, or increased, viability as compared to an individual homozygous for the dominant characteristic (*AA*). Dobzhansky (1947), and Reed and Reed (1948) have investigated some configurations of chromosomes in *Drosophila* which seem to be disadvantageous to flies possessing them in double dose (i.e., homozygous for them). These disadvantageous chromosomal arrangements are prevented from complete elimination, however, because individuals *heterozygous* for the arrangements are better adapted to survive under certain environmental conditions than are homozygotes for the advantageous arrangement. It is as though *Aa* individuals were more viable than *either AA* or *aa* individuals. (See further discussion of these experiments on pp. 459–464, and of "The role of heterozygotes," pp. 457–469.)

At times, also, a mutation which produces a visible characteristic of neither advantage nor disadvantage to its possessor may be acted upon by natural selection because of associated effects of the same gene. Thus a structural change harmless in itself may be associated with lowered viability. Natural selection will reduce the proportion of the population having the lowered viability and in doing so will necessarily reduce *pari passu* the proportion of the population having the harmless structural feature. (See also p. 350.)

Another variable of importance is the role of chance in the form of genetic drift (pp. 349–351). We recall that the effect of drift varies with varying population size, being particularly effective when populations are small, as in isolated animal communities, or following a severe winter which has killed large numbers of the population.

Mutation pressure, selection pressure, varying effects of mutations, genetic drift, and many other factors combine in varying proportions to produce the type and degree of evolutionary change observable in any one animal group at any given time in its history. Further discussion of these factors will be found in the following chapters.

Mutations with Large Effects

From the foregoing discussion the reader will have gained the impression that a single mutation always produces a small effect—a small increment in length of leg of an ancestral horse, for example. It is true that small effects characterize most well-known mutations, but evidence is accumulating that there are other mutations which have more far-reaching effects. Thus, there seem to be genes controlling the *rates* at which various parts of the body increase in size. If a mutation occurs in one of these genes the relative size of the part of the body affected may be greatly altered as a result of that single mutation. Suppose, for example, that at a certain point in the evolution of the horse a mutation occurred in a gene controlling the rate at which the legs increased in length as the body increased in size. Such a mutation might determine, perhaps, that as the body doubled in size the length of the legs would increase two and a half times (instead of merely doubling as they had formerly done). Since, as we know, the body did increase in size during horse evolution, such a mutation would explain the fact that the size increase was accompanied by a disproportionate lengthening of the legs—such a lengthening as was observed to occur.

According to this idea the cumulative action of many little mutations, each adding its increment to length of leg, can be replaced by a single mutation altering the rate at which the leg increases in length as the body increases in size. Such unequal growth of one part of the body relative to another is called **allometric growth.** Allometry (heterogony) presents possibilities for explanation of some types of evolutionary change with economy in number of mutations postulated. Mathematical formulation of the principles involved, additional examples, and further discussion of the application of allometry to horse evolution will be found in Chapter 18.

In this connection we may mention that one investigator, Goldschmidt (1940) dissented completely from the idea that "little" mutations can ever be accumulated sufficiently to account for major evolutionary change. He divided evolution into "microevolution" (evolution of subspecies or geographic races) and "macroevolution" (evolution of species, genera, and so on). He contended that, while "little" mutations can provide the raw materials for the degree of diversity represented by subspecies, mutations of an entirely different order of magnitude ("systemic mutations") must be invoked to explain macroevolution (p. 503). The origin of large evolutionary changes receives further attention later (pp. 502–506). We may note at this time, however, the difficulty of distinguishing clearly between "little" and "systemic" mutations. Is a change in a single gene controlling the rate of growth of a part of the body a "little" mutation or a "systemic" mutation? Perhaps we may best describe it as a little mutation with a big effect. It seems unlikely that a sharp line can be drawn between "little" mutations and "systemic" mutations; increase in knowledge will probably lead to discovery of a complete spectrum of "sizes" of mutation. Nevertheless Goldschmidt rendered service to evolutionary thinking by emphasizing the importance of mutations which can produce far-reaching change.

Conclusion

Owing to the particulate nature of Mendelian inheritance, inherited characteristics are combined and recombined in great variety. This phenomenon underlies some of the diversity characteristic of evolutionary change. Really new inherited characteristics arise as mutations (defined broadly); hence these form the principal raw materials from which evolutionary change is constructed. The fate of the mutations which occur is determined by many factors, including the laws of chance (in genetic drift), and natural selection. Genetic drift may cause a mutation to be lost from a population or, alternatively, to become established in that population without regard to considerations of advantageousness and disadvantageousness. Natural selection tends to preserve mutations which in any way contribute to the ability of their possessors to produce a disproportionately large share of the next generation.

In this chapter we have summarized some of the highlights of modern thinking as to the means and methods of evolutionary change. The remaining chapters are devoted largely to exposition and discussion of these principles and of correlated ones, with a view to more complete understanding of forces operative in evolution.

References and Suggested Readings

Agar, W. E., F. H. Drummond, O. W. Tiegs, and M. M. Gunson. "Fourth (final) report on a test of McDougall's Lamarckian experiment on the training of rats," *Journal of Experimental Biology,* 31 (1954), 307–321.

Blum, H. F. *Time's Arrow and Evolution,* 2nd ed. Princeton: Princeton University Press, 1955.

Castle, W. E. "Influence of certain color mutations on body size in mice, rats and rabbits," *Genetics,* 26 (1941), 177–191.

Darwin, C. *The Origin of Species by Means of Natural Selection.* 1859. (Modern Library series, Random House, New York; and Mentor Book MT294, New American Library, New York.)

Dobzhansky, Th. "Adaptive changes induced by natural selection in wild populations of *Drosophila,*" *Evolution,* 1 (1947), 1–16.

Dobzhansky, Th. *Genetics and the Origin of Species,* 3rd ed. New York: Columbia University Press, 1951.

Emerson, S. "The induction of mutations by antibodies," *Proceedings of the National Academy of Sciences,* 30 (1944), 179–183.

Goldschmidt, R. *The Material Basis of Evolution.* New Haven: Yale University Press, 1940.

Guyer, M. F. *Being Well-Born,* 2nd ed. Indianapolis: The Bobbs-Merrill Company, 1927. (Pages 269–278 summarize the Guyer and Smith investigation.)

Guyer, M. F., and E. A. Smith. "Studies on cytolysins. I. Some prenatal effects of lens antibodies," *Journal of Experimental Zoology,* 26 (1918), 65–82.

Guyer, M. F., and E. A. Smith. "Studies on cytolysins. II. Transmission of induced eye defects," *Journal of Experimental Zoology,* 31 (1920), 171–223.

Guyer, M. F., and E. A. Smith. "Further studies on inheritance of eye defects induced in rabbits," *Journal of Experimental Zoology,* 38 (1924), 449–475.

Hardin, G. "The competitive exclusion principle," *Science,* 131 (1960), 1292–1297.

Huxley, J. S. *Problems of Relative Growth.* New York: The Dial Press, 1932.

Huxley, J. S. *Evolution: The Modern Synthesis.* New York: Harper & Brothers, 1942.

Jepsen, G. L., E. Mayr, and G. G. Simpson (eds.). *Genetics, Paleontology and Evolution.* Princeton: Princeton University Press, 1949.

Keeler, C. E. "The association of the black (non-agouti) gene with behavior in the Norway rat," *Journal of Heredity,* 33 (1942), 371–384.

Lamarck, J. B. P. A. *Histoire Naturelle des Animaux sans Vertèbres,* 2nd. ed. Paris: J. B. Baillière, Libraire, 1835. (Vol. 1, *Introduction,* contains a statement of his theory of evolution; theory first published in 1809 in his *Philosophie Zoologique.*)

Lerner, I. M. "The concept of natural selection: a centennial view," *Proceedings, American Philosophical Society,* 103 (1959), 173–182.

McDougall, W. "Fourth report on a Lamarckian experiment," *British Journal of Psychology,* 28 (1938), 321–345, 365–395.

Muller, H. J. "Our load of mutations," *American Journal of Human Genetics,* 2 (1950), 111–176.

Reed, S. C., and E. W. Reed. "Natural selection in laboratory populations of *Drosophila,*" *Evolution,* 2 (1948), 176–186.

Rensch, B. *Evolution Above the Species Level.* New York: Columbia University Press, 1960.

Simpson, G. G. *The Meaning of Evolution.* New Haven: Yale University Press, 1949.

Simpson, G. G. *The Major Features of Evolution.* New York: Columbia University Press, 1953.

Sturtevant, A. H. "Can specific mutations be induced by serological methods?" *Proceedings of the National Academy of Sciences,* 30 (1944), 176–178.

Tax, S. (ed.). *Evolution after Darwin. Vol. I, The Evolution of Life.* Chicago: University of Chicago Press, 1960.

Thompson, D'Arcy W. *On Growth and Form,* 2nd ed. Cambridge: Cambridge University Press, 1942.

CHAPTER 16

NATURAL SELECTION IN ACTION

In the preceding chapter we presented a summary of the theory of natural selection, and in the following chapters we shall develop the theory in more detail. At the present time we may ask the question: Granted that natural selection seems logical and probable, can we actually *see* it in operation? In Chapter 20 we shall describe some experiments in which natural selection was observed to operate in the laboratory. In the present chapter we shall discuss mainly observation of natural selection at work in a state of nature.

Protection from Predators

As we have seen, predatory animals constitute one factor in "the struggle for existence"; to live and leave offspring, organisms must survive predatory attacks. Some animals survive by running away. Others survive by being inconspicuous: by camouflage or protective coloration.

By way of example we may cite the common observation that mammals (e.g., mice) living on light-colored soils are themselves light colored, while inhabitants of dark-colored soils are dark colored. An example of a light-colored race of *Peromyscus* was described above (pp. 322–323). In this case an island of white sand is populated by an almost white race obviously descended from darker-colored mice inhabiting neighboring woodlands. How did the light-colored race arise? We may hypothesize that the light color protects the mice from attack by predators, especially owls. If so, mice having mutations (or other genetic variability) making for light coat color would be expected to survive on the island in larger proportion than would mice having darker coloration. Thus the lighter-colored mice would contribute a larger proportion of genes to the next generation than would the darker-colored mice. If this trend continued for many generations, the present almost white race of mice could be accounted for. We note that in this explanation predators utilizing vision for hunting occupy a key position. Granted that light coat color causes the mouse to blend with the light background to our eyes, does it also do this in the eyes of predators? Does "protective coloration" actually protect?

In order to answer this question Dice (1947) performed a series of experiments with *Peromyscus* differing in shade, utilizing owls as predators. A darkroom was divided into halves by a low partition on one side of which light-colored soil covered the floor, on the other side dark-colored soil. Both dark-colored and light-colored mice were placed in both halves of the room. The owl lived in a nest box near the ceiling in the middle of the room. Would the owl catch more dark-colored than light-colored mice on the light soil, and more light-colored than dark-colored ones on the dark soil? At first there seemed to be no tendency of this kind. Gradually the experimenter reduced the dim light intensity used during the tests until finally there was no light at all. Still the owls caught mice. Evidently, then, they were not using the sense of sight in their hunting. Probably they located the mice by hearing their movements. Marks on the soil indicated that in the darkness they used their wings to sweep in mice located by hearing.

The problem was, then, to force the owls to rely on the sense of sight. The experimenter did this by covering the floor of the room with an artificial "jungle," a sort of latticework of light timber arranged so that owls could reach through the meshes and catch mice when the light intensity was sufficiently high so that the mice could be seen. This "jungle" simulated the plants and bushes under which mice normally live. In a series of trials under these conditions 107 conspicuous mice (dark-colored on light soil, and light-colored on dark soil) were captured but only 65 concealingly colored ones were. Dice found that "in every experiment in which the predator was evidently using sight to capture his prey, the concealingly colored individuals enjoyed more than a 20 percent advantage over the conspicuous animals in escaping capture." And he concluded: "such a high rate of selection, should it be applied to a natural population, would undoubtedly result in a very rapid change in the frequencies of the genes producing the character under selection."

Previous experimenters, using different predator and prey organisms, had obtained similar results (Dice, 1947).

Industrial Melanism

We see all around us plants and animals whose adaptations to the conditions of life we ascribe to natural selection. For the most part these adaptations were perfected long before there were human observers to record the process. Only seldom in the world around us will conditions have changed rapidly enough and recently enough so that biologists can obtain actual records of the changes and the forces effecting them. Usually it will be environmental changes produced by man that will lead to evolutionary change discernible within historic times. One of our best observed examples of natural selection in a state of nature concerns an effect of the Industrial Revolution upon the color of moths.

Most people are acquainted with the fact that albinos (individuals completely lacking pigment) occur from time to time in most kinds of animals including man himself. Fewer people are acquainted with *melanics,* individuals having heavier pigmentation than their fellows. Difference in a single pair of genes is commonly involved in the difference between normal pigmentation and melanism (pp. 376–377). Such melanism is found in many animals, including many species of moths. Usually the proportion of melanic individuals is very low, but in certain regions the proportions have become high within historic times. These are predominantly regions in which pollution of the atmosphere by large industrial centers has altered the appearance and color of, for example, the tree trunks upon which the moths normally rest during their daytime period of inactivity. Kettlewell (1958) stated that in England some seventy species of moths are now in process of increasing the proportion of darker individuals in their populations. Of these the peppered moth (*Biston betularia*) has been most intensively studied. Fig. 16.1 shows the normal light and the melanic form of this moth against a normally lichened tree trunk in a region free from pollution, while Fig. 16.2 shows the same two forms on a blackened tree trunk, upon which no lichens grow, in an industrial region (near Birmingham, England). Evidently, to the human eye the light form is inconspicuous and the dark form conspicuous against the background of lichens, and the reverse is true against the blackened trunk. Does this difference in visibility also apply to visibility by birds, the principal predators of these moths?

Kettlewell has demonstrated by careful observation, recorded photo-

FIG. 16.1. Dark-colored (melanic) and light-colored "typical" specimens of the peppered moth (*Biston betularia*) at rest upon a lichen-covered tree trunk. (Photograph by courtesy of Dr. H. B. D. Kettlewell.)

FIG. 16.2. Light-colored "typical" and dark-colored (melanic) specimens of the peppered moth (*Biston betularia*) at rest upon a lichen-free, blackened tree trunk in an industrial region. (Photograph by courtesy of Dr. H. B. D. Kettlewell.)

graphically, that birds do search out and eat motionless moths on tree trunks, a fact that had been doubted. This being true, does coloration which renders moths inconspicuous to our eyes also serve to protect them from being seen by birds? Careful observation indicates that the coloration is of protective value. Thus Kettlewell and his colleagues kept eighteen moths under continuous observation. Nine were of the light form, nine of the dark, and they were all on blackened tree trunks. During the day of observation all nine of the light individuals were found and eaten by birds but only three of the dark individuals were. On another occasion a pair of redstarts and their young were observed for two days in a polluted locality. Light and dark moths had been reared by the experimenters and were released in equal numbers. During the two days forty-three of the light individuals were found and eaten but only fifteen of the dark ones were. On the other hand, similar observations in unpolluted countryside yielded results which were just the reverse. Again the light and dark indi-

viduals were released in equal numbers but in this case 164 dark individuals were observed to be eaten, while only twenty-six of the light ones
were. Thus it seems that coloration which renders the moths inconspicuous to our eyes has the same effect in the eyes of birds.

In addition to experiments in which predation by birds was directly observed, experiments were performed in which large numbers of light and
of dark male moths were released into a countryside (Kettlewell, 1955,
1956). These males were marked so that they could be identified if they
were caught subsequently. After a time the males in the region were attracted to lights, or to cages containing females, and were trapped. In
this way the investigator could determine whether or not more of the released males of one kind or the other had fallen victim to predators. During two different summers hundreds of marked males were released into
the polluted countryside near Birmingham. The proportion of dark moths
recaptured was twice as high as the proportion of light moths recaptured,
demonstrating that more of the unconcealingly colored individuals had
been killed by predators. The same conclusion, based on converse findings, was drawn from similar experiments in an unpolluted region. Here
it was the light-colored males which were protected: three times as many
of them as of dark-colored ones were recaptured. Kettlewell noted that
to human eyes the light individuals were less easily visible on lichen-
covered tree trunks than the dark individuals were on blackened trunks.
But in both instances blending with the background afforded some protection to the moths.

The most common melanic form of the peppered moth differs from the
normal light form by possession of a dominant gene. The first melanic
specimen on record was caught near Manchester in 1848. For many years
following that date black specimens were rare; but by 1900 they had become common in many localities, forming as high as 83 percent of the
population in some localities. At the present time black individuals constitute at least 85 percent of the population in all industrial areas of England; in some places the percentage reaches 98. Here, then, is an instance
in which man's activities have altered an environment and a species has
altered its characteristics in response to the changed conditions. Evidently
what happened was this: Since, as we have seen, melanic individuals are
in less danger of death from bird predation than are light-colored ones,
they had a tendency to survive in greater numbers in the polluted regions, and to pass on their genes to a greater proportion of offspring.
Hence in polluted regions the dominant gene for melanism increased in
frequency as the generations passed until the present high percentages
were reached.

Not only have the melanics increased in numbers, they have apparently become blacker. Comparison of specimens caught many years ago with modern ones indicates that formerly the melanic specimens had more white markings than do modern melanics (Kettlewell, 1958). Probably this "improvement" in matching black backgrounds has been brought about by natural selection acting on genes which modify the effect of the main dominant gene.

It is of interest that in no populations do the melanics constitute 100 percent of the population. Why is this? Perhaps, as Kettlewell suggests, the *heterozygous* melanics have some advantage over both homozygous melanic and homozygous light individuals. Heterozygote superiority has been mentioned previously (pp. 346–347) and will be discussed more fully below (pp. 457–468). It forms the basis for balanced polymorphism in, for example, fruit flies having the M-5 chromosome (p. 459), ebony fruit flies (p. 457), and the chromosome types of *Drosophila pseudoobscura* (p. 460).

Other forces may also be at work to maintain a balanced polymorphism of light and dark forms. Working with a different species of moth, Kettlewell (1957) found that in a certain unpolluted region the light individuals were inconspicuous when at rest but were much more visible when flying than were the dark individuals. Thus the respective advantages of the two types would tend to maintain an equilibrium in their respective numbers; neither would completely supplant the other.

The example just given is also of interest in that it demonstrates that melanic forms may have an advantage in environments unaffected by industrialization. Nevertheless most localities in which the percentage of melanism is high are either located near industrial centers or in portions of eastern England subject to "long continued smoke fall-out carried by the prevailing south-westerly winds from central England" (Kettlewell, 1958).

We have emphasized the importance of predation in the natural selection of melanic individuals. Other forces may also be at work. There are physiological differences between melanic and normally colored individuals. Thus Ford (1940) found that larvae of melanic moths withstand partial starvation better than do larvae of normally colored ones. Behavioral differences manifesting themselves in differences in success in mating also seem to be present (Kettlewell, 1957). Evidently, however, any advantages conferred by the gene for melanism were offset in normal countrysides by the added conspicuousness to birds. When, however, man blackened the environment then natural selection led to the establishment of the melanic form in the changed environment.

Additional evidence that coloration is, in part, at least, controlled by predators using the sense of sight is afforded by the studies of Cain and Sheppard (1954; and Sheppard, 1955) on bright-colored, polymorphic European snails of the genus *Cepaea*. In this case the predator is a song thrush. The investigators found that the color patterns of snails most commonly found and eaten varied with the background. Interestingly enough, no such correlation existed in localities in which snails were preyed upon by rabbits rather than by birds. Apparently color as such was not involved in the locating of snails by rabbits.

Mimicry

Another situation in which natural selection can be seen at work in the predator-prey relationship is that in which organisms resemble, not their backgrounds or surroundings, but each other. The simplest example is that in which an edible species resembles an inedible one, a situation emphasized by Bates and hence called **Batesian mimicry.** If one species of butterfly is unpalatable to birds, another species which is palatable would find it of advantage to resemble the unpalatable one and thus be spared from predation by birds. This being so, natural selection would favor the acquisition by edible species of markings and behavioral traits which would cause them to resemble inedible species.

Sometimes two or more inedible or unpalatable species resemble each other; this is called **Müllerian mimicry.** Fig. 16.3 presents a striking example; the insect has remarkable resemblance to a wasp, yet is a *moth*. Beebe and Kenedy (1957) reported that they found this moth unpalatable to a lizard, a bird, and three species of ants. Wasps are also highly inedible. Of what advantage is it for two inedible species to resemble one another? According to the theory of Müllerian mimicry the advantage stems from a reduction in the number of "lessons" required by a young bird in learning to avoid inedible species. Once a bird has learned not to eat wasps it has automatically also learned not to touch the Ctenuchid moth shown in Fig. 16.3. Thus moth individuals are not destroyed by the bird in learning that they are inedible. Conversely, if a bird learns that the moth is unpalatable it will also avoid wasps, and such avoidance will be of advantage to wasps. Thus Müllerian mimicry is of advantage to both, or all, species concerned, while Batesian mimicry is of advantage only to the edible species (the mimic) which resembles the inedible one (the model). In actuality the sharpness of distinction between Batesian and Müllerian mimicry is reduced by the fact that there are all degrees of edibility and palatability.

The most widely known example of mimicry in North America is that of the Monarch and Viceroy butterflies. The striking similarity of these actually unrelated species is evident in Fig. 16.4. This is usually cited as an example of Batesian mimicry, the Monarch being said to be inedible, the Viceroy edible. This conclusion has been challenged, however, on the ground that the Viceroy is also inedible. Brower (1958a) in an extensive series of experiments with captive jays, found that the Monarch is indeed unpalatable to these birds, and also that the birds do not distinguish be-

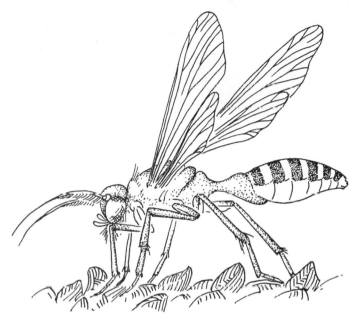

FIG. 16.3. Müllerian mimicry: a moth which mimics a wasp. (Drawn from a photograph in Beebe and Kenedy, "Habits, palatability and mimicry in thirteen Ctenuchid moth species from Trinidad, B.W.I." Zoologica, Vol. 42, 1957, pp. 147–158, Plate II.)

tween the Monarch and the Viceroy. Thus birds that had learned to avoid the Monarch also avoided the Viceroy. Brower found that birds which had not been given experience with Monarchs ate Viceroys but that on the whole Viceroys seemed to be less palatable than were other species of butterflies tested (e.g., Tiger Swallowtails). Hence this example seems to fall somewhere between classical Batesian and classical Müllerian mimicry.

Brower (1958b) tested other cases of mimicry with her captive jays. She demonstrated one example of classical Batesian mimicry. The butterfly *Battus philenor* was unpalatable to the birds; having had experience with

FIG. 16.4. Mimicry. Monarch butterfly, the model (upper); Viceroy, the mimic (middle); a relative of the Viceroy showing a color pattern more usual for the group to which the Viceroy belongs (lower). Stippled areas of the Monarch and Viceroy are brown in color. (Drawn by Halcyon W. Hellbaum; from Guyer, *Animal Biology*, Harper & Brothers, 1948, p. 105.)

this model, the birds tended to avoid two other species which mimicked it in markings. These latter two species, however, were completely palatable to birds which had not had experience with the unpalatable model.

Mimicry is a widespread phenomenon among insects. In view of experiments such as those cited we may conclude that resemblances evident to human eyes are also effective in deceiving such predators as birds. Hence development of resemblances of this kind will be favored by natural selection. While, as we have seen, some mimicry is remarkably detailed, more general resemblances and partial similarities will also have selective value insofar as they reduce the chance of attack by predators. There is experimental evidence (e.g., Brower, 1958c) that birds have some ability to generalize—once having learned to avoid an unpalatable model they will avoid other species that to our eyes have some, but not striking, resemblance to that model.

So far we have been discussing **protective** mimicry, mimicry which protects from predators. There is also the possibility that mimicry may be **aggressive.** If, for example, a predator resembles its prey, that predator may be able to approach its victim more easily than it could otherwise do. Some predatory flies lay their eggs in colonies of bees; when the larval flies emerge they feed upon the immature stages of the bees. If, as is sometimes the case, the fly resembles the bees, its entrance into the bee colony to lay its eggs may be facilitated. The bees may not be "suspicious" of the beelike fly. Brower, Brower, and Westcott (1960) have discussed this question, citing a probable example. In this case the adult fly attacks and feeds upon adult bumblebees. The authors concluded that the resemblance of the fly to the bee, extending even to the tone of its buzz, probably makes capture of the victim easier than it would otherwise be. The authors demonstrated that protective mimicry of the Batesian variety is also involved in this instance. Toads which had learned to avoid bumblebees (unpalatable because of their stings) also avoided the mimicking flies, whereas toads lacking experience with bumblebees usually ate the flies readily.

Conclusion

In this chapter we have summarized investigations which demonstrate that protective coloration, including mimicry, does protect. The results demonstrate that when predators utilize the sense of sight, prey organisms which, for example, blend with the background are afforded sufficient protection so that their greater success in survival and reproduction can account for origin of evolutionary changes, as postulated by the theory of natural selection. And in the case of industrial melanism we see differential predation as a factor which has altered the nature of populations within historic times.

References and Suggested Readings

Beebe, W., and R. Kenedy. "Habits, palatability and mimicry in thirteen Ctenuchid moth species from Trinidad, B. W. I." *Zoologica,* 42 (1957), 147–158.

Brower, J. VZ. "Experimental studies of mimicry in some North American butterflies. Part I. The Monarch, *Danaus plexippus,* and Viceroy, *Limenitis archippus archippus,*" *Evolution,* 12 (1958a), 32–47.

Brower, J. VZ. "Experimental studies of mimicry in some North American butterflies. Part II. *Battus philenor* and *Papilio troilus, P. polyxenes,* and *P. glaucus,*" *Evolution,* 12 (1958b), 123–136.

Brower, J. VZ. "Experimental studies of mimicry in some North American butterflies. Part III. *Danaus gilippus berenice* and *Limenitis archippus floridensis,*" *Evolution,* 12 (1958c), 273–285.

Brower, L. P., J. VZ. Brower, and P. W. Westcott. "Experimental studies of mimicry. 5. The reactions of toads (*Bufo terrestris*) to bumblebees (*Bombus americanorum*) and their robberfly mimics (*Mallophora bomboides*), with a discussion of aggressive mimicry," *American Naturalist,* 94 (1960), 343–355.

Cain, A. J., and P. M. Sheppard. "Natural selection in *Cepea,*" *Genetics,* 39 (1954), 89–116.

Dice, L. R. "Effectiveness of selection by owls of deer-mice (*Peromyscus maniculatus*) which contrast in color with their background," *Contributions, Lab. of Vertebrate Biology, Univ. of Michigan,* No. 34 (1947), 1–20.

Fisher, R. A. *The Genetical Theory of Natural Selection.* 2nd ed. New York: Dover Publications, Inc., 1958. (Chapter 7 is a discussion of mimicry.)

Ford, E. B. "Genetic research in the Lepidoptera," *Annales of Eugenics,* 10 (1940), 227–252.

Kettlewell, H. B. D. "Selection experiments on industrial melanism in the Lepidoptera," *Heredity,* 9 (1955), 323–342.

Kettlewell, H. B. D. "Further selection experiments on industrial melanism in the Lepidoptera," *Heredity,* 10 (1956), 287–301.

Kettlewell, H. B. D. "The contribution of industrial melanism in the Lepidoptera to our knowledge of evolution," *British Assoc.: The Advancement of Science,* No. 52 (1957), 245–252.

Kettlewell, H. B. D. "A survey of the frequencies of *Biston betularia* (L.) (Lep.) and its melanistic forms in Great Britain," *Heredity,* 12 (1958), 51–72.

Sheppard, P. M. "Evolution in bisexually reproducing organisms," In J. Huxley, A. C. Hardy, and E. B. Ford (eds.). *Evolution as a Process.* London: Allen & Unwin, Ltd., 1955. Pp. 201–218.

Sheppard, P. M. "The evolution of mimicry; a problem in ecology and genetics," *Cold Spring Harbor Symposia on Quantitative Biology,* 24 (1959), 131–140.

Sheppard, P. M. *Natural Selection and Heredity.* New York: Harper & Brothers, Torchbook 528, 1960. (Mimicry is discussed in Chapter 10.)

CHAPTER 17

GENETIC FACTORS IN THE

ORIGIN OF DIVERSITY

POLYMORPHIC SPECIES

Examples of genetic diversity encountered in a state of nature are afforded by polymorphic species. These are species in which an individual may possess one or two or more possible sets of 'characteristics. The polymorphism of moth species in which both light-colored and dark-colored individuals occur was discussed in the preceding chapter in connection with industrial melanism. Additional examples are represented by the "color phases" of some birds and mammals. Most of the individuals of our common little screech owl are speckled gray in coloration, but occasionally reddish individuals appear. These are said to be in "the rufous phase." Again, most of the fox squirrels of the American Middle West have a reddish coloration, but occasionally melanistic (dark) individuals occur. Most of the black bears of North America have glossy black coats, but brown individuals are also found—"cinnamon bears." In some regions the cinnamon individuals may be fairly common. Examples might be multiplied almost indefinitely, but we shall find convenient as a focal point for discussion the polymorphic condition of a rodent which occurs in vast numbers in parts of Europe and Asia: the common hamster. This hamster belongs to the same genus as does the golden hamster from Iran, recently popularized as a pet in the United States. The European hamster is larger, and important as a source of fur, much as is the muskrat in this country. Great numbers of hamsters are trapped annually in Russia.

"Normal" hamsters vary from gray to grizzly brown in appearance, but black individuals frequently occur. In some regions the black (melanistic) individuals are rare, in other regions they occur with varying frequencies, the extreme being reached in localities having populations in which nearly all individuals are black.

Genetic experimentation has demonstrated that the color difference between a normal and a black hamster depends upon a single gene. Thus, inheritance is of the type discussed in the first part of Chapter 15. Melanism (blackness) is dominant to normal pigmentation (Gershenson, 1945). Accordingly, gray hamsters are homozygous (see p. 333) for a recessive gene; we may indicate their genetic formula as *mm*. Black hamsters may be homozygous for the corresponding dominant gene (i.e., *MM*), or they may be heterozygous (i.e., *Mm*). It is probable that the color phases of other animals mentioned above depend upon similar genetic mechanisms, but in most cases the genetic analyses necessary to demonstrate the point have not yet been made.

MENDELIAN INHERITANCE

Single-Gene Differences

What will be the result of mating homozygous black hamsters to gray ones? The homozygous black individuals have the formula *MM,* the gray individuals the formula *mm*. Thus the cross becomes: *MM* × *mm*. Each germ cell (sperm or ovum) produced by the black parents will contain one of the *M* genes; each germ cell produced by the gray parent will contain an *m* gene. The basis of this separation of members of pairs of genes so that each germ cell receives but one member is expressed in Mendel's "law of segregation" (see below). As a result, each offspring produced by the fertilization of an ovum by a sperm will be of the formula *Mm,* i.e., will be heterozygous. Since black coloration is dominant to gray, all these F_1 (first filial generation) offspring will be black (Fig. 17.1).

$$MM \times mm$$

$$\text{germ} \left\{ \begin{matrix} M \to m \\ \diagdown \ \nearrow \\ \diagup \ \diagdown \\ M \to m \end{matrix} \right\} \text{germ cells}$$

F_1 offspring *Mm, Mm, Mm, Mm;* all have black coloration.

Suppose that the *Mm* males are now mated to the *Mm* females. What will be the result in the next, or F_2 generation? As we noted in a pre-

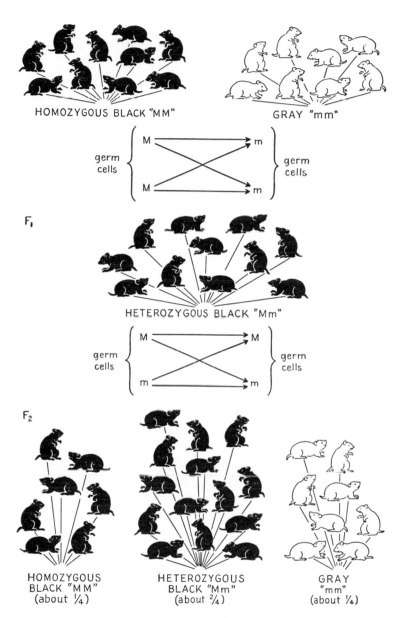

HOMOZYGOUS BLACK "MM"

GRAY "mm"

germ cells { M ⟶ m
             M ⟶ m } germ cells

F_1

HETEROZYGOUS BLACK "Mm"

germ cells { M ⟶ M
             m ⟶ m } germ cells

F_2

HOMOZYGOUS
BLACK "MM"
(about ¼)

HETEROZYGOUS
BLACK "Mm"
(about 2/4)

GRAY
"mm"
(about ¼)

FIG. 17.1. Mendelian inheritance of melanism (black color) in the European hamster.

ceding chapter (p. 333), heterozygous individuals produce germ cells of two kinds in approximately equal numbers. About half of the sperms produced by the *Mm* males will contain *M;* about half will contain *m.* Similarly, half of the ova produced by *Mm* females will contain *M;* half will contain *m.* The reason is that sperms and ova arise from cells which contain the *pair* of genes *Mm.* In such a paired arrangement the number of *M*'s equals the number of *m*'s. Accordingly, when the members of these pairs separate in the formation of germ cells, *M*-bearing germ cells and *m*-bearing ones should be about equal in number.

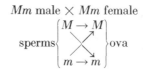

We may now ask: What are the chances that an *M*-containing ovum will be fertilized by an *M*-containing sperm cell? The question may be answered in three stages: (1) What are the chances that any given fertilization will involve an *M*-containing *ovum?* Since half the ova are *M*-containing this chance is 1 in 2, or ½. (2) What are the chances that any given fertilization will involve an *M*-containing *sperm cell?* Again, since *M*-containing sperm cells and *m*-containing ones are equal in number, the chance that an *M*-containing one will be involved is ½. (3) What, then, is the chance that both an *M*-containing ovum and an *M*-containing sperm cell will be involved? The probability that two independent events will occur together is the *product* of the probabilities of their occurring singly. Thus the chance that an *MM* fertilized ovum will occur is the chance that an *M*-containing ovum will be involved (½) multiplied by the chance that an *M*-containing sperm will be involved (½); ½ · ½ = ¼. A similar situation arises when two coins are tossed together. What are the chances that both will come up "heads"? The chance that one coin will be "heads" is ½; the chance that the other coin will be "heads" is ½. Thus the chance that both will be "heads" is ½ · ½ or ¼.

Similarly, what are the chances that an *m*-containing ovum will be fertilized by an *m*-containing sperm? The answer is exactly the same as in the case just described. The chance that an *m*-containing ovum will be involved is ½; the chance that an *m*-containing sperm will be involved is also ½. So the chance that an *mm* fertilized ovum will arise is ½ · ½ or ¼.

We have seen that the chances that offspring will be *MM* are ¼, and the chances that they will be *mm* are ¼. Thus on the average ¼ of the offspring may be expected to be homozygous black, ¼ to be homozygous gray. The remaining $\frac{2}{4}$ will be expected to be heterozygous black: *Mm*. Such individuals can arise in two ways: (1) by an *M*-containing sperm cell's fertilizing an *m*-containing ovum (chances of this $\frac{1}{2} \cdot \frac{1}{2} = \frac{1}{4}$); (2) by an *m*-containing sperm's fertilizing an *M*-containing ovum (chances of this $\frac{1}{2} \cdot \frac{1}{2} = \frac{1}{4}$). Since the chance that two mutually exclusive events will occur is the sum of the chances that either event will occur alone, the chances that *Mm* offspring will arise is $\frac{1}{4} + \frac{1}{4}$ or $\frac{2}{4}$.

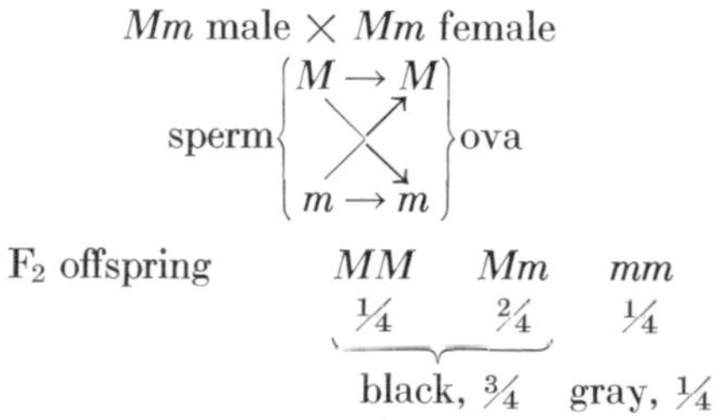
Mm male × Mm female
M → M
sperm
ova
m → m
F2 offspring
MM
Mm
mm
1/4
2/4
1/4
black, 3/4
gray, 1/4

The above results are sometimes expressed as ratios. The fundamental ratio among offspring of parents both of whom are heterozygous is 1:2:1 (1 homozygous dominant to 2 heterozygotes to 1 homozygous recessive). When dominance is present, this fundamental ratio is masked, since homozygous dominants (*MM*) look like heterozygotes (*Mm*). Thus on the basis of phenotype (p. 333) the ratio becomes 3 black-colored offspring to 1 gray one (Fig. 17.1).

Sometimes dominance is not present. In such cases the 1:2:1 ratio is the ratio of phenotypes as well as the ratio of genotypes. For example, when red snapdragons (*RR*) are crossed with ivory ones (*rr*) the F_1 offspring (*Rr*) are pink in color. Pink may be regarded as intermediate between red and ivory, a sort of diluted red. Evidently in this case having one *R* gene results in less red pigment than does having two *R* genes. When the F_2 offspring are produced by mating these pink heterozygotes together (*Rr* × *Rr*), the ratio of $\frac{1}{4}$ red (*RR*) to $\frac{2}{4}$ pink (*Rr*) to $\frac{1}{4}$ ivory (*rr*) is obtained. Similarly, Blue Andalusian fowls are heterozygotes (*Ww*). When Blue Andalusians are mated together the ratio obtained is: $\frac{1}{4}$ black (*WW*) to $\frac{2}{4}$ blue (*Ww*) to $\frac{1}{4}$ splashed white (*ww*).

We should emphasize that these 1:2:1 and 3:1 ratios, so prominent in writing concerning Mendelian inheritance, depend upon the operation of the laws of chance as set forth above. The ratio expresses the ideal or perfect outcome when two types of sperms fertilize two types of ova. Ratios obtained in actual experiments approach the ideal ratio but seldom conform to it exactly. On the whole, the larger the number of offspring produced, the more closely will the ideal ratio be approached. As is well known, Mendel himself experimented with garden peas. During the course of his experiments he produced about 20,000 individuals as offspring of heterozygous parents. The ratio he obtained from them was 2.996:1.004, certainly a near approach to the ideal 3:1.

During some years of teaching an elementary course in heredity the present author has utilized the coin model mentioned above. Students are asked to toss two coins and record the number of times both coins come up heads; the number of times one coin comes heads, the other tails; and the number of times both come up tails. To date, a cumulative total of over 57,000 such tosses has been amassed. Adding together the tosses in which there is *at least* one head (as in combining the *MM* and *Mm* groups above) we obtain a ratio of 2.987:1.

Thus we see that the distribution of genes from parents to their offspring is dependent upon the operation of the laws of probability (chance). The 1:2:1 ratio (and its modification the 3:1 ratio) is the ideal ratio approached when two equally numerous kinds of sperms fertilize two equally numerous kinds of ova.

In our examples so far we have noted that genes occur in pairs in the genotypes of parents, while in germ cells produced by those parents the members of pairs are separated so that each germ cell receives but one gene of each pair. This means that while genes occur in pairs in the body (somatic) cells of animals, they occur singly in the mature reproductive cells. What is the explanation? To answer this question we must learn something of the behavior of the **chromosomes** which contain the genes.

Meiosis

As a specific example, let us take the heterozygous black, male hamster just mentioned. His body cells contain chromosomes arranged in pairs; one member of each pair came from his mother, one from his father. Early in his embryonic development certain cells were set aside to form the sperm cells which he would require when he reached sexual maturity. These primordial germ cells are called **spermatogonia.** They contain chromosomes in pairs just as do the body cells. At the top of Fig. 17.2 we see spermatogonia containing a long pair of chromosomes and a short pair. (For sake of simplicity only two pairs are shown.) One member of each pair is white, one is shaded. The white member may be thought of as the one derived from the mother, the **maternal** one, the shaded member as the one derived from the father, the **paternal** one. Somewhere on each chromosome there is a **centromere** or spindle fiber attachment. This is represented as a large dot in the diagram.

The spermatogonia, originally few in number, multiply by the ordinary process of cell division, mitosis. For sake of simplicity in the diagram only one of these mitoses is indicated, and this is done without including all the

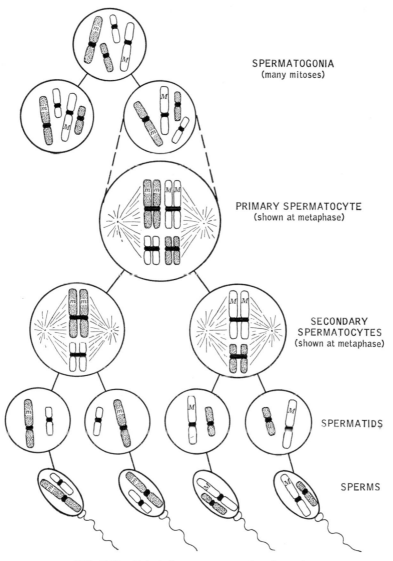

SPERMATOGONIA
(many mitoses)

PRIMARY SPERMATOCYTE
(shown at metaphase)

SECONDARY
SPERMATOCYTES
(shown at metaphase)

SPERMATIDS

SPERMS

FIG. 17.2. Meiosis (spermatogenesis) in the male.

stages in the process (see Fig. 5.2, p. 83). Eventually each resulting spermatogonium becomes a **primary spermatocyte.** By this time each chromosome has duplicated itself. The two resulting duplicate chromosomes **(chromatids)** are for the time being held together by the centromere

(Fig. 17.2). As the primary spermatocyte prepares to divide, the chromosomes come together in pairs; e.g., the two chromatids representing the
maternal "long chromosome" pair with the two chromatids representing
the paternal "long chromosome." This pairing is called **synapsis** and during
it the chromatids are frequently twisted around each other instead of
lying smoothly side by side as shown in the diagram. At this time part of
one chromatid may be exchanged with part of another one. This exchange
is called **crossing over** and has important genetic consequences, as we
shall see below.

Eventually each primary spermatocyte divides to form two **secondary
spermatocytes.** In this division each centromere remains intact, carrying
with it its two chromatids. Thus, in terms of our diagram, each secondary
spermatocyte receives the chromatids representing one "long chromosome"
and one "short chromosome." The chromatids representing the maternal
"long chromosome" (white) go to one secondary spermatocyte, those
representing the paternal "long chromosome" (shaded) go to the other. It
is important to note that what the "long" chromatids do in this respect does
not influence what the "short" chromatids do. In the diagram of the primary spermatocyte we have shown the maternal "long" chromatids on
the right, the paternal ones on the left, and the paternal "short" chromatids
on the right, the maternal ones on the left. This is a matter of chance.
About half the time this arrangement would be expected; about half the
time the maternal members of both "long" and "short" chromosomes
would line up on the same side, the paternal members of both on the other
side.

Each secondary spermatocyte divides to form two **spermatids.** In this
division each centromere splits so that the chromatids separate, one
"long" chromatid and one "short" one going into each spermatid. Each
spermatid undergoes a metamorphosis, developing a swimming tail, and
becomes a mature **sperm** cell. We note that each sperm cell contains only
half as many chromosomes as did the spermatogonium and that one member of each pair of chromosomes present in the spermatogonium is present
in the sperm cell. The number of singly occurring chromosomes in a
mature germ cell (e.g., sperm) is called the **haploid** number. In our
diagram the haploid number is 2. On the other hand, the number of
chromosomes occurring in pairs in primordial germ cells, and in body
cells, is called the **diploid** number. In our diagram the diploid number is
4. The process we have described is called **meiosis;** it results in the production of haploid germ cells from diploid primordial cells.

As noted above, we have pictured meiosis in a heterozygous black, male hamster. Let us suppose that he inherited the gene for melanism (*M*) from his mother, the gene for grayness (*m*) from his father, and that these genes are in the "long chromosomes" (Fig. 17.2). When each chromosome duplicates itself to form a pair of chromatids the genes are duplicated, too (as shown in the primary spermatocyte of Fig. 17.2). In the figure the maternal "long chromosomes," with their duplicated *M* genes, are shown going to the secondary spermatocyte on the right, the paternal "long chromosomes," with their "*m*" genes, to the secondary spermatocyte on the left. Then when the chromatids separate, each of the pair of spermatids on the right receives a maternal chromosome containing *M,* and each of the pair of spermatids on the left receives a paternal chromosome containing *m*. As a result, half the sperm cells in such a heterozygous male receive maternal chromosomes containing gene *M,* half receive paternal chromosomes containing gene *m*. It will be readily appreciated that the hamster in which this occurred might have inherited *m* from his mother and *M* from his father, in which case the *m* gene would have been contained in the maternal chromosome, the *M* gene in the paternal one. But the genetic results would have been the same: half the sperm cells would contain *M,* half would contain *m*.

Meiosis in females differs from meiosis in males only in details. The primordial germ cells are called **oögonia.** These multiply by mitosis. Eventually each daughter oögonium increases in size, and the chromosomes duplicate themselves and pair in synapsis, forming a **primary oöcyte** stage (Fig. 17.3). Whereas the primary spermatocyte divides into two secondary spermatocytes of equal size, the primary oöcyte divides into two cells of very unequal size: the **secondary oöcyte** and the **first polar body.** The secondary oöcyte contains practically all the cytoplasm of the primary oöcyte, the polar body containing only enough cytoplasm to enclose the chromosomes. Despite the unequal partitioning of cytoplasm, the secondary oöcyte and the polar body contain equivalent chromosomes: in our example each contains the chromatids representing one "long chromosome" and one "short chromosome" (Fig. 17.3).

When the secondary oöcyte divides, the cytoplasmic division is again unequal, the products being the large **ovum** and the tiny **second polar body.** But, as shown, each receives one chromatid of each pair contained in the secondary oöcyte. The polar bodies disintegrate; hence each primary oöcyte gives rise to but one ovum. This ovum contains one chromosome for each pair of chromosomes contained in the oögonium from which it arose. Thus meiosis in the female resembles meiosis in the male in that haploid germ cells are produced from diploid primordial cells.

Fig. 17.3 pictures meiosis in a heterozygous, black female hamster, which inherited the gene *M* from its mother, the gene *m* from its father. In the figure the paternal "long chromatids" with gene *m* are shown as

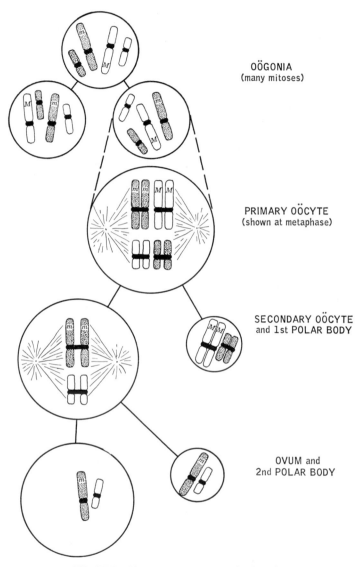

OÖGONIA
(many mitoses)

PRIMARY OÖCYTE
(shown at metaphase)

SECONDARY OÖCYTE
and 1st POLAR BODY

OVUM and
2nd POLAR BODY

FIG. 17.3.   Meiosis (oögenesis) in the female.

passing into the secondary oöcyte, the maternal "long chromatids" with gene *M* as being discarded in the first polar body. The result is that the ovum shown contains *m*. But the fate of the chromosomes when the primary oöcyte divides is determined by chance. Thus it is as likely that the paternal "long chromosome" will be discarded in the first polar body as it is that the maternal one will be. In this case the secondary oöcyte, and hence the ovum, would contain M. Hence in the long run half the ova produced by such a heterozygous female may be expected to contain M, half to contain m.

As a result of meiosis in both sexes haploid germ cells are produced. When a sperm cell (haploid) fertilizes an ovum (haploid) the two cells fuse and the diploid number is restored (Fig. 17.4). The fertilized ovum undergoes mitosis, dividing into two cells each with the diploid number. Such mitoses continue and eventually an embryo takes shape, the cells all

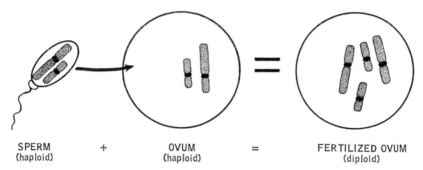

| SPERM | + | OVUM | = | FERTILIZED OVUM |
| (haploid) | | (haploid) | | (diploid) |

FIG. 17.4. Fertilization. Haploid germ cells (gametes) unite to form a diploid ovum (zygote).

containing the diploid number of chromosomes derived from the fertilized ovum. Some of the cells in the embryo are set aside as primordial germ cells, which in time undergo meiosis, and so the cycle is continued generation after generation.

Returning to the genetic implications of meiosis, we note that the behavior of the chromosomes in this process provides the mechanism for Mendel's "law of segregation" (p. 376)—the means by which each germ cell receives but one member of each pair of genes. The chromosomes also provide the mechanism for the Mendelian "law of independent assortment." This is the principle that different pairs of genes are independent of each other in the manner in which they are distributed to the germ cells.

Independent Assortment

As an example we shall employ the guinea pig, a form whose genetics is more thoroughly known than is the genetics of the European hamster.

Two pairs of contrasting characteristics in guinea pigs are (1) black versus white and (2) short hair versus long. Individuals heterozygous for both pairs of characteristics are black and have short hair. This shows that the gene for black (*B*) is dominant to the gene for white (*b*), and the

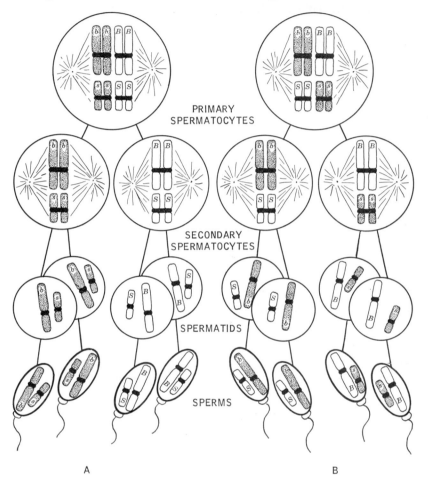

FIG. 17.5. Chromosomal basis of the independent assortment of genes in meiosis.

gene for short hair (*S*) is dominant to the gene for long hair (*s*). Fig. 17.5 is a diagram of meiosis in a doubly heterozygous, black, short-haired male. As with the hamster, the diagram is simplified by showing only two pairs of chromosomes, a long pair and a short pair. It is assumed that the male inherited blackness and short-hairedness from his mother, the opposite characteristics from his father. Thus the gene *B* is in the maternal (white) "long chromosome" and the gene *S* is in the maternal "short chromosome." In the diagram the spermatogonia have been omitted, the first stage shown being the primary spermatocyte. The pairs of chromatids are shown in synapsis. In Fig. 17.5A they are lined up in such a manner that the paternal pairs of chromatids are on the left in both cases. As a result two kinds of sperm cells are produced in equal numbers: (1) those containing the maternal "long chromosome" (with gene B) and the maternal "short chromosome" (with gene S); (2) those containing the paternal "long chromosome" (with gene b) and the paternal "short chromosome" (with gene s).

It is to be noted, however, that the arrangement of chromatid pairs in synapsis is a chance affair. Sometimes they will line up as shown in Fig. 17.5A, but they are equally likely to line up as shown in Fig. 17.5B, with the pair representing the paternal "long chromosome" on the left, the pair representing the paternal "short chromosome" on the right. As a result of this arrangement sperm cells containing one maternal chromosome and one paternal one are formed, with the accompanying Bs and bS combinations of genes.

The two arrangements of chromatid pairs are equally likely to occur, hence the four kinds of sperm cells shown in Fig. 17.5 will occur with equal frequency: BS, bs, Bs, and bS. By a somewhat comparable operation of the laws of chance in female meiosis, a doubly heterozygous, black, short-haired female will produce ova of these same four types.

What offspring will be expected when doubly heterozygous males and females are mated to each other? In other words, what combinations of the four types of sperms with the four types of ova will occur? This is diagrammed in Fig. 17.6 in the form of a "checkerboard" having four squares on a side. Across the top are placed the four types of ova, along the left-hand margin the four types of sperms. Each square in the diagram represents a fertilized ovum; in each case the genetic formula (genotype) is indicated without drawing the enclosing chromosomes. The squares are numbered. At the bottom of the diagram are shown the four expected types of offspring with the numbers of the squares corresponding to each. We note that nine of the sixteen fertilized ova contain at least one B and at least one S and so give rise to black, short-haired offspring; while three of the sixteen contain at least one B but are homozygous ss, and hence result in black, long-haired offspring. Similarly, three of the fertilized ova are homozygous bb but have at least one S; they have the phenotype white, short-haired. Finally, one of the sixteen fertilized ova is homozygous bbss and hence gives rise to a white, long-haired individual.

We may note that this 9:3:3:1 ratio is merely two 3:1 ratios multiplied together. Considered alone, the mating of heterozygous black females to heterozygous black males results in an expected ¾ black offspring and ¼ white (as with melanism in hamsters; see p. 379). Similarly, considered

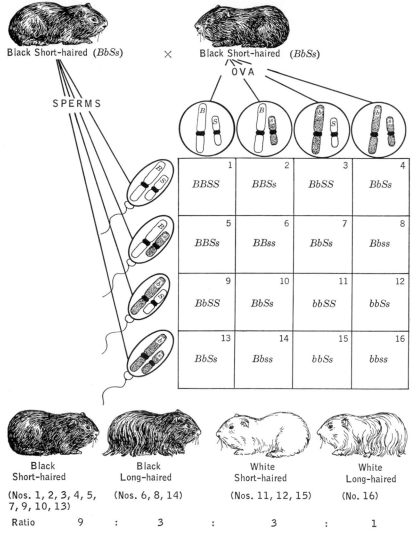

FIG. 17.6. The effect of independent assortment of genes in determining the offspring to be expected when doubly heterozygous guinea pigs are mated to each other.

alone, the mating of heterozygous short-haired females to heterozygous short-haired males results in an expected ¾ short-haired offspring and ¼ long-haired. Combining these expectations:

¾ (black) + ¼ (white)
¾ (short) + ¼ (long)

---

⁹⁄₁₆ (black, short) + ³⁄₁₆ (white, short) + ³⁄₁₆ (black, long) + ¹⁄₁₆ (white, long)

When additional pairs of contrasting characteristics are considered, still more complicated ratios are obtained. Another pair of characteristics in guinea pigs is rough hair versus smooth hair. The gene for rough (R) is dominant. Thus when heterozygous rough guinea pigs are mated together ¾ of the offspring are expected to be rough-haired, ¼ smooth. What will be expected when *triply* heterozygous black, short, rough (BbSsRr) guinea pigs are mated together? We may answer the question by the checkerboard method (c.f., Fig. 17.6), noting that in this case *three* pairs of chromosomes are involved, and that the females will produce *eight* types of ova, the males *eight* types of sperms. Or we may answer the question by multiplying the 9:3:3:1 ratio already obtained by another 3:1 ratio:

⁹⁄₁₆ (black, short) + ³⁄₁₆ (white, short) + ³⁄₁₆ (black, long) + ¹⁄₁₆ (white, long)
¾ (rough) + ¼ (smooth)

The reader will find working this out completely an instructive exercise. We may note that the first and largest item will consist of offspring showing all three dominants (black, short, rough) and that ⁹⁄₁₆ · ¾ or ²⁷⁄₆₄ of the offspring will be expected to be of this type.

Still more complicated ratios result when more than three pairs of contrasting characteristics are being considered. Since in actuality every individual is heterozygous for many pairs of genes (p. 466) the amount of genetic diversity produced by the "shuffling" of chromosomes, with their contained genes, is enormous. This is part of the raw material for evolutionary change.

Lethal Genes

We note that these more complicated ratios are elaborations of the 1:2:1 ratio (and its modification the 3:1 ratio). These ratios may be modified in various ways. For example, one homozygote or the other may be **lethal.** A lethal gene is one which kills fertilized ova or embryos homozygous for it. Such homozygotes are not hatched or born, or at best they die young. Yellow mice, for example, are always heterozygous (for present purposes we may designate their genotype as "Yy"). When yellow mice are mated together the following results are obtained:

yellow × yellow

$$\underline{Yy} \qquad \underline{Yy}$$

$$\text{sperm} \left\{ \begin{matrix} Y \to Y \\ \times \\ y \to y \end{matrix} \right\} \text{ova}$$

$$\left(\dfrac{YY}{\frac{1}{4}} \right) \qquad \dfrac{Yy}{\frac{2}{4}} \qquad \dfrac{yy}{\frac{1}{4}}$$

dies   2 yellow: 1 normally colored

In this case the $1:2:1$ ratio is changed to a $2:1$ ratio. Here it is the homozygous state of the dominant gene which is lethal.

Sometimes the homozygous condition of the recessive gene is lethal. In corn, for example, there is a recessive gene (w) which results, in homozygotes, in failure to produce chlorophyll; the seedling is white and dies as soon as the food stored in the seed is exhausted. Heterozygous corn (Ww) is green just like homozygous corn (WW). When heterozygous corn is self-pollinated ($Ww \times Ww$) the following results are obtained: $\frac{1}{4}$ WW (green): $\frac{2}{4}$ Ww (green): $\frac{1}{4}$ ww (white). The white seedlings wither, leaving only the green ones. If the ww individuals did not sprout at all we should know of the presence of the gene w only through its effect in reducing the proportion of viable seeds produced. Doubtless many recessive lethals are known only through their effects in reducing fertility.

Later on we shall have occasion to mention genes which affect viability without being completely lethal (pp. 450–454). Genes which in homozygotes are lethal, or lower viability, are widespread in natural populations. The most abundant mutations produced by irradiation (X rays, etc.) are changes in genes causing them to become lethal or to reduce viability.

Interaction of Genes

In the example of the $9:3:3:1$ ratio in guinea pigs the pairs of genes were independent both in inheritance *and in effect*. The color of an individual, for example, had no effect upon whether it was short-haired or long-haired. At times, however, pairs of genes may be independent in inheritance *but not* be independent in their effect upon the phenotype. An example of such an interaction of genes is afforded by **epistasis,** a situation in which one pair of genes prevents or hides the expression of another pair of genes. This interaction of genes assumes various forms. We shall mention but one example.

In dogs there is a dominant gene, *B,* for black hair color; its recessive, *b,* results in brown color, in homozygotes. Another dominant gene, *I,* inhibits the action of the genes just mentioned causing the coat to remain unpigmented, white, despite the presence of genes *B* or *b.* Dogs having the genotype *ii* will be colored if the proper genes for color are present. Thus a brown dog has the genotype *iibb.* Some white dogs have the genotype *IIBB.* What would be expected from matings of dogs of these genotypes? As a result of meiosis the brown dog produces germ cells having the constitution *ib,* the white dog produces germ cells of *IB* constitution. The resulting fertilized ova have the genotype *IiBb,* and give rise to white dogs, because of the presence of *I.*

When these F_1 white dogs are bred together the offspring shown in Fig. 17.7 are expected. We note that twelve of the 16 combinations contain at least one *I* and hence result in white dogs. Of the four combinations which are homozygous *ii,* three contain at least one *B,* and hence are black, while one is homozygous *bb* and hence brown. Thus the 9:3:3:1 ratio (p. 388) has been modified to a 12:3:1 ratio.

Epistasis is not the only type of gene interaction. The expression of many genes is modified by the action of other genes. An example of such **modifier genes** is afforded by the genes affecting the size of the pigmented areas of hooded rats. Hooded rats are white with black heads and shoulders and a black stripe down the middle of the back and tail. They are homozygous for a recessive gene, *h.* But in addition to this gene there are other genes which determine the size of the pigmented areas—whether, for example, the black stripes down the back shall be narrow or broad. Such interaction of genes is very common, in fact it is probably the rule. When we speak of a gene "for" a certain characteristic we mean that without the gene the characteristic can not develop but we do not imply that the gene in question works alone in producing the characteristic.

A type of gene interaction which is very common is the *addition* of the effect of one gene to that of another. Genes which have cumulative effects of this kind are called **multiple genes** or **polygenes.** Many quantitative characteristics have polygenes as their genetic basis.

Suppose, for example, that a certain species of plant has a tall variety and a dwarf variety, the tall variety averaging 34 inches in height, the dwarf variety 10 inches. Thus the difference between them is 24 inches. We shall also suppose that the dwarf variety has the genotype *aabb,* the tall variety the genotype *AABB.* In this case each "capital letter" gene contributes a certain increment in height. If the effect of each "capital letter" gene is the same, each one contributes 6 inches *increase* in height over the height of the dwarf variety having the *aabb* genotype. What will be expected from a cross between the two varieties?

As shown in Fig. 17.8, the F_1 offspring from the cross will have the genotype *AaBb*. Each "capital letter" gene adds 6 inches to the 10 inches

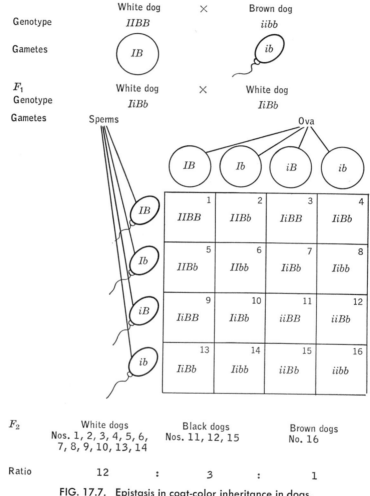

		White dog	×	Brown dog	
Genotype		*IIBB*		*iibb*	

Gametes *IB* *ib*

F_1
Genotype

	White dog	×	White dog
	IiBb		*IiBb*

Gametes Sperms Ova

	IB	*Ib*	*iB*	*ib*
IB	1 *IIBB*	2 *IIBb*	3 *IiBB*	4 *IiBb*
Ib	5 *IIBb*	6 *IIbb*	7 *IiBb*	8 *Iibb*
iB	9 *IiBB*	10 *IiBb*	11 *iiBB*	12 *iiBb*
ib	13 *IiBb*	14 *Iibb*	15 *iiBb*	16 *iibb*

F_2

White dogs	Black dogs	Brown dogs
Nos. 1, 2, 3, 4, 5, 6, 7, 8, 9, 10, 13, 14	Nos. 11, 12, 15	No. 16

Ratio   12   :   3   :   1

FIG. 17.7. Epistasis in coat-color inheritance in dogs.

which the *aabb* genotype would produce. Consequently these F_1 plants are 10 + 6 (for the *A*) + 6 (for the *B*) or 22 inches tall.

The F_2 offspring produced by these F_1 parents are shown in the "checkerboard" and summarized in the graph at the bottom of Fig. 17.8. We note that $\frac{1}{16}$ of the F_2 offspring are expected to be as tall as the original tall variety, $\frac{1}{16}$ as short as the original dwarf variety. The rest of the offspring are intermediate, the mean or average height being 22 inches. Connecting the tops of the columns in the graph results in an approximation to a normal frequency curve. Many of the quantitative characteristics determined by polygenes exhibit such a normal distribution. The greater

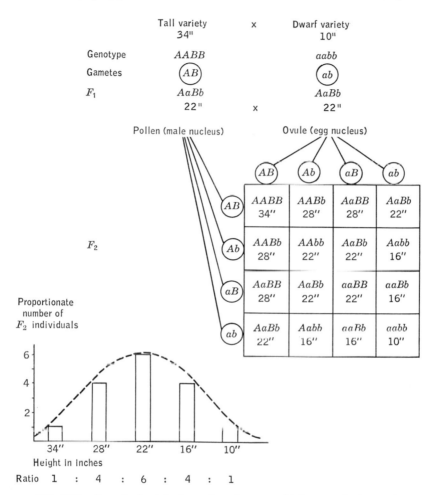

FIG. 17.8. Quantitative inheritance based upon multiple genes (polygenes).

the number of pairs of genes involved the closer the approximation to the typical bell-shaped curve. For sake of simplicity we have assumed that the difference in height between the two varieties depends upon but two pairs of genes; obviously such differences might be dependent upon three, or four or more pairs of genes.

Polygenic characteristics are very common, though the genetic basis of only a few of them has been analyzed. The difference in pigmentation between Negroes and "whites" seems to depend upon several pairs of genes with cumulative effects, inheritance following a pattern like that of our hypothetical tall and dwarf plant varieties.

Linkage and Crossing Over

So far we have been discussing pairs of genes which are independent in inheritance even though they may not be independent in their effects upon the phenotype. The reason the genes considered were independent in inheritance was because each pair was contained in a separate pair of chromosomes (Fig. 17.5). But since the number of gene pairs far exceeds the number of chromosomes, it is obvious that many genes must be contained in each chromosome. The genes in one chromosome do not exhibit the independent assortment discussed above; they are said to be **linked** to each other.

A hypothetical example of such linkage is represented in Fig. 17.9, showing a pair of chromosomes in a cell. The maternal (white) member of the

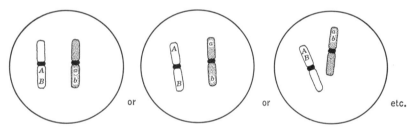

FIG. 17.9. Chromosomal basis of linkage. Genes may be linked in various ways, close together or far apart, on the chromosomes, as shown.

pair is shown as containing the dominant genes *A* and *B*, the paternal (shaded) member as containing the corresponding recessives, *a* and *b*. Fig. 17.9 may be taken as representing the constitution of a spermatogonium. What will be the result of meiosis of such a cell? Fig. 17.10A shows what will *usually* happen (starting with the primary spermatocyte, having each chromosome represented by a pair of chromatids). As a result of meiosis half the sperm cells contain *A* and *B,* half contain *a* and *b*.

In our discussion of meiosis, however, we mentioned (p. 382) the fact that during synapsis part of one chromatid may be exchanged with part of another one. As the chromatids separate following synapsis cross-shaped configurations called **chiasmata** can frequently be observed. Such a chiasma is shown in the primary spermatocyte of Fig. 17.10B. If the chromatids break and recombine at the point where they cross each other, chromatids having the constitution (*Ab*) and (*aB*) will be produced. Such exchange of genes between homologous chromosomes is called **crossing over.** As a result of crossing over in our example a *few* sperm cells having the constitution (*Ab*) and (*aB*), respectively, will be produced.

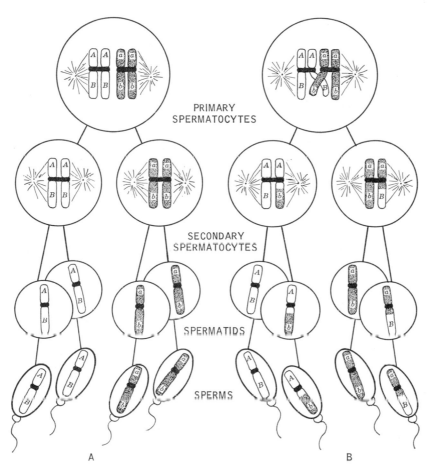

FIG. 17.10. Effect upon linkage of (A) meiosis without crossing over, and (B) meiosis with crossing over.

We see, accordingly, that a group of linked genes tends to behave as a unit in inheritance but that crossing over tends to disrupt this unit. The chromosomes may be thought of as long chains of genes. Crossing over leads to a regrouping of genes in the chain and hence is one of the forces making for genetic diversity.

MUTATIONS

Changes in the genetic materials are known as mutations in the broad sense of that term. They may be conveniently divided into those which produce visible changes in the chromosomes and those which do not. Mutations involving visible changes in the chromosomes are called chromosomal mutations or perhaps better **chromosomal aberrations.** Mutations which do not involve such visible changes and which are presumably chemical changes in single genes are called gene mutations (pp. 400–402).

Chromosomal Aberrations

Chromosomal aberrations are of two main types: (a) changes in structure of individual chromosomes, and (b) changes in number of chromosomes.

Turning our attention to structural aberrations, we may note that a piece of a chromosome may become detached and lost. Such a loss is called a **deletion** or **deficiency.** The diagram in Fig. 17.11A represents a normal chromosome. The dot near the center represents the centromere to which the spindle fiber attaches. The letters of the alphabet represent genes. The second diagram shows a deletion. The part of the chromosome containing genes *D, E,* and *F* has become detached. Since it has no spindle fiber attachment this fragment will probably be lost, though it might possibly become attached to another chromosome.

Deletions are harmful to their possessors. If an individual is heterozygous for a small deletion (i.e., has one normal chromosome and one deficient one, Fig. 17.11) that individual will probably be viable but is likely to be abnormal in some way. For example, the missing genes *D, E,* and *F* on one chromosome are likely to be compensated for, but usually not completely so, by the corresponding genes in the other chromosome. On the other hand, homozygosity for a deletion is likely to be lethal (e.g., both chromosomes of a pair like the second one in Fig. 17.11B). Normal viability requires that the full complement of genes be present.

The opposite of a deletion is a **duplication** or **repeat.** In Fig. 17.11C the section of chromosome containing the genes *B* and *C* is present twice. The repeated section may have come from another chromosome that suffered a deletion. Duplications do not necessarily lower the viability of their possessors, although they may result in abnormalities of structure or function. It is possible that repeats of this kind have been important in the evolution of chromosomes—that chromosomes were originally small and that in the course of evolutionary history they have increased in size by the formation of repeats, accompanied by gene mutations of the contained genes.

Sometimes the number of genes in a chromosome is not changed but the order or sequence of genes is altered. Such an **inversion** is shown in

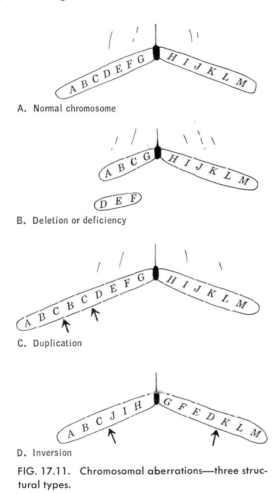

A. Normal chromosome

B. Deletion or deficiency

C. Duplication

D. Inversion

FIG. 17.11.   Chromosomal aberrations—three structural types.

Fig. 17.11D, where the middle section of the chromosome, involving genes *D* through *J*, has become reversed or inverted. Since all the genes are present in normal number, the effects of inversions are not so drastic as are the effects of deletions and duplications. Effects on the phenotype may be produced, however, because of what is known as **position effect.** A gene in one location on a chromosome does not necessarily have the same action it would have in another position. (Gene *D,* Fig. 17.11D, when located next to gene *K* may not have the same action it would have when located next to gene *C.*)

Inversions have another interesting genetic effect: they tend to suppress crossing over (p. 395). In a heterozygote for an inversion (an individual having in a certain pair one "normal" and one inverted chromosome) normal pairing at synapsis is difficult and hence the likelihood of crossing over is reduced. Thus inversions tend to cause chromosomes to remain intact. This might have evolutionary significance since if a chromosome came to contain a superior arrangement of genes it might be of advantage *not* to have the arrangement destroyed through crossing over. At times experimenters deliberately introduce inversions into their experimental stocks so that the chromosome in which they are interested may remain intact (pp. 460–464).

Crossing over involves exchange of parts of homologous chromosomes, chromosomes which constitute a pair. Sometimes part of a chromosome may become detached, and then become attached to another chromosome which is not homologous to the first. This is known as **translocation.** If nonhomologous chromosomes *exchange* parts the exchange is known as **reciprocal translocation.** A case is illustrated in Fig. 17.12; two chromosomes (not homologous, as evidenced by the differing genes) are shown as exchanging their entire right "arms." Reciprocal translocation of this type seems to have been important in the formation of varieties within some species of plants.

The second class of chromosomal aberrations involves changes in number of chromosomes. Rarely a whole chromosome may be lost and the organism still survive. But loss of chromosomes is usually lethal, as we have noted that loss of pieces of chromosomes (deletion) is likely to be. Increase in number of chromosomes may occur at times and may have genetic and evolutionary significance.

A gamete may come to possess an extra chromosome by *an error* in meiosis. In Fig. 17.3, p. 384, normal meiosis is shown. Suppose, however, that when the secondary oöcyte divided to form the ovum and second polar body, the short pair of chromatids failed to separate and that both were retained in the ovum. Such failure of chromatids to separate and be distributed normally is called **nondisjunction.** As a result the ovum would contain one long chromosome and two short ones. When fertilized by a normal sperm the fertilized ovum would contain two long chromosomes but *three* short ones. Such an individual is called a **trisomic** (Fig.

17.13). Such increase in chromosome number by addition of one or more single chromosomes is called **aneuploidy;** it seems to have been important in producing varieties of plants.

Suppose that both pairs of chromatids in the secondary oöcyte of Fig. 17.3 failed to separate. As a result the second polar body would be

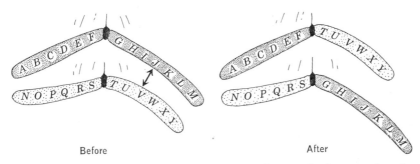

Before   After

FIG. 17.12.   Reciprocal translocation of entire right "arms" of two nonhomologous chromosomes.

empty of chromosomes, the ovum containing two long chromatids and two short ones. Such an ovum would be *diploid,* instead of haploid, containing as many chromosomes as the oögonium and the other cells of the body contain. When such a diploid ovum is fertilized by a normal haploid sperm the resulting fertilized ovum has three of each kind of

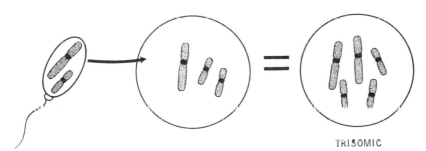

TRISOMIC

FIG. 17.13.   Production of a trisomic fertilized ovum (zygote). Nondisjunction of "short" chromosomes (see Fig. 17.3) resulted in an ovum containing two of them. This ovum was fertilized by a normal sperm cell.

chromosome, and is called a **triploid** (Fig. 17.14). Diploid sperm cells may also arise by suppression of normal meiosis. When a diploid ovum is fertilized by a diploid sperm cell a **tetraploid** is the result (Fig. 17.14). Increase in chromosome number by addition of complete haploid sets is called **polyploidy.** In our diagrams a haploid set has consisted of two chromosomes, one long one and one short one. The actual number varies from species to species, however. The somatic (body) cells of man each contain forty-six chromosomes, for example. These are comprised of twenty-three pairs. Following meiosis each sperm and ovum contain twenty-three single chromosomes. Thus in man a haploid set of chromo-

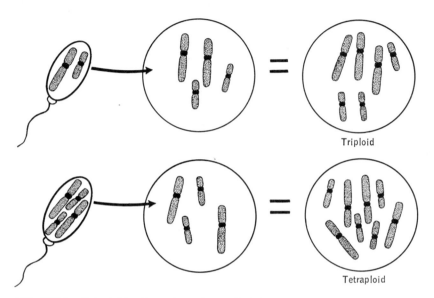

Triploid

Tetraploid

FIG. 17.14. Polyploidy. Formation of a triploid fertilized ovum when a haploid sperm cell fertilizes a diploid ovum (upper diagrams). Formation of a tetraploid fertilized ovum when a diploid sperm cell fertilizes a diploid ovum (lower diagrams).

somes numbers twenty-three. In the fruit fly, *Drosophila,* a haploid set numbers four.

Polyploidy seems to have been important in the evolution of plants, as discussed below (pp. 418–420).

Gene Mutations

Evidence accumulates that genes consist of molecules of deoxyribose nucleic acid (DNA). These are very large molecules having complex structure. When the molecular structure is altered the result is a gene mutation. On the whole, gene mutations produce more fundamental changes than do chromosomal aberrations, and hence are of more importance to evolution.

Genes exert their control of living processes by controlling the nature or production of enzymes. As we have seen, enzymes catalyze all living processes. Since this is true in embryos as well as in adults, the developmental processes depend upon enzymes and hence upon genes. (This is not to minimize the importance of the environment in which the embryo develops, but in the last analysis the capability of an embryo to respond to environmental stimuli is determined by genetic constitution.) Changes in genes result in changed enzymes which, in turn, result in changes in metabolism and developmental processes. Hence mutations may affect any aspect of metabolism and development.

Because they are most easily observed, we think most frequently of *structural changes* resulting from mutation. An insect's eye is changed in color, or a wing is changed in shape, for example. Changed enzymes during embryonic development have resulted in these changes in morphology.

At least as important as changes in structure, however, are changes in function, *physiological changes*. These are usually less easily observed and measured than are structural changes, but they may be of even greater significance to their possessors. Mutations, for example, have given rise to strains of the bread mold, *Neurospora,* unable to utilize the sugar lactose as a source of food (Bonner, 1948), or to manufacture various vitamins and amino acids as normal strains do (Beadle, 1946, 1959). The "temperature races" of *Drosophila funebris* have no structural differences distinguishing them but are characterized by different tolerances to external temperatures (pp. 453–454). These races doubtless arose by mutation.

A special case of physiological effects of mutation is afforded by development of resistance to disease, or to antibiotics. The colon bacillus, *Escherichia coli,* is susceptible to streptomycin. Demerec (1950) has found that on the average one in many millions of cells undergoes a mutation to streptomycin resistance. Such individual cells can live and multiply in medium containing streptomycin. Indeed some of these strains must have streptomycin in order to live—they have become "streptomycin addicts." Doubtless the development of strains of houseflies resistant to the insecticide DDT has also occurred through processes utilizing mutations.

Many other examples of physiological effects of mutations might be given. Probably there is no aspect of metabolism that can not be altered, for better or for worse, by mutation. Of great importance for evolution are the *viability and fertility aspects* of mutations. We have already referred to lethal genes. These are genes, arising originally by mutation of "normal" genes, which result in death of homozygotes. Death results from some lack, probably in most cases a physiological or metabolic lack. Lethality is viability reduced to zero; other mutations reduce viability less drastically. In our discussion of natural selection (pp. 450–469) we shall enlarge upon the viability relationships of mutations. Mutations may also affect fertility. Since success in natural selection is measured by relative numbers of offspring produced, fertility effects of mutations are of great importance to evolution.

Since structure and function are so intimately related, a single mutation may frequently affect both, or it may affect more than one structure or more than one physiological process. Examples of such *pleiotropic genes,* arisen by mutation, were given in Chapter 15 (pp. 350–351). Evidence accumulates that it is the genotype as a whole, all the genes working together, which determines the phenotype. Hence we may anticipate that alteration of one gene may have far-reaching effects upon developmental and metabolic processes.

References and Suggested Readings

Beadle, G. W. "Genes and the chemistry of the organism," *American Scientist,* 34 (1946), 31–53.

Beadle, G. W. "Genes and chemical reactions in *Neurospora,*" *Science,* 129 (1959), 1715–1719.

Bonner, D. M. "Genes as determiners of cellular biochemistry," *Science,* 108 (1948), 735–739.

Demerec, M. "Reaction of populations of unicellular organisms to extreme changes in environment," *American Naturalist,* 84 (1950), 5–16.

Gershenson, S. "Evolutionary studies on the distribution and dynamics of melanism in the hamster (*Cricetus cricetus* L.). I. Distribution of black hamsters in the Ukrainian and Bashkirian Soviet Socialist Republics (U.S.S.R.)," *Genetics,* 30 (1945), 207–232.

Sinnott, E. W., L. C. Dunn, and Th. Dobzhansky. *Principles of Genetics,* 5th ed. New York: McGraw-Hill Book Company, 1958.

Snyder, L. H., and P. R. David. *The Principles of Heredity,* 5th ed. Boston: D. C. Heath & Company, 1957.

CHAPTER 18

GENETIC CHANGE AND

EVOLUTIONARY CHANGE

In the preceding chapter we noted that genes act by determining the presence or the nature of enzymes. Enzymes, in turn, control the processes of metabolism and of development. Hence, changes in genotype result in changed enzymes and so in changed phenotype—and changed phenotypes are the raw materials of evolution. Consequently understanding of the nature of gene action is important to understanding of evolution.

Gene Action

We have mentioned a strain of the bread mold, *Neurospora,* lacking the ability to utilize lactose in its nutrition (p. 401). Normal *Neurospora* can use this compound sugar; an enzyme called lactase splits lactose to the simple sugars glucose and galactose. The strain unable to do this was produced by irradiation (Bonner, 1948). Chemical analysis showed that organisms in this strain did not possess lactase, or that if it was present it was not in its active form. The lactase-less strain differed from normal ones by mutation of a single gene.

In Chapter 5 we discussed the fact that most metabolic processes in the body involve a long chain of chemical reactions each one of which is catalyzed by an enzyme. One such chain of reactions, involving a whole series of intermediate chemical substances each synthesized under the influence of the appropriate enzyme, results in the production of the brown pigment in the eye of the fruit fly, *Drosophila.* (The wild-type eye color is a shade of red resulting from the mixture of red and brown pigment.) If one of the enzymes in this series is not produced or is changed in some way so that it does not perform its usual function, the chain is "broken" and no brown pigment is produced. Such a change in an enzyme may result from mutation of the gene upon which it is dependent for its presence or its specificity. As a result of mutation of one of the genes connected with the chain of enzyme-controlled reactions the eye is left with only bright red pigment, the resultant eye color being called vermilion. The mutated gene (whose effect is to suppress brown pigment formation) is called a gene "for" vermilion eye. But note that its effect is through alteration of one step in a series of enzyme-controlled chemical reactions occurring in the body of the fly during its embryonic development. Similarly, mutation of another gene will cause failure to produce both brown and red pigment, the eye being left white in color.

Important for evolution are those genes that control the *rates* of metabolic processes and the *times* in the life history at which the processes occur. This aspect of gene action is complementary to that discussed in the preceding paragraph since the so-called **"rate-genes"** doubtless act by means of control of enzymes. From the standpoint of evolution we are particularly interested in rate-genes expressing their effect during the course of embryonic development, since the phenotype of the adult is a resultant of the forces (genetic and environmental) that have acted on it during its embryonic life. Natural selection acts, not on the genes themselves, but upon what those genes produce, or as Waddington (1959) has expressed it, "natural selective pressures impinge not on the hereditary factors themselves, but on the organisms as they develop from fertilized eggs to reproductive adults." This is important. Too often we think of individuals as adults only; the individual is an organism, and hence subject to natural selection, from the time it is a fertilized egg onward.

An easily visualized example of a rate-gene in action is afforded by the research of Ford and Huxley (Huxley, 1932) on eye color in the crustacean *Gammarus* (an amphipod or "scud"). Early in embryonic life these creatures have bright red eyes. At about the end of the first week of development deposition of melanin (dark brown pigment) begins in the eyes. This continues at such a rapid rate that three or four days later the eyes appear black. The investigators discovered a mutation which causes the eyes of adults to be red, with a faintly brownish cast. They showed that in this case deposition of pigment did not begin until the young were 4 weeks old, and that then it proceeded so slowly that by the time sexual maturity was reached the original red color was but slightly modified. Here we see one mutation with the two effects listed above: it affected the time at which the reaction occurred and it affected the rate of that reaction.

Of the metabolic processes operative during embryonic development particular interest centers on those affecting *growth* of the parts and organs of the developing individual. Parts and organs grow at different rates, hence genes controlling these relative rates must have great potency in determining the nature of the resulting adult. If so, mutations of genes concerned with differential growth could be highly important in producing the variability upon which natural selection operates. Most of the examples of differential growth rates known at present have not been analyzed genetically. We can scarcely doubt, however, that rate-genes, probably complex systems of them, are involved.

DIFFERENTIAL GROWTH RATES (ALLOMETRY)

The study of differential growth rates of the kind just mentioned is called **allometry** (or originally by Huxley, heterogony). Although we may seldom think of it, the fact that different parts of the body grow at different rates, and that these rates change from time to time, is a matter of everyday observation. A glance at Fig. 4.14 (p. 66) will remind us that in the human fetus the head grows much more rapidly than does the rest of the body, the legs especially having a slow rate of growth. After birth the situation changes. An adult man is far from being a newborn baby with all parts of the body increased equally in size. Such an adult would be a most ungainly creature: enormous head, large trunk, and short, crooked legs. After birth the head continues to increase in size but at a decelerated rate, while the lower portions of the body, particularly the legs, grow at an increased rate.

Differential growth of one part as compared to another is common in the animal kingdom. Fig. 18.1 shows an example among males of a certain species of beetle. In this species small males have large forelegs as compared to males of most beetles. But larger males of the species have forelegs that are proportionately much larger than are those of the smaller males. In other words, a *little* increase in body size is accompanied by much increase in foreleg size. Thus the growth rate of the forelegs must be greater than that of the body as a whole.

In many cases the differential growth rate of one part as compared to that of another is sufficiently precise so that a mathematical statement of it may be made. The formula employed is: $y = bx^k$ (or $\log y = k \log x + \log b$). In this formula, x is the size or dimension used as a basis for comparison, frequently the general body size; y is the size or dimension of the part of the body being compared; b is the "initial growth index," i.e., a constant expressing the size of y when x is 1; k is a constant indicating the

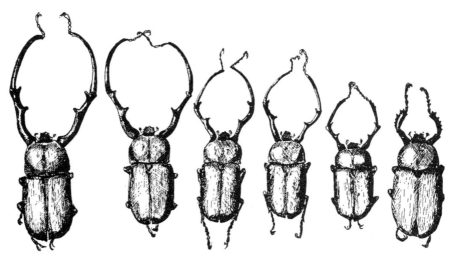

FIG. 18.1. Allometry (differential growth) exhibited by forelimbs of male beetles of the species *Euchirus longimanus*. Specimen at extreme right is a female; other specimens are males arranged in order of increasing size. (After Champy; from Huxley, *Problems of Relative Growth*, Methuen & Co., Ltd., 1932, p. 56.)

ratio that y bears to x (e.g., the ratio of the size of the organ being compared to the size of the body as a whole).

In Fig. 18.2 we present a hypothetical but true-to-life example of the manner in which differential growth works. Fig. 18.2A represents a small rhinoceroslike animal with a tiny horn on its nose. As indicated, the horn is 2.5 cm. long, and the length of the head measured from the base of the ear to the tip of the snout is 25 cm. Since we wish to study changes in length of horn as the head increases in size, we designate length of head as x in the above allometry formula, length of horn as y. Thus, at the outset $x = 25$, $y = 2.5$. For the purposes of this example we arbitrarily decide that the value of the constant k shall be 2. If k were 1, the horn would increase in length at the same rate as that at which the head increased in length. A k value of 2 provides that the horn shall increase in length more rapidly than does the head.

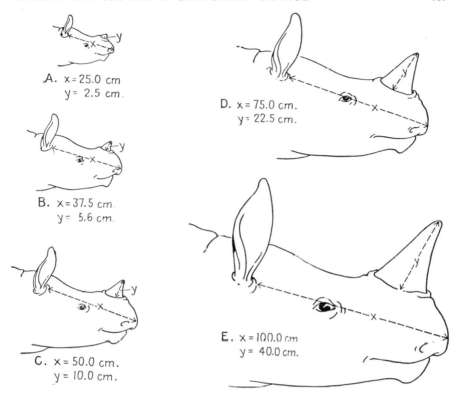

A. x = 25.0 cm
   y = 2.5 cm.

B. x = 37.5 cm.
   y = 5.6 cm.

C. x = 50.0 cm.
   y = 10.0 cm.

D. x = 75.0 cm.
   y = 22.5 cm.

E. x = 100.0 cm
   y = 40.0 cm.

FIG. 18.2.   Positive allometry of the nasal horn of a hypothetical rhinoceroslike mammal.

The initial growth index, b, can now be determined by substituting the values of x, y, and k in the formula:

$$y = bx^k$$

$$b = \frac{y}{x^k}$$

$$b = \frac{2.5}{25^2} = \frac{2.5}{625}$$

$$b = .004$$

We are now in position to utilize the formula in determining the horn sizes which will accompany increase in length of head. We may inquire what will be the change in length of horn when the length of the head increases from 25 cm. to 37.5 cm. (Fig. 18.2B); x is now 37.5 cm.

$$y = bx^k$$
$$y = .004 \cdot 37.5^2$$
$$y = 5.6 \text{ cm.}$$

Fig. 18.2C shows the increase in horn length when the head length has increased to 50 cm. The length of the horn is calculated using the same constants as before but assigning x a value of 50. We note that y now equals 10 cm. In other words, while the head has doubled in length, the horn has become four times as long as it was at the outset.

D and E, Fig. 18.2, show the increase in horn length with additional increase in length of head. In E the length of the head has increased to four times its original length, but the horn is sixteen times as long as it was at first.

Our hypothetical example assumes added significance when we note that Fig. 18.2 may be interpreted in one or all of three different ways. (1) The series of heads shown may represent stages in the growth and development of an *individual* rhinoceroslike animal. In this case A is the head of a young, perhaps newborn, animal, and the succeeding diagrams show stages in the animal's development as it becomes adult. In other words, the diagrams may represent an ontogenetic series (cf. "ontogeny"). (2) On the other hand, the series of heads may represent adult individuals of varying sizes. In this case A would represent an adult of a dwarf species of rhinoceroslike animal, E an adult of a relatively giant species, the intervening forms being adults of species of intermediate size. (3) Or again, the series of heads may represent an evolutionary series. In this case A would represent an adult of a prehistoric ancestor, E would be its modern descendant, and the intervening forms would be intermediate steps in the sequence of forms leading from A to E. Such series of fossils, marked by increasing size, are frequently encountered; we recall particularly the evolutionary sequences leading to the modern horse and to the modern elephant (pp. 197–216). Thus the series of diagrams in Fig. 18.2 may represent a phylogenetic series (cf. "phylogeny").

Let us turn from a hypothetical example to one based on actual data. In our discussion of the evolution of the horse (pp. 197–206) we noted that during evolution the facial or preorbital portion of the skull increased in length disproportionally to the increase in size of the skull as a whole (Fig. 10.3, p. 199). The same trend is noted in the ontogeny of modern horses. Line A in Fig. 18.3 shows the increase in length of face as compared to length of brain case (cranium) in modern horses of different sizes and ages. The lowest point on the line represents a foetal horse; other points represent colts and adults of varying sizes. As the cranium increases in length the face increases in length at a somewhat faster rate ($k =$ about 1.5) until a cranium length of about 15 cm. is reached (in colts 6 to 8 months old). From that point on $k = 1$; in other words, growth is *isometric,* face and cranium increasing in length at the same rate.

Line B (Fig. 18.3) represents allometry in the phylogenetic line leading to the modern horse. Here the growth ratio, k, seems to be slightly greater than it is in the ontogeny of the modern horse (about 1.8). But each point

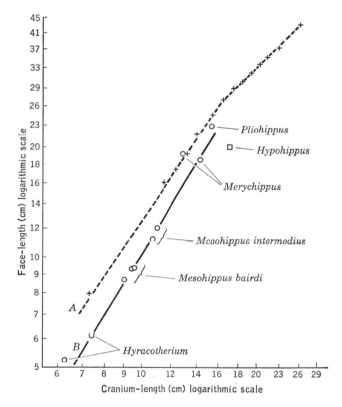

FIG. 18.3. Allometry of facial length in horses. Line A: allometry in the ontogeny of the modern horse. Line B: allometry in the ancestral line leading to the modern horse. Plus signs indicate modern horses (*Equus*); open circles indicate prehistoric horses. (Redrawn from Reeve and Murray, "Evolution in the horse's skull," *Nature,* Vol. 150, 1942, p. 402.)

on the graph is based on a single specimen; the difference from 1.5 might not be found to be significant if a larger number of specimens were measured. Reeve and Murray (1942) pointed out that simple allometry of face growth to cranium growth seemed to prevail until about the time of *Merychippus,* when a change in skull proportions occurred "by an increase in size of the facial rudiment at a very early stage of growth." In terms of the allometry equation this may have represented an increase in the initial growth constant, b (Simpson, 1953a). We recall that *Merychippus* initiated many adaptations to life on dry plains. Accordingly, the change in b seems to have occurred in connection with the acquisition of hypsodont (continuously growing, high-crowned) molar teeth. From *Pliohippus* on through the ancestral species of *Equus* facial growth and cranium growth may well have been nearly isometric as they are in later stages of the ontogeny of *Equus* (upper portion of line A, Fig. 18.3) but we need more data on this point.

By way of contrast to the line leading to *Equus,* the "forest horse," *Hypohippus,* is included in Fig. 18.3. Note that the point representing it falls at some distance from either of the two lines. *Hypohippus* did not have hypsodont teeth; its face was only three quarters as long as that of a modern horse having the same cranium length (Reeve and Murray, 1942).

What has allometry to do with evolution? As noted previously, genes control the rates at which developmental processes, including those of growth, occur in the body. Thus, for example, genes would control the rate at which the horn of our hypothetical rhinoceroslike animal (Fig. 18.2) would grow; other genes would control the rate at which the length of the head as a whole would increase. In the example shown we need only suppose that the genes controlling growth of the horn determine that the horn shall grow at a more rapid rate than the rate of growth of the body as a whole. Then, if for any reason the head becomes larger, the horn will automatically become disproportionately larger, as shown in the figure.

As a result of this phenomenon some of the burden is removed from the back of natural selection. We need no longer ask: Is it important for a large rhinoceros to have a proportionately much longer horn than a small rhinoceros has? Nor need we attempt to imagine how, in evolutionary history, a horn could be increased in length by gradual accumulation of mutations each of which increased length by a small amount. Perhaps the only matter of sufficient importance to be acted on by natural selection was the matter of total body size, including head size. Perhaps it *was* important for the animals to become larger. Judging by the number of evolutionary lines in which increase in size is found, this supposition seems highly probable. If so, natural selection would favor the production of larger and larger animals. In this event, and if the animals possessed a horn growth rate greater than the growth rate of the body as a whole, the disproportionately longer horn would develop automatically as a sort of by-product. Just so long as having a longer horn was not positively detrimental, natural selection might not be directly involved in the matter of horn length. Theoretically, the time might come when the horn would become so large as to be a positive handicap. Then natural selection would tend to eliminate possessors of the oversized horns. Among prehistoric animals some instances are observed of animals possessing horns and other structures so huge that they seem to have passed the point of maximum usefulness. The huge spread of antlers possessed by the Irish stag affords a case in point. Whether or not the excessive antler development contributed to the animal's extinction is still the subject of lively debate. But we may feel reasonably confident that the tendency of these big stags to develop disproportionately huge antlers represented the culmination of such a process of differential growth as we have been discussing. (See Huxley, 1932, for discussion of allometry of antlers.)

We may well mention in passing that the observed tendency of a part or organ to change progressively in size is sometimes given as an example of what is called **orthogenesis,** evolution in a straight line. In such a terminology the steady increase in length of horn in our rhinoceroslike animal would form an example of an orthogenetic series. Orthogenesis as a descriptive term indicating the occurrence of progressive changes is sometimes useful. But, unfortunately, it has at times been endowed with an occult meaning and presented as an evolutionary force in its own right, as though there were some inner force in animals tending to cause them to evolve in straight lines. Further discussion of orthogenesis is not appropriate here; readers are referred to Jepsen (1949) and Simpson (1953a), for more extended treatment of the controversial subject. We recall that the "line" leading from *Hyracotherium* to *Equus* (Fig. 10.7, p. 204) frequently cited as an orthogenetic line, was in reality singled out for attention from among many other lines actually existing. We may quote with approval Simpson's conclusion that much apparent orthogenesis is "a product rather of the tendency of the minds of scientists to move in straight lines than of a tendency for nature to do so" and note further that at least some of the progressive series which *are* observed are explicable as the result of differential growth rates. Other progressive series are explicable as the result of operation of natural selection on organisms living in a stable environment or an environment that is changing with a constant trend (e.g., becoming increasingly dry). Under such conditions natural selection promotes more and more perfect adaptation to that environment and the resulting changes may take the form of a progressive series. Natural selection operating in this manner is sometimes called "orthoselection." (See also "Directive Forces in Evolution," pp. 496–500.)

Returning to the subject of the evolution of the preorbital portion of the horse skull (Fig. 18.3), we note that the increase in relative length as the horses increased in size can be explained by a tendency of the face to increase in length faster than does the cranium. Up to a certain size, small horses have short faces, larger horses have disproportionately longer ones. This is true today; it was true in prehistoric times. The observed evolutionary trend through at least the larger *Mesohippus* (Fig. 18.3) can be explained without assuming any change in the genes concerned. The larger the horse the longer the face. Thus, if by evolutionary change we mean change in the genes, genetic change, we can not say that the horses underwent evolutionary change in facial length until the *Merychippus* stage was reached. Before that, increase in length of face had been an automatic accompaniment of increase in body size. Genetic change was evidently introduced with *Merychippus,* however, connected with development of hypsodont teeth (p. 200).

The changes in the feet of horses resulting in the one-toed condition characteristic of modern horses presents a somewhat similar situation. We recall (Fig. 10.7, p. 204) that there were many lines of three-toed horses, one of which eventually gave rise to the one-toed genus. It has been shown (work of Robb, summarized by Simpson, 1944) that the relationship between the growth rate of the lateral digits and that of the cannon bone remained constant among these three-toed horses ($y = 1.5x^{.97 \text{ to } .98}$, in which y is the length of the lateral digits, x is the length of the cannon bone). There was no evolutionary, i.e., genetic, change among them; changes in proportionate length of digits were the automatic accompaniment of whatever changes in size of foot (typified by changes in size of cannon bone) occurred. But in the one-toed horse line there *was* an abrupt change in proportion, as compared to the proportions of three-toed ancestors. This change took the form of a sudden *relative* decrease in the length of lateral digits as compared to the length of the cannon bone. The change is expressed in the allometry formula by a reduction of the constant b to about half its former value: $y = .76x^{.99 \text{ to } 1.00}$. Once inaugurated, this changed value has continued and is found to apply to modern adult horses of various sizes, and to size changes encountered in the ontogeny of modern horses.

Viewed in the light of allometry, horse evolution assumes quite a different complexion from what it has in other lights. According to this view, the important evolutionary change at first was in size. It is doubtless of advantage to a horse to be large. For one thing, large animals do not fall so easy prey to predators as do small ones. Thus natural selection would tend to favor genetic changes (mutations) making for increase in size. As the horses became larger their faces became longer, not because of any genetic changes, but because genes controlling rate of facial growth determined greater rate of growth than that characterizing the body as a whole. Eventually, at the *Merychippus* stage, hypsodont teeth evolved in connection with change in diet. This change in tooth structure necessitated changes in the facial skeleton. At that time genetic changes occurred, but since then there has evidently been little further change in the relative lengths of face and cranium.

Similarly, in most horse lines the three toes retained about the same proportions to each other. But in the line leading to the one-toed horses a sudden genetic change occurred, with the result that there was an abrupt decrease in relative size of the lateral digits. Presumably this change was favored by natural selection in connection with the development of efficient foot structure adapted for rapid movement on dry plains (see pp. 197–198).

Thus we see that allometry removes the necessity for postulating large numbers of more or less independent mutations, each affecting some particular structure of the body and each acted on by natural selection. In the evolution of the face and legs of the horse two principal genetic changes seem to have occurred: (1) increase in growth rate of the face, inaugurated at the *Merychippus* stage; (2) decrease in growth rate of the lateral digits when the horses reached a functionally one-toed state. Once inaugurated, these changed growth rates persisted.

So far we have emphasized cases in which the growth rate of a part has been greater than that of the body as a whole. This is called positive allometry and is exemplified in Fig. 18.2. In positive allometry the constant k is greater than 1. If the value of k is 1, growth of the part proceeds at the same rate as does growth of the whole. This is called isometric growth. If the growth of the horn in our rhinoceroslike animal had been isometric, when the head increased in length fourfold (Fig. 18.2E), the horn would also have increased in length fourfold, i.e., would have been 10 cm. long. If the value of k is less than 1, i.e., is a fraction, the part in question increases in size more slowly than does the body as a whole. This process is called negative allometry. If this had been true of our rhinoceroslike animal, the horn of the largest animal (Fig. 18.2E) would have been even less than 10 cm. long; it would have been relatively shorter than it was in the smallest individual (Fig. 18.2A). Negative allometric growth may help to account for the relative reduction in size observed in some organs during evolutionary history. Recall that k is slightly less than 1 in the allometry formula describing the relationship between lateral digits and cannon bone in the feet of three-toed horses.

Finally, we should note that changes in the genes controlling growth rates would constitute mutations having large effects. The effects might even be so large that the mutations could rank as examples of the "systemic mutations" postulated by Goldschmidt (1940) as necessary if drastic evolutionary change is to occur. Yet in themselves these mutations might be ordinary gene mutations requiring no special rubric of "systemic." In Fig. 18.2 we have presented a hypothetical example of horn evolution involving a gene which determines that the horn shall grow in length faster than the head increases in length. Suppose that in an immediate descendant of animal A that gene underwent a mutation, the effect being to lower the rate of growth so that the horn increased in size more slowly than did the body as a whole. That is, the mutation changed the allometric growth rate from positive to negative. Then, through isolation, genetic drift, and other forces discussed on earlier pages, two populations might become established, one population possessing the unchanged gene, the other the mutated one. If body size increased in both populations, we should find them coming to differ greatly in the character of the nasal horn. The population with the unchanged gene would develop long horns, as shown in Fig. 18.2. On the other hand, the population with the mutated gene would develop relatively short horns; indeed, as the animals became large the horns might have become reduced to mere blunt, bony calluses (Fig. 18.4A). What a difference in the end products of the two evolutionary lines! And all, conceivably, the result of a single mutation occurring early in evolutionary history.

For sake of simplicity we have confined our discussion of allometry to single dimensions, e.g., *length* of horn. But material objects have three dimensions, and growth in one dimension is not always proportional to growth in the other two. In drawing Fig. 18.2 we have actually shown the horn increasing in breadth as well as in length, although the point was not mentioned previously. Suppose growth in length had been positively allometric, as shown, but growth in breadth had been isometric, relative to increase of head length. The result would have been a much slenderer horn (Fig. 18.4B) than that shown in Fig. 18.2E. Or again, we have shown the head itself increasing in height in approximate proportion to the increase in length. This conception need not have been true. The growth rate in height might have exceeded the growth rate in length. In that case E would have had a much higher "forehead" than that shown. Conversely, the rate of increase in height might have been lower than the rate of increase in length, in which case E would have had a slender head. The third dimension, not represented in our flat diagram, may also change at a rate different from the rates by which the other two dimensions change. Little

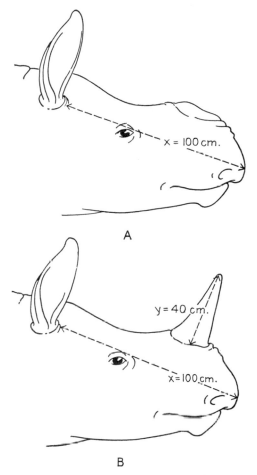

FIG. 18.4.   A, negative allometry of the nasal horn of a hypothetical rhinoceroslike mammal. B, positive allometry in length of nasal horn coupled with isometric growth in width (cf. E, Fig. 18.2).

imagination is needed to picture some of the great variety of shapes and proportions possible when growth in these three dimensions varies.

In closing this phase of our discussion we may well mention the Cartesian coordinate method utilized by D'Arcy Thompson (1942) for representing simultaneous change in two dimensions. Fig. 18.5 shows one of his most famous examples. The figure at the right approximates the outline of a huge marine sunfish of most unusual proportions. Almost circular in profile, the fish seems to be mostly head, the relatively short body and tail fin being excessively broad, vertically. A close relative is the fish shown at

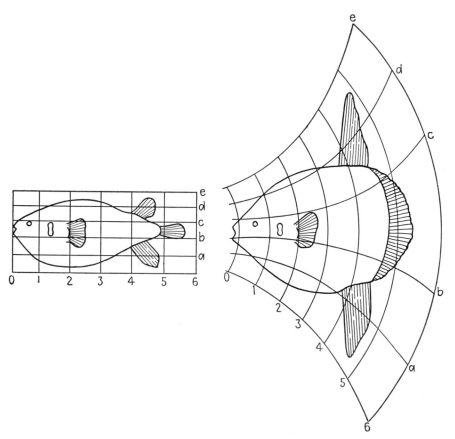

FIG. 18.5.   Transformation of the body outline of a teleost fish, *Diodon* (left), to give the outline of the sunfish, *Orthagoriscus* (right). The outline of *Diodon* was inscribed in a framework of rectangular coordinates and the latter were then distorted in a regular manner as indicated. (Redrawn from Thompson, *On Growth and Form,* Cambridge University Press, 1942.)

the left, a creature of smaller size and more "usual" proportions, resembling the presumed ancestor of the fantastic sunfish. If this outline of a "normal" fish is inscribed in a grid of rectangular coordinates, as shown, and then this system of coordinates is distorted in the regular way indicated at the right, the result is the shape possessed by the weird sunfish. What does such distortion of a system of coordinates mean in terms of biological processes? The diagram would be interpreted to indicate that a center of very active growth in the vertical dimension developed in the tail region, and that the growth rate declined progressively from tail to head. Presumably these changed growth rates arose as the result of mutation occurring in the evolutionary line leading to the strange sunfish. Consequently, as the descendants increased in size the posterior regions of the body increased in height more rapidly than did the anterior regions, with the result observed.

The reader is referred to D'Arcy Thompson's stimulating classic, *On Growth and Form* (1942), for other and more complicated applications of the method, including that to changes in skull shape encountered in the evolution of the horse. The method offers admirable description of observed trends, but the physiologic and genetic forces at work in production of the trends remain largely undetermined. This condition should not be permitted to continue. D'Arcy Thompson's studies offer real challenge to anyone interested in evolution of animals as *wholes*. That this technique of analysis is not being entirely neglected is indicated by its application to changes in skull shape in evolutionary lines of prehistoric mammals (e.g., Colbert, 1935; Patterson, 1949).

In conclusion, we would not convey the impression that allometry offers the key to *all* evolutionary change. But it illustrates how evolution can occur by means of mutation of genes controlling growth rates during embryonic development. For example, suppose that in the evolution of a rhinoceroslike animal a large nasal horn would be useful. How can we visualize the action of natural selection in providing such a horn? Natural selection might favor the possessors of a mutation that increased the rate at which the horn grew as the embryonic head increased in size. Such a genetic change, once inaugurated, might ultimately have far-reaching effects if the evolution of the species involved great increase in body (head) size.

Furthermore, allometry aids in explaining the development of neutral or nonadaptive characteristics, those which have little or no significance in the lives of their possessors. Natural selection itself can only account for characteristics which are useful. But a horn, or a spine on the thorax of a beetle, may become disproportionately long as the body itself becomes larger, even though the lengthening is of no value to its possessor. We need only suppose that the genes controlling growth of the horn or spine determine a disproportionately high rate of growth. So long as the lengthening remains neither beneficial nor harmful natural selection will not operate either for or against the rate-gene. As noted previously, other indifferent or nonadaptive traits may be accounted for by the side effects of pleiotropic genes (pp. 350–351) or by the random fixation of genes through genetic drift (pp. 349, 439).

POLYPLOIDY IN EVOLUTION

In the preceding chapter we discussed the essentials of the genetical phenomenon of polyploidy, that type of chromosomal aberration in which the number of chromosomes is increased by multiples of the haploid number (pp. 399–400). What role has polyploidy played in evolution?

Polyploids may arise in various ways from diploid ancestors. Perhaps the easiest way to visualize is that by means of the production of diploid germ cells by these ancestors. Ordinarily germ cells contain one haploid set of chromosomes. But sometimes owing to abnormality in the process of germ cell formation the full number of chromosomes characteristic of the parent's cells finds its way into one germ cell. Thus, a parent whose diploid number is eighteen will ordinarily produce germ cells containing nine chromosomes (i.e., nine chromosomes comprise one haploid set in this species). But occasional germ cells may be produced which contain all eighteen chromosomes. If a diploid ovule of this kind is fertilized by a diploid pollen grain (also containing eighteen chromosomes), the result is a fertilized ovum containing thirty-six chromosomes. These thirty-six chromosomes will comprise four haploid sets (two from the male parent and two from the female) and the resultant individual will be a tetraploid. A tetraploid is likely to differ from its diploid ancestors in a number of ways, presenting quite an altered appearance. Many tetraploids are entirely fertile among themselves, or self-fertile (we recall that production of both pollen and ovules by a single plant is not unusual). But most important of all, there is frequently a high degree of *sterility* between the polyploid and its diploid progenitors. Thus reproductive isolation arises at one stroke, and without the aid of spatial isolation. This point is of interest since usually, as we have emphasized elsewhere (pp. 473–474), spatial isolation is important in the first stages of species formation.

Polyploidy has formed a common means of speciation in plants. Multitudes of wild species are polyploids, as are many of our cultivated plants: cotton, wheat, oats, tobacco, potato, banana, coffee, sugar cane, many of our cultivated flowers, and so on. Indeed, plant breeders are today constantly employing artificial means of inducing polyploidy to create new varieties. There is historical interest in the fact that some of the "mutations" discovered by De Vries in the evening primrose (*Oenothera lamarckiana*) were subsequently found to be polyploids, rather than to have arisen through changes in individual genes (gene mutations) (pp. 337–338).

Frequently polyploidy is linked with hybridization in the production of new varieties and species. The hybrid produced by crossing two diploid species of plants may be partially or completely sterile if it has only the

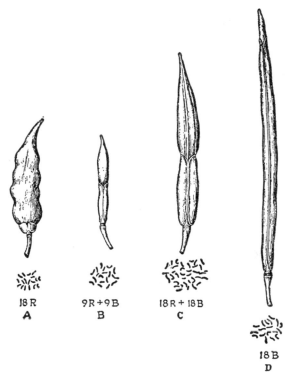

18 R
A

9R + 9B
B

18 R + 18B
C

18 B
D

FIG. 18.6. Seed pods and chromosomes of radish (A), of cabbage (D), of their diploid hybrid (B), and of their tetraploid hybrid, *Raphanobrassica* (C). R, radish chromosomes. B, cabbage chromosomes. (After Karpechenko; by permission from *Principles of Genetics*, by Sinnott, Dunn, and Dobzhansky, p. 370. Copyright 1950. McGraw-Hill Book Company, Inc.)

same number of chromosomes as do the parental species (i.e., is itself diploid). If, on the other hand, the hybrid is a tetraploid, containing *both* sets of chromosomes from *both* parents, it is likely to be fully fertile and to be reproductively isolated from the diploid parental species. Hence, it will "breed true." An instructive example is the tetraploid hybrid between the radish and the cabbage, produced by Karpechenko (Dobzhansky, 1951;

Sinnott, Dunn, and Dobzhansky, 1958). The radish (*Raphanus*) and the cabbage (*Brassica*) both have a diploid number of eighteen, a haploid number of nine. The hybrid is a tetraploid, having received two haploid sets of radish chromosomes and two haploid sets of cabbage chromosomes (total: thirty-six) (Fig. 18.6). Since the hybrid is infertile with both parent species it forms a new species; this has been named *Raphanobrassica* by combining the names of its parents. The hybrid is intermediate between its parents in many characteristics; the intermediate structure of its seed pod is clearly evident in Fig. 18.6. Unfortunately *Raphanobrassica* seems to have no commercial future, since it combines the root of a cabbage with luxuriant leaves resembling those of a radish!

If space permitted, other examples of polyploidy as a means of evolution in plants might be described. Many polyploid species have arisen in a state of nature, and frequently it is possible for botanists to decide which diploid species were their ancestors. The matter has been "clinched" in a few cases by actually "resynthesizing" the polyploid, starting with the diploid species suspected of being its parents.

Although polyploidy is most important in the evolution of plants (for discussions see Dobzhansky, 1951, and Stebbins, 1950), it has been of almost no importance in animal evolution. It is found in few animals and among that few only in some types which have forsaken reproduction involving two sexes (bisexual) for reproduction in which a single individual produces both ova and sperm (hermaphroditism) or for reproduction by means of unfertilized eggs (parthenogenesis). Apparently the sex-determining mechanism of animals cannot function properly when polyploidy occurs.

In sum, we find that plants possess in polyploidy one means, and perhaps the only means, by which a new species can arise in one step, achieving reproductive isolation in the absence of spatial isolation. Mayr (1949) has termed this phenomenon "instantaneous speciation."

GENETIC ASSIMILATION AND THE BALDWIN EFFECT

In Chapter 15 we stressed the importance of natural selection operating upon randomly occurring mutations, and in subsequent discussions we shall emphasize this action again (pp. 450–480). While this is the most generally recognized means of evolutionary change, many investigators suspect that it is not the only means. The perfection with which organisms are adapted to their environmental niches has led these people to despair of explaining adaptation upon a basis of natural selection operating on chance mutations alone. As is repeatedly emphasized, the mutation process is random in the sense that mutations occur without reference to whether or not they are "needed." How could the delicately adjusted adaptations that organisms are observed to possess actually have arisen through such a haphazard process? That question disturbs many thinkers on the subject. There are answers (the probability of even a chance occurrence is high, given a long enough period of time), nevertheless some means by which the reaction between organism and environment could lead to the production of hereditary change would be welcome. As indicated earlier (p. 341), this is the appeal of the Lamarckian idea of the inheritance of acquired characters. Is it possible that there are indeed means by which an adaptation at first individually acquired may become hereditary?

What does the genetical constitution (genotype) produce in an individual? It produces a bodily constitution (phenotype) which enables the individual to live in a certain range of environments. A species of mammal, for example, may possess such a genotype that if the animal lives in a hot climate the coat of hair will be relatively thin or sparse, while if it lives in a cold climate the coat will be thicker. The range of coat densities possible to the animal represents the latter's **"norm of reaction"** (Dobzhansky, 1951) or **"reaction range"** (Simpson, 1953b). Some species have such a genotype that the norm of reaction is broad; depending upon the environment, the coat may be very sparse or very thick. Other species have such a genotype that the range is narrow, only relatively sparse or relatively thick hair being possible. It is important to note that a change in the genotype may produce a change in the norm of reaction. On the whole, dogs have genotypes causing development of a certain range of densities of hair. In some varieties, however, this range has been sharply restricted, with the result that they either can not develop heavy coats in cold climates, or they have such heavy coats that they experience discomfort in hot climates. Without doubt both types arose by genetic change from an ancestor with a broader norm of reaction, as their wild relatives the wolves presumably have today.

Now let us imagine a situation in which a species of mammal living in the Temperate Zone finds open to it an opportunity to live in arctic regions. It will be able to do so if its genotype is such that the reaction range is sufficiently broad so that both the coat density appropriate to the Temperate Zone and the coat density needed in the new environment can be produced. We will suppose this to be the case and that the species extends its range into arctic regions. What will happen then? As generations pass, changes in the genotype may occur so that the heavier coat originally produced in reaction to the environment becomes "hereditary," as we usually use that term. We may think of it in this way: if it is desirable for the animal to have a thick coat it will be desirable for the animal to be *born* with such a coat, or with the capacity to develop it even before the stimulating effect of cold weather is felt. Accordingly, natural selection will favor changes in the genotype which will narrow the norm of reaction toward the upper end of the range of coat densities originally possible. Waddington (1953–1960) has spoken of the embryonic development of organisms as being **canalized** or buffered "in the sense that even though it may become somewhat modified in response to an environmental stress, it also exhibits a tendency to reach its normal end-result in spite of disturbing circumstances." In our example the "normal end-result" is a thicker coat of hair; "canalizing selection" will favor genotypes which give rise to it (Waddington, 1953b). As a result, remote descendants in the arctic might no longer be able to produce the sparser coats possible to their Temperate Zone ancestors. Heavy coats have now become hereditary, in the sense that they are produced without any action by the external environment.

We have visualized this change as having been accomplished by what is known as the "genetic assimilation of an acquired character" (Waddington, 1953–1960). At first the heavier coat had to be acquired by each generation, but eventually the genotype changed, narrowing or "funneling" the reaction range so that only heavy coats were produced.

How does this "genetic assimilation of an acquired character" differ from the inheritance of acquired characters in the Lamarckian sense? There is no thought that the acquired character (denser fur) in some manner changes the germ plasm directly; rather the idea is that genetic variability already present is made use of in producing the hereditary change. The range of variability already present is narrowed so that, in our example, only the thicker coats are produced.

What if still heavier coats, outside the original reaction range, might prove advantageous to our arctic immigrant? A genetic change might occur making possible heavier fur than the original genotype could produce. Such a genetic change would be to all intents and purposes a mutation or series of mutations. Hence we see that genetic assimilation and mutation are to be thought of as coexistent, and sometimes cooperating, means by which genetic variability may be supplied to natural selection.

Another instructive example is afforded by the fact that animals are frequently born with thickened skin on areas of the body which will later be subjected to friction in the course of the animals' normal activities.

Thickened skin on the sole of the human foot, calluses on the "knees" of the forelegs of the wart hog, calluses on the front and rear ends of the body of an ostrich are examples. The skin on all these areas is found to be thickened before birth. How can the origin of such hereditary thickenings be explained? It is noteworthy that while these thickenings are hereditary they are of such a nature that they would have been produced in direct response to the environment if they had not been. Use of the human foot, for example, causes the skin on the sole to thicken.

How can we visualize the origin of an inherited thickening of the skin at a point where friction will later be applied? In the first place we may note that the ability of the skin to thicken in response to friction is undoubtedly determined by the genotype. If we knew more of the genetics of the trait we should probably find that different genotypes vary in the amount of friction needed to "trigger" the production of a certain amount of thickening. Let us imagine an ancestral population in which the individuals are born with thin skin on the soles of the feet. It would be of advantage to develop thickening as rapidly as possible after birth, i.e., in response to a very small amount of friction (or none at all!). As a possible intermediate step we may visualize a situation in which genotypes resulting in production of maximum thickening in response to minimum friction would be favored. The next step would be elimination of the need for any stimulation whatever by friction, for as Medawar (1951) has stated, "if it is advantageous to have thickened feet at all, it will be advantageous to have them ready made when the foot is first put to the ground." How can this last change be brought about? Formerly friction "pulled the trigger." Now that it has become advantageous to have thickening developed before birth, natural selection will favor a genetic change which will result in the taking over by some internal factor of this function of pulling the trigger. This factor may be some inducing force operative upon the localized areas of the skin as they develop in the embryo. Perhaps the original norm of reaction included the possibility that thickening might arise as a result of either external or internal stimuli; if so, development has now become canalized so that the internal stimulus is the one regularly operative. Or perhaps the internal factor which now acts as a trigger arose as the result of one or more mutations. In any case, the adaptation which formerly had to be acquired by each individual for itself (**exogenous adaptation** or **accommodation**) has become hereditary in the sense that no external force is any longer necessary to call it into existence. White and Smith (1956) have called this phenomenon *ontogenetic assimilation*.

Waddington (1953, 1956, 1960) has performed experiments affording evidence that genetic assimilation of an acquired character is possible. For example, if pupae of the fruit fly, *Drosophila,* are subjected to a heat shock a certain proportion of them will fail to develop the cross-veins normally present in the wings. By selecting cross-veinless individuals as parents and continuing the treatment and selection in each generation Waddington produced a strain in which the percentage of individuals responding to the heat shock was very high. "It is therefore actually possible to select for capacity to respond to the environment." Eventually strains were produced which lacked the cross-veins even when the pupae were not given heat shocks. The trait originally induced by the environment had become genetically assimilated. In this case it is possible that mutations for cross-veinlessness occurred in the stock and were selected. But Waddington pointed out that such an explanation is not necessary and is rendered un-likely by the fact that the cross-veinless strain differed from the original stock by differences in several genes rather than in one gene pair only.

In a second series of experiments (Waddington, 1956) an abnormality of the thorax called bithorax was induced by subjecting *Drosophila* eggs to ether vapor. Again, selection resulted in strains having increased sensitivity to the external stimulus. Three different strains were produced in which some form of the bithorax phenotype occurred even in the absence of the ether treatment. Two of these strains differed from the original stock by single-gene changes; these may have arisen as dominant mutations appear-ing at the right time to satisfy requirements imposed by the artificial selec-tion. The third strain, showing greater phenotypic change, differed from the original stock by more complex genetic differences and was interpreted by Waddington as an instance of genetic assimilation of the acquired character bithorax.

Genetic assimilation as a possible factor in evolution is an idea of such interest that it will undoubtedly be investigated extensively. An allied con-cept is that which has come to be known as **"the Baldwin effect."** Various forms of the concept have been advanced, sometimes independently, by a number of investigators; the history of it was summarized by Simpson (1953b). According to this idea, an organism may invade an environ-ment if it is adaptable enough to do so (if its genotype gives a norm of re-action making possible the necessary exogenous adaptation). In other words, it may meet the requirements of the environment by adjustments or accommodations it is able to make in response to that environment. This is valuable; the animal has gained a "toe hold" in the new environment and is able to live there, but each generation is under the necessity of developing its own adaptive characteristics. How much better it would be if the animals could be *born* with them. Eventually genetic changes may occur which mimic the adaptive characteristics each generation has been acquiring for itself. Since it will be desirable for the organism to be relieved of the necessity of acquiring these characteristics in every generation, natural selection may be expected to favor individuals which are born with them. So in time hereditary characteristics may replace the individually acquired ones. "Characters individually acquired by members of a group of organisms may eventually, under the influence of selection, be reenforced or replaced by similar hereditary characters" (Simpson, 1953b).

As commonly conceived the theory is that the organism lives in the environment to which it can accommodate and "waits" for appropriate chance mutations to occur. An experimental instance of the Baldwin effect operating with chance mutations seems to have been afforded by Waddington's experiment on the bithorax phenotype (1956). The experimenter "required" the strain to have this phenotype. He enforced the requirement by subjecting the eggs to ether vapor. Eventually, apparently in two instances as noted above, what seem to have been dominant mutations appeared giving rise to the required phenotype.

But in addition it is conceivable that the genetic change involved in the Baldwin effect may be the genetic assimilation of an acquired character we have been discussing. If so, we note that the environment is thought to be concerned with the *instigation* of the genetic change (through canalization of development) as well as with the final fate of the change. Genetic assimilation of acquired characters forms a possible additional means (supplementing the mutation process) of supplying grist to the mill of natural selection.

References and Suggested Readings

Bonner, D. M. "Genes as determiners of cellular biochemistry," *Science,* 108 (1948), 735–739.

Colbert, E. H. "Siwalik mammals in the American Museum of Natural History," *Transactions of the American Philosophical Society,* new series, 26 (1935), 1–401.

Dobzhansky, Th. *Genetics and the Origin of Species,* 3rd ed. New York: Columbia University Press, 1951.

Goldschmidt, R. *The Material Basis of Evolution.* New Haven: Yale University Press, 1940.

Huxley, J. S. *Problems of Relative Growth.* New York: Dial Press, 1932.

Jepsen, G. L. "Selection, 'orthogenesis,' and the fossil record," *Proceedings, American Philosophical Society,* 93 (1949), 479–500.

Mayr, E. "Speciation and systematics." In G. L. Jepsen, E. Mayr, and G. G.

Simpson (eds.). *Genetics, Paleontology, and Evolution*. Princeton: Princeton University Press, 1949. Pp. 281–298.

Medawar, P. B. "Problems of adaptation," *New Biology*, No. 11. Baltimore: Penguin Books, Inc., 1951. Pp. 10–25.

Patterson, B. "Rates of evolution in Taeniodonts." In G. L. Jepsen, E. Mayr, and G. G. Simpson (eds.). *Genetics, Paleontology, and Evolution*. Princeton: Princeton University Press, 1949. Pp. 243–278.

Reeve, E. C. R., and P. D. F. Murray. "Evolution in the horse's skull," *Nature*, 150 (1942), 402–403.

Schmalhausen, I. I. *Factors of Evolution. The Theory of Stabilizing Selection*. Philadelphia: The Blakiston Company, 1949.

Simpson, G. G. *Tempo and Mode in Evolution*. New York: Columbia University Press, 1944.

Simpson, G. G. *The Major Features of Evolution*. New York: Columbia University Press, 1953a.

Simpson, G. G. "The Baldwin effect," *Evolution*, 7 (1953b), 110–117.

Sinnott, E. W., L. C. Dunn, and Th. Dobzhansky. *Principles of Genetics*, 5th ed. New York: McGraw-Hill Book Company, Inc., 1958.

Stebbins, G. L., Jr. *Variation and Evolution in Plants*. New York: Columbia University Press, 1950.

Thompson, D'Arcy W. *On Growth and Form*, 2nd ed. Cambridge: Cambridge University Press, 1942.

Waddington, C. H. "Genetic assimilation of an acquired character," *Evolution*, 7 (1953a), 118–126.

Waddington, C. H. "The evolution of adaptations," *Endeavour*, 12 (1953b), 134–139.

Waddington, C. H. "The 'Baldwin effect,' 'genetic assimilation' and 'homeostasis,' " *Evolution*, 7 (1953c), 386–387.

Waddington, C. H. "Genetic assimilation of the *bithorax* phenotype," *Evolution*, 10 (1956), 1–13.

Waddington, C. H. "Evolutionary systems—animal and human," *Nature*, 183 (1959), 1634–1638.

Waddington, C. H. "Evolutionary adaptation." In S. Tax (ed.). *Evolution After Darwin. Vol. I, The Evolution of Life*. Chicago: University of Chicago Press, 1960. Pp. 381–428.

White, F. N., and H. M. Smith. "Some basic concepts pertaining to the Baldwin effect," *Turtox News*, 34 (1956), 51–53, 66–68. Chicago: General Biological Supply House.

⌒

CHAPTER 19

POPULATION GENETICS AND

EVOLUTIONARY CHANGE

In Chapter 17 we discussed some of the principles of Mendelian inheritance revealed by experiments in which matings were arranged by the experimenter. What happens when members of a population are free to interbreed as they may, rather than according to some plan of an experimenter? In our discussion of this question we shall refer constantly to a unit which we shall call "the population." We shall use this term to mean a Mendelian population, defined by Dobzhansky (1950) as "a reproductive community of sexual and cross-fertilizing individuals which share in a common gene pool." The term *deme* is sometimes used for such a population, but since the term is also applied to local communities characterized in other ways than that of reproduction within the group we shall not employ it.

GENETIC EQUILIBRIUM

It will be convenient to begin our discussion by referring again to the melanistic hamsters (pp. 376–379). As the result of the cross diagramed in Fig. 17.1 (p. 377) an F_2 generation was produced consisting of ¼ homozygous black (*MM*), ²⁄₄ heterozygous black (*Mm*), and ¼ homozygous gray (*mm*). If these F_2 individuals interbreed *at random* what types of offspring will be expected in the next (F_3) generation, and in what proportions will the various types be expected to occur? For present purposes we shall assume that there is nothing about the melanistic condition which affects an individual's mating and that no preference is exercised dependent upon color of the coat. Under such conditions a melanistic individual would be equally likely to mate with another melanistic one or with a gray one, *if* the two were present in equal numbers. Similarly, a gray hamster would be equally likely to mate with a melanistic one or with a gray one, if the two were present in equal numbers. But in this instance the two types are not present in equal numbers; there are three times as many black individuals as there are gray ones. The same principle of random mating will hold, however: the chances of an individual's mating with one type or the other will be in proportion to the relative frequency with which the types occur. Or, in terms of this specific example, the chance of any individual hamster's mating with a black individual will be ¾, the chance of its mating with a gray individual will be ¼. It is necessary, however, to go one step further and to distinguish between homozygous black hamsters and heterozygous ones. We have seen that the F_2 offspring are as follows: ¼ are *MM*, ²⁄₄ are *Mm*, ¼ are *mm*. Accordingly, the chance that any individual hamster will mate with an *MM* individual is ¼; the chance of mating with an *Mm* individual is ²⁄₄ or ½; the chance of mating with an *mm* individual is ¼.

We can now rephrase the question: What will be the nature of the offspring from a population consisting of ¼*MM* individuals, ½*Mm* ones, and ¼*mm* ones? (We shall assume that no sex differences are involved, that these proportions are true of both males and females.)

The answer may be obtained by making a "checkerboard" diagram in which the male parents are listed along the left-hand margin, the female parents across the top.

In the body of the diagram are placed the different types of offspring produced and their relative frequencies. The frequencies are obtained for each square by multiplying the fraction representing the proportion of

		Female Parents		
		¼*MM*	²⁄₄*Mm*	¼*mm*
Male Parents	¼*MM*	¹⁄₁₆*MM*	²⁄₁₆ { ¹⁄₁₆*MM* / ¹⁄₁₆*Mm*	¹⁄₁₆*Mm*
	²⁄₄*Mm*	²⁄₁₆ { ¹⁄₁₆*MM* / ¹⁄₁₆*Mm*	⁴⁄₁₆ { ¹⁄₁₆*MM* / ²⁄₁₆*Mm* / ¹⁄₁₆*mm*	²⁄₁₆ { ¹⁄₁₆*Mm* / ¹⁄₁₆*mm*
	¼*mm*	¹⁄₁₆*Mm*	²⁄₁₆ { ¹⁄₁₆*Mm* / ¹⁄₁₆*mm*	¹⁄₁₆*mm*

males of the constitution concerned by the fraction representing the proportion of females of the constitution concerned. Thus the frequency in the square in the upper left-hand corner is $\frac{1}{4} \cdot \frac{1}{4}$ or $\frac{1}{16}$. The upper row represents the offspring to be expected when the MM males, constituting $\frac{1}{4}$ of the total males, mate with the three different types of females in proportion to the relative frequencies of the latter. The diagram shows that $\frac{1}{16}$ of the matings will occur between MM males and MM females, $\frac{2}{16}$ between MM males and Mm females, $\frac{1}{16}$ between MM males and mm females. The other two horizontal rows are to be interpreted similarly.

The offspring from some of the matings are all of one type—shown in the corner squares of the diagram. In four other squares two types of offspring occurring in equal numbers are shown. An example is the middle square of the top row; here MM males are mated to Mm females.

offspring: MM, MM, Mm, Mm

In such a mating MM offspring and Mm offspring are to be expected in equal numbers. Hence, the $\frac{2}{16}$ of the offspring arising from such matings resolves itself into $\frac{1}{16} MM$ offspring and $\frac{1}{16} Mm$ offspring.

The central square of the diagram represents a still more complex situation, in that both parents are heterozygous, $Mm \times Mm$. As we noted earlier, offspring from such parentage are expected to appear in a $1.2.1$ ratio; hence the $\frac{4}{16}$ of this square is resolved into $\frac{1}{16} MM$, $\frac{2}{16} Mm$, and $\frac{1}{16} mm$, as indicated.

If now we assemble the results shown in the diagram, we find that $\frac{4}{16}$ of the offspring will be expected to be MM, $\frac{8}{16}$ will be Mm, $\frac{4}{16}$ will be mm. This is our $1:2:1$ ratio again. The proportions of the different types of individuals are the same in the F_3 generation as they were in the F_2. Evidently, then, our artificial population is in *equilibrium;* so long as random mating occurs the proportion of $\frac{1}{4} MM$ to $\frac{1}{2} Mm$ to $\frac{1}{4} mm$ may be expected to continue generation after generation.

Gene Pool

There is a simpler and more direct way of working the problem discussed above. Let us concentrate upon the genes, rather than upon the combinations of genes in the various parents. Turning our attention to the male parents we note that ¼ of the effective sperm cells are produced by *MM* individuals; these sperm cells will all contain gene *M*. Two-fourths of the effective sperm cells are produced by *Mm* individuals; half of these (or ¼ of the total number of sperms) will contain gene *M*. As a result, *half* the total number of sperm cells will contain *M* (¼ from *MM* males plus ¼ from *Mm* males). The other half of the sperm cells will contain gene *m* (¼ from *Mm* males plus ¼ from *mm* males). In the female parents the situation is exactly comparable. Half the ova will contain gene *M* (¼ derived from *MM* females plus ¼ from *Mm* females), and half of the ova will contain gene *m* (¼ from *Mm* females plus ¼ from *mm* females).

As a result we can considerably simplify our checkerboard diagram as follows:

Ova

		½ M	½ m
Sperms	½ M	¼ MM	¼ Mm
	½ m	¼ Mm	¼ mm

The fraction in each square is obtained by multiplying the fraction of ova having the gene in question by the fraction of sperms having it.

Assembling the results from the chart we find that the offspring occur in the proportions ¼*MM*, ²⁄₄*Mm*, ¼*mm*—the same result we obtained with the more complicated diagram.

We may even go one step further in our simplification. It is not really necessary to separate the sperms from the ova in our thinking. Grouping the two together we have a "gene pool" in which half the genes (regardless of whether they are in sperms or ova) are recessive, *m,* half are dominant, *M*. In such a gene pool the equilibrium of ¼*MM*, ²⁄₄*Mm*, ¼*mm* will be maintained as long as random mating occurs (i.e., as long as choice of mates is entirely a matter of chance and hence obeys the mathematical laws of probability).

An instructive model of such a gene pool is afforded by a box containing red and blue beads (corresponding to gene *M* and gene *m* respectively) in equal numbers. If without looking you reach into the box and pick up two beads at a time, you may, obviously, pick up two red ones (*MM*), a red and a blue one (*Mm*), or two blue ones (*mm*). If you do this enough times you will obtain a good approximation of the ratio: ¼ both beads of the pair red, ²⁄₄ one bead red and one blue, ¼ both beads blue.

Hardy-Weinberg Formula

We have just noted that offspring derived from a gene pool in which half the genes are dominant, half recessive, are expected to consist of $\frac{1}{4}$ homozygous dominants, $\frac{2}{4}$ heterozygotes, and $\frac{1}{4}$ homozygous recessives. In terms of the genes we have used for illustration we may write this as: $1MM + 2Mm + 1mm$.

Suppose we now write MM as M^2, and mm as m^2. Our statement then becomes: $M^2 + 2Mm + m^2$. Such a statement should begin to stir dormant memories of something we encountered in high school algebra, or more recently as college freshmen. Probably memories will be still further stimulated if we express it with a's and b's: $a^2 + 2ab + b^2$. Maybe we can now recall that this is the result of multiplying $(a + b)$ by itself: $(a + b)^2$. In other words, $a^2 + 2ab + b^2$ is the expansion to the second power of the binomial $(a + b)$. Evidently the $1:2:1$ ratio we have been discussing is a special case of such an expansion.

Instead of employing a's and b's we may follow custom and use p's and q's, those letters we are proverbially admonished to "mind."

$$\text{Let } p = \text{ the frequency of gene } M$$
$$q = \text{ the frequency of gene } m$$

Then if random mating occurs, the offspring resulting can be calculated by use of the formula

$$(p + q)^2 = p^2 + 2pq + q^2.$$

We may note that this formula is an algebraic equivalent of the small checkerboard diagram (p. 430). Along the left side of the latter we listed the genes carried in the sperm cells together with fractions expressing their frequency: $\frac{1}{2}M + \frac{1}{2}m$. This is equivalent to $p + q$. Along the top we listed the genes carried in the ova together with fractions expressing their frequency: $\frac{1}{2}M + \frac{1}{2}m$. This, also, is equivalent to $p + q$. Filling in the squares of the checkerboard involved multiplying the frequencies of the two kinds of genes carried in the sperm cells by the frequencies of the two kinds of genes carried in the ova: $(\frac{1}{2}M + \frac{1}{2}m)(\frac{1}{2}M + \frac{1}{2}m)$. This is equivalent to $(p + q)(p + q)$ or $(p + q)^2$. Obviously, then, the binomial is *squared* because two parents are involved in the production of offspring.

This formula is referred to as the Hardy-Weinberg formula, from the names of the two men who first realized its application to the problems of population genetics.

Let us apply the formula to the situation we have just been discussing, a gene pool in which the numbers of dominant and recessive genes are equal. In such a situation

$$p = \text{the frequency of gene } M = \tfrac{1}{2}$$
$$q = \text{the frequency of gene } m = \tfrac{1}{2}$$

(Note that $p + q = 1$ or unity, standing for the total number of genes. This must always be so since the number of dominant genes plus the number of recessive genes must equal the total number of genes.)

Substituting the numerical values in our formula we obtain

$$
\begin{aligned}
(p + q)^2 &= p^2 + 2pq + q^2 \\
&= (\tfrac{1}{2})^2 + 2 \cdot \tfrac{1}{2} \cdot \tfrac{1}{2} + (\tfrac{1}{2})^2 \\
&= \tfrac{1}{4} + \tfrac{2}{4} + \tfrac{1}{4} \\
&= \tfrac{1}{4}MM + \tfrac{2}{4}Mm + \tfrac{1}{4}mm
\end{aligned}
$$

(Recall that p represents gene M in this case, hence p^2 means M^2 or MM. Similarly pq means Mm, and q^2 means m^2 or mm.)

Thus the Hardy-Weinberg formula affords a means of calculating expectation with regard to offspring without recourse to the checkerboard diagrams previously employed.

So far in our discussion we have confined attention to a situation in which the number of dominant genes equals the number of recessive genes —in which $p = q$. It will be recalled that this situation arose in an experiment in which homozygous, black hamsters were mated to gray ones. The first-generation (F_1) individuals were all black but heterozygous. When these F_1 individuals were interbred, their offspring (F_2) fell into the following groupings: $\tfrac{1}{4}$ homozygous black: $\tfrac{2}{4}$ heterozygous black: $\tfrac{1}{4}$ gray (Fig. 17.1, p. 377). Then when the F_2 individuals were allowed to mate at random we discovered that the 1:2:1 ratio appeared again in the next (F_3) generation and continued through subsequent generations. That is, an equilibrium had been reached.

While situations in which the number of dominant genes equals the number of corresponding recessive genes are common enough in genetics laboratories, they are seldom encountered in a state of nature. There it is much more common for one gene to preponderate in frequency, the other gene being much rarer. Are the principles we have been discussing applicable to such situations?

Suppose we have a population of hamsters in which the gene pool consists of 90 percent M genes and 10 percent m genes. If random mating occurs, what proportion of the offspring may we expect to be black, what proportion gray? The Hardy-Weinberg formula permits easy solution of the problem.

$p =$ frequency of $M = .90$ (writing the percentage as a decimal fraction)

$q =$ frequency of $m = .10$

$$(p + q)^2 = p^2 + 2pq + q^2$$
$$(.9)^2 + 2 \cdot (.9) \cdot (.1) + (.1)^2$$

.81   .18   .01

81% MM   18% Mm   1% mm

99% black   1% gray

We see, then, that under such conditions only 1 percent of the offspring will be expected to be gray—only one hamster in 100. If random breeding occurs in subsequent generations, the gene pool may be expected to remain the same (90 percent M genes, 10 percent m genes) generation after generation, with the result that gray hamsters may be expected to appear about once in 100 individuals indefinitely. The genetic bases for the occasional appearance of albino individuals among normally pigmented ones, of black sheep among white ones, of cinnamon bears among black ones, of rufous screech owls among gray ones, and so on, are doubtless of this type.

We noted earlier (p. 376) that black hamsters appear with varying frequencies in various regions of Europe and Asia; in some places they are rare, in some places common, even approaching 100 percent of the population. Thoughtful students will readily appreciate that if, knowing the nature of the gene pool, we can calculate the proportion of gray hamsters that will appear, we can reverse the process and calculate the nature of the gene pool if we know the number of gray hamsters occurring. For example, in a certain region 16 percent of the hamsters are gray ones. In what proportions do dominant and recessive genes occur in that gene pool?

The gray hamsters are represented by the q^2 of the Hardy-Weinberg formula. Accordingly $q^2 = 16\%$ or $.16$, $q = \sqrt{.16} = .4$ or 40%. Thus 40 percent of the genes are recessive (m); consequently the remaining 60 percent must be dominant (M).

Having determined the nature of the gene pool we can now do one other thing not possible by direct observation—estimate the proportion of the hamsters that are heterozygous. These are represented by the $2pq$ of the Hardy-Weinberg formula. Substituting the values of p and q, we find: $2 \cdot (.6) \cdot (.4) = .48$ or 48%. Thus, in such a population we may expect that 48 percent of the hamsters are heterozygotes, "carriers" of the gene for gray color. There is interest in obtaining this statistic in view of the role which heterozygotes are observed to play in evolution (see pp. 457–468).

One word of qualification must be added concerning the correctness of calculating the nature of the gene pool from the proportion of individuals exhibiting (and therefore homozygous for) a recessive characteristic. The procedure is only valid insofar as conditions of random mating actually prevail in the population and insofar as the recessive characteristic in question does not affect fertility and viability. Obviously if gray hamsters were less viable than black ones calculations based on the number of gray hamsters which managed to survive would give an incorrect idea concerning the nature of the gene pool.

So far we have confined attention to situations in which an equilibrium is already present. We have seen that an equilibrium tends to persist generation after generation. But such an equilibrium is the antithesis of evolution; "evolution means change," to quote the statement with which this book opens. When changes occur what effect will the tendencies embodied in the Hardy-Weinberg formula have upon them?

Suppose we imagine the formation of an artificial and arbitrary population of hamsters: A thousand black hamsters, half of them homozygous, half heterozygous, become isolated in some way—marooned on an island, perhaps. What may be expected in future generations of such a population?

The original population has the frequency 50 percent *MM*, 50 percent *Mm*. All the genes contributed by the *MM* individuals are *M*, but only half the genes contributed by the *Mm* individuals are *M*. Thus the frequency of *M* in the gene pool will consist of 50 percent of the total number of genes, contributed by the *MM* parents, plus one-half the genes contributed by the *Mm* parents. The latter contribute 50 percent of the total number of genes; one half of this 50 percent, or 25 percent, are *M* genes.

$$\begin{aligned}
\text{Thus, } p &= 50\% + 25\% = 75\% \text{ or } .75 \\
q &= 25\% \text{ or } .25 \\
(p + q)^2 &= p^2 + 2pq + q^2 \\
&= (.75)^2 + 2 \cdot (.75)(.25) + (.25)^2 \\
&= .5625 + .375 + .0625 \\
56.25\% \ &MM + 37.5\% \ Mm + 6.25\% \ mm
\end{aligned}$$

We note immediately that a change has occurred in the population. There is a somewhat larger proportion of homozygous, black hamsters than there was among the parents, and the proportion of heterozygous animals has been somewhat reduced. In addition, a small group of gray hamsters has appeared, although none of the parents were gray. Since this change from the parental generation has occurred it is evident that the original population was not in a state of genetic equilibrium. What is the situation among the offspring?

We answer this question by computing the frequencies of the dominant and the recessive genes, i.e., the values of p and q: 56.25 percent of the individuals have only M genes, and consequently contribute that percentage of M genes to the pool; 37.5 percent of the individuals are heterozygous, half their genes being M, half m, and thus contribute one-half of 37.5 percent, or 18.75 percent, of M genes, as well as 18.75 percent of m genes. The 6.25 percent consisting of gray hamsters are homozygous mm and hence contribute only m genes, doing so in proportion to their frequency in the population.

$$\text{Thus, } p = .5625 + .1875 = .75 \text{ or } 75\%$$
$$q = .1875 + .0625 = .25 \text{ or } 25\%$$

We notice immediately that these values of p and q are exactly the same as those for the original population (see above). Substituting them in the Hardy-Weinberg formula will form a mere repetition of the calculation by which we determined the constitution of the first-generation offspring. Evidently, therefore, the population is now in a state of equilibrium and, as long as unmodified random mating occurs, may be expected to continue 56.25 percent MM, 37.5 percent Mm, and 6.25 percent mm generation after generation.

Our hypothetical example has demonstrated that when a population is not in genetic equilibrium with regard to a pair of genes it tends to attain such an equilibrium in one generation of random mating.

Significance of Genetic Equilibrium for Evolution

So far in this chapter we have devoted attention to the manner in which the laws of chance or probability operate upon gene distribution in ways tending to preserve the *status quo*—to maintain an unchanging equilibrium as generations pass. We have noted that not only is there a tendency to maintain such an equilibrium but if the equilibrium is upset there is a tendency to establish quickly a new equilibrium. Evidently this tendency to equilibrium forms a sort of inertia which must be overcome if evolutionary change is to occur.

Stating the matter so may give the impression that equilibrium is entirely detrimental, and obstructive of progress. We should note, therefore, that the equilibrium tendency is *conservative*, in the best sense of that much abused word. It tends to conserve gains which have been made in the past and to prevent too rapid change. "Taking chances" is the price of real achievement and progress in the life of a species, as in the life of a human individual. But a species, or a man, who continually gambled everything upon single spins of the wheel of fortune would lead a precarious existence. Genetic equilibrium helps to insure that a species will not "put all its eggs in one basket" in undergoing evolutionary change. Radical change may lead to progress; it may also hustle a species down a blind alley to speedy extinction.

A further conservative function of the equilibrium tendency arises from the manner in which it keeps a store of recessive genes continually in existence even though individuals homozygous for those genes rarely appear. As we noted earlier (p. 349), there is no tendency for recessive genes to "die out." This fact should be clearly evident from the examples showing the workings of the Hardy-Weinberg law. In the last example, while only about 6 percent of the hamsters are gray, over 37 percent of them "carry" the gray gene (i.e., are heterozygous). These heterozygous individuals thus form a reservoir of "gray" genes which can be drawn upon in producing future gray individuals. If there is no advantage to be gained from being gray, this matter remains of little importance, but if at any time or under any conditions grayness, or any associated physiological effect, becomes an asset, the reservoir of "gray" genes may assume great significance for the species. We have mentioned this matter of the importance of heterozygotes before (pp. 346–347) and shall return to it again (pp. 457–468).

Having established a foundation of understanding concerning the tendency to genetic equilibrium we shall now turn our attention to the forces which tend to modify or upset that equilibrium and hence to lead to evolutionary change.

MUTATION PRESSURE AND GENETIC EQUILIBRIUM

In earlier chapters we have emphasized mutations as the raw material of evolution. It will be recalled that mutations are changes in genes and that, having occurred, they are inherited in accordance with the Mendelian principles we have been discussing.

We noted (p. 337) that the Dutch botanist, Hugo De Vries, first emphasized the importance of mutations in evolution. Indeed, he proposed a "mutation theory" of evolution intended not only to supplement but in large measure to supplant the Darwinian theory of natural selection. But that was before the principles of genetic equilibrium we have just been discussing were understood.

Before discussing in more detail the role of the laws of probability in determining the fate of mutations, we should note that the occurrence of mutations does have a tendency to disturb any equilibrium which may exist. To refer to our hamsters again, every time a gene which originally produced black coat color undergoes a chemical change so that it now conditions the appearance of gray coat color, the gene pool has been altered through decrease by one in number of *M* genes and increase by one in number of *m* genes. Obviously, if such changes occurred frequently, considerable modification in the ratio between numbers of *M* and *m* genes might arise. But actually **mutation pressure,** as it is called, is observed to be of low order of magnitude. Accurate data on this point are difficult to obtain. In the fruit fly, *Drosophila,* the genetically best-known animal, it is estimated that mutations of one kind or another are present in from 1 to 10 percent of the germ cells produced in every generation. Individual genes, however, vary greatly in frequency of mutation. With some kinds one out of every thousand genes, on the average, may undergo mutation. Other kinds of genes may be so stable that only one in a billion will mutate. Accordingly, there must be great variation in the efficacy of mutation pressure in disturbing genetic equilibrium. Some genes may mutate so frequently that, under particular circumstances, the constitution of the gene pool is considerably altered from the equilibrium which would otherwise prevail. For example, imagine a gene pool consisting of 50 percent *M* genes and 50 percent *m* genes, and having a mutation rate such that one in every thousand *M* genes mutates to *m*. It can be demonstrated mathematically that in one generation the gene pool will be shifted to 49.95 percent *M* genes and 50.05 percent *m* genes. This is a small change, but if the same trend continued generation after generation a considerable difference in frequency of the two genes would eventually be accumulated. Indeed, if the trend continued long enough the *M* genes would be entirely replaced by *m* genes, assuming that the change from *M* to *m* was unopposed. Actually the trend would be opposed by what is known as *reverse mutation,* the mutation of *m* genes to form *M* genes. This would also occur at a rather constant rate, although, judging by evidence available, at a rate lower than that by which *M* mutates to *m*. Thus there are two opposed mutation rates: (1) the rate at which *M* changes to *m* and (2) the rate at which *m* changes to *M*. The combined action of the two rates is to change the gene frequency until a point is reached at which the number of *M* genes changing to *m* genes in any generation balances the number of *m* genes changing to *M* at that time. At this point an equilibrium is established. So we see that while mutation pressures by and of themselves may alter genetic equilibriums their ultimate net effect is to establish equilibrium, even though it is a different equilibrium from that which would otherwise prevail. (The reader is referred to Chapter 3 of

Dobzhansky's *Genetics and the Origin of Species,* 1951, for more complete discussion of mutation pressure and genetic equilibrium.)

In this connection we may note that a new mutation may not produce a detectable effect until several generations following the actual occurrence of the change in the gene. This is true when a dominant gene mutates to form a completely recessive one. Let us imagine a population of black hamsters all homozygous *MM.* What will be the fate of a single mutation which occurs in this stock? Suppose that in this case the mutation occurs in a sperm-forming cell in a male. As a result one or more of his sperms contains gene *m* instead of the gene *M* possessed by all his other sperm cells. If an *m*-containing sperm functions in fertilization, it must necessarily fertilize an *M*-containing ovum (there are no others). When this occurs an individual of the formula *Mm* is produced. This individual, like its parents, is black; the "new" gray gene has still not produced a visible effect. The *Mm* individual must mate with an *MM* individual of the opposite sex. As we saw on page 429, such a mating (*Mm* × *MM*) is expected to result in offspring that are half *Mm,* half *MM.* Again, these offspring are all black although half of them are heterozygous. Still we have no gray hamsters! How can we obtain gray hamsters? These can only arise if an *Mm* female mates with an *Mm* male. As we saw earlier, one-fourth of the offspring of such a mating are expected to be gray (*mm*) (p. 379). Thus the actual occurrence of a recessive mutation must necessarily be separated from the production of an individual showing the visible effects of that mutation by at least two generations.

Generation I	Heterozygous Black Hamster *Mm*	×	Homozygous Black Hamster *MM*	
Generation II	*MM* Black	*MM* Black	*Mm* × *Mm* Black ↓ Black	
Generation III		*MM* Black	*Mm* Black	*Mm* Black	*mm* Gray

It will be noted that in order to produce a gray individual in the fewest possible generations we have made use of a brother-sister mating in Generation II. Such matings are not uncommon among lower animals. In modern human societies the nearest approach to them consists of first-cousin marriages. These could also bring a recessive gene "to light" in the minimum number of generations if the *Mm* individual in Generation I had a brother or sister of the same constitution, and an *Mm* offspring of the latter married one of the *Mm* individuals shown in the diagram.

We mention this matter to emphasize the fact that recessive mutations may occur and be carried by a population as a sort of hidden store, with only occasional homozygous recessive individuals being produced to display the phenotypic effect of the gene. Yet this time lag between the occurrence of the new mutation and the appearance of an individual showing its phenotypic effect occurs only when the new mutation is completely recessive. If a normally occurring recessive gene mutates to form a dominant gene (e.g., *m* to *M*), a visible effect is produced in first-generation offspring. Here we may recall that most European hamsters are gray, hence the "black gene" must have arisen in just this way.

In an earlier discussion (pp. 346–347) we noted that frequently mutations classed as recessive are not completely so—that they produce *some* effect in heterozygotes even though the dominant member of the pair may produce the principal effect. When this is the case, an effect of the "recessive" mutation will be manifested in the first generation following the change in the gene. As we noted, evidence is accumulating that frequently, perhaps usually, it is the heterozygous state rather than the homozygous one that is important in evolution.

GENETIC DRIFT

Let us return in imagination to the population of black hamsters all of which are *MM* except for the one *Mm* individual. We saw that the only mating possible for the latter is to an *MM* individual. We then stated that such a mating (*Mm* × *MM*) is expected to produce offspring that are half *Mm*, half *MM*. Now that statement is true *on the average*, but such theoretically expected ratios are merely expressions of the operation of the laws of probability, as in flipping coins. If parental pairs of *MM* × *Mm* constitution give rise to 200 offspring, about 100 of them would be *MM*, about 100 *Mm*. But let us suppose that this single pair of parents had only *two* offspring—at least, two which lived to reproduce in their turn. Such a situation commonly prevails in populations that are stationary in numbers from generation to generation. If the parents produce only two offspring which live to reproduce, what effect will that fact have upon the fate of the mutation, *m*, in which we are interested?

$$MM \times Mm$$

$$\text{germ cells} \left\{ \begin{matrix} M \to M \\ \diagup\hspace{-0.3em}\diagdown \\ M \to m \end{matrix} \right\} \text{germ cells}$$

The four arrows in the diagram represent the four possible combinations of germ cells. Probability of occurrence is the same for all four combinations. Two combinations result in *MM* offspring, two in *Mm* offspring. Thus the chance that the *first* offspring will be *MM* is ½, and the chance that the *second* offspring will be *MM* is also ½. Hence, the chance that both of two offspring will be *MM* is ½ · ½ or ¼. But if both the offspring are *MM*, an event of great significance has transpired: the *m* gene has been irrevocably lost. The population will revert to its original all-*MM* constitution and remain so until such time as a fresh mutation from *M* to *m* occurs. We note, moreover, that the chance of losing a mutation in this way is not a small one; it is one chance in four, or 25 percent.

But what other constitutions may the two offspring possess? The chance that the first offspring will be *Mm* is ½, the chance that the second offspring will be *Mm* is also ½. Thus the chance that both of the two will be *Mm* is ½ · ½ or ¼. It is to be noted that in this case the number of *m* genes is doubled; the parents, only one of which possessed the *m* gene, have been replaced by two offspring both of which possess the gene.

The chance that the first offspring will be *MM* is ½, the chance that the second will be *Mm* is ½. Hence, the chance that the two will have the designated respective constitutions is ½ · ½ or ¼. Finally, the chance that the first offspring will be *Mm* is ½, the chance that the second will be *MM* is ½, the chance for the combination being ½ · ½ or ¼. Thus the chance that either one of the two offspring will be *MM* and the other *Mm* is ¼ + ¼ or ½. These combinations represent retainment of the *status quo:* the parents, *MM* × *Mm,* are merely replaced by two offspring having the same constitutions as themselves. The frequency of the *m* gene has neither increased nor decreased.

In sum, we find that, owing to the operation of chance in the reproduction of a relatively stationary population, we may expect "new" mutations to be lost from the population about 25 percent of the time, to be doubled in frequency about 25 percent of the time, and to remain unchanged in frequency about 50 percent of the time.

Suppose we assume that the second possibility is the one which occurs—that the parents are replaced by two offspring, both *Mm* in constitution. If these two are of opposite sex, they may mate together, thus making possible the actual appearance of gray offspring, as diagramed above (p. 438). But the chances of their mating together are not large; if they do not do so they obviously must mate with *MM* individuals. The result would be two matings like those of the original parents:

Original parents $MM \times Mm$

1st generation $MM \times Mm$ $Mm \times MM$

In the case of each of these first-generation matings the chances with regard to two offspring are the same as they were for the original parents. Both may be MM (the m gene being lost as far as that mating is concerned); both may be Mm (the frequency of the m gene being doubled); one may be MM, the other Mm (the frequency of the m gene remaining unchanged).

For the sake of illustration, let us suppose that the second possibility materializes in both cases, that the offspring from each mating are both Mm.

Original parents $MM \times Mm$

1st generation $MM \times Mm$ $Mm \times MM$

2nd generation Mm Mm Mm Mm

On this supposition we see that the frequency of the m gene has doubled again. Two individuals possessed it in the first generation; four possess it in the second generation.

We might continue on into a third generation, following the matings of the four second-generation individuals. But the principle involved should be evident without more extensive illustration. In small populations, producing small numbers of offspring per mating, the frequencies of mutant genes may fluctuate either up or down according to chance. This chance fluctuation in gene frequencies has been termed genetic "drift" by Sewall Wright, who has emphasized its role in evolution. Owing to chance, gene frequencies may "drift" either up or down. In our illustration, the frequency of gene m might continue to increase generation after generation; if so, actual gray hamsters (mm) would soon appear, and their breeding would accelerate the spread of the m gene. If this trend continued to its culmination, the m gene might reach a frequency of 100 percent; i.e., a population entirely composed of gray hamsters might result. Or the trend in the other direction might set in at any time: matings in which offspring possessing the m gene were possible but not inevitable might fail to produce such offspring. As a result the frequency of the m gene would decline. If the decline were of sufficient magnitude, the m gene might be lost entirely from the population, all the hamsters being homozygous for black coloration. In the former case we should say that the recessive gene had become fixed, by chance; in the latter case that the dominant gene had become fixed. When fixation occurs the drift becomes irreversible, but at any point before fixation is reached reversal of drift may occur.

A model to illustrate the operation of "drift" was constructed by Dubinin and Romaschoff (described in Dobzhansky, 1941, p. 162). In this model the gene pool was represented by 100 marbles in a bowl. Each marble bore a different number. In order to simulate the loss of 25 percent of the mutant genes described above (p. 440) the investigators discarded from the bowl twenty-five marbles, taken at random. In order to simulate the doubling in frequency of 25 percent of the mutant genes (p. 440) they withdrew twenty-five more marbles at random and then replaced them, accompanying each marble by a second one bearing the same number. In this way the total number of marbles remained 100, but 25 percent of the numbers designating individual marbles were lost, and 25 percent of the designating numbers were doubled in frequency. This procedure represented the action of chance in the production of one generation of offspring. The process was then repeated time after time. As the "generations" passed it was found that fewer and fewer different numbers remained in the bowl, until finally all 100 marbles came to bear the same number. This culmination was reached in from 108 to 465 "generations," in different experiments.

In order to demonstrate the influence of size of population upon drift Dubinin and Romaschoff repeated the experiment with a gene pool consisting of but 10 marbles. In this case "homozygosis" (all marbles having one number) was attained much more rapidly than it was in the larger gene pool, only fourteen to fifty-one "generations" being required. This observation emphasizes the point that drift is primarily a phenomenon characteristic of small breeding populations.

Instructive as is the model just described, the present author felt that a model mimicking more closely the actual conditions of bisexual reproduction might have enhanced value. He also wished to avoid the artificial regularity imposed by discarding 25 percent of a gene pool, and doubling another 25 percent, at each generation. Accordingly, he devised a simple model in which chance was free to operate in two phenomena at each generation: (1) in arranging of matings and (2) in production of offspring from these matings (Moody, 1947). In the model, individuals were represented by pairs of beads tied together; two red beads stood for a homozygous dominant individual (*MM*); two blue beads for a homozygous recessive (*mm*); a pair consisting of one red and one blue bead represented a heterozygous individual (*Mm*).

The model began with a small population conforming to the Hardy-

Weinberg equilibrium; 3*MM* : 6*Mm* : 3*mm*. To represent them, three pairs of red beads, six pairs consisting of one red and one blue bead, and three pairs of blue beads were placed in a box and thoroughly mixed. Then the pairs were withdrawn at random, two at a time. Two pairs withdrawn together constituted a "mating," arranged at random. The "matings" actually obtained at one trial were: *MM* × *Mm*; *MM* × *mm*; *MM* × *Mm*; *Mm* × *Mm*; *Mm* × *mm*; *Mm* × *mm* (Fig. 19.1).

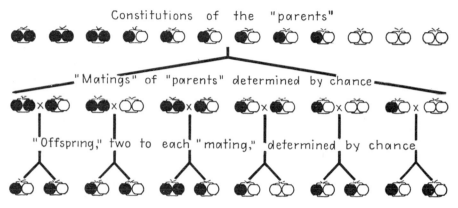

FIG. 19.1. Model of genetic drift, employing red and blue beads. Production of one "generation" only is shown. "Matings" of "parents" occurred by chance. Chance also determined the nature of the two "offspring" resulting from each "mating."

Then chance was allowed to operate in determining the two offspring to arise from each "mating." For example, from the *Mm* × *mm* "mating" two types of offspring are possible, *Mm* and *mm*. The *mm* parent must contribute an *m* gene; this could be coupled with either an *M* gene or an *m* gene from the *Mm* parent. To permit chance to operate in deciding whether in each case the latter would contribute *M* or *m*, a bowl containing equal numbers of red and blue beads was used. One bead was withdrawn from the bowl at random; if the bead was red, that meant that the *Mm* parent contributed an *M* gene (and the offspring was therefore *Mm*); if the bead was blue, that meant that the *Mm* parent contributed an *m* gene (and the offspring was therefore *mm*). This drawing was done twice, once for each of the two "offspring." The bowl of beads was used in the same way to determine the contribution of a heterozygous parent in the other matings listed. When both parents were heterozygous, as in the fourth "mating" listed, two beads were withdrawn from the bowl at a time, since both parents might contribute either an *M* (red bead) or an *m* (blue bead), the offspring being either *MM* (two red beads), *Mm* (one red and one blue bead) or *mm* (two blue beads). In "matings" like the second listed, in which both parents were homozygous, the offspring must necessarily both be of one constitution (*Mm,* in this instance); hence, no drawing of beads was needed.

In an actual experiment the offspring derived from the "matings" listed above gave the following totals: 1*MM,* 10*Mm,* 1*mm* (Fig. 19.1).

The process was then repeated to produce a second generation. One pair of red beads, ten pairs consisting of one red bead and one blue bead, and one pair of blue beads were put in the box, mixed, and withdrawn at random, two pairs at a time. Thus "matings" were arranged by chance. Then the two offspring from each "mating" were determined, using the bowl of red and blue beads as described above.

The process was repeated "generation" after "generation." Sometimes the number of blue beads increased, sometimes the number of red beads did so. Sometimes beads of one color almost disappeared, the population coming to consist of 11*MM* and 1*Mm* individuals. Then there would be a "rally" on the part of the *m* genes, which became more numerous again. The model demonstrated the tenacity with which the laws of probability expressed in the Hardy-Weinberg formula tend to maintain equilibrium even in such a tiny "population." Yet eventually "drift" won out, and one gene was entirely lost. The first time the experiment was tried, fixation of one gene did not occur until the 134th generation; members of that generation were all *MM* (12 pairs of red beads). That the large number of generations was of no real significance, however, was attested by another running of the experiment in which the same result was achieved in seventeen generations. These results are given in the accompanying table, study of which will make clear that complete elimination of the blue beads might easily have occurred in even fewer generations.

What has genetic drift to do with evolution? As noted previously (p. 350), it affords a means by which inherited characteristics can become established in a population without regard to their usefulness. When the size of the population is small some genes may be lost or reduced in frequency by chance, others may be increased in frequency by chance. Thus the nature of the population is changed without involving the matter of usefulness. In our discussion of classification (Chap. 14) we noted that the structural differences between species, and especially those between subspecies, are frequently small. Commonly, also, these differences do not seem to be of importance to their possessors. What difference does it make to a mouse whether the margins of its dorsal tail stripe are clearly drawn or indistinct (see p. 316)? Genetic drift affords a means by which

TABLE 19.1. Results of One Demonstration
of the Genetic Drift Model

Generation No.	Distribution of Individuals MM	Mm	mm
Parents	3	6	3
1	3	4	5
2	4	2	6
3	2	5	5
4	2	9	1
5	6	5	1
6	7	5	0
7	8	4	0
8	9	3	0
9	10	1	1
10	10	2	0
11	10	2	0
12	11	1	0
13	11	1	0
14	11	1	0
15	11	1	0
16	11	1	0
17	12	0	0

isolated populations may come to differ from each other in characteristics which are of no practical importance in the lives of the animals concerned.

We have mentioned repeatedly that drift is a phenomenon of small populations. That it is such may at first glance seem to restrict its action to inhabitants of oceanic islands and members of other small, isolated communities. Yet, as noted earlier (p. 350), even large, widely ranging assemblages of animals are commonly at least partially divided into smaller breeding groups. A species of field mouse, for example, may range over an entire state and include millions of individuals. If the principles of random mating prevailed, any given individual would be equally likely to mate with any other individual, of opposite sex, among those millions. Yet that is not the condition which actually obtains. An individual living in one river valley is more likely to mate with an individual in the same valley than with an individual in another one. An individual in one patch of woods is more likely to mate with another individual in the same wood lot than with an individual in woods separated from it by open country. Furthermore, field studies reveal that many animals establish rather definite "home ranges" beyond the limits of which they seldom stray and within which they repel intruders of the same species and sex. Thus the territory within which an individual is likely to secure a mate is still further restricted.

We should also note that many species of animals pass through "bottle-necks" in their yearly life cycles. Among insects, especially, winter is likely to constitute a bottleneck. In a given region there may be thousands of individuals of a certain species throughout the summer, yet only a relatively few may survive the winter to become progenitors of the next summer's population. If the few which survive the winter happen to possess some genetic characteristic in greater frequency than the general population of the preceding summer did, the population of the second summer may differ considerably from that of the first summer. Thus Spencer (1947) found that the fruit flies, *Drosophila,* of a certain small community possessed an unusual frequency of a recessive mutation named "stubble," affecting the length of bristles. In these flies great seasonal fluctuations in number of individuals occur, the parents of a given summer population consisting of a few individuals who succeed in surviving the winter indoors. Since the "stubble" gene seems not to be of significance in the lives of the flies, the explanation for its having attained a considerable frequency of occurrence in this particular locality seems to be genetic drift. By chance, an unusual proportion of the few individuals surviving a winter possessed the "stubble" gene; hence the gene occurred with increased frequency among their offspring, the next summer's population.

In somewhat similar manner an "error of sampling" may occur when, through migration, a small group from a large population establishes a sub-population in a new locality. The "founders" of the new population may not be entirely typical of the large population from which they came. Suppose, for example, that a large population has in its gene pool equal numbers of genes M and m (i.e., $p = 0.5$ and $q = 0.5$; p. 432). As we noted previously, such a population would be expected to consist of $\frac{1}{4}MM$ individuals, $\frac{2}{4}Mm$ individuals, and $\frac{1}{4}mm$ individuals. Now if ten members of this population migrate to an island, these founders of the island population may, by chance, not exhibit that $1:2:1$ ratio. Perhaps five will be *MM,* four will be *Mm,* and one will be *mm*—or any other chance combination you can imagine. In the extreme case all ten might be *MM* (or, alternatively, *mm*), in which case the island population descended from the ten individuals would lack completely one of the genes under consideration. In this manner the gene pool of the island population might be very different from the gene pool of the population from which the founders came. This **founder principle,** as it is called, may help to explain how small, isolated populations have come to possess the unusual characteristics they sometimes exhibit, as compared to characteristics shown by large populations of their relatives, and how large populations descended from a few immigrants may differ from the population from which the immigrants came (Mayr, 1954; Sheppard, 1960).

Genetic Drift and Natural Selection

We have noted that chance may lead to increased frequency of occurrence of a gene, without regard to usefulness. In this connection it is only fair to state that differences of opinion exist as to the importance of genetic drift in producing the variations in gene frequency actually found in small populations, and especially as to the importance of drift in giving rise to the first steps in evolutionary change. Some investigators conclude that the differences between even small populations arise through the action of natural selection rather than through the action of chance in genetic drift.

This point of view was set forth by Ford (1949), who described the spread of a gene through an isolated population of moths. In 1928 the frequency of the gene was 1.2 percent; by 1939 it had risen to 9.2 percent, and in 1940 to 11.1 percent, after which it fluctuated between 6.8 and 4.3 percent. The isolated population fluctuated in numbers between 1000 and not over 8000, but the fluctuations in population size did not affect the frequency of the mutant gene under study. Ford concluded, "It has been possible to show that the chances are less than one in a hundred that the observed variations in the gene-ratio could be produced by random survival, indicating that they must be due to the influence of selection, varying in direction and intensity from year to year. This is the first time that these alternatives have been studied experimentally, and the result gives no support to the view that random survival plays a significant part in evolution in populations of 1000 individuals or more." Furthermore, he feels that populations of smaller size than this are not permanent, are particularly liable to extinction, and hence are not likely to contribute significantly to evolution.

Doubtless the conditions of effective population size vary from animal to animal; an effectively small population of butterflies may not have the same size range, in absolute numbers, as an effectively small population of mice, for example. Extremely small populations are sometimes recorded. Thus Miller (1950) recorded a unique dwarf species of fish confined entirely to a single hot-spring hole in Death Valley. "Since every fish is in view at one time, reliable estimates of the total population are possible. The number of individuals of this species fluctuates between about 50 and 400. At times the minimum effective breeding population may thus fall below 50 individuals. No doubt the Sewall Wright effect has been a very significant factor in the evolution of this remarkable species, which is one of the most distinctive in the genus." (We suffer from a plethora of terms; "random variation of gene frequency," "genetic drift," "random survival," "Sewall Wright effect" all refer to the same phenomenon.) This example is an extreme one in that evolution has proceeded so far that the inhabitants of this spring are regarded as constituting a distinct species. It is not certain that the effective breeding population is abnormally small, however. We should note in this connection that the number of individuals of importance to genetic drift is not the total number in the population but only the portion of the latter which actually contribute genes to the next generation. Immature, sterile, aged, and infirm individuals are not part of the "effective breeding population." Furthermore, in many species the effective breeding population is restricted in size during certain seasons of the year, particularly, in the Temperate Zone, during the winter. It is this minimum size of effective breeding population which is important in determining the occurrence of random variations in gene frequency.

Elementary students are frequently dismayed by what seem to them flat contradictions, such as those contained in this discussion of genetic drift. We should realize, however, that such differences of opinion are inevitable in a *growing* science. It behooves us not to be dogmatic in the present state of knowledge. We know too little about the genetic constitutions of animals and the varied effects of single genes, about the size of effective breeding populations actually found in nature, about the effectiveness and action of barriers, and particularly about the relationships of animals to their environments, i.e., the ecology of animals. Evolution does not occur in a vacuum. The animal is an integral part of a community of plants and animals played upon by a variety of inanimate environmental factors: temperature, humidity, climate, seasonal changes, nature of the soil, and so on. Until all these animate and inanimate factors in the environment of an animal are understood we cannot have a complete picture of the demands-of-life faced by that animal, and hence of the opportunities for operation of natural selection. We have intimated (p. 324) that in the case of wood lots three miles apart it is difficult to imagine environmental differences sufficient to give rise, through natural selection, to the observed differences in mouse inhabitants. That is true, but there are many environmental factors involved which are yet unanalyzed. Also, recent experiments in natural selection (pp. 460–464), give evidence of the subtlety and rapidity with which natural selection can, upon occasion, operate. We remember, too, that genes producing structural changes may also affect viability, that the latter effect may be of importance even if the structural change is not (pp. 452–455), and that the genetics of most wild animals is almost totally unknown. All these and other unanswered questions should make us wary of dogmatic statements that natural selection is not, or cannot be, the basis of some particular observed change.

Perhaps we shall be nearest the truth if we think of genetic drift and natural selection as partners in producing the varied gene combinations observed to arise in isolated subpopulations. Whether or not chance may be operative in determining gene frequencies in the early stages of evolutionary change, everyone will agree that upon its usefulness will depend the final fate of the gene as a contributor to evolution. As Wright (1948) has stated it: "Nonadaptive differentiation is obviously significant only as it ultimately creates adaptive differences."

References and Suggested Readings

Dobzhansky, Th. *Genetics and the Origin of Species*, 2nd and 3rd eds. New York: Columbia University Press, 1941 and 1951.

Dobzhansky, Th. "Mendelian populations and their evolution," *American Naturalist*, 84 (1950), 401–418.

Ford, E. B. "Early stages in allopatric speciation." In G. L. Jepsen, E. Mayr, and G. G. Simpson (eds.). *Genetics, Paleontology, and Evolution*. Princeton: Princeton University Press, 1949. Pp. 309–314.

Mayr, E. "Change of genetic environment and evolution." In J. Huxley, A. C. Hardy, and E. B. Ford (eds.). *Evolution as a Process*. London: Allen & Unwin Ltd., 1954. Pp. 157–180.

Miller, R. R. "Speciation in fishes of the genera *Cyprinodon* and *Empetrichthys*, inhabiting the Death Valley region," *Evolution*, 4 (1950), 155–163.

Moody, P. A. "A simple model of 'drift' in small populations," *Evolution*, 1 (1947), 217–218.

Sheppard, P. M. *Natural Selection and Heredity*. New York: Harper & Brothers, Torchbook 528, 1960.

Spencer, W. P. "Genetic drift in a population of *Drosophila immigrans*," *Evolution*, 1 (1947), 103–110.

Wright, S. "Evolution in Mendelian populations," *Genetics*, 16 (1931), 97–159. (Contains the mathematical background of much of modern evolutionary theory.)

Wright, S. "On the roles of directed and random changes in gene frequency in the genetics of populations," *Evolution*, 2 (1948), 279–294.

CHAPTER 20

NATURAL SELECTION: I

In the preceding chapter we emphasized the point that populations have a tendency to remain in genetic equilibrium but that various forces tend to upset this equilibrium. Of these forces we discussed mutation pressure and genetic drift, saving for later consideration the most potent force of all: natural selection. In Chapters 2 and 15 we discussed the general principles of natural selection, and in Chapter 16 we saw examples of it at work in a state of nature. Now we turn our attention to some of the factors involved in natural selection and some of the ways in which it operates to produce evolutionary change.

MUTATIONS AS RAW MATERIALS FOR NATURAL SELECTION

Let us look more critically at mutations and ask whether they really possess the qualifications for the important role assigned them in the modern theory of natural selection.

Critics of the idea have emphasized the point that most of the mutations we study in our laboratories are harmful, not beneficial. The multitudinous mutations to which students of genetics in *Drosophila* devote themselves are almost all of the nature of abnormalities and malformations. Even when no marked structural abnormality is involved, mutations frequently reduce the viability, or fertility, of their possessors. Since, as we have noted (p. 355), the leaving of disproportionately large numbers of offspring is the principal hallmark of success, reduced viability and fertility are at least as detrimental as are malformations of structure.

Nevertheless the fact that not all mutations are harmful is emphasized by the increasing use man makes of mutations to *improve* cultivated plants. In this case mutations are induced by subjecting plants to irradiation, such as that from X rays, radioactive cobalt, and even ultraviolet light. Some of the mutations obtained have resulted in barley having increased stiffness of the straw (Gustafsson, 1947); penicillin-producing mold giving greatly increased yields of antibiotic (Raper, 1947); wheat having increased resistance to rust; peanuts having thicker shells and higher yields than usual; and many other things. (For a popular account see Manchester, 1958.) In a state of nature such mutations might be expected to occur, though infrequently. When they did occur, however, if they afforded some advantage to their possessors we might expect natural selection to favor them much as man does when he selects them for propagation.

In Chapter 17 we mentioned the strains of houseflies that have become resistant to the insecticide DDT, and the strains of the colon bacillus, *Escherichia coli,* that have become resistant to streptomycin (Demerec, 1950). When this antibiotic is added to a culture of *E. coli* most of the bacteria are killed. But on the average one cell in many million has a mutation which enables it to survive, and hence to give rise to a streptomycin-resistant strain. Indeed, some of these mutations produce strains which cannot live in the absence of streptomycin; they have become streptomycin-dependent. It has been demonstrated that the mutations occur spontaneously and not because of the streptomycin treatment. The streptomycin simply acts as an agent of natural selection favoring the rare cells which possess what, under these circumstances, has become a favorable mutation. Note that under most circumstances in a state of nature a mutation causing a bacterium to be dependent upon streptomycin would be a most unfavorable mutation. This points up the fact that circumstances determine in many cases whether a mutation is harmful or beneficial to its possessor (see below).

As Dobzhansky and others have pointed out, the fact that great numbers of the mutations we observe today are deleterious is the outcome of the historical process of evolution. We mentioned previously that a given mutation occurs "spontaneously" at a rather constant, though low, rate. There is no reason to doubt that this has been going on throughout geologic time. Each mutation has "popped up" time after time as the eons have passed. Consequently, the favorable mutations have for the most part long since been incorporated into the structure of the species. The "normal" characteristics which we observe today are the accumulated favorable mutations of past ages; natural selection has incorporated them into the warp and woof of the species. But the deleterious mutations have also put in an appearance time after time. Since they *are* deleterious, however, they have been rejected by natural selection every time they have appeared. But owing to the mutability of the genes they still continue to appear from time to time. Consequently they are the mutations which come to the attention of modern observers—the deviations from normal, "normal" being comprised of the sum of favorable mutations accumulated in the past.

If the point of view just expressed is valid, we should seldom expect to observe favorable mutations in modern animals which are truly successful in their particular environmental niches. They are successful because they already incorporate most, if not all, the favorable mutations of which their genes are capable. If we really wish to observe favorable mutations, our search should follow two lines: (1) We should examine animals placed in conditions to which they have not been adapted by the historical process of evolution. (2) We should study animals which are not well adapted for life in their environments, i.e., which are not at their "adaptive peaks."

Turning to the first line of approach, we may expect that mutations which are deleterious in some environmental conditions may not necessarily be so under all conditions. We have noted the mutations of *E. coli* which are unfavorable in an environment lacking streptomycin, but are favorable in an environment containing streptomycin. We have mentioned that many of the mutations of *Drosophila* reduce the viability of the individuals exhibiting them. Timofeeff-Ressovsky (1940) investigated the viability of a number of mutations, using hatching rate of eggs as a yardstick. He found that when the flies were raised at a temperature of 25° C. most of the mutations lowered the viability, though two increased the viability slightly. Furthermore the viability varied with changes in temperature. One mutation gave above-normal viability in flies raised at 25° but slightly below normal viability at 15° and 30°. Another mutation gave slightly subnormal viability at 15° and much more markedly lower viabilities at the higher temperatures. A third mutation showed just the reverse relationships: poor viability at 15°, better at 25°, almost normal at 30°. Such results demonstrate that environmental factors are influential in determining whether a given mutation shall be harmful or beneficial to its possessor.

As yet only a few instances are known of mutations that increase viability of *Drosophila* above that of normal, wild-type individuals. Perhaps one reason for lack of data on this point is that the appropriate tests have not been made, and the appropriate environmental factors have not been detected and then varied. Such data as we have, however, indicate that mutations which are deleterious under some conditions may be neutral or beneficial under others. If the climate should change, so that *Drosophila* flies in a certain region must exist, for example, under more elevated temperatures than prevail today, some of the mutations and gene combinations which are now deleterious might then become beneficial and might consequently be favored by natural selection. In the course of time the mutation conferring increased viability at high temperatures might be incorporated into the population as "standard equipment."

Or suppose the presently prevailing temperature conditions do not change. Individuals possessing a chromosomal structure conveying increased viability at high temperatures are *preadapted* (see p. 13) for invasion of environments having higher temperatures than the general population could tolerate. Some such preadaptive mutations must have been involved, for example, in the successful invasion of hot springs, such as those in Yellowstone National Park, by animals and plants now found living in them. Mutations conferring increased viability at low temperatures would correspondingly preadapt their possessors for invasion of colder environmental niches than the niche to which the general population is adapted. In correspondence with this thought, Timofeeff-Ressovsky (1940) found that flies of *Drosophila funebris* from southern Europe have greater viability at high temperatures and lower viability at low temperatures than do flies from northwestern Europe. Equally interesting were flies from eastern Europe and neighboring sections of Asia; these flies have greater viability at both high and low temperatures than do flies from northwestern Europe, viability at intermediate temperatures being the same (Fig. 20.1). This observation correlates well with the fact that eastern Europe and adjoining portions of Asia have higher summer temperatures and lower winter temperatures than does northwestern Europe. Thus flies inhabiting the eastern regions must be adapted to withstand both extremes instead of only one.

We mentioned previously (p. 351) that many, if not most, mutations have more than one effect on the organism. One of these effects is frequently a change in viability, and it is often of more importance to the organism than are effects more noticeable to observers. Thus the success of a mutation in becoming established in a population may depend upon the mutation's effect on viability, the visible bodily changes involved being more or less incidental accompaniments. We mention this matter because it helps to explain how characteristics of no evident significance to an animal may nevertheless become established in the species. To give a hypothetical example: If a certain mutation changed the color of an insect's eyes from red to black and increased viability at low temperatures,

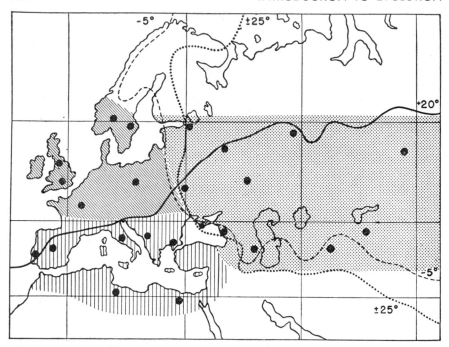

FIG. 20.1. Approximate distribution of three "temperature races" of *Drosophila funebris.*
Solid line (+20°) is the isotherm of July; dashed line (−5°) is the isotherm of January;
dotted line (±25°) is the isoline of a difference of 25°C. between the mean temperatures
of July and January. (After Timofeeff-Ressovsky; from Allee, Emerson, Park, Park, and
Schmidt, *Principles of Animal Ecology,* W. B. Saunders Company, 1949, p. 117.)

it might eventually be found that mountaintops in the region were inhabited by a black-eyed race of the insect. Such a race would have arisen, not
because there was any advantage in being black eyed, but because there
was advantage for a mountain dweller in having increased viability at low
temperatures.

   The second line of investigation likely to yield evidence of favorable
mutations involves study of animals not already at their "adaptive peaks."
We shall seldom find such relatively poorly adapted animals living in a
state of nature. Natural selection will have seen to that. But we can produce such animals experimentally, and then observe what natural selection does to them. Dobzhansky and Spassky (1947) produced populations of this kind in the form of stocks of *Drosophila* homozygous for one
or another of certain chromosomes known to contain recessive genes or
gene complexes which reduced viability and produced other deleterious
effects. Homozygotes for one such chromosome (designated PA748) had
very low viability, were slow in developing to the adult stage, and had

small, crumpled wings, elongated, cylindrical abdomens, and sometimes short and crooked legs. Obviously these flies were far below their "adaptive peak." Stocks of flies homozygous for this chromosome were established in culture bottles and raised generation after generation. The culture bottles became overcrowded and were deliberately kept that way to provide a restrictive factor making for natural selection. In the later generations of the experiment natural selection was further abetted by keeping the cultures at a temperature high enough to be deleterious. From time to time, as the generations passed, flies were removed and the PA748 chromosomes they carried were tested to determine whether there had been any improvement in the genes present. It was found that by the tenth generation viability had clearly improved and that by the fiftieth generation it was almost normal. Improvement in the speed of development from egg to adult occurred more slowly, but at some time between the thirty-eighth and fiftieth generations it had become normal. (We recall that rate of development may constitute an important factor in the relative success of a species. See p. 357.) By the fiftieth generation, also, the wings and legs had become normal, though the elongated, cylindrical abdomen had remained unchanged. Evidently appropriate mutations for rectifying the abnormalities of the abdomen had not occurred.

All told, Dobzhansky and Spassky performed this experiment with strains of flies homozygous for seven different chromosomes having deleterious effects. Of each strain two stocks were established: one received X-ray treatment; the other was left untreated. It was thought that the radiation might increase the rate at which mutations occurred and hence the rate of evolutionary change. The X-ray treatments seemed to have no particular advantageous effect, however. Ten of the fourteen experimental stocks showed improvements in the genetic contents of the respective chromosomes concerned. Three stocks remained unchanged as the generations passed, and one actually deteriorated. This is exactly the sort of result which would be expected if improvement depended upon the chance occurrence of suitable mutations for natural selection to act upon.

The results in terms of viability alone are summarized in Fig. 20.2. It will be noted that eleven of the stocks improved in viability—some very markedly, some only slightly. Two stocks declined slightly in viability; one remained unchanged.

Parallel with the stocks just mentioned the authors kept "balanced strains" in which the chromosomes under study were "protected" from the action of natural selection by the presence of normal genes in the other chromosome of the pair. Of the chromosomes possessed by these stocks six

remained unchanged or improved slightly, while eight deteriorated markedly. Six of the latter chromosomes eventually came to possess lethal genes
or gene combinations.

Evidently in the balanced strains, as in the homozygous ones, both advantageous and harmful mutations occurred. In the homozygous strains
the deleterious mutations were "weeded out" by the action of natural
selection, which at the same time favored individuals possessed of favor-

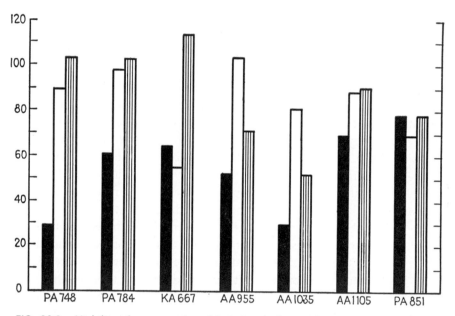

FIG. 20.2. Viability of seven strains of fruit flies before and after fifty generations of
homozygosis for deleterious genes. Black columns: initial viability before start of the
experiments. White columns: viability of homozygous untreated stocks after fifty generations. Shaded columns: viability of homozygous X-ray-treated stocks after fifty generations. Vertical axis: percentages of viability, relative to normal viability. (Redrawn
from Dobzhansky and Spassky, "Evolutionary changes in laboratory cultures of Drosophila pseudoobscura," Evolution, Vol. 1, 1947.)

able mutations. In the balanced strains, however, since natural selection
did not operate, deleterious mutations, including lethal ones, could become
established.

We have placed emphasis upon this investigation because it affords a
particularly instructive example of natural selection operating under experimental conditions. We might wish that the individual genes whose
mutation resulted in the improvements recorded could have been identified. But that would have entailed a colossal task. As it is, few readers

probably have any conception of the magnitude of the investigation we have summarized so briefly. The authors state that 410,784 flies were classified and recorded! And those must have constituted but a small fraction of the total number of flies raised. While we may not be able to "put a finger on" the individual mutations whose occurrence led to the improvements cited, we cannot doubt that such favorable mutations occurred, and that natural selection utilized them for the improvement of the strains.

THE ROLE OF HETEROZYGOTES

Slightly differing experiments in natural selection have revealed the importance of heterozygotes in evolution. Pioneer experimentation in this field was that of L'Héritier and Teissier (1937), who designed a type of cage for rearing *Drosophila* which made possible the maintenance of a large population over an extended period of time. Experiments began with populations of around 4000 individuals, all of which possessed a certain mutation. A few normal, "wild-type" flies were then introduced into the cage. Thus competition was established between normal individuals and individuals possessing a mutation. Nature was allowed to take its course as time passed and generation followed generation.

In some experiments the flies originally present possessed a malformation of the shape of the eye, called "bar eye." The population was "infected" by addition of a few normal flies. At first the population was practically 100 percent bar eyed. But in the ensuing competition the proportion of bar-eyed flies declined (Fig. 20.3). At first the decline was rapid, but as the number of bar-eyed flies decreased the rate of decline lessened. By the end of 235 days, in one experiment, bar-eyed individuals constituted only about 28 percent of the population, the remaining 72 percent being normal eyed. By the end of 426 days the bar-eyed flies constituted only about 1 percent of the population. They continued at or below this very low frequency as long as the experiment lasted. Here is another example of natural selection operating under experimental conditions. In this case the bar-eyed flies were clearly less well adapted than were normal flies and hence lost out almost completely in competition with the latter.

Another mutation in *Drosophila* is "ebony," the most evident effect of which is darkening of the body color, from the normal gray. L'Héritier and Teissier performed the same experiment starting with ebony flies. As shown in Fig. 20.3, the proportion of ebony flies declined rapidly at first; by the 235th day it had reached about 28 percent, the remaining 72 percent consisting of normal flies. But the further course of the experiment differed from that in which bar-eyed flies were in competition with normal ones. Instead of almost disappearing, ebony flies continued to constitute around 15 percent of the population as long as the experiment continued; i.e., an equilibrium of about 85 percent normal flies and 15 percent ebony flies was established. Why was there this difference between the two experiments? Why did not the ebony flies disappear almost completely, as the bar-eyed ones had? Evidently the normal flies were more efficient or better

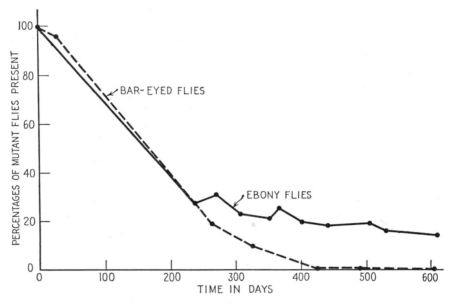

FIG. 20.3. Natural selection operating in (1) competition between normal fruit flies and bar-eyed ones (dashed line) and (2) competition between normal fruit flies and ebony flies (solid line). (Based on data of L'Héritier and Teissier, 1937.)

adapted than were the ebony ones. Yet after the initial decline ebony individuals continued to form a substantial "minority group."

Since "ebony" is a recessive mutation, all flies actually exhibiting this darkened body color are homozygous for the recessive gene, i.e., are *ee* in genetic constitution. Evidently such flies were at a disadvantage in competition with normal flies. Many of the homozygous recessive individuals (*ee*) which appeared in any generation, however, were the offspring, not of homozygous recessive parents, but of heterozygous parents (*Ee*). It will be recalled that when two such parents mate (*Ee* × *Ee*) one-fourth of their offspring are expected to be homozygous recessive (*ee*). It seems likely, then, that ebony flies continued to appear generation after generation because they continually arose from heterozygous parents. The latter did not exhibit the ebony trait in their own bodies, although they carried the recessive gene for it. Evidently these heterozygous parents (*Ee*) were at no disadvantage in the competition, as compared to homozygous normal parents (*EE*). Indeed, there is evidence that heterozygotes had one advantage over homozygous normal individuals. In an independent investigation Timofeeff-Ressovsky found that, while homozygous ebony flies had lower viability than did homozygous normal flies, individuals heterozygous for the ebony gene had actually higher viability than did homozygous normal flies. This phenomenon is probably a form of **"hybrid vigor" (heterosis),** by virtue of which hybrids are frequently larger, stronger, and more vigorous than are purebred strains. The hybrid corn so prevalent on modern farms is a familiar example of hybrid vigor, as is the mule, which possesses some superiorities over either of its parents, the horse and the donkey.

In sum, we see that in the experiment involving competition between ebony and normal flies both negative and positive natural selection (p. 357) were at work. Negative selection tended to eliminate the homozygous recessives, i.e., the ebony flies. Positive selection tended to increase the proportion of *heterozygous* flies. The result of the opposing forces was eventual establishment of an equilibrium at a point at which the strength of the negative selection against recessive homozygotes equaled the strength of the positive selection favoring heterozygotes. In the experiment cited, the equilibrium was reached when about 85 percent of the flies had normal color (some being homozygous, some heterozygous), and 15 percent had ebony color. In each generation this 15 percent of ebony flies arose largely as a "by-product" of the matings of the favored heterozygous flies.

Experiments corroborating the one just described were performed by Reed and Reed (1948). Instead of concentrating on a single mutant gene, these authors used a strain containing a chromosomal constitution which conferred semisterility and poor viability, amounting almost to lethality. Obviously, flies homozygous for this M-5 chromosome were at an enormous disadvantage. When flies possessing this chromosome were placed in competition with substantially normal flies the proportion of individuals having the chromosome declined with great rapidity. By the end of two months natural selection had completed its main task, and approximate equilibrium had been reached. Although the chromosome in question conferred such great disadvantage upon flies homozygous for it, it was not eliminated from the population. Retention was due to the fact that flies heterozygous for the chromosome were actually more successful than were homozygous "normal" flies.

A comparable situation was found to exist in populations of *Drosophila pseudoobscura* studied by Dobzhansky (1947, 1950). As background for understanding of this study, it is necessary to recall that genes are arranged in a straight line down the length of a chromosome (a string of beads is a useful analogy if not applied too literally). No one has yet seen the genes, but there are ways of determining their locations relative to each other. Within recent years the value for genetic studies of the relatively huge chromosomes found in the cells of the salivary glands of *Drosophila* larvae has been appreciated. These "giant chromosomes" are characterized by an arrangement of cross-banding so varied in configuration and arrangement of bands that each portion of each chromosome is identifiable under the microscope. Furthermore, investigations, description of which is outside the province of this book, have revealed that certain bands are associated with the presence of certain genes. This is not to say that the bands *are* the genes, but merely that the sequence in which the bands occur along the chromosome may be taken as visual indication of the sequence in which the genes occur in that chromosome. In the cells of *Drosophila* there are four pairs of chromosomes; these are numbered for convenience, one of the larger pairs being referred to as the third chromosomes. In the investigation mentioned, Dobzhansky concentrated attention on the third chromosome of *Drosophila pseudoobscura*. He found that in some individuals the bands, and hence the genes, on this chromosome were arranged in one sequence, in other individuals in other sequences. **Inversions** of longer or shorter sections of the chromosome were frequent. For example, if we represent bands, or genes, by letters, we might have a chromosome with the structure *A B C D E F G H I J*. This might be called the "standard" arrangement and be found in some individuals of a race or species. Some other individuals might have the same genes in this chromosome but have them arranged differently: the section *C D E F* might be turned around, inverted, perhaps. Then the whole chromosome would have the sequence: *A B F E D C G H I J*. If both members of this pair of chromosomes in an individual had the inverted arrangement, the individual would be called an "inversion homozygote." If the individual possessed one uninverted or "standard" chromosome and one inverted chromosome, that individual would be termed an "inversion heterozygote."

In the third chromosome of *Drosophila pseudoobscura* at least twenty-one different gene sequences have been identified. Not all of these are possessed by individuals in any one portion of the range covered by the species. There are, however, definite geographic trends in the distributions of the arrangements, some arrangements being common in one locality, rare in another.

In one locality, Piñon Flats, on Mount San Jacinto in southern California, four such arrangements are found. They are identified by the symbols ST, CH, AR, and TL, the meanings of which need not concern us. The point of particular interest at present is that the relative frequencies of these arrangements fluctuate with the seasons. As shown in Fig. 20.4, in March of each year about 52 percent of the chromosomes found in these flies are ST chromosomes, about 23 percent are CH ones, about 18 percent AR, and about 7 percent TL. As the spring progresses these frequencies change for the first three mentioned, while the frequency of the TL chromosome fluctuates but little. The ST chromosome rapidly diminishes in frequency, while the CH and AR chromosomes correspondingly increase. Fig. 20.4 shows the maximum frequency of AR as reached in May, that of CH in June. In the latter month the ST chromosome is at its lowest frequency. Following its peak, the AR chromosome declines somewhat in frequency, while the CH

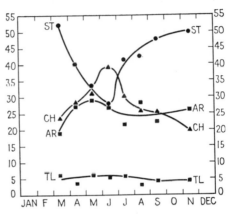

FIG. 20.4. Changes in frequencies of four different gene arrangements in third chromosomes of the fruit-fly population of Piñon Flats, California. Vertical axis: frequencies, in percentage. Horizontal axis: successive months. Combined data for six years of observation. (Redrawn from Dobzhansky, "Adaptive changes induced by natural selection in wild populations of Drosophila," Evolution, Vol. 1, 1947.)

chromosome declines much more rapidly and to much greater extent. Contrariwise, the ST chromosome increases rapidly in frequency until by November it has practically the same frequency it had in March.

How can we account for seasonal fluctuation of this kind in gene arrangements of chromosomes? Parenthetically we should note that these flies, of whatever gene arrangement, all look alike as far as external visible characteristics are concerned. Only microscopic examination of the chromosomes in salivary glands of the larvae reveals any differences. The differences obviously are of a most subtle nature. But subtle or not, they evidently are important in the lives of the flies, important enough so that natural selection acts upon them. It seems reasonable to conclude that the differences have something to do with either viability or fertility, or both. It would seem, for example, that under conditions prevailing in the spring months carriers of CH chromosomes have some advantage over carriers of ST chromosomes, leaving more surviving progeny on the average and thus leading to the observed increase in frequency of CH chromosomes, with concomitant decrease in frequency of ST chromosomes. Following the same line of thought, we may conclude that conditions during the summer favor carriers of ST chromosomes; hence their numbers increase. The same summer conditions are evidently unfavorable for carriers of CH chromosomes, with resulting decline in numbers. Perhaps differences in temperature are concerned in the matter. Specifically we might interpret the graph (Fig. 20.4) as indicating that during the heat of summer carriers of ST chromosomes are at a relative advantage (and hence increase in numbers rapidly), while carriers of CH chromosomes are at relative disadvantage (and hence decline in numbers).

To test interpretations of the kind suggested, Dobzhansky set up experiments in natural selection, using population cages much like those of L'Héritier and Teissier (see p. 457). In one experiment several hundred flies having two different gene arrangements in the desired proportions were placed in a cage. Within a single generation the population increased to the maximum compatible with the amount of food available—usually to between 2000 and 4000 flies. The experimenter recorded that the numbers of eggs deposited were tens to hundreds of times greater than the numbers of adult flies that hatched. "The competition for survival is intense." Once a month samples of eggs were taken and the salivary gland chromosomes of larvae hatching from them were studied. In this way changes in the relative frequencies of the different gene arrangements were traced.

It was found that when population cages were kept in the cold ($16\frac{1}{2}°$ C.) no changes in frequencies of gene arrangements occurred. The original relative proportions continued generation after generation. At this temperature there is evidently little if any difference in advantageousness among the various gene arrangements.

When the cages were kept at room temperature or higher (25° C.), however, progressive changes occurred until a definite equilibrium was established. Fig. 20.5 shows the results of one such experiment. The population was established in March. In this population 10.7 percent of the third chromosomes were ST, 89.3 percent were CH. As the graph shows, the frequency of ST chromosomes nearly doubled in the first month and continued to rise rapidly in succeeding months (it is to be emphasized that the temperature throughout this time remained constant, at 25° C., i.e., the passing months did not bring temperature changes for the flies). An equilibrium was reached by about the end of December (the graph, Fig. 20.5, does not include the concluding months of the experiment). In experiments involving ST and CH chromosomes equilibrium was reached when about 70 percent of the chromosomes were ST, about 30 percent of them CH. The rapid increase in relative number of ST chromosomes in a population maintained at a high temperature affords evidence that the conclusion concerning the relative advantage of the ST arrangement in the heat of summer (see above) is valid.

Of equal interest with this conclusion is the fact that an equilibrium is eventually established. If the CH chromosome confers a disadvantage at high temperatures why does it not disappear entirely? Following mathematical analyses by Sewall Wright the experimenter concluded that the CH chromosomes do not disappear entirely because flies heterozygous for them (i.e., having one CH third chromosome and one ST third chromosome—written: ST/CH) are more successful than are either

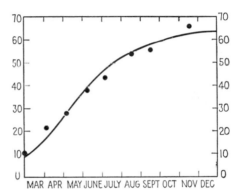

FIG. 20.5. Frequency of ST chromosomes (in percentage) in an experiment in which the ST gene arrangement was in competition with the CH gene arrangement at the temperature of 25°C. (Redrawn from Dobzhansky, "Adaptive changes induced by natural selection in wild populations of *Drosophila,*" *Evolution,* Vol. 1, 1947.)

flies homozygous for CH (i.e., CH/CH) or flies homozygous for ST (i.e., ST/ST). It will be recalled that this is the explanation reached for the experimental results obtained by L'Héritier and Teissier and by Reed and Reed. Evidently ST/CH heterozygotes are characterized by that hybrid vigor previously referred to (p. 459) and hence have an advantage over *both* kinds of homozygotes (ST/ST and CH/CH). As Dobzhansky expressed it, "The populations at equilibrium contain the greatest possible proportions of the well adapted heterozygotes compatible with the lowest possible proportions of the relatively ill adapted homozygotes."

It is of interest that in one experiment no equilibrium was reached. This experiment involved the relatively rare TL chromosome (Fig. 20.4), placed in competition with the ST chromosome. The latter "won out" entirely, the TL chromosome virtually disappearing from the population. Evidently, then, the ST/TL heterozygote enjoys no advantage over the ST/ST homozygote (or, of course, over the TL/TL homozygote), and hence the TL chromosome eventually disappears. Why then does the TL chromosome persist in appearing with a constant though low frequency in the Piñon Flats population (Fig. 20.4)? The answer was given by another experiment in which the TL chromosome was placed in competition with the AR chromosome. In this case an equilibrium *was* established, at a point where about 80 percent of the third chromosomes were AR, about 20 percent TL, indicating that AR/TL heterozygotes have an advantage over AR/AR homozygotes and TL/TL homozygotes. This advantage of the heterozygotes would be sufficient to keep the TL chromosome from disappearing from the Piñon Flats population, even though ST/TL heterozygotes had no advantage over their respective homozygotes. TL chromosomes "form adaptively valuable heterozygotes with AR but not with ST chromosomes present in the same populations."

One aspect of natural selection evident in this experiment of Dobzhansky's, as well as in that of Reed and Reed (pp. 459–460), deserves especial emphasis. That is the *rapidity* with which changes are produced. Traditionally students of evolution have assumed that natural selection must operate very slowly—that time in the bountiful quantities provided by geologic history must be available for detectable results to be achieved. This was an assumption, but one generally accepted. In contrast to this view are these recent experiments in natural selection, in one of which (Reed and Reed) natural selection accomplished the greater part of its work within two months, and in the other of which natural selection operated with comparable rapidity, to produce changes with changing seasons of the year. Such rapidity and delicacy of control by natural selection came as a distinct, though welcome, surprise. To be sure, these experiments and observations deal with one particular, rapidly breeding organism. But even so, the number of generations required for production of significant change is small.

We have described Dobzhansky's experiment in some detail, partly because of its trail-blazing nature, partly because it is typical of results obtained subsequently by other investigators. Succeeding investigations have illuminated many facets of heterozygote superiority. What factors are involved? We have seen that temperature is one; food supply has been found to be another. The adaptive values of different gene combinations differ with differing foods (differing species of yeasts and bacteria).

Hence "the types of food predominant in a given region may be important in determining the chromosomal composition of the *Drosophila* populations which inhabit this region" (da Cunha, 1955). Spiess and others have studied the physiological properties of homozygotes and heterozygotes for different gene arrangements, investigating the effect of the latter on such things as egg-laying capacity, longevity, wing-beat frequency, and wing dimensions. These investigations and a multitude of others were summarized by da Cunha (1955).

In this connection we should note that the chromosomal structures investigated constitute another example of **balanced polymorphism.** The polymorphism discussed earlier (pp. 366–376) dealt with structures visible to the unaided eye; the present polymorphism is revealed only with the aid of a microscope. But it is nonetheless real. Previously we have noted cases of polymorphism connected with action of predators (e.g., in industrial melanism). The present polymorphism is maintained by virtue of heterozygote superiority (which indeed, as we noted, may also be involved in industrial melanism). Just *what* is superior about a heterozygote? In most cases the necessary investigations have not been made to answer the question. But interestingly enough man himself provides an example of balanced polymorphism maintained in this manner, a case in which the question of what is superior has been determined. Persons suffering from a severe disease known as **sickle-cell anemia** are homozygous for the gene concerned. Heterozygotes for the gene are not diseased but are detectable by virtue of the fact that their red blood cells will "sickle" (assume unusual shapes when deprived of oxygen). Only a small proportion of sickle-cell homozygotes live to reproduce and pass on the gene. Yet in some sections of Africa the gene remains at a fairly high level of frequency in the gene pool. Why does not the gene disappear? Evidently, as in the experiments described above, it would not disappear if heterozygotes enjoyed some advantage. In this case Allison was able to show what the advantage is. "The sickle-cell heterozygote is relatively resistant to malignant tertian malaria and has as much as a 25 per cent better chance of attaining adulthood than the normal homozygote in parts of Africa where malaria is hyperendemic" (Allison, 1959; see also Allison, 1955). Thus the gene remains in a balanced state, the point of equilibrium being established by the tendency of the genes to be lost through low viability of homozygotes, counteracted by the tendency of the genes to increase in number by virtue of the fact that heterozygotes survive better, and thus presumably reproduce more, than do persons lacking the gene entirely (homozygous "normals"). The small proportion of sickle-cell anemia patients produced in each generation is a price the population pays for increased ability to survive the ravages of malaria.

Genetic Homeostasis

Closely linked to heterozygote superiority is the concept of genetic homeostasis. While this term has unfortunately been used in more than one sense (Waddington, 1953), the usage pertinent to our discussion is as a name for the *self-regulating* ability of a population which enables it to survive environmental change or diversity. The population is said to be "buffered" against change. The idea is analogous to that of the physiological homeostasis of the human body. If one kidney is destroyed or removed, for example, the other kidney will adjust and compensate for the lost organ, and the body will continue to function normally. This ability to adjust to change and so to continue normal life is homeostasis. The idea of genetic homeostasis is that populations possess a capability of self-regulation so that they can continue normal existence under a variety of environmental conditions and so survive environmental vicissitudes which would destroy populations less capable of "rolling with the punch."

We may expect that natural selection will favor the development and maintenance by a population of such homeostasis. We note that genetic homeostasis has much in common with the Baldwin effect (pp. 420–425) and with the canalization of embryonic development (pp. 421–422). All three refer to self-regulating properties permitting normal existence in varied environments. Natural selection favoring the development of such properties has been termed **stabilizing selection** (Schmalhausen, 1949), or **canalizing selection** (Waddington, 1953).

Evidence is accumulating that populations *heterozygous* for many gene pairs are better buffered against change than are populations composed of homozygotes. This evidence comes both from experiments with such laboratory forms as *Drosophila* (see Beardmore, Dobzhansky, and Pavlovsky, 1960) and from experiments with domestic animals (largely summarized in Lerner, 1954). Apparently both wild populations and successful breeds of domestic animals have a high degree of heterozygosity for genes which are deleterious when homozygous. If attempts are made to rid the population of these genes the population becomes less viable, or fertile, or able to withstand environmental change. Lerner, for example, described a series of experiments with a hereditary abnormality of chickens known as "crooked toes." The genes for this are probably present in all stocks of chickens. The experimenters attempted by selection and inbreeding to produce a strain of birds free from the gene, but met with only partial success since "the fitness of the . . . line has continually dropped and only a few survivors are available each year for reproduction." On the other hand, selection and inbreeding were successful in establishing an almost pure-breeding line having the crooked-toes character; in this line the reproductive capacity was not diminished as it was in the other line.

The crooked-toes example is illustrative of the evidence accumulating that successful, viable populations, wild or domestic, normally consist of individuals having a high degree of heterozygosity. Experimental evidence even suggests that viability can be increased by increasing the degree of heterozygosity artificially, by inducing new mutations with irradiation (see Dobzhansky, 1959). (Such results may have fascinating implications for the question of the possible genetic effect of irradiation of mankind, from natural and artificial sources, e.g., atomic bomb fallout. But such discussion is outside our present field of consideration.)

We may note that the view of population structure just described contrasts with the view formerly held that most wild populations consist of individuals homozygous for most of their genes, which are regarded as the "normal" genes. If this were true most mutations would be harmful to homozygotes and, if they produced a phenotypic effect in heterozygotes, to heterozygotes also. (We have noted previously that many if not most mutations do have some effect upon heterozygotes, p. 347.) This "classical hypothesis" made possible the separation of "good" genes from "bad" genes. According to the "balance hypothesis" (the terms are Dobzhansky's, 1959), on the other hand, "good" genes are those which contribute to the fitness of individuals heterozygous for them, almost regardless of their effect in individuals homozygous for them.

We say "almost" in this last sentence because we must not forget that there *are* genes which are harmful to both homozygotes and heterozygotes. Thus the majority of *lethal* (pp. 389–390) mutants in *Drosophila* are harmful in heterozygotes, even though many mutations that stop short of lethality, when individuals are homozygous for them, form adaptively superior heterozygotes. And in cases not involving lethality heterozygotes for a given pair of genes may be inferior to one or both of the homozygotes (*Aa* inferior to *AA* and/or *aa*). What determines whether *Aa* will be inferior or superior? Many factors are involved, some genetic, some environmental. A gene pair does not operate in a vacuum; it is part of the complete genotype of the individual. Its effects are conditioned by the other genes present. This integrated genotype is the totality that produces the phenotype upon which natural selection operates. Thus all the genes of the individual may be involved in determining in any given instance whether *AA* or *Aa* or *aa* shall be adaptively superior.

We see, therefore, that there are elements of truth in both the "classical" and the "balance" hypothesis of population structure. Yet increasing evidence suggests that natural selection favors a balanced population structure composed of many genotypes in which the genes interact to produce a high average of such qualities as superior viability, fertility, and adaptability to change.

What are the advantages of such a population structure? (1) Most of the individuals in a population of this kind have the superior qualities just listed even though a small proportion may be abnormal by-products. (2) The population has genetic reserves upon which it can draw if adaptation to differing conditions becomes necessary or desirable. As we noted earlier, genes which are deleterious in some environments may not be so in others. In other conditions they may be positively advantageous. Thus by keeping these genes and gene arrangements from disappearing natural selection is providing a race or species with reserves upon which it may draw if and when conditions change. Referring again to the experiment with *Drosophila* (Fig. 20.4), we recall that the CH gene arrangement is relatively disadvantageous in summer months, although it contributes largely to the building up of the population in the spring. Suppose that by fall of some year the CH chromosome should have disappeared entirely, instead of merely being decreased in frequency. The effect would be to deprive the stock of a gene arrangement which would evidently be of distinct advantage to the species when spring came again. Similarly, if the ST arrangement died out in the spring, the species would have lost a genetic constitution valuable for the increase of its numbers during summer and early fall. Consequently, the genetic mechanism (heterozygote superiority) which leads to a balanced polymorphism, keeping both ST and CH in the population, makes a distinct contribution to the success of the species as it faces the changing seasons. Other genes and gene arrangements kept from disappearance by the means described may not be brought into play by the changing seasons but may be in readiness for use if longer-range changes occur in the environment, or if the species attempts to invade a different environmental niche. Thus the species may be well adapted to one environment and yet not lose the hereditary plasticity which will enable it to adjust to environmental change or to invade different environmental niches.

In sum, what does natural selection favor? We have spoken previously of the positive action of natural selection in favoring certain mutations or characteristics. Now we can appreciate that the matter is really more complex than such a statement implies. To a considerable extent the Mendelian population, rather than the individual, is the unit upon which natural selection operates. Such a population has a great variety of genotypes present. Natural selection will favor the development of an aggregate of genotypes which will react to produce for the population a high level of adaptive and homeostatic properties, with resultant high efficiency in reproduction.

THE ROLES OF ISOLATION

We have seen that large, random-breeding populations have a tendency to maintain a genetic equilibrium which is the antithesis of evolutionary change (pp. 427–436). We have likened such equilibrium to an inertia which evolutionary processes must overcome if change is to be effected. Since the equilibrium is connected with large population size, any factors which tend to break up large populations into smaller ones are likely to contribute to evolutionary change. Thus isolation, and factors giving rise to it, are important in evolution.

Types of Isolation

Geographic isolation is the most easily visualized type. It exists when two populations, or two parts of one population, are separated by some geographic barrier (examples listed on p. 272). The effectiveness for evolution of this, or any other, type of isolation resides in the fact that it prevents, or greatly reduces, exchange of genes between the populations so isolated. Such isolated populations are more or less completely "out of touch with each other," genetically, and hence the occurrence of new mutations, genetic drift, the action of natural selection, etc., in one population has no effect on the other populations.

As a corollary of the fact that isolation is important only as a means of impeding gene interchange we should note that the only isolation of importance is that concerned with the *breeding* of animals. Most species of higher animals have definite periods of breeding; it is isolation during these periods which counts. Many migratory birds, for example, collect into great flocks and range over vast territories, yet when the breeding season approaches individuals return to the same locality, even the same dooryard, where they themselves were hatched. The prolonged and hazardous migration undertaken by individual salmon in returning to spawn in the stream where they began life is another classic example. It is the relative isolation of these local breeding groups which affects gene distribution and hence is important for evolution.

The local populations just mentioned are frequently not separated from each other by mountain ranges, deserts, and other obvious geographic features. As we noted earlier (p. 445), *distance* is in itself a barrier—if not a complete one, at least one that in practice is effective (see Wright, 1943). Its effectiveness arises in large part from what we may call the homing or territorial tendency of animals. It is the exception rather than the rule for animals to carry on their reproductive activities far from the region in which they themselves first saw the light of day. As mentioned previously (p. 445), individual animals commonly establish more or less clearly delimited home territories. They do not usually stray far from these, at least at the time of breeding. Whatever the psychological concomitants, "home" evidently has significance in the lives of most animals. Even such able travelers as birds commonly use their wings to return home, if removed from it by some accident such as a storm, rather than to travel to some other locality and establish a new place of residence, as Mayr has remarked.

Environmental isolation is a term which the author feels may be more evident in meaning than is the commonly used term "ecological isolation" or the synonymous "habitat isolation" of Moore (1949). As the term implies, populations that are environmentally isolated live under different environmental conditions, at least during the breeding period. A fish and a seed-eating bird are environmentally isolated even though they live in the same locality. Similarly, an insect which inhabits only coniferous trees is environmentally isolated from an insect which inhabits only deciduous trees, even though both live in the same wood lot. Beetles which spend their lives burrowing in the ground are environmentally isolated from beetles which spend their lives on trees.

We note that, whereas geographic isolation depends upon separation in *space,* environmental isolation depends upon separation resulting from differences in the food, habits, and physiological requirements of animals.

We may well ask: Do we ever find the one type of isolation without the other? Do animals ever occupy somewhat different positions in space without at the same time being faced with somewhat different environmental conditions? Conversely, are animals ever faced with differing environmental conditions while occupying the same position in space? Certainly differences in position in space usually, if not always, involve differences in environment, and differences in environment involve differences in position in space. The fish in a lake is not occupying the same position in space as is the bird flying overhead. An insect on coniferous trees is not occupying the same position in space as is an insect on deciduous trees. A beetle burrowing in the ground is not occupying the same position in space as is a beetle living on trees. Geographic isolation and environmental isolation thus go hand in hand. Sometimes one predominates, sometimes the other. If the main difference between the territories occupied by two species is difference in location, environmental conditions being similar, we say that the species are geographically isolated. In doing so, we merely overlook what environmental differences there are. If, on the other hand, the main differences between the territories occupied by two species are differences in environmental conditions (ground dwelling versus tree living, for example), we say that the species are environmentally isolated. In this case we overlook the fact that the two species are also geographically isolated in the sense of not occupying the same position in space—in the vertical dimension of space rather than in its horizontal dimension. All sorts of intermediate conditions exist. Moore (1949) has well said, "The distinction between geographical and habitat isolation is merely quantitative."

We have labored this point at some length because of the occurrence of a prolonged but rather footless debate as to which is more important in evolution, geographic isolation or environmental (i.e., ecological) isolation. The controversy has centered around the query as to whether environmental isolation can promote evolutionary change in the absence of geographic isolation. If, as we have maintained, the one never occurs without some degree of the other, the point of the query vanishes. It is then apparent that isolation (i.e., nonbiological isolation; see below) always entails some separation in space, this being accompanied by greater or lesser differences in environment. (See Mayr, 1947, 1949, for further discussion of this matter.)

Under the term **reproductive isolation** we group a great variety of biological restrictions to gene interchange. The two types of isolation just discussed prevent individuals from coming into contact or reduce the likelihood of their doing so. But suppose individuals *do* come into contact, will interbreeding, with consequent interchange of genes, occur? Many factors may prevent exchange of genes and thus constitute means of biological isolation.

In some cases interbreeding is not *possible*. At least two types of factors may be involved: (1) The anatomies of the two populations may be so unlike that copulation between males of one population and females of the other is impossible. This so-called mechanical isolation is sometimes encountered in insects with highly complex genital organs. A comparable situation exists in those plants in which the flower structure is such that cross-pollination cannot occur. (2) The breeding seasons of the two species may not coincide. Flowers of one population of plants may open and then disappear before the flowers of another population mature. One population of insects in which adults live but a few days may be effectively isolated from another population if the periods of emergence of adults in the two do not coincide.

In other cases interbreeding is possible but does not occur (sexual or psychological isolation; ethological isolation). In many insects copulation is preceded by rather elaborate courtship behavior. Closely related species may differ in details of this ritual. Females readily accept only males which observe the punctilios of courtship behavior characteristic of their species. This behavior may be the expression of a form of *preference* in the choice of mates. It clearly seems to be such in higher animals. Thus related species of deer mice (*Peromyscus*) are found not to interbreed in a state of nature, although some will do so readily enough when placed in cages together, i.e., when possibility of choice is removed.

That this tendency to selective or preferential mating may be a potent force is suggested by experiments of Reed and Reed (1950). We noted (p. 459) an earlier experiment by these investigators in which it was found that when two genetic types of fruit flies were placed in competition an equilibrium was reached, the more deleterious genetic type not being completely eliminated from the population. Quite otherwise were the results of another experiment in which fruit flies having the mutant gene for "white eye" were placed in competition with normal wild-type (red-eyed) flies. In twenty-five generations the white-eye gene disappeared from the population completely. The investigators determined that white-eyed flies were not less *viable* than were wild-type individuals. Tests indicated, however, that the mating behaviors of white-eyed and red-eyed flies were strikingly different. Both red-eyed and white-eyed females "preferred" to mate with red-eyed males. The strength of this preferential mating was determined, and expressed mathematically, calculations showing that it was sufficient to account for the disappearance of the white-eye gene in the number of generations within which that elimination was observed to occur. (See also "Hybridization: Disadvantageous," pp. 474–477.)

Reproductive isolation may exist even in cases in which matings between populations take place. (1) Fertilization may not occur as a result of the mating. Sperm cells may fail to reach the eggs, or if they reach them may not enter and fertilize them. In plants, pollen tube growth may be arrested before the ovule is reached. (2) Fertilized eggs may be formed, but the hybrid individuals may prove to be inviable. This inviability may express itself at any time: as soon as the fertilized eggs are formed, early in embryonic development, later in embryonic life, or after birth but before sexual maturity is reached. (3) Hybrids may live to sexual maturity but may be sterile so that they cannot pass on the genes they have received. Mules, hybrids between horse and donkey, form well-known examples of this type of isolation (although rare fertile individuals occur).

All of the isolating mechanisms we have enumerated, geographic, environmental, and reproductive, may result in isolation which is complete or partial in its effectiveness. And obviously several of them may be operative simultaneously in any given situation to prevent or reduce gene interchange between populations.

Action of Isolation

With regard to their function in evolution we may group the three types of isolation into two categories: (1) geographic-environmental; (2) reproductive. The two play different roles in evolution (Mayr, 1959).

Geographic-environmental isolation causes two populations or subpopulations to be separated so that each goes its own way in acquiring mutations, and in being acted upon by such forces as genetic drift and natural selection. Two geographically separated populations are said to be **allopatric.** We should note that isolation between two allopatric populations may not always be complete. If it is not, neighboring populations may interbreed in regions in which they come into contact (frequently the case between neighboring subspecies, pp. 320–321). Or individuals may migrate from one population to another. If interbreeding occurs in either of these ways the gene pools of the two populations will not remain as completely separate as they would under conditions of complete isolation. The effect of this mingling of genes may be small or large, depending upon the extent to which isolation is incomplete. (See Wright, 1931; also discussion of effects of hybridization, pp. 474–481.)

We conclude that at least some degree of geographic-environmental isolation is necessary as a first step in the development of genetic diversity between populations. So long as the gene pool remains undivided, two differing populations cannot arise from it. (As an exception to this statement we recall the action of polyploidy, pp. 418–420.) Conversely, when the gene pool does become divided, by geographic-environmental factors, the allopatric populations so produced may become differentiated in ways which give rise to reproductive isolation. Following the development of reproductive isolation the populations may come into contact (e.g., by migration) and still retain the integrity of their respective gene pools. Two populations living in the same area are said to be **sympatric.** Sympatric populations must always be reproductively isolated from each other if they are not to merge into a single amalgamated population.

Apparently, then, geographic-environmental isolation is primary: the first steps in species formation will not be taken without it (except in the case of polyploidy). The attainment of reproductive isolation is, as previously noted (pp. 314–317), the most conspicuous sign that the species level of evolutionary change has been reached.

HYBRIDIZATION IN EVOLUTION

Since the primary role of isolation is the prevention of hybridization, it is now appropriate to inquire further into the evolutionary significance of interbreeding between populations and of the failure of this to occur. Paradoxically, hybridization is important in evolution when it occurs and when it does not.

Hybridization: Disadvantageous

We may consider first the importance of the failure of hybridization to take place. As noted, different species do not usually interbreed or if they do interbreed they do not usually produce viable hybrids. Moreover, when viable hybrids between species are produced they are generally sterile or of such low fertility that the amount of reproduction is negligible. What is the value to a species of failure to produce "successful" hybrids?

Usually species as we find them under natural conditions are well adapted for particular environmental niches. Suppose that hybrids are produced between two such species, A and B. These hybrids will ordinarily possess some of the characteristics of species A, some of species B. Consequently, in most cases the hybrids will not be so well adapted for life in the environmental niche occupied by species A as is species A itself. Neither will they be so well adapted for the niche occupied by species B as is species B itself. In other words, the hybrids will usually "fall between two stools." Accordingly, in such cases hybrids would represent biological wastage. We may anticipate, therefore, that species which produced hybrids under these circumstances would be wasting their energies and hence would be at a disadvantage in competition with species that concentrated on production of nonhybrid offspring.

At this point we come upon a debate of long standing, participated in by Darwin himself in fact (Mayr, 1959). There is abundant observational evidence that isolating mechanisms arise as the more or less incidental accompaniment of adaptive changes mainly concerned with such matters as better adaptation to environment, reduction of competition, and the like. The question is, will natural selection act directly to cause populations to develop isolating mechanisms? Will natural selection favor genetic factors that have as their sole or main effect the production or intensification of isolating mechanisms (such as hybrid sterility, preferential mating, and the like)?

We have noted above that one means by which reproductive isolation, and hence failure to hybridize, is achieved is through exercise of "choice" or "preference" in mating (selective or preferential mating). Koopman (1950) found that he was able to obtain intensification of the tendency to selective mating exhibited by fruit flies of the two sibling species *Drosophila pseudoobscura* and *D. persimilis*. These two are so similar that they cannot be told apart by external structure. Yet when hybrids between them are produced, the male hybrids are sterile, and the female hybrids when mated with males of either parent species "lay the usual number of eggs, but the larvae arising from these eggs have such poor viability that in competition with the larvae of the pure species, as in population cages, they never reach the adult state." Obviously, then, such hybrids are worthless to the species, representing true biological wastage. Actually hybrids between *pseudoobscura* and *persimilis* have never been found in a state of nature. The species are somewhat isolated from each other ecologically, preferring slightly different environments, but when they do occur together sexual isolation of the selective mating type tends to prevent production of hybrids. Using a modified L'Héritier-Teissier population cage, Koopman demonstrated that in artificial mixed populations of *pseudoobscura* and *persimilis* the number of hybrid individuals could be made to decline rapidly by removing the hybrids which were produced. This had the effect of removing from the gene pools of the two species genes contributed by individuals which tended *not* to mate with members of their own species. Thus the tendency of each species to mate within its own species (homogamic mating) was intensified; consequently the number of hybrids produced decreased markedly in the course of a few generations. Koopman ascribed this decline to the action of natural selection in the population cages since he concluded that the poor viability and sterility of hybrids and their offspring would have prevented their contributing to future generations even if he had not removed them. (See also Merrell, 1953.)

Similar results were obtained by Knight, Robertson, and Waddington (1956) who employed ebony-bodied and vestigial-winged stocks of *Drosophila melanogaster*. Males and females of both stocks were placed together so that they could either mate with their own kind or cross-mate, as they "wished." But in each generation only offspring of homogamic (pure-breeding) matings were used as parents for the next generation. As generations passed, production of hybrids declined, indicating that some degree of sexual isolation between the stocks had been produced by selection.

Hence the results cited seem to indicate that under experimental conditions, at least, selection will intensify one of the mechanisms of reproductive isolation: selective mating.

Moore (1957) has pointed out that factors increasing reproductive isolation would be of value to the populations concerned only in those regions where the populations were actually in contact. (No advantage to a frog living in Vermont would accrue from having a genetic constitution whose only function would be to render impossible hybridization with a Florida frog with which it would never actually come into contact anyway.) Blair (1955), investigating two species of frogs with overlapping ranges, noted that the greatest difference in mating call and the greatest difference in size between the two species occurred in the region where their ranges overlapped. He concluded: "The existence of the greatest size differences as well as the greatest call differences where the two species are exposed to possible hybridization supports the argument that these potential isolating mechanisms are being reenforced through natural selection."

Such reenforcement is not always encountered, however. Thus Volpe (1955) found that reproductive isolation between two species of toads was *weaker* in areas where the ranges overlapped than it was in other regions (judging from the results of laboratory experiments on artificial hybridization). He cited other investigations yielding similar results.

Perhaps some of the conflicting results arise from differences in the animals being investigated; production of hybrids is not detrimental to all species and under all conditions (see below). Natural selection, if it *does* act to favor development of isolating mechanisms, will only do so under conditions in which hybridization is detrimental. In most instances we know too little of the environmental requirements placed upon species to be able to draw valid conclusions on the extent to which hybridization would be detrimental.

Our tentative conclusion may be that natural selection may under special circumstances favor genetic mechanisms having as their principal function the prevention of hybridization, but that usually such functions arise as a by-product of the genetic changes by which two isolated populations become adapted to their respective environments. (In *Rana pipiens,* Vermont frogs and Florida frogs will *not* produce viable hybrids if the experimental attempt is made. Apparently adaptation to development in cold and warm environments, respectively, has carried with it genetic changes which result in constitutions so unlike that hybridization is not possible. Moore, 1955, 1957.)

Hybridization between species is less frequent in animals than it is in plants. Nevertheless, instances of natural hybridization between animal species are not lacking (see Stebbins, 1959, for a review of the literature in this field). Among vertebrates some hybridization has been found in all groups but seems perhaps to be most common—at least, it has been most studied—in fresh-water fishes (cf. Hubbs, 1955; Hubbs, Walker, and Johnson, 1943), amphibians (cf. Blair, 1941, and investigations cited above), and birds (e.g., Sibley, 1954).

Hybridization: Advantageous

Since, as we have noted, hybrids *are* sometimes produced we may now ask the question: Under what circumstances might production of hybrids be of advantage in evolution? We have noted that the usual disadvantage faced by hybrids arises from the fact that they are generally not so well adapted for the environmental niche occupied by either parent species as is that parent species itself. In other words, the hybrid is at a disadvantage in competition with its parents and the latter's nonhybrid progeny. Under what circumstances might this situation not be true? It would not be true if there were available to the hybrid other environmental niches than those occupied by the parental species. These other niches would be expected to present somewhat differing living requirements from those presented by the niches occupied by the parental species. Accordingly, some of the combinations of characteristics possessed by the hybrids might prove to be "just the thing" to enable the hybrids to enter and occupy the new niche. They would afford one means of *preadaptation* (see pp. 12–13).

Viewed in this light, hybrids are "experiments" in preadaptation; but the experiments will succeed only if suitable environmental niches are available.

Many examples have been found of hybrids between plant species occupying successfully environmental niches unlike those of the parent species. A frequently cited example is afforded by two species of spider-wort studied by Anderson and Hubricht (1938). In the Ozark Mountains one species, *Tradescantia canaliculata,* grows in full sunlight on the tops of cliffs. The other species, *Tradescantia subaspera,* grows in the woodland shade at the base of the cliffs (Fig. 20.6*A*). In some places where there is

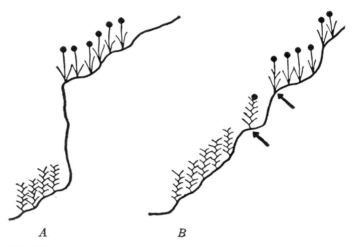

A   B

FIG. 20.6. Environmental isolation of two spiderworts, *Tradescantia*. One species grows on the tops of cliffs, the other at the foot of the cliffs. Hybrids are found where the slope is gentle (*B*), permitting the species to come into contact. (After Anderson and Hubricht; by permission from *Principles of Genetics,* by Sinnott, Dunn, and Dobzhansky, p. 354. Copyright 1950. McGraw-Hill Book Company, Inc.)

a gradual slope connecting the top of a cliff with its base, e.g., in ravines, the forest-dwelling species has extended its range upward and the cliff-top species has extended its range downward. When the two species meet hybrids are produced (Fig. 20.6*B*). The hybrids combine characteristics from the two parental species and apparently are successful because the environment is intermediate between that optimal for the forest-dwelling species and that optimal for the cliff-top species. We may speak of it as a "hybrid environment." As a matter of fact, most of the known examples of species hybrids which have become established in nature have done so when man has "hybridized the habitat" in Anderson's phrase (1949). By this we mean that most of them have arisen in locations where man has upset natural conditions by his cultivating, pasturing of domestic animals, lumbering operations, and so on. Anderson notes that most of the abundant hybrid irises produced spontaneously in southern Louisiana have arisen on patches of land that have been badly overgrazed by domestic animals. Such "hybrid habitats" present living conditions for which the parent species living in undisturbed environments are not adapted. Thus hybrids are offered opportunities they would not otherwise receive. At times, such varied collections of hybrids are produced that students of the subject refer to them as "hybrid swarms." We should note, also, that hybridization of the habitat may be produced by agencies other than man. Climatic changes and such natural catastrophes as floods, volcanic action, and particularly glaciation leave in their wake changed conditions offering possible opportunities for hybrids. Thus, through preadaptation, followed by postadaptation under the spur of natural selection, hybridization may have played a part in the historical process of evolution.

Introgressive Hybridization

What is the effect of hybridization upon the parent species themselves? Apparently hybrids form a means by which genes of one species may be transferred to another species. Let us consider again the two species of spiderwort (Fig. 20.6). The hybrids will breed not only among themselves but also with the two parent species (the latter process being called by geneticists "backcrossing"). The hybrids possess some genes derived from the forest-dwelling species, some genes from the cliff-top species. When, for example, the hybrids breed with the cliff-top species they may pass on to the latter some genes *received from the forest-dwelling species.* The reverse, of course, could occur also. Thus the hybrid may serve as a go-between, passing on genes received from one parental species to the other parental species. This process is called **introgressive hybridization.** As a result of it, genetic variability will be increased over what it would otherwise have been. Genetic variability, as we have seen, furnishes the raw materials upon which natural selection acts. Thus introgressive hybridization may in some cases provide raw materials for evolutionary change. The importance of introgressive hybridization in evolution is being actively investigated at the present time. Wide differences of opinion prevail concerning its frequency of occurrence and its effects. Anderson (1949) has postulated that under some conditions introgressive hybridization may be at least as potent a force in introducing genetic variability into a species as is the occurrence of new mutations. Readers are referred to Anderson (1949), Stebbins (1950), and Sibley (1954) for more complete discussion of the subject.

A particularly instructive case in animals has been studied by Sibley (1954). The investigation involved two species of the red-eyed towhee (Fig. 20.7). The collared towhee (*Pipilo ocai*) lives in various localities

FIG. 20.7. Two species of towhees from Mexico: collared towhee, *Pipilo ocai* (above), and spotted towhee, *Pipilo erythrophthalmus* (below). (After Stebbins and Sibley; reprinted by permission from *Evolution, Genetics, and Man*, by Dobzhansky, 1955, p. 186. John Wiley & Sons, Inc.)

in southern Mexico, primarily in coniferous woodland. The spotted towhee (*Pipilo erythrophthalmus*) lives primarily in oaks and brushy undergrowth in northern Mexico. In at least one locality on the Mexican plateau the species live together without interbreeding. But in other localities the local populations present combinations of the characteristics of two species, a fact suggesting that these populations are composed of hybrids between the latter. These hybrid populations vary greatly from locality to locality. Sibley concluded that "the patterns of variation suggest that the two species, originally ecologically separated, were brought into contact when forests were cleared for human purposes." The investigation was not of a nature to disclose whether any of the hybrid populations are better adapted to their "hybrid habitats" than either parental species would have been. This is a possibility. Sibley noted that in some localities with hybrid populations the numbers of towhees present were unusually large. This suggests that the hybrids were at least a successful group. At any rate, this example shows how hybridization can produce variability among populations, a variability which might be acted upon by natural selection.

References and Suggested Readings

Allee, W. C., A. E. Emerson, O. Park, T. Park, and K. P. Schmidt. *Principles of Animal Ecology.* Philadelphia: W. B. Saunders Co., 1949. (Sec. V deals with evolution.)

Allison, A. C. "Aspects of polymorphism in man," *Cold Spring Harbor Symposia on Quantitative Biology,* 20 (1955), 239–255.

Allison, A. C. "Metabolic polymorphisms in mammals and their bearing on problems of biochemical genetics," *American Naturalist,* 93 (1959), 5–16.

Anderson, E. *Introgressive Hybridization.* New York: John Wiley & Sons, Inc., 1949.

Anderson, E., and L. Hubricht. "Hybridization in *Tradescantia.* III. The evidence for introgressive hybridization," *American Journal of Botany,* 25 (1938), 396–402.

Beardmore, J. A., Th. Dobzhansky, and O. A. Pavlovsky "An attempt to compare the fitness of polymorphic and monomorphic experimental populations of *Drosophila pseudoobscura,*" *Heredity,* 14 (1960), 19–33.

Blair, A. P. "Variation, isolating mechanisms, and hybridization in certain toads," *Genetics,* 26 (1941), 398–417.

Blair, W. F. "Size difference as a possible isolation mechanism in *Microhyla*," *American Naturalist,* 89 (1955), 297–301.

da Cunha, A. B. "Chromosomal polymorphism in the Diptera." In M. Demerec (ed.). *Advances in Genetics,* Vol. 7. New York: Academic Press, Inc., 1955. Pp. 93–138.

Darwin, C. *The Origin of Species by Means of Natural Selection,* 1859. Modern Library series, Random House, New York; or Mentor Book MT294, New American Library, New York.

Demerec, M. "Reaction of populations of unicellular organisms to extreme changes in environment," *American Naturalist,* 84 (1950), 5–16.

Dobzhansky, Th. "Adaptive changes induced by natural selection in wild populations of *Drosophila,*" *Evolution,* 1 (1947), 1–16.

Dobzhansky, Th. "The genetic basis of evolution," *Scientific American,* 182 (1950), 32–41.

Dobzhansky, Th. *Evolution, Genetics, and Man.* New York: John Wiley & Sons, Inc., 1955.

Dobzhansky, Th. "Variation and evolution," *Proceedings, American Philosophical Society,* 103 (1959), 252–263.

Dobzhansky, Th., and B. Spassky. "Evolutionary change in laboratory cultures of *Drosophila pseudoobscura,*" *Evolution,* 1 (1947), 191–216.

Fisher, R. A. *The Genetical Theory of Natural Selection,* 2nd ed. New York: Dover Publications, Inc., 1958.

Gustafsson, A. "Mutations in agricultural plants," *Hereditas,* 33 (1947), 1–100.

L'Héritier, Ph., and G. Teissier. "Élimination des formes mutantes dans le populations de Drosophiles," *Comptes Rendus Société de Biologie,* 124 (1937), 880–884.

Hubbs, C. L. "Hybridization between fish species in nature," *Systematic Zoology,* 4 (1955), 1–20.

Hubbs, C. L., B. W. Walker, and R. E. Johnson. "Hybridization in nature between species of American cyprinodont fishes," *Contributions, Laboratory of Vertebrate Biology, University of Michigan,* No. 23 (1943), 1–21.

Knight, G. R., A. Robertson, and C. H. Waddington. "Selection for sexual isolation within a species," *Evolution,* 10 (1956), 14–22.

Koopman, K. F. "Natural selection for reproductive isolation between *Drosophila pseudoobscura* and *Drosophila persimilis,*" *Evolution,* 4 (1950), 135–148.

Lerner, I. M. *Genetic Homeostasis.* New York: John Wiley & Sons, Inc., 1954.

Manchester, H. "The new age of 'atomic crops,'" *Reader's Digest* (November, 1958), pp. 135–140; *Popular Mechanics* (October, 1958), pp. 106–110, 282–288.

Mayr, E. "Ecological factors in speciation," *Evolution,* 1 (1947), 263–288.

Mayr, E. "Speciation and systematics." In G. L. Jepsen, E. Mayr, and G. G. Simpson (eds.). *Genetics, Paleontology, and Evolution.* Princeton: Princeton University Press, 1949. Pp. 281–298.

Mayr, E. "Isolation as an evolutionary factor," *Proceedings, American Philosophical Society,* 103 (1959), 221–230.

Merrell, D. J. "Selective mating as a cause of gene frequency changes in laboratory populations of *Drosophila melanogaster,*" *Evolution,* 7 (1953), 287–296.

Moore, J. A. "Patterns of evolution in the genus *Rana.*" In G. L. Jepsen, E. Mayr, and G. G. Simpson (eds.). *Genetics, Paleontology, and Evolution.* Princeton: Princeton University Press, 1949. Pp. 315–338.

Moore, J. A. "Abnormal combinations of nuclear and cytoplasmic systems in frogs and toads." In M. Demerec (ed.). *Advances in Genetics,* Vol. 7, New York: Academic Press, Inc., 1955. Pp. 139–182.

Moore, J. A. "An embryologist's view of the species concept." In E. Mayr (ed.). *The Species Problem,* Pub. No. 50, American Association for the Advancement of Science, Washington, D.C., 1957. Pp. 325–358.

Raper, K. B. "Penicillin." In *The Yearbook of Agriculture 1943–1947.* Washington: United States Department of Agriculture, 1947. Pp. 699–710.

Reed, S. C., and E. W. Reed. "Natural selection in laboratory populations of *Drosophila," Evolution*, 2 (1948), 176–186.

Reed, S. C., and E. W. Reed. "Natural selection in laboratory populations of *Drosophila*. II. Competition between a white-eye gene and its wild type allele," *Evolution*, 4 (1950), 34–42.

Schmalhausen, I. I. *Factors of Evolution. The theory of stabilizing selection.* Philadelphia: The Blakiston Co., 1949.

Sibley, C. G. "Hybridization in the Red-eyed Towhees of Mexico," *Evolution*, 8 (1954), 252–290.

Sinnott, E. W., L. C. Dunn, and Th. Dobzhansky. *Principles of Genetics,* 5th ed. New York: McGraw-Hill Book Co., Inc., 1958.

Stebbins, G. L., Jr. *Variation and Evolution in Plants.* New York: Columbia University Press, 1950.

Stebbins, G. L., Jr. "The role of hybridization in evolution," *Proceedings, American Philosophical Society,* 103 (1959), 231–251.

Tax, S. (ed.). *Evolution after Darwin. Vol. I, The Evolution of Life.* Chicago: The University of Chicago Press, 1960.

Timofeeff-Ressovsky, N. W. "Mutations and geographical variation." In J. Huxley (ed.). *The New Systematics.* Oxford: Oxford University Press, 1940. Pp. 73–136.

Volpe, E. P. "Intensity of reproductive isolation between sympatric and allopatric populations of *Bufo americanus* and *Bufo fowleri," American Naturalist,* 89 (1955), 303–317.

Waddington, C. H. "The 'Baldwin effect,' 'genetic assimilation' and 'homeostasis,' " *Evolution,* 7 (1953), 386–387.

Wright, S. "Evolution in Mendelian populations," *Genetics,* 16 (1931), 97–159. (Contains the mathematical background of much of modern evolutionary theory.)

Wright, S. "Isolation by distance," *Genetics,* 28 (1943), 114–138.

Wright, S. "Adaptation and selection." In G. L. Jepsen, E. Mayr, and G. G. Simpson (eds.). *Genetics, Paleontology, and Evolution.* Princeton: Princeton University Press, 1949. Pp. 365–398.

NATURAL SELECTION: II

So far in our study of natural selection as an evolutionary force we have stressed its operation upon mutations, emphasizing the importance of heterozygote superiority in maintaining a balanced polymorphism contributive to genetic homeostasis. We have inquired into the role played by geographic-environmental isolation in the instigation of genetic change between populations, and have discussed the attainment of reproductive isolation, in its various forms, as an indication that the species level of differentiation has been reached. We have noted that while absence of hybridization between species is the rule, and is favored by natural selection, at times hybridization may form a means of increasing genetic variability and thus of providing grist to the mill of natural selection.

In the present chapter we shall continue our inquiry into evolution by natural selection, emphasizing the forces operative in species formation (speciation) as well as in production of the adaptive differences by which the higher categories differ from each other. We shall discuss briefly the ancillary theory of sexual selection, and shall then pull the threads together in an outline of the factors and forces operative in producing evolutionary change. Brief discussion of directive forces in evolution and of rates of evolutionary change will conclude the chapter.

SPECIATION

Evolution may be divided, conveniently but somewhat arbitrarily, into two types or patterns: (1) **phyletic evolution,** and (2) **speciation.** Phyletic evolution means evolution in a line or lineage. Species *A,* living in a certain region, in the course of time undergoes change so that the descendants are sufficiently unlike their distant ancestors to be considered a different species. *Mesohippus* evolving into *Miohippus* may be taken as an example. Species *A* has become species *B*. Typically, species *A* will have disappeared in the process, leaving species *B* in its place. Similarly, as time goes on species *B* may evolve into, and be replaced by, species *C,* and so on. This phyletic pattern of evolution along a time axis is abundantly evident in the sequences of fossil forms studied in earlier chapters.

If, however, instead of tracing a historical sequence through time in this manner we concentrate attention on one period in the earth's history, we see evidences of the second pattern of evolution. This consists of the more nearly "simultaneous" (in terms of geologic time) production of groups of species, the type of evolution to which Mayr (1949) has insisted that the term speciation be restricted. In this second pattern of evolution species *A* gives rise to two or more species, perhaps to a whole cluster of them, usually, if not always, originating in separate territories. These daughter species may or may not replace species *A*. This type of evolution occurs when a species ranges widely over a large territory various portions of which are separated from other portions by distance and perhaps also by other geographic-environmental isolating mechanisms. Under such conditions the original species becomes divided into subpopulations. As mentioned in our discussion of isolation, each subpopulation is free to undergo independent evolution, through action of genetic drift and natural selection. The result will be differing populations of animals inhabiting isolated territories.

Because of the effectiveness of the barriers producing isolation, animals inhabiting oceanic islands afford particularly instructive examples of this phenomenon. One such example is diagramed in Fig. 21.1, which represents the varieties or races of the golden whistler found on various of the Solomon Islands. The varied colorations and patterns of plumage which have developed in these isolated populations are evident. We may well conclude that we are seeing the results of genetic drift plus, perhaps, some measure of natural selection. Here is an example of the formation of varieties or geographic races comparable to the subspecies of *Peromyscus* discussed earlier (pp. 320–325), and, on reduced scale, to the races of man (pp. 250–255).

Most biologists believe that the same process carried one step further leads to the formation of distinct species. As we have noted before, the "step further" is the development of reproductive isolation. If, while isolated, two subpopulations accumulate sufficient genetic differences so that they will no longer exchange genes if and when they come into contact, those subpopulations have become separate species.

As the subpopulations develop genetic differences contributing to reproductive isolation, they are also developing genetic differences connected with the varying living conditions which face them. That is, they are becoming adapted to somewhat different habitats and environmental conditions. If living conditions are similar, the subpopulations may be expected to develop similar adaptations even while they are accumulating differ-

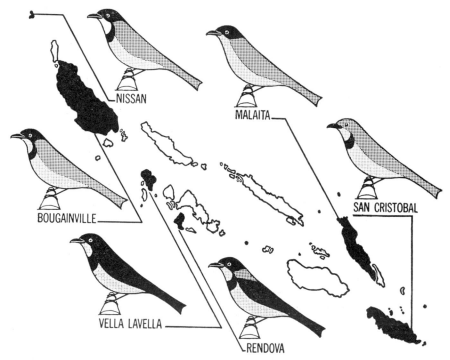

FIG. 21.1. Geographic races of the golden whistler (*Pachycephala pectoralis*) on various of the Solomon Islands. The races differ in black, white, and colored markings. Dark gray areas represent green markings, light gray areas yellow markings. (Redrawn from Dobzhansky, "The genetic basis of evolution," *Scientific American*, Vol. 182, 1950, p. 41.)

ences in, for example, plumage and in neutral or nonadaptive characteristics. If living conditions are dissimilar, on the other hand, the adaptations acquired by subpopulations will lead to greater differences between them.

What will happen when two such subgroups expand their ranges and come into contact with each other? Because of the reproductive isolation developed they will not interbreed, but to the extent to which they are adapted to the same conditions of life they will come into *competition* with each other. What will happen as a result of this competition? (1) One species may be so much more efficient or better adapted that it will succeed in monopolizing the environmental niche, with resultant extinction of the less well-adapted species. Since the writing of Gause (1934) it has been recognized that two species cannot occupy the same environmental niche in the same region. Since it is extremely improbable that the two species would have exactly the same degree of adaptation to the niche, one species is certain to replace the other, if they remain unchanged. This has been called the "competitive exclusion principle" (Hardin, 1960). (2) One or both species may change somewhat to lessen the direct competition between them. If both are seed-eating birds, for example, one species may specialize in a certain type or size of seeds, the other in another type or size (cf. our discussion of the three species of ground finches on the Galápagos archipelago, pp. 294–295). Thus competition spurs on evolutionary divergence begun when the species were spatially isolated from each other. In this connection we may note that competition in areas in which two species come into contact may cause populations of the two species in those areas to develop increased or accentuated differences from each other. Rivalry stimulates the development of differences. By contrast, in areas in which the two species do not come into contact the differences between them may be less. Brown and Wilson (1956) have emphasized the importance of this phenomenon, called "character displacement," in speciation.

The amount of divergence resulting from the processes involved in speciation will depend upon many factors, one of the most important being the number of environmental niches open for invasion. If many environmental niches are open, the final result of the process may well be *adaptive radiations* such as the remarkable ones we described for Darwin's finches on the Galápagos archipelago (pp. 292–296) and for the drepanid birds on the Hawaiian Islands (pp. 296–304).

To add concreteness to the discussion, let us imagine the sequence of events which probably produced the adaptive radiation of Darwin's finches. The ancestor was a finch from Central or South America. When this finch arrived there were doubtless no other land birds on the archipelago. This ancestral finch found the archipelago a favorable home and so spread widely through the islands, continuing to rely on its traditional diet of seeds. As time went by, the finches living on one island came to differ from those living on another. Both genetic drift and natural selection probably operated to this end. Of greatest importance among the accumulated differences were those which resulted in reproductive isolation. Eventually islands became overpopulated with their respective species, and the inhabitants of each island attempted to find new territories. Thus the stage of direct competition between species formed in isolation was reached. For example, most of the larger islands now have all three species of the seed-eating ground finches (Fig. 13.3, p. 295). If our interpretation is correct, each of these originated in isolation from the others and then extended its range so that it came into competition with the others. As we noted previously, all three can live together in the same territory because they have become specialists in eating seeds of different sizes. Perhaps differences between them were at first slight, but "character displacement" occurred as a result of the competition, increasing the differences in the size of the beaks.

The number and variety of seeds available are limited. Owing to the fortunate circumstance that these birds were first on the islands, a variety of environmental niches were unoccupied: insect-eating, woodpeckerlike, cactus-feeding, and so on. Thus the competition caused some species to forsake the ancestral diet of seeds and start concentrating on these other means of sustenance. Since the species were already reproductively isolated from each other, mutations occurring in one would not be transmitted to others. Hence mutations adapting their possessors for insect eating were accumulated in one species, mutations making possible a woodpeckerlike manner of feeding were accumulated in another, and so on, all without danger of loss through interbreeding. In this way each species followed its own independent route to adaptation for its own particular environmental niche. (Much more complete discussion of this subject will be found in Lack, 1947, 1949; and Mayr, 1942, 1949.)

A similar process of speciation doubtless occurred among the drepanids of Hawaii. In this case the ancestor was a nectar feeder. If our interpretation is correct, this ancestor spread throughout the islands. Then, because of the isolation of the several islands, the subpopulation on each island accumulated genetic differences resulting in reproductive isolation. The species thus formed subsequently migrated to other islands and came into competition. This competition stimulated invasion of niches other than that of nectar feeding, and the remarkable adaptative radiation in beak structure was the result. (For more complete discussion see Amadon, 1950.)

While oceanic archipelagos afford particularly instructive examples of this process, doubtless the same sequence of events occurred on continents long ago. But there the major environmental niches have long since been filled, and species find few opportunities for important evolutionary change. "On continents evolution is usually in the later, more stabilized stage of minor adaptations and specializations" (Amadon, 1950).

We have emphasized three factors in the process of speciation, operative in the order named: (1) spatial isolation; (2) development of genetic diversity sufficient to insure reproductive isolation if and when the species come into contact (this genetic diversity may or may not include visible structural differences); (3) divergence in characteristics if the species, already reproductively isolated, come into competition for food, nest sites, or other essentials of life. The spatial isolation considered primary is tantamount to the geographic-environmental isolation we discussed earlier. In some cases the main isolating factor may be an environmental one (e.g., differences in food habits), but enough "space" must also be involved to insure that the two populations do not come into contact and interbreed (prior to the development of reproductive isolating mechanisms).

Lack (1947, 1949) presented as an example of the necessity for initial spatial separation the case of the finch inhabiting Cocos Island (Fig. 13.2, p. 288). This finch is so unlike the other Darwin's finches that it is placed in a separate genus, suggesting that it has been on the island for a long time. Yet this genus contains but one species, which is not even divided into subspecies. Lack wrote, "Cocos resembles the Galápagos in providing varied habitats and in having a great paucity of other land-birds, but it differs in one essential respect: it is a single island, not an archipelago. Hence there has been no opportunity for the geographical isolation of populations and hence no evolution of new species or of an adaptive radiation." The one species present has presumably undergone progressive evolution of the replacing or phyletic type described on page 484. Adaptive radiations of birds occur on archipelagos but not on single oceanic islands; such radiations formerly occurred on continents, which are large enough so that means of geographic isolation other than stretches of ocean are operative. Obviously for other animals than such accomplished travelers as birds smaller barriers and distances will suffice to produce the needed isolation. The point is that some effective means of spatial isolation seems essential as an initial step in speciation, and indeed in almost all evolutionary change.

Effect of Population Size

Our discussion of speciation has emphasized the breaking up of large populations into relatively small, isolated subpopulations. Students of the subject are now generally agreed that optimal conditions for evolutionary change are provided by such conditions (see Wright, 1949). Our preceding discussion will have made evident that a large population not divided in this way would not be favorable for evolutionary change, since random breeding of large numbers of individuals results in population equilibrium, resistant to change. Change in conditions, or increase in severity of natural selection, acting on such a large population might result in some shift in gene frequencies, changing them to a new equilibrium which would then be maintained as long as the new conditions persisted (Wright, 1931). But the change would be slow, and would be reversible whenever conditions altered again. Thus, while some increased adaptation might be brought about by this means, no considerable evolutionary change would be produced.

Conversely, very small populations are not favorable for evolutionary change. They are too likely to lose genes by chance, through the action of genetic drift, thus reducing their reserves of hereditary variability and consequently their possibilities for further change. Owing to genetic drift, also, members of a very small population may all come to possess genetic characteristics which are of no particular value or are even deleterious. Thus observers of species inhabiting small oceanic islands find, on the one hand, reduced variability among them and, on the other, possession of a variety of seemingly nonadaptive characteristics. The disharmonic nature of the fauna of oceanic islands (p. 283) frequently results in absence of competitors for a given environmental niche. Therefore, relatively ill-adapted animals can continue to exist—even animals so ill adapted that they would not succeed in the stiffer competition characterizing life on continents. Zimmerman (1948) recorded the unusual number of flightless insects on the Hawaiian Islands and explained them as mutant forms which can survive under conditions of reduced competition found on oceanic islands. The influence of size of population on variability was clearly demonstrated in the observation of an isolated colony of butterflies over a prolonged period by Ford (1949). For the first few years specimens remained rare; it was noted that those taken were very constant in appearance. In later years the species increased greatly in numbers; "an extraordinary outburst of variation took place while the numbers were rapidly increasing, and many of the more extreme aberrations were deformed." The author continued, "When the population became stabilized again at the new and high value, uniformity was restored, yet the constant form which was then established differed in appearance from that which existed before the outburst of variability."

Populations broken up into subpopulations provide a means by which nature can make "experiments," to employ a figure of speech suggested by

Muller (1949), without risking the fate of the entire species on the outcome of one experiment.

SEXUAL SELECTION

Darwin considered that the development of the so-called secondary sex characteristics could not be adequately explained by his theory of natural selection. The primary sex characteristics are, of course, the male and female reproductive organs. But in addition to the latter, males usually differ from females in a variety of bodily structures. The bright plumages and elaborate songs of many male birds, contrasted with the duller plumages and relative tunelessness of the females, form a familiar example. Among mammals it is the male lion that develops a mane, the male goat that possesses a beard, the male deer that displays many-pronged antlers. Darwin felt that such differences between the sexes are not vital enough to the welfare of the species to arise through the operation of natural selection. Hence, he advanced the supplemental theory of **sexual selection** to explain their development.

Although one would not expect it from the abbreviated title by which the book is usually known, the theory is set forth in detail in Darwin's book *The Descent of Man*. Bodily characteristics with which the theory is concerned may be divided into two main types: (1) those of use in combat between rival males and (2) those used for display purposes. Both types might be useful under conditions of competition between males for mates.

Male birds or mammals are sometimes observed to fight for possession of a particular female, although the number of species in which this struggle occurs has probably been much overestimated in the past. When such combats do occur, males with superior implements of warfare might be expected to be most successful, becoming the fathers of a disproportionate share of the next generation. The male offspring of such fathers might be expected to inherit their fathers' superior fighting equipment, and if the process continued long enough males of that species might become quite unlike the females in terms of bodily equipment specifically connected with fighting.

But how about the development of features concerned with display—bright colors, ornate plumages, songs, posturing, dancing, and the like? The theory accounts for their development by assuming that females possess aesthetic sense and employ it in deciding which suitor to accept. Thus the male with the brightest colors, the most intricately ornamental plumage, the most beautiful song, the most skill in courtship wins the female, in competition with his less endowed brethren. In consequence, he fathers a disproportionate share of the next generation, the males of which inherit their father's superior attractions. If females continue generation after generation to select as mates the brightest-colored or otherwise most ornamental males, male pulchritude may be expected to increase in the species.

Despite the fact that Darwin marshaled a great array of circumstantial evidence in support of the theory, sexual selection is generally considered to have but limited applicability. Combat between two males, for example, when it does occur, is seldom to the death, an eventuality which would, of course, permanently eliminate one potential father. Furthermore, according to the theory, after the fight is over the victor wins the female. Although evidence is difficult to accumulate on such matters, it seems that the female not infrequently goes off with the vanquished combatant rather than with the victorious one. Moreover, in species in which the individuals are monogamous, pairing for a season or longer, sexual selection would work only if there were more males than females. If the sexes were equal in number, every male would eventually find a mate regardless of his prowess in combat. In species in which polygamy is the rule sexual selection might be expected to be more effective, since the successful males would amass the largest "harems" of females, or would otherwise mate with the largest number. It is noteworthy that some of the most elaborate displays are possessed by male birds which are polygamous (e.g., the argus pheasant). Under such circumstances, since one male may mate many times, other males not at all, a high premium is placed on elaborate display. Such cases are perhaps our best example of sexual selection in the Darwinian sense.

What we have said about combat applies also, in the main, to the matter of display on the part of the males for the benefit of the watching females. Evidently some of the display of bright and ornate plumages or other male adornments, accompanied by the courtship ritual appropriate to the species, does have the effect of arousing the female so that she will accept the male. But there is little evidence that females sit in judgment upon the quality of ornamentation or posturing of males of their own species and decide upon that basis which male to accept. Indeed, "in most monogamous birds, display begins only after pairing up for the season has occurred" (Huxley, 1938). And in polygamous species, so long as the courtship behavior is adequately exciting and orthodox for the species, the females usually are rather passive in the matter of which individual male is accepted. On the other hand, evidence accumulates that females detect small irregularities in the courtship behavior and that even seemingly minor irregularities may be sufficient to cause a female to refuse a male. As mentioned earlier (p. 472), such refusal appears to form a means by which interbreeding between closely related species is prevented. Thus differences in courtship ritual form one of the means of *reproductive isolation*. We mention the matter here because it has bearing on one a priori objection sometimes raised to the theory of sexual selection: that the theory presupposes that females possess a discriminating power which we can hardly grant their having, particularly if they are insects. Evidence cited earlier indicates that female insects have surprising powers of discrimination.

Returning to such matters as the bright colors and songs of male birds, we note that investigators have found that many of these features do not have as their principal function the pleasing of females. Some bright colors are warning or threatening devices. Observation and experiment on the common robin of England have demonstrated that the red breast, conspicuously displayed during the breeding season, is a device for threatening other males which might seek to invade the territory the individual has claimed for himself. The same is true of conspicuous plumages of other birds that establish home territories. The songs of male birds serve the same purpose. Song has "its prime function as a 'distance threat' to rival males and its secondary function as an advertisement, so long as the singer is unmated, to unmated females" (Huxley, 1942). There is nothing to prevent, of course, bright colors from serving *both* as warnings to rivals and as lures for possible mates. We readily appreciate that if the establishment of home territories is advantageous to the species, in terms of welfare of the young, characteristics which aid in the establishment and maintenance of the territorial system will be furthered by *natural* selection.

Some of the conspicuous characteristics ascribed at times to sexual selection may serve a variety of functions in the lives of their possessors. Some of the functions are: (1) **recognition characters,** means by which a female recognizes a male of her own species; (2) **warnings** to rivals or to other animals that the possessor is dangerous; (3) **mimicry,** either Batesian or Müllerian (pp. 370–373). All such categories, and others we have not mentioned, fall within the province of *natural* selection since they affect either the survival or reproductive success of their possessors. In fact, we may expect that natural selection will tend to favor any factor or characteristic that increases effectiveness in reproduction. Another such factor consists of the means of stimulating females to reproductive activity. In birds, especially, mating and reproduction are largely under control of the higher cerebral centers, psychological stimulation (as by bright colors, mating displays and dances) being necessary to induce ovulation. This being so, natural selection would favor development and maintenance of the means of stimulation, no recourse to sexual selection in the Darwinian sense being necessary. This is not to say that sexual selection does not exist or is not important, but only that its range of operation may be more restricted than it was formerly thought to be (see Huxley, 1938, for more extensive discussion).

PULLING THE THREADS TOGETHER

We now summarize in outline form the main factors and forces making for evolutionary change.

I. SOURCES OF VARIABILITY
  A. NEW MUTATIONS. These include gene mutations and chromosomal mutations or aberrations (pp. 396–402). Aside from the "instantaneous speciation" possible to plants by *polyploidy* (pp. 418–420), chemical changes in genes seem on the whole to produce more far-reaching changes than do chromosomal aberrations.
    1. EFFECTS. (a) *Structure,* (b) *physiology,* (c) *viability,* (d) *fertility,* and other aspects of the organism and its life may be affected by mutation. One gene may affect several aspects (be *pleiotropic*), and conversely many genes may affect any one aspect. Effects may be small or large. Some of the large effects may be the result of mutations occurring in genes controlling *differential growth rates* of different parts of the body (pp. 405–418).
    2. MUTATION PRESSURE. New mutations are produced at a continual, though low, rate, thus providing raw materials for evolutionary change.
  B. NEW COMBINATIONS OF GENES
    1. MENDELIAN RECOMBINATION. Accumulated genetic variability inherited from preceding generations constitutes a store of genetic diversity which in bisexual organisms is constantly shuffled and reshuffled into everchanging combinations (pp. 331–336).
    2. INTROGRESSIVE HYBRIDIZATION. Under some circumstances one population may obtain genes from another through hybridization (pp. 479–481) when (a) the ranges of the species overlap or (b) migration occurs.
  C. NORM OF REACTION OR REACTION RANGE of a genotype. The fact that a genotype confers upon an organism some degree of flexibility in this respect enables the organism to accommodate to various environmental conditions to which it may subsequently attain genetically based adaptation (*genetic assimilation,* pp. 420–424; *Baldwin effect,* pp. 424–425).

II. FORCES OPERATIVE UPON THE VARIABILITY PRESENT IN A POPULATION

   A. TENDENCY TO EQUILIBRIUM

      1. MECHANISMS OF MENDELIAN INHERITANCE tend to establishment and maintenance of equilibrium in a population; this is expressed by the Hardy-Weinberg formula (pp. 431–435).

      2. GENETIC HOMEOSTASIS, based upon heterozygote superiority, tends to conserve genetic variability present in a population, while the population itself remains in equilibrium (pp. 466–469).

      3. STABILIZING SELECTION is an aspect of natural selection tending to maintain the status quo of a population already well adapted to its environment. Stabilizing selection (pp. 466–469) may operate by (a) weeding out ill-adapted deviates and (b) favoring production of a genotype which confers upon its possessors high adaptability to environmental change, i.e., a genotype characterized by *homeostasis* and the tendency of embryonic development to be *canalized* (pp. 421–422).

   B. FACTORS AND FORCES TENDING TO DISTURB EQUILIBRIUM

      1. ISOLATION. Populations are isolated from each other primarily by *geographic-environmental* factors (pp. 469–471) involving some element of isolation in space. Such isolation may be reenforced by, and in later stages of speciation even supplanted by, various physiological and behavioral adaptations which prevent interchange of genes between populations. These mechanisms of *reproductive isolation* include selective mating (pp. 471–472). Within isolated populations or subpopulations the following forces may be operative—

      2. GENETIC DRIFT. Especially if the subpopulation is small, *chance* may increase or decrease the frequency of a gene or genotype (p. 444). If the genotype increased in frequency in this manner has elements of superiority, the way is paved for the action of

      3. NATURAL SELECTION. Natural selection will act in these subpopulations upon the store of genetic variability submitted to it, tending always toward production of populations having large capacity for reproduction. This will mean in most, if not all, instances a population adapted to its environment and well "buffered" to withstand some range of environmental diversity.

         a. *Post-adaptation.* Insofar as the characteristics which become established in a subpopulation are of value to their possessors, they will usually have the effect of adapting the subpopulation to its particular environmental niche.

         b. *Tendency to expansion of range.* A successful subpopulation will usually tend to increase in numbers and hence to expand its range. Doing so will bring it into competition with other subpopulations. If reproductive isolation has been developed by two subpopulations while isolated, interbreeding will not occur and the subpopulations will have attained the species level of differentiation. One species may then supplant the other or, alternatively, the two species may change their ecological requirements sufficiently so that they no longer compete (pp. 486–488).

c. *Preadaptation* (prospective adaptation, Simpson, 1953). At times a subpopulation may attain adaptations of wider applicability than merely to the environmental niche in which it lives at the time. If so the population may take up life in a different environment. Usually this can only happen if the new environmental niche is unoccupied.

d. *The measure of success.* Success in evolution is measured by magnitude of genetic contribution to the next generation. Successful populations or subpopulations are those which (1) are, or become, so well adapted to life under conditions prevailing that they continue generation after generation to fill completely the environmental niche in which they live, or (2) possess, or become possessors of, adaptations enabling them to invade new environmental niches. The first type of successful population will continue to be successful so long as environmental conditions remain substantially unchanged. The second type, capable of change to meet new conditions, may be expected to give rise to evolutionary changes of larger magnitude than those attained by populations that merely become better adapted to prevailing conditions. Obviously, however, a given population may be both well adapted to one environmental niche and possessed of attributes which would enable it to enter some other niche if opportunity offered. Probably most populations adapted for life in one niche do not retain sufficient genetic plasticity to permit them to enter a radically different niche or are not presented with opportunity to enter a radically different one, even though they may have the necessary capacity for change. Historically, those populations both possessed of the requisite genetic plasticity *and* afforded the opportunity to invade radically different niches have been the ones that have made large strides in evolutionary change.

DIRECTIVE FORCES IN EVOLUTION

What determines the direction evolution shall take? This is a large question the answers to which are imperfectly known. Space will permit only brief consideration of two important factors concerned: (1) the directive effect of preceding events and (2) natural selection.

Directive Effect of Preceding Events

We may think of the first factor as the directive action of past history. The future is always in part determined by the past. To illustrate our meaning let us devise a little game of words. The rules of this game are simple:

words must be made entirely from letters used in preceding words. How many English words can be made from the twenty-six letters of the alphabet? The weight of paper required for manufacture of an unabridged dictionary gives graphic evidence of their vast number. Let us now pick one of the longer words from this dictionary: "disestablishmentarian." How many other words can be made from the letters in this one? The number is large but is much smaller than the number of words we can make from the letters of the entire alphabet. By picking the word "disestablishmentarian" we have eliminated the future possibility of constructing words that include the letters *c, f, g, j, k, o, p, q, u, v, w, x, y, z.*

From the letters remaining to us we now elect to construct the word "misadministrate." In doing so we have lost the letters *b, h,* and *l;* they can no longer be used in our game. The next word we make, from the letters in "misadministrate," is "semianimate." In doing this we have lost *d* and *r* from our stock of letters. From the letters remaining we now make the word "stamina," losing *e* in the process. Our next word may be "maintain"; if so, we have lost *s.* Next, perhaps, we construct "taint," losing *m* by doing so. Next may come "tint," with loss of *a* from our stock of letters. The number of words we can construct from the three letters remaining to us is extremely limited. The point we wish to make is that this limitation is imposed by past events—by the decisions made each time we chose to construct a certain word rather than some other one possible to us at the time. If we had chosen differently the letters remaining for use at the end of the game would have been different ones from the *i, n,* and *t* of our example. Looking over the course of our game as a whole we might be impressed by the fact that our example exhibits a progressive tendency to emphasize the importance of *i, n,* and *t.* But this emphasis is only a product of decisions made during the course of the game, not of any innate importance or superiority of *i, n,* and *t* themselves. Thus we see that past events exercise a directive or channeling action upon subsequent events.

How does this fact apply to the evolution of life? Here also past events influence the course of subsequent history. On page 90 we noted the fundamental importance of the element phosphorus (in phosphates of adenylic acid) in mobilizing and transporting the free energy needed for all living processes. Why do living organisms concentrate on phosphorus for this function? "Does the unique behavior of phosphorus in this case depend upon very special properties, such that even quite similar elements could not serve as substitutes; or is this unique function to be attributed to events in evolutionary history which caused the accidental 'selection' of phosphorus for this rôle?" (Blum, 1955). Blum suggested that the phosphorus-adenylic-acid system of free energy transport was a very early step in the origin of life (recall our discussion on pp. 90–91) and that this fact explains why subsequent forms of life have concentrated upon that special system rather than upon some other system which might have served the same purpose. We may compare this to our word game; in choosing "disestablishmentarian" at the outset we chose to concentrate on certain letters to the exclusion of others.

Again, Blum (1955) has pointed out the possible significance of the fact that all amino acids entering into the formation of proteins are of the "left-handed" variety, i.e., their solutions rotate the plane of polarized light to the left. Yet both "right-handed" and "left-handed" amino acids are readily synthesized in the laboratory. Why are living organisms composed of "left-handed" ones only? We cannot give a definite answer but we may reasonably conclude that historical events underlie that answer. Perhaps the first proteins simply *chanced* to be formed of "left-handed" amino acids only. Or perhaps the first proteins were formed under conditions in which, for some reason unknown to us, "left-handed" amino acids were the ones predominantly available. Lacking any reason for thinking that "right-handed" amino acids *could* not be built into proteins, we see here another probable instance of the determination by past events of subsequent ones.

Many other examples might be given but enough has been said to indicate that inclusion of chemical compounds in the body is determined, not alone by their suitability, but also by the past history of life. This may well be true of the genes themselves, composed of deoxyribose nucleic acid (DNA). Because of the strategic importance of genes and their mutations the particular chemical properties of DNA are of great significance to evolution. Genes may undergo a variety of chemical changes (mutations) but the variety is not endless. Limitations are set by the chemical structure of DNA, just as limitations on the number of words that can be made from the letters in "stamina" are set by the variety of letters in that word. And not all the chemical changes possible to DNA (probably enormous in number) would constitute mutations capable of actual existence, just as not all combinations of letters from "stamina" constitute actual words.

Furthermore, not all the chemical changes that a gene *can* undergo are equally likely to occur. The point is an important one but the underlying reasons cannot be explained in an elementary discussion (see Blum, 1955). Briefly, the reasons relate to the fact that different chemical changes have different energy requirements. Changes requiring little energy of activation occur more readily, and hence more frequently, than do changes requiring investment of greater amounts of energy. As a result a gene will give rise more frequently to some mutations than it will to other mutations possible to it. This fact in itself reduces the randomness of the raw materials available for the construction of evolutionary change.

Thus it turns out that, strictly speaking, mutations are not random after all. On previous pages we have called them random, but the randomness consists of their occurring without reference to the adaptive requirements of the organisms in which they occur. Conceivably, indeed, a sequence of "most probable" mutations might in itself become a directive force in evolution, resulting, perhaps, in a progressive series of changes of the type sometimes cited as an example of orthogenesis (pp. 411–412). The point has not been established, however, and remains at present no more than an interesting speculation.

In summary, our discussion has shown that past events, by determining at each step in the evolution of life that an organism shall have one structure or attribute and not another, channel and restrict the courses which future evolution may take. At any given time in evolutionary history the raw materials available for the building of further change are not entirely random in nature. Their nature has been determined by preceding events in that history.

Natural Selection

Added to this channeling action of past events is the further directive force of natural selection. Previously we have discussed the action of natural selection in sorting the raw materials presented to it; we mention it here to stress the importance of that sorting action as a directive force in evolution. Natural selection always promotes *adaptation*. Though its action varies in rate and intensity, its trend is always to cause animals to become more perfectly adapted to their environments. Thus it constitutes the main active force directing the course of evolution.

We might inquire at this point, "Is natural selection a force directing evolving organisms into pathways of *progress?*" That depends upon how we define "progress." If progress consists in becoming more perfectly adapted to the needs of life, whatever they may be, then natural selection always promotes progress. Sometimes progress in this sense may lead to loss of structures possessed by ancestors. Thus parasites frequently lose the sense organs possessed by their free-living ancestors. Is this progress? It is perfection of adaptation, since the sense organs are not needed and their continued formation would constitute waste of the organism's metabolic energies. Hence it is progress of a kind.

But we usually think of progress in terms of increase rather than decrease in complexity of structure. Especially are we prone to think of
progress in terms of increasing mental development. We are rather anthropomorphic about the matter. In our judgments of lower animals, the
more they approach *us* in endowments the more progressive are we likely
to consider them. Perhaps after all there is justification for such a point of
view. Unquestionably we ourselves are the finest product yet produced by
the evolutionary process. Has natural selection been a major directive force
in progress defined as this "upward trend" in evolution?

As noted above (p. 18), a progressive step in such a trend depends upon
two things: (1) an opportunity open and (2) an organism capable of taking advantage of that opportunity. For example, the phenomenon of the
emergence of vertebrates from the water to take up life on land depended
upon (1) presence of a dry-land environment as yet unexploited by vertebrates and (2) presence of vertebrates (the Crossopterygii) capable of
making the change (pp. 15–17, 157–162). Natural selection in its varied
aspects supplied the stimulus causing certain Crossopterygii to forsake the
water and causing their descendants to become more and more perfectly
adapted to life on land. Thus when the nature of opportunities open is
such that more complex structure and greater mental endowments are
needed, natural selection in its role of promoting adaptation is found to be
promoting progress in the sense of our second, more restricted, definition
of the word.

RATES OF EVOLUTIONARY CHANGE

Two groups of factors are involved in determining the
rate of evolutionary change: factors within the organism and factors external to the organism.

Internal Factors

Of the internal factors involved, primacy must be accorded the *rate* with
which mutations occur, since mutations are the raw materials of evolutionary change. Other things being equal, we should expect a population in
which mutations occurred at a high rate to change more rapidly than would
a population having a low mutation rate. In the former population the genetic equilibrium would be much more radically modified (p. 436) by occurrence of new mutations than in the latter population. Unfortunately,
positive evidence of the actual importance of this factor in determining

rates of evolution in specific groups of organisms is almost completely lacking. Different evolutionary lines are observed to differ in rate of change, and one evolutionary line may be observed to undergo alteration in rate of change during the course of its history. But there is little clear evidence that differences or changes in mutation rate underlie the differences and changes in rate of evolution. Indeed, there is some evidence to the contrary (cf. Stebbins, 1949). At the same time we must remember that our present actual knowledge of mutation rates in wild populations of plants and animals is still very fragmentary.

An interesting discovery in this connection is that of genes which increase the rates at which other genes undergo mutation. The possible evolutionary significance of such genes is discussed by Ives (1950), who describes a high-mutation-rate gene in *Drosophila*. This gene has the effect of increasing the mutation rates of other genes about tenfold. Such genes increase the rate of supply of "raw materials" and hence might under some conditions affect the rate of evolution.

External Factors

On the whole, evidence available seems to indicate that differing rates of change are more dependent upon external factors than they are upon internal ones, always provided, of course, that the mutation rate is *adequate* to furnish the raw materials. Analysis of factors involved in determination of rates of change is outside the province of an elementary discussion. Readers are particularly referred to the basic treatment accorded the subject by Simpson in his *The Major Features of Evolution* (1953) as well as his more general discussion in *The Meaning of Evolution* (1949a). Statement of a few general principles and conclusions which seem justified by present knowledge must suffice us here.

Such quantitative studies as have been possible on rates of evolution among prehistoric animals seem to indicate that there is an average rate of evolution approximated by many evolutionary lines. Simpson has used the term **horotelic** to designate average rate of evolution. Other evolutionary lines group themselves around a lower mean rate of evolution, termed **bradytelic.** Clearly, cockroaches, mentioned on a preceding page (p. 164) as having undergone little change since the Pennsylvanian period, are bradytelic. Many forms have changed little over long periods of time during which other forms underwent great changes. Oysters were practically the same 200 million years ago as they are today. The opossum has changed but little from the closing days of the dinosaurs down to the present.

The term **tachytelic** has been assigned evolutionary lines in which the mean rate of evolution is above the average, or horotelic, rate. Apparently there are no evolutionary lines in which rate of change remains permanently at the tachytelic level. This exceptionally rapid evolution *is* exceptional in that in any given line it is "effective only during certain crucial relatively short evolutionary episodes" (Simpson, 1949b).

What causes a line which has been evolving at its average, or horotelic, rate to make a sudden evolutionary spurt and become for a time tachytelic in its evolution? We have suggested that the answer is probably not to be found mainly in increased rate of mutation. Rather it seems to lie in the field of what Simpson terms the "organism-environment relationship." We observe that the *large* evolutionary changes are usually concerned with the adaptation of animals to environment; i.e., the changes are in the nature of adaptive responses. Throughout our discussions, for example, we have referred repeatedly to the emergence of vertebrates from life in the water to life on land. This was certainly one of the largest evolutionary changes in all history. The bodily changes involved were clearly associated with meeting the needs of the new environment. Similarly the changes involved in the evolution of horses, elephants, and many other groups not cited in our brief discussion have been of a nature to adapt animals to conditions of life facing them. Accordingly, it seems that change in environment is a primary factor in the speeding up of evolution. This change in environment may occur in one of two ways: (1) The environment in which the species is living may change, e.g., as a result of geologic change, or (2) the species may enter a new environment, not previously available to it, or with the demands of which it was not previously able to cope. The entering of new environmental niches seems to have provided the stimulus for the most radical, and rapid, evolutionary changes.

Mega-Evolution

On page 361, we noted Goldschmidt's division of evolution into "microevolution" (that of subspecies) and "macroevolution" (that of species and genera, and perhaps also of higher categories). Simpson (1953) has proposed the additional term "mega-evolution" for really large-scale evolution, such as that of families, orders, classes, and phyla. It is evolution at these levels that claims the chief attention of students of the fossil record. Unfortunately, on the other hand, most experimental studies of the evolution of living animals must perforce concentrate on differences between subspecies, species, and at times genera. But principles revealed by these studies can, with caution, be applied to explanation of origin of the larger differences between families, orders, classes, and phyla. The large evolutionary changes, connected as we have seen with major changes of environment, constitute the most important accomplishments of evolution. Accordingly, brief consideration of mega-evolution will form a fitting climax to our discussion.

Evidence accumulates that *extent* of evolutionary change and *rapidity* of evolutionary change are connected. So far as we can judge from the geologic record, large changes seem usually to have arisen rather suddenly, in terms of geologic time. This fact has been one of the reasons why a special type of large mutation, "systemic mutation," has been postulated by Goldschmidt (1940) as necessary to account for the large changes observed in evolution. By "systemic mutation" Goldschmidt meant a complete repatterning of the chromosomes—"the arrangement of the serial chemical constituents of the chromosomes into a new, spatially different order; i.e., a new chromosomal pattern." Chromosomal aberrations (pp. 396–400) qualify as systemic mutations under this definition. But are chromosomal aberrations of great importance in producing major evolutionary change? While we have seen that new species of plants may arise suddenly by polyploidy (pp. 418–420), it is noteworthy that chromosomal aberrations frequently produce less marked effects upon their possessors than do gene mutations. In other words, the *arrangement* of the genes present usually makes less difference than does the *nature* of the genes present, whatever their arrangement in the chromosomes. Hence most students of the subject regard gene mutations as of more importance to evolution than are those "systemic mutations" known to us (i.e., chromosomal aberrations).

What explanation other than that of "systemic mutations" can we find for rapid occurrence of large changes? As noted before, rapid change may be expected to occur when an organism faces the demands of a new environmental niche radically different from the one formerly occupied. Under such conditions the severity of natural selection will be greatly increased, with resultant increase in rate of evolution. We recall recent experimental evidence (pp. 460–464) indicating that natural selection can, upon occasion, operate with surprising swiftness. Organisms faced with radically new conditions of life will adapt rapidly to those conditions under the stimulus of a severe natural selection operating upon the raw materials provided in the form of mutations and other types of genetic variability. We recall, also, that such factors as differential growth rates may magnify the effects produced by single mutations.

Another pertinent observation is the fact that fossil forms intermediate

between large subdivisions of classification, such as orders and classes, are
seldom found. This situation is not true of reptiles and birds, where, as we
have seen, *Archaeopteryx* occupies an almost perfectly intermediate position. Likewise, it is not true of reptiles and mammals, where the therapsid
reptiles grade into the primitive mammals almost insensibly. But it is true
in many instances. We have, for example, presented the insectivores as the
ancestral group from which the other orders of placental mammals arose.
There is good basis for doing so, yet no forms have been discovered that
are intermediate, for example, between insectivores and the flesh-eating
mammals of Order Carnivora, between insectivores and rodents (Order
Rodentia), or between insectivores and most other orders of mammals.
Does this lack mean that such intermediate forms never existed, that each
order arose by a sudden jump (saltation) from the insectivores? Or is the
lack simply due to the incompleteness of our knowledge of fossil animals?
Two schools of thought have arisen on this matter; the reader is referred to
Simpson (1953) for the pros and cons of the controversy. That author has
marshaled evidence in support of the view that intermediate or transitional
forms existed (recall that some have been found) but that most of them
remain unknown to us because of incompleteness of the geologic record.
He quoted (1949a) a pithy statement of the matter by H. E. Wood to the
effect that "the argument from absence of transitional types boils down to
the striking fact that such types are always lacking unless they have been
found."

Why are such transitional types still largely absent from our collections
of fossils? The answer proposed by Simpson relates to the matter of rate of
evolution and constitutes the reason for bringing the subject of the gaps in
the fossil record into our discussion. The answer will summarize the best
conclusions which are available at the present writing concerning the causa-
tion of large evolutionary changes. To make the matter as concrete as possible, we shall present it in terms of a specific example, that of bats, Order Chiroptera. Bats resemble insectivores in many ways but differ from
them by having wings. Bats have existed since at least the beginning of
the Cenozoic era, and the early bats had wings as well developed as are
those of their modern descendants. No transitional forms with partially
developed wings are known as fossils. If we grant that bats did not arise by
a single "systemic mutation" converting certain insectivores into bats
"overnight," how can we explain the observed facts?

In the first place, it seems clear that bats did *not* arise by a long process of
accumulating slight changes in structure over a great span of time. Bat evolution has been bradytelic in the extreme since early in the Cenozoic era

but there must have been a tachytelic phase in the evolution of bats prior to that time. Such a spurt in evolution, involving change from one way of life to another, has been termed by Simpson "quantum evolution."

Can we imagine the conditions which would lead to quantum evolution among certain arboreal insectivores, giving rise to bats? One environmental niche is that of *flying insect-eaters*. That it is not an easy niche to enter is attested by the fact that only three vertebrates have entered it: small pterosaurs (Fig. 3.1, p. 22), some birds, and bats. Pterosaurs had either disappeared or were about to disappear at the time bats were evolving. At any rate, bats would fill the niche much more efficiently than would these flying reptiles. Birds are highly efficient occupants of the niche, but most insectivorous birds do their insect feeding by day (as, probably, the pterosaurs did also), while bats are active by night. The environmental niche found open by these early arboreal insectivores was, then, that of nocturnal, flying insect-eaters. We recall that they were already insect-eaters, and probably nocturnal, so the change called for was primarily development of the power of flight.

Most of the arboreal insectivores of that day had no capability for entering the vacant niche. But somewhere there must have existed a small group of them, a subpopulation, in terms of our previous discussion, that underwent rapid evolution in developing wings. We recall that division of a population into subpopulations affords optimal conditions for evolutionary change. In some such subpopulation genetic variability of types previously enumerated (pp. 494–495) must have combined to alter the structure of the forelimb toward that of a wing. This alteration may have been spread through the subpopulation by genetic drift; it was certainly favored by natural selection. Probably, though not necessarily, the modified forelimb was first used for gliding from tree to tree; various vertebrates have achieved one type of structure or another for gliding through the air. But gliding does not provide the means for entering the flying insect-eater niche. The ancestors which essayed to enter this niche could have done so only by developing forelimbs capable of true flight. Anything less would have been too little. Insect-eaters in transition between life in trees, including, perhaps, gliding from tree to tree, and life involving true flight would have been in a most unstable position, not well adapted for any environmental niche. Consequently, for them natural selection must have operated with extreme severity, resulting in rapid perfection of the flight mechanism.

Now we can understand why our fossil collections contain no transitional forms between insectivores and bats. If our interpretation is correct, this evolution occurred rapidly, in terms of geologic time, and in only a small population of animals. That small population lived under conditions which did not favor fossil formation. Perhaps no fossils of that small group ever were formed; if some were formed, they have not yet been discovered.

In terms of bat evolution we have summarized what seems to the author the best current thinking concerning the production of major evolutionary change. This explanation stresses the importance of small populations' entering new environmental niches and accordingly being subjected to severe natural selection. This combination of factors results in rapid change to a new type of organism. Once the niche has been "conquered" the pressure of natural selection relaxes. Consequently, the perfecting of details of adaptation proceeds at a slower rate. A slower rate also characterizes the accumulating of the partly adaptive and partly nonadaptive changes which eventually results in the subdivision of the descendants of the new type of organism into subspecies, species, and other subordinate groupings of classification.

References and Suggested Readings

Amadon, D. "The Hawaiian honeycreepers (Aves, Drepaniidae)," *Bulletin, American Museum of Natural History,* 95 (1950), 155–262.

Blum, H. F. *Time's Arrow and Evolution,* 2nd ed. Princeton: Princeton University Press, 1955.

Brown, W. L., Jr., and E. O. Wilson. "Character displacement," *Systematic Zoology,* 5 (1956), 49–64.

Darwin, C. *The Origin of Species by Means of Natural Selection,* 1859. Modern Library series, Random House, New York; or Mentor Book MT294, New American Library, New York.

Darwin, C. *The Descent of Man and Selection in Relation to Sex,* 1871. Modern Library series (bound in one volume with *The Origin of Species*), Random House, New York.

Dobzhansky, Th. "The genetic basis of evolution," *Scientific American,* 182 (1950), 32–41.

Ford, E. B. "Early stages in allopatric speciation." In G. L. Jepsen, E. Mayr, and G. G. Simpson (eds.). *Genetics, Paleontology, and Evolution.* Princeton: Princeton University Press, 1949. Pp. 309–314.

Gause, G. F. *The Struggle for Existence.* Baltimore: Williams & Wilkins Co., 1934.

Goldschmidt, R. *The Material Basis of Evolution.* New Haven: Yale University Press, 1940.

Hardin, G. "The competitive exclusion principle," *Science,* 131 (1960) 1292–1297.

Huxley, J. S. "Darwin's theory of sexual selection and the data subsumed by it, in the light of recent research," *American Naturalist,* 72 (1938), 416–433.

Huxley, J. S. *Evolution: The Modern Synthesis*. New York: Harper & Brothers, 1942.

Huxley, J. S. *Evolution in Action*. New York: Harper & Brothers, 1953.

Ives, P. T. "The importance of mutation rate genes in evolution," *Evolution*, 4 (1950), 236–252.

Lack, D. *Darwin's Finches*. Cambridge: Cambridge University Press, 1947.

Lack, D. "The significance of ecological isolation." In G. L. Jepsen, E. Mayr, and G. G. Simpson (eds.). *Genetics, Paleontology, and Evolution*. Princeton: Princeton University Press, 1949. Pp. 299–308.

Mayr, E. *Systematics and the Origin of Species*. New York: Columbia University Press, 1942.

Mayr, E. "Speciation and systematics." In G. L. Jepsen, E. Mayr, and G. G. Simpson (eds.). *Genetics, Paleontology, and Evolution*. Princeton: Princeton University Press, 1949. Pp. 281–298.

Muller, H. J. "Redintegration of the symposium on genetics, paleontology, and evolution." In G. L. Jepsen, E. Mayr, and G. G. Simpson (eds.). *Genetics, Paleontology, and Evolution*. Princeton: Princeton University Press, 1949. Pp. 421–445.

Simpson, G. G. *The Meaning of Evolution*. New Haven: Yale University Press, 1949a.

Simpson, G. G. "Rates of evolution in animals." In G. L. Jepsen, E. Mayr, and G. G. Simpson (eds.). *Genetics, Paleontology, and Evolution*. Princeton: Princeton University Press, 1949b. Pp. 205–228.

Simpson, G. G. *The Major Features of Evolution*. New York: Columbia University Press, 1953.

Simpson, G. G. *Principles of Animal Taxonomy*. New York: Columbia University Press, 1961.

Stebbins, G. L., Jr. "Rates of evolution in plants." In G. L. Jepsen, E. Mayr, and G. G. Simpson (eds.). *Genetics, Paleontology, and Evolution*. Princeton: Princeton University Press, 1949. Pp. 229–242.

Tax, S. (ed.). *Evolution After Darwin. Vol. I, The Evolution of Life*. Chicago: The University of Chicago Press, 1960.

Wright, S. "Evolution in Mendelian populations," *Genetics*, 16 (1931), 97–159.

Wright, S. "Adaptation and selection." In G. L. Jepsen, E. Mayr, and G. G. Simpson (eds.). *Genetics, Paleontology, and Evolution*. Princeton: Princeton University Press, 1949. Pp. 365–398.

Zimmerman, E. C. *Insects of Hawaii. Vol. 1, Introduction*. Honolulu: University of Hawaii Press, 1948.

CHAPTER 22

WHAT OF IT? AN OPEN

LETTER TO STUDENTS

Those of you who specialize in science will find it hard to understand religion unless you feel, as Voltaire did, that the harmony of the spheres reveals a cosmic mind, and unless you realize, as Rousseau did, that man does not live by intellect alone. We are such microscopic particles in so immense a universe that none of us is in a position to understand the world, much less to dogmatize about it. Let us be careful how we pit our pitiful generalizations against the infinite variety, scope and subtlety of the world.

—WILL DURANT*

This chapter will be devoted to a brief discussion of the bearing of evolution on some other facets of our intellectual lives—particularly on religion. Such a discussion does not constitute an integral part of a scientific treatise on evolution. If this book were being written for scientists, or primarily for advanced students of biology, this last chapter would not be included. But I realize that for many of my readers this book will constitute the only formal excursion into evolutionary literature, and that for them evolution is of most interest as it relates to other aspects of their lives. Of these other aspects religion is the one usually considered most affected by "belief in" evolution. Experience has taught me that when a scientist follows his natural inclination to treat evolution objectively, without reference to such matters as religion, his silence on the subject is frequently misinterpreted as indifference or hostility to religion. Accordingly, after long consideration, I have decided to doff the cloak of scientific objectivity, to sit down at your elbow, so to speak, and to talk over with you some of

* From a commencement address; quoted from *The Reader's Digest,* 74 (June, 1959), 94–96.

the implications of evolution for your outlook on life in general, including religion. Although I lay no claim to having originated most of the ideas and viewpoints, I shall write this chapter largely in the first person as a constant reminder that the opinions expressed are personal ones. If some of you find my viewpoints helpful, my inclusion of this discussion will have been justified. Yet you have complete freedom to ignore any of the ideas which seem to you unfruitful or unacceptable.

Evolution and Religion

One question about evolution is in the minds of a large proportion of the students who study the subject with me. Occasionally they say something about it in class, or when they stop to see me after class, but for the most part they wonder about it in private or in the small circle of their "bull sessions." This is the question of the relation of evolution to the stories of creation contained in the Bible. As children at home and in their churches they learned about how things started; now at college they hear an entirely different story. That is a really unsettling experience when it involves the book which forms the principal document of our religion. In the light of scientific discoveries must we discard the Bible and with it our religion?

The whole difficulty here lies in the fact that we try to use the Bible in ways for which it was never intended. *It is a book of religion, not a book of science.* If that fact becomes thoroughly established in our minds most of our difficulty vanishes. The Bible as we know it is the work of many writers, writing at widely diverse periods in human history. The contributions of these multitudinous writers are almost inextricably mixed, although modern Biblical scholars have done much to untangle the intertwining strands. All of the writers had this in common: they were interested in religion, not science, and they did their writing long before *anyone* knew anything about modern science. If in writing of religion they had occasion to refer to science they inevitably did so in terms of the science known in their day. So if we piece together these scattered references to the physical world we obtain a picture of the world and solar system as these people thought them to be. And by reading other writers who wrote at the same periods, in Babylonia, for example, we learn that these ideas of the world were widely current at the time.

As Fosdick (1924) has pointed out, to a considerable extent these people relied on their senses and thought that the universe was as it seemed to be. They thought the earth was flat and that a sea lay under it (Psalm 136:6; Psalm 24:1–2; Genesis 7:11). They thought that the heavens were like a tent or an upturned bowl above the flat earth (Job 37:18; Genesis 1:6–8; Isaiah 40:22; Psalm 104:2). They thought that the earth was stationary (Psalm 93:1; Psalm 104:5) and that the sun, moon, and stars moved through the heavens for the special purpose of illuminating the earth (Genesis 1:14–18). They thought that there was a sea above the sky (Genesis 1:7; Psalm 148:4) and that there were windows in the sky through which the rain came down (Psalm 78:23; Genesis 7:11). They thought various other things that we know to be incorrect, but this sample will suffice.

I hope you will take your Bibles and read the references given above. If you do I am sure you will be struck by one thought—that the references to the nature of the universe are purely incidental to the writers' main objectives in writing. The fact that the passages reveal something of the writers' ideas of the universe is entirely secondary and of no consequence to the writings themselves. Many of the references are to the great religious poems which we call the Psalms. Their authors were writing of religion; if in doing so they made an inaccurate allusion to the nature of the universe that is a fact of no real importance. Their writing stands or falls on the basis of its worth to religion, not of its worth to science.

What we have just been saying seems pretty obvious, doesn't it? It seems so obviously true to me that I often wonder how anyone can think otherwise. Yet people have thought otherwise, vehemently; and some people still do. Take the matter of the earth's being stationary, for example. When the Copernican astronomy became established, with its proof that the earth revolves (instead of the sun, moon, and stars revolving around the earth as they seem to do), various religious leaders were extremely upset. Father Inchofer, for example, "went off the deep end" as follows: "The opinion of the earth's motion is of all heresies the most abominable, the most pernicious, the most scandalous; the immovability of the earth is thrice sacred; argument against the immortality of the soul, the existence of God, and the incarnation should be tolerated sooner than an argument to prove that the earth moves" (Fosdick, 1926). And even such a generally wise religious leader as Martin Luther attacked Copernicus in these intemperate words: "People gave ear to an upstart astrologer who strove to show that the earth revolves, not the heavens or the firmament, the sun and the moon. Whoever wishes to appear clever must devise some new system, which of all systems is, of course, the very best. This fool wishes to reverse the entire science of astronomy, but sacred Scripture tells us that Joshua commanded the sun to stand still, and not the earth."

What was the matter with such people? They failed to make the differentiation I am recommending to you. They failed to recognize that the Bible is a book of religion but not a book of science.

This conflict over whether or not the earth revolves seems remote and unreal to us today (though there is at least one religious sect in the United States which still maintains that the Bible must be regarded as scientific authority on this point). For the most part the church long ago adjusted itself to the new findings of science concerning the physical universe and has found essential religion but little affected by the adjustment.

This point brings us to evolution—a relative newcomer in the history of science, so far as general attention is concerned, at least. Most people had thought little about the subject before 1859, when Darwin published his *Origin of Species*. Then the storm broke all over again! Religious leaders who had become entirely reconciled to the Copernican astronomy, despite its contradiction of Scripture, maintained that the stories of creation in Genesis must be accepted as literal history. What peculiar inconsistency they showed in recognizing that the Bible is not a scientific book in matters of astronomy and yet refusing to recognize that the Bible is not a scientific book in matters of biology! The conflict during the latter part of the nineteenth century was bitter and is not yet completely dead. Yet again, for the most part religious leaders are recognizing the Bible for what it is, a book of religion, but not a book of science (not even of biology). And again, essential religion is but little affected by the adjustment.

Since many people still maintain that they regard the creation stories in Genesis as literal history, however, we may be interested to look at them a little. Perhaps you are surprised that I write of them in the plural: the creation "stories." Most people do not realize that the early chapters of Genesis contain two such stories and that they differ greatly. This situation arose from the fact mentioned earlier that the Bible had many authors, writing at different times, and that these varied writings were assembled together without indication of the sources of the various portions and without much attempt to remove inconsistencies and contradictions. By dint of painstaking sleuthing Biblical scholars have done much to unscramble the various portions.

The Pentateuch (the first five books of the Bible) is "a composite production, made out of sources old and new, which have been blended, brought up to date, and supplemented" (Moffatt). One of the sources was the Judahite or "J" narrative written as the religious book of the kingdom of Judah. The northern kingdom of Israel also had its narrative, usually called the "E" narrative. When the kingdoms were subsequently united their two sacred books were combined, and supplemented from other sources. Although neither the J nor the E narrative was written earlier than the ninth century B.C., both tell of the founding of the Jewish nation centuries earlier. The E narrative starts with Abraham, but the J narrative begins with the creation. This most ancient account of creation is now found in our Bible in the second chapter of Genesis—Genesis 2:4b–23, beginning "in the day that the Lord God made the earth and the heavens. . . ." I hope you will read this passage. According to this account God made the earth suitable for life ("watered the whole face of the ground") and then "formed man of the dust of the ground." Then he planted a garden for the man Adam to live in, creating a variety of trees for his use and enjoyment. Following that God created the beasts of the field, and the fowls, and brought them to Adam to name. Afterward God created Woman from one of Adam's ribs. Note that in this account man was created *before* the lower animals were, and that the creation was not represented as divided into separate days.

When the J and E narratives were united and added to, the ancient Judahite account of creation was left intact but ahead of it was placed another and differing account of creation: Genesis 1, and 2:1–4a. This later account is the familiar one divided into six days. In this narrative plants were created first (on the third day) and then the sun, moon, and stars were created (certainly an improbable sequence!). Then water-dwelling animals and fowls were created, followed on the next day by beasts and "creeping things." Finally on the sixth day man was created ("male and female created he them"; no mention here of Adam and his rib).

So we find together in these first two chapters of Genesis two entirely different stories of creation, conflicting in detail and chronology at practically every point. Both of them cannot be the literal history of what occurred, so why regard either of them as being that?

Why were these accounts of creation written? Were they intended as textbooks of instruction in the *facts* of creation? Partly, perhaps, and to that extent they are outmoded. But mainly their emphasis is *religious,* not historical. "In the beginning *God* created the heavens and the earth." These early writers were striving to impress the thought of a divine Creator of all things, and the later writers at least were especially intent upon establishing the point that all this was the work of *one* God, not many gods, as most other people of that time believed. In describing the creative work of this omnipotent Deity they wrote in terms of such scientific ideas as were prevalent in their day. Somewhat similar accounts of creation are found in ancient Babylonian documents, but with this important difference: the latter are full of the quarrels of many gods, the fear of primeval dragons, and the like. "When one turns from this welter of mythology to the first chapter of Genesis, with its stately and glorious exordium, 'In the beginning God created the heavens and the earth,' one feels as though he had left miasmic marshes for a high mountain with clean air to breathe and great horizons to look upon. Here a victory was gained for pure religion for which we never can be too thankful" (Fosdick, 1924).

Yes, the first chapters of Genesis are great religion. Why worry about the fact that they are not valid science? The Bible is a book of religion, not a book of science. Acceptance of its religion is in no way dependent upon acceptance of such scientific allusions as it chances to contain. It is just as possible to worship a God who works through natural laws, slowly evolving life on this planet, as it is to worship a God who creates by sudden command. In fact, is not our concept of the Creator immeasurably heightened when we understand more and more of the intricate workings of this marvelous universe? Such a Creator is of far greater stature than would be a miracle worker who created things once and for all back in 4004 B.C.

I know the question in the minds of many of you who have followed me to this point: "Does not science prove that there is no Creator?" Emphatically, science does *not* prove that! Actually science proves nothing about *first causes* at all. As we mentioned in an earlier chapter, science deals with phenomena that can be studied by the physical senses, particularly the sense of sight, aided by all manner of methods of extending those senses: microscopes, telescopes, varied measuring devices, and so on. As we perfect these "tools" and become more and more adept in their use and in the interpretation of the data which they supply we learn more and more about the facts of the universe. But we do not arrive at the first causes of those facts. Science enables us to determine that "phenomenon Z" is caused by "phenomenon Y," for example. Further research may demonstrate that "phenomenon Y," in turn, is caused by "phenomenon X." But what causes "phenomenon X"? Researchers work on the problem and eventually discover "phenomenon W," which is a necessary precursor of "phenomenon X." Or perhaps they discover a "phenomenon W" and a "phenomenon V" both of which are necessary if "phenomenon X" is to occur. Now we have to determine the causes of "phenomenon V" and "phenomenon W." And so we go back, step by step discovering more and more causes of causes, but not arriving at first causes ("phenomenon A" of our hypothetical series). Will science, as such, *ever* arrive at first causes ("phenomenon A")? That, of course, is a question we cannot answer. If it ever does, science will then be in position to prove whether or not there is a Creator. But that time is certainly far removed from the present. Until it arrives science can neither prove that there is a Creator nor prove that there is not a Creator.

If your question had been: "Do not many scientists believe that there is no Creator?" I should have answered, "Yes." But that is quite another matter from science's proving that there is no Creator. Scientists, like other fallible human beings, *believe* many things not proved by science. If we took a poll of bankers or bakers, machinists or farmers we should find that many of them do not believe in a Creator either. What we *believe* to be true is determined by numerous factors, conscious and subconscious, many of which have nothing to do with scientific demonstration. This statement is as true of scientists as it is of other people. Scientists are not a race apart; they had impressionable childhoods, molded by varying influences, and lead private lives, too. Accordingly, in matters of *belief* they are much like other people. Many of them believe in a Creator; many of them do not. But if they are thoughtful and honest they readily recognize that their belief one way or the other is not equivalent to scientific demonstration.

All right, the question is in your mind; why not ask it? How about me, do I believe in a Creator? As I mentioned earlier, this letter is intended to give you an idea of how things look to me, so the question is not out of order and I shall answer frankly, "Yes, I do." Then, of course, you want to know, "Why?" Probably it would be impossible for me to answer that question fully even if space permitted. Certainly a powerful influence in the direction of belief in God was exerted by the deeply religious home in which I grew up. Suppose we change the question slightly and ask: "Granted that science cannot *prove* either that there is or that there is not a Creator, has my study of science contributed in any way to belief in a Creator?" Again let me warn you that my answer is a purely personal one and that many persons, some of them more profound than myself, will consider it totally inadequate. But after all, this is *my* letter! The more I study science the more I am impressed with the thought that this world and universe have a definite *design*—and a design suggests a *designer*. It may be possible to have design without a designer, a picture without an artist, but *my* mind is unable to conceive of such a situation.

Evidences of design are everywhere about us; the forces producing the design are the so-called "laws of nature," many of which science has disclosed to us, many of which still await discovery. The greatest aspect of design visible to us is in the ordered movement of the stars and planets in this solar system, and in other solar systems extending on and on through space—a design almost incomprehensibly large. At the other extreme we find all matter composed of invisible atoms, each of which in turn is a solar system almost inconceivably small, with electrons swinging in orbits around the atomic nuclei somewhat as planets circle about the sun. And everywhere in between these extremes we find evidence of design. Atoms are arranged in definite patterns to form molecules. The electron microscope has shown us how molecules arrange themselves in perfect patterns to form crystals. While design is most regular and easily seen in the inorganic world, it is also apparent in living things. The outward patterning observable in the bodies of plants and animals is a reflection of inner patterning of organs, tissues, and cells, and this patterning in turn is a reflection of patterning of genes in chromosomes. And the genes are composed of complex but regular arrangements of atoms. And so it goes—everywhere there is design. Everything is conforming to definite forces acting upon it, is obeying natural laws applicable to its particular state. Whence come these natural laws? There we find the Creator.

It may seem to you that we have drifted rather far from the subject of evolution, but in reality we have not. Evolution is part of the great design, or better it is the way in which certain parts of the design are being produced. The principles of evolutionary change discussed in previous chapters are the means employed by the artist to paint the picture—to create the design. In other words, the design was not completed in its entirety at some distant time in the past; it is not completed even yet. The process is a continuing one and the end is not in sight.

Now I am perfectly well aware that some students of evolution conclude that there is no design in evolution, that the whole process is haphazard, without direction or goal. They point to the many evolutionary blind alleys up which animals have gone, only to become extinct. They emphasize the fact that evolution is not steadily progressive, that progress is frequently followed by retrogression. They stress the point that animals do not seem to evolve according to an established pattern, that how animals evolve depends upon the opportunities which chance to befall them. All these things are matters of observation, yet may not they in themselves form part of the pattern? Why should we assume that the laws of the universe, including those of evolution, must be so organized as to reach a goal by what seems to our human minds the most direct route? And why should we conclude that if the natural laws do not seem to be leading toward a goal by what seems to us a direct route, there is no goal at all?

Admittedly these are matters of speculation. Perhaps the universe, including evolution on this planet, has no design and no goal. But exercising the prerogative of voicing my own opinion here, I submit that the point is far from proved. My own "hunch" is that all organic evolution is following a pattern which constitutes one portion of the great design of the universe. Of course, I cannot *prove* that such is the case, any more than those who hold the opposite view can *prove* their position.

A word seems appropriate at this point concerning the statement sometimes made that the universe and everything in it arose by *chance*. The statement usually carries the implication that if a thing occurs by chance it obeys no laws, follows no design, whatsoever. As should be clear to you from our previous discussions, such an implication reveals a fundamental misunderstanding of the nature of chance. Chance itself follows statistical laws—the laws of probability which we saw to be so fundamental in Mendelian inheritance (pp. 376–389), in population genetics (i.e., Hardy-Weinberg law, pp. 431–435), and hence in evolution. These laws are clearly as much a part of the design of the universe as is the law of gravitation. They express the regularities with which phenomena occur. Probable events occur frequently, less probable events occur less frequently. But even highly improbable events do occur. We are told, for example, that on a roulette wheel at Monte Carlo red once came up thirty-two times in a row. The probability of such an occurrence is about one in four billion. Yet this high degree of improbability did not prevent the occurrence from happening. Similarly, some new evolutionary developments may have been dependent on very "improbable" combinations of genes and mutations. It was doubtless "improbable" that a climbing or gliding insectivore would become possessed of limb structure suitable for flight (pp. 504–506). Yet, as with the roulette wheel, the improbable event did occur, and having occurred altered all subsequent evolutionary history of the group by making possible the origin of bats.

We should note that the occurrence of highly improbable phenomena is not a "breaking" of the laws of chance. The laws of chance provide for improbable phenomena as well as for probable ones, and even predict the frequency with which improbable events may be expected.

I suspect that one reason some people doubt the existence of a design or pattern in the universe, and all of us discern the pattern so dimly, if at all, is because we are part of it. If we imagine a dab of paint on a canvas endowed with the sense of sight, we readily appreciate that this bit of paint would find it well-nigh impossible to see the painted landscape of which it was a minute part. It might well deny that it was part of any landscape, any design, at all!

Not only is our perspective likely to be faulty; our knowledge and understanding of the universe are strictly limited by the nature of our sensory equipment and minds. We frequently overlook these limitations. If, for example, you look at a postage stamp through a compound microscope you see only a tiny bit of the stamp, greatly magnified. In your small field of view you see irregular and apparently meaningless blotches of colored ink on a light background. If you move the stamp other patches of ink come into view. Moving the stamp further you see still different ink spots. But these spots do not seem to "add up to" anything. If you never saw a postage stamp except through the high powers of a microscope you might feel entirely justified in concluding that postage stamps have no pattern, that their surface is covered with ink spots distributed at random, forming no design. Here and there, on the other hand, you might by careful study detect arrangements of spots suggesting that a pattern really exists. Yet you would probably not be able to determine the actual nature of the design. We are much in that position as we look at the universe and at evolution. What we perceive and what we understand are strictly limited by the nature of our sense organs and of our minds. If we had different sense organs and different minds our perceptions and understandings might be quite other than they now are. So it behooves us to be cautious about concluding that if we see no pattern in the universe there must necessarily be no pattern. The design may be there; in fact we see evidences that it is. Yet our sense organs and minds may have such limitations that we can no more perceive the complete scope and nature of the design than a student viewing a postage stamp with high-power magnification can make out the face engraved upon it.

What is the outcome of the matter? Personally, it is that I am impressed with *design* permeating all things great and small. For me, design necessitates a designer. And I suspect that the design has a goal—an objective which gives significance and meaning to the whole. But I would not presume to state that I know what that objective is, and I suspect that I am not mentally equipped to comprehend it.

We are touching here on important matters. It is essential for each of us to feel that his life has significance. A sense of being part of a great pattern or plan contributes mightily to one's feeling of personal significance. I have testified to belief that the universe and everything in it is characterized by design and goal. Perhaps some of you are unable to follow me in this belief. Does that mean that you must regard your own life as without significance, as meaningless and without goal or objective? Not at all. As we shall mention shortly, there has been added to biological evolution in the case of man an entirely new form of evolution: *social evolution*. Social evolution is dependent upon learning and the passing on of acquired wisdom from generation to generation. Whether or not you agree with me that the universe and organic evolution give evidence of purpose and plan, you will recognize readily enough that this new evolution, under human control, is characterized by purpose and plan, "because man has purposes and he makes plans" (Simpson, 1949). The quotation is from the pen of a distinguished contributor to evolutionary thinking who does not agree with the point of view I have expressed—that the universe gives evidence of being characterized by pattern and goal. Nevertheless he finds pattern and goal in man's social evolution sufficient to confer significance upon human life. His discussion merits thoughtful reading.

Looking at Man and His Future

If space permitted I should like to discuss at some length the influence of evolution upon our conception of man and upon human institutions and society. I must content myself with but a few points, however. In the first place, what is the influence of evolutionary thinking upon our ideas concerning man himself? Succinctly, it changes our viewpoint so that we regard man no longer as a "fallen angel" but instead as a "risen animal." Some people, mostly of an older generation, are sincerely distressed by this changed viewpoint. For them there was comfort in the thought that man once was perfect, and that his principal task is to regain that perfect state. Then along came knowledge of evolution, demonstrating that the first men were not perfect at all. The more we learn of prehistoric men and their predecessors the more we appreciate the fact that they were less "perfect" in the higher human attributes than are we. This means that man, as found from the dawn of civilization down to the present, represents the finest fruit of the evolutionary process. It does not necessarily mean that no finer fruit will ever be produced, but if superior types of man do arise they will be a new development, not a reversion to a perfect human state once existent but subsequently lost. Accordingly it seems to me that evolution forms the optimistic viewpoint from which to look at man. From this viewpoint we may well believe that the great days for humanity are yet ahead of us, not behind us.

In the preceding paragraph I spoke bluntly of man as a "risen animal." You may have thought that in so doing I was casting aspersion upon man. Not at all; the emphasis is upon the "risen." In other words, we do not regard man as "just an animal"; he is an animal who has achieved heights attained by no other inhabitant of this planet. His use of tools has enabled him increasingly to adapt his environment to himself, instead of adapting himself to his environment. His development of spoken and written language has made possible the development of a *social inheritance* which forms a unique addition to his biological inheritance. Through this social inheritance the ideas and achievements of past generations are handed on to descendants, so that one generation builds upon the achievements of its predecessors in a manner totally unlike anything possible to lower animals. Because one generation does thus build on the achievements of its predecessors we have the possibility of *social evolution,* an evolution independent of biological evolution. The importance of this new evolution cannot be overemphasized. It is a unique achievement of man, and it enables him increasingly to control his own destinies.

We noted in earlier chapters that biological evolution varies from animal to animal and from time to time. Some animals, like the cockroach, remain virtually unchanging for vast periods of time while other animals undergo great changes. Still other animals, whose ancestors were highly developed, become simpler in structure, losing many of the ancestral structures—particularly animals which develop parasitic modes of life. Evolution, then, does not always mean *progress,* in the sense in which we usually employ the word, for any particular species (but see p. 499). Yet viewed as a whole the broad trend of evolution has been progressive, producing ever higher types of organisms. Thus progress seems to be part of the design to which I referred earlier. But it is not constant in rate, and it does not involve all forms of life equally. While some forms progress, others retrogress, and others travel down evolutionary blind alleys until they become extinct. At any given time in the earth's history it would be practically impossible for an observer to tell which forms were progressing and which were moving toward extinction. With the wisdom of hindsight we see that in the latter days of the Mesozoic era the dinosaurs were heading for extinction, while the future belonged to the descendants of the insignificant little mammals. But would an observer living at the time have drawn any such conclusion? It seems most unlikely.

So it is with human evolution. Some human societies remain almost static for centuries, others progress rapidly, still others retrogress. By analogy we may feel confident that some societies will develop into something higher while others, possessing the seeds of their own destruction, will become extinct. But as observers of the current scene we are as little likely to be able to "pick the winner" as would have been our hypothetical observer of the late Mesozoic scene. Thus while we may feel confident that progress will be achieved, we cannot feel confident that it will necessarily be achieved through one particular form of society which we may regard as "best." Perhaps *our* social and economic system is in the evolutionary blind alley, peoples of some other cultures being on the road to progress. If it sounds like heresy to suggest that the people with the most and best machines, the most potent engines of destruction, and the most devastating bombs are not surely on the road to progress, recall that the dinosaurs were the most powerful destroyers in their day also! As a student of evolution I find strange fascination in that most controversial of the Beatitudes: "Blessed are the meek: for they shall inherit the earth" (Matthew 5:5). Perhaps the future will demonstrate that this and its companion—"all they that take the sword shall perish with the sword" (Matthew 26:52)—were correct prophecies.

Though we cannot predict with certainty that ours is the society which is on the road to progress, our knowledge of biological and social evolution does provide us with inklings as to what may constitute the hallmarks of progress. First we may note a grave error made by some of the immediate followers of Darwin. Darwin himself stressed the struggle for existence. One phase of this struggle is between individuals for supremacy and survival. Emphasis on this phase led to a school of thought called Social Darwinism, in which great emphasis was placed upon the value of struggle for supremacy between individuals and between societies. This was the "nature red in tooth and claw" concept applied to human life and society. According to this view, ruthless economic competition, the exploitation of "inferior peoples," and warfare constituted the accepted means of evolutionary progress. "Might makes right" and "the devil take the hindmost." So in the decades following publication of the *Origin of Species* the idea of natural selection was taken as justification for all manner of exploitation, economic and military. Those who were strong proved to themselves that they were "the fittest" by exploiting the weak. Cutthroat competition and the exploitation of colonial peoples were the order of the day. No wonder evolution fell into disrepute with sensitive and thoughtful people.

Fortunately a reaction set in. Kropotkin was a leader in this with his *Mutual Aid; A Factor of Evolution* (1917), and other voices were heard calling attention to the fact that *cooperation* is as valid a factor in evolution as is competition (see Allee, 1951; Montagu, 1950, 1952). On an earlier page (p. 355) we mentioned the "survival value" of cooperation, for animals living together in societies. Man is such an animal. Clearly, cooperation between individuals in a society is of the highest value for the success of that society. In fact, we may anticipate that that society will be most successful which achieves the most perfect state of cooperative living. For man, then, cooperation is clearly a hallmark of progress.

How inclusive must this cooperation be? In the time of the Biblical patriarchs the members of one family cooperated together, but each family was more or less continually at war with other families. In later times families joined together to form cities, but each city-state was more or less constantly at war with every other one. Eventually the city-states joined to form confederations and these finally became nations. Each change enlarged the circle within which cooperation was operative. We have now reached the stage when it seems imperative that for the good of mankind nations shall join into super-states, enlarging the cooperative circle still further. Just at present we seem destined to have two such cooperative circles, one labeled "the East," the other "the West." The two circles are pitted against each other, but this conflict seems unlikely to be a permanent condition. By some means, peaceful or otherwise, the circles will merge to form one—the "One World" of Wendell Willkie.

Man has become so powerful in controlling his own social evolution, including the invention of means for his own destruction, that nothing short of complete cooperation by all peoples on our "shrinking planet" will suffice. If any people or society finds itself unable to adapt to such cooperative living on a global scale we may predict that that people or society will go the way of the dinosaurs, leaving the earth to those peoples who can make the adjustment. Natural selection is not dead; but in the modern world natural selection is placing a premium on ability to live cooperatively, not competitively.

Each of us is naturally interested that *his* society shall be among the survivors. It is not pleasant to imagine a future in which our particular race or nation shall have no part. How can we help to insure that our group shall not be eliminated by natural selection? Evidently, since social evolution is so largely under human control, we can contribute most by supporting all measures which further cooperative living on this earth.

Perhaps all peoples will be able to make the adjustment to cooperative living on a global scale. On the other hand, being as pessimistic as possible for the moment, we may ask: What will happen if *no* peoples can make the necessary adaptation? Then we may feel sure that mankind as a whole will become as extinct as the dinosaurs (probably through self-destruction), leaving our environmental niches free for exploitation by some other form of life. What form of life? We should have as great difficulty predicting that as a dinosaur would have had predicting that the mammals would inherit his place on earth.

But such pessimism is untimely. Possibly the way of progress will be found to lie through some form other than man. We have reason to doubt that this will be the case, however. Increasingly man controls his own evolution, especially his social evolution. Development of cooperative living is one process in that social evolution. We may feel confident that man, or at least some groups of men, will develop the qualities necessary for cooperation on the scale required. If so, there now seems no ascertainable limit to man's supremacy. Each of us can make his own contribution toward creating a mental and spiritual climate in which the necessary cooperation can thrive. "Cooperation begins at home" but it must not end until it encompasses the earth. Each of us can contribute to this end.

In closing this letter on an optimistic note I may be laying myself open to the accusation of being a "Pollyanna." After all, none of us can really foretell the future—most especially the distant future. But optimism seems at least as warranted as pessimism, especially when we recall the brief space in which our social evolution has been operative. In Chapter 7 we spoke of a hypothetical time-lapse movie of earth history. You will recall that the movie runs continuously for a year, but that of that year man has been in existence for only about twelve *hours,* and civilization has occupied only the last five or six *minutes.* Much social evolution has occurred in that five or six minutes; we may feel confident that much more will occur before man's time on earth equals that of many of his predecessors. Our social evolution is near its beginning, not its ending. Knowledge of evolution, then, gives us the perspective for optimism. We say that these are "dark days"; thoughtful reading of history will convince us that most days have been "dark" in the sense we have in mind. But out of the darkness has come progress in the past. That fact gives us optimism that progress will also characterize the long trends of the future.

References and Suggested Readings

Allee, W. C. *Coöperation Among Animals,* rev. ed. New York: Henry Schuman, Inc., 1951.

Fosdick, H. E. *The Modern Use of the Bible.* New York: The Macmillan Company, 1924.

Fosdick, H. E. *Adventurous Religion.* New York: Harper & Brothers, 1926.

Genesis, the first book of the Bible, Chapters 1 and 2.

Kropotkin, P. A. *Mutual Aid; A Factor of Evolution.* New York: Alfred A. Knopf, Inc., 1917.

Montagu, M. F. Ashley. *On Being Human.* New York: Henry Schuman, Inc., 1950.

Montagu, M. F. Ashley. *Darwin: Competition and Coöperation.* New York: Abelard-Schuman, Ltd., 1952.

Persons, S. (ed.). *Evolutionary Thought in America*. New Haven: Yale University Press, 1950.

Simpson, G. G. *The Meaning of Evolution*. New Haven: Yale University Press, 1949.

Sullivan, J. W. N. *The Limitations of Science*. New York: Viking Press, 1933. Also Mentor Book MD35, New American Library, New York.

INDEX